CAMBRIDGE LIBRAI

Books of enduring sc

Classi

From the Renaissance to the nineteenth century, Latin and Greek were compulsory subjects in almost all European universities, and most early modern scholars published their research and conducted international correspondence in Latin. Latin had continued in use in Western Europe long after the fall of the Roman empire as the lingua franca of the educated classes and of law, diplomacy, religion and university teaching. The flight of Greek scholars to the West after the fall of Constantinople in 1453 gave impetus to the study of ancient Greek literature and the Greek New Testament. Eventually, just as nineteenth-century reforms of university curricula were beginning to erode this ascendancy, developments in textual criticism and linguistic analysis, and new ways of studying ancient societies, especially archaeology, led to renewed enthusiasm for the Classics. This collection offers works of criticism, interpretation and synthesis by the outstanding scholars of the nineteenth century.

Grammar of the Latin Language

Henry John Roby (1830–1915) was a Cambridge-educated classicist whose influential career included periods as a schoolmaster, professor of Roman law, businessman, educational reformer and Member of Parliament. His two-volume *Grammar of the Latin Language* went through seven editions during his lifetime. It provides in-depth analysis of Latin phonetics, noun and verb construction, and syntax and morphology, taking a descriptive approach. Drawing examples from the corpus of classical writings dating from circa 200 B.C.E. to 120 C.E., this first volume (1872) discusses sounds and syllable quantities, noun and verb inflexions, and the basic elements of word formation, organized according to noun and verb stems. Appendices include pronoun tables, lists of weights and measures, and a chronological compilation of inscriptions from the republican era. A work of remarkable breadth and depth, Roby's book remains an essential resource for both historical linguistics and the study of Latin grammar.

Cambridge University Press has long been a pioneer in the reissuing of out-of-print titles from its own backlist, producing digital reprints of books that are still sought after by scholars and students but could not be reprinted economically using traditional technology. The Cambridge Library Collection extends this activity to a wider range of books which are still of importance to researchers and professionals, either for the source material they contain, or as landmarks in the history of their academic discipline.

Drawing from the world-renowned collections in the Cambridge University Library, and guided by the advice of experts in each subject area, Cambridge University Press is using state-of-the-art scanning machines in its own Printing House to capture the content of each book selected for inclusion. The files are processed to give a consistently clear, crisp image, and the books finished to the high quality standard for which the Press is recognised around the world. The latest print-on-demand technology ensures that the books will remain available indefinitely, and that orders for single or multiple copies can quickly be supplied.

The Cambridge Library Collection will bring back to life books of enduring scholarly value (including out-of-copyright works originally issued by other publishers) across a wide range of disciplines in the humanities and social sciences and in science and technology.

Grammar of the Latin Language

From Plautus to Suetonius

VOLUME 1

HENRY JOHN ROBY

CAMBRIDGE
UNIVERSITY PRESS

CAMBRIDGE UNIVERSITY PRESS

Cambridge, New York, Melbourne, Madrid, Cape Town, Singapore,
São Paolo, Delhi, Dubai, Tokyo

Published in the United States of America by Cambridge University Press, New York

www.cambridge.org
Information on this title: www.cambridge.org/9781108011228

© in this compilation Cambridge University Press 2010

This edition first published 1872
This digitally printed version 2010

ISBN 978-1-108-01122-8 Paperback

A GRAMMAR

OF THE

LATIN LANGUAGE

FROM PLAUTUS TO SUETONIUS

BY

HENRY JOHN ROBY,

M.A. late FELLOW OF ST JOHN'S COLL. CAMBRIDGE.

PART I. containing :—

BOOK I. *SOUNDS.*
BOOK II. *INFLEXIONS.*
BOOK III. *WORD-FORMATION.*
 APPENDICES.

SECOND EDITION.

London:
MACMILLAN AND CO.
1872

Table of Contents.

PREFACE.

Gereral Observations.

Compass of the book:

Observations on Book I.; particularly on Pronunciation, p. xxx.

BOOK I. SOUNDS.

BOOK III. WORD-FORMATION.

APPENDICES.

Preface.

General Observations.

As the present work differs in many respects from other grammars in use, it may be desirable that I should briefly note some of the more important changes which I have made, and in some cases discuss the grounds of the change. In the work itself I have refrained from dissertation, and aimed at giving the facts of the language in as few words as possible. If facts are stated with their real limitations, they either explain themselves, or at least afford a sound basis for theory to work on. If they are grouped according to their natural affinities and arranged on natural principles, the briefest statement is the most illustrative.

I have called the book, *A Grammar of the Latin Language from Plautus to Suetonius*. Now first, by *Grammar*, I mean an orderly arrangement of the facts which concern the *form* of a language, as a Lexicon gives those which concern its *matter*. The ordinary division into four parts seems to me right and convenient. The first three Books on Sounds, Inflexions, and Word-formation, are often comprehended under the general term *Formenlehre*. The fourth Book, on Syntax, contains the *use* of the inflexions and of the several classes of words. I have given much greater extension than is usual to the treatment of Sounds and Word-formation, and on the other hand, have cut away from the 2nd and 4th Books several matters which do not properly belong to them. For instance, numerals and pronouns are often included in Book II. in a way which conceals the fact, that it is only so far as their inflexions are peculiar, that they demand specific notice. Again, the use of prepositions and conjunctions is often discussed in the Syntax; whereas, so far as the use depends not on the class to which a word belongs, but on the meaning of the individual, the discussion belongs to lexicography. The error lies in thinking, that because certain words

b

are more general than others in their application, they are therefore
formal. However, there is no doubt a convenience in including
some of these matters in a Grammar, and accordingly I have put
them, or some of them, in the Appendices to this or the second
volume. Further, I have not attempted to twist the natural arrangement of the facts so as to make it suitable for persons who are first
learning the language and cannot be trusted to find their own way.
There are plenty of other books for that purpose.

Secondly, it is a Grammar of the *Latin* language. It is not a
Universal Grammar illustrated from Latin, nor the Latin section of
a Comparative Grammar of the Indo-European languages, nor a
Grammar of the group of Italian dialects, of which Latin is one.
I have not therefore cared to examine whether the definitions or
arrangement which I have given are suited to other languages of
a different character. A language in which, like Latin, the Verb is
a complete sentence, or in which e.g. **magnus** can be made to denote *great men* by a change in the final syllable, may obviously
require very different treatment from one in which, like English,
the verb requires the subject to be separately expressed, or the
adjective *great* requires, in order to gain the same meaning as
magni, the prefix of the definite article, or the addition of the
word *men.* I have confined myself, with rare exceptions, strictly
to Latin, and this for two reasons. First, Latin is the only
language which I have studied with sufficient care to enable me to
speak with any confidence about its Grammar, and I have learnt
in the process how little trustworthy are the results of an incomplete examination. Greek I have referred to in Books I. and III.
because of its close connexion with Latin, and I could rely, for the
purposes for which I have used it, on Curtius' *Griechische Etymologie.*
The Italian dialects, other than Latin, I have studied but little.
Such results, as can be drawn from the scanty remains which we
have, will probably be found in Corssen's pages, but I hesitate to
regard them as sufficiently solid to allow one to rest any theories of
Latin Grammar upon them. My second reason for declining frequent
reference to other languages, is the belief that such reference is incompatible with a natural treatment of my own proper subject. Each
language has its own individuality, and this is distorted or disguised
by being subjected to a set of general categories, even though

guarantied by Comparative Philology. It is no doubt true that progress in the knowledge of language is to be attained only, as in other sciences, by the constant action and reaction of theory and observation; of the comparison of phenomena in different languages with the special investigation of each for itself. I have chosen the latter part of the work, without supposing that all the secrets of Latin etymology could be discovered by so limited a view. But it is true all the same, that if one's eyes are but armed or practised (and some study of Comparative Philology alone can arm them), a closer and longer gaze detects something which might otherwise be overlooked.

Lastly, this is a Grammar of Latin *from Plautus to Suetonius*. That is to say, I have confined my statements of facts and lists of words or forms (except with distinct mention) to the period from the commencement of Latin literature to the end of the silver age, i. e., roughly speaking, to the three centuries from cir. 200 B.C. to cir. 120 A.D. There are but few inscriptions before 200 B.C. What there are I have of course taken into account. On the other hand, the imperial inscriptions which come within this period are not yet conveniently accessible in trustworthy texts. The silver age I take to end at latest with Tacitus and Suetonius[1], and I am convinced that this is as real a division with the line drawn at the right place, as literature admits of. It is quite remarkable how many forms and words are wholly confined to later writers or are used in common with only one or two rare instances in Pliny the elder, Suetonius, &c. Nor can any subsequent writer be fairly regarded as within the pale. The literature of the second century p. Chr. is but small. Aulus Gellius and Fronto are near in time, being indeed contemporaries of Suetonius' later life, but their claims are vitiated by so much of their language being conscious antiquarianism. The lawyers Javolenus, Julianus, Pomponius, Gaius, &c. have perhaps the strongest claim, for they naturally, as lawyers, use a somewhat older style than their age would imply. Their inclusion however would not noticeably affect the statements. But it is intolerable to find frequently given, in modern Grammars, without a word of warning, forms and words which owe their existence to Apuleius or Tertullian— imaginative antiquarian Africans, far removed indeed from insig-

---

[1] Suetonius' *Lives of the Cæsars* date about 120 A.D., though he lived to cir. 160 A.D. Teuffel, *Gesch. Röm. Lit.* § 324.

nificance, and not at all wanting in interest, but certainly not representative of the ordinary or normal language of the Romans. Some other writers, e.g. Justin, Florus, &c. are of too uncertain an age, and too unimportant, to be worth considering. Writers of the third and fourth century, however good, are quite inadmissible. Nor am I at all disposed to attach weight to a mention of a word or form in Priscian or other Grammarians, unless accompanied by a clearly intelligible quotation from an author before 120 A.D., or thereabouts. I do not mean that distinct proof can or need be alleged e.g. for every person of every tense of an ordinary verb; but any typical form not shewn to have been used in the period here taken, ought to be excluded from a Grammar of Classical Latin, or mentioned only with the authority affixed. E.g. indultum is usually given as the supine of indulgere, but neither it nor its kin (indultor, &c.) are found before Tertullian; and this fact is seen to be important when it is observed that they deviate from the regular analogy of stems in -lg (§ 191, 3), and that their occurrence is in fact contemporaneous with the use of indulgeri as a personal passive. Again, I have said in § 395 that quercus has no dative singular or dat. abl. plural. But Servius uses (and the form seems right enough) quercubus (*Neue*, i. p. 376). It should be understood therefore that a statement in the following pages that a form or word is not found, does not necessarily mean more than that it is not found within the classical period. A form or word first found in subsequent writers may be legitimate enough, and the absence of authority for it may be only accidental, but in such cases the subsequent use does not appear to me to add anything to the evidence for its legitimacy; i.e. it does not make it more probable that Cicero or Livy, or Horace, or Quintilian, or even Plautus might have used it. The character of the formation and the probability that, if no objections had been felt to lie against it, it would have been used by some now extant author, who wrote before 120 A.D., form the real turning-points of such a discussion. And to gain a firm basis for the discussion we must have the facts of the normal Latin usage clear from later and inferential accretions. Corssen has made his wonderful collection of facts much less useful than it might have been, by not distinguishing *always* between later and earlier forms. Of course an exclusion of the later forms from a book like his is not at all to be desired; but it is thoroughly misleading to put together words first found in the 4th century of the Christian Era, along with well-known words belonging to the ordinary language of the Romans. To take one instance—(hundreds might be given); he adduces (*Beitr.* p. 107; *Ausspr.* i. § 77) nine substantives in -ĕdĭn (ĕdŏn, as I call it), which he says are from verbs with -e stems, and stand beside six adjectives in -ĭdo, from six of the same verbs. Now the six adjectives are all well accredited. But of the nine substantives, two only (**torpedo, gravedo**) are well accredited; one more (**pingvedo**) occurs once in Pliny the elder, and then not again till the 4th century: one other (**frigedo**) is quoted by Nonius from Varro; three others are first found in Apuleius, two more not until the 4th century p. Chr. Now these last five words are probably mere creations of a later age in conscious imitation of the earlier words, and, it may be, imitating them, *because* they were rare. But as soon as we get to conscious imitation by literary speculators, the value of the words as evidence of the proper development of the language is gone.

[Another instance may be taken. Gustav Meyer, in an interesting essay on *Composition in Greek and Latin* in Curtius *Studien* v. 1. p. 42, quotes from Corssen 11². 318, as proofs "that the weakening of a, o, u to i in compounds was not always the rule" (nicht von je her überwiegend üblich), the examples **sacrosanctus, Sacrovir, Ahenobarbus, primogenitus, mulomedicus, albogalerus, albogilvus, merobiba, sociofraudus, vicomagister**, and says that "these justify the supposition that originally the o-stems entered unaltered into composition." I take these words in order.

Sacrosanctus is not an ordinary compound, but its precise components are not clear. I have suggested (§ 998) that it is possibly a spurious compound. For in Pliny 7. § 143 we have **resistendi sacroque sanctum repellendi jus non esset.** Probably sacro is an ablative, *by a sacrifice;* or *victim;* or *curse.* **Sacrovir** is only known as the name of a Hæduan in Tacitus. The origin of the name is obscure. Is it Roman at all? The first **Ahenobarbus** of whom we have any historical account held office about 200 years B.C., though the family traditions carried the origin of the name to the battle of Lake Regillus. **Primogenitus** appears to be first found in Palladius: (in Pliny 11. § 234, I find (in Detlefsen and Jan's editions) only

primis genitis). **Mulomedicus** is in Vegetius; **albogalerus** in the extracts of Paulus from Festus. **Merobiba** and **sociofraudus** are each found once only in Plautus. They are evidently compounds framed on the spur of the moment and not part of the ordinary stock of the language. Moreover **sociofraudus** must retain the **o** after **i**. **Vicomagister** appears to be found only in the barbarous **Curiosum urbis Romæ regimen**, which is referred to the end of the 4th century p. Chr.

Of the whole number of ten words, one only (**Ahenobarbus**) can be taken as an instance of some weight for the matter in question.]

My authorities then are the writers of the classical period as above defined; and I have not knowingly admitted, without distinct mention, any word which they have not used, or made any statement which their writings critically examined do not justify. But Donat and Priscian have so long reigned over Latin Grammar, and Latin Grammar has so impregnated literary speculation, that it is next to impossible, if it were desirable, to emancipate oneself from their influence. Still it is important to decline to recognize them as authorities for the grammatical usage of classical Latin, except where they may be taken to be witnesses to facts. They no doubt had access to some writings which are now lost, and they often transmit the theories of older grammarians; but they no doubt also sometimes misunderstood them, they avowedly regarded Greeks as their supreme authorities, they lived when Latin had long ceased to be pure, and they probably would have regarded a statement by Cæsar or Pliny of what ought to be said, as of more importance than the actual fact of what Cæsar or Pliny did say. But it is to the usage, not to the grammatical theories, of good writers that we should look for our standard of right. And for my part, if canons of grammar are to be laid down, I prefer Madvig to any xxii Roman whatever, and believe Ritschl and Mommsen know a great deal more about the Duellian inscription (§ 467) than Quintilian did.

The arrangement adopted requires a few words.

In Book I. I have thought it important to give a sketch, however slight, of the analysis of vocal sound and of the laws of phonetic change. The special Latin phenomena are treated at some length; but I have been desirous rather that the instances given should be tolerably certain, than that all possible instances should be included. In most grammars these phenomena are collected and arranged under the heads of *Omission, Contraction,* &c. If any one desires such an arrangement, he can make it for himself, by simply turning to those heads under each letter. But as the primary division of the matter it seems to me much more natural and fruitful to make each particular letter the centre of discussion. Whether it be changed or inserted or absorbed must ultimately depend on the sound it represents and on the relations of this sound to others. The ordinary procedure is the same as if a treatise on chemistry arranged all the phenomena of chemical action under such heads as *Explosion, Solution, Combination,* &c. Schweizer-Sidler's arrangement by the affections of *groups* of letters is rational enough, but not, I think, very convenient.

I have distinguished with some care between instances of *correspondence* and *representation* (see note on p. 24). The distinction of these two classes of phenomena is ignored in many of the earlier grammars, and is still not unfrequently forgotten. Yet the distinction is of great moment. In questions of pronunciation *representation* gives very important evidence, while *correspondence* witnesses at most to the pronunciation of primæval or at least præ-historical times. On the other hand, in discussing the affinities of language, *correspondence* bears the whole weight of the argument, and *representation* can only mislead.

The arrangement of the letters has been adopted as the one which best brings into connexion allied sounds. Gutturals have a tendency to pass into dentals, and dentals into linguals; and these classes should therefore come in this order. Labials form a class somewhat apart from the rest, and I have therefore put them first, out of the way. The relations of the nasals are on the whole more with the labials, gutturals, and dentals respectively than with one another. The order of the vowels is that given by Ritschl, and is the same to a great extent as that given by Corssen. It is without doubt, so far at least as it is common to these two authors, the order of development in the history of the language. Any one referring to Bell's *Visible Speech* (p. 73), will see that the order has a physiological side also, in so far that the vocal cavity of the mouth is progressively diminished from a in this order to ı.

I have not followed Schleicher and others in the treatment of Latin vocalization according to what for brevity I may call Sanskrit principles. This method applied to Latin seems to me to fail both in basis and result. Corssen's elaborate treatment of vowel-intensification in the first volume of his new edition is not more satisfactory; and on this point I can refer to Curtius (*Studien*, I. 2, p. 294) who, commenting on Corssen's sanguine view of the result of his medley collection of long vowels in root-syllables, suffixes and endings, points out that vowel-intensification is " after all only a name for the fact that we often meet with a long vowel, when we expect a short one." The parts of my Grammar which deal with *contraction, hiatus, change of vowel quantity*, &c., are far from being what I should like; but there is a great difficulty in arriving at any satisfactory conclusions, owing to our ignorance of the precise quality and quantity of the vowels, which were, or may be regarded as having been, the components of the long vowel or diphthong, *at the time* when the long vowel or diphthong first arose. Our knowledge of the language begins at a later period, when this process was already over, and we have therefore not facts enough for the historical method. I have little right to speak on such a matter, but I venture to think that the greatest light upon this branch of philology is now to be expected from strengthening the theoretical side of this investigation, but strengthening it not so much by the study of literature and grammar as in Sanskrit, but by a more accurate study of the physiological conditions, and by a closer contact with nature as exhibited in groups of dialects of living tongues. But the application to Latin must in any case be difficult.

In Book II. I have regarded the main division as twofold only, Nouns and Verbs. Adverbs, Prepositions, Conjunctions, have place here only as being originally parts of nouns or verbs. Numerals, as I have said before, have no right to a separate place at all: they are either adjectives or substantives or adverbs, and should be classed accordingly. (For convenience they are also given, in the ordinary arrangement, in Appendix D.) Pronouns are similarly referable to the other classes.

Understanding by a *declension* a mode of forming the cases by a separate set of inflexions, 1 have made two declensions only instead of five. The distinction of the stem is subordinate to this. At the same time it did not appear worth while to separate such forms as **filiabus** from the more usual forms, and put them under the head of the second class, to which they strictly belong. Pronouns are in their main features clearly words of the first class; but, as the genitive singular is differently formed throughout, they are here kept together in a separate chapter. **Qvis** of course belongs to the second class, but here again convenience seemed to forbid its separation from **qvi**.

The ordinary separation of substantives from adjectives, and the gradually growing tendency to confine the term *noun* to substantives, seem to me, in Latin at any rate, thoroughly wrong and misleading. The difference between substantives and adjectives is almost entirely syntactical, and, even as such, not so great as is generally assumed. What slight inflexional differences there are, will be found noted (cf. §§ 352, 403). The modification of adjectives to express degree in a comparison has clearly as little right to be put in Book II., instead of Book III., as the formation of diminutives, or any other common derivatives, which the language allowed to be formed very much at pleasure from any stem, because it retained a consciousness of the meaning of the suffix. (In Appendix C I have for convenience sake treated the matter more in the ordinary way.)

The formation of participles, &c. ought no doubt to be put in Book III.; but they have so much bearing on the inquiry into the nature of the verbal stem, that I have preferred to leave them as usual in Book II. The formation of the several parts of verbs has been treated under the appropriate heads. The endeavour to form the verbs into classes by combined consideration of their present and perfect and supine stems, as is done in Vaniçek's Grammar, after the analogy of Curtius' Greek Grammar, seems to me to lead to inconvenience without much compensatory advantage. Chapter xxv XXX. contains a list of so-called irregular verbs in alphabetical order, as being that which is far the most useful for ordinary reference.

I have followed the *Public Schools Primer* in putting generally the future instead of the imperfect next to the present tense.

It is very common, perhaps invariable, to prefix to Book II. a classification of the Parts of Speech. So far as this bears on

Book II. I have briefly touched it. But in the main it is of a syntactical nature, and in Book IV. it will therefore be found.

It may surprise some readers to see so imperfect an explanation of the meaning and origin of the inflexions of nouns and verbs. Where I have seen my way tolerably clearly, I have briefly stated the view which appeared most probable, but in many cases I have preferred merely to mention views entertained by others; in some cases I have stopped short at the facts, and left the origin untouched. This indeed seems to me, at any rate at present, the proper position of a Latin grammarian. What can be deduced from the facts of the historical language comes fairly within his province, but more than this can only be done by the light derived from other languages. And greater agreement among philologers is necessary before any theory of the precise origin and meaning of these inflexions can claim more than a very subordinate place in a grammar of historical Latin.

In Book III. will be found fuller lists of Latin words, arranged under their endings, than I have seen in any other grammar, except Leo Meyer's (which has too the advantage of containing lists of Greek words as well as of Latin). My lists are distinguished from his in two ways. His embrace a great many words, often without notice, which are only found in writers after the silver age; and the arrangement is more subjective and consequently less convenient than that which I have adopted. There is no doubt that almost any arrangement made on some principle brings together words which have a claim for common consideration and thereby may give rise to useful result. The ordinary arrangement, when of an etymological character, has been to class compound endings under xxvi the first part of the suffix, not the last[1]. This seems to me wrong both as matter of convenience and theory. A word is not so easy to find, because the analysis is more uncertain: and the practice contradicts the essential character of a (Latin) suffix, that

---

[1] Key's *Grammar* is an exception. See his tables in pp. 26, 28, 8, 39.

it is applied *at the end* of a word.   Of course if we were quite certain what is suffix, what is root, either arrangement (i.e. by the first part of the suffix or by the last) would be in some sort natural. But when to the uncertainty, which in many words there is on this point, is added the fact, that though some compound suffixes are apparently used as if they were simple, and are appended at once to a root or simple stem, yet in the majority of cases the last part only of the suffix is to be regarded as truly suffixal in the feeling and apprehension of the people, the safest plan seems to be that followed in the present volume; viz. giving all the words of any importance and certainty, and arranging them under the final suffix, or that final part which, if anything, would be the suffix, or which is at least parallel to what is suffixed in other stems.

There are other principles of division which are followed in some grammars either with or without the above. One is the separation of substantives from adjectives and enumeration of the suffixes under these supreme heads. Besides the general objection to such a division, which I have spoken of before, the lists will shew, that in far the majority of instances the suffixes or endings belong to both classes, and the separation of them is cumbrous and misleading.

Another division is according to the part of speech from which the derivatives are formed. This again is liable to the same objections. Many substantives are not so different from adjectives as to render it desirable to establish any sharp distinction between their respective progenies. And though some suffixes are particularly or exclusively applied in derivatives from verbs, others in derivatives from nouns, or, subordinately, from substantives or adjectives, many have no such particular or exclusive attachment.

To treat the ' derivation of adverbs' as coordinate to the derivation of nouns and verbs, is the same as it would be to treat so the derivation of the several persons of a verb or cases of a noun. So far as an adverb is formed with derivative suffixes &c., of the same kind as adjectives, they may belong here, but most adverbs are merely cases of nouns.

Many words formed, so far as we know, directly from a root are, as I have implied (see also § 748), included in these lists. Where any tolerably certain indication of the meaning of these roots was

known to me, it has been given; but to add either Sanskrit homo-
nyms or investigations into doubtful etymologies would have been
unsuited to my plan.

I have also added to the lists a considerable number of proper
names, chiefly of persons. No attempt has been made to be exhaustive in this matter, those only as a rule being given, which are
either clearly intelligible and therefore instructive derivatives, or
which are names of well-known or at least not merely private
persons. There is however probably somewhat more vacillation
in the extent to which this enumeration has been carried, than there
is in the case of appellatives.

The list of derivative verbs is fuller than I have hitherto seen,
though in no way exhaustive as regards stems in **a**. Still here as
in nouns it brings into strong light the comparative prevalence of
different classes. And this is a matter which is commonly left with
little notice.

The Chapter on *Composition* deviates considerably from ordinary treatment. In the first place, the lists are tolerably complete,
except in the case (1) of very common classes, e.g. words compounded with numerals or with -fĕro, and the like; and (2) of some
momentary formations found in Plautus or Petronius or the like.
The result is to shew that, except with prepositions, there was no
great development of Composition in Latin,—certainly nothing
approaching the Greek. Secondly, I have ventured to lay down
(§ 979) more broadly than is usual, at least in Latin Grammars,
the principle that Composition is simply welding together in one
word two words conceived as standing in ordinary syntactical
relation with each other. The welding however is a welding of
stems, and the changes of letters are simply in accordance with the
xxviii general habits of the language and require no separate treatment.
Thirdly, the form of the compound word is given by the necessity
which produced it. If an adjective was wanted, an adjective was
formed; if a verb, a verb; and a suitable derivative or stem suffix
was appended, which might or might not be like that possessed by
the simple words. No doubt much of this view is identical with
the ordinary division into *composita determinativa, constructa, pos-*

sessiva[1]; but it seems in the ordinary treatment to be regarded rather as a special and adventitious characteristic of some particular classes than as the natural result of the determining cause of all Composition. The compounds with prepositions used absolutely may however, at least with our present notions of prepositions, be a separate class.

Many will doubtless think the lists of words, derivative or compound, needlessly full. But I do not fear the charge from those who desire to study as a whole the formation of Latin words, or to ascertain the meaning or use of particular suffixes, or the laws of combination and change of the several vowels and consonants, or the etymology of particular words. I have indeed found these lists of much use in testing various etymological and phonetic theories which I have seen in other writers or which have occurred to myself. I have especially borne the possibility of this use in mind when the multitude of instances forced me to make a selection only. Indeed many of the instances inserted have been in fact the answers I have found to various doubts which occurred to me respecting the possibility or the behaviour of certain groups of sounds or of certain elements of composition. Nonconformists have a special right to a place in such a representative assembly.

The *interjections* I have tried to identify with inarticulate sounds of emotion. But a greater knowledge of phonetics and more acquaintance with the habits of peoples of southern Europe than I possess is required to do this clearly and fully.

---

[1] I worked the matter out for myself with the hint given by this division. But L. Tobler's book (*über die Wortzusammensetzung*, Berlin, 1868) is well worth reading.

Observations[1] on Book I.;

particularly on

Pronunciation.

THE account which I have given of the several letters took its origin in the desire of finding a tolerably firm basis for forming a judgment of the real sound of each. But any inquiry of this kind presupposes some acquaintance with at least the leading divisions of articulate sound, so far as they are actually heard from the lips of Europeans and Western Asiatics. For this reason I have prefixed to the discussion of Latin sounds, a brief account of articulate sound in general, omitting, however, many of the finer distinctions, and many of the sounds (chiefly Asiatic and Slavonic) which there seems little room for supposing were known to, or at least represented by, Greeks or Romans. Etymology becomes a science only when its physiological conditions are understood and applied, and I believe no greater service could be rendered to Comparative Grammar, than the publication of a brief and clear Grammar of Phonetic, with illustrations (a) from misformations of sounds, such as are now heard from individuals; (b) from varieties of sound in living languages and dialects; and (c) from well-ascertained facts in the history of words. To write such a book would require, besides knowledge and caution, an acute and trained ear, as well as sensitive and flexible organs. Few possess these qualifications. I cannot pretend to any of them. At present, the only book which can be named as combining these different parts of the discussion in relation to the ancient languages is Max Müller's *Lectures*, Vol. II. But it is not nearly full enough.

---

[1] A few copies of these Observations and of Book I. were privately distributed in April 1871. Some verbal corrections, and one addition (p. xli.), have been since made.

Some other books which I have used are named in the note to ₓₓᵢᵢ
p. 1[1]. But to these must be added Alex. J. Ellis' elaborate
work (not yet finished) on *Early English Pronunciation* —a work
with which I did not become acquainted till after Book I. was
stereotyped, and of which I have consequently made hardly any
use in that book (except in the list of vowels). When I see
the admirable mode in which English pronunciation is there discussed, I feel how very imperfect, nay almost perfunctory, by the
side of it is any inquiry into Latin pronunciation, which has yet been
made. And yet Mr Ellis' inquiry is into the pronunciation of a
language, still living, and familiar, and only five or six centuries old.
An inquiry into classical Latin is into a pronunciation which has
not been uttered by any accredited representative within the last
seventeen hundred years. Still, I persuade myself, that the pronunciation which I have given, may be taken to be one which would
at least have been intelligible to Cicero or Cæsar, and which would
not have differed from his own, more than the pronunciation of
educated men in one part of England would differ from that heard
in other parts.

I have assigned little weight to the accounts of pronunciation
given by Roman grammarians, except so far as they imply the
non-existence, at the time, of sounds which the letters might on some
other grounds be supposed to have had. Some isolated statements made by Cicero and Quintilian are worth careful notice; but
to describe sounds properly requires a large acquaintance with
possible and actual sounds, and who in the ancient world had that?
It is absurd to see loose statements of writers of uncertain age,
but probably between A.D. 200 and 600, and often nearer the
latter than the former, taken as authenticated evidence of the pronunciation of Cicero and Cæsar, and conclusions deduced from
them by writers who have themselves a loose knowledge of sounds,
and that derived only from books, not from close study of the human
voice itself. Assuming that the Roman spelling was in the main
phonetic, i.e. that it varied with the sound, (though doubtless the
change in the spelling lagged behind the change of sound,) I am

---

[1] On the pronunciation of Greek a pamphlet by Friedrich Blass,
über die Aussprache des Griechischen (1870), has lately come to me. It
will be found well worth reading.

xxxi sure that the only safe guide is the actual history of the letters, aided by a knowledge of their possible and likely sounds.

I have thought it would be convenient if I put together here some of the facts and arguments upon which my view of the Roman pronunciation is based, instead of leaving them to be collected from the accounts of the several letters in Book I. Some points I have treated at greater length than others, because there is not that general agreement which would permit of my using more dogmatic brevity. Prof. Max Müller has recently (*Academy*, 15 Feb. 1871) thrown doubt on what he fairly states to be the conclusion almost all scholars have come to with respect to the Latin c. [He has since (*Academy*, 15 Dec. 1871) explained that his arguments were only intended to shew that the evidence for ce = ke, &c. was weaker than that for ca = ka, &c., and that he himself is in favour of pronouncing c always as k.] Prof. Munro has in a privately circulated pamphlet[1] replied to his arguments on this question, besides expressing his own opinion on most other points of Latin pronunciation. My own argument was written before I saw Mr Munro's remarks, but I have since taken one or two hints from them. I am glad to find my views on the pronunciation of Latin generally accord closely with those of one whose fine taste and many-sided scholarship need no commendation from me. I have mentioned candidly my difference on some points, though I am well aware how probable it is that I am wrong.

The question, What was the Roman pronunciation? is quite distinct from the question, Shall we adopt it? Prof. Müller's argument has a tendency to confuse them. I quite admit that a change in our pronunciation of Latin is inconvenient, but the inconvenience is greater in imagination than in reality, and will be soon overcome, whilst the benefit to any student of philology will be very great. With our English pronunciation of the vowels, of j, v, c, g, r and others, the development of the language becomes an inextricable riddle, and the student naturally gets into the fatal habit of dissociating letters from sounds. Nor can it be said that we

---

[1] The reply to Prof. Müller's arguments is now reprinted in *Academy*, March 15, 1871. [Mr Munro has since (Oct. 1871) published this pamphlet under the title *A few remarks on the pronunciation of Latin*, and added a *Postscript*.]

shall not be approaching to the pronunciation of continental nations. We shall approach them considerably at once, and if, as seems to me probable, they change their pronunciation eventually, we shall be coincident with them in proportion as we and they respectively have succeeded in ascertaining the truth. Nothing short of that can or ought to be the common goal and place of meeting. Argument from some supposed superiority of one sound, as sound, to _{xxxii} another, seems to me worthless: the question is one of historical fact, not of æsthetical selection [1]; and we shall do better in speaking Latin as the Romans spoke it, if we can but discover how, than in either indulging fancy or being swayed by associations, which are none the less delusive because they are habitual.

I assume throughout, until the contrary be proved, that a letter has but one sound, except so far as it is necessarily altered by its position as initial or medial or final. The phenomenon presented by most letters in English of sound and sign having but a fortuitous connexion is, I believe, nearly unique.

On v consonant.

The following are the reasons for the pronunciation of **v** consonant as Eng. **w**, or perhaps sometimes as French **ou** (in *oui*), and not as the labio-dental **v**.

1. The same letter was used without any distinction for the vowel and the consonant sound. There is no doubt that the vowel sound was English **oo**. ' By a slight appulse of the lips the vowel oo becomes the consonant **w**' (Bell, p. 151). '**W** is often considered to be a vowel, but is not so' (Ellis, p. 580). At the same time the Romans were quite alive to the distinction. The emperor Claudius proposed a new letter, and Quintilian thought it would have been desirable to have one. For (he says) neither **uo**, as his teachers wrote, nor **uu**, as was written in his own time, expressed the sound actually heard; which he compares to the digamma (I. 27. 26; XII. 10. 29, quoted in Book I. p. 29).

---

[1] If the matter were really one of taste, I should not be afraid of putting the questions: Is a sibilant or buzz a finer sound than a mute or semivowel? Are *seas* and *cheese* pleasanter sounds than *keys*, *sin* and *chin* than *kin*; or *veal* and *vain* more expressive than *weal* and *wane?*

The later grammarians, e.g. Terentianus Maurus, dwell at greater length on this difference.   This makes it probable that the sound was rather **w** than French **ou**.   Comp. Gell. XIX. 14 with *id.* X. 4.

2. A sound practically identical with **w** is generally considered to be the sound of **u** when following **q**.   It is probable, indeed, as Mr Ellis says, that **qu** in Latin represents only a xxxiii labialised guttural, not a clearly pronounced **kw**, for it never lengthened the preceding syllable: but then the nearest approach to such a labialised **k** is **kw**, certainly not **kv**. (Comp. Quint. XII. 10, § 29.)

3. The vowel **o**, when following **v** (consonant or vowel), was retained till the Augustan age and later, though after other letters it had usually changed to **u**; e.g. servos, later **servus**; quom, later (in 4th century) **quum**.   Compare this fact with Bell's statement: ' When **w** is before **oo**, the combination is rather difficult from the ' little scope the organs have for their articulative (i.e. consonantal) ' action: the **w** is in consequence often omitted by careless speak- ' ers, *wool* being pronounced *ool*, *woman*, *ooman*, &c.' (Bell, p. 171). It is worth notice, that in English the pure Italian **a** was retained after **w** in several words (*water*, &c.), and in the 17th or 18th century gave way to its present usual sound of a**w** (Ellis, 187-8).

4. **u** and **v** were frequently passing into one another: compare **miluus** and **milvus**, **relĭcŭum** and **reliqvum**; **genua** sounded as **genva**, **pituita** as **pitvita**, **tenuia** as **tenvia** (§ 92).

Again **v** is vocalised in **soluo** for **solvo**, **acuæ** (Lucr.) for **aquæ**, **siluæ** for **silvæ**, &c. (§ 94. 2).   So **solvo** has **solūtus**, **volvo**, **volŭtus**, just as **acuo** has **acŭtus**.

5. **v** between two vowels constantly falls away, not sapped by a slow decay, but as it were melted before the eye and ear of the people.   Compare **amaveram**, **amaram**; **audiveram**, **audieram**; **cavitum**, **cautum**; **ævitas**, **ætas**; **juvenior**, **junior**; **reversum**, **rur-** **sum**; **providens**, **prudens**, &c. (§ 94).   This phenomenon, repeatedly occurring, seems hardly explicable, except on the assumption of the **v** being a vowel, or the closest approach to a vowel.

6. **v** in Latin never (except in **nivis**, and the compounds **bi-** **vium**, **tri-vium**, &c.) follows short **i**.   Now there is no difficulty

in pronouncing Engl. **iv**, but **iw** is very far from easy. Indeed **v** after any short vowel is not common in Latin. I have only noticed the following instances: **avis, avus, Bavius, bovis, brevis, cavus, exuviæ, induviæ, favus, fluvius, gravis, Jovis, juvenis, levis, ne-vis** (§ 728), **novem, novus, ovem, ovis, pluvia, pover** (= **puer**), **simpuvium**; and the verbs **caveo, faveo, juvo, lavo** (also **luo**), **moveo, paveo.** (The syllable preceding **v** is in all accented.) The cause of this rarity is the great tendency to fusion of two vowels when only separated by a **v.** (See preceding paragraph, and comp. Schleicher, *Deutsche Sprache,* p. 159, ed. 2.) xxxiv

7. Consonantal **v** is never found before a consonant (Prisc. 1. 23) or final; but always before a vowel. This is quite as it would be if **v** be equal to **w**; for **w** scarcely gains any consonantal power, if indeed it be not absolutely unpronounceable[1], except before a vowel; but **v** is as pronounceable after as before a vowel. Thus **sive** (older **seive**), **neve** when they drop the final e become **seu, neu,** not **siv, nev**[2]. Compare this with Italian, where (the labio-dental) **v** is frequent before a consonant in the middle of a word; e.g. *avro* (habebo), *covrire* (cooperire), &c.

8. The English name of the labio-dental voiced fricative is **vee**. This name is derived from **vau,** the term applied to the digamma, with which the Latin **f,** on account of its symbol ϝ, and the Latin consonantal **u,** on account of its sound, were identified (cf. Quint. XII. 10. § 29). But in classical times, at any rate, **v** consonant and **v** vowel (like **i** consonant and **i** vowel) were not distinguished either in symbol or name. Nor were they by Terentianus Maurus. Priscian (1.20) speaks of the name **vau** being given it from its resemblance to the digamma. But had the sound of English **v** belonged to it, at the time when the other letters received their name, it would have been called **ev.** For it is the law of Roman nomenclature[3] to denote vowels by their sounds, mute consonants by sound-

---

[1] [Mr Ellis says (*Acad.* 15 Jan. 1872), that **w** after a vowel, and without a vowel following it, *can* be pronounced after some practice.]

[2] Marius Victorinus (p. 2465) stands alone, I believe, in thinking that **obverto, obvius** should be **ovverto, ovvius.**

[3] The names of all the letters are given in Pompei. *Comm. ad Donat.* Vol. v. p. 1c1, Keil. Cf. also Serg. IV. p. 478. I cannot bring myself to believe that Mr C. B. Cayley, *Philol. Soc. Trans.* for 1870,

ing a vowel after them, be, ce, de, ge, &c.; continuous consonants by a vowel before them (e.g. ef, el, em, en, er, es), probably because in this way each consonant gets its fullest and most characteristic sound (Prisc. I. 8); the explosives being chiefly distinguishable when they precede a vowel (§ 274), the continuous consonants having when final an opportunity of being prolonged at pleasure. Varro is said to have given va as the name and sound
xxxv of the digamma. If the Romans had named their consonantal use of u, they would have denoted it similarly by va or ve (pronounced wa, we), as w like h only obtains its full sound *before* a vowel.

9. The labio-dental f differs from the labio-dental v only as p from b, t from d, s from z, th (in *thin*) from th (in *then*), &c.; i.e. the former is whispered, the latter is voiced. The Saxons and (formerly at least) Welshmen do not make this difference, or rather they sound the voiced consonants nearly as the voiceless (e.g. *pet* for *bed*); we give to each of the symbols, s and th, both the sounds. With so great similarity between f and v is it likely that the Romans, if their v was a labio-dental, would not have confused them or noticed the resemblance? Yet (*a*) no inscription substitutes F for v (Corssen, *Ausspr.* I. p. 136); and (*b*) the Roman writers (at any rate before the 4th century[1]) seem not to have noticed this close resemblance, although (as was said before) the symbol F was the ordinary symbol of f, and was borrowed from the digamma to which the Roman v *corresponded.* Quintilian's description (XII. 10, § 29) of the Roman f indicates strongly its dental and voiceless character. I am inclined to think that no more is meant by his words than 'blown out between the intervals of the teeth with no sound of the voice[2].' In the next sentence he speaks of the 'Æolic letter which we utter in seruum, ceruum,' but seems in no way

pp. 5—16 (the only paper which I have ever seen on the question of the names of the letters), is right in thinking that the Latin names have not been assigned on phonetic principles. Comp. App. A. xxiii.

[1] Marius Victorinus (p. 2464) speaks of the 'cognate letters b, f, m, p, u,' which is of course in some sort correct on any supposition.

[2] Some think that a still harsher articulation than the ordinary English f is here meant, and no doubt this is possible enough, but, considering that Quintilian regards it as quite peculiar, some emphasis of expression is not unnatural. Even in English f and v are different enough from any other consonants.

conscious of any close similarity of it to f. Terentianus Maurus (*v.* 227) describes f quite correctly as uttered 'with a gentle breathing while the under lip is pressed against the upper teeth,' and speaks of v consonant at considerable length, but never suggests any resemblance to f.

10. The ordinary and regular mode of expressing the Latin v in Greek is by ου[1], and no distinction is made whether it be a vowel or consonant. On the other hand, Latin v is never used in the transcription of a Greek word, except as a vowel, usually for ο or ου (cf. § 90. ii.).

But Latin v consonant is sometimes expressed in Greek by ο, and sometimes by β. Now ο was an occasional descendant from a digamma (cf. § 91, and Curt. *Gr. Etym.* II. 145 = 500, ed. 2), and is certainly, next to ου, the nearest vowel sound to the Latin u. This use of ο therefore tends to confirm the inference which may be drawn from the use of ου, viz. that Latin v consonant was the consonantal sound nearest to the vowel u; and that is Engl. w.

The expression of the Latin v consonant by β is one of the main arguments upon which the theory, which makes Latin v = English v, rests. The argument proceeds, as I understand, thus: 'Greek β either had the sound of Engl. v, or, if not, it had a 'sound, say b, nearer to v than to w. And it is probable that Greek 'β had the sound of Engl. v, for it has this sound in modern 'Greek. [As Greek β is constantly used to represent Latin v, it is 'probable therefore that Latin v had the sound of English v].'

Now the extent to which β was used to represent Latin v is commonly taken to have been much greater than it really was. Nothing but an undoubting acquiescence in an accredited belief could have caused so vigilant and industrious a philologer as Corssen to treat the question in the superficial way which he has done (*Aussprache*, I. 311, ed. 2). He gives no authority for the instances in which v in proper names is represented by β, and he quotes, as instances of the same in words which are not proper names, two only from inscriptions (date not specified: they are from Lycia), three

---

[1] The sign Ȣ (originally a Υ put with its foot in the middle of the ο) is not found in inscriptions or coins till the end of the second century p. Chr. (Franz, *Elem. Epigraph. Græc.* p. 246).

from Suidas, and four from Lydus. Lydus was a Byzantine, and not born before A.D. 490; Suidas is later, and indeed is often put as late as the 11th or 12th century p. Chr. Both therefore are witnesses of little weight in such a question; and when we remember that in the 4th century p. Chr. there was a frequent confusion between Latin **v** and Latin **b** (which began as early as the 2nd century but not before[1]), we see that the use by any writers later xxxvii than the 4th century of a β for **v** is no evidence whatever of the sound of **v** in the age of Cicero or of Quintilian.

The Greek writers of most importance for this matter are Polybius (2nd cent. B.C.), Diodorus Siculus (1st cent. B.C.), Dionysius of Halicarnassus and Strabo (Augustan age), Josephus and Plutarch (latter half of 1st cent. p. Chr.), Appian (middle of 2nd cent. p. Chr.), Dio Cassius (end of 2nd or beginning of 3rd cent. p. Chr.). I have examined these attentively, though not exhaustively, and collected a large number of instances of transcription of Latin words, principally proper names. I have since examined Benseler's most painstaking dictionary of Greek proper names, and the result is in both cases the same; viz. that, except in one writer, the instances of **v** consonant being represented by β are few absolutely, and very few relatively to the instances of its being represented by ov. The one exception is Plutarch, and, so far as I have noticed, most instances commonly quoted have or might have been taken from him. He has β for **v** frequently, though not as often as he has ov. The same name appears with β in some of his Lives, in others with ov. Other names are always written one way.

But this matter has been so little noticed that some details may be interesting. I have looked particularly through (1) all Plutarch's lives of Romans, and that of Pyrrhus (in Sintenis' edit., Teubner series); (2) the first five books of Polybius (Hultsch's edit.), i.e. all that is preserved in a continuous narrative; and (3) Books IV.—VI. of Dionysius of Halicarnassus (in Kiessling's edit., which in these books rests on a better collation of the most important MS. than in the first three).

---

[1] See § 72. Corssen, *Aussprache*, I. 131 sq.; Schuchardt, I. 131; Göschen's *Pref. to Gaius*, p. xxxii. ed. Lachmann; and Naber's edit. of Fronto, *passim*. So Priscian (*Part.* 23 = III. 465, Keil) makes the strange statement, that 'all words beginning with **vi** are written with **v**, 'except **bitumen, bilis** and the compounds of **bis**.'

The result is as follows, the numbers being possibly not strictly accurate, but at any rate accurate enough for the present purpose[1].

(1) In Plutarch there are of names of persons (almost all Romans), or places, or peoples, 50 written with ου, and 43 with β; and the occurrences of these names are, in all, 323 with ου, 180 with β. Of these **Valerius, Valeria, Valens, Ventidius, Verginius, Vespasianus, Vibius, Vindicius, Vinius, Vitellius, Volsci** occur at least 5 times each (**Valerius** and **Volsci** nearly 50 times each), and always with ου; **Fulvius, Fulvia, Varro, Verres** occur at least 8 times each, xxxviii and always with β. Others, e.g. **Veii**, occur both with ου and β; **Volumnius** (in Brutus) always with β, **Volumnia** (in Coriolanus) always with ου; **Octavius** 16 times (chiefly in Crassus and Pompeius) with ου, 30 times (chiefly in Gracchi and Marcellus) with β; but **Octavia** (in Antony) 22 times with ου, and only twice (in Marcellus) with β; **Servilius** 9 times with ου, twice with β; **Servilia** once with ου, 14 times with β. Yet other writers have ου in the names which Plutarch writes with β only. For instance, no one else (according to Benseler's *Lex.*) writes Βάρρων (except once Dionys. Hal. I. 14) or Βέρρης.

(2) In the first three books of Polybius I find 10 names, making in all 20 occurrences, all with ου; not a single instance of β. In the 4th and 5th books I find no instance of either. On turning to the extracts from Polybius' lost books I find nothing in those from the 6th and 7th; but in the 8th Ουαλέριος once, Λίβιος four times.

(3) In Books IV. to VI. of Dionysius I find 21 names written with ου (besides Αὐεντῖνος), and the occurrences are 184, **Valerius, Volsci,** and **Servilius** being exceedingly frequent. There are 5 names only in which v is represented by β; **Nævius, Flavus** (written in the two best MSS. φλαβιος), **Servius, Pulvillus,** and **Elva,** the last only occurring twice, the others once.

How much of this comparative frequency of β in Plutarch is due to the author, how much to his copyists, how much to his editors, I do not know. The text of Polybius and Dionysius may,

---

[1] I have not included instances where neither ου nor β are used, e.g. in Plutarch, Φαώνιος, Νοέμβριος, Σκαιόλας: nor instances of u after q (cf. § 90, 2); though both these speak for a light value being given to v.

I suppose, be fairly trusted as far as the editors are concerned. And it may be noted that the most trustworthy part of the text of the most trustworthy author (Polybius) gives no instance of β.

Now in this representation of v by β something doubtless is due to the source of the Greek writer's narrative in each case. Something also to the instinctive desire of assimilating a word to Greek forms; hence the frequent use of β before -ιος, e.g. Λίβιος (in Plutarch once only Λίουιος), Φλάβιος, Ὀκτάβιος, Φούλβιος, &c. Something again is due to phonetic reasons. Thus while ου is (in Plutarch) initial in 34 names and medial in 16, β is initial in 17 and medial in 26. In 15 of these 26 β follows λ or ρ, and in the rest it is between vowels; which are exactly the positions in which xxxix a German b is pronounced like Germ. w[1]. It will be seen that the instances from Dionysius are all thus disposed of. As regards Plutarch it is perhaps not inappropriate to remark that he expressly tells us he was not a good Latin scholar (*Vit. Demosth.* 2, p. 846), and secondly, that he was a Bœotian; and the relations of the Bœotian dialect to the digamma were such as to make it possible that his native pronunciation or habits may have had something to do with this peculiarity. But all the MSS. of these authors are, I suppose, posterior by many centuries to the time of confusion of v and b; and this fact, while not at all impairing their testimony when they represent v by ου, is strong against its trustworthiness when writing β. For there is no apparent reason why a copyist, if he found β written, should have changed it to ου, while the change of ου (for consonantal v) into β would be in accordance with the tendencies either of pronunciation itself or of its expression. A reference to Benseler's lexicon will shew at once a number of words, written earlier with ου, which in Byzantine writers received a β. Or look to the names of consuls, &c. given from various authorities side by side in the *Corpus Inscript. Latin.* I. 483 sqq., and it will be seen how persistently the *Chronicon Paschale* of the 7th century

---

[1] Schleicher (*Deutsche Sprache*, p. 212, ed. 2) says: 'b and g we 'write in accordance with the old language, but pronounce these sounds, 'when medial, between vowels, as w and [voiced] ch, consequently as 'spirants not as momentary sounds...e.g. *graben*, *sagen*, as *grâwen*, '*sâchen*...The b also in the combinations lb, rb is pronounced as w: 'e.g. in *gelber*, *farbe*, but not when the l and b belong to different 'words, e.g. *stulbein*, *harbeutel*.'

writes β where Dionysius or Diodorus or Dio has ου, and how often the v of the Inscriptions gives place in the Latin of the 4th century to b; e. g. **Calvus** to **Calbus**, &c.

Again, the MSS. of the New Testament, are, I believe, the earliest MSS. existing (except some papyri and the Herculaneum rolls), and the following facts may therefore be of use. The name **Silvanus** occurs four times (2 Cor. i. 19; 1 Thess. i. 1; 2 Thess. i. 1; 1 Pet. v. 12). In St Peter Vat. alone (against Sinait. Alex.) has Σιλβανος. In St Paul Vat. like the rest (and Ephr. in 2 Cor., being lost in 1, 2 Thess.) has Σιλουανος: two bilingual MSS. Clar. Boern. (cent. 6 and 9) with the transcripts Sang. Aug. and (once) the second hand of No. 67, are the only MSS. late or early, as Mr Hort informs me, which are known to spell the word with β. The Latin version of Clar. (though not of Boern.) has **Silbanus**. The solitary instance of Σιλβανος in the Vatican is probably (as Mr Hort suggests) only one of several indications of the Vatican scribe being familiar with Latin; the confusion of v and b being common in early as well as late Latin biblical MSS.; e. g. the Codex Vercellensis of the Gospels (middle of 4th cent,; i. e. same date as the Vatican).

[Dittenberger, who has written two interesting papers on the representations of Roman names in Greek inscriptions, says on this point (*Hermes* VI. 303) 'ου is older' than β as a representative of v 'and in republican times is found almost exclusively, whereas β. 'comes most into use later, without however ever getting completely 'the upper hand; for even in Constantine's time there are inscriptions 'in which Latin v is represented by ου.' The only instances of β which he mentions are Βαλεριος (Attic. 2nd cent. B.C.); Βιβια for **Vibia** (at Delphi); Φουλβιος (Naples, 71 B.C.) once, against two instances of initial and three of medial ου in the same inscription; Λαιβιλλος (Ephesus, not before Hadrian's time) with Ουειβιον and Ουαρον in same inscriptions. The name of **Varus**, he adds, is commonly Ουηρος, much less frequently Βηρος. On the other hand, in Italian inscriptions not uncommonly, but in those only, occurs Σεουαστος for Σεβαστος.]

What then was the value of β? Not, I think, that of the labiodental **v**. For the only argument that is brought for this value is that it has this value in modern Greek. I do not doubt that some

Greek speakers give it this sound, but I am not disposed to admit that all those who think they hear this sound are right. The truth is there is a labial **f** and **v**, as well as a labio-dental **f** and **v**, and by those who are not familiar with the labial the sound is often taken for that of the labio-dental. Mr Ellis (p. 518) says of an eminent modern Greek, ' The letters β, φ seem to be naturally pronounced ' by Prof. Valetta as a labial **v** and **f**, but when he became particularly ' emphatic he made them the labio-dental **v** and **f**.' Mr Geldart (*Journ. of Philology* for 1869, II. p. 159) says, 'β is pronounced in ' Greece not like our **v** but like the German **w**, only much more ' strongly and explosively, if one may use the word. It is not ' sounded by bringing together the lower lip and the upper teeth, ' but by compressing the two lips together. So too φ, and the con- ' sonantal sound of **v**. are pure lip-letters, and very different in ' point of formation from **f** or **v**.' (See also Appendix A. xviii.) It is obvious that a sound like this stands in at least as close a relation to the English **w** as to the English **v**.

Here then we meet with a solution of the difficulties presented by the confusion of Latin **v** with **b**, by the occasional representation of Latin **v** by β, and by the historical substitution of the labio-dental **v** in the Romance languages for the Latin **v**. The phonetic pedigree of the Romance **v** might be at once stated as: 1. **u** vowel; 2. French **ou**, pronounced as in **oui**; 3. English **w**; 4. Labial **v**; 5. Labio-dental **v**. But I do not assert that this represents an historical succession in a single line. It is very probable that the labial **v** existed dialectically in Italy (and probably in Greece) in classical times, and that this accounts for such instances of the tran-
xli scription of Latin **v** by β, as may be really the writing of Polybius, Dionysius of Halicarnassus, and others[1] (e.g. Βέσβιον ὄρος for **Vesuvius**[2]), and such vacillation in names of places as may be really due to the ancient authors (e.g. **Labici**, Cic. *Agr.* 2.35; so also Greek writers generally; but **Lavici**, Liv. 2, 39; 3, 25; 4, 45). In and after

[1] Some few instances in inscriptions between the battle of Actium and the end of the 4th century p. Chr. are mentioned by Franz (*Elem. Epigraph. Græc.* 'p. 248). I have not the means now for further inquiry. [See above, p. xli.]

[2] [The Neapolitan dialect of modern Italian is characterised among other things by ' its extremely frequent interchange of **b** and **v**.' (Diez, *Gram.* I. 83.)]

the 3rd century this sound encroached upon the domain of the **w** [and **b**], and rendered e.g. **verba** indistinguishable from **berba**. But because the Greek β may very possibly have had this sound, and may have been used for Latin **v**, it does not follow that Latin **v** had this sound, but only that in the want of an exact representative β came near enough to be used. I see no reason whatever for supposing that in classical times educated persons pronounced the letter **v** (**u**) (except in certain positions) otherwise than as the vowel **oo**, either with a pause after it, or running on to a succeeding vowel, (as in French **oui**,) or as English **w**. The first of these modes was the usual sound of **v** when called a vowel, the third when called a consonant. After **q** it may have been a mere sign of the labialisation of the guttural, an effect which most people would not distinguish from **w**. And possibly the same may be its purport sometimes after **g, l, r, s**. (See §§ 89 ; 94, 2, and Append. A. xx.—xxii.) With a short **i** following, **qv** made a sound which the Greeks represented by κυ, i.e. κ followed by the 12th vowel (see below). The rise of **b** out of **v** in a few cases is noted in § 76, and this was probably negotiated by a labial **v**, which perished in the transaction.

Corssen appears to think such a sound as the Engl. **w** to be too weak for **v** generally, and points to its having expelled the preceding consonant in some words. But the words in which this took place, leaving evidence in historical Latin behind it, are very few[1], **viginti** from **duo** (§ 76), **nivis** from **nigv-is**, shown by **ninguit** and **nix**, **vixi** compared with **vivo** (§ 129), possibly **reduvia** with **ungvis**. Others are evidenced only by comparison with Greek or Sanskrit stems. That these changes may have been produced by the mediation of a labial **v** is likely enough, but they seem to me to be part or rem- xlii nants of the changes which constituted the separation of the Latin language from its common stock, and to prove nothing for the pronunciation of **v** in the days of Cicero and Quintilian, unless indeed *guard* (once, I suppose, pronounced *gward*) compared with *ward*, &c. shews that **w** is in English pronounced as **v**. That Corssen should also consider (*Aussprache*, I. 315) the omission of **v** in such words as **sos** for **suos**, **savium** compared with **svavium**, &c.,

---

[1] Corssen does not mention such words as **sēvoco, seviri** ; and they are only instances of the usual habit of **sed, sex**; see §§ 93, 2 ; 113.

or the absorption of v in fautor for favitor, nuper for novum per, as proofs that v had not a 'weak vowel sound like the English w,' but a consonantal tone like the Germ. w[1], is to me very surprising. I draw the precisely opposite inference. (See above, 5, p. xxxiv.)

[Mr A. J. Ellis has written in the *Academy* for 15 Jan. 1872[2] a very interesting paper on the letter v, to which I am desirous of directing my readers' attention, as containing a great deal of authentic information and the results of an almost unrivalled power of phonetic discrimination in reference to this subject. He points out that, whereas, when oo is followed by another vowel, English speakers naturally pronounce a w, other nations do not; Italian *uomo, uopo,* and French *ouais, ouate, ouest, oui* being distinguishable by an attentive hearer from English *wa(r)m, wa(r)p, way, wattle, west, we.* The case of oo before a vowel is parallel to that of ee. 'The initial short and stressless elements ee, oo do not occur at the 'ccmmencement of diphthongs in English, as to my ears they do in 'Welsh[3], and as they may once have done in Latin. Those nations 'who use short ee, oo habitually give them consonantal syllabic value.' He objects to the notion, that Latin v was equivalent to English w, mainly on the ground that it is, so far as he knows, not familiar to the lips of any European people except the English. 'The final 'inference would seem to be that I, V (in Latin) should be considered 'as vowels capable of becoming the stressless elements of diphthongs, 'so long as II, VV initial are not found; that after these were found '(and probably some time before they crept into writing, which 'always lags after speech) y and labial v were employed, when I, V 'were the initial (not the *final*) stressless elements of diphthongs;

---

[1] Corssen means by the Germ. w the labio-dental English v. The *south* Germ. w is, according to Mr Ellis, the labial v (see App. A. xviii.). But this is not known to all Germans, though Rumpelt (*Deutsch. Gram.* I. 322—327 note) seems groping for it. See also p. 319, where he argues for the old high German w or uu having had the sound of English w.

[2] Prof. M. Müller's remarks in *Acad.* 15 Dec. 1871, and the reply of Prof. Munro in *Acad.* 1 Jan. 1872, should also be read.

[3] 'In ia, ie, io initial, Welshmen conceive that they pronounce ya, 'ye, yo, and similarly in wi, wy they believe they say (Engl.) we, wy. 'This is doubtful to me, because of the difficulty all Welshmen expe- 'rience at first in saying ye, woo, which they generally reduce to e, oo.' Ellis, *Engl. Pron.* p. 746 n.

'and that later in some words, especially in provincial pronuncia-
'tion, y passed into dzh (English j) in Gaul (subsequently French j)
'and parts of Italy, and gh (Spanish j) in Spain; that v either
'remained provincially as labial v, or became dentalised into labio-
'dental v as being the firmer form and corresponding to the fa-
'miliar f. But there seems to be no time during which English w
'can be interpolated. As a matter of practical convenience, English
'speakers should abstain from w in Latin, because no continental
'nation can adopt a sound they cannot pronounce. As a question
'of date, if the spelling vv is used, the pronunciation of labial v or
'labio-dental v at pleasure may be employed, most of the Germans
'taking labial v, and the rest of the world dental v.' (*Acad.* pp.
36, 39 somewhat abridged.)

I cannot say that the fact of w being a difficult and now rare or
non-existent sound in Southern Europe is to my mind decisive against
its having been the sound of Latin v in the time of Cicero. For
that sound, whatever it was, did (as Mr Ellis agrees in thinking)
historically give place to other sounds, and is not now the sound of
the character v either in Italy or in France at least. And I can
detect nothing in English inconsistent with Roman phenomena, and
a great deal wonderfully identical. At the same time such a pronunciation as *ou* in French *oui* does apparently correspond equally
well with the early Roman phenomena; and it has existing Southern
usage in its favour as against English w. And I am quite content
to think that a labial v was provincially contemporary and in the
end generally superseded it. (This really differs little from what I
have said before; see §§ 61, 88 and supr. pp. xlii. xliii.) But "as a
matter of practical convenience," I venture to give a different
recommendation from Mr Ellis. I am confident that the labio-
dental v is a very misleading pronunciation of Latin v, and wholly
inconsistent with the Roman phenomena until some late period[1].
English people will practically be very near the truth, if they pronounce v in Latin for some centuries after Christ as w. If the
French pronounce it as ou (in *oui*), the Italians as u (in *uomo*), and the

[1] Comp. Prof. Munro, *Acad.* 1 Jan. 1872, p. 17: 'Let Latin v be
'English or South-German w, or the French ou in oui, only not English
'or Romance v.'

Germans as labial **v**, there will probably be no greater difference than was often heard in the streets of Rome in the days of Cicero. The close resemblance of English **w** to these French and Italian sounds is shewn most strongly by the existing doubt as to whether Welsh **w** is a vowel or a consonant, and by the uncertainty of English orthoepists to which class to refer English **w** (Ellis, *Eng. Pron.* p. 185). Its close resemblance to labial **v** will not be doubted by those who hear a South German pronounce English words. If the English hearer expects a **v**, he thinks he hears a **w**; if he expects a **w**, there is difference enough to make him think he hears a **v**.]

On F.

On the sound of **f** I have already spoken (p. xxxvi).

The facts adduced in this first book and in § 766 of the third book would be almost enough to shew that **f** was not a sound of the Indo-European original alphabet, but of a much later and more special source. The number of words, in which it occurs as initial, is not very large, but the number in which it occurs, as initial of a suffix or after a vowel, is exceedingly small—four or five only. (Of course compounds must for such a purpose be separated into their members; e.g. in **æstifer f** is *initial*.) A few more are named by Corssen (*Krit. Nachtr.* p. 193 sqq. *Aussprache*, I. 140 sqq. ed. 2), e.g. **Alfius, Orfius, Ufens, Aufidus**, but these are proper names and probably not Latin. Certainly such a rare occurrence of **f** in suffixes goes far to shew that the sound did not exist at the time when these suffixes first assumed shape and use. It may well be that -**bro** is of the same stock as **ferre** *to bear*, but, if so, they are collateral relatives, and -**bro** is the earlier of the two. Similarly the verbal tense-suffixes -**bam**, -**bo**, &c., the derivative noun-suffixes -**bulo**, -**bili**, -**bo**, the case-suffix -**bi** in **tibi**, -**bis** in **nobis, vobis**, -**bus** xliii in nouns, may very possibly have correspondents in Latin (or Umbrian or Oscan[1]) beginning with **f**, but I should be inclined to

---

[1] Is it certain that the signs in Umbrian, Oscan, &c., for which we write **f**, had the sound which we ascribe to the Latin **f**, and not rather a labial sound? [Compare what Mr Ellis says (*Acad.* 15 Jan. 1872): 'After some recent experience I feel doubtful of all assertions respecting 'f as well as **v**. Certainly **f** is a comparatively rare sound, and labial **f** 'may prove more common than is generally supposed.']

regard such words with **f** as in a collateral not a parental relation to those with **b**. And thus **amavi** would not be for **ama-fui**, but it may contain a suffix from the same root as **fui**.

On C before æ, e, i, &c.

That **c** before **e** or **i** was in Latin not pronounced as either Engl. **ch**, i.e. **tsh** (so in Italian), nor as **s** (so in French and English), nor as **ts** (so in German), nor in fact noticeably different from **k**, may be inferred from the following arguments.

1. Closely connected forms exhibit perpetual alterations of the letter following **e**, without any sign of a variance in the sound of **c** when followed by **e** or **i**. Can Vergil in writing **replictus**, instead of the usual **replicitus**, have made so great a change as hardening **s** or **sh** or **ch** into **k**? If a final **e** be omitted, could the effect have been to harden these dentals or palatals into **k**? Yet **dic, duc, sic, hunc** stand for **dīce, dūce, sīce, hunce**. **Hosce** is common, but is never abbreviated into **hosc**: that is to say, **c** is frequently added when it would, if a sibilant, be indistinguishable, it is not added, when its presence would have been audible! Can **decem** have been pronounced **dechem** or **detsem** or **desem**, and yet its derivative ordinal have been sounded **dekumus**, and then, at the same time with that, **dechimus**, &c.? **Kailius** became **Cælius**: did the **c** change its sound when the diphthong **ai** was changed into the diphthong **ae**? or did it wait until the diphthong **ae** gave place to the single vowel **e** (§ 262)? Compare **audacter** (Quint. I. 6, § 17) with **audaciter**; **difficulter** and **difficultas** with **difficile**; **capio, recipio, cepi, captum, receptum**; **cano, cecini**; **acer, acris**; **locus, loci, loco, locŭlus, locellus**; **lacus** with its genitives **laci** and **lacus**, and dat. pl. **lacŭbus** and **lacĭbus**; **piscis, pisciculus, piscosus**; **qverqvetum** with **qvercetum**; **præqvoquis** contracted into **præcox**, and **præcox** with its genitive **præcocis**; **fax** with its old nom. **faces**; &c. I am aware that the substitution of a guttural for a palatal (**dic** = **dik**, for **dice** = **diche**) may be paralleled xliv from Sanskrit *as now pronounced*, but the change of sound is marked by a change of letter, and the palatal letters are not dependent for their sound on one vowel rather than another. But in classical Latin the change supposed is not justified, so far as I know, by any

analogy. Changes of consonantal sounds are frequent, but they are rarely caused by any change of the subsequent vowel: and the change of sound is frequently shewn by a change of the spelling, e.g. in **veh-ere**, **vec-tum**, which is the nearest analogy that I know.

2. The letter c was used in early times in words which were afterwards spelt, some with c, others with g; and some instances of this use remain in early inscriptions (see §§ 56, 104). Whether these words were at the time pronounced with the flat guttural, or whether the sharp and flat guttural were not clearly distinguished (cf. App. A. vii.), it is not easy to say. But k was also in use, and is found in a few inscriptions, generally before a, but also before o, and (in one inscription regarded on this account by Mommsen as Græcising) before e; e.g. **kalendas, korano, dekembres**; and it was the regular abbreviation for the prænomen **Kæso** and for **kalendas** (§ 103). It is not likely that, if c before e and i was pronounced otherwise than before a, o, and u, no attempt should have been made to retain k for the guttural. Yet such an idea does not appear to have occurred to any of the reformers of Latin orthography—neither to Accius nor to Lucilius nor to Claudius Cæsar, in the name of each of whom (see however § 946 n.) c occurs before one of these supposed influential vowels. Quintilian (I. 7, § 10) speaks of the desire on the part of some grammarians to write k before a, (not before o and u also,) but his remark on this seems clearly to imply that c had but one sound. "**k** quidem in nullis verbis utendum puto, nisi quæ significat, etiam ut sola ponatur. Hoc eo non omisi, quod quidam eam, quotiens a sequatur, necessariam credunt, cum sit c littera quæ ad omnes vocales vim suam proferat." *'k should not in my opinion be used in any word except in those for which it can stand by itself as an abbreviation. I mention this because of the opinion of some persons that* k *must be used if the vowel* a *follow it, though* c *is a letter the sound of which is heard before all vowels.'*

3. But with these facts must be considered, in order that xlv their full force may be seen, the fact that there is no hint in any ancient writer whatever of c having more than one sound, since the early times mentioned in the last paragraph (Schneider, *Lat. Gr.* I. 244, 247; Corssen, *Aussprache*, I. 48). And this is the more remarkable, because there are many parts of their writings in which

such a variety of sound could hardly help being noticed, if it had existed. For instance Quintilian (1. 4, §§ 7—9) first refers to the discussion of the grammarians whether the Romans lacked some necessary letters, and then to the counter question whether some were superfluous, and speaks of k and q. In 7 § 28 he is speaking expressly of what is written one way and pronounced another, and instances this very letter c as used to denote **Gnæus** (cf. infr. § 104). Terentianus Maurus (who is generally thought to have lived at end of 3rd century p. Chr.), referring to the fact that the names of the three letters c, k, q contained each a different vowel (ce, ka, qu; comp. App. A. xxiii.), says expressly, as I understand him, that k and q are alike in sound and are both superfluous, because it matters not whether c, k, or q be used, whichever of the vowels follow (vv. 204—209)[1].

See also Diomed. pp. 423, 424, ed. Keil; Priscian Inst. 1. 14. 17; pp. 12, 13, ed. Hertz; Servius, p. 422, ed. Keil; Pompeius, v. 110, ed. Keil; Max. Vict. p. 1945, Putsche; and others quoted in Schneider, *Lat. Gr.* 1. p. 292 sqq.

4. c is invariably represented in Greek transliteration by κ, be the vowel that follows what it may; and κ is invariably represented by Latin c[2]. Now Greek κ has never been, and is not either

---

[1] The lines stand thus in Lachmann's edition, but the whole passage, beginning at v. 85, should be read:

> k perspicuum est littera quod vacare possit;
> et q similis, namque eadem vis in utraque est;
> quia qui locus est primitus unde exoritur c,
> quascunque deinceps libeat jugare voces,
> mutare necesse est sonitum quidem supremum,
> refert nihilum, k prior an q siet an c.

i. e. *Whatever vowels you please to utter after forming the guttural contact for* c, *you must change accordingly the last part of the sound* (*i.e. the vowel part of the syllable* ca, cu, ce &c.), *but it matters not whether the former part (i. e. the consonant) be* k *or* q *or* c. [Marius Victorinus in the passage (1. 6) quoted by Prof. M. Müller (*Acad.* 15 Dec. 1871) had this passage of Terentianus before him. Both, I think, in the words 'supremum sonitum (sonum)' are referring, not to the opening of the organs as distinguished from the closing of them in the pronunciation of mutes, but to the names of the letters, which were symbols of the pronunciation. (See § 57). In Marius 'distento rictu' refers to the vowel a (in ka), 'producto rictu' to the vowel u (in qu).]

[2] Except possibly in a few early words, the spelling of which may be accounted for from c being once the common sign of both the sharp and flat guttural.

d

xlvi palatalised or assibilated before any vowel, but is the sharp guttural mute[1].

Against this argument it may be urged that as the Latin c coincided in sound with κ before a, o, u, it was only natural for the Greeks to use κ for c before e and i, unless the sound before e or i was clearly different from the sound of κ and was readily expressible by some other Greek letter[2].

Now the actual sounds given to c before e or i in words derived from Latin are (1) Engl. ch (= tsh) by the Italians and Wallachians. (2) Engl. th (sharp) by the Spaniards. (3) s (sharp) by the other Romance peoples (and the English). (4) The Germans pronounce it in Latin words as ts. Further it may be argued on physiological grounds that it may have been sounded as ky, or Germ. ch, or sh; these being possible mediating sounds between the sharp guttural mute and the various existing sounds of Latin c. (See v. Raumer, *Gesam. Schriften*, pp. 40—43, 90—95; Schuchardt, I. 164; Ellis, p. 204, quoted in App. A. xxv.; Max Müller in *Academy* for Feb. 15, 1871.) Could these sounds have been represented in Greek?

The sound of s could easily and accurately have been expressed by Greek σ.

sh could be expressed by either σ, σσ or σι (cf. Mullach, *Gram. d. Griech. Vulgarsprache*, p. 115).

th (sharp) would be expressed far more nearly by σ than by κ. The sound of sharp th is now expressed in modern Greek by θ, but it is not clear when θ first obtained this sound.

ts could easily be expressed by τσ or τζ (see below). I regard this value for Latin c, until at least some very late period, as utterly inadmissible. No combination was so thoroughly alien to the Romans, who never tolerated a dental mute before a sibilant in the

---

[1] The Tzakonians say τζε for και (see below, p. li.). Mr D. Bikelas (in the *Academy* for 15 March, 1871) says, 'in many of the Greek 'islands κ is pronounced like Italian c before the vowels ε, ι, v.'

[2] Prof. Max Müller says: 'Unless we admit that c in Cicero was 'pronounced either exactly like ζ or exactly like σ—and this nobody 'maintains—nothing remained to the Greeks but to use k as the nearest 'approach to the modified c.' Surely this is going too far. He himself explains the fact that the Germans wrote z or tz for c, as proving, not that z or tz was the exact pronunciation of c, but that they came nearer to c than did the Germ. k, or ch. (*Academy*, 15 Feb. 1871, p. 146.)

same word. (**Etsi** is of course two words.) Nor did the Greeks xlvii either.

Germ. **ch** is a sound which, so far as I know, has never yet been actually proposed as a value of Latin **c** before **e** and **i**. In modern Greek χ expresses it exactly, but χ is not generally supposed to have had this sound, at any rate till late Imperial times (cf. Curtius, *Gr. Etym.* p. 371, ed. 2). It is enough for the present to wait till some spark of evidence for such a sound is produced. It can never be a formidable claimant.

Engl. **ch** = **tsh** was expressed in Greek by τζ by Procopius in the sixth century p. Chr. (in the word τζουρουλόν, now *Tchorlu*, and others in Benseler's Lexicon), and probably in the Ravenna documents of the same time, e.g. ακτζιο, δονατζιονες, for **actio, donationes** (Corssen, I. 65 sq.; Ellis, p. 529). So in modern Greek τζ is used to represent either **ts**, or **sh**, or **tsh** (Engl. **ch**) or **zh**, i.e. French **j** (Mullach, p. 115). Compare the Tzakonian dialect, Mullach, p. 94 sqq., M. Schmidt in Curtius *Studien*, III. 349. Prof. Max Muller objects to the supposition of ζ having been possible, 'because ζ was 'looked upon as a double consonant, and in the middle of a word 'would have made a preceding short vowel long.' This argument is no doubt good in reference to verse in the Augustan age: I am not sure of its being applicable to prose even then, if **ci** had really been sounded as **chi**, and I believe it has little or no weight as applied to transliteration in the 2nd or 3rd century, when yet κ represented **c**. (See Prof. Munro's account of an Algerian inscription in Donaldson's *Varronianus*, p. 522, ed. 3; Mullach, p. 71; Luc. Müller's 2nd Appendix to his *De re metrica*.) But is not the prosodiacal argument as good against the supposition of **ci** being = **tshi**, as it is against its being represented by ζ? (cf. v. Raumer, p. 40); and is there any trace whatever of a tendency, at a time when quantity was felt, to make the first syllable in e. g. **cecidi** long?

There remains one theoretical sound for **ce**, viz. **kye**. Here it is necessary to discriminate. It is possible I believe to articulate **ke** at the same part of the mouth as **ka**, but neither English nor Germans nor, so far as I know, any other European people do so. **ke** is palatal and **ka** is guttural, but the difference is imperceptible. But the real question is, had Latin **ke** either a full **y** sound or a slight **y** sound, such as is sometimes heard in Engl. *kind, card*? Mr Ellis

xlviii several times (e.g. p. 525, comp. 204) suggests that it had, but he
nowhere defines the time to which he is referring, and he seems to
think the distinction of **ke** and **kye** is too slight for us to rely upon
its being noticed. I can only say that the distinction is one which
seems to me obvious enough, far more obvious than many which I
find noticed by Roman grammarians; and I cannot trust my ear
or tongue to find or make any clear distinction between sounds
which Ellis discriminates, viz. a palatalised **k** (as heard in the occasional pronunciation of *kind*, &c.) and a full **ky**. But be that as it
may, if the distinction was not obvious, surely we need not trouble
ourselves about it; if it was, then would not the Greek $\kappa\iota$ have
been a tolerable representative? Yet no Greek gives us $\kappa\iota\eta\nu\sigma\omega\rho$
for censor, or $K\iota\kappa\epsilon\rho\omega\nu$ for Cicero.

5. Latin **c** was represented by Gothic **k**, and the early Latin
words, received into High German, were all spelt with a **k**, whatever vowel followed; e.g. **Cæsar**, *Kaiser;* **carcer**, Goth. *karkara,*
Germ. *kerker*. Later adoptions into German were spelt differently,
e.g. **census**, Germ. *zins;* **cancelli**, Germ. *chanzella*, &c. (Prof.
Max Müller accounts for this as due to the early poverty of the
German alphabet, not to the identity or similarity of the sounds; and
as regards Gothic, partly to this cause, partly to a (supposed) habit
of taking letter for letter without regard to distinctions of sound,
partly to the possibility of Ulfilas having received the words through
the Greek.)

But the argument most pressed, for **c** having sometimes a different
sound from **k**, is the confusion which existed between **ci** before a
vowel and **ti** before a vowel. Now first, whatever force there may
be in this argument, it is one which cannot justify our attributing
an altered sound of **c** to **ce**, **ci**, &c. when before a consonant.
Secondly, it seems tolerably clear (Corssen, I. 50—67) that many
instances of the miswriting are due to the confusion not of two
sounds but of two distinct suffixes **-cio, -tio**; and that there is no probable instance of **ti** for **ci** before at least the end of the 4th century
p. Chr.; and only seven instances of **ci** for **ti** in inscriptions before
the 7th century p. Chr.[1] Further, of these seven instances, three

---

[1] Corssen points out (II. p. 1003) that Mommsen speaks to the
same purport (Liv. *Cod. Veron.* p. 175). 'Numquam in libro Vero-

(periciæ, ocio, prudencius) are not of early times, and are given by
collectors who lived at a time when the spelling ocio at least was
usual; one (renunciationem) is from a notoriously bad collector: a
fifth (disposicionem) is from a late Neapolitan inscription containing several misspelt words[1]; the remaining two (terminac[iones],
defenciones) are from an inscription at Medjana in Africa of the
time of Alexander Severus (222—235 p. Chr.). Even if these last
be rightly copied, (which is not certain,) an inference from African
spelling or pronunciation in the 3rd century to ordinary Roman
spelling and pronunciation in (say) the Augustan age would be
about as justifiable as an inference from the usage of words or
constructions in Apuleius or Tertullian to that of Cicero or
Quintilian. It is curious that the grammarian (Pompeius), whom
Prof. Max Müller quotes as his authority for saying that ' we
' know for certain that in the 5th century it was considered wrong
' not to assibilate ti before a vowel,' was also an African, from
Mauretania, and as regards his age all that is tolerably certain is
that he did not live before the 5th century, and not later than the
end of the 7th century (Keil, *Gram. Lat.* v. p. 93. See also
Teuffel, *Gesch. d. Röm. Litt.* p. 982). And again, another African,
Commodianus, of the 3rd century, has in an acrostic the word *cum*
for the initial word of the line which is to give the last letter but
three of concupiscen*t*iae[2] (L. Müller, *De re metr.* p. 262, quoted by
Corssen, II. 1003).

　　Thirdly, what does this confusion really prove as to the pronunciation of ci before a vowel, at the time, be it what it may,
when the confusion existed? Prof. M. Müller says: ' The only
' point where these two letters (c and t) can possibly meet is the
' assibilation. Ti may go as far as tsi, but unless ki also went as
' far as tshi, the two could not have met, and no Roman whether in
' Italy or Africa could have attempted to write renuntiatio by

nensi commutatas reperies litteras c et t, quod qui ante septimum
sæculum obtinuisse sibi persuadent, ne (*assuredly*) ii vehementer errant.'
[See also to the same effect Mommsen's Preface to his edition of the
Digest, p. xl.]
　　[1] Some of these remarks are due to Prof. Munro's pamphlet.
' [2]. Prof. Munro tells me that this line should be read, ' Tum pro die
tuo vigila,' in order to harmonize with the imperatives and antitheses
before and after. [Haupt has independently made the same correction.]

'renunciatio' (*Academy*, p. 146). I reply (1) by referring to Prof. Müller's instructive Lectures, II. p. 168, where, quoting Marsh, he says, 'We are told by careful observers that the lower classes in '(French) Canada habitually confound t and k, and say *mékier*, '*moikié* for *métier*, *moitié*.' Quintilian (if the MSS are correct, I. II. 5, ed. Halm) speaks of that 'fault of pronunciation by which 'c and g are softened into t and d' (comp. Schuchardt, III. 81, sq.). (2) I refer to an authority whom Prof. Müller will respect—Mr Ellis (quoted in App. A. xxv.), who explains distinctly how the confusion of t with c arises, and in the stage of ky, ty, *before* either is assibilated; and v. Raumer (who seems to me to have inspired M. Muller in his argument generally) says the same (*Gesam. Schriften*, p. 92). (3) I venture to go still farther, and, while fully admitting the theoretical possibility of palatalised k and t (ky, ty) having been the mediator between ce, ci and the modern assibilated pronunciations, such as s, ts, or th, I hesitate as to its reality. For, as Corssen says (I. 49), there is not a spark of positive evidence for it: and, if c once became t, the change of t to s is far too common a phenomenon in Latin to *necessitate* an explanation, which applies only to t before i (cf. § 191 and infr. p. lxii.). It must be remembered that the palatalisation of c into ch = sh in French is before the vowel a[1]. (Diez, I. 249, considers here the intermediate step to have been a guttural aspirate, Germ. ch.)

To sum up; as there is not one particle of trustworthy evidence, before at least the fifth or sixth century, for any other pronunciation of c than that of the sharp guttural, except the few reminiscences of the sound of g, two African inscriptions, and the [doubtful text of the] African acrostic of the 3rd century with the doubtful inferences deduced from them, I am unable to see how it can be any defence of so thoroughly confusing a pronunciation of the Latin of Cicero and Quintilian, as arises from sounding c as s, that it is theoretically possible for the Romans to have made a difference in ci compared with ca, which was yet so small that no grammarian noticed it, and no writer attempted to express it.

---

[1] So in English the pronunciation of c as ky took place only (?) before a; e. g. *card*, *kind* (= *kyaind*), *sky* (= *skyai*).

On g before æ, e and i.

That g in Latin was not pronounced as English j (= dzh), and that it was always hard before all vowels, may be inferred from the following arguments. (Compare also the discussion of the sound of c before the like vowels.)

1. Closely connected forms exhibit perpetual alterations of the vowel following g, without any evidence of a desire to change g before e or i; e.g. malignus for maligenus; gigno for gigeno; tegmen for tegimen; tignum compared with tigillum, &c. Similarly rego, regis, regit becomes rectum (for regtum); reg- makes regis, regi, regum, regulus, and rex (for reg-s, rec-s); ager, agri; fuga, fugæ, fugax, fugio, fugitivus.

2. In Greek g is always represented by γ; and γ is represented by g. It is true in modern Greek γ before ε and ι is Eng. y; but it is by no means certain when γ first gained this sound. And moreover the sound of y is not that of Engl. j.

3. There is no trace to be found in the grammarians of any different sound of g before the several vowels. This is the more noticeable, because they speak of the effect of g and c, upon a preceding n, in converting the dental into the guttural nasal. But they make no allusion to any difference in the g. Yet the instances adduced contain the lingual as well as the labial vowels, e.g. angvis, ingenuus, anceps, Longinus, angulus, angens. It is no doubt not impossible that this change in the sound of n should be made before palatals such as Engl. ch and j; but we do not make it in English. I infer that the Latins had (in these cases at least, and if in these, why not in others?) c and g hard, whether e and i, or a, o, u followed.

4. There is no evidence of g having such a sound as Engl. j before the 4th or 5th century p. Chr., according to Schuchardt; before the 5th century, according to Corssen. Diez (I. 268) infers from the Anglo-Saxon alphabet that g was the guttural flat mute up to the 7th century. The omission of g before i, in major for magior, does not appear to imply the assibilation of g. For it takes place

lii before **v** as much as before **i**, e.g. **nivis** for **nigvis**, **malo** for **magvolo**; and **g** is too commonly omitted before consonants to make its omission before semiconsonants unnatural. There is evidence in the 4th and 5th centuries of its having the sound of Engl. **y** (=ɟ), e.g. **magestates** for **majestates**, βειεντι for **viginti**. Possibly this sound of **g** may have existed dialectically earlier.

On dentals; especially **ti** before a vowel.

On the pronunciation of **ti** we have a distinct statement by Isidore in the beginning of the 7th century p. Chr., viz. that before a vowel **tia** should be sounded as **zia**. And Pompeius (v. pp. 104, 286, ed. Keil) and Consentius (v. p. 395, ed. Keil) appear to say the same. But these are apparently not much, if at all, earlier witnesses; and accordingly **donationem, donationes,** are represented in Ravenna Greek of the 6th century by δωναζιονεμ, δονατζιονες. And since the 6th century, according to Corssen, instances occur of a similar assibilation, in which the **i** was not preserved, e.g. **constantso, constanzo** are written for **constantio.** Schuchardt (I. 104. 150) thinks that assibilation began as early as the 2nd century p. Chr., but did not become general till a much later period. In Umbrian and Oscan it appeared before the first Punic War, and the origin of such forms as **formonsus** is probably to be found in **formontios** (see § 813). On **di** before a vowel see § 154.

A final **d** was often pronounced as **t** (§ 150); and Quintilian's words (I. 7, § 5) imply, I think, that there was no difference in the pronunciation of **ad** and **at**, though the difference in spelling appears to have continued long. But **d** is rarely final (§ 155), and Velius Longus (beginning of 2nd cent. p. Chr.) speaks of **apud** and **sed** being pronounced with **d** (p. 2231, Putsche).

Mr Munro calls attention to the fact that the continental **t** (and therefore of course **d**) is more dental than with us. Mr Ellis (*Phil. Soc. Trans.* 1867, *Suppl.* p. 12) describes the European dental as formed by pressing the tongue against the teeth, whereas in English the tongue scarcely reaches the gums. (See however *Eng. Pron.* p. 477, n.) But I do not think this can affect the question of the

interchange of **d** and **t**. That interchange depended on the tendency ᴵⁱⁱⁱ
to drop the sound of the voice at the end of the word, as the
Germans do now, e.g. *unt* for *und* (Brücke, pp. 38. 46. See also
below, App. A. vii.).

On **bs**, **x**, **bt**, &c.

That **bs** is = **ps**, not **bz**, follows from the general law of Latin, that
the former of two consonants is made conformable to the latter, and
from the fact that **s** was the sharp hiss. Some instances are found
of **araps, urps, pleps** (Neue, I. p. 137).. Compare also **scribo,
scripsi, scriptum** (cf. § 78). Plutarch writes ἱερὸν ὀψεκουέντης
for **templum obseqventis** (*Fort. Rom.* 10).

Similarly **x** is for **ks**, not **gz**. Compare **rego, rexi, rectum.
Reg-si** first becomes **rec-si**, then is written **rexi**.

So also **obtulit** was pronounced **optulit**: **optimus** is for **ob-timus**,
(see Quint. I. 7. 7). And usually with the prepositions in composition, we shall be justified in thinking that, even where MSS. and
inscriptions vary much in their spelling, the assimilation, entire or
partial, was expressed in pronouncing; the spelling, as is natural,
oscillating between the claims of etymology and sound; e.g. **apparere,
adparere; imperium, inperium;** &c.

On **n** before gutturals; **gn.**

The pronunciation of **n** as **ng** before a guttural (**c, g, qu**) is clear
from Nigidius Figulus, *ap. Gell.* XIX. 14. 7. No mention is made of
the absorption of the **g**. And in the Greek to which it is compared
the γ is written twice, ἄγγελος.

Gn is (or was) in Germany, I believe, pronounced like **ng** + **n**, i.e.
dignus is sounded **ding-nus**. In Italian and French it is like **ny** in
din-yus. There appears to be no allusion to such pronunciations
in any of the Latin writers, although they frequently discuss **ng**.
This seems decisive against the above-named pronunciations of **gn**, at
least in the absence of any other evidence for them. (See Schneider,
Lat. Gr. I. 272; Corssen, II. 262, ed. 2; and below, p. lxxx.)

On s.

^{liv}   Corssen maintains (*Ausspr.* I. 294) that s had in Latin three sounds:

(1) Sharp (i.e. a hiss) as initial, and medial before and after other consonants, except n.

(2) Soft (i.e. flat = Engl. z) between two vowels, as now in the Romance tongues, and after n.

(3) Dull and faint at the end of words.

Of the sound of s as s sharp there is the strongest possible proof. For (*a*) it maintains its place before sharp consonants in st, sp, sq, sc, and it does not maintain its place before flat consonants, e.g. d, m, n, l, r (§ 193.2). And (*b*) it changed a flat consonant preceding it to a sharp. It may be said that consul, mons, ars show flat consonants preceding. But consul was abbreviated cos, which shows the evanescence of the n. Mons, ars (from stems monti-, arti-) are instances of the refusal of the Romans, when sacrificing something, to sacrifice all. The ti had already gone: it was necessary at least to write n and r to preserve the individuality of the words. But the pronunciation is a different thing. I conjecture that both n and r were in these cases *whispered*, not voiced (cf. App. A. viii.—x.). This necessity made the Romans unwilling to permit the retention of n and r, when there was no further reason. A whispered r exists in Icelandic (written hr, Ellis, p. 544). A similar whispered r may be presumed in words like prorsum, sursum, which became prosum, susum, by r assimilating to s. But that r as a general rule was voiced, appears clearly from its pathology and influence.

The third sound, attributed by Corssen to s, is inferred from the frequent omission of s in writing, and from its non-pronunciation in early verse (§ 193. 5). I do not know what precise sound Corssen means to give it, nor what it could have, different from s or z, but, this difficulty over, I have nothing to object.

But the second sound seems to me very doubtful. I cannot estimate properly the value of the argument from the Romance languages[1]. Their list of sounds is not so closely accordant with that

---

[1] Mr Payne (*Phil. Soc. Trans.* 1868—9, p. 419) doubts the s between two vowels having a z sound in French in the 13th or 14th centuries.

attributed either by Corssen or myself to the Romans, as to render lv
it necessary to suppose any identity of pronunciation in this case.
In Italian particularly s has a very different character from what it
had in Latin. Witness the combinations sb, sm, sg, sd, sn, sl, sr,
&c. There remain three other arguments which appear to me, if
they prove anything, to prove that s written was s sharp.

(1) The fact that r supplanted s in many words is justly adduced (p. 280) as a proof that s was in these words pronounced
like z. But why this should prove that s was pronounced as z in
other words, in which this change did not take place, is far from
clear. I draw exactly the opposite inference. If s had in these
words been pronounced like z, it would have passed to r as in
other words. This rhotacism swept over the language like an
epidemic, and seized those instances of s as its victims which were
predisposed to it by the sound; and it is surely most probable that
it seized all such. Reason for discrimination I see none.

(2) Another argument (p. 281) is that an s between two
vowels, which in some forms was changed to r, in other forms of
the same stem was omitted. I cannot see what this proves, except
that the flat s which changed to r was sometimes omitted. But
the question is, what was the sound of an s which was not omitted,
and which did not change to r?

(3) The last argument brought by Corssen (p. 284) is that s
after n was pronounced, in certain words at least, as if between
two vowels, the n being omitted, and, consequently, it would have
the ordinary sound of s between two vowels, i.e. z (see § 168. 3).
On this matter I would refer to the extract from Mr Bell given
in App. A. § v. It will be remembered that Cicero tells us that ns,
nf lengthened the preceding vowel (§ 167). Now s and f agree in
being voiceless continuous consonants. And voiceless consonants
are just those ' before which n is so short, as scarcely to add any
' appreciable quantity to the syllable.' I conclude from these facts that
s was a voiceless consonant in this case also; that the n was scarcely
audible; but that to compensate for this, the Romans lengthened
the preceding vowel, i.e. dwelt longer on the preceding vowel, to
signalize the fact of the syllable being more than the vowe + s.

lvi Greek transcriptions show that it was the *vowel*, not merely the syllable, that was lengthened.

[Mr Munro contends for s having had the flat sound 'in the 'comparatively few cases in which s not representing a real ss 'comes between two vowels.' He points to the fact that 'in 'Italian there are most suggestive exceptions to s being soft' (flat) 'between two vowels: in *cosa, riso*, etc.; and in the adjective ter-'mination -oso it is sounded, as' sharp s. 'The Italian too is strongly 'supported by late Greek; we find κασσος (casus), κουριοσσος '(curiosus), φαμωσσα (famossa), ἐξκουσσατος (excusatus), εξκουσ-'σατεύειν (excusare) and the like. What is the meaning of this σσ, 'if there was no difference between the s of casus (cassus) and căsa, 'of rosus (rossus) and rŏsa?" (*Few Remarks*, pp. 13 and 26.) If indeed the Italian representatives of all the words enumerated in § 193. 3. *c.*, which are not really referable to *a*, or *b* of that section, and if no other words with Latin s have a flat s between two vowels, the coincidence would be so striking as perhaps to justify Mr Munro's inference. I do not know whether this is so or not. An intimate knowledge of Italian in its whole development is requisite to enable due weight to be given to an argument from pronunciation which seems to spring over many centuries.]

Curtius has made the origin of the long vowel in the nominative case of certain classes of Greek substantives the subject of an instructive essay (as indeed all he writes is instructive), *Studien*, II. 159—175; and has put forth a theory of the pathology of these cases, which has considerable bearing on the Latin long vowel before **ns**, a fact which he naturally notices in this connexion. I am not sure that in setting out the different moments of the change from e.g. πατέρς to πατήρ, γνώμονς to γνώμων, φέροντς to φέρων, σαφέσς to σαφής (p. 169), he means to imply any chronological interval, even the smallest, between the stages of the change. But there seems to me to be an unreality about it, which makes me unable, at least without explanation, to adopt his theory. He describes the process thus: '**n, r, s** before a final s make the preceding 'vowel long; and thereby becoming weak themselves, run a risk of 'passing, as it were, into the preceding vowel, as is the case in the 'accusative plural (μούσας, musas, for μουσανς, musams). But in-'stead of so doing, they draw the following s to themselves, assi-

' milate it to themselves, take, as it were, the duration of the s, and
' so recover their full sound of **n, r, s.**' The unreality of this lies
first in speaking of **n, r, s** as going through successive stages of
weakness and recovery, and secondly in the notion of assimilation
itself.   The fact is, I suppose, that in Greek and Latin the vocal n
and voiceless s were incompatible.   The Latin generally, after its
wont, and the Greek in some instances (e. g. μούσας, δούς), made the
former of the two give way to the latter; **n** became voiceless, and
the vowel was lengthened by the involuntary dwelling upon it in
consciousness of the obscuration of one of the normal sounds of the
word.   In Greek generally the **n** won the day, and the so-called
assimilation of **ns** to **nn** is, in reality, the voice dwelling longer on
the **n** and not uttering the **s** at all, the previous vowel having been,
as before, prolonged in anticipation of the loss.   If I may use
metaphorical language, the voice may be said to lengthen the vowel
just as a leaper presses the ground more firmly before a spring.
The speaker is aware of a difficult combination of sounds approaching, and instinctively spreads the time required for the vowel
+ **n** + **s** over two of them, because he knows he cannot apportion it
strictly and preserve them all.

In Latin **homons** became **homos**, and the **s** was then dropped; lvii
partly perhaps, because otherwise a confusion with the acc. plur. of
o nouns would be imminent, partly from the slight hold a final s
had in the early language.   But in by far the majority of -**on** stems
(cf. §§ 449, 450) the **o** was naturally long.   The stems in -**r** and -**l**
(which were voiced consonants) repudiated the sharp nominative
sign **s**.   Stems in -**s** with a short preceding vowel and not neuter
are rare.   In some we have a long vowel in the nominative (e. g.
Cerēs, arbōs), in others a short vowel (e. g. **venŭs, vetŭs, lepŭs,
cinĭs**).   Of stems in -**t** with short vowel, only **abies, aries, paries**
lengthen it in nom. sing.

Origin of ss.

It passes now for a recognized and certain theory among most philologers that ss is in many words the result of a *progressive* assimilation (§ 31. n.). This assimilation is alleged in (*a*) the supine stem; and (*b*) in superlatives and ordinals. It is always assumed by Bopp, Curtius[1], Corssen, L. Meyer, Schleicher.

(*a*)   Corssen, who especially has defended this theory against all comers (*Beitr.* 419, 426 sq.), holds that, e.g. tond-tum became tons-tum, and then tons-sum, afterwards tonsum; and that in such cases as mer-sum, lap-sum, &c., where there is no dental at the end of the stem, the change of t to s is due to a false analogy.

Now to this theory there are, as it seems to me, two fatal objections: (1) tons-tum is a perfectly stable sound, and if this form had once arisen, no further change (except perhaps to tostum) would have occurred; (2) there is a *whole class* of stems forming their supine in -sum (§ 191. 3), for which the theory utterly fails to account.

I have not a word to say against the possibility of Corssen's first step; viz. that tond-tum became tons-tum. Neither Greeks nor Romans tolerated two dental mutes coming together. It was important to show the existence of the suffix, and yet tond-tum, if left to the ordinary law, would have become simply tont-tum, and the double t would have been sounded like one only. The Greeks therefore softened the former of the two mutes into s; e.g. ἀνυτ-τός, ἀνυστός; ἀδ-τέον, ἀστέον; πειθ-θῆναι, πεισθῆναι. (Curt. *Gr. Gr.* § 46. See also § 50.) The Romans also adopted this course in cases in which it was important to preserve the t (e.g. in est for edit (edt), *eats*); and where an r follows immediately, because an s immediately before an r is hardly pronounceable; e.g. tond-trix becomes tons-trix (not tond-srix, tonsrix); and compare mulctrum with mulsum. There is therefore nothing against, but much to favour, the first step of Corssen's theory, if dental stems only were concerned. Tond-tum, mit-tum may well have become tons-tum, mis-tum; but why should

lviii

---

[1] Curtius says, 'στ is in all Greek dialects one of the most favourite 'groups. I only know at the most of one instance of its passing into 'σ...The passage of st into s is in Latin as frequent as it is strange in 'Greek.' (*Studien*, I. 1, p. 241—2.)

any further change have occurred? If, as Curtius says (*Erläut. zu*
§ 147), 'it is a prevalent law of speech that difficult combinations
' of sounds are more bearable, if they have arisen from others yet
' more difficult, language setting limits to the change of sounds in
' order to make their origin more patent,' still less is it likely that,
when change has secured an easy combination, a causeless further
change should be made. The combination st is one of the com-
monest in the language[1]; e.g. **fastus, festus,** § 787; **arista, costa,
prætexta,** &c. § 788; **angustus, funestus,** &c. § 789; **astus, cæstus,**
&c. § 800; **fustis, hostis, pestis,** &c. § 803; **agrestis,** &c. § 808;
egestas, potestas, § 811; **equester, pedester,** &c. § 903; **post, ast;
ostendo, abstineo, sustento,** &c.; **est, estis; venisti, audisti,** &c.;
stella, sturnus, sto, sterno, antistes, &c. Nor, so far as I am aware,
is there a single clear instance of **st** passing into **ss** or **s**[2]. There is
no necessity whatever for assuming that os, ossis, or the old form
ossu, are formed from ὀστέον. The root of os may have had a **d** or
t; in which case this instance would only exemplify the very same
difference between the Greek and Roman method of dealing with
double dentals, which we are here discussing. Corssen indeed
brings forward **adgretus, egretus,** quoted by Festus as old forms of
the past participles; **comestum** is also found in one or two places[3]
as well as **comesum**; and ostensa is found as well as **ostenta.**
Now **adgretus** and **egretus** are of course, if genuine, simply in- lix
stances of the preservation of the starting-point common to all
theories: **comestum** is, I believe, the only instance of a perfectly

[1] Leo Meyer calls it 'a combination for which our languages
(i.e. Greek and Latin) have a general and strong predilection.' (*Vergl.
Gr.* I. 243.)
[2] Even in the later imperial times there seems little evidence of such
a change. See Schuchardt, I. 145. III. 75.
[3] [They are (see Neue, II. 442) Cato, *R.R.* 50, 'comesta' (but in 58
'comesæ'); Val. Max., 9, 12, Ext. 6; and the African physician (referred
by Teuffel to Hadrian's time) Cælius Aurel., *Chron.* II. 1. Priscian, X.
28, 30, quotes 'comestum' from Cic. *Clu.* 62, § 173, where the oldest
MS. has 'comesum.' Diomedes, pp. 363, 387, ed. Keil, condemns the
formation 'comestum,' but adds a quotation from an obscure 'Didius de
Sallustio, comesto patrimonio.' If this is the Declamatio in Sallust., the
MSS. give **comeso.** In a passage of Varro (*Menip. Sat.* 523, ed.
Bücheler) quoted by Nonius, p. 152, we have 'acinis electis et **comestis.**'
(In Varr. *R.R.* I. 2, § 11, we have 'comesa' or 'comessa.')]

possible way of dealing with the double dental in these forms,
but may be equally well regarded as the sister, not the mother, of
comesum: ostenta may be an instance of the same, but is probably
to be regarded as belonging to ten-ēre, while ostensa belongs to
tend-ēre. (On infestus, &c., quoted by Corssen, see my note on p.
220. On hæsum, hausurus see below, p. lxv.) It can hardly be
said that there is any evidence for the change of st into s or ss.

My second objection to Corssen's theory is this. All the verbs
which form their supine in -sum may be divided into three classes;
the first, stems of which the final consonant is a dental mute, viz.
t, d; the second, stems in which the final stem consonants are l or r
preceding g, l, or r; the third consisting of a miscellaneous list of
verbs, all of which are however characterised by the active perfect (if
they have one) being in si (§ 705). Now this third class, not a large
one (lapsum, jussum, pressum; parsurus, mulsum from mulcere;
fixum, fluxum; mansum; censum, hæsum, hausurus), but containing
stems ending similarly to other verbs which have -tum, exhibits
probably the result of various laws, and the -sum may be partly
due to a kind of attraction exercised by the perfect. At any rate
no light on its origin is derivable from Corssen's theory. But the
second class, which is quite as numerous, is pervaded by a law: *all*
words of the character named have the supine in -sum. And yet
this is utterly alien from Corssen's theory. No one will suppose
that sparg-tum, mulg-tum, fall-tum, curr-tum became spar-sum,
mul-sum, fal-sum, cur-sum by passing through the stage of spar-s-
tum, mul-s-tum, fal-s-tum, cur-s-tum. (Torreo with stem tors-
made torstum, then tostum, and there stayed.)

Two other grounds for hesitation in accepting Corssen's theory
may be mentioned. (1) It supposes a *progressive* assimilation,
whereas this is very rare indeed in Latin[1]. But I admit that it is
possible. Its probability however is very small. Moreover (2),
the fact should be noticed that stems ending in s originally do not
follow the change prescribed by Corssen; e. g. ges-tum does not
become ges-sum. But there are three verbs in which such a change

---

[1] It is rare in other cognate languages too, if I may judge from
Schleicher's *Compendium.* (For the definition of *progressive* and *regres-
sive* assimilation see note to page 12. Kühner (*Ausf. Gr. Gr.* § 64,
Vol. I. p. 209, ed. 2) reverses the usual application of these terms).

appears to be found; censeo, haurio, hæreo. Now censeo is originally a t- stem (comp. κεντέω), and is perhaps a secondary derivative from census, which would in that case be the participle of a lost consonant verb. Hausurus is quite anomalous. I find it only in Verg. *A.* IV. 383, and an imitation in Stat. *A.* I. 667, twice in Silius, and possibly once in Seneca (see p. 247). Hausturus (Cic.) and haustus show the regular supine stem. Hæreo is, I suspect, an r stem (comp. αἱρέω, though h in Latin does not usually *correspond* to an aspirate in Greek), and owes its supine stem (hæsurus, hæsito) to the long penult (comp. curro, verro).

[Mr Nettleship (*Academy* 1 March 1872) brings, against my theory and in favour of a progressive assimilation of st into ss, the words jussus (for justus) from jus; assus, assura apparently participial formations (as-tus, as-tura) from a stem as- which in ārēre, aridus follows the ordinary law; pustula with another form pusula (or pussula?) which had it been formed from stem pus + ulo would have been purula. Now jussus is from a stem jou-, as I believe, §§ 76. 2; 705, though why it has jussus and not jutus I cannot explain. Possibly the desire to avoid comparison with the participle of juvare may have had something to do with it: (see also p. lxiv). Assus, assura I take from a root ār- and parallel them to hær-, hæsum. Pustula, in texts accessible to me, I find only in Cels. 2. 1; 3, 22, ed. Daremberg; Sen. *Ep.* 72. § 75, ed. Haase; Mart. 8. 51. 6; 11, 98, 4. ed. Schneidewin; Vitruv. 7, 2. § 9 ed. Rose. Also pustulatum Suet. *Ner.* 44, ed. Roth.; Mart. 7, 86. On the other hand I find pusula in Cels. v. 26. § 31, 28. §§ 6, 10, 15 (eleven times), 16, 17; Sen. *Ir.* 3. 43; Pliny (ed. Detlefsen) xx. § 44; and at least eleven other places, besides XXXVII. §§ 77, 98, ed. Jan.; in Martial. 14, 167; Colum. VII. 5. § 15; Paul. ap. Fest. p. 99, s.v. Hetta, ed. Müller; and pusula in Tibull. 2. 3. 10, ed. L. Müller q. v. p. xxii.; also pusulatum Dig. 19. 2. 31; pusulosum Cels. 5. 26. 31; Colum. 7. 5. 17. I believe pusula to be the earlier form of the two, and to be from the Greek φῦσα, φυσαλλίς. Pustula, if not due to copyists, is probably formed from the Latin pus.]

The theory which I oppose to Corssen's is, taking the dental stems as instances, that tt, dt became first ts, ds, and then ss or s. This theory fulfils the really necessary conditions of truth as completely as Corssen's fails. For the first step is equally applicable to all stems, inasmuch as it supposes the suffix only to be primarily

e

affected: the second step is inevitable if the first be admitted. **Ts, ds** are utterly unstable (in Latin), and must become entirely sibilant.

The only objection which I can see to this theory is that the phonetic cause of the change of **dt, tt, lgt, bt,** &c. into **ds, ts, lgs, ps,** &c. is not apparent. But neither is the phonetic cause of the change of **dt** to **st**. Possibly a good phonetician, like Mr M. Bell or Mr Ellis, may find a reason for the change where others cannot. I content myself with referring to the fact that in Greek τ before ι frequently changed to **s** (e. g. φησί, Dor. φατί), φάσις by the side of φάτις; εἴκοσι, Dor. εἴκοτι; ἀναισθησία from ἀναίσθητος (Schleicher, *Vergl. Gr.* § 148; Curtius, *Gr. Gr.* § 60); and sometimes before υ; e. g. σύ, Dor. τύ, Lat. **tu** (but also σοῦ, σοί); and to the word **ipse**, which is generally taken to be for **ip-te**; **noxa** for **noc-ta**; **capsa**, *a box*, from **capere**; &c. (See App. A. xxvi.)

A double **t** is found in a few words; e. g. **Attius, blatta, cette, Cotta, cottidie, quattuor, gutta, matta, sagitta, vitta, futtilis, littera, Mettius, mitto,** and, it may be, some others. The question is perhaps one rather of spelling than of pronouncing. But, considering the frequency of suffixes commencing with **t**, the paucity of words with double **t** is striking. As I hold, the Romans had two ways of avoid-
lxi ing it; they changed **tt** either into **ts** or into **st**. The first produced an unstable combination, and therefore passed on into **ss** or **s**. This was the course usually adopted. The second produced a stable combination, but was (in Latin) used only where the first would occasion further difficulties of pronunciation. (Comp. §§ 151. 2; 152. 3.)

(*b*) The double **s** in the superlative form of most adjectives is also supposed by Corssen (see esp. *Ausspr.* II. 550 sqq. 1022, ed. 2) and many philologers to have arisen out of **st**. The superlative is formed from the comparative stem in **ios**, by adding, as is supposed, **tŭmus** (or **tĭmus**), and compressing **ios** to **is**, as in **magis** for **mag-ios** (*Ausspr.* II. 215). My objection to this is the same as in the former case, the extreme improbability of a stable combination like **st** changing to **ss**. Corssen states that his theory of this change rests principally on his explanation of the two words **sinistimus, sollistimus,** as being superlatives. But, even granting that these are superlatives, such a fact would only show that a superlative *might*, not that it *must*, be so formed. Here again, as I conceive, the Latins had two modes of forming the superlative; either by a suffix -**ŭmo**, or by a compound suffix -**tŭmo**. It is agreed that some superlatives are

formed by the simple addition of a suffix (without a dental) -mo or
-ŭmo to the positive or comparative stem (see § 754; Corssen, I.
780); e.g. primus, minimus, plurimus, &c.   I think that the easiest
way of explaining the formation of the ordinary superlative is by
adding the same suffix -ŭmo to the comparative, and regarding the
double s as accentual and phonetic only, i.e. as representing the
length of the syllable and the sharp sound of the s.   It is possible
to explain the superlative of words in 1 or r, as having the same
suffix, but attached to the stem of the *positive*, and to give a similar
explanation of the double 1 or r.   But the suffix may have been
appended to the *comparative*, and then a strong contraction have
taken place, facilios-imus, facilisumus, facilsimus, facillimus.   This
presumes indeed a progressive assimilation.   But 1 and r seem to
me the only sounds in Latin which show signs of such an influence; comp. velle for volere, turris by the side of τύρσις (Corssen, *Beitr.* p. 402), and the evident incompatibility of 1 and r with
a final s; e.g. consul for consuls, pater for paters.   Corssen considers miserrimus to be for misersimus, and that for misertimus;
'for t after r and 1 is frequently changed to s' (*Ausspr.* II. 552);
but with this I cannot agree.   I do not remember any instance of lxii
t after a *simple* r or 1, preceded by a short vowel, becoming s.   The
instances are after rr, ll, and haurio, hæreo; on which see above, p. lxv.

Corssen accounts for the s in ordinal numbers on a similar
hypothesis to that which he applies to the superlative forms; e.g.
vigesimus for vigenstimus, for vigentitimus.   As in the case of the
supine form I suppose nt-t to have become nt-s, and then necessarily
ns-s, and easily ns or s only.   (Cf. §§ 757. c. 168. 3.)

Besides the above-named classes of formations we find ss also (*c*)
in the old futures; e.g. prohibessit, levassit; (*d*) in arcesso, capesso,
&c.; (*e*) in verrucossus, &c.; (*f*) in essem, amavissem, amavisse,
&c.; (*g*) in assis, bessis, tressis, &c.; (*h*) to represent Greek ζ.
The cases of double s in prohibessit, &c. are explained in § 622;
and here I have the authority of Corssen in supposing the double s
to be due to accentual considerations (*Ausspr.* II. 563, ed. 2).   For
arcesso, &c. see § 625; for verrucossus, §§ 168. 3. 813.   Essem, &c.
are, I imagine, cases of a natural union of s with a suffix beginning

with s, §§ 609, 610. Assis is of uncertain origin, unless it be a masculine formation from the same stem as æs, but retaining its s and therefore defending it with a double s.

The double s used to represent the Greek ζ, at least in early times (§ 189), was perhaps really from the Dorian $\sigma\sigma$. Whether this ss represented the sound of s or sh (which Curtius once attributed to $\sigma\sigma$) is not, as it seems to me, certain. Sh appears to my tongue and ears a more natural result of ky, ty, which are regarded as the origin of $\sigma\sigma$ in Greek, than s (Curt. *Gr. Gr.* § 57). But see above, pp. liii, liv.

It appears to be generally conceded that the sound of sh was not unknown in Italy. According to Mommsen the Etruscans had it (*Unter-Ital. Dial.* p. 6); the Greek alphabet of Cære had it (p. 15); the Umbrian had it (p. 22); perhaps also the Sabellian (p. 24) and Oscan (p. 26). Moreover, of the Romance languages Portuguese and French have this sound (written ch), and Ital. and Wallach. c before i and e, and Spanish and Provençal ch are sounded as (English ch; i.e. as) tsh. (See Diez, *Gram.* Vol. I.)

On the assumption made in the above explanations that ss may stand merely for s, or at least for s when some letters or syllables have been extruded, I will only observe that the fact that the early Romans wrote no double letters (§ 58) seems to me a very important one. For, when first the Romans took to writing them double, what clue did they follow? It is possible that they followed the pronunciation, as an Italian now makes a difference between such sounds as āto and atto—a difference which Englishmen do not make. (Comp. also Ellis, *Early Engl. Pron.* p. 56.) I am not sure whether Quintilian's language (quoted in note to p. 58) should be taken to imply a real difference in pronunciation, though the word dixerunt looks like it[1]. But, when the practice of writing double

---

[1] Mr Munro (in his note on Lucr. III. 545) quotes Servius on *Æn.* I. 616: '*applicat:* secundum præsentem usum per *d* prima syllaba scribitur: secundum antiquam orthographiam, quæ præpositionum ultimam 'litteram in vicinam mutabat, per *p*: secundum vero euphoniam per *a* 'tantum;' and adds, 'i.e. only one *p* was sounded. In this, as in so 'many other points, it is clear that the artificial modern Italian pronun-'ciation is directly contrary to that of the old Latins, with whom causa 'and caussa, excisus and exscissus, were identical in sound.' In his note, Lucr. III. 504, he points out the striking instances of mamma,

letters came in, it is surely very probable that they were guided, at least to some extent, by etymological theories; and thus, though I regard the supposition that **levasso** arose by *assimilation* from **levaviso** as unsound, I think it by no means unlikely that the notion of a syllable being dropt justified to the popular apprehension the spelling **levasso**[1].·

On the vowels, especially o and e.

The exact determination of the quality of the vowels is a problem which scarcely admits of satisfactory solution. Descriptions of vowel sounds are worth very little, and the ancients had no full list of customary or possible vowels, derived, either from observation of provincial pronunciations, or from analysis of vowel sound, so as to assign to any particular vowel its nearest representa- lxiv tive. Still less had they any such definitions of vowels as Mr Bell's system affords, and his *Visible Speech* exhibits. It is quite possible that the same letter did not always represent the same quality of vowel; indeed, when we see one letter supplanted eventually by another, we may be sure (as I have said before) that the sound had been already supplanted, before the letter was changed.

But there seems no ground for doubting that a, u, i were what they are now in Italian, the distinction between the Germ. a and Ital. a being relatively unimportant. o and e are intermediate vowels, o being somewhere between a and u, e somewhere between a and i. Modern Italian which, as the local representative of Latin, has perhaps the right to maintain its identity, until a reason for inferring a difference is brought forward, has two sounds of each of these vowels. They will be found included in the list on p. 9, the close sounds being further from a and nearer respectively to i and u than the open sounds. Illustrations of the present use of these sounds in connection with their Latin original are given in Diez,

mămilla; offa, ŏfella; tintīno, tintinnabulum; Porsenna, Porsĕna; Catillus, Catīlus; and perhaps **currus, cŭrulis**; quattuor, quăter; littera, lītura. See also on III. 1044. And comp. ŏmitto, ŏperio, § 784.
1 A similar account may be given of **dissicio, porricio** for **dis-jicio, por-jicio**: cf. § 144, 2 and 143. (I doubt these being analogous to ἄλλος for **alius**, &c. on which see Curt. *Gr. Etym.* p. 592 sqq. ed. 2.)

Gram. Vol. I. ed. 3; (see also Schuchardt III. p. 161 sqq.). The most important facts seem to be these:

Open **e** arises (1) from short **e**, (2) from **e** before two consonants, (3) from **æ**:

close **e** arises (1) from short **i**, (2) from **i** before two consonants, (3) from long **e**; and (4) is usually heard when **e** is final.

Open **o** arises (1) from short **o**, (2) from **o** before two consonants, (3) from **au**; and (4) is heard (without exception?) when **o** is final:

close **o** arises (1) from short **u**; (2) from **u** or **y** before two consonants; (3) from long **o** in the suffixes **one, oso, ore,. ojo** (though this last is identical with **orio** which has open **o**).

From most of these rules there are more or fewer individual exceptions, especially (perhaps in accordance with the real length or shortness of the vowel) from the rules relating to the vowel before two consonants: and both **e** and **o** have the close sound frequently, when the former of the two consonants is **n**. Moreover it appears that Italian grammarians are not always agreed as to whether a particular word has the close or open vowel[1].

lxv   Two points here are noticeable. The first is that both **e** and **o** are often written in Italian where the Romans had **i** and **u**, and in this case the **e** and **o** have the close sound, i.e. a sound nearer to **i**, **u** than the open sound is. If the cultivated Latin dialect had been the parent of the Italian, we should have had here a reversal of the early tendency by which **o** became **u**, and **e** became **i** (§§ 196, 213, 234). But, as the Italian has sprung not from the cultivated language, but from one or more rustic provincial dialects[2], the explanation is simpler,—the old sounds having been preserved, if the close sounds were original, or, more probably, having advanced only half, and not the whole, distance towards **i** and **u**. In either case we gain little if any light on the question, how **o** and **e** were pronounced in the cultivated language of, say, the Augustan age.

The second point is that long **e** and (though less decisively) long

---

[1] I am not acquainted with Italian myself. My notion of the Italian sounds is mainly derived from Mr Ellis's book.

[2] [This is from Schuchardt: see also Diez, *Gram.* i. 6. Mr Munro says (*Few Remarks*, p. 29), 'I on the other hand hold it to be 'demonstrable that the Romano-Tuscan is the child of *cultivated* Latin 'falling to pieces, and caught up and *subdued* by German mouths.']

o in Latin generally receive in Italian the close sounds, short e and o receive the open sounds. The inference which may be drawn from this is confirmed, as Schuchardt[1] maintains, in the case of e, by the fact that æ is often miswritten for ĕ, and i for ē; by the language of the grammarians, who describe ĕ as having the sound of a diphthong (apparently æ), ē as having the sound of i; and by the same difference in quality accompanying the difference in quantity in the e of the Greeks, Kelts, Germans, English (Schuchardt, I. 461 sq.). In the case of the o sounds the miswriting is not so decisively one way. And though Marius Victorinus (p. 33, ed. Keil) says, ' O, ut e, geminum vocis sonum pro con- 'dicione temporis promit...Igitur qui correptum enuntiat, nec ' magno hiatu labra reserabit, et retrorsum actam linguam tenebit : 'longum autem productis labiis, rictu tereti, lingua antro oris 'pendula, sonum tragicum dabit ; cujus observationis et in e litera ' similis pæne ratio est :' yet other grammarians (Sergius in Donat. IV. p. 520, ed. Keil; Pompeius V. p. 102, ed. Keil), probably copying from Donatus, speak of ŏ as being expressed at the extremity of the lips (**primis labris exprimitur**), and ō as sounding within the palate (**intra palatum sonat**), which apparently would make ō to be a sound nearer a, and ŏ to be nearer u. And the Greek ω[2] never lxvi became so completely u as η became i (Schuchardt, II. p. 146), though the Germans and English, it may be added, give to their long o a sound nearer to u, and to their short o a sound nearer to a.

It is not easy to draw with much confidence any argument from this to the pronunciation of the Romans in the classical period. For (1) Italian is (as has been already remarked) not the child of classical Latin, but of one or more unsubdued dialects, [or, if the child of cultivated Latin, has grown up under foreign influences ; (see above, p. lxx)]. (2) The inference from misspellings is by no

---

[1] In reading Schuchardt it is well to remember that his distinction of 'clear' and 'dull' corresponds with 'open' and 'close' in the o sounds, with ' close' and ' open ' in the e sounds. His use of accents in Italian words is different from Diez's (see II. p. 146 n., but also III. 213).

[2] Mr Ellis says (p. 523), that Prof. Valetta (Greek) pronounced Greek (o and ω) and English with a clear 7th vowel (Ital. open o), and did not seem to be aware of the 8th vowel at all.

means clear in the case of o, and is not very weighty in the case of e. For æ is frequently miswritten for long e, and i for short e ; and many instances of æ for short e are probably due to mistaken etymology (e.g. præces, sæcundum, quæstus for questus). (3) The grammarians quoted (Schuchardt, III. 151, 212) are none of them earlier than the 4th century[1]; and three centuries are a long interval, when delicate distinctions of sound have to be caught. (4) The analogy of other languages is proof only of what was possible, not of what was actual, still less of what was actual at a particular time. And long·e and long o, even if they changed at all, may yet very well have been open e and open o in the mouths of Cicero and Quintilian. Mr Ellis's investigations into English pronunciation show a similar direction and at least as great an extent of change within the period from the 16th to the 19th century. The whole section of Mr Ellis's book (chap. III. § 6) is highly illustrative of the question, but some of his words describing the change may be quoted. ' The long vowels have altered more than the short vowels. The ' voice being sustained, there was more time for the vowel-sound to ' be considered, and hence the fancy of the speaker may have come ' more into play. This has generally given rise to a refining process, ' consisting in diminishing the lingual or the labial aperture. The ' lingual aperture is materially diminished in the passage from a long ' Italian a (2nd vowel) successively to Somersetshire a (13th vowel), lxvii ' to open e (15th vowel), to close e (16th vowel); and again in the ' passage from open e to Ital. i. The change of long open o (7th ' vowel) to long Ital. u (10th vowel) was a similar refinement, con- ' sisting first in the elevation of the tongue, and corresponding ' narrowing of the labial passage, producing long 9th vowel, and ' secondly in the narrowing of the pharynx. The change from open ' o to close o consisted simply in narrowing the pharyngeal cavity.' (Ellis, p. 232.)

This tendency of long vowels is a tendency working through long periods of time, and is not at all inconsistent with Mr Bell's assertion, 'that the tendency of all vowels is to *open* in prolongation' (*Principles*, p. 34, comp. 122). This latter physiological tend-

---

[1] Terentianus, quoted by Pompeius (*Keil.* v. p. 102), does not bear out the quotation, at least if the poem of Terentianus Maurus is meant.

ency accords with the following line of argument, which seems to me to furnish us with some evidence as to the quality of o and e in Latin. It has two premises; (1) the representation of Latin vowels in Greek, and of Greek vowels in Latin; (2) the components which under crasis, contraction, &c., gave rise to ω and η or a.

The details of the representation[1] will be found under that head in Book I. Chap. 9 (viz. o in §§ 208, 218, 219; e in §§ 229, 239). The facts of Greek contraction, &c., may be found in Greek Grammars (e.g. Kühner's *Ausführliche Gram.* ed. 2, §§ 50, 51. Curtius, *Gr.* §§ 36—38. Comp. also *ib.* § 42).

Now the very introduction of the new symbols ω and η probably implied a sound different in quality as well as in quantity from o and ε respectively. And this is confirmed by the fact that the name of o was ου, not ω, and of ε was ει, not η; in other words that, as the voice dwelt on the sound of o, it naturally uttered ου, and as it dwelt on ε, it uttered ει. In the same way, when the vowels ε and o were lengthened in compensation, as it is called (see below, § 273. 4), for an omitted consonant, they become ει and ου. But when ao and oa are contracted, we get ω in Attic: when αε is contracted, we get a; from εα, usually η in Attic. From these facts I infer that ω and η differed in quality from o and ε by being nearer a, and not by being nearer the u and i sounds; i.e. ω and η were opener, not closer than o and ε. But η was perhaps nearer to ε than ω was to o. lxviii

But Latin ŏ represents Greek ω, and ω represents Latin ŏ. Both Latin ŏ and Latin ŭ represent Greek o; Greek o represents Latin o; and both o and ου represent Latin ŭ (as well as Latin v, cf. §§ 90, 91). This seems to imply that Greek o was between Latin ŏ and Latin u. Again Latin ē represents Greek η, and η represents Latin ē. Latin ŏ represents Greek ε, and Greek ε represents both Latin ĕ and often Latin ĭ. This seems to imply that ε was between Latin ĕ and Latin ĭ; but perhaps, considering the sphere of ι, ε was nearer to Latin ŏ, than o was to Latin o. [It is

---

[1] *Correspondence*, i. e. Etymological representation (see p. 24, n.) is not here concerned. And to this head belong the suffixes of inflexion, e. g. *Hecuba*, Ἑκάβη.

possible that the Greek ϵ, when used apparently to represent Latin i,
is really a representative of the older vowel e (cf. §§ 234, 239) which
older vowel may have remained dialectically for a long time].

In the stricter Doric oo gives ω, ao and oa give a[1]; $\epsilon\epsilon$, $a\epsilon$ and
ϵa give η. This is probably to be accounted for by supposing
o and ϵ to have been opener in Doric than in Attic or Ionic, and
perhaps a to have inclined more to the o sound than it did in
Attic. But the language with which we compare Latin is the
language of Polybius, Dionysius, Diodorus, &c., and this is an
Attic dialect, though a late one.

Now, without professing to be able to assign any absolute quality
to the ancient vowels, I may, if this argument be sound, express
their *relative qualities* by a tabular arrangement. I take a, aw,
Fr. au, u to represent four *regions* of labial vowel sound, and
a, ê, é, i to represent four *regions* of lingual vowel sound. Then
we may arrange Attic, Doric, Latin somewhat as follows:

Labial	a		aw		Fr. au	u
Attic	a		ω		o, ov	
Doric		a	ω, o		ov?	v?
Latin	a		$\bar{o}$ $\breve{o}$			u

Lingual	a	ê		é		i
Attic	a		η	ϵ, $\epsilon\iota$		ι
Doric	a		η ϵ			ι
Latin	a		$\bar{e}$ $\breve{e}$			i

It should always be borne in mind, in comparing the transcrip-
lxix tion of a word in different languages, that each can supply only
what it possesses, and therefore if the sounds are not the same (and
the whole range never is the same), the representation of them can
be but approximate. Hence the Latin u and the Greek o may
sometimes be representative of one another. But generally Gr. o
and o go together, and ov represents Latin u. That ov should in
the Roman period represent u even exactly, is no obstacle to its
having earlier represented the long sound of the Greek o. This

----

[1] The Doric substitution of a for ω is reproduced in the Cumberland
quarter, and Somersetshire *cord* with 2nd vowel instead of 6th; the
Ionic substitution of η for a by the Somersetshire *Bath* with the 13th
vowel instead of the 2nd. (Cf. Ellis, p. 67.)

change is analogous to that which has befallen η, which is now
identical with long ῑ. And both are but instances of the same law
as that which we find to have prevailed in English. So ει (at least
before consonants, § 229) was in the Roman period a long ῑ, but
earlier a long ε. Whether both ει and ου had, at first, the slight
diphthongal termination which we hear in our ordinary Southern
English long **a** (= ει), and **ō** (= ου), is not easy to say positively,
but it looks probable enough on the mere face of it.

On the diphthongs **ai, ae, oi, oe, ui.**

The Latin **æ**, the ordinary representative of the Greek αι, became eventually hardly, if at all, distinguishable from e, just as αι
was confounded with ε. Originally it was doubtless a diphthong.
And this seems to have been the case in Varro's time; for he states
(*Lat. Ling.* v. § 97, Müll.) that in the country **edus** was used, in
the city **ædus**, 'with the addition of **a** as in many words;' (see
also VII. § 96, Müll). Speaking, not writing, must be meant.
Now a diphthong with so small an interval between its limiting
vowel-positions easily passes into a single intermediate sound. It
may be assumed that this sound, if it differed from e, lay on the
side nearer **a** and not on the side nearer **i**. So that if Latin **e** be
represented by the Italian open e, perhaps the English **ă** (13th
vowel) may be taken (in *quality*) for **æ**. The sounds are quite near
enough to be readily confused, and yet are in themselves distinct.
A Saxon (says Mr Ellis, p. 58, 106) would pronounce the English
words *had*, *head*, with the substitution of the Italian open e for the
vowel in each. If the Latin e be represented by the English open e,
we get a somewhat greater distinction (and that is desirable) between Latin **æ** (13th vowel) and e (15th vowel).

The sound of **œ** is somewhat perplexing. Mr Ellis has suggested lxx
(*Trans. Phil. Soc.* 1867, Supp. p. 65, and *Early Eng. Pron.* p. 529)
that Greek οι was originally **ui** with the first element preponder-
ating, Latin **œ** was originally **ue** with the second element preponder-
ating. This seems possible enough for the Greek, as *o* had frequently that approximation to our **w**, which is here presumed (see
App. A. xii.). But the Latin sound is much more doubtful. It is

true that œ is the successor of Latin oi and the representative of
Greek οι, and that both oi and œ passed frequently into u, e.g.
coirare, cœrare, curare; mœrus, murus; mœnia, munia; pœna, punire,
&c.; but I am not aware of any indication that Latin o had any
such approximation to our w; and œ never alternated with ui. The
passage of oi and of œ into u seems to imply that at that time the
first, not the second, element, the o, not the i or e, was in the pre-
ponderance. In imperial times œ became confused with e and æ,
and then the second element may have been preponderant. And
this was the case also in the words which in very early times
were spelt with œ, e.g. lœbertas, oloes (cf. §§ 264, 363, 366), and
afterwards were written with i. I am inclined to think that the
diphthongal sound implied by the letters o and i, or o and e, (with
their Latin sounds) is the safest conclusion, and that in the words
which the ordinary language spells with œ (e.g. amœnus, cœpi,
mœnia, fœdus, Pœni, pœna, obœdio) the stress should be laid on the
o rather than the e.

ui as a diphthong occurs (besides an interjection or two) only in
huic, cui. In both of these words it represents an earlier oi, e.g.
hoic, quoi. In Quintilian's time (I. 7. § 27) cui and qui appear to
have been pronounced alike. Probably the sound was French oui.
In the dative of -u stems, e.g. gradui, the vowels would probably
be pronounced separately, when both written. But a diphthongal
pronunciation may have led to the omission of the i. On the pronunciation of -aius, oius, -eius, see § 138.

On a supposed sound like ü.

There are three cases in which it appears more or less probable that the Latins had a modified sound of a short vowel similar
to that of French u or Germ. ü, especially when it inclines, as it
does in some parts of Germany, more to i than to u.

(1) The first case is in the combination qui-, which is generally
represented in Greek by κυ, though sometimes by κυι or κοι. Cf.
§ 90. 2. And in some Latin words qui- is descended from cu- or
co-; e.g. Quirinus from cures, esquiliæ from æsculus, inquilinus
from incola, sterquilinium (§ 934) from stercus. So Tarquinius

from the Etruscan **Tarchun** (Schuchardt, II. 277). The labialisation of the guttural, which is expressed by **qu**, affected the following vowel, and the result was a pronunciation like **kü** instead of **kwi**.

(2) The second case is that of **i** after **v**, which is noticed by several of the grammarians in almost the same words. Priscian (*Part.* § 24, 25 = III. p. 465, Keil) lays down generally, that words beginning with **vi** followed by **d, t, m, r** or **x** appear to have the sound of the Greek *v*, and instances **video, vim, vis, virgo, virtus, vitium, vix,** and says most people gave the same sound to **fi**. But I see no other authority for such a statement, the only examples quoted by Diomedes, Servius, Sergius and Cledonius being **vir**, to which Velius Longus adds **virtus**, and the Appendix to Probus (IV. p. 198, Keil) adds **virgo** and **virga**. (Cf. Schuchardt, II. 219. Schneider, I. 19 sq.). I notice this because **vir** and its probable kin are almost the only words in which short **i** occurs before **r**, and some peculiarity of the sound of **i** in these words is therefore not unnatural (cf. § 184, 3).

(3) The third case is that of the vowel in the penultimate of superlatives and ordinal numbers, which was **u** in the earlier language, and **i** usually in the subsequent language. Jul. Cæsar is said to have first written **i**. The variation in spelling remained for long. Quintilian (I. 7. 21) expressly says that the sound of **i** in **optimus** was intermediate between **i** and **u**, and this view is confirmed by the later grammarians.

But on the other hand there are difficulties. (1) It may be said that, if the sound of this vowel had been that of the French **u**, the Latin **y**, which was the Greek *v*, would have been often used to represent it. But from Schuchardt's collections (II. 224, 225), it appears that it is rarely found in this termination. Indeed it is more common in **gyla, Sylla** (Schuchardt, II. 198, 205). Its rarity, how- ever, may be accounted for by the natural shrinking of the Romans from writing their own words with a foreign letter. (2) The Greek transcription of these words is, so far as I am aware, uniformly by *ι*, not by *v*. [Dittenberger (*Hermes*, VI. 296) says that in inscriptions we find earlier only *o*, later *ov* or *ι*, never *v*]. (3) Quintilian dwells on the beauty of two Greek sounds, *φ* and *v*, and expressly says the Romans have not got them (xii. 10, § 27). (4) The later grammarians, except Marius Victorinus, do not suggest the **y** sound for this vowel, though Priscian does almost in the same sentence suggest it for **i** after *v*.

I do not see much likelihood or possibility of **u** changing to **i**, without some such intermediate step. But yet it may be, that the vowel was not specifically **u** or specifically **i**, but simply an unaccented vowel in a suffix, which for a time was, under the influence of the following labial, retained at the stage of **ŭ**, but afterwards was carried away by the general drift and became **i**. In this case the precise quality of the vowel need never have been very sharply defined, and the representation of it by one of the five vowel signs was approximate only. Or, indeed, the relation of the two sounds in this and in many other cases may be more analogous to the *correspondence* of sounds in different languages. **U** may have belonged to one dialect and **i** to another, and the eventual substitution of **i** may have been mainly the triumph of the second dialect. Thus Mr Ellis (p. 473, n.) speaks of the Peak in Derbyshire having two distinct pronunciations of e.g. *sheep*, and one of these is a sound which one Southerner might interpret one way and another another. Thus *sheep* might be sounded with the 16th vowel, or the 18th or the diphthong 3 to 18. We shall not be far wrong, if we print **proximus** or **proximus** according to the best evidence we may have respecting the particular author in whose text it occurs, or the period at which each author wrote, and then pronounce accordingly either **u** or **i** lightly. But our English sound (the 3rd vowel) is, I suppose, entirely out of the question, though I expect many English speakers often utter it in these as in many other unaccented syllables.

Miscellaneous: chiefly on vowel pronunciation.

There are one or two other points respecting the pronunciation of vowels which may here be mentioned.

lxxiii   The length of the *vowel* should be preserved, as much before two consonants, as before one or more. In the cases of **ns, nf** a vowel originally short was lengthened by position (§ 167). Mr Munro takes Priscian's statement[1] (II. 63), that the vowel before gn ·was always long, as meaning that the gn makes it long by nature: but I cannot agree to this. Priscian could on his principles come to no other conclusion; for he held that gn begun the final syllable (II. 8) and that gn made a preceding syllable common, i.e. allowed a short vowel to remain short (I. 11; II. 12). Hence, finding all words which ended in gnus had the penultimate long, he concluded the *vowel* must be long. But, I believe, gn did not belong to the last syllable; the g belonged to the penultimate[2]. And, as in Greek such a syllable with a short vowel (e.g. ἔγνων) is always long by position, although at one time it was supposed that occasionally it remained short, there seems no reason for assuming in general the *vowel* to be lengthened. In ignavus, &c. where the n is omitted, the i may be lengthened in compensation. Many words no doubt had, or were supposed to have, a naturally long vowel, e.g. regnum from rĕg-, rex, instead of from rĕg-ĕre; but tignum, signum, magnus, &c. (comp. tĭgillum, sĭgillum, măgis) probably have a short vowel. The Latin words Egnatia, Egnatius occur not unfrequently in Greek with ε. (See Benseler's *Lexicon*).

[Mr Munro has replied (*Few Remarks*, p. 26 sqq.) to these observations at length. But I am still unconvinced. I do not think Priscian or those from whom he copied were at all incapable of substituting a theoretical conclusion for an actual observation. Very much better orthoepists than he was have stated rules, which their own ear, if emancipated from prejudice, would have told them were not true, or not universally true. This particular statement may very likely not be of Priscian's own discovery, but I should require further evidence before I should think it properly attributable to a good authority four or five centuries earlier; and less time will not give us a contemporary statement. A statement like that of Cicero's about ns has very different weight.

But I have endeavoured to show (p. lix.) how ns lengthened the

---

[1] Priscian is, I think, unsupported in this statement.

[2] See § 272. The Verona palimpsest of Livy, which was probably written in the 4th cent. p. Chr., and consequently before Priscian's time, always divides words with gn occurring at the end of a line between the g and n, so as to give the g and n to separate syllables (Mommsen, *Cod. Liv. Ver.* p. 164).

preceding vowel. I do not see, why **gn**, if pronounced as hard **g**
followed by the dental nasal, could have done so, any more than
any other mute followed by a nasal. If Priscian's statement is true,
then I should argue that probably **gn** was pronounced like **ng-n**
or like **ny**, (Spanish ñ.) And this statement of Priscian has, I see,
actually been brought forward by C. Brugman (in Curtius *Studien*,
IV. 105—108) to prove that **gn** was **ng-n**. But against this sound of
gn is the fact that no Roman grammarian, so far as I am aware, al-
ludes to such a sound of **gn**, though the occasions for so doing
were obvious (see p. lvii.).

I did not refer before to Mr Munro's arguments in support of
his view derived from the long **I** in **sIgna, dIgna**, "in inscriptions
of high authority not likely to err on such points," and "from
regni and **regno** with the apex," because the long **I** is certainly
sometimes misplaced, and I expect the apex is too. And it is not
at all clear to my mind why one stone-cutter puts long **I** or apex,
and another omits them, or on what grammatical authority the
stone-cutter who did put them acted. But until we get further
volumes of the Berlin edition of the Inscriptions, I deem it wise to
postpone any positive opinion on this as well as on some other
points.

Mr Munro has I think missed my meaning when I refer (p.
lxxix. n.) to the mode in which syllables are divided in the Verona
palimpsest of Livy. I endeavoured to account for Priscian's statement
by his theory of syllables. And I adduced the Verona palimpsest
to show that this theory was apparently not that of more ancient
authorities. Rightly or wrongly, I do at present hold that a
Roman did not pronounce **i-gnominia, i-gnota, co-gnatus, re-gnum,
gi-gno**, but **ig-nominia, ig-nota, cog-natus, reg-num, gig-no**.

For we have to account for the Romans writing **inglorius, congredior**, but **ignotus, cognatus**. Now **gl** and **gr** are, and were
readily pronounceable in an initial position. **Gloria** and **gradior**
were so written whether in or out of composition. But **gn** is not
easily so pronounced, and therefore **gnomen, gnatus**, became **nomen,
natus**. Accordingly I divide **inglorius, congredior**, as **ing-glorius,
cong-gredior**, the **ng** being a single sound, viz. the guttural nasal
(see § 162). Had the Romans retained the **n** of the prepositions
before **gn**, they would have felt bound to pronounce **ing-gnotus**,

eong-gnatus, but would practically have pronounced ing-notus, cong-natus. But they did not retain the n and write ingnotus, congnatus, but ignotus, cognatus. What is the explanation? Does this represent a pronunciation ing-notus, cong-natus, or inyotus, conyatus? Mr Munro (and I agree with him) holds that it does not. I account for it by supposing the Romans to have reduced the mass of consonants, the whole of which they were unable to pronounce, by omitting as usual (§ 31) the former n, that of the preposition, rather than the later and radical n. And then I divide the consonants according to phonetic laws, and pronounce with the ordinary sounds of the consonants ig-notus, cog-natus. That the vowel i may *here* be lengthened, as an n is omitted, I have said above is quite possible. But it is very remarkable that Cicero, only a few lines before he calls attention to the lengthening of the vowel before ns, nf, refers to this very phenomenon without giving a hint that the vowel was lengthened. His words are: 'noti' erant et 'navi,' et 'nari,' quibus cum 'in' præponi oporteret, dulcius visum est 'ignoti, ignavi, ignari' dicere, quam ut veritas postulavit (*Or.* 47). The context shews that 'dulcius' here has no distinctive reference to any peculiar pronunciation.

I see no ground for thinking that the Romans pronounced according to the etymology, and therefore neither did they (before Greek-following systematisers like Priscian gave artificial rules) divide the words in writing according to the etymology, which is all that Mommsen means in his words quoted by Mr Munro.

It is hard to believe that the i in gigno was 'long by nature.'

In reference to Egnatius, I will quote some of Mr Munro's remarks. 'The words Egnatia, Egnatius, are no more Latin than 'Diögnetus, Polÿgnotus, Prögne, Cÿgnus: the town is Peucetian, 'alien to Greeks, not Latins; and Mommsen tells us that the native 'name is Gnathia, the genuine Latin form Gnatia; and certainly 'our two oldest authorities Horace and Mela know no other 'form'.]

Of course a short vowel before two consonants (unless lengthened as above) should be pronounced with its usual short quantity.

In English we are in the habit of changing, or pronouncing ob-

f

scurely, short vowels in unaccented syllables, e.g. in the first syllable
of *appear*, *together*, &c., and in the final syllable of *mention*, *goodness*,
cabbage, *futile*, *honour*, &c.   In Latin the pronunciation may be
presumed to have been, as in Italian, more distinct; and though
changes of the vowels occur, we shall be safest in following the
spelling, which represents, though no doubt sometimes laggardly,
the pronunciation.

lxxiv   The pronunciation of a final vowel before an initial vowel is
somewhat uncertain. But that it was not omitted, but either lightly
pronounced separately, or formed into a diphthong with the initial
vowel, seems both in oratory and poetry to be the right conclusion,
both from the language of Cicero (*Orat.* 13. § 77; 14. § 150 sqq.),
and Quintilian (IX. 4, § 33; XI. 3. 34), and from the fact that the
vowel was written, not omitted. (See Corssen, *Ausspr.* II. pp. 770
—793).   The chief points of usage in this matter in Latin verse are
given (after Luc. Müller) in §§ 288—291. (I have there used the terms
elided and *elision* in conformity with general usage and for brevity.)

The modern analogies are thus stated by Mr Ellis (p. 324).
‘ In common French discourse the final *e* and many medial *e's*
‘ may be said to be entirely elided..... When singing, the French
‘ not merely pronounce these *e's*, but dwell upon them, and give
‘ them long and accented notes in the music.   This recognition is
‘ absolutely necessary to the measure of the verse, which, depending
‘ solely upon the number of the syllables in a line, and having no
‘ relation to the position of accent, is entirely broken up and
‘ destroyed when these syllables are omitted.   And yet when they
‘ declaim, the French omit these final *e's* without mercy, producing
‘ to English ears a hideous, rough, shapeless, unmusical result,
‘ which nothing but a consciousness of the omitted syllables can
‘ mass into rhythm.’ Again (p. 329 n.), ‘ In German and French
‘ poetry the omission of the vowel is complete and absolute.   It is
‘ not in any way slurred over, or rapidly pronounced in connection
‘ with the following vowel, as is the case in Italian and Spanish
‘ poetry, and even in Italian singing.   The Germans, like the Greeks,
‘ do not even write the elided vowel.   The Latins wrote the elided
‘ vowel, as the Italians do, and may therefore have touched it briefly,
‘ as in the English custom of reading Latin verse; whereas it is
‘ the German custom to omit such vowels altogether, even in reading

' Latin verse. Except in a few instances as *l'*, *t'*, &c. the French do
' not make the elision of a final e before a following vowel, and in
' old English the vowel was written even when elided.' Mr Ellis
thinks Chaucer sounded, at least usually, his final e's.

Final **m** before an initial vowel was, according to Quintilian (IX.
4. 40), sounded, though slightly: ' Etiamsi scribitur, tamen parum
' exprimitur, ut *multum ille* et *quantum erat*, adeo ut pæne cujus-
' dam novæ litteræ sonum reddat. Neque enim eximitur, sed lxxv
' obscuratur et tantum in huc aliqua inter duas vocalis velut nota
' est, ne ipsæ coeant.' Mr Ellis (*Phil. Soc. Trans.* 1867, *Suppl.* p. 20)
suggests that the **m** may have simply nasalized the preceding vowel,
as is the case with **m** frequently in Portuguese and French, and with
n always in the latter language.

The omission of the *initial* vowel in **est** is mentioned in § 721.
Perhaps also the same may have taken place in **istuc**, &c. (§ 375).

The chief rules of accentuation are given in Book I. Chap. XIII.
I confess to entertaining some doubts as to a short syllable, when
followed by an enclitic, receiving the accent, e.g. **primáque.** As
the Romans would not have accented **primaque** on the penult, if it
had been one word, I do not see why the **i** should have lost the
accent by the addition of the enclitic. But the grammarians no
doubt are against me, and I cannot pretend to any great confidence
in my own judgment in matters of accentuation and quantity.

Division of words into Syllables.

The general doctrine given (in §§ 14—16, 272—274) is, I
think, in fair accordance[1] with the teaching of Mr Bell and
Mr Ellis. To a pamphlet of the latter I owe the first hint of

[1] But the mode of representing the pronunciation is often different
from what they appear to recommend. For instance, Mr Bell (*Visible
Speech*, p. 119; and comp. Ellis, p. 55 note) says *critical* is pronounced
cri-ti-cal not *crit-ic-al.* I am quite aware that his ear is far better than
mine, but I cannot think, if we are to assign the **t** to one syllable
more than the other, that it would be generally felt to belong to
the second syllable. However, write the division how we may, I do
not mean more in what I say of Latin pronunciation of mutes than
that the consonant was pronounced as much with the vowel before it
as **t** is (invariably I believe) in this word *critical*. And this is not the
notion which I get from the ordinary statement.

what I believe to be the truth.   Their views will be found in Bell's
Visible Speech, p. 69 sq., *Principles of Speech*, p. 87 sq.; Ellis's *Early
English Pronunciation*, p. 51 sqq.

The application of this doctrine to Latin brings me at once into
collision with the doctrine faithfully transmitted from Priscian
(Lib. 2), and even with the same doctrine as modified by Krüger
(*Lat. Gr.* §§ 32, 33) and Madvig (*Bemerkungen*, p. 17).   Madvig's
lxxvi account of both is as follows (*Lat. Gr.* § 13): ' A consonant be-
' tween two vowels belongs to the last vowel, and with this it is
' combined in pronunciation.   Of two or more consonants the last,
' or, if they can begin a Latin word, the two last, belong to the
' following vowel, the remaining consonant or consonants to the
' preceding vowel (**pa-tris, fa-scla, ef-fluo, perfec-tus, emp-tus**).
' The double **x** is best united with the preceding vowel.   In words
' compounded with prepositions the final consonant of the preposi-
' tion is not separated from it (**ab-eo, ad-eo, præter-eo**, also **prod-eo,
' red-eo**).

' According to a generally spread custom' [this is Priscian's doctrine and is the only one which has ancient authority in its favour]
'words are in many books so divided, that all consonants which
'in Greek can begin a word, and all mutes with liquids (even
'though they could not begin a Greek word, e.g. **gm**), and similar
'combinations of two mutes (e.g. **gd** as **ct**) are drawn to the syllable
'following (**i-gnis, o-mnis, a-ctus, ra-ptus, Ca-dmus, i-pse, scri-psi,
' Le-sbos, a-gmen, Da-phne, rhy-thmus, smara-gdus**).'

I assert, on the contrary, that the Roman pronunciation tended
to unite a consonant with the preceding, not with the following,
vowel; and I have briefly mentioned in § 273, and need not here
repeat, the indisputable facts of Latin etymology and prosody, which
seem to me to justify this inference.   I have in § 274, p. 89, briefly
noted (in some words of Mr Bell's) the probable basis of the ordinary doctrine, and will now remark on some objections which may
possibly be urged to three of my four arguments.

1.   It may be said that the retention of **o** after **v** (instead of
allowing the change to **u**, § 93) shows a connexion with the following, not with the preceding, vowel.   Unquestionably it does, and
the reason is that the vowel **u** only becomes consonantal at all by its

rapid pronunciation before a following vowel. **V** (= **w**) is not a consonant standing independently between two vowels (as it ought to have been to invalidate my principle), but a vowel, which, if it be distinctly pronounced as such, does not necessarily affect either the preceding or subsequent sounds, but, when coming before a different vowel, naturally gains a semiconsonantal character. **W** is hardly pronounceable at the end of a syllable. See above, p. xxxiv.

2. It may be said that a change of the final sound of a word is sometimes caused by the initial sound of a *word* following; e.g. lxxvii ἀμ-πέδον for ἀνα πέδον; **imprimis** for **in primis**; and that therefore such a change does not imply the union in one syllable of the consonants so affecting each other. I do not deny that sounds in different syllables may affect one another; the law of assimilation or dissimilation does undoubtedly extend over several syllables, and in some languages, I believe, prevails much more largely than it does in Latin; but when we find, as we do in Latin, such changes frequent and regular, almost invariable indeed, in the case of contiguous consonants, and very rare, in the case of separated consonants, it seems to me difficult to suppose that these contiguous consonants were separated in speech. And such instances of the influence of initial sounds of a word on the terminal sound of a preceding word rather show that the two words run into one another in pronunciation. This is confirmed (*a*) by the express statement of the Latin grammarians, that prepositions with a case had no separate accent (§ 299): (*b*) by their being constantly written as one word in inscriptions (Corssen, *Aussprache*, II. 863—872); (*c*) by the change of vowel in (for instance) **illico** for **in loco** (Ib. p. 869).

3. It may be said that the prosodiacal law, of a syllable being long if its vowel has two consonants after it, applies just as much when these two consonants are in different words, as when they are in the same word as the vowel; and therefore, if the lengthening of the syllable proves that the consonants are in the same syllable, it proves also that the initial consonant of a word must be regarded as in the same syllable as the end of a preceding word. This is so, no doubt, but how else is the fact to be accounted for? The Romans did not arbitrarily invent the laws of prosody: these laws

must in substance rest on sounds actually heard. Part of the
solution of the apparently strange confusion of word with word is,
I think, to be found in the fact that words were not divided in
writing, and that consequently a law strictly applicable to consonants in the same word was applied also to consonants in different
words, partly from a real confusion in rapid speech, partly from a
want of distinction in writing. When both consonants are in the
second word, the Romans were much more reluctant (cf. § 293) to
lxxviii admit in theory, because they were less liable to produce in practice, the same prosodiacal effect. The confusion of two words
here supposed finds an analogy in French, when the final consonant
otherwise mute is revived in order to be pronounced, not with its
own word, but with the following word. (Comp. also Ellis, *Early
Eng. Pron.* p. 56.)

To the 4th argument I do not see what answer can be made.

Madvig (*Bemerk.* pp. 17, 26. *n.*) points to the vowel **e** being
found in **perfectus, nomen** compared with **i** in **perficio, nominis,** and
considers it to be due to the syllable being closed in the first two
words, open in the last two. And it may be urged that on my
theory, though **perfect-us** compared with **perfic-io** may admit of
explanation, there are not two consonants to account for the **e** in
nomen. True, but neither is there a closed syllable to account for
mare compared with **maris**; and still more clearly in words like **iste,
ante,** compared with **istic, antistes,** &c. (see § 234, 3), the open
syllable exhibits the **e,** but becoming closed takes **i** instead. The
true explanation of the **e** in **nomen,** I am not at all sure of: it might
perhaps be held to be the result of the suffix having once been, as
some philologers (e.g. Leo Meyer, II. 263) suppose, **ment** (for **mant**),
in which case the **e** has remained as in **eques** for **equets,** &c. But
it is enough to observe that on examining carefully the laws of
change as set forth (more systematically than I have elsewhere seen)
in § 234, 3, it will be found that **nomen, nominis** is quite consistent
with other words, and that these laws, be their basis what it may,
do not depend on the syllable being open or shut.

The following is a summary statement of the probable pronunciation of educated Romans in the period from Cicero to
Quintilian, say 70 A.C. to 90 P.C. (The references in brackets are
to pages of the preface or sections of the book where arguments
are given.)

I. VOWELS:

The long and short sounds of a vowel were probably identical in
quality. In English they are always different.

> ā as in Italian, i.e. as in *father;* not as in *fate.*
>
> ă the same sound shortened, as in French *chatte;* not as in *hat.*
>
> ŏ as Italian open o, nearly as in *dot.*
>
> ō as Italian open o, or the Cumberland pronunciation of *home,*
> a sound nearer to English *aw* than is the ordinary o in *dote,*
> or in the ordinary English *home.* (pp. lxix.—lxxv.)
>
> ŭ as in Italian, i.e. as French *ou* in *poule,* nearly as in *pull;*
> not as in *lull.*
>
> ū as in Italian, i.e. oo in *pool;* not with a prefixed *y*-sound, as
> in *pule, mule.*
>
> ĕ as Italian open e; nearly as in *pet, met.*
>
> ē the same sound lengthened; not as in *peat,mete.* (pp.lxix.—lxxv.)
>
> ī as Italian ì, i.e. as in *machine;* not as in *shine, pine.*
>
> ĭ the same sound shortened: but practically the ordinary·
> English short ĭ may be used, as in *pin.*
>
> y as Germ. ü, but inclining to ĭ, e.g. *Müller,* which is nearer
> *Miller* than *Muller.*

This pronunciation of ō and ē is recommended, partly because it appears more probably to be right than the sound of
French au and French é: partly because the ordinary English
long o and long a, which might be otherwise used, are usually
diphthongs (see § 21).

A long vowel was pronounced long, and a short syllable short,
whether by itself or before one or more consonants, e.g. lūx, lūce;
pắter, pắtre; mäter, mätre; amänt, regŭnt, &c. (pp. lxxviii. lxxxi.)

A vowel before ns or nf was pronounced long (§ 167).

In unaccented syllables, each vowel probably had its proper sound, instead of their being all alike reduced as commonly in English to the sound in *mention*, *paper*, *label*, *turban*, &c. (pp. lxxxi. lxxxii.)

When **est** followed a vowel or **m**, the **e** was omitted (§ 721).

lxxx ## II. DIPHTHONGS.

The right rule for pronouncing diphthongs is to pronounce the constituent vowels as rapidly as possible in their proper order. (See a more exact account in App. A. xi. xii.)   This will give as follows:

au as in Germ. *haus*, i.e. a broader sound than **ow** in *cow;* not as **au** in *cause*.

eu as in Italian *Europa*, i.e. as **ow** in Yankee *town*.

ae nearly as (the single vowel) *a* in the Somerset pronunciation of *Bath*, *i.e.* as in *bat* lengthened. (p. lx.v.)

oe as a diphthong. (p. lxxv.)

ei nearly as in *feint*, but with the stress on the latter vowel; not as long English **i**. (Cf. § 267.)

ui (in *huic*, *cui*) as French *oui*. (p. lxxvi. and § 222.)

The diphthongs **ou** (§ 251) and **oi** (§ 263) are found only in early Latin.

III. CONSONANTS :

c always hard, as **k** in *kitty;* not as **c** (= **s**) in *city*. (pp. xlvii—liv.)

g always hard, as **g** in *give;* not as in *gin*. (p. lv.)

ng as **ng + g** i.e. as in *anger* (i.e. *ang-ger*); not as in *hang-er*. So **nc**, **nq**, as **ng + c**, **ng + q**. (p. lvii.)

j as English **y**, in *year;* not as English **j** in *jeer*. (§ 138.)

v as English **w** in *wine*, or French **ou** in *oui;* not as **v** in *vine*. (pp. xxxiii.—xlvi.)

qu as in English, e.g. *queen*. But **quu** should be avoided, and e.g. **quom** or **cum** uttered. On **qui-** see p. lxxvi.

r always trilled, never vocalized as commonly in English when
a vowel does not follow. (See App. A. xiii.—xvii.) Thus
per should be sounded as in *perry*, not as in *pert;* **ēre** as
English *ā-ry*, not *airy:* **īre** as (English) *ee-ry*, not *eary.*

s always sharp as in *hiss;* not (like z) as in *his.* (pp. lviii.— lxxxi
lxi.) The mispronunciation by Englishmen occurs most
when **s** follows e or n.

bs as **ps**, not as **bz**. (p. lvii.)

x always as **ks**, as in *axe;* not **gz**, as in *exact.* (p. lvii.)

ti always **tee** (long or short as the case may require), not (as
before a vowel, e.g. **natio**) as *sh* or *she.* (p. lvi.)

ph, ch, th were not like English f, German ch, ¦English th,
but as **p+h**, **k+h**, **t+h**: sounds somewhat difficult to
Englishmen, but often heard from Irishmen (§ 132).

In prepositional compounds assimilation in pronunciation appears
to have been usual in certain cases :

ad was completely assimilated to all consonants, except **b**,
f, and **m**. (§ 160. 9.)

sub, **ob** were completely assimilated to **c**, **f**: and became **sup**,
op, before sharp consonants. (§ 78.)

com was completely assimilated to **l**, **r**; became **co** before **gn**
and **h**; and became **con** before all other consonants, except labials. (§ 85. 4.)

in was completely assimilated to **l**, **r**, and became **im** before
labials. (§§ 168. 1. 2; 176. 1; 184. 1.)

per was completely assimilated to **l**. (§ 176. 1.)

On other cases see Book I.

The other consonants in Latin were probably pronounced as
we now pronounce them. But final **m** was sometimes not sounded,
or perhaps gave only a nasal sound to the vowel. (p. lxxxii.)

An observance of the Latin rules for accentuation does not involve much which is different from the usual English practice
(p. lxxxiii). On the division of the words into syllables, see §§ 15,
232; pp. lxxxiii.—lxxxvi.

A few examples will show plainly the great difference between the ordinary English, and what is here represented to be the Roman, pronunciation. To express the pronunciation I have thought it best to follow no exact system, but to select, where possible, common English words or syllables. I have however used **ah, æ, eh,** and **ò** for what I suppose to be the true sounds of Latin **a, æ, e,** and **o** as defined above; **èrr** for the sound in *herring*, not in English *err;* **ay** for the ordinary English long **a.**

Pronounce	as	not as
cerno, crēvi	kĕrr-nò, kreh-wee	sur-no, kree-vie
cīvītātēs	kee-wi-tah-tāce	sigh-vi-tay-teez
exercĭtui	eks-ĕrr-kĭt-oo-ee	eg-zur-sit-you-I
fāgīs	fah geese	fay-jis
fiĕri	fee-ĕrr-ee	fire-eye
fūmāre	foo-mah-rĕh	few-Mary
infrā	een-frah	in-fray
jăciunt	yăhk-i-oont	jăs-i-unt or jay-si- unt, jay-shi-unt
jŏvĭs	yò-wĭs	joe-vis
nātio	nah-ti-ò	nay-shi-o
obscūrior	òps-koo-ri-orr	obz-kyoor-i-or
paucæ	pow-kæ	paw-see
rērum	reh-room	rear-um
scīre, cīre	skee-rĕh, kee-rĕh	sīre-y
sciscĭtari	skis-ki-tah-ree	sis-si-tare-eye
vēni, vīdi, vīci	weh-nee, wee-dee, wee-kee	vee-nigh, vie-die, vie-sigh
[urbs	oorps	urbz]

The division of syllables in the above is, in order not to embarrass the reader, accommodated in the main to the ordinary view.

Observations on Book II.

Noun-stems ending in e.

I BELIEVE the general doctrine of grammarians may be represented to be, that the stems commonly forming the fifth declension have
the genitive and dative singular, except occasionally in poetry, in eī;
that the eī is a dissyllable; and that the e is usually long, e.g. diēī,
but short, if it follows a consonant, e.g. fidĕī. And accordingly
it is common enough to find modern writers using such words as
materiēī, and referring (e.g. Corssen, II. 723) without hesitation
to words like faciēī, notitiēī, amicitiēī, as if they were of common
and undoubted occurrence. Now, putting aside the Latin authors
subsequent to the silver age, into whose usage on this point I have
made but little investigation, and speaking of the older period, that
which alone I regard in this volume, I believe all the above parts
of the ordinary doctrine to be quite unfounded. I do not profess to
have read through all the writers of the gold and silver ages with
a view to this inquiry, but I have used such other means as were
available, and have had the point before me for some years. The
result is stated in §§ 340—343, and 357 and 360. The kernel of the
whole matter is to be found in Gellius, IX. 14, and in Quintilian's
significant question (v. 6. § 26) quoted in the note to p. 116; and
the inf rence, which may be thence drawn, is confirmed by Neue's
collection of the facts of actual usage. The great mistake commonly made is in starting from the assumption, derived from Roman
grammarians, that a dissyllabic eī is the regular ending, and consequently only noticing what are supposed to be deviations. In
§§ 357, 360 will be found all the instances that I have been able to
collect of the use of a genitive or dative singular of an e stem at all.
It will be seen that dies, res, spes, fides and plebes, are the only
words which are found in these cases, except quite sporadically.

lxxxiv Of these, only dies has i before e, and the i here is a vowel of the root, not part of a derivative suffix, as in notities, &c.   As for the rule concerning the quantity of the e, diei alone when dissyllabic has always an e long (as indeed a short e between two i's would be utterly unstable in Latin): rei is used with e long in Plautus and Lucretius, with ĕ short in Plautus, Terence, and Horace: fidei has e long in Ennius, Plautus, and Lucretius; ĕ short in Manilius and Silius.   There are, so far as I can find, no other instances in verse of a genitive and dative singular in ei.   The dissyllabic nature of ei can be shown only by express mention or by verse.

Now, putting together the following facts, (1) that at least in many words the stems in e are collateral to stems in a; (2) that an. antique genitive of -a stems, in āī, was preserved in poetry by occasional usage for some time; (3) that in Cicero's time the genitive and dative of the -e stems were written either with e or with i; (4) that ei was an accredited spelling of either an intermediate sound between e and i, or of long i: (5) that the use of any genitive or dative sing. of these stems is decidedly rare, except in three or four words, and that Quintilian regarded the form, at least as regards progenies, as either non-existent or disputed;—putting these facts together, we may conclude that while ei may very possibly have been one mode of spelling the ending of the genitive and dative, it was probably monosyllabic, except in poetic and antiquarian writers.   There is, however, no reason to doubt that, after Gellius' time, this was the ordinary spelling, and possibly, under the deceptive influence of diei, fidei in the old phrases bonæ fidei, and plebei (in tribunus plebei, plebeiscitum), and the monosyllabic stems re-, spe-, the ei was regarded as dissyllabic.   I have given in the paradigms of the declension (§ 343) what I suppose Cicero or Livy would have given.

It may perhaps be the most convenient course in modern times to continue to write ei, but we should pronounce it as a diphthong (§ 267), and use such forms as little as may be.   It is impossible to suppose, considering the words[1], that the rare occurrence of the genitive and dative is not in some degree the result of a felt difficulty: and some of the instances which do exist are probably

---

[1] e. g. acies.   I have not hit upon any place in Livy where the genitive or dative of this word is used.

due to copyists who restored the ordinary spelling of their time, lxxxv
not to the writing of the authors of the gold or silver age themselves.

Noun-stems ending in ɪ and in a consonant.

In determining which are ɪ stems and which are consonant
stems, I have followed principally the clue given by the genitive
plural, and, in the case of neuter substantives or of adjectives, that
of the nominative and accusative plural also. But I have also
taken into account, especially where evidence on the above points
was either non-existent or vacillating, the use of - is in the nom.
or accus. plural of masculine and feminine nouns, and of course,
in the few nouns which exhibit it, -im in the accus., and the more
frequent ī in the abl. singular. Many writers have considered words
like **ars, mens,** &c., which do not exhibit the ɪ in the nominative
singular, as having, either in this case or in the singular number
generally, passed into the consonant declension, or as having two
stems, a consonant stem and an ɪ stem. But the thorough-going
distribution of the words of the third declension, adjectives included, between consonant stems and ɪ stems, and the enumeration
of all the words (except very numerous derivatives), with mention
of any peculiarities they may show, have not, so far as I am aware,
been done before. And this has brought into light two important
points, stated respectively in § 406 and in § 408, compared with
§ 435.

1. The first of these points is that the difference between retaining or omitting the ɪ in the nominative singular is due to
phonetics and not to etymology. The ɪ was evidently so weak
ın this final syllable, that, with rare exceptions, it was retained
only when the nature of the preceding consonants was such as
to be powerfully affected by an adjoining **s.** Thus stems in **-mi,
-vi, -qvi, -gvi, -ni, -li, -ri, -si,** retain the ɪ with rare exceptions.
The exceptions show the extent to which the stem would have been
disguised, if this protective influence had not been exerted. Thus
nix is hardly recognizable as of the same stem as **nigvis** or **nivis**;
præcox, though looking very different, really stands to **præcoqvis** in

lxxxvi the same relation that cŏcus does to coqvos. Ci generally drops i, but sci retains it, clearly because fascis would otherwise have been confused with fax. Ti generally dropped it, notwithstanding that this occasioned the loss of the t also. I presume, the close affinity of the continuous dental sharp s to the explosive dental sharp (t) rendered the former a sufficiently clear symbol of the real stem. But this clearness could not last, if other consonants were also to be absorbed by the nominative suffix; and therefore sti and -di retain the i, and thereby retain their distinctive consonants; restis is not allowed to become res, nor pedis to become pes. Assis, semissis, bessis (cf. App. D. p. 449), are found both in the full form, and as as, semis, bes, the abbreviation being the natural result of constant usage. Again, where t is preceded by a short vowel, the omission of the i would confuse stems having a short vowel, with stems having a long vowel. Hence nătis does not become nas, because nas would presume a stem năti-; sītis is, by the retention of its i, preserved from an identity with the commonly occurring word sīs. On the other hand, intercus, compos, compared with cutis, potis, show the tendency allowed to operate, because the desire of shortening a long word prevailed over the risk of confusion—a risk which is indeed less when a word has a prefix than when it is a simple stem. But the confusion is evident, where such principles have been disregarded. Princeps may fairly enough represent principis, but then præcipitis should not have been allowed to sink into an apparently analogous præceps. Ennius indeed, and another old poet, seem to have been deceived by the nominative, and used præcipim, præcipe, for accus. and abl.[1] Clear evidence of the antipathy of n, l, and r to an adjoining final s is afforded by the nominative of such consonant nouns as had stems ending in these sounds. It would not have been well to cut all such words down, as supellectilis was cut down, simply through this, to (supellectils, supellects) supellex. Who could have borne messis becoming mes, tussis becoming tus?

Corbis and orbis retained their i, probably because otherwise they might be confused with p stems. Thus urbs was doubtless

---

[1] This is by no means the only instance in which the very early poets (Greeks by origin) seem to have simply blundered.

pronounced **urps**, but there appears to have been an unwillingness lxxxvii
so to write it, lest the last evidence of the **b** stem should vanish.
For, it must be remembered, though the Romans knew nothing of
the modern theory of stems, yet they were struck by the apparent
anomaly of writing, e.g. **urps** in the nominative and **urbem** in
the accusative.

It is probable that the ı has a very different origin in some
of these words from what it has in others; in some it may be
original, in others a weakened **a** (or **o** or **e**); in others it may
have been inserted in order to give more distinctness and indepen-
dence to a puny stem, and ward off the dangers of an overbearing **s**.
This appears to be the case in **canis**, **juvenis**. **Senex** found another
way out of this difficulty.

The stems with nom. in -es, I have thought best to class
with the ı stems, as those with which they have most resemblance.
I am well aware that they are often supposed properly to have
their *stem*, not merely their nominative case, in -es (cf. e. g.
Schweizer-Sidler *Lat. Gr.* § 50, and see Leo Meyer, Corssen, &c.),
but this appears to me far from certain (see § 405). And in a case
of obscurity I have preferred to be guided in my arrangement by
the balance of objective facts.

2. In §§ 408, 435, I have pointed out some striking differences
between the words which have ı stems, and the words which have
consonant stems. While fully admitting the probability of some
of both classes of stems being as original as stems in **a** and **o**, I
am inclined to regard the second class of nouns as on the whole
of later birth than the first class, and the majority of these stems as
being weakened forms of **o** and **a** stems, the so-called ı stems having
been for phonetic reasons arrested at an intermediate stage, the
consonant stems showing the latest and furthest stage. As the
words increased in length by the addition of derivative suffixes,
they under the influence of the Latin accentuation first thinned the
final vowel, then dropped it altogether. This final vowel was,
it is true, originally very important as the sign of gender, but as
the language grew older, the imagination which saw sex in inani-
mate objects grew duller, and first the distinction of male and
female became unimportant in such matters, and then the distinc-

lxxxviii tion of sex and no sex. The new derivatives which were the offspring of the rational faculty were names of abstractions, not of
things, and they were by the process of their formation descriptions,
not pictures. Thus the gender became masculine or feminine
according to some distant analogy, instead of present vision; and
it was recognized not by one special and invariable suffix for
each sex (o or a), but by the character of the derivative suffixes
themselves; e.g. ōn masculine, -iōn feminine; -tŏr masculine, -trīc
feminine, &c.; -ŭs or -ĕs neuter. So again some suffixes were
confined primarily at least to adjectives, e.g. -tĭlĭ: others to substantives, e.g. -ōn, -iōn.

Gossrau (*Lat. Gr.* § 86, p. 92) has called attention to the connection of the genitive plural with the accent, and proposed the
following rules: '(1) All pari-syllables, as belonging to the 1 de-
'clension, have -ium. (2) All words, which with the ending in
'-ium need not draw the accent forward from the syllable on which
'it falls in the genitive singular or nominative plural, have ium;
'others have um. Or the rule may be thus stated: all words which
'in the genitive singular have the penultimate syllable long have
'-ium, those which have it short have -um. This rule,' he adds,
'is good also for all adjectives.' But there are some considerable
exceptions, as he acknowledges, to these rules.

In my opinion the only truth, contained in these rules, is what
I have before referred to; viz. that the consonant stems are to a
considerable extent stunted 1 stems, the Roman law of accentuation
exerting a constant influence to shorten the word at the end, and
this particularly, when the penultimate syllable is short.

Verbs with vowel stems.

Some readers will probably be surprised at seeing the final vowel
of some verb-stems marked as short; e.g. domă-, monĕ-, facĭ-, and
others of the classes to which these belong. My reasons for regarding them as short are these.

To take first the case of e stems[1]. (1) A few verbs with e

---

[1] A very competent comparative philologer, Grassmann, has already
taken a similar view, and on much the same grounds (Kuhn's *Zeitschrift*, XI. p. 89).

radical (all but two, -ole, and -vie being monosyllabic stems) have lxxxix -ĕtum in the supine (§ 692). But the great mass of the rest have -Itum (§ 693). A few omit the vowel altogether (§§ 700—709). Short I is a very frequent substitute for ĕ, especially in unaccented syllables (§ 234). The occurrence therefore of a short i in the great majority of suffixes from verbs with e stems is strongly suggestive of the shortness of the final stem e.

(2) There is a numerous class of adjectives with stems in -do (§ 816). Most of these are derived from verbs, and all but a few of these are from verbs with e stems. In all these cases there is a vowel preceding the -do, and this vowel is short I. In no instance is there a long vowel, unless radical, preceding -do, and in no instance is the adjective derived from a stem with ā or ē or ū or I. This again points to a connection of I-do with shortness of the stem vowel of the e verbs.

(3) The perfect of verbs with e stems which have -Itum in the supine is in -uI, never in -ēvI. And the same perfect is found in a great many other verbs of the like stems, which have no supine or other word of this formation in use. Now it seems difficult to account for the general prevalence of uI (instead of ĕvI) in e verbs, compared with -āvI in a verbs, unless from the *quantity* of the vowels being different. The difference in *quality* between a and e, when these vowels come before u, does not seem of a kind to account at all for the nearly universal solution of the one vowel and maintenance of the other. Verbs which, as monosyllables and as having radical e, have the best claim on *à priori* grounds to e long, have ĕvI in the perfect, accompanying ĕtum in the supine. But ĕ + u seems calculated to pass into eu and then into u without difficulty.

These facts together seem to me to make strongly for the shortness of the ĕ in mone- and such like verbs. Nor do I see any argument[1] for its length, which is not drawn from facts which, to say

---

[1] Gellius indeed speaks (VII. = VI. 15) as if 'calescit, nitescit, stupescit, et alia hujuscemodi multa' had e long, and 'qviescit' e short. Those who consider this a proof of the characteristic vowel of e verbs being long naturally, may explain how 'quiescit' came to be (according to Gellius) short. [In Greek inscriptions we have from verbs with e stems Οὐαλεντος, Πουδεντος though the nominatives were written Οὐαλης,

the least, are perfectly compatible with this theory. I conceive the
xc length of e in parts of the present stem, e.g. monēs, monēmus,
monētis, monēre, and similar parts of the passive verb, to be explicable by a contraction of the final e with the initial vowel of this
suffix, monĕ-ĕre = monēre. For the existence of the initial vowel
of the suffix, I refer to the consonant stems. (For Corssen's theory
respecting these consonant stems, see § 743.)

The analogy of Greek stems appears to confirm the same
view. There the e is unquestionably short, e.g. φιλέω; and
wherever a long vowel appears in its stead, a contraction has taken
place.

I might refer to the quantity of the e in the half compounds,
e.g. pudefacis, but the evidence is not decisive. All the instances
will be found collected in § 994. The majority of them have
e short, and of the dozen which are found with a long e, three
(experge-, rare-, vace-) are not from e stems, one (sve-) is from
a verb with radical e, four others (liqve-, pate-, putre-, tepe-) are
also found with e short; and the remaining four (conferve-, contabe-,
perfrige-, obstupe-) are each used once only, and that in writers
(Plaut., Ter., Lucret.) whose use in such a matter can hardly be regarded as decisive. The probable solution of this occasional lengthening may be sought in a wrong inference from the length of the e in
monemus, monere, or in a fancy that, e.g. perfrige-facio is contracted
for perfrigēre facio. Anyhow the evidence from these compounds
on the whole inclines considerably in favour of the theory of the
final e of the stem being short.

There are a few verbs with a stems which seem to me to have ă
short. They will be found named in §§ 645 and 688. The
greater number of them are markedly distinguished from ordinary
a verbs by the same characteristics as have been noticed in most e
verbs, viz. a perfect in -ui (instead of avi), and a supine in -itum
(instead of ātum). Some of these show indications of having their
natural character eventually overborne by the analogy of the others.
Hence we have micui and dimicāvi, enecui and enecāvi, -plicui

Πουδης (for Valens, Pudens, cf. § 167); Ουαλεντεινος, Φλωρεντια; just as
much as Κρησκεντος, Πραισεντα which are from consonant verbs.
(Dittenberger, Hermes VI. 308.)]

and -plĭcāvi. Dă- retains its radical short quantity throughout, except in das; stă- is, as regards the present stem, swept into the strong current of the derivative verbs; sonă- gives place to a verb sŏn-; or it may perhaps be held that sonĭs, sonĕre are really attempts xci at preserving the proper quantity without the apparent anomaly of a short ă. [Lavĕre, lăvi, lautum or lōtum with compound (dīluo for dīlauo) points to a stem lau-; but there is also lavātum pointing to lavā-: the common point of origin may well have been lăvă-]. Răf- and să- deviate in other ways. On inqvam, see § 561.

The argument from the supine will be best appreciated by an examination of Book II. Chap. xxiv. It will be seen how few are the cases in which a vowel is found before tum in the supine, without the other parts also showing a vowel stem. (See § 698, also fruĭturus and ruĭturus.) Nor are the instances many more in which, if the above principles be adopted, the quantity of this vowel does not correspond with the quantity of the final stem vowel. (Corssen supposes in the case of e stems a shortening of an original ē; in the case of the a stems the coexistence of a verb of the 3rd conjugation. *Ausspr.* II. 292—295 ed. 2.)

The verbs like facio, capio, &c. are generally regarded as having an inorganic i inserted in some parts, whilst in others what is considered its real consonant stem is shown. I have ventured to consider these verbs to be vowel verbs with stem ending in -i. For, as far as I understand the laws of vocalization in Latin, the phenomena are exactly those which would be found, if they had this stem ending: i would maintain its place before a labial vowel (o or u), and would be omitted before i; comp. adice for adjice, &c. (§ 144). But when s becomes r, i would of course become ĕ, and this completely accounts for what otherwise seems such strange variation as capio, capĭs, capĭt, capiunt, capiebam, capias, capies, capĕre, capĕrem[1], &c. The imperative singular cape from a stem capi- is evidently analogous to mare from a stem mari-, and may be accounted for in the same way, whatever that be (see § 196). It may be remarked that a final i is very rare in Latin words (see §§ 280, 243, 4). Such

---

[1] Comp. Grassmann in Kuhn's *Zeitschrift*, XI. p. 50.

instances as do occur are all due to poetic shortenings of original long vowels.

Some of these verbs exhibit this ĭ short in the supine. In others it is omitted, as is the case in many vowel verbs. Any short vowel in this position would almost inevitably have become ĭ, and the omission of ĭ in, or adjoining to, suffixes is far from being uncommon.

[Just as the current of the derivative verbs with -ā stems, swept with it some verbs whose stem was properly in -ă, so some verbs with ĭ stems were made occasionally to assume the character of verbs with ī stems. Thus e.g. cupĭ- has cupīvĭ, cupĭtum and once cupīret; morĭ- has morīrĭ; aggredĭ- has aggredīrĭ, aggredĭmur; fodĭ- has fodīrĭ; orĭ- has orīmur, adorīris; potĭ- has potĭtus, potīrer, potīrĭ. (See Chap. xxx.) Comp. also § 657.]

xcii   I am not confident as to the quantity of the final stem vowel in such verbs as sentĭ- (sentio, sensĭ, sensum). I have sometimes marked it long as usual. It may be, these verbs are instances of a semi-perversion by the analogy of more regular ĭ stems, e.g. audĭo, audīvĭ, audītum; or the ĭ is here distinctly realized as a suffix of inflexion only, a mark of the *present* stem, instead of the verb stem. In verbs which have reduplicated perfects, or perfects in -sĭ, the same distinction is practically recognized.

Concluding Remarks.

I have stated in different parts of the book such obligations as I thought necessary to mention in a book of this kind, which can rarely be formed by independent research from the original authorities directly. But I desire here expressly to recognize the debt I owe to Ritschl, Corssen, Neue, and Curtius, to all of whom I hope, at a future time, to express renewed obligations for further information. Many of the statements about Latin inscriptions of the Republican period are taken from Ritschl, and taken with the confident belief that, though they may not prove always right, it is exceedingly improbable that I should be able to correct him. Some of his writings on Inscriptions are not easily accessible. I look forward with much interest to their republication in his *Opuscula*, as well as to the new edition of his Plautus, and the promised Grammar of old Latin, if indeed the last is not put off to the Greek Kalends. The statements about later inscriptions, and some respecting Republican inscriptions, are chiefly founded on statements by Corssen or Brambach (*Die Neugestaltung der lateinischen Orthographie*, 1868). These of course cannot claim anything like the weight of Ritschl's statements, which are the outcome of years of skilled and careful labour. To Corssen I am the more anxious to acknowledge my frequent obligations, because his very prominence in the field of Roman phonetics has made it necessary for me, in some cases, to express and vindicate my dissent from his views. The second volume of the new edition of his *Aussprache* did not reach me in time to make much use of, except in occasional reference and correction. Curtius' very careful identification of Latin and Greek roots has been followed almost implicitly to this extent, that I have xciii rarely suggested an identity which he has not approved, though I have frequently omitted some which were either superfluous for the purpose in hand, or appeared to me to admit of some doubt.

Neue's *Formenlehre* (1300 closely printed pages without an index) has enabled me to give a more complete, and at the same time a briefer, account of Latin inflexions than will be found in other Grammars. It seemed to me useless, as a general rule, to encumber my book with references to the passages where a particular form occurs, when this work has been done exhaustively already, and the result can be easily obtained by any scholar who seeks to test a matter himself. On the other hand Neue's book is quite unreadable by the majority of students, and is, in fact, not so much a grammar itself, as a quarry from which grammars will be built. I hope greatly to improve my own 1st and 3rd Books when the corresponding parts of Neue's work are published. It may be useful to add that, being mainly a collection of references, it is accessible to a great extent by students who have little knowledge of German. I have tested his references in a great many cases, and rarely found them inaccurate. Of course, later critical editions of authors will sometimes alter his results.

Madvig's Grammar (3rd Germ. edit.) has not been of so much service to me in this volume, as in the Syntax. In that my obligations to him are paramount to all others. To Key's Grammar I certainly owe much in the way of suggestion, but how much

I cannot tell, as I have often used it for many years, and in such a case it is impossible to distinguish between ideas which have been more or less borrowed, and those which have been obtained by independent inquiry with eyes turned in the same direction.   But there is no recent Latin Grammar, that I know of (except Madvig's in the Syntax), which is based on so fresh a study of the facts, or has done more in awakening a more scientific treatment.   I have also read some of his other Philological papers, and sometimes got useful hints even from those with whose general arguments and conclusions I am quite incompetent to deal.

Gossrau's elaborate, but not, as I think, very happily conceived Grammar, and Schweizer-Sidler's *Formenlehre*, were not published till my first two books were in print.   And two English books, Peile's *Introduction to Greek and Latin Etymology*, and Ferrar's *Comparative Grammar*, vol. I., did not come into my hands till still later.

xciv

I have intended to use always the best texts of the Latin authors. What I have used are Cicero by Baiter and Kayser, and the larger edition by Baiter and Halm; Sallust by Jordan; Cæsar by Kraner and Dinter; Livy by Madvig; Curtius by Hedicke; Pliny the elder by Detlefsen, so far as it had appeared (now 3 vols. containing Books i.—xxii.), and Jan for the rest; Quintilian by Bonnell, and latterly the edition by Halm; Plautus by Ritschl, and Fleckeisen, with Wagner's *Aulularia;* Terence by Wagner and Umpfenbach; Lucretius and Horace by Munro, to whose notes on Lucretius I am often indebted ; Vergil by Ribbeck, whose grammatical index has been of much service to me.   For most other books I have used the editions in Teubner's series.

Of some plays of Plautus which have had no recent critical editors, and of Cato and Varro, *de re rustica,* I have made less use than I should have done, had I been able to regard the text as in a fairly trustworthy condition.

I have the pleasure of expressing my thanks to my friend, the Rev. Professor Joseph B. Mayor, who has kindly read over most of the proof sheets, and by whose criticisms I have always benefited : and to the Rev. J. H. Backhouse, who read and commented on the proof sheets of the book when in an early stage. The draft he saw (an enlargement of my *Elementary Latin Grammar*, published in 1862) has however been twice superseded since, and I can only regret that the present book has not passed under his most accurate eye.

There are several real or apparent inconsistencies, especially in the printing of the volume, which I mention, lest they should deceive any one. I have by no means always distinguished (as I think it desirable to do in a grammar) the consonant v from the vowel u; nor always marked the suffixes or parts of suffixes with hyphens, nor always marked the quantity of vowels, nor been rigid in spelling, especially in cases of assimilation, e.g. qvanqvam or qvamqvam, &c., nor named a word always according to its form at the same stage of the language, e.g. proxumus and proximus; com, cum, con; &c. Nor have I been always consistent in noticing or not noticing very exceptional occurrences of words or forms, or rare occurrences in extinct writers (e.g. the early dramatic poets); or the non-use of particular cases of nouns, where the non-use was probably accidental, and the like. In some cases I have had a reason for the apparent inconsistency, but in others it has been unintentional. I fear too that there are some unintentional omissions and misplacements of words in the lists in Book III.

The second part containing the Syntax is half printed, and will be ready, I hope, in a few months. References made here to sections bearing numbers higher than 999 are to the Syntax.

I have now only to add that I shall be thankful to any one who may take the trouble, either privately or publicly, to point out any mistakes I may have made.

H. J. ROBY.

LONDON, *May*, 1871.
(*Published* 7 *July*, 1871.)

In this second edition I have silently corrected the errors which have been pointed out to me and those which I have myself noticed. Some additions also have been made, though these had to be kept within narrow limits owing to the book being stereotyped. Both corrections and additions, though not inconsiderable in number, are mostly of slight moment, and none, I think, involve any change of principle. A thorough revision of the book has been out of the question. Such time as I have to spare for studies of this kind, has been fully taken up with the preparation of the Syntax. Nor indeed could a re-examination of the subject-matter be so usefully undertaken now, as after a few more years have brought further criticism and further aids from without.

The additions made to the Preface have been included in square brackets. A few verbal corrections have been made without notice. I have marked in the margin the pages of the first edition.

I am glad to be able to refer my readers for a fuller exposition of many points of phonetics and philology to the second edition of Mr Peile's able and interesting *Introduction to Greek and Latin Etymology.*

I have the pleasure of acknowledging corrections kindly sent to me by the Rev. John E. B. Mayor, of Cambridge; Henry Nettleship, Esq., of Harrow; Charles C. Tancock, Esq., of Exeter College, Oxford; and especially by Professor George M. Lane, of Harvard College, Massachusetts, who favoured me with a long list of corrections, of which many might have escaped my notice, and all have been of much service.

The second Part has been delayed partly by increased official work, but chiefly by my having recast and enlarged the doctrine of the cases. I hope now a few months will complete it.

H. J. R.

92, KENSINGTON GARDENS' SQUARE, LONDON. W.
14 *Octob.* 1872.

BOOK I.

SOUNDS.

BOOK I.

SOUNDS.

CHAPTER I.[1]

ELEMENTS OF SPEECH; and particularly CONSONANTS.

THE human voice may be regarded as a continuous stream of
air, emitted as breath from the lungs, changed, as it leaves the larynx,
by the vibration of two ligaments (called **chordæ vocales**) into
vocal sound, and either modified by various positions, or interrupted or compressed by various actions, of the uvula, the tongue,
and the lips. In a whisper the ligaments do not vibrate, but otherwise the description holds good.

Interruption by complete contact, or compression by approximation of certain parts of the organs, or vibration of the tongue
or uvula, produces *consonants.*

Modification, without interruption or compression, and without
vibration of the tongue or uvula, produces *vowels.*

CONSONANTS.

Consonants admit of a fourfold classification, according to

1. the completeness or incompleteness of the contact;
2. the accompaniment or absence of vocal sound;
3. the position of the organs, where the contact takes place;
4. the passage of the breath through the mouth or nose.

[1] In this and the next two Chapters, much use has been made of
Lepsius' *Standard Alphabet* (1863); Max Müller's *Survey of Languages*
(1855) and *Lectures* 2nd series; Melville Bell's *Principles of Speech*
(1863); Brücke's *Physiologie der Sprachlaute* (1856).

I—2

1. (*a*) If the contact is complete, so as to cause an entire in- 3 terruption of the passage of the breath, we get *mutes* (*explosive* consonants, *checks*, &c.); as p, b; k, g; t, d.

(*b*) If the contact is only partial, i.e. if the organs do but approximate more or less closely to each other, we get a continuous sound caused by the friction of the breath against the parts. These sounds are called *fricative* consonants (*continuous, spirants, flatus, breathings*, &c.); as s, z; sh, zh (French j); th; f, v; &c.

2. (*a*) Again the contact or approximation may be made with 4 the vocal chords wide apart, in which case a whisper only takes place. These consonants are called *sharp* or *voiceless* (*breathed, hard, surd*, tenues, &c.); as p, k, t, s, sh, th (in *thin*), f, wh, h (in *huge*), rh (as r in French *theatre, fiacre*), &c.

(*b*) If the contact or approximation is made, with the vocal chords close to one another, the consonants are called *flat* or *voiced* (*soft, blunt, sonant*, mediæ, &c.); as b, g, d, z, zh, th (in *then*), v, w. y, r, &c. The chords being thus ready to vibrate usually do vibrate, causing voice, either during the approximation, or, in the case of a mute, the instant that the contact is released. But the sound of the voice is not essential, as, in whispering, a rustle in the throat takes its place. (See App. A. vii.)

3. Again the parts of the mouth which are put in contact or 5 approximation or movement are very various, and the sound is modified accordingly. For the purposes of classification in European languages five parts may be especially distinguished; viz. the lips, the throat (or rather the soft palate just above the larynx), the hard palate, the teeth, and the tongue.

(*a*) Consonants formed at or with the lips are called *Labial;* viz. p, b, m, w, and labial f, v. The ordinary f, v are *labio-dentals*, being formed by the under lip and upper teeth.

(*b*) Consonants formed in the throat (or soft palate) are called *Guttural;* viz. k (c, q), g, ng, ch (in *loch*).

(*c*) Consonants formed at the hard palate are called *Palatal*, of which some approach nearer to gutturals, some to dentals: such are y, ch (in Germ. *Ich*, or h in Engl. *huge*), sh, French j. (The Italian c (in *cima*) i.e. English ch (in *church*), and Italian g (in *giro*) i.e. English j (in *join*), which are sometimes classed as *palatals*, appear to be really double consonants; viz. ch = tsh; j = dzh where zh is French j.)

(*d*) Consonants formed at or just above the teeth are called *Dental;* viz. **t, d, n; th; s, z**.

(*e*) Two other consonants, called *Lingual* consonants or *liquids* (or *trills*), are **r, l**. **r** is caused by the breath passing over the tip of the tongue, which is more or less vibrated: **l** is caused by the breath passing over the sides of the back of the tongue, which is then removed from its position to complete the sound. For an **r** (common in France), caused by vibration of the uvula, see App. A.

4. If the uvula be lowered so as to obstruct the passage of the 6 air through the mouth, but allow it to vibrate in the cavities of the nose, a *nasal* sound is produced. If the organs are otherwise in the positions required for **b, d, g**, but the air passes into the nose, the nasal consonants **m, n, ng** (a single sound as in *sing*) are respectively produced. (The palatal **n** has much the same sound as a dental **n**.)

The nasals resemble the *explosive* consonants in requiring a vowel before and after to give the full effect; they resemble the *continuous* consonants in the possibility of continuing the sound, which is however that of the first half only of the consonant.

5. The semivowels **w** and **y** will be best described after the 7 vowels (§ 23).

Another letter has yet to be noticed, viz. **h** (**spiritus asper**). This is a mere expulsion of breath through the perfectly open glottis, i.e. with the vocal chords apart, not approximated and vibrating. **h** stands to the vowels, as **p** to **b**, **k** to **g**, &c.

(If **h** is breathed immediately after an explosive consonant we get sounds, represented in Greek, viz. $\phi = \mathbf{p} + \mathbf{h}$, $\chi = \mathbf{k} + \mathbf{h}$, $\theta = \mathbf{t} + \mathbf{h}$, and in Sanscrit (**g** + **h** &c.). A strong articulation of consonants e.g. by Scotchmen or Irishmen gives a similar sound.)

There is also a very slight sound heard before any initial vowel, and best caught when two vowels come together, but are pronounced separately, as in *go over*. This is rarely expressed by any letter. It is the **spiritus lenis** of the Greeks.

The principal sounds in European languages may be tabulated 8 as follows, the letters being supposed to be sounded as in English, except where it is otherwise stated.

| | EXPLOSIVE. | | NASAL. | FRICATIVE. | |
	Sharp.	Flat.	Usually flat.	Sharp.	Flat.
LABIAL.	p	b	m	{ wh[1] { labial f	w[1] labial v
LABIODENTAL.				ordinary f	ordinary v
GUTTURAL.	k	g hard	ng	⌈ ch in │ Scotch *loch* { (Germ. ch after ⌊ a or o)	g in Germ. *tage*
PALATAL.				⌈ h in *huge* │ (nearly Germ. ch { after i or e) │ ⌊ sh	y nearly g in Germ. *wiege* zh (French j)
LINGUAL.				⌈ whispered r { Welsh (?) ll	r l
DENTAL.	t	d	n	⌈ s { th ⌊ (in *thin*)	z th (in *then*)

It may be added that s, z, and sometimes sh and French j are called *sibilants*.

CHAPTER II.

COMBINATION OF CONSONANTS.

SINGLE consonants may be sounded either before or after a vowel. But the semivowels y and w are sounded only before a vowel.

A continuous consonant has always the same sound whether its vowel be before or after: but an explosive consonant has not the same. The full pronunciation of an explosive consonant requires both the closing and opening of the organs. Thus in ap only half the p is properly sounded: in pa we have the other half. The full pronunciation is heard in apa, or, as commonly written, ap-pa. In ap-ka the first half of p and the second half of k is sounded.

Writing consonants double has either an *etymological* origin, when it is done to preserve the memory of distinct sounds now lost; e.g. ac-cedo for ad-cedo; ἄλλ-ος compared with ali-us; &c., or a *phonetic* origin, as in English it is used to distinguish a short accented vowel from a long one, e.g. *kite, kitten;* &c. In either case the consonant is wholly pronounced once only.

[1] The continuous part of the sound wh is really a *blowing*, the continuous part of w is the vowel u.

Two or more consonants may be pronounced with only one 10
vowel, but the possible combinations are somewhat different, when
the vowel is *before* the consonants and when it is *behind* them.
When the vowel is sounded after the consonants, the combination
may be called *initial;* when the vowel is before the consonants, *final.*

(The Germans give the name *Anlaut, Inlaut, Auslaut* (on-
sound, in-sound, out-sound) to the sound of a consonant with the
vowel following, on both sides, and preceding, respectively.)

An *Initial*[1] combination may not consist of a liquid or nasal 11
followed by any other consonant, except that an m may be followed by n, nor of a fricative, except a sibilant, followed by an
explosive: nor of two explosives unless the former of the two be a
labial or guttural, the latter a dental. Semivowels are never followed by any consonant.

Of the rarer combinations may be given as instances:
Greek, τλάω, πτύω, κτείνω, ψεύδω, ξαίνω, μνῆμα, φθίνω, χθές.
German, *Pfanne, Pflaum, Pfropf, Zerren* (i. e. *tserren*).

A *final* combination may not consist of a nasal preceded by any 12
consonant, except a liquid; nor of a liquid preceded by any consonant,
except that l may be preceded by r; nor readily of two explosives
or two fricatives, unless the latter of the two be a dental: e. g. **akp,
apk, atk, atp,** seem harsher than **akt, apt;** and (taking **th** as in
English and **ch** as in German) **athf, asf, athch, afch,** than **afth, afs,
achth, achf.**

Instances of the rarer combinations are
English, *film, kiln, strength, watch, texts, cringed.*
German, *kopf, dumpf, obst, balgst, birgst.*

Neither in initial nor final combinations are sharps pronounceable 13
before flats, or readily flats before sharps. When they occur together in writing, the former of the two, if a sharp, is usually changed
in speaking into the corresponding flat; if a flat, into the corresponding sharp. Sometimes the latter is changed, to suit the former,
which is retained: e. g. **obst** is either pronounced **opst,** or **obzd.**
(But *midst, striv'st, hugg'st* are pronounced without this change.)

Nor can either an initial or final combination contain more explosives than two, with or without a fricative before or after each.

A syllable is such a sound or combination of sounds as can be 14
uttered with one breath. It may consist of a vowel (or diphthong)
only, or of a vowel (or diphthong) combined with one or more
consonants.

A word consists of as many syllables, as it has vowels separately
pronounced.

---

[1] The languages of the Græco-Latin and Teutonic stocks are alone
regarded in the following statements.

A single syllable may contain a vowel with two or more con- 15 sonants on each side of it. Two consecutive syllables may therefore, if the first ends and the second begins with a combination of consonants, bring together in the middle a twofold aggregation of consonants.

The aggregation of consonants in the middle of a word is limited only by the necessity of its being capable of precise division into a pronounceable final combination followed by a pronounceable initial combination.

But in ordinary pronunciation a consonant between two vowels is uttered partly with both. The real division of the syllables is therefore neither before nor after the consonant, but in the middle of it, i.e. after the closing of the organs and before the opening.

Accordingly a valid aggregation of consonants in the middle of a word must be such that some one of the consonants shall fitly close the first syllable, and also open the second syllable: e.g. **actra** is divisible into **act-tra**; but **act-pra** is not divisible into **act-tpra** or into **actp-pra, tpra** not being a possible initial combination, nor **actp** a possible final combination.

The division of a word into syllables is in modern languages 16 decided rather by the etymological than by a phonetic division. So far as this phonetic principle is disregarded, the word is either resolved not into separate syllables, but into separate words, or else a vowel is lightly interposed between the consonants by the opening of the organs to complete one consonant before uttering the next; e.g. **actpra** becomes **actĕpra** or **acĕtĕpra.**

On the division in Latin, see Chap. XI.

CHAPTER III.

VOWELS AND COMBINATIONS OF VOWELS.

THE shape of the mouth determines the quality of the vowel. 17 There are two great agents in modifying vowel sound, the tongue and the lips. The tongue by the elevation of its hinder part towards the palate diminishes internally the oral channel: the lips being protruded lengthen the oral channel and contract the external aperture.

The purest and simplest vowel is Italian **a**, English **ah.** The 18 extremes are Italian **i** (i.e. English **ee**), being the vowel with the narrowest channel: and Italian **u**, English **oo**, the vowel with the longest channel and narrowest external aperture. Of these **a** is formed nearest to the guttural point of contact; **i** at the palato-dental point; **u** at the labial.

Other vowels, i.e. other modifications of vowel sound, may be 19 regarded as intermediate either between **a** and **i** (*lingual* vowels), or between a and u (*labial* or *round* vowels), or partaking in some degree of the characters of both lines. Each vowel also may be *wide* or *close*, according as the pharynx (i.e. the cavity at the back of the tongue above the larynx) is more or less expanded.

It is difficult to put any precise limit to the number of possible vowels, most nations, and, indeed, most individuals, differing more or less from one another in vowel pronunciation. But the vowels most worth notice for an English student of Latin are given in the following list. All may be either long or short. (Ellis's palæotypic symbols and Bell's names are subjoined to each. Most of the parallelisms are from Ellis.)

1. Germ. a (*a*. 'Low back wide'). Scot. *măn;* Germ. *mănn, mähnen.*

2. Ital. a (a. 'Mid back wide'). Engl. *father;* Ital. *mătto, măno;* Fr. *chătte.*

3. A common Engl. vowel (ə or ɟ. 'Mid mixed' or 'Mid back'). Engl. *ŭp, sŏn, does;* nearly *tailor, paper;* long in *urn, word, fern, bird;* nearly Fr. *que je me repente.*

4. Ital. close o (*uh*. 'High mixed wide round'). Ital. *croce, dolce, Roma.* It sounds to English ears between 3 and 9, but nearer 9.

5. Engl. short o (ɔ. 'Low back wide round'). Engl. *odd, doll, John, dog.*

6. Engl. aw (A. 'Low back round'). Engl. *awed, tall, pawn;* Austrian a; short in Engl. *august.*

7. Ital. open o (o. 'Mid back wide round'). Cumberland *home;* Ital. *uomo;* French short o, e.g. *homme;* Germ. short o, e.g. *gold.*

8. French au (*o*. 'Mid back round'). Engl. *ŏmit, window, home* (but cf. § 21); Germ. long o, e.g. *gross.*

9. Engl. short u (*u*. 'High back wide round'). Engl. *pull, book, wood.*

10. Ital. u (u. 'High back round'). Engl. *brute, rule, do, mood;* short in French *poule, coupe.*

11. French eu (œ. 'Mid front wide round'). Fr. *peur, jeune;* Germ. ö, e.g. *böcke, Göthe.*

12. French u (y. 'High front wide round'). Devonshire *combe, you;* French *du, hutte;* Germ. ü, e.g. *lücke, Müller.*

13. Engl. short a (æ. 'Low front wide'). Engl. *hăt, măn;* long in (sometimes) *half, ask,* and in Somersetshire *Băth.*

14. Ital. open e (E. 'Low front'). Scot. *ell, pet;* Ital. *bello, letto, bene, Galileo;* Germ. ä, e.g. *Väter;* Fr. *même.*

15. Engl. short e (e. 'Mid front wide'). Engl. *ell, pet, men;* Scot. *ill, pit;* Germ. *fett, eben;* Fr. *elle, les.*

16. Ital. close e (*e*. 'Mid front'). Engl. a in a*erial;* Ital. *quello, detta, remo;* Fr. *é,* e.g. *été.*

17. Engl. short i (*i*. 'High front wide'). Engl. *shin, fit, pity;* the long sound is heard in singing and in Icelandic.

18. Ital. i (i. 'High front'). Engl. *machine, feet;* Scot. *pity;* the ordinary Fr., Germ., and Ital. i.

Of these 5 to 18 may be arranged tabularly from their common base **a** to each of the extremes:

Labial.		Labio-lingual.	Lingual.	
Wide	Close	**Wide**	Wide	Close
5	6		13	14
Engl. short **o**	Engl. **aw**		**Engl.** short **a**	Ital. open e
7	8	11	15	16
Ital. open **o**	French **au**	French **eu**	Engl. short **e**	Ital. close e
9	10	12	17	18
Engl. short **u**	Ital. **u**	French **u**	Engl. short **1**	Ital. **1**

A *diphthong* is the sound made by the voice while passing from 20 one vowel position to another. The precise sound varies according to (1) the quality of the limiting vowels; (2) the distance between them; (3) the evenness of the rate of speed. The most usually recognized diphthongs are formed when the passage is from an open to a close position, i.e. when the initial position is nearer to **a**, and further from **1** or **u** than the final position is.

The following may here be noted, the limiting vowels being 21 denoted by their numbers in the list given above. (Ellis' symbol is added in brackets. On diphthongs with Engl. **r** see Appendix A.)

2 to 10 (au). Germ. *haus, laut*.
3 to 10 (əu). Engl. *now, bough, house, loud*.
8 to 10 (oou). Southern Engl. long o, the second element being faint, e.g. *no, bone, hose*.
13 to 10 (æu). Cockney *town*.
15 to 10 (eu). American *town ;* Ital. and Span. Eur*opa*.
2 to 18 (ai). Engl. ay (*yes*), a broad sound of I, *Isaiah;* Germ. *hain, Kaiser, theil;* Ital. ai (with first element prolonged), *daino, laido;* French ai (with second element prolonged), *faience*.
3 to 18 (əi). Engl. long i, e.g. *fine, eye, buy, die*.
13 to 18 (æi). Cockney and Scotch long i.
16 to 18 (eei). Southern Engl. long **a**, the second element being faint ; e.g. *fate, fain, feint*.
5 to 18 (ɔi). Engl. oi, e.g. *boil, boy, oyster*.
7 to 12 or 18 (oy or oi). Germ. eu, e.g. *heute, euch*.

A diphthong sometimes gives way to an intermediate **vowel**, 22 which yet is often written as a diphthong. Comp. Germ. **au, ai** with French **au, ai**. Again, an intermediate vowel is sometimes resolved into a diphthong; e.g. Cockney **au** for **ō**.

The sounds represented in English by **w** and **y** when initial 23 are usually called *semivowels*. They easily arise when the voice passes from a closer to a more open vowel position; i.e. **w** in passing from **u** or **o**, **y** in passing from **1** or **e**, backwards towards **a**. The consonantal character (compare Engl. **we** with Fr. **oui**) is produced by very slight pressure of the lips in the case of **w**, of the tongue and palate in the case of **y**, followed by instant separation.

CHAPTER IV.

LAWS OF PHONETIC CHANGE[1].

i. PHONETIC change in words is either *voluntary*, e. g such as 24 is made for the purposes of inflexion, or *involuntary*. The latter alone is the subject of the following statements.

ii. Involuntary phonetic change is the result of a struggle be- 25 tween the physical tendency to reduce the effort of articulation, and the intellectual or instinctive desire of preserving any parts of the word which are characteristic of its meaning. The latter acts mainly by way of resistance.

e. g. **ab** is much seldomer changed in composition than **sub**, because of the danger of confusion with **ad**.

In the passive voice forms like **amabaris, amaberis, amareris** are shortened into **amabare**, &c., but **amaris** is not shortened to **amare** lest it should be confused with the present infinitive.

iii. The normal condition of these forces is one of apparent 26 equilibrium, but really of slow conflict, which however is called into greater and more perceptible activity, when a new sound or syllable is added to the word, as is done by inflexion or derivation or composition in order .to adapt the word to a modification or enlargement of the conception.

Sudden phonetic change.

iv. Such an addition may produce phonetic changes in two 27 ways: (1) by its adding to the length or weight of the word; and (2) by its bringing into contact sounds, which do not then admit of easy articulation in their integrity.

---

[1] The illustrations throughout this Chapter are meant as illustrations only, not as in any way exhausting the phenomena. Many of the facts are stated more fully as regards Latin in the sixth and following Chapters.

v. So far as such an addition lengthens a word, there is a 28 tendency to counteract this in other ways, especially

1. by omitting short unaccented vowels; e. g. **audacter** for **audaciter**; **jurgium** for **jurigium**; **disciplina** for **discipulina**, &c.

2. by omitting entire syllables; e. g. **homicīdium** for **hominicidium**; **veneficium** for **venenificium**; **viginti** for **dvi-decen-ti**; **corpulentus** for **corporulentus**; **voluntas** for **voluntitas**, &c.

Compound verbs rarely retain the reduplication in the perfect; e. g: **tango, tetigi,** but **contingo, contigi.**

So in French **semet ipsissimum** becomes in old Provençal *smet essme;* in Provençal *medesme;* in old French *meisme;* in modern French *même.* **Maleaptus** becomes Prov. *malapti;* Ital. *malato;* French *malade.*

In English *Cholmondeley* is pronounced *Chumley; Brighthelmstone, Brighton; Wymondham, Wyndham; Towcester, Towster; Marjoribanks, Marchbanks; Cirencester, Cicester;* &c.

3. by slurring over the final syllable, which in Latin is always unaccented; e. g. **amavēre** for **amavērunt; amatŏr** for **amatōr,** &c. Each of these changes may again bring incompatible sounds into contact.

vi. The incompatibility of neighbouring sounds may be abso- 29 lute, or only relative to other combinations ready at hand to replace them. That is, it may be impossible to pronounce two neighbouring sounds, or, at least, it may be much easier to pronounce other sounds nearly allied to the more difficult sounds.

Thus we have **suggero** as well as **succurro,** though **subgero** contains no such incompatibility as **subcurro** does.

vii. Sounds are incompatible either from requiring very different 30 positions of the organs, or from being respectively voiced and voiceless (flat and sharp).

viii. When two incompatible sounds would otherwise come 31 together, usually the difficulty is foreseen, and instead of the organs being left, after pronouncing the former, to do what they can with the latter, the anticipation works a change in the former, or at least acts so as to preserve the latter. (But the reverse is sometimes the case[1].)

---

[1] When the former of the two consonants or vowels is changed to suit the latter, the assimilation is called *regressive;* when the latter is changed to suit the former, *progressive.*

The former is either made compatible with the latter by partial assimilation, or by complete assimilation, or the former is omitted altogether, or other changes are made.   And the change thus produced may propagate effects still further back.

ix. The phenomena are naturally divided into four classes, according to the nature of the sounds brought into contact :

1. Consonant + consonant ; 2. vowel + consonant ; 3. consonant + vowel ; 4. vowel + vowel.

1. CONSONANT + CONSONANT :

(*a*) Partial assimilation.

Thus, voiced are changed to the corresponding voiceless consonants ; e. g. sub-porto to supporto ; scrib-tus to scriptus ; ag-tus to actus ; aug-si to auc-si (auxi), &c.

Again a nasal of one organ is changed to that of another ; e. g. com-tero to contero ; exim-de to exinde ; in-pero to impero, &c.

Analogous to this is the change of an explosive to a continuous consonant as seen in lg, rg, ll, rr, changing a *following* suffixed t to s ; e. g. mulg- mulsum ; curro, cursum, &c.

(*b*) Complete assimilation is found, chiefly, either (*a*) when both consonants belong to the same organ, or (β) in the case of prepositions in composition ; (γ) rarely otherwise.

e. g. (*a*) cessi for ced-si ; fossus for fod-sus ; pos-sidere for por-sidere ; summus for sub-mus ; gemma for gen-ma ; sella for sed-la ; puella for puer-la ; columella for columen-la ; &c.

(β) ad in compounds ap-pello, accurro, aggero, afficio, assideo, arrideo, allicio, &c.

ob in oppono, occurro, officio, oggannio, &c.; sub in suppono, summoveo, succurro, sufficio, suggero, &c.

ec- in effero, effugio, &c.; dis in diffugio, &c.; com in corruo, collido, &c.

(γ) pressi for prem-si (pren-si) ; flamma for flag-ma, &c.

(*c*) Omission : the preceding vowel is often lengthened :

(*a*) *Medial:* before c ; e. g. hoc for hodce.

Before nasals ; e. g. exāmen for exăg-men ; jūmentum for jŭg-mentum ; cæmentum for cæd-mentum ; semestris for ses-mestris ; pono for posno ; lūna for luc-na ; dēni for dĕc-ni ; satin' for satisne ; &c.

Before t; e.g. nītor for gnictor (§ 110); autumnus for auctumnus.

Before d; e. g. jūdex for jusdex.

Before s; e. g. sustollo for substollo; ostento for obstento; asporto for absporto.

Before l; e. g. quālus for quas-lus.

Before j; e. g. dījudico for disjudico; rējectus for redjectus; pējero for perjĕro; mājor for magjor.

Before v; e. g. brĕvis for bregvis (§ 129).

The middle of three consonants is frequently omitted; e. g. fulmen for fulgmen: fultus for fulctus; mul-si for mulgsi; pars for parts. Comp. pergo for perrigo; surpuit for surripuit, &c.

(β) Initial: e. g. lamentum for clamentum; lis for stlis; bonus for dvonus; Janus for Djanus; nitor for gnitor, &c.

(γ) In *final* syllable; e. g. cor for cord; lac for lact; consul for consuls; equĕs for equets; pes for peds, &c.

(*d*) Dissimilation: e. g. in order to avoid the recurrence 36 of l, the suffix alis is frequently changed after l to -aris; e. g. puerilis, but puellaris, &c. Similarly Parilia from Pales.

(*e*) Insertion; e. g. sumptus for sum-tus; hiemps for hiems, 37 &c.

So also in early Latin; e. g. Alcumena for Ἀλκμήνη; Tecumessa for Τέκμησσα; Æsculapius for Ἀσκληπιός.

In Greek ἀνδρός for ἀνέρος; μεσημβρία from μέση ἡμέρα.

In French *chambre* from *camera*; *tiendrait* from *tenir*; *humble* from *humilis*; *nombre* from *numerus*.

In German *wesentlich, namentlich* for *wesenlich,* &c.; *Fändrich* for *Fänrich*; *aendlich* (in rustic dialect) for *ähnlich*; in Dutch *Hendrick* from *Henricus,* &c.

(*f*) Transposition: 38

(*a*) of two consonants; e. g. mixtus for misctus (as some think: but cf. § 635). So in Greek ἔσχατος for ἔξατος, superlative of ἐξ; English *wasp,* dialectically *waps.*

(β) of liquid (r, l) with succeeding vowel; e. g. stra-, sterno; spre-, sperno; cre-, cerno. So in Greek καρδία for κραδία; δρακ-, δέρκω; &c. dulcis compared with γλυκύς; in English, *purty* for *pretty; burn* for *bren; firth* and *frith; Althorp* pronounced *Altrup;* &c.; and all terminations in -bre, -cre, -gre, -tre; -ble, -cle, -gle, -tle, pronounced ber, cer, ger, ter; bul, cul, gul, tul.

(*g*) The combinations ᵭt, and (almost always) tt appear to have been unbearable; hence they are usually changed to ss, apparently by the latter letter being changed to s and then the former assimilated to it; e.g. cessum, missum for ced-sum, mit-sum from ced-tum, mit-tum. (But mitto, quattuor, &c. are allowed.)

2. VOWEL + CONSONANT.   39

(*a*) The vowel ĕ is substituted or retained before r (also br, tr) in place of ĭ; e.g. părio, pepĕri, compĕrio compared with cădo, cecĭdi, concĭdo; fĕro, refĕro with lĕgo, collĭgo; funus, funĕris with homo, homĭnis; anser, ansĕris with ales, alĭtis; regeris from regis; &c.

In fieri, fierem (for fĭri, fĭrem) e is inserted (or not absorbed) before r. So in English *mire, fire* pronounced *mier, fier.*

(*b*) If a precedes two consonants, of which the first is l, a is changed into u instead of into e; e.g. salsus, insulsus, compared with cantus, concentus; calco, conculco, with tracto, contrecto, &c.

ll prefers e; e.g. vello, vulsum; pello, pulsum; &c.

Before a single l, ŏ is changed to ŭ (or retained) instead of being changed to ĭ (unless i follow; cf. § 41); e.g. popolus, populus; ἐπιστολή, epistula; compared with homo, homĭnis; λέγομεν, legimus, &c.

(*c*) ĕ is found before two consonants, where ĭ is found before a single consonant; e.g. scando, conscendo compared with cano, concino; nutrimentum compared with nutrimĭnis; biceps with bicipĭtis; &c.

(*d*) ŭ was preferred to ĭ before m (at least before Cæsar's time); e.g. maxumus, documentum, drachuma, &c.

3. CONSONANT + VOWEL.   40

(*a*) The vowel i when following c, g, t, d assibilated the preceding consonant in late Latin, and languages thence derived. Hence we pronounce *nation, nashon; musician, musishon.* The Italians pronounce c as English ch, in *Cicero;* gi as English j, in *collegiato, religione,* &c., and have *Marzo* from Martius; *palazzo* from palatium; *mezzo* for medius, &c.

The French have assibilated c before other vowels; e.g. *chambre* from camera; *chien* from canis; *cheval* from caballus; &c.

(*b*) The vowel ŏ was retained (to avoid confusion) after the consonantal v (§§ 93, 213) for a considerable time after it had given place in other words to ŭ; e.g. equos, quom, servos, &c. were not changed to equus, quum, servus, &c. till long after domĭnos (nom. sing.), &c. had given place to dominus, &c. In English *want, was, war,* &c. the sound of a has been partially assimilated to w.

4. Vowel + Vowel.　　　　　　　　　　　41

(*a*) Though 1 has a liking for u (or earlier o) before it, yet if i follows, i also precedes: hence **similis, facilis**, compared with **simulo, simultas, facultas; inquilinus** from **incola; Æmilius, familia, exsilium**, compared with **æmŭlus, famulus, exul**, &c.

(*b*) A similar assimilation is seen in **bene** for **bone; soboles** for **suboles; socordia** for **secordia; solvo** for **se-luo** (Curtius).

In German this principle has a much wider application, under the name of *Umlaut*, when a, o, u of the stem are changed to ä, ö, ü in consequence of an i or e in the termination, e.g. *Glas, Gläser; Schloss, Schlösser; Kuh, Kühe; Kunst, künstlich; flog, flöge;* &c.

x. The usual changes are sometimes foregone from dread of 42 some characteristic part of the word being obscured. Hence (1) sometimes an unstable combination of sounds is preserved, especially where it is the result of previous changes: (2) sometimes the incompatibility of sounds is removed by other methods than those usual.

(1) Thus **ars, puls, amans, frons** are allowed to remain because they are for **arts, pults, amants, fronds** or **fronts**; while **pater, consul** have thrown away the **s**, and **homo, sermo** for **homons, sermons** have thrown off **ns**. In **fers** (so also in **vis** for **vils**) the **s** is preserved as the sign of the second person.

(2) In **tonstrix** for **tondtrix** the suffixed **t** is preserved, because **tonsrix** would be contrary to Latin pronunciation; **tonsor** for **tondtor** follows the ordinary rule by which **dt** becomes **ss** or **s**.

In **pietas, societas, ebrietas**, &c., the o of **pio-, socio-, ebrio-**, is changed to **e** instead of to **i** (as in **bonitas**, &c.), because **piitas** would have become **pitas**, &c.

Gradual Phonetic Change.

xi. The more gradual phonetic changes, not caused by any 43 sudden derangement of the balance, take place mainly according to the following laws or tendencies:

1. A position of the organs requiring greater exertion is changed for one requiring less exertion.

2. The change is either between sounds of different characters (sharp, flat, nasal, fricative) uttered at the same part of the mouth; or

3. A sound made in the more forward part of the mouth is substituted for one which should have been made further back.

xii. The result of these tendencies (when uninfluenced by the 44 neighbouring sounds) is that

(*a*) Explosive sounds change to fricative, not the reverse[1].

c = k to c = s; e.g. centum (= kentum), Fr. *cent.*

k to ch Fr., (sh Engl.); e.g. caballus, Fr. *cheval.*

g to y; e.g. *Geist,* Berl. *Jeist;* Germ. *Gestern,* Engl. *yester-*day.

t to s; e.g. Indo-Europ. Lat. tu, Doric τυ, Attic συ.

g to Fr. j; e.g. pagina, Fr. *page.*

d to l; e.g. δάκρυ, Lat. lacruma; 'Οδυσσεύς, Ulixes.

d to th; e.g. οὐδέν, modern Greek δέν, pronounced as English *then.*

b to v; e.g. habere, Ital. *avere.* So Greek β = b has become in modern Greek a labial fricative, between our v and w.

p to v; e.g. sapere, Fr. *savoir;* faba, Fr. *fève.*

So the three aspirates χ, θ, φ, once pronounced k + h, t + h, p + h, are in modern Greek fricative; viz. ch Germ., th, f. And the Latin h and f are representatives of earlier aspirates.

(*b*) Gutturals change to palatals and dentals, not the reverse. 45 Thus c = k changes to c = Eng. *ch;* e.g. Cicero (Κικέρων) to Ital. *Cicero:* caseus, Germ. *Käse,* Engl. *cheese.*

hard g to g = Engl. j; e.g. gyrus, Ital. *gire.*

The labials conform apparently to no definite law.

(*c*) Of the liquids &c., r appears to be older than l, Greek 46 and Latin often giving l where Sanscrit has r. In the Romance languages they interchange both ways; e.g. peregrinus, Ital. *pellegrino;* Tibur, Ital. *Tivoli;* lusciniolus, Ital. *rossignuolo;* apostolus, Fr. *apôtre;* &c.

N also passes into either, and sometimes vice versa; e.g. Bononia, Ital. *Bologna;* venenum, Ital. *veleno;* lamella, Provençal *namela;* hominem, Span. *hombre;* tympanum, Fr. *timbre.* In Greek, ἐλθεῖν is in Doric ἐνθεῖν; φίλτατος, φίντατος; &c.

m appears to be earlier than n; e.g. Sanscrit damam, (Lat. domum), Gr. δόμον; rem, Fr. *rien,* &c.

s changes to later r in Latin; and to the rough breathing in Greek; e.g. arbosem, arborem; Sansc. saptan, Lat. septem, Gr. ἑπτά, &c.

[1] See Curtius, *Gr. Etym.* p. 385, ed. 2.

H in Latin becomes in French almost always inaudible: l is often omitted or sounded as y; final s is not sounded; and the nasals merely give a twang to the vowels.

(*d*) In the case of the vowels a appears to have been earlier 47 than o and e, and changes through them respectively to u and i. Thus Sanscrit frequently has a, where Greek and Latin have the more forward vowels. In Latin the order of priority is a, o, u, e, i, not the reverse. (See § 196.)

xiii. By a similar laxness of pronunciation parasitical sounds 48 often arise, the organs assuming a position for one sound in the effort to reach or leave the position required for another sound.

Thus from Latin **vastare** comes Ital. *guastare;* from **vadium**, *guage;* from **vespa**, French *guêpe;* &c. The same was perhaps the case with **vivo** compared with **vic-si**, as if from **vigvo**; (see § 129 *c*).

So in English a parasitical d becomes attached to n in the vulgar pronunciation of *gown* as *gownd; drowned* as *drownded*[1].

Y is by some speakers inserted before i (=ai) in *guide* pronounced *gyide; kind, kyind; sky, skyi;* &c.: and before u, e.g. *duty,* usually pronounced *dyooty; music, use,* &c., always pronounced *myoosic, yoos;* &c. But see App. A. xx, xxv.

After a broad a = ah or er, a slight raising of the tip of the tongue suggests to some speakers a vibration, and an r is the result; e.g. *Emma Ann* becoming *Emma ran,* &c.

xiv. The difficulty of uttering a particular sound varies with 49 different individuals, sometimes from want of practice, sometimes from organic defect; and where there is no absolute incapacity or even difficulty, there is often a greater tendency for the organs to assume one position, and consequently to pronounce one sound, rather than another.

Thus in English we have persons pronouncing *rake* for *lake; lake* for *rake* (cf. Aristoph. *Vesp.* 45); *thin* for *sin; dound* for *round; wun, gween,* for *run, green; hat* for *at,* and *at* for *hat; wine* for *vine,* and *vine* for *wine;* &c. Foreigners often pronounce *tree* and *dat* for *three* and *that*

xv. As with individuals, so with tribes and nations. Certain 50 sounds and certain classes of sounds are preferred or avoided, are frequently or never pronounced. In this way the same word may, when tribes separate from a common stock, assume gradually a

---

[1] Prof. Key considers this tendency to have been widely operative in language. *Essays,* p. 204 foll.

somewhat different shape (even apart from inflexions) in one tribe from what they bear in another, each tribe fixing differently an ambiguous or intermediate sound, or developing it in a different way.   A few illustrations only can be given, (1) of the absence or presence of certain sounds in nations[1]; (2) of the different shapes the same root assumes in different languages.

1.   (*a*)   The dentals appear to be the easiest sounds, for they are usually the first uttered by children and they are the most universal. But it is said the voiced dental **d** does not occur in Chinese, or in the Mexican and other American languages.   51

(*b*)   Several of the Polynesian languages have no gutturals; and several of the North American have no labials.   In the language of the Sandwich Islands the gutturals and dentals are indistinguishable.   " It takes months of patient labour to teach a Hawaian youth the difference between **k** and **t**, **g** and **d**, **l** and **r**."   *Steel* is pronounced nearly as *kila; Cook* as *tute;* &c.

(*c*)   Again the sharp and flat sounds are not distinguished in any Polynesian dialect.   So the Welsh often pronounce sharp for flat; e.g. *pet* for *bed:* and the inhabitants of Saxony are said not to know the distinction.   Cf. App. A. vii.

(*d*)   The Sanscrit has aspirated flat mutes (**b**+**h**, **g**+**h**, **d**+**h**); the ancient Greek had aspirated sharp mutes **p**+**h**, **k**+**h**, **t**+**h**; the Romans had neither.

(*e*)   The labio-dentals denoted in English by **F** and **V** are absent from Hottentot and Australian languages, and probably from ancient Greek.   **F** is absent also from Finnish, Lithuanian, Tamil, Burmese, &c.

(*f*)   **R** is absent altogether from some American and Polynesian dialects: **L** is absent from Zend, Japanese, and several American and African tongues.   The Chinese substitute **l** for **r**, saying, e.g. *Eulopa* for **Europa**, and (avoiding the pronunciation of two consonants together), *Ki-li-sse-tu* for *Christ.*

(*g*)   The Arabic and cognate languages have peculiar guttural and gutturo-dental consonants.   The Indian languages have a peculiar palatal class.   The Hottentots accompany the pronunciation of other letters with peculiar clicks.

2.   The variation of the same root in languages of the same stock is best illustrated by the law which Grimm (following in Rask's track) showed to prevail between the Sanscrit, Greek and   52

---

[1] These statements are chiefly from Max Müller, *Lectures, Second Series,* p. 167, &c.

Latin together, compared with the Gothic and low German dialects, cn the one hand, and the old High German and its stock on the other, the one having an aspirated mute or fricative, where the second has a flat mute, and the third a sharp, and so on. *Initial* mutes exhibit the law most clearly, being freest from the influence of neighbouring consonants, and dentals most regularly. The English is here taken as the representative of Gothic, and the modern German as representative of high German.

Greek θ	θυγάτηρ,	θήρ,	θύρα,	μέθυ.
Latin f		fera,	fores.	
English d	*daughter*,	*deer*,	*door*,	*mead.*
German t, or th = t	*tochter*,	*thier*,	*thor*,	*meth.*

Greek δ	ὀδούς,	δαμᾶν,	δύο,	ἔδειν,	ὕδωρ.
Latin d	dens,	domare,	duo,	ĕdere,	unda.
English t	*tooth*,	*tame*,	*two*,	*eat*,	*water.*
German z or s	*zahn*,	*zähmen*	*zwei*,	*essen*,	*wasser.*

Greek τ Dor. τυ Att. συ, τρεῖς,			τό.	
Latin t	tu,	tres,	tenuis, is-tud,	frater.
English th	*thou*,	*three*,	*thin*, *that*,	*brother.*
German d	*du*,	*drèi*,	*dünn*, *das*,	*bruder.*

Similarly a Greek aspirate often corresponds to a Latin s.

xvi.   It results from the action of these laws, both those of 53 sudden and those of gradual change, that while the same word may under different influences give rise to variously modified forms, the same form may also eventually result from different original combinations of sounds.

e. g. *page* in English is in its different senses derived respectively from Greek παιδίον and from Latin **pagina.**

From the three Latin words **mare, major, mater** come three French words all pronounced alike; viz. *la mer, le maire, la mère.*

xvii.   The introduction of foreign words into a language is 54 subject to special phonetic conditions. One nation has rarely got just the same set of sounds as another, or allows the same combinations. Consequently in adopting a foreign word by the sound an approximation more or less clumsy has to be made, and a greater divergence is sometimes caused by the tendency to approximate to a familiar indigenous word, especially if it seem to afford an intelligible etymology.

e.g. the Romans had **Hercules** for Ἡρακλῆς; and in early Latin **tecīna** for τέχνη; **Clutĕmestra** for Κλυταιμνήστρα.

The English pronunciation of such words as *pure* (*pyoor*) is said to be from an attempt to imitate the French *u*.

As errors caused by what has been called Popular Etymology may be quoted *Jerusalem artichoke* for *Girasol* which comes from **gyrus** and **sol**: *walnut*, which is from Angl. Sax. *wealh-knut*, i.e. foreign or Italian *nut*.

xviii. The use of letters reacts on the sounds. They rarely fit 55 each other precisely to start with; and the pronunciation has a constant tendency to change, while the spelling remains. The letters then become symbols of different sounds from those proper to them, and sometimes are supposed to carry, and thence do carry these new sounds into other words. In the case of foreign names the want of correspondence in the alphabets is an additional cause of error to that named in the preceding paragraph.

CHAPTER V.

LATIN ALPHABET IN GENERAL[1].

THE alphabets of all Italian peoples were borrowed immediately 56 from that of the Dorian Greeks of Italy and Sicily. The Roman or Latin alphabet was probably obtained from the trading colony of Cumæ. Its oldest form, as collected from coins and inscriptions, dating between the end of the Samnite wars (272 B.C. = 482 U.C.), and the end of the second Punic war (201 B.C. = 553 U.C.), contained the following twenty letters; **A, B, C, D, E, F, H, I, K, L, M, N, O, P, Q, R, S, T, V, X.**

The Romans appear never to have used the three aspirates which the Greek alphabet contained, Θ, Φ, Ψ (= **X**): and there is but slight evidence of their having at first taken **Z**.

In the course of the century, 300 to 200 B.C., a modified form of **C**, viz. **G**, was introduced, in order to distinguish the flat from the sharp guttural; and **K** was used only in very few words. **Z**, if it ever had been in use, had passed out again. In Cicero's time or somewhat earlier, the characters **Z** and **Y** were used in writing words borrowed from the Greek.

The Romans devised a very simple nomenclature for the letters, 57 the vowels being denoted by their own sound, the explosive consonants and **h** by a vowel after them, the fricative consonants by

---

[1] See Corssen, *Aussprache*, i. 1 foll. ed. 2.

a vowel before them. The vowel used for this purpose was e, excepting that the gutturals k and h were called ka, ha, q was called qu, and x was called ix.

The consonants were not, so far as we know, written double 58 before Ennius (who is said to have introduced the practice), the first inscription containing doubled letters being A.U.C. 565: but from that period the practice began, and, if we judge from inscriptions, became predominant about the time of the Gracchi, and constant twenty years later. Plautus could have used the doubled letters only in his last years, if at all.

To denote the length of a vowel several methods were tried. 59 (1) They doubled the vowel[1]. This method introduced into Latin by the tragic poet Accius prevailed in inscriptions from about 130 to 75 B.C. It was also used by other Italian nations, but neither in Oscan nor Latin was o doubled. After Cicero and Cæsar's time the double i had a different meaning, the second i being a semiconsonant; e.g. Pompeijus, &c.

(2) The length of an i was often denoted by writing the diphthong ei, but also and most usually since Sulla's time by making the i taller than the other letters. In imperial times this sign appears to have sometimes stood between two vowels to denote the semiconsonant I (i.e. J). In later times, e.g. even in Domitian's reign, in some Spanish inscriptions the tall I is used indiscriminately for long and for short vowels, and also for the semiconsonant.

(3) Since about the time of Cicero's consulate, a long vowel was frequently denoted by an accent, e.g. Júlió: but this too came gradually to be misapplied.

The Emperor Claudius attempted to introduce three new cha- 60 racters; viz. an inverted digamma (ꟓ) for v when used as a semiconsonant: a reversed Greek sigma (ꟗ) for the combination bs or ps: and the sign of the Greek spiritus asper (Ⱶ) for the middle sound between i and u; that is, according to inscriptions in which we find it used, merely to represent the Greek v (not for the doubtful vowel in $max^{u}_{i}mus$, &c.). The first and the last of these new signs are found in inscriptions of this reign; the antisigma, as it was called, is not found.

The following table contains the letters of the Latin alphabet 61 with their signs and probable pronunciation, as inferred chiefly from the facts respecting the several letters given in the ensuing Chapters.

---

[1] Probably this is the meaning of the double u which occurs regularly in the gen. sing. and nom. and acc. plur. of u stems in MSS. of Pliny, &c.; e.g. vagituus, specuus.

Old signs (other than in next col.)	cir. 80 B.C. (Ritschl. tab. LXIX.)	Modern signs.	Name.	Pronunciation.	Greek letter for same sound.
ΛΛΛΛΛ	A	A a	a	*ah*	A
⟨B B	B	B b	be	*b*	B
⟨	C	C c	ce	*k*	K
▷	D	D d	de	*d*	Δ
ƐE ‖	E	E e	e	{ Ital. open *e?*	H for *ē* (E as Ital. close *e*)
⟨F F ⟨'	F	F f	ef	*f*	(cf. § 98)
C G	G	G g	ge	*g* (*give*)	Γ
	H	H h	ha	*h* (*hat*)	‛
	I	I i	i	{ *ee* (*feet*) *y* (*yes*)	I
⟨		K k	ka	*k*	K
L	L	L l	el	*l*	Λ
ΛΛΜ	M	M m	em	*m*	M
Ν	N	N n	en	{ *n* *ng*	N Γ
◇ ∩◯	O	O o	o	{ Ital. open *o?*	Ω for *ŏ* (O as Engl. *ŏmit*)
Γ	P	P p	pe	*p*	Π
Ϙ	Q	Q q	qu	*k*	K
R Ρ	R	R r	er	*r* (trilled)	P
Ϟ⟨	S	S s	es	*s* (sharp)	Σ
T Τ	T	T t	te	*t*	T
	V	U u ⎫ V v ⎭	u	{ Engl. *oo:* Engl. *w* (or Fr. *ou* in *oui*)	OY: F, later OY
Ⅴ					
X	X	X x	ix	*x*	Ξ
Y		Y y (Ypsilon)	*u* Fr.		Y
		Z z (Zeta)	(cf. § 195)		Z

Modern.	Pronunciation.	Greek.	Modern.	Pronunciation.	Greek.
AI ai	*ay* (= *yes*)	earlier AI	EU eu	Ital. *eu*	EY
AE ae	(cf. § 258)	later AI	OI oi	nearly *oi* (*boil*)	earlier OI
EI ei	Engl. (*fate*)	EI	OE oe	(cf. § 263)	later OI
AU au	Germ. *au* (*haus*)	AY	UI ui	as Fr. *oui*	(cf. § 222)
OU ou	Engl. *o* (*note*)	OY			

The Greek υ was Fr. *u.* (It did not correspond to Latin **u**, which Greek expressed by ου). The Greek ω was probably the sound of English **aw.** It must be remembered that the contraction of *oo* in Greek gives ου, not ώ; of εε gives ει, not η. Moreover the name of *o* was οὖ; of ε was εἶ. On the English ŏ and ā being really diphthongs, see § 21.

CHAPTER VI.

LATIN ALPHABET IN DETAIL.

LABIALS AND LABIODENTALS[1].

P.

CHARACTER: in the oldest inscriptions Γ (but not after cir. 620 62 U.C.), then Γ, last **P.**

SOUND: always the sharp labial mute; English **p.** Never aspi- 63 rated, except in Greek words; e.g. **sphæra, philosophus.**

POSITION: never final, except in **volup** (for **volupe**). It can 64 stand immediately in same syllable

    1. before **l** or **r**; e.g. **plaudo, prandeo,** &c.

    2. after **s**; e.g. **spatium, splendor, sprevi,** &c.

REPRESENTATION: (i) of Greek 1. π (ps for ψ): e.g. πνευμα- 65 τικός, **pneumaticus;** Πτολεμαῖος, **Ptolemæus;** ψάλλω, **psallo;** &c.

    2. rarely β; e.g. θρίαμβος, **triumpus** (later **triumphus**).

    3. frequently φ; e.g. πορφύρα, **purpŭra;** Δίφιλος, Πάμφιλος, Φιλονείκης, **Dipŭlus, Pampĭlus, Pĭlŏnīces;** Φαρνάκης, **Parnaces;** &c. almost always in inscriptions before cir. 660 U.C. (see § 132).

---

[1] In the following account of each letter, the term *Representation* has been confined to the way in which one language transcribes the words borrowed from another : *Correspondence* to the etymological correspondence, *i.e.* the shape which the same stem, though forming perhaps a verb in one and a noun in another language, assumes in sister languages. The instances of *correspondence* are almost all selected from Curtius, *Griech. Etym.* 2nd ed. *Influence* is used for the way in which a letter affects others, *weakness* for the way in which it is affected by others. The *sound* is inferred from the facts here collected. Throughout, great help has been obtained from Corssen's *Aussprache,* &c., and in some parts from Luc. Müller's *De re metrica.*

(ii) in Greek by π; e.g. **Papirius**, Παπείριος (also Παπίριος); **capitolium**, καπιτώλιον; **Spurius**, Σπόριος; **Appius**, Ἄππιος; &c.

CORRESPONDENCE: 1. to an original Indo-European p.   66

2. to Greek π; e.g. **răpio**, ἁρπ-άζω; **septem**, ἑπτά; **păc-iscor, pang-o, pig-nus**, πήγ-νυμι, aor. ἐπάγ-ην; **pater**, πατήρ; **imple-o, plenus**, πί-μ-πλη-μι, πλήθω; **pannus**, πῆνος; **pullus**, πῶλος; **palma, palámē**; **nĕpos, neptis**, ἀνεψιός, **pisum**, πῑσος; **pilleus**, πῖλος; **pluo, plĕo, plúvo**; **pūs, puteo, pūtris**, πύον, πύθω; **pulmo**, πνεύμων, πλεύμων; &c.

3. to Greek φ; e.g. **căput, căpillus**, κεφαλή; **ops**, ἄφενος.

4. to Greek β in **pasco**, βόσκω.

5. rarely to Greek κ. So probably **lŭpus**, λύκος; **spŏlium**, σκῦλον; **sæpes, præsepis**, σηκός.

Possibly these Latin words may have been borrowed from the Umbrian or Oscan, in which p often corresponds to an original k.

SUBSTITUTION: p is often a substitute for b; e.g. **sup-porto** 67 for **sub-porto**; **op-timus** for **ob-timus**; **scrip-si, scrip-tus** from **scrīb-o**; **op-sides** (in early inscriptions) for **ob-sides**; &c.

INFLUENCE: 1. before p the prepositions **sub, ob, ad** become 68 **sup, op, ap** in pronunciation, though not always in writing; e.g. **supporto, op-portunus, ap-pello**; &c. Possibly this was the original form of **sub, ob** (compare **super**, ἐπί).

2. requires a preceding nasal to be m, not n; e.g. **impar, com-porto**; &c. **ru-m-po** compared with **fu-n-do**.

WEAKNESS: 1. changed (cir. 650 U.C.) to b before l in the 69 word **publicus**, for **poplicus**, from **populicus** (old form **pouplicos**). So **Publius** is Πόπλιος in Polybius and Dion. H.).

2. becomes m before a nasal suffix; e.g. **som-nus** compared with **sŏp-or, sōp-io**. And comp. **trĕpĭdus** with **trĕmo**.

INSERTION: 1. P is naturally pronounced in passing from 70 m to t or s or l; e.g. **sum-p-tus, sum-p-si; em-p-tus, em-p-si; tem-p-to** for the (etymologically better) form **ten-to; hiem-p-s** for **hiems; exem-p-lum**, from **exĭm-ĕre; tem-p-lum**, comp. τέμενος. In **am-sancti, am-p-lus**, the p may be for b in **amb-**.

2. In late imperial language we have **dam-p-num, calum-p-niare**, &c.

B.

CHARACTER: similar to modern B.   71

SOUND: the flat labial mute; English b.   72

In later Latin inscriptions, not frequently before the 4th century A.D., words were written with v for b, chiefly between vowels (e.g. **devitum, sivi, Lesvia, verva**), and b for v (e.g. **bolo, berba, bixit**; hence **Danubius** for the earlier and correct **Danuvius**), one or both having then perhaps the sound of labial v.   The confusion is also found in the MS. of Gaius, and in the Florentine MS. of the Digest. **Flabio, Jubentius** are rare instances from the 2nd century after Christ. **Besbius** (cf. § 90. 3) for Vesuvius in Pompeian inscriptions.

POSITION: Final only in ab, sub, ob.   73

It can stand immediately in same syllable before 1 or r; e.g. **blandus, brĕvis, brūma,** &c.

REPRESENTATION (i) in Greek by β; e. g. **Aboriginum,** 74 'Αβοριγίνων; **Umbrici,** 'Ομβρικοί; **Bovillani,** Βοΐλλανοί; &c.

(ii) of Greek: 1. ordinarily β; βάσις, **basis**; Βοιωτοί, **Bœoti**; &c.

2.   For φ and π Ennius always used b, at least in the words **Burrus** for Πύρρος, and **Bruges** for Φρύγες (Cic. *Or.* 48, § 160). Probably Ennius was following the etymological correspondence (see next section).

CORRESPONDENCE: 1. to an original Indo-European b or bh, 75 or, in the middle of a word, to an original dh.

2.   to Greek β; e.g. **brevis,** βραχύς; **bulbus,** βολβός; **balare,** βληχάομαι.

3.   to Greek π; e.g. **ab,** ἀπό; **buxus,** πύξος; **carbasus,** κάρπασος; **lambo, lăbium,** λάπτω, λαφύσσω.

4.   medial b to Greek φ (frequently); e.g. **amb-,** ἀμφί; **ambo,** ἄμφω; **lăbor,** ἀλφ-άνω; **umbo, umbilicus,** ὀμφαλός; **nŭb-es,** νέφ-ος; **orb-us,** ὀρφ-ανός; **sorb-eo,** ῥοφέω; **glūbo,** γλύφω; **scrībo,** γράφω. So probably the derivative suffix -ber (comp. fero) to -φόρος (φέρω); e.g. **salū-ber, candēla-brum.**

5.   medial b to Old Italian f; e.g. **trĭbus,** Umbr. **trefu; stabulum,** Umbr. **stafu; tibi,** Umbr. **tefe; sibi,** Oscan **sifei.**

SUBSTITUTION: 1. It is in several words a substitute for an 76 earlier **dv.** Thus **bis, bellum, Bellona, Bellius, bŏnus** are for **dvis, dvellum, Dvellona** (so in S. C. de Bacchan. 568 A.U.C.), **Dvellius, dvonus (dvonoro** i.e. **bonorum** in epitaph on Scipio, son of Barbatus, cir. A.U.C. 500). C. Duellius the consul of 494 A.U.C. is said to have been the first of the family called Bellius[1] (Cic. *Or.* 45, § 153).

2. In a few words, it stands for medial **v** in order to avoid the combination **uu**. Thus **bubīle, bubulcus** from **bovīle, bobulcus**, when o was giving place to u (§ 213); **deferbui** from **deferveo**; **jūbeo** from a root **jou-** (comp. old perf. **jousi, jūro**).

INFLUENCE : It requires the preceding nasal to be **m**; e. g. com- 77 **buro** compared with **conduco**; **im-buo** with **in-duo**; **im-berbis**, com**bĭbo**, &c.

WEAKNESS: 1. Before a sharp (**s** or **t**), **b** is sometimes changed 78 to **p**; e. g. **scrip-si, scrip-tus** from **scrib-o**; **op-sequi** for **ob-sequi**; **op-tineo** for **ob-tineo**, &c. In compounds with **sub, ob**, the inscriptions before cir. 650 U.C. have **p**; later inscriptions and MSS. oscillate. So occasionally **urps, pleps** for **urbs, plebs**. But in **os-tentum, sus-cipere, sustuli, asporto**, &c. **b** in **obs, subs, abs** is omitted.

2. Before **c, g, p, f, sub** and **ob** are assimilated; e. g. **suc-curro, oc-cumbo, suggero, suppono, suffero**, &c.

3. Before **f, ab** takes the form **au**; e. g. **aufugio, aufero** (but **abs-tuli, ab-latum**); or **b** is dropped; e. g. **afui, afōre.** (On **af** see § 97 n.)

4. In **ōmitto, ōperio, oportunus** (if they are compounds) the **b** is omitted. [Some consider the dat. abl. in -**īs** to have arisen from an omission of **b** (or **bh**), **fīliis** being for **fīliabus**.]

5. **b** becomes **m** before a nasal suffix; e. g. **sum-mus** for **sub-mus** (for **sup-imus**); **scam-num** compared with **scab-ellum**; **sam-nium** (ἡ Σαυνῖτις Polyb.) with **Sabini**. So perhaps **glōmus** is for **glōb-mus**.

M.

CHARACTER: In a few of the oldest inscriptions before 500 U.C. 79 the modern shape with the middle strokes not reaching to the bottom is found, but not afterwards. The usual form has the four strokes of equal length and all inclined, not vertical. Verrius Flaccus (in Augustus' time) wished to use only half the ordinary letter as its sign at the end of words before an initial vowel, on account of its faint sound.

SOUND : the labial nasal; English **m**.　　80

At the end of words it appears to have been scarcely audible.

POSITION : very frequently final: viz. 1. in accusative and 81 neuter nominative singular, and in genitive plural of nouns: 2. in

---

[1] In Polybius, I. 22, 23, we read Βίλιος; (but the MSS. have Λίβιος or ᾽Ατίλιος Λίβιος). Diodorus (XI. 68) has Δουίλλιος.

1st person singular of verbs; 3. in some adverbs; e.g. **tum, quam, nam, clam, autem, enim, partim,** &c.

Never before or after another consonant as the commencement of a syllable.

REPRESENTATION: (i) in Greek by μ; e.g. **Marcius** by Μάρκιος, 82 **Viminalis** by Οὐιμινάλιος; &c.

(ii) of Greek μ; e.g. Μαραθῶν, **Marathon**; πραγματικός, **pragmaticus**; &c.

CORRESPONDENCE: 1. to Indo-European m.　　83

2. to Greek μ; e.g. **sĭmul, sĭmilis,** ἅμα, ὁμοῖος, ὁμαλός; **vŏmo,** ἐμ-έω (Fεμ); **mol-lis,** μαλᾰκός; **me,** με, ἐμέ; **magnus, măgis,** μέγας, μέγιστος; **mel,** μέλι, **mŏr-ior, mor-tuus, mar-ceo,** μᾰρ-αίνω, βροτός (for μροτός); **mĭnuo,** μινύθω; **ŭm-erus,** ὦμος; &c.

3. but in inflexions final m corresponds to Greek ν; so in the acc. sing. and gen. pl. of nouns and in the 1st pers. sing. of verbs: e.g. **nāvem,** ναῦν; **musarum,** μουσῶν; **sim, siem,** εἴην; **ferebam,** ἔφερον.

SUBSTITUTION: 1. for p or b before a nasal suffix; e.g. **som-** 84 **nus,** comp. **sŏp-or, sōp-io; scam-num** compared with **scab-ellum; Sam-nium** with **Sab-ini; sum-mus** with **sub** or **sup-er.**

2. for n before a labial; e.g. **im-pello** for **in-pello;** &c. Compare **ru-m-po** with **fu-n-do.**

INFLUENCE: 1. often occasions the assimilation or omission 85 of a preceding consonant, especially if three consonants would otherwise be together: e.g. **flam-ma (flag-); exā-men** for **exag-men; jŭ-mentum (jŭg-); tor-mentum (torquēre); lū-men (lūc-ēre); ful-men (fulg-ēre); cæ-mentum (cæd-ere); rā-mentum (rād-ere); sum-movere, sum-mus (sub); contā-minare (contag-); sē-mestris (sex).**

But **seg-men** from **sec-āre; ag-men** from **ag-ĕre;** &c.

So n becomes m; e.g. **im-motus** for **in-motus; īmus, immo** for **inīmus, inĭmo** (superlative from preposition **in**).

2. prefers a short ŭ (instead of ŏ or ĭ) before it; e.g. **doc-u-mentum (doc-e-); monumentum (mon-e-).** So till Cæsar's time **decŭmus, facillŭmus, durissŭmus, maritŭmus,** &c. Similarly **æstŭmo, lacrŭma,** and in Greek words the short inserted vowel is u; e.g. **Alcŭmena, drachŭma, Tecumessa** (compared with **tecina,** &c.).

WEAKNESS: 1. Final m having a faint sound fell away; in 1st 86 pers. sing. of present, and perfect indic. and future in -bo of all verbs; e.g. **amo, amavi, amabo;** the words **sum** and **inquam** alone retaining it. Cato is said to have written **recipie, dice**, &c. for **reci-piam, dicam** (**recipiem, dicem?**). Cf. Quintil. I. 7, § 23; IX. 4. § 40.

2. In nouns early inscriptions frequently omit final m, but not regularly. Thus in the oldest Scipionic inscription **Luciom** is found by side of **Corsica, oino** (for **unum**), **Scipione, optumo** (all accusatives), **duonoro** (for **bonorum**). The omission is rare in the legal inscriptions, and in others also after 620 U.C., but is found in the vulgar wall inscriptions at Pompeii; and towards the end of the third century after Christ becomes frequent again (even in words which are not nouns; e.g. **mecu, dece, oli** for **mecum, decem, olim**).

Non is for **nœnum** (**ne-oinom**, i. e. **ne-unum**).

3. Before a vowel, a final syllable in m was disregarded in verse : and **com** in composition dropped its m; e.g. **co-ire, cohibeo, coheres, coopto**; **cōgo** (**com-ago**), **cōperio** (**com-operio**), **cōmo** (**com-emo**). But m is retained in **cŏmes, com-itium, cŏmitor**; **cŏm-ĕdo**.

So **circu-itus**; but **circum-ago**.

4. Before most consonants except the labials p, b, m, m becomes n ; e.g. **an-ceps, prin-ceps, nunc** (**num-ce**), **tantundem** (**tantum**), **ean-dem, eorun-dem, con-sul, con-fero, con-jux, con-venio, septen-trio, aliquan-diu**, &c. So **quoniam** for **quom jam**.

In a few compounds of com m is omitted; e.g. **co-gnosco, co-gnatus, cō-necto, cōnitor, cōnīveo, cōnubium**. So in old time **cosol** for **consul** and this form was retained in the abbreviation **cos**; also in inscriptions **cosentiont**, &c. Cf. §§ 168, 167, 2.

5. m before r became b; e.g. **hībernus** is for **hiemrinus** (cf. χειμερινός). So in Greek βροτός from root μορ-, **morior**.

V as Consonant.

CHARACTER: always **v**, whether as vowel or consonant. 87 (Throughout this article **v** is used for the consonantal sound, **u** for the vowel.)

SOUND: as the English **w**, or perhaps, at least originally, the 88 more vocal Fr. ou in **oui**.

POSITION: always before a vowel. Not after any consonant, 89 except q, g, s, l, r; e.g. **qvis, pingvis, svavis, salvus, servus**.

REPRESENTATION: (i) in Greek[1], 1. usually by ου (which 90 was also the usual representation of **v** as vowel); e.g. **Servius**, Σερ-

---

[1] The Oscan v was represented in Greek by the digamma ; e. g. Joveis, ΔιουϜει; Clovatius, κλοϜάτωι; tovtiks, τοϜτο. Quintilian says Æolicæ litteræ, qua 'servum,' 'cervum'que dicimus, etiam si forma a nobis repudiata est, vis tamen nos ipsa persequitur (xii. 10. 29).

οὔιος; Venusia, Οὐενουσία (Polyb.); Veii, Οὐήιοι; Volsci, Οὐόλσκοι (Strab.), Οὐολοῦσκοι, (Dion. H., Plut.), Οὐόλοσκοι (Plut.); Qvintilius Varus, Κουιντίλιος Οὐᾶρος (Joseph.); Juvenalia, Ἰουουενάλια; Qvadratus, Κουάδρατος (Dio Cass., *Epit.*); Æquum Faliscum, Αἰκουουμφάλισκον; Svessula, Σουέσσουλα (Strab.); &c.

2. after q, before ī, also by υ or ο; e.g. Qvintus, Κόιντος (Polyb., Diod., Dion. H.), Κύιντος (Dio Cass.); Qvintilius, Κοιντίλιος (*Mon. Ancyr.*), Κυιντίλιος (Dio C.); Nonis Qvintilibus, Κυιντιλίαις Νόνναις (Plut.); Aqvīnum, Ἀκυῖνον (Strab., Plut.); &c.
But qvī=κυ, e.g. Aqvillius, Ἀκύλλιος; Qvirīnus, Κυρῖνος; Qvirītes, Κυρῖται (but Κυιρῖται, Dio); Aqvileia, Ἀκυληία; Tarqvinius, Ταρκύνιος.

3. by β rarely, except in Plutarch, who has for Flavius Φλάβιος (also Φλαούιος); Livius, Λίβιος (also Polyb.); Varro, Βάρρων; Fulvius, Φούλβιος; Servilia, Σερβιλία, (Servilius, Σερουίλλιος); Voconius, Βοκώνιος; &c. So Pulvillus, Πολβίλλος; Flavus, Flavius, Φλάβος, Φλάβιος, also Φλαούιος (Dion. H.); Vesuvius, Βέσβιος (Dio C. App.), but Οὐεσουούιος (Diod.); Beneventum, Βενεβεντόν (Appian), but Βενεουεντόν (Appian, Strabo), Beneventana, Οὐενοαντανή (Polyb.). Nerva and Severus in contemporary inscriptions are Νερουα, Νερβα; Σεουῆρος, Σεβῆρος. In and after the sixth century after Christ β appears frequently for v. Compare § 72.
(ii) of Greek. V as consonant is never found in transferring a Greek name into Latin, the digamma, which alone had the same sound, not being in use in the time of the Roman writers.

CORRESPONDENCE: 1. to original Indo-European V: sometimes 91 (e.g. in first four instances given infr. 3) to G (where Greek has β).

2. to Greek ϝ, which often fell away without altering the word, sometimes was replaced by ο or υ; e.g. ævum, αἰϝές, ἀεί; ŏvis, ὅϝις; ăvis, οἰωνός (οϝιωνος); ŏvum, ὠϝόν; silva, ὕλη (for ὑλϝα); svāvis (for svad-vis), svadus, ἡδύς (for σϝηδυς); vallus, Ϝῆλος; vellus, villus, Ϝέριον, εἶρος; vĕhere, Ϝόχος; vēnum, vēn-eo, ὦνος; vēr, Ϝέαρ, ἦρ; verbum, Ϝερέω, ῥῆμα; vesper, Ϝέσπερος; vestis, Ϝέν-νυμι, ἐσθής; vĕtus, Ϝέτος (*a year*); vĭdere, Ϝιδεῖν, (Lac. βιδεῖν;) οἶδα; vīginti, Ϝείκοσι, Bœot. Ϝίκατι, (Lacon. βείκατι); viŏla, Ϝίον; vĭtulus, Ϝιταλός; vītex, vī-men, Ϝιτέα; vŏmere, Ϝεμ-εῖν; volvo, Ϝελύω, εἰλύω.

vah, væ, ὀά, οὐαί; vīnum, οἶνος; vicus, οἶκος. The noise of frogs is represented by κοάξ, which Ovid imitates by ' sub aqua sub aqua maledicere temptant.' (*Met.* VI. 376.)

Arvum, ἀρόω, ἄρουρα; nervus, νεῦρον; vĕreor, οὖρος, *a watcher* (Ϝορ-).

3. to Greek β; e.g. vĕn-io (bēto, perbīto, Osc. benust = venerit), βαίνω; vivo βίος, βιόω; vŏro, βιβρώσκω, βορά; ervum, ὄροβος; severus, σέβας, σέβομαι ; vŏlo, βούλομαι.

SUBSTITUTION: In verse the vowel u is sometimes hardened into 92
the consonant **v**. Thus in Plautus, **tvos, svos, tvi, svi**; &c., **fvit,
pver, pvella, dvorum**, (comp. above § 76 **dvonoro, dvello**); in dactylic
poets, **svo** (Lucr. twice); **genva** (Verg., Stat.); **pītvīta** (Hor.),
patrvi (Stat.), **sinvatis, sinvatur** (Sil.). Also **larva, larvatis** (Hor.),
for **lārua, lāruatis** (Plaut.); **milvus** and **reliqvus** after the 8th cent.
U.C. for the earlier **mīlŭŭs, rēlĭcŭŭs**. In **tenvis, tenvia, tenvior**, the
consonantal **v** seems to be the regular pronunciation: Statius's use
is peculiar. See § 142.

INFLUENCE: 1. The vowel **ŏ** when following **v** (consonant 93
or vowel) was retained till the Augustan age and later, though after
other letters it had usually changed to u; e.g. **servos**, nom. sing.,
æqvom, &c. **Vorto** and derivatives are said by Quintilian (i.7.25),
to have been changed to **verto**, &c. by Scipio Africanus (i.e.
minor), but the forms with **e** are not usually found in republican inscriptions.

2. medial **v** causes omission of preceding consonant; e.g. **sē-
vŏco** for **sed-voco**; **sēviri** for **sexviri**; **pavi** from **pasco** (for **pas-sco**).

3. The consonantal character of **v** is shown by its use in metre
(*a*) in not causing elision, e.g. **dicerĕ verba**:

(*b*) in lengthening with another consonant a preceding short
vowel. Comp. **volvo, vŏlutus**. But it has not this effect when following **q**; e.g. **äqva**.

WEAKNESS: 1. **v** between two vowels usually fell away, or 94
resumed its vowel power and formed a diphthong or long vowel
with the preceding vowel: the succeeding vowel was absorbed in
either case.

(*a*) in perfect suffix; e.g. **amāram** for **amāvĕram**; **flēram** for
flēveram; **nōram** for **nōvĕram**; **plui** for **plūvi**; **audieram** for **audīvĕ-
ram**; **amasse**, for **amavisse**; **petiit, petīt** for **pĕtīvit; fōvi** for **fŏv-vi**; &c.

(*b*) **nauta** for **nāvīta**; **auceps** for **ăvĭceps**; **cautor** for **căvĭtor**;
cauneas for **cave ne eas** (Cic. *Div.* II. 40); **Gnæus** for **Cnaivos**;
prædes for **prævĭdes**; **ætas** for **ævitas**; **præco** for **prævīco** (voc-āre),
horsum for **ho-vorsum**; **hornus** for **ho-ver-nus**; **cunctus** for **co(m)-
vinctus**; **prūdens** for **prŏvĭdens**; **Juppiter** for **Jŏvĭpater**; **jūcundus**
for **jŏvĭcundus**; **jūnior** for **jŭvĕnior**; **ūpĭlio** for **ŏvĭpĭlio** (cf. βουπό-
λος); **nūper** for **nŏvumper**; **oblītus** for **oblīvitus**; **rursum** for re-
versum; **brūma** for **brĕvīma**; **nōlo** for **nĕvŏlo**; **neu, seu** for **neve,
sive** (**neve, seve** old).

So in Plautus, **Jŏvem, ŏvis, bŏves, brĕvi**, and (after Greek model)
nāvem are monosyllables, and **ăvonculus, oblīvisci** trisyllables.

2. **v**, after any other consonant than **q, g, s, l**, or **r**, was vocalised:
e.g. **vacuus** for (old form) **vŏcīvos**. (Plautus wrote always **vacivos**
or **vocivos**.) Compare **conspicuus, arduus, annuus, noctua**, with
longinqvus, curvus, fulvus. (But also **sŭŭs, irriguus, patrŭus**.)

Poets, rarely after Augustan age, sometimes vocalised a (usually) consonantal **v**. Thus **sŭădeo, sŭēsco** (Lucr.); **sŭērunt** (Cic.); **sŭētus** (Lucr., Hor.); **consecue** (Lucr.), **adsecue, obsecuum** (Plaut.); **ăcŭāī, ăcŭæ** (for **aqvæ**) Lucr. So also **sŏlŭo, dissŏlŭo,** &c. (Lucr., Cat., and elegiac poets); **vŏlŭo** (elegiac); **sĭlŭæ** (Hor.). **decuria, centuria, cŭria** are by some supposed to be for **dec-vĭr-ia, cent-vĭr-ia, co-vĭr-ia.**

3. **v** fell out in some few words; e.g. **săvium** for **svavium**; **tĭbĭ, te** for **tvĭbĭ, tve**; **ungo, tingo, urgeo** for **ungvo, tingvo, urgveo.** (In slave names, e.g. **Publipor, Marcipor, por** is for **puer,** probably the **e** being extruded).

So also **qum, qur** is sometimes written for **quom, quor,** or **cum, cur.**

4. Apparently an initial **v** has fallen off in some words beginning with **r** and **l**; e.g. **rŏsa,** ῥόδον, Æol. βρόδον; **rīgare,** βρέχειν; **radix,** ῥίζα, Lesb. βρίσδα; **lăcer,** ῥάκος, Æol. βράκος; **lŭpus,** Germ. *wolf*; **laqueus,** βρόχος. (Compare our pronunciation of *wreck, wreak, wrong, wrought,* &c.)

5. **v** after **d** hardened to **b,** and then **d** fell off; e.g. **duellum, bellum,** &c. (see § 76).

In a few words medial **v** changed to **b**; e.g. **deferbui, bubile**; see § 76. 2, and compare the examples in § 90. 3.

6. On the confusion in late Latin of **v** and **b** see § 72.

F.

CHARACTER: before 500 U.C. sometimes |', which is also 95 found in (later) cursive writing; e.g. the wall inscriptions at Pompeii. (See also E, § 226.) The sign F is the Æolic digamma, which the Latins adopted instead of 8, which form was used by the Etruscans, Umbrians, and Oscans.

SOUND: a sharp labio-dental fricative formed between the upper 96 teeth and under lip: English F. The dental element appears to have been predominant.

POSITION: never final except in the old rarely used form of **ab,** 97 viz. **af**[1]. Can stand in the commencement of a syllable before **l** or **r**; e.g. **fluo, frango;** but not after a consonant.

REPRESENTATION: 1. in Greek by φ; e.g. **Fabius,** Φάβιος; 98

---

[1] This word, apparently an Italic form of the preposition **ab,** is found only before consonants, chiefly in Republican inscriptions; e.g. **af Capua, af vobeis, af solo.** Corssen holds **af, ab** and **au** (see § 78. 3) to be all three of distinct origin (*Ausspr.* 1. 152—157, ed. 2).

Fortuna, Φορτοῦνα; **Furius**, Φούριος; **Fidenæ**, Φιδήνη; **præfectorum**, πραιφέκτων (Polyb.) &c. Quintilian (I. 4, 14) says the Greeks used to pronounce the Latin **f** with an aspiration, and instances Cicero's ridiculing a witness for not being able to pronounce the first letter of **Fundanius**.

2. of Greek φ, not until 4th century after Christ. So in the MS. of Gaius, **elefantis**, **chirografis**, &c.

CORRESPONDENCE: 1. to an original Indo-European **bh** and **dh**. 99

2. to Greek initial φ (which was π followed by an aspirate, not English **ph** or **f**); e.g. **fa-ri**, **fā-ma**, φάναι, φήμη; **fŭr**, φώρ; **fĕro**, φέρω; **fluo**, φλύω (*bubble*); **frātĕr**, φράτηρ (*clansman*); **fu-i**, φύω; **fŏlium**, φύλλον; **farcio**, φράσσω; **fŭga**, φυγή; **frĭgo**, φρύγω; **fāgus** (*beech*), φηγός (*oak*); **fallo**, σφάλλω; **fungus**, σφόγγος; **funda**, σφενδόνη.

3. to Greek β (rare); e.g. **frĕmo**, βρέμω; **fascīno**, βασκαίνω; **fŏd-io**, βόθ-ρος.

4. to Greek χ (which was κ followed by an aspirate[1]); e.g. **frio**, χρίειν; **fel**, χολή; **fă-mes**, **fă-tisco**, χῆτος, χᾰτίζω; **frēnum**, χᾰλινός; **fŭnis**, σχοῖνος.

5. to Greek digamma, later an aspirate; e.g. **frango**, Ϝρήγνυμι, ῥήγνυμι; **frĭgeo**, **frīgus**, ῥῑγέω, ῥῖγος.

6. to Greek initial θ (which was τ followed by an aspirate, not English *th*); e.g. **fĕ-mina**, θῆ-λυς; -**fen-do**, θείνω; **fĕra**, θήρ, Æol. φήρ; **fŏris**, θύρα; **fū-mus**, **sub-fi-o**, θυμός, θύω, θύελλα; **fingo**, **fĭg-ura**, θιγγάνω, θίγμα. Also to medial θ in **rūfus**, ἐρυθ-ρός.

SUBSTITUTION: 1. for **d** in preposition **ad**; e.g. before **af-** 100 **fero**, **af-fătim**, &c.

2. In **ef-fĕro**, **ef-fatus** for older **ecfero**, **ecfatus**, the first **f** may perhaps be only a mark of a long syllable for **ēfero**, **ēfatus**.

INFLUENCE: 1. requires a preceding nasal to be **n**; e.g. **in-** 101 **fero**, **con-fero**, &c. **an-fractus** for **amb-fractus**.

2. **nf** lengthens a preceding vowel; See under N (§ 167. 2).

WEAKNESS: Parts of the stem **fu-** are supposed to have been 102 modified and used as a verbal suffix, viz. **ama-vi** to stand for **ama-fui**; **ama-bam** for **ama-fuam**, **ama-bo** for **ama-fuio**. But see Preface.

---

[1] In English we substitute **f** (in speaking) for the guttural **gh** in *laugh, cough, trough.*

CHAPTER VII.

GUTTURALS AND PALATALS.

K, C.

CHARACTER : as above, except that c was in early inscriptions 103 sometimes angular ⟨.

k went out of use at an early period, probably before the decemviral laws, almost entirely, except in a few old abbreviations; e. g. in republican inscriptions, K. for Kæso; k. k. for kalumniæ causa; XVIR. SL. IVDIK. for Decemvir stlitibus (litibus) judicandis; K. or KAL. for Calendæ ; INTERKAL. for intercalares ; MERK. for Mercatus ; and in later times K for caput, cardo, castra, carus, and KAR. for Carthago. In early inscriptions the words Kastorus (Castoris), Korano (Coranorum ?) ; Kæl. for Cælius ; Dekem. for Decembres also occur. There was a tendency with some grammarians in Quintilian's time (I. 7, 10) to use k always before a.

SOUND: K always as the sharp guttural mute : i. e. English k. 104

C was used indiscriminately for both the sharp and flat guttural mute, till the beginning of the sixth century U.C., when a modified form (G) was introduced for the flat sound. A few instances, probably accidental, are found in later inscriptions. For Gaius and Gnæus the abbreviations always followed the old form, viz. C. Cn. C had not the sound of s (as in English). Nor does ci before a vowel appear to have been pronounced as sh, except provincially, before the 6th or 7th century after Christ (see § 110. 4).

POSITION: never final, except in a few words from which a 105 short ĕ has fallen off : dic, duc, fac, ac, sic, hic, illic, &c. for dice, duce, &c. Also usually lac for lacte (nom. sing.).

It can stand in the commencement of a syllable (1) before l, r ; e. g. clamo, crimen, &c. : (2) after s ; e.g. scindo, scribo, &c.

REPRESENTATION : (i) in Greek by κ always; e.g. Campani, 106 Καμπανοί; Lucius Cæcilius, Λεύκιος Καικίλιος ; centurio, κεντυρίων; Curius, Κόριος ; Cornelius, Κορνήλιος (all in Polybius): pontifices, ποντίφικες ; Numicius, Νομίκιος ; Cicero, Κικέρων ; Compitalia, Κομπιτάλια; &c.

(ii) of Greek 1. κ; e. g. λυγκός, **lyncis**; Κίλιξ, **Cilix**; Κύ-κλωψ, **Cyclops**; Περδίκκας, **Perdiccas**; Κίμων, **Cimon**; Κάδμος, **Cadmus**; &c.

2. also in early times χ; e. g. **Bacas**, (i. e. **Baccas**) for Βάκχας in the (so-called) *S. C. de Bacanalibus*, A. U. C. 568; and in later inscriptions **Cilo** for Χίλων; **Antiocus** for ʼΑντίοχος; &c. But the h was usually written in Cicero's time (*Or.* 48. § 160).

CORRESPONDENCE: 1. to an original Indo-European **k.**   107

2. to Greek κ; e. g. **arx, arceo**, ἄρκιος, ἀρκέω; **decem**, δέκα; **dico, maledic-us**, δείκνυμι, δίκη; **decet**, δοκεῖ; **centum**, ἕκατον (i. e. ἕν-κατ-ον *one hund-red*); **socer**, ἐκυρός; **cadus**, κάδος; **calare, calendæ, nomenclator**, κᾰλεῖν, κλή-τωρ; **cerebrum**, κάρα; **caput**, κεφ-αλή; **cluo, cli-ens, inclutus**, κλύω, κλυτός; **canis** (for **cvanis**), κύων; **specio**, σκοπεῖν; **cuculus**, κόκκυξ, *cuckoo*; **scipio**, σκῆπ-τρον; &c.

3. to Greek π (cf. § 118); e. g. **voc-are, vox**, ἔπ-ος εἶπον, ὄψ (stem Ϝεπ-); **oc-ulus**, ὄπ-ωπ-α, ὤψ; **sucus, sapio**, ὀπός; **jecur**, ἧπαρ.

SUBSTITUTION: 1. for g before a sharp; e. g. **actus** from **ag-o**; 108 **punctus** from **pungo**; **rexi = rec-si** from **reg-o**; &c.

2. for **h** before **t**; e. g. **trac-tus** from **trah-o**; **vec-tus** from **veh-o**.

3. frequently written for final consonant of **ob, sub, ad, id**, in composition before **c** or **q**; e. g. **oc-curro, suc-curro, ac-curro, ic-circo, quicquid, acquiro**. So also **ecce, ecquis** for **en-ce, enquis**.

4. **cu** for **quo**; e. g. **cum, cuius, cui, cur**, &c. for **quom, quoius, quoi, quor**, &c.; **cotidie** for **quotidie**; **quicumque** for **quiquomque**; **alicubi** for **aliquobi**; **ecus, cocus, hircus, æcus, anticus, oblicus**, for **equos, coquos, hirquos, æquos, antiquos, obliquos** (all in nom. sing.); **secuntur, locuntur** for **sequontur, loquontur**. Both forms were in use from the later part of the republic, till after the middle of the first century after Christ, when **quo-** began to give place to **quu**, the forms with **c** however remaining also, and being often found in our earliest MSS. **Quum** appears to be not earlier than the fourth century after Christ; and to have been sounded as **cum**.

INFLUENCE: 1. changes a preceding flat consonant in prepo- 109 sitions and pronouns to **c**; e. g. **ac-curo, ic-circo**, &c. § 108).

2. occasions omission of preceding dental; e. g. **ac** for **atc, atque**; **hoc** for **hodce**.

3. changes preceding **m** to **n** (sounded here as the guttural nasal § 162); e. g. **hunc, nunc, tunc**, for **hum-ce, num-ce, tum-ce**; **anceps** for **am-ceps**; **prin-ceps** for **primi-ceps**; **sinciput** for **semi-caput**; &c.

WEAKNESS: 1. c is omitted before **m, n, t,** the preceding 110 vowel being lengthened to compensate; e. g. lŭ-na, lu-men, compared with lūc-eo; dē-ni (for dĕcĭni) from dĕc-em; quīnī (for quincini) from quinque; lāna, lānugo compared with λάχ-νη; arānea with ἀράχνη; līmus, *slant*, with lĭcīnus, *crumpled*, oblīq-uus, λέχρις, λικ-ριφίς; pī-nus for pĭc-nus (pĭc-, nom. pix), vă-nus compared with vac-uus; au-tumnus from aug-eo; dūmēta for dumec-ta; sētius for sectius; nītor for gnic-tor, comp. nixus, geniculum.

2. c is often omitted when preceded by **l, r, n,** and followed by a consonant; e. g. ar-tus for arc-tus; far-tus for farc-tus; ful-tus for fulc-tus; ul-tus for ulc-tus; quin-tus (usually) for quinc-tus; nac-tus as well as nanc-tus; nasturtium for nās-torctium; fulmentum from fulc-ire; mul-si, mulsum from mulc-ēre, &c.

3. Initial c is sometimes omitted before **l, r, n**; e. g. lāmentum compared with clāmare; læna with χλαῖνα; ălăpa with κόλαφος (a Syracusan word?); raudus, rūdus with crūdus; nīdor with κνῖσα.

4. **ci** (before a vowel) is often confused with **ti** in the spelling of derivative suffixes, partly from doubts as to the etymology of a word, partly from the palatilisation of both ci and ti (= sh) in times when the MSS. were written. ci for ti does not appear, till an African inscription in 3rd century after Christ; and not numerously before Gallic inscriptions and documents of the 7th century after Christ. ti for ci is not certainly found before end of 4th century after Christ. In certain proper names (e. g. Marcius, Martius) both forms appear to have existed as separate names with different origin, and then to have been confused.

The following appears according to inscriptions to be the correct spelling of certain disputed words: dĭcio, condĭcio, solacium, patricius, tribunicius;

contio, nuntius (and derivatives), fētialis, indūtiæ, ōtium, negōtium, sētius.

Both suspicio and suspitio, convicium and convitium are found in good MSS.; neither in inscriptions.

X.

This character is a mere abbreviation for **cs.** It is first found in 111 a single **sexto,** referred to times before the second Punic war, and afterwards not until *S. C. de Bacc.* 186 B. C. (The inscriptions before this date are but few.)

In inscriptions at all times (perhaps from regarding x as a mere guttural like Greek χ) xs is often found instead of x; e. g. exstrad, (in *S. C. de Bacc.*), **taxsat, lexs, proxsumus, exsigito, deixserit,** by side of **exigatur, exterarum, taxet,** &c. in laws of Gracchus' time. So in Greek Σέξστος and Σέξτος. In the Augustan age and subsequently, the simple **x** is the more frequent.

INFLUENCE: Words beginning with **s**, if compounded with **ex**, 112 usually dropped the **s**, but the retention is not unfrequent; e. g. **exilium**, also **exsilium; expecto**, also **exspecto;** &c.

WEAKNESS: Before semivowels, liquids, nasals, and flat mutes, 113 **sex and ex** in composition usually dropped **x**; e. g. **sēvīri, sējūgis, sēmestrīs, sēdecim, sēni, ēduco, escendo** (but **exsto** or **exto**); **ēvādo, ējuro, ēmergo, elicio, ēnormis.** So also **e** for **ex** out of composition, after (rarely in inscriptions before) Augustan age.

Before **c**, **sex** became **ses** ; e. g. **sescenti.**

Before **f**, **ex** sometimes became (or reverted to) **ec;** e.g. **ecfari, ecficio.**

Before **l** and **m** a medial **x** was sometimes omitted ; e. g. **tēla** for **texula; subtēmen** for **subteximen; subtīlis** for **subtexilis; māla** for **maxula; paulus** for **pauxillus; āla** for **axula;** &c.

Q.

CHARACTER : In one or two very old inscriptions **Q** is like 114 the Greek Koppa with a short vertical stroke: its normal form in the best period was with a horizontal stroke to the right.

SOUND : the same as **k**, the sharp guttural mute. It is always 115 followed by the consonantal **u**, except in some old inscriptions where it is immediately followed by the vowel **u** (§ 119). **Qu** was probably sounded as it is in English, i.e. as **kw**, and was regarded in prosody as a single sound. But see App. A. xx.

POSITION : never final, or followed immediately (with or with- 116 out the consonantal **u**) by any consonant: nor preceded immediately in the same syllable by any consonant except **s**; e.g. **squama.**

REPRESENTATION : (i) **q** in Greek by κ: **qu** by κου, κυ, or κο; 117 see § 90.

(ii) of Greek. **Q** is not used in writing any Greek word.

CORRESPONDENCE : 1. **qv** to original Indo-European **kv** (so 118 Lepsius, Donaldson, Grassmann, L. Meyer); or to **k**, to which a parasitic **v** very early fastened itself (Curtius, Corssen). Some languages exhibit the labial, some the guttural.

2. to Greek π, Oscan p; e.g. quo-d? quo? qua-ntus? qva-lis? πό-θι, πού, πό-σος. πο-ῖος, Ionic κόθι, κοῦ, κόσος, κοῖος; qvinque, πέντε, Æol. πέμπε (cf. πέμπ-τος), Osc. pomptis; cŏqvo (also written qvŏqvo), cŏqvīna, πέπω, (Oscan?) pŏpīna; linqvo, re-līqv-us, λείπω; sĕqv-or, ἕπ-ω; ĕqvus, ἵππος; torqv-eo, τρέπω. Probably also in-qvĭlinus, cŏlōnus, cŏlere, πέλω, πολεύω, πόλος.

3. to Greek τ, Osc. Umbr. p; e.g. quis, τίς, Osc. Umbr. pis; quisquis, Osc. pit-pit; -que, τε; quattuor, τέσσαρες, Æol. πίσυρες, Umbr. petur.

4. to Greek κ; e.g. quĭ-squĭl-iæ, κο-σκυλ-μάτια; quiesco (cu-bo, cūnæ), κεῖμαι, κοίτη; oc-cŭl-o (oquoltod for occulto *S. C. de Bacc.*), clam, cēlare, καλύπτω, κρύπτω.

SUBSTITUTION: Q is found before u in inscriptions (rarely be-   119 fore A.U.C. 620), in words which commonly have c; e.g. pequnia (frequently), pequlatus, qura, mirqurios (for mercurius). Quer-quetum also was found for quercetum.

INFLUENCE: 1. changes a preceding d to c; e.g. ac-quiro for   120 ădquiro; quicquam, quicque, quicquid for quidquam, &c.

2. changes a preceding m to n; e.g. con-queror, con-quiro, con-quiesco; an-quiro; tan-quam, nunquam. Before -que, and usually in compounds, as quiquomque or quicumque, utrumque, utrimque, quotiescumque, the m is generally *written*.

WEAKNESS: 1. When ŏ was changed to u, qu passed into c;   121 e.g. ĕcus for ĕqvos; cŏcus for qvŏqvos; cum, cur for qvom, qvor; see under C § 108. 4. So perhaps stercus for sterqvos, comp. ster-qvĭlinium; cænum, cūnire for quenum, comp. inqvīnare. But sometimes q is found without v; e.g. qum, qur, &c. See above § 119.

2. Before a consonant qu changed to c; e.g. coctum, coxi (=coc-si) from coqu-o; relic-tus from relinquo.

3. Q fell away in certain forms of the pronoun qui (stem quo-), and, as the short ŏ past into ŭ, the semiconsonantal u then fell away also. Hence ŭbi, ŭti, ŭter, unde, for quŏbi, quŏti, quoter, quonde.

So văpor for quapor, comp. καπνός.

4. -qve and -pe appear to have been collateral forms. Cf. § 517, and above, § 118. 3.

G.

CHARACTER: a slightly modified C. The earliest inscription   122 in which it is found is that on Scipio Barbatus, inscribed probably soon after 500 U.C. Plutarch ascribes its invention to a Spurius

Carvilius, who, if the freedman of Sp. Carvilius Ruga is meant, kept a school probably twenty or thirty years later. See under **C** (§ 104).

SOUND: the flat guttural mute—English hard **G**. There ap- 123 pears to be little, if any, evidence of its ever having the soft sound (*g* in *gentle*) at least before the sixth century after Christ.

POSITION: never final. As initial it stands before vowels and 124 the liquids l, and r, and in a few words before n; e.g. glans, grus, gnarus, &c. (See below § 129. 3.)

REPRESENTATION: (i) in Greek, by γ; e.g. Verginius, Οὐερ- 125 γίνιος; Sergius, Σέργιος; Gaius, Γάιος; Gnæus, Γναῖος; Gabii, Γάβιοι; Gellius, Γέλλιος; &c.

(ii) of Greek γ; e.g. Γραϊκός, Græcus; Φρύγες, Phryges; 'Αναξαγόρας, Anaxagoras; &c.

CORRESPONDENCE: 1. to original Indo-European g, and me- 126 dial gh.

2. to Greek γ; e.g. ăgo, ἄγω; ăger, ἀγρός; arg-entum, argilla, ἄργυρος, ἄργιλος; gaudeo, γαῦ-ρος, γη-θέω, γά-νυμαι; gigno, gĕnus, γίγνομαι, γένος; gus-tare, γεύ-ομαι; gnosco, γιγνώσκω; genu, γόνυ; urg-eo, εἴργω (Ϝεργ-); rego, ὀρέγω; fulg-eo, φλέγω; vig-eo, ὑγι-ής; mulg-eo, ἀμέλγω; garrio, garrulus, γῆρυς, γηρύω; &c.

3. g medial, or before r, to Greek χ; e.g. ango, ἄγχω; rigo, βρέχω; anguis, anguilla, ἔχις, ἔγχ-ελυς; lingo, λείχω; grando, χάλαζα; gratus, gratia, χαίρω, χάρις; unguis, ὄνυξ (ὀνυχ-); &c.

4. to Greek κ; e.g. viginti (but vicies), εἴκοσι, Bœot. Ϝίκατι; gubernator, κυβερνήτης; mūgio, μυκάομαι; Gnossus, Κνωσσός; gummi, κόμμι; Saguntum, Ζάκανθα (Polyb.).

5. to old Umbrian k; e.g. Iguvini, Umbr. Ikuvini; tergeantur, Umbr. terkantur. (The old Umbrian like old Latin had no separate character for g as distinguished from k.)

SUBSTITUTION: for c in the word nec; e.g. neg-o, neg-otium, 127 neg-lego. So probably glōria, from cluere.

INFLUENCE: 1. turns to g the final consonant of sub, ob, and 128 ad; e.g. suggero, suggredior; oggannio; agger, aggredior, aggravo, agglomero, agnoscor (for ag-gnoscor), &c.

Ex in composition before g appears as e (perhaps for eg- from ec-); as e-gelidus, egero, egredior, &c.

2. always gives a guttural clang (as English ng) to a preceding nasal; e.g. con-gero, in-gredior, &c. were sounded as conggero, ing-gredĭor, &c.

WEAKNESS: 1. Medial g before a sharp consonant (t or s) ¹²9 is changed to c; e.g. punc-tum, punxi (=puncsi) from pung-o; auc-tum, auxi from aug-eo; mulctrum from mulg-eo; &c.

2. Medial g drops away in several cases, viz.

(*a*) after 1 or r and before s; e.g. mul-si, mulsum from mulgeo; mer-si, mersum from mergeo; spar-si, sparsum from sparg-o; &c.

(*b*) after u; e.g. flu-o compared with fluc-tus; struo with struc-tus; fruor with fruc-tus, frŭges; sŭ-men from sug-o; jŭmentum from jungo (jug-); ŭ-mor compared with ὑγ-ρός.

(*c*) before v; e.g. vīvo (for gvigvo) compared with vic-tus, vīxi (cf. Engl. "the *quick* and dead"); nivis with nix, ninguit (*it snows*); conīvēre with conixi, nixus, nic-to; brĕvis (for bregvis) with βραχύς; lĕvis with ἐλαχύς; mălo from măg-vŏlo.

before m in a few words; e.g. contă-minare, comp. contăg-es; flă-men, *a priest*, comp. flag-rare, fulg-ēre, flamma; examen for exagmen; sŭ-men for sŭg-men; u-mor for ug-mor (cf. ὑγ-ρός); stĭmulus for stig-mulus (comp. in-stīg-are). (But augmen, coagmentum, fragmen, sagmen, tegmen, &c. preserve the g.)

(*d*) before i in derivatives with stem mag-; e.g. măjor, majestas for măg-ior, mag-iestas; and perhaps in ajo for ag-io, comp. ad-ag-ium.

3. Initial g before n was rarely retained in classical times; e.g. nascor, natus for gnascor (i.e. gen-a-scor), gnatus (which is found in Vergil and in compounds cognatus, prognatus, &c.); nosco for gnosco (which is found in *S. C. de Bacc.* and also in compounds cognosco, ignotus, ignominia); nārus (C. *Or.* 47) for gnārus (so often written: also in comp. ignarus); năvus for gnăvus; nixus for gnixus (from gĕnu, *the knee*); norma compared with γνώρ-ιμος. (Comp. English pronunciation of *gnaw, gnat, gnarl, knee*.) In the proper name Gnæus (which abbreviated is written Cn.) the g remained.

Also before 1; e.g. lact-is compared with γάλακτ-ος.

H.

CHARACTER as above.   130

SOUND: the rough breathing, as in English.   131

Ph, ch, th, were not sounded either as in English or as in German; but as p+h, k+h, t+h; i.e. a rough breathing immediately after an ordinary p, k, t.

POSITION: never final, either of a word (except a few interjec- [132] tions) or syllable; and never before a consonant.

After the consonants **p, c, t, r** it is found chiefly in Greek words. Inscriptions of the 7th century U.C. give it, though rarely until cir. 660 U.C. After cir. 700 U.C. they give it regularly; e.g. **philosophus, Achilles, Thyrsis,** &c. Cicero (*Or.* 48, § 160) says that at one time he spoke as the old Romans did, **pulcros, Cetegos, Kartaginem, triumpos**: afterwards he conformed to the ordinary practice, and said **Phryges, Pyrrhus** (not **Bruges, Burrus,** as Ennius wrote); but still **sepulcra, coronas, lacrimas, Otones, Matones, Cæpiones.** Catullus wrote an epigram (LXXXIV) ridiculing the pronunciation of **chommoda** for **commoda, hinsidias** for **insidias.** See Gell. II. 3, XIII. 6, where Nigidius is quoted: "Rusticus fit sermo, si aspires perperam." According to Quintil. I. 5, 20, some inscriptions had **choronæ, chenturiones, præchones.**

REPRESENTATION: (i) In Greek, by the sign of the rough [133] breathing; e. g. **Horatius,** 'Ορáτιος; **Hernici,** "Ερνικες; **Hostilius,** 'Οστίλιος; &c.

(ii) Of Greek rough breathing; e.g. 'Hρόδοτος, **Herodotus;** ἥρως, **hēros;** 'Ροδόπη, **Rhodope;** Πύρρος, **Pyrrhus;** &c.

ph, ch, th respectively for φ, χ, θ; e.g. 'Αμφίπολις, **Amphipolis;** Xίος, **Chios;** Θεσσαλοί, **Thessali;** θάλαμος, **thalamus;** &c.

CORRESPONDENCE: 1. to original Indo-European **gh.** [134]

2. Initial **h** to Greek χ; e.g. **pre-hendo,** χανδáνω; **helvus,** χλό-η, χλῶ-ρος; **hĕri, hes-ternus,** χθές (where the θ is parasitical); **hiemps, hīb-ernus,** χιών, χειμών, χειμερινός; **hir** (old word used by Lucilius for *hollow of hand*), χείρ; **hirundo,** χελιδών; **hīra, hilla, hāru-spex** (but see § 136. 4), χόλιξ, χορ-δή; **hio, hisco,** χαίνω, χάσκω; **hortus, cors** (for cohors), χόρτος; **hŭmi,** χαμαί.

Medial **h** to Greek χ in **veh-o, vec-tus,** ἔχω, ὀχέω.

3. to a Sabine **f** [1]; e.g. **hædus,** Sab. **fædus; hariolus,** Sab. **fariolus; hărēna,** Sab. **fasena; hordeum,** Sab. **fordeum; hircus,** Sab. **fircus; hostis,** Sab. **fostis.** Quintilian attributes **fordeum, fœdos** (**fædos,** Halm) to the old Romans (I. 4. 14).

So **forctus** and **horctus** are said to have both been used with the meaning of **bonus;** and **horda** to have been an old form for **forda,** *pregnant.* Perhaps **horreum** is connected with **far.**

INFLUENCE: none. [135]

---

[1] So Spanish has **h** for Latin **f**; e. g. *hijo* for *filius.*

WEAKNESS: 1. changes (or reverts?), *after* a vowel, to c (before 136
t or s); e.g. vĕh-o, vectus, vexi (=vec-si); trăh-o, tractus, traxī.

2. h was not a consonant, so as to affect the quantity of a
preceding syllable or prevent the elision of a preceding final vowel;
e.g. inhibet; tŏllit hŭmō; tŏllite hŭmō.

3. H between two vowels dropped out, and the vowels if like
one another coalesced. Thus Plautus uses dehibeo, præhibeo, for
which afterwards dēbeo, præbeo. So comprehendo, comprendo;
cŏhors, cors; ahĕnus, aē-nus; vehĕmens (always two syllables only
in verse), vēmens; nĭhil, nil; mĭhi (and not very frequently), mi,
existed side by side. Dehinc as monosyllable sometimes in Augustan verse. Mehercŭles as trisyllable (mercules) in Phædrus.

Incoho is an older form for which inchoo is found as early as
the second century after Christ at least.

4. In several words the pronunciation appears to have been
uncertain, and the spelling varied accordingly; e.g. hărundo,
hărēna, hēres, hŏlus, hordeŭm; aruspex, ĕdĕra, ei (interjection), ĕrus,
erciscundæ, ŭmĕrus, ūmor (the preferable spelling is here given).
Gellius (II. 3) speaks of h being formerly found in hallucinor,
heluor, honera, honustum. Late inscriptions insert and omit h
almost at random; e.g. hădītus, hii, hauctoritas; ŏmĭni, ăbĭtat,
inospita. In modern Italian h is not sounded.

In foreign proper names both spellings often occur; e.g. Hiberus,
Iberus; Hirpini, Irpini; Hannibal, Annibal; &c.

J i.e. I as consonant.

CHARACTER: same as the vowel I. In the middle of words 137
Cicero is said to have written the i twice; e.g. Aiiax, Maiia. In-
scriptions of the imperial time, rarely any of earlier date, use a tall
I for the consonantal i between two vowels. The form j is modern.

SOUND: As English **y**. In the middle between two vowels it 138
probably gave a sound to the preceding vowel, as if forming a
diphthong with it, besides its own sound of y. Thus Aiiax or Ajax
would be sounded as (English) Ay-yax; Pompeiius or Pompejus as
(English) Pompa-yus; quojus as Engl. quoy-yus; cujus as Engl.
cwee-yus.

For j after consonants in verse see below, § 142. 2.

POSITION: never final. I is consonantal (1) when it stands 139
as initial, before any of the vowels a, e, o, u, in Latin words (except
iens from īre, *to go*); e.g. jacio, jeci, Jovis, jugum, &c.

(2) when it stands between two vowels, in Latin and some
Greek words, viz.:

aj-; Gajus (but in Martial, nom. Gāǐŭs; voc. Gāǐ), Trajanus, Bajæ, Cajeta, bajulus, major, ajo; Achaja, Maja, Ajax, Grajus.

ej-; Aquileja, Veji, pulejum, legulejus, plebejus, jejunus, pejor, ejus, ejulo, mejo, pejero; and proper names, as Pompejus (voc. Pompei as trisyllable in Ovid; as disyllable in Hor.).

oj-; quojus, Troja, Bojos (acc. pl.).

uj-; cujus, hujus. In tenuia, tenuior, assiduior, i is a vowel, u consonantal. For compounds of jacio see below.

REPRESENTATION: (i) in Greek by ι; e.g. Junius, 'Ιούνιος; 140 Julius, 'Ιούλιος; Vejos (acc.), Οὐηίους; Gajus, Γάιος; Pompejus, Πομπήιος; Appulejus, 'Αππουλήιος; &c.

(ii) of Greek ι, which sometimes forms a diphthong with the preceding vowel; e.g. Αἴας, Ajax, or (Cic.) Aiiax; Τροία, Troja; &c.

CORRESPONDENCE: 1. to an original Indo-European j.   141

2. to Greek ζ (perhaps Engl. *dy*); e.g. jugum, ζύγον; Juppiter, Jovis, Ζεύς (i.e. Δjευς); jus, *broth*, ζω-μός.

3. to Greek δ; e.g. ja-m, δή.

4. to Greek rough breathing; e.g. jĕcur, ἧπαρ; jŭvenis, ἥβη.

SUBSTITUTION: 1. for di, gi (the i first becoming j, and then 142 pushing out the preceding consonant); e.g. major for magior; Janus for Dianus.

2. In verse the vowel i becomes sometimes hardened to j. Thus in Plautus in scjo, djes (scio, dies); filjo, otjum: in the dactylic poets, arjetat, arjetibus (Verg. Stat. Sil.), abjete, parjete, parjetibus (Verg. Sil.), filjorum (or fivuīorum), steljo, omnja, precantja (Verg.); vindēmjator, Nasīdjeni, and (in alcaics) consiljum, principjum (Hor.); abjegnæ (Prop.), antjum, promuntorjum (Ovid, but see § 940); ludjum (Juv.). So also in words compounded of semi- (e.g. semjanimus, semjesus), unless the i be really elided (e.g. sem-animis, semesus). In Statius tĕnŭja, tĕnŭjore (or tĕnvia, tĕnviore?) appear to occur; for tenvja, &c. seem impossible.

In conubium probably the u is short in the numerous cases, in which the metre has been supposed to require conubjum. (See Luc. Müller, p. 258, and Munro on Lucret. iii. 776.)

INFLUENCE: 1. caused the omission of a preceding conso- 143 nant; e.g. pējor for pĕd-ior, *lower* (compare pes-simus, pessum); pējĕro for perjero (in good MSS.), later per-jūro; dī-judico, trā-mitto, &c. for disjudico, transmitto (cf. 168. 3); rējectus, rējecto, for red-jectus, red-jecto; sējŭgis for sexjugis; Jānus for Djānus (for Dianus); see § 160. 2

The effect attributed to **j** by the old grammarians that it lengthens a preceding vowel is usually explicable either by the absorption of a consonant, or by the vowel being long independently; but the pronunciation (§ 138) may have had some effect; e.g. in **hoius, quoius (hūjus, cūjus).**

2. At a late period of the language it caused, (when followed by a vowel,) the assibilation of a preceding **c, g, t, d**; viz. **ci, ti = chi,** or **shi; gi, di = ǰi** (either with French or English pronunciation of j). This assibilation is not proved for any period of Latin proper before the 3rd or 4th century after Christ. Instances of it are found in old Umbrian and Oscan.

WEAKNESS : 1. **j** was vocalised (rarely), when occurring be- 144 tween two vowels, and absorbed the succeeding vowel ; e. g. **bīga** for **bī-jŭga.**

2. Before another **i** in the compounds of **jacio**, it was omitted ; e.g. **ădĭcio, cōnĭcio, prōĭcio, dēĭcio** : but the preposition remained usually long, though, in and after Ovid, sometimes short ; e. g. **ădĭcī.** Sometimes the vowels were contracted ; e.g. **rēĭce** (Verg.), **ēĭcĭt** (Lucr.) : and in the Augustan and præ-Augustan period **jacio** in composition was sometimes written **jecio** (e. g. **rejěcit, adjěcit**) instead of **ĭcio. Dis-jacio** became **dissĭcio; porjacio, porrĭcio.** So **ajo, ăis, ăit.**

In the same way the **ĭ** of **capio, fugio,** &c. dropped away before **-is, -it**; e.g. **capĭs, capĭt** (for **capiis,** &c.).

3. In late imperial inscriptions **z** is sometimes written for **j**; e.g. **Zesus, Zanuari** for **Jesus, Januari**: or **Gi**; e. g. **Gianuaria, Giove** for **Januaria, Jove.**

CHAPTER VIII.

DENTALS AND LINGUALS.

T.

CHARACTER : as above, but with the top stroke sometimes 145 slanting, and sometimes mainly or entirely to the right or left of the vertical stroke.

SOUND : the sharp dental mute : English **t.** 146

POSITION : frequently final, being so used in verbal inflexions 147 of the third person. Also in some conjunctions.

As initial it can stand immediately before **r**, and in the oldest language also (rarely) before **l**; e.g. **tlatum, stlis.** In Greek words before **l** or **m**; e.g. **Tlepolemus, Tmessus.** It can also stand immediately after an initial **s**; e.g. **sto, stravi**: and in Greek words after **p**; e.g. **Ptolemæus.**

On its aspiration see under **H** (§ 132).

REPRESENTATION: (i) in Greek by τ; e.g. **Titus,** Τίτος; **Pala-** 148 **tium,** Παλάτιον; &c.

(ii) (*a*) of Greek τ; e.g. Αἰτωλοί, **Ætoli;** Μιλτιάδης, **Miltiades**; ἄστρον, **astrum**; &c.

(*b*) of Greek θ, in early period (see § 132); e.g. Κόρινθος, **Corintus;** θέατρον, **teatrum**; θίασος, **tiasus**; &c.

(*c*) of Greek δ, only in two or three of the oldest inscriptions; e.g. Ἀλέξανδρον, **Alixentrom;** Κασσάνδρα, **Casenter.** (Comp. Quintil. I. 4, 16.)

CORRESPONDENCE: 1. to original Indo-European **t.** 149

2. to Greek τ; e.g. **ten-do, ten-eo,** τείνω; **taurus,** ταῦρος; **tu, tuus,** τύ Dor. (σύ Att.), τεός; **tuli, tollo, tolerare,** τολ-μάω, τλῆ-ναι; **terminus,** τέρμα; **tero, ter-es, trua,** τείρω, τρίβω, τρῦμα; **torr-eo,** τέρσομαι; **sto, sisto,** στάσις, ἵστημι; **di-sting-uo,** στίγ-μα, στίζω; **sterno, strā-tus, tŏrus,** στορ-έννυμι, στρώ-μνη; **stella** (for ster-ula), ἀστήρ (ἀστερ-); **tĕgo,** στέγω; **et,** ἔτι; **peto, præpes,** πέτομαι, πί-πτω; **pateo,** πετ-άννυμι; &c.

3. **st** sometimes to Greek σπ; e.g. **stŭdeo,** σπεύδω; so **talpa,** σπάλαξ (also σκάλοψ); **turgeo,** σπαργάω (the **s** having fallen off as in **tego,** στέγω); &c.

SUBSTITUTION: 1. for **d** (in the preposition **ad**) before **t**; e.g. 150 **at-tineo** for **adtineo,** &c. Also, in the old language, **cette** for **cĕdite,** from imperative **cĕdŏ.**

2. for final **d** in a few words (in inscriptions) in and after the 8th century U.C.; e.g. **aput, aliut, quitquit, it;** and in and after, rarely before, 4th century after Christ, **set, at** (for preposition **ad**). **Haut** is found in republican inscriptions. **Ut** is probably for **quod.**

3. For confusion of **ti** with **ci** see under **C** (§ 110. 4).

INFLUENCE: 1. changes a preceding **b, g** to **p, c**; e.g. **scrip-tum** 151 from **scrib-o;** **ac-tum** from **ăgo**[1]. So the prepositions **ad, ob, sub**

---

[1] Lachmann (Lucr. p. 54) generalizing from Gellius' statements (IX. 6, XII. 3), lays down the following rules for the *quantity* of the vowel in past participles and frequentatives. Stems in **b, g, d** and **u** (for

were changed (in pronunciation, though the spelling varies); e.g.
at-tineo, optimo, supter, &c.

2. A preceding **d** or **t** is softened to **s** before a suffix commencing with **t**, if it was important to preserve the suffixal **t**; e.g.
tons-trix from **tond-eo** (**tonsrix** was almost unpronounceable); **ras-trum** from **rād-o**; **eques-tris** from **equit-**, nom. **eques**; **est**, *eat*, for **edt** (i.e. **edit**, the **t** being preserved as the sign of the 3rd pers.).
(See below (§ 152. 3) for another course which the language adopted in order to avoid the double dental.)

3. retains a preceding original **s**, which before a vowel has passed into **r**; e.g. **us-tus** from **ur-o**; **tos-tus** (comp. **tes-ta**) from **torr-eo**; **mæs-tus** from **mærere**; **arbus-tum** from **arbos, arbor**; **hones-tus** from **honos, honor**; **sceles-tus** from **scelus, sceler-is**; &c.

4. requires the insertion of **p**, if **m** would otherwise have preceded it; e.g. **em-p-tus, prom-p-tus** from **emo, sumo**. The **p** is involuntarily pronounced, as the organs change from pronouncing **m** to pronouncing **t** (or **s**, § 70).

WEAKNESS: 1. Initial **t** fell off before **l**; e.g. **lis** for **stlis**; 152 **locus** for **stlocus**; **latum** for **tlatum**.

2. Drops away or is assimilated before **s**; e.g. **mīsi** from **mitto**; **percussi** from **percutio**; &c.

At the end of a word one **s** only is retained, and the preceding vowel, if short, usually remains so; e.g. **virtūs** for **virtut-s**; **regens** for **regent-s** (originally **regentis**, § 245. 2); **sors** for **sort-s**; **equĕs** for **equet-s** (**equit-**); **compŏs** for **compot-s**; **damnās** for **damnāt-s**; &c.
But **pariēs, abiēs, ariēs** for **pariĕt-s**, &c.

3. The initial **t** of a suffix is changed (but see § 151. 2) to **s** after **t, d, lg, rg, ll, rr**, and in a few other cases, the last letter of the stem being then assimilated or omitted; e.g. **cāsum** for **cad-tum**; **divisum** for **divid-tum**; **messum** for **met-tum**, **mer-sum** for **mergt-um**; **pul-sum** from **pello**, (but in **expultrix** compared with **expulsor** the **t** resumes its place in order to prevent the combination **sr**).

So also **vicensumus** or **vicēsimus** for **vicent-tŭmus**; **tricensumus** or **trigēsimus** for **trigent-tŭmus**; **pes-simus** for **ped-timus**; &c.

On **eques-tris** for **equet-tris**, see above § 151. 2.

4. **tn, tm** were not allowable combinations in Latin. (*Ætna* is Greek.) Hence e.g. **vicē-nus** for **vicent-nus**; **sexagēnus** for **sexagint-nus**; &c.

gu) lengthen the preceding vowel (e.g. **āctus, strūctus** from **ăgo, struo**) : in **c**, shorten it (e.g. **dĭctus** from **dīco**); in **p, t**, are short except **mĭssus, sēnsus**: in **m, n, l, r, s, h**, retain quantity of present tense.

5. Final **t** had a weak position. Thus it fell off:

(*a*) in Umbrian; e.g. **habe, facia** for **habet, faciat;**

(*b*) in the oldest Latin inscriptions of Picenum; e.g. **dede** for **dedet** (i.e. **dedit**). (This is the only word in 3rd pers. sing. which occurs in these inscriptions.)

(*c*) in vulgar inscriptions on walls of Pompeii; e.g. **ama, valia, parci** for **amat, valeat, parcit,** (but the **t** is much oftener retained);

(*d*) frequently in inscriptions of fifth century after Christ and later; e.g. **fece, quiesce, militavi, vixi,** for **fecit, quiescit, militavit, vixit,** &c.

6. **nt** fell off in 3rd pers. plur. perf. in Cato, Sallust, dactylic poets, &c. (Cic. *Or.* 47, § 157); e.g. **scripsēre, amavēre** for **scripserunt, amaverunt.**

In late inscriptions sometimes **fecerun, vivon,** &c. are found for **fecerunt, vivont (vivunt).**

7. A long vowel preceding a final **t** was shortened; e.g. **amăt** compared with **amās, amātis; amarĕt** compared with **amarēs, amarētis;** &c.

D.

CHARACTER : as above.   153

SOUND : the flat dental mute : English **d. di** before a vowel, 154 at and after the end of the 4th century after Christ, was pronounced ' **cum sibilo,**' i.e. probably as **ji** or as **j,** with English or, perhaps, French sound of **j.** (See below under **Z,** § 195.)

POSITION : final only in **sed, haud, ad, apud,** and the pro- 155 nouns **id, quod, istud, illud, aliud.** (Often final in early Latin, see below § 160. 6.)

Never immediately precedes another consonant in same syllable, except in a few Greek words, and **Drusus** (said to be from the Gallic, Suet. *Tib.* 3); and see § 158.

REPRESENTATION : (i) in Greek by δ; e.g. **Decius,** Δέκιος; 156 **Cædicius,** Καιδίκιος; **Domitius,** Δομίτιος; **Fidenæ,** Φιδήνη ; &c.

(ii) of Greek δ; e.g. δρέπανον, **Drepanum;** Δημοσθένης, **Demosthenes;** δίαιτα, **diæta** ; &c.

CORRESPONDENCE : 1. to an original Indo-European **d,** and 157 (medial) **dh.** The final **d** of the ablative corresponds to an original **t.**

2. (*a*) to Greek δ; e.g. dŏmāre, δαμάζω; daps, δάπτω, δεῖπνον; densus, δασύς; dŏmus, δέμω, δόμος; dexter, δεξιός; dăre, dător, δοτήρ, δίδωμι; dŏlus, δόλος; duo, dis-, dŭbius, δύο, δίς, δισσός; ĕdo, es-ca, ἔδω, ἐσ-θίω; dens, ὀδούς (ὀδοντ-); op-pĭdum, pe(d)s, πέδον, ποδ-, (πούς); scindo, σχίζω, σχίδαξ; unda, ὕδωρ; &c.

(*b*) to Greek medial θ; e.g. fīdo, fīdes, πείθω, πίστις; gaudēre, γηθεῖν; va(d)s, vad-imonium, ἄεθ-λον.

SUBSTITUTION: 1. for tv before r in words derived from 158 quattuor; e.g. quadraginta, quadra, quadrupes, quadriduum (not quatriduum), &c.

2. once (in a very old vase inscription) for final t: fecid for fecit. (The Oscan had sometimes the 3rd pers. sing. in d.) So in the *Mon. Ancyr.* adque, aliquod, for atque, aliquot. In late imperial inscriptions occasionally capud for caput; reliquid for reliquit; &c.

INFLUENCE: 1. requires a preceding consonant to be flat; e.g. 159 sub-duco, ab-do, &c.

2. changes preceding m to n; e.g. con-do (for com-do), &c.

3. changes a following t to s, and then is assimilated or omitted; e.g. divi-sum for divid-tum; scan-sum for scand-tum; fossa from fŏd-io; &c. (For d before tr see below.) In the præ-Ciceronian language cette for cĕdite is found.

WEAKNESS: 1. Initial d before v dropped off, the v be- 160 coming b; e.g. duonus becomes bonus. See § 76.

2. Initial d before j dropped off; e.g. Jŏvis for (old) Diŏvis; Jānus for Diānus; jŭvenis, Jūnius from stem diu-; jacio compared with διώκω, διάκτωρ; &c.

3. Before the initial tr of a suffix, d changed to s. (The t was retained because sr was unpronounceable.) e.g. tonstrix for tond-trix; claus-trum for claud-trum; rās-trum for rād-trum; ros-trum for rŏd-trum; frus-tra for fraud-tra; &c.

4. Before the initial m, l, n of a suffix, d fell off or was assimilated; e.g. cæ-mentum from cædĕre; rā-mentum from rād-ere; rā-mus compared with rādix; &c.

scā-la (for scand-la) from scand-ĕre; nītela or nītella for nītē-dula.

fī-nis (for fid-nis) from fĭndo; mercennarius for mercednarius.

5. Before s, d is assimilated or falls away; e.g. ces-si for ced-si; ten-si for tend-si; &c. See also § 159. 3.

At the end of a word, the d being assimilated, one s only remains, and the preceding vowel, if short, remains so; e.g. incŭs for incŭds; hērēs for hērēds; lapis for lapids; compĕs for compeds; [pĕs, văs (from stems pĕd-, văd-), are long as being monosyllables].

6. Final **d** fell off at an early period from the ablative case of which it appears to have been the characteristic. It is not found in any inscription later than the *S. C. de Bacc.* 186 B.C. and is not found constantly even in the earliest inscriptions. The Oscan shows this **d**: the Umbrian and other Italian dialects (Volscian, Sabellan) do not, though some inscriptions are much older than the Latin. Plautus probably used it or not as he chose.

This ablatival **d** has dropped off also from the adverbs **supra, infra** (**suprad, infrad**), &c., and probably from **interea, postea**, &c.; also from the particle **red**, and the prepositions, **sed, prod, antid, postid**, except sometimes in composition; e.g. **sed-itio, red-eo, prod-est, antidhac** (for **antehac**); &c. So also **facilumed** (*S. C. de Bacc.*), for later **facillime**.

The pronouns **me, te, se** (both accusative and ablative) were in early times **med, ted, sed**.

Of the final **d** of the imperative (also retained in Oscan), one example remains in Latin; **estod** (Fest. p. 230): perhaps also **facitud** for **facito**.

7. In the particle **red** in composition, the **d** was frequently either assimilated, or fell off, the vowel being lengthened to compensate. Thus **reddo, rĕcido**, or **reccido, rĕjectus** always: **redduco** or **rēduco** in early poets including Lucretius; **rēlĭquiæ, rēligio, rēlicuus** in Lucr.; (**rĕliquiæ**, &c. in iambic &c. (Plaut. Ter. Phædr. Sen.); **rĕllĭcus** in Persius and later poets;) **rēceptus, rēlictus** (Lucil.); **rellatus** and **rĕlatus** (Lucr.). The perfect stem has always a long first syllable in **repperi, reppuli, rettuli, rettudi**, probably as a joint effect of the original **red** and the loss of the reduplication. In other words the **d** is lost without compensation.

8. The preposition **prod** always drops the **d** in composition except before a vowel; e.g. **prodeo, prodest**, but **prōsum, produco**. But the **o** is always lengthened, except in a few words, viz. **prŏcella, prŏnepos, prŏneptis, prŏtervus**, and before **f** (except **prōfero, prōficio, prōfligo, prōflo**); usually **prōpago** (noun and verb), **prōcuro**, and, rarely, **prŏpello, Prŏserpina**. (In Greek words **prŏ** is always short, except **prōlogus** and sometimes **prŏpino**.)

9. **D** in the preposition **ad** is usually assimilated to a following **p, c, g, t, l, r, n**; e.g. **apparet, accipio, aggero, attinet, alloquor, arripio, annuo** (but **adnepos**). It is usually omitted before **gn, sp, sc, st**; e.g. **agnosco, aspicio, ascisco, asto**. It always remains before **b, j, v, m**; e.g. **adbibo, adjuvo, advena, admiror**; and in inscriptions before **q, f, s**[1]; e.g. **adquiro, adfero, adsigno**.

---

[1] The retention of the **d** is not a proof of the pronunciation, as we see from the pun in Plaut. *Pœn.* i. 2. 67. **MI. Adsum apud te eccum, AG. Ego elixus sis volo.** The pronunciation was **assum**.

For the more usual atque, ad-que is found in the Mon. Ancyr.
and frequently in other inscriptions.

10.   Final **d** in old Latin sometimes changed to **r**. Thus in **ad**
in composition, chiefly before **v** and **f**; e.g. **arvocatos, arvorsum,
arveho, arvena**; **arfines, arfari, arfuisse**. Hence **arbiter** from **ad-**
beto, arcesso for **ad-cesso**.

So also **meridies** for **medi-dies** (according to the Romans);
Ladinum on old coins for **Larinum**; **apor** (in Festus) for **apud**.
Comp. **aud-io, aur-is** *ear*.

11.   In **quicquid, quicquam, cette** (for **cĕdite**), **d** is assimilated.

In **quo-circa** (for **quod-circa**, comp. **idcirco**), **hoc** (for **hodce**), **d**
is omitted.

For the more usual **haud**, are found **haut**, and in early Latin
(and in mss. of Livy and Tacitus) before consonants **hau**. (For
aput, set, &c. see § 150, and for the practical omission of **d** in **apud**
in the comic poets, see § 295. 4.)

N.

CHARACTER: as above.   161

SOUND: both (1) dental, and (2) guttural, nasal.   162

1.   as dental nasal usually, like English **n**.

2.   as guttural nasal ("**n adulterinum**") before a guttural (**c, q,
g. x**); sounded like English **ng**, (or **n** in *inky*, *finger*). Varro (*ap.*
Prisc. I. 39) said the oldest Roman writers followed the Greek in
writing **g** for **n** before **c** and **g**; e.g. **aggulus** for **angulus** (comp.
Greek ἀγκύλος); **agguilla** (comp. ἔγχελυς); **agcora** (comp. ἄγκυρα);
agceps for **anceps**; **aggens** for **angens**; **iggerunt** for **ingerunt**.

POSITION: final, only 1. in nom. acc. sing. of neuter nouns in   163
-men, and a few others; e.g. **gluten** (n), &c.; **tibicen, cornicen,
tubicen, fidicen** (for **tibicinus**), &c.

2.   in some adverbs; e.g. **in, an, sin** (for **si-ne**), **quin** (for **qui-ne**),
tamen; also **viden, audin**, &c. (for **vides-ne, audis-ne**).

3.   in Greek words; e.g. **splen, sindon**, &c.

Never after another consonant in an initial combination (§ 11),
except in a few words which in the older language began with **gn**
(see § 129. 3).   Never initial before another consonant.

Frequent before **t** and **s** at end of a word (§ 271).

REPRESENTATION: (i) in Greek by ν, or, before gutturals, by   164
γ; e.g. **Faunus**, Φαῦνος; **Numitor**, Νεμέτωρ; **Cincius**, Κίγκιος; **uncia,
ουγκία** or οὐγγία; **Longus**, Λόγγος; &c.

(ii) of Greek ν, or, before gutturals, γ; e.g. γνώμων, gnomon; Πᾶν, Pan; Σειρήν, Siren; Ἀγχίσης, Anchises; σπογγία, spongia; Coruncanius, Κορογκάνιος (Polyb.); &c.

CORRESPONDENCE: 1. to an original Indo-European n.   165

2. to Greek ν, or, before gutturals, γ; e.g. animus, anima, ἄνεμος; gĕna, γένυς; an-hēlo, ἀνά; in, ἐν, εἰς (for ἐνς); māneo, me-mĭn-i, mens, &c., μένω, μέ-μον-α, μέν-ος, &c.; Nĕro (a Sabine word), ἀνήρ (ανερ-); nŏvus, νέος (νεϜος); ānas (anat-s), νῆσσα; nix, nĭv-is, nin-guit, νίφετός, νίφει; nun-c, νῦν; unguis, ὄνυξ; nuo, co-nīveo, νεύω, νυστάζω, &c.

SUBSTITUTION: 1. For m before all but labial consonants; e.g.   166 con-cors, con-gero, conjux, &c. (see under m, § 86. 4).

2. nn for nd. There is some evidence for forms distennite, dispennite for distendite, dispendite (Pl. *Mil.* 1407); and tennitur for tenditur (Ter. *Ph.* 330).

INFLUENCE: 1. causes c, s, t, d, m to fall out before it; e.g.   167 lŭ-na for luc-na; pōno for posno; vicēnŭs for vicentnus; fī-nis for fid-nis (findo); septenus for septem-nus; novēnus for novem-nus, &c.

2. ns, nf lengthened the preceding vowel. See Cic. *Or.* 48, § 159: "'Indoctus' dicimus brevi prima littera, 'insanus' producta, 'inhumanus' brevi, 'infelix' longa; et ne multis, quibus in verbis eæ primæ litteræ sunt, quæ in sapiente atque felice, producte dicitur, in ceteris omnibus breviter." So Consus, Consualia, consules (acc.), consilia, Considius, are written Κῶνσος, Κωνσουάλια, κωνσούλας, κωνσίλια, Κωνσίδιος (Dionys. Hal.); Consentia, Κωνσεντία (Appian), Κωσεντία (Strab.); Constantinus, Κωνσταντῖνος (Dio Cass.); census, accensus, κῆνσος, ἄκκηνσος (Inscr.); Censorinus, Κηνωρίνος (Mon. Ancyr. App.); Ramnenses, Titienses, Ῥαμνήνσης, Τιτιήνσης (Plut.). [Compare with Centenius, Κεντήνιος (Polyb., App.); Centuriones, Κεντυρίωνες (Polyb.).]·

WEAKNESS: 1. changes to m before a labial (p, b, m), though   168 the change is not always marked in writing; e.g. imperator, imperium (sometimes inperium); compleo (conpleo), imbuo, commuto, immortalis (often inmortalis); &c.

2. in drops its n in composition before gn; e.g. i-gnavus, i-gnarus, i-gnosco, i-gnominia. (Compare § 86. 4.)

3. Before s it frequently falls away, sometimes is assimilated:

(*a*) in adjectival suffixes; e.g. formosus for formonsus (Verg.); verrucossus, imperiossus (Augustan inscript.); Maluginesis (ib.);

Thermeses (also **Thermenses, Termenses,** in some inscr. A.U.C. 683); **Pisaureses** (very old inscr.). Cicero is said to have written **Megalesia, Foresia, Hortesia.** So Ὁρτήσιος for **Hortensius.** In late inscriptions also in pres. part.; e.g. **doles, lacrimas** for **dolens, lacrimans,** &c.

(*b*) numeral suffixes; e.g. **quoties, vicies, millies,** &c., **vicēsimus, millesimus,** &c. are post-Augustan forms for **quotiens, viciens, vicensumus** (or **vicensimus**), &c.

(*c*) in stems; e.g. **cēsor,** in præ-Aug. inscriptions for **censor; mostellaria** from **monstrum** (**mostrum,** Verg.); **tosillæ** (C. *N. D.* 2. 54) for **tonsillæ; trimestris** for **trimenstris; tūsus, passus, fressus,** also **tunsus, pansus, frensus.** So **elephas** for **elephans; trastrum** (Verg.) for **transtrum.**

4. **n** final (or **ns**?) falls away always in nom. case of stems in -on; e.g. **homo, cardo** (**homŏn-, cardŏn-**), **sermo, oblivio** (**sermōn-, obliviōn-**), &c. So **ceteroqui, alioqui,** for præ-Augustan **cæteroquin,** &c.

INSERTION: 1. **Athamans, Indigens** in Augustan inscriptions 169 for **Athamas, Indiges,** &c. Also **thensaurus** (**tensaurus**?) in Plautus for θησαυρός.

2. in verbal forms; e.g. **tango** (see Book II). So also **conjunx, conjugis** from **jug-, jungo.**

L.

CHARACTER: always as above, after 570 or 580 A.U.C. Before 170 that the earlier form (with the bottom stroke not horizontal but forming an acute angle with the other), once exclusively used, was still in use.

SOUND: as in English.   171

POSITION: final only in a few nouns in nom. and neuter acc. 172 cases sing. It can stand immediately before a mute at the end of a syllable; e.g. **sculptus, calx,** &c.; and immediately after **p, b, c, g** at beginning of a syllable; e.g. **pluma, blandus, clamo, glans,** &c.

REPRESENTATION: 1. in Greek by λ always; e.g. **Publius** 173 **Lentulus,** Πόπλιος Λέντουλος (Polyb.), Πούπλιος Λέντλος (Appian); **Popillius,** Ποπίλλιος; **Latini,** Λατῖνοι; &c.

2. of Greek λ; e.g. χλαμύς, **chlamys;** Φυλλίς, **Phyllis;** Ἑλένη, **Helena;** &c.

CORRESPONDENCE: 1. to an original Indo-European **l** or **r.** 174 [Some (e.g. Schleicher) consider **l** to arise always from a weakening of an original **r**].

2. to Greek λ; e.g. ălius, ἄλλος; dulcis, γλυκύς; volvo, ἐλύω (Ϝελ-); oleum, ἔλαιον; calx, λάξ (for κλαξ); lāna, λάχνη; lĕgo, λέγω; leo, λίς, λέων; luo, λύω; lăvo, ad-luo, λούω; ŭlŭlo, ὀλολύζω; fallo, σφάλλω; pŭlex, ψύλλα; ulna, ὠλένη; vŏlo, βούλομαι; &c.

3. to Greek ρ (rarely); e.g. vellus, villus, ἔρος (ionic), ἔριον; balbus, βάρβαρος; lilium, λείριον.

4. to Greek δ; e.g. lacruma, δάκρυον; levir, δᾱήρ; ŏleo, ŏdor, ὄζω (perf. ὄδ-ωδ-α), ὀδμή.

SUBSTITUTION: for m, d, n or r before l. See next section. In 175 composition com- generally became con-, sometimes col-; e.g. collegium; &c. In inscriptions conlegium, conlega till about end of Augustus' reign; then collegium, &c. (Momms. *Ephem.* I. p. 79.)

In usually remained. Ad generally became al; e.g. alloquor, &c.

INFLUENCE: 1. Assimilates to itself or omits a preceding 176 c, d, n, r, s, x, an intervening short vowel being omitted; e.g. paullus for pauculus; lapillus for lapid-ulus; sella for sĕdŭla; corolla for corōn-ŭla; Catullus for Catōn-ŭlus; Hispallus for Hispānulus; Asellus for Asin-ulus; prēlum for pren-lum (from premo); agellus for ager-lus; quālus for quas-lus (comp. quăsillus); āla for ax-la (or axilla); vēlum for vex-lum (or vexillum).

2. 1 preferred ŏ or ŭ before it; e.g. salto, insulto, compared with tracto, detrecto; pocŭlum with pulcĕr (old polcer); &c. (§ 204. 2, *e.*)

ll preferred e; e.g. vello compared with vulsus; fiscella with fiscīna; &c. (§ 213. 5.)

3. caused the omission of a preceding initial t or guttural; e.g. latus for tlātus (tollo); lis for stlis; lōcus for stlōcus; lamentum compared with clamo; lac (lact-) with γαλακτ-; or the insertion (or transposition) of a short vowel between; e.g. scalpo, sculpo compared with γλάφω, γλύφω; dulcis with γλυκύς (for δλυκύς).

4. caused the omission of a preceding short vowel after c or p; e.g. vinclum, saeclum, periclum, hercle, disciplina, maniplus, for vincŭlum, &c.; publicus for populicus.

5. threw off a following s; e.g. consul for consuls, sōl for sols, &c. vigil for vigilis. In velle a succeeding r is assimilated (vŏlĕse becoming volere, volre, velle).

6. lg, ll, changed a following suffixed t into s; e.g. mulg-, mulsus; vell-, vulsus.

7. changed a subsequent l, in suffix -āli, into r; e.g. famularis, palmaris, vulgaris compared with talis, animālis, frugālis, augurālis, edūlis, &c.

So also a preceding l is changed into r; e.g. cæruleus from cælum; Parilia from Pales.

WEAKNESS: In some words the spelling varied between a single 177 and double l, viz.:

1. if 1 (not being a case-inflexion) followed l, the grammarians held that single l should be written; e.g. mille, mīlia (Mon. Ancyr. has millia); Messalla, Messālīna; villa, vīlicus; but stillicidium (not stilicidium) usually. So inscriptions give both Amulius and Amullius; Petilia, Petillius; Popilius, Popillius; &c., but -ilius is much more frequent than -illius in most words; Pollio however is more frequent than Polio.

2. the suffix -ēla is in good MSS. written -ella after a short syllable; e.g. lŏquella, quĕrella, mĕdella; suādēla, tūtēla, corruptēla.

R.

CHARACTER: usually as above, but in early inscriptions the 178 right hand lower limb is very short.

SOUND: the sound made by vibration of the point of the 179 tongue: rather the Italian or German r, than the English.

POSITION: frequently final; viz. in nom. and neut. acc. sin- 180 gular of nouns, and in 1st and 3rd persons singular and plural of passive verbs. It can stand immediately before any final consonant; e.g. ars, arx; and immediately after an initial mute.

REPRESENTATION: 1. in Greek, by ρ; e.g. Roma, 'Ρώμη; 181 Trebia, Τρεβία; Tiberius, Τιβέριος; Hernici, Ἐρνικες; Brutus, Βροῦτος; &c.

2. of Greek ρ; e.g. κρατήρ, crater; ῥήτωρ, rhetor; Πάρις, Paris; &c.

3. of Greek λ; e.g. κανθήλιος, cantērius.

CORRESPONDENCE: 1. to an original Indo-European r. 182

2. to Greek ρ; e.g. ar-ma, ar-mus, ar-tus, ars, ἀρ-, ἀραρίσκω, ἄρθρον, ἄρτιος; āro, arvum, ἀρόω, ἄρουρα; rătis, rē-mus, ἐρέσσω, ἐρέτης, ἐρετμός; ardea, ἐρωδιός; ŏrior, ὄρνυμι; rāpa, ῥάπυς, ῥάφανος; rĕpente, ῥέπω; frīgus, ῥίγος; rădix, ῥίζα; rixa, ἔρις (ἐριδ-); rīvus, ῥέω, ῥεῦσις; sero, sertum, series, servus, εἴρω (ἐρ-, ἐρ-), σειρά, ὅρμος; &c.

3. to Greek λ (rarely); e.g. grando, χάλαζα; hirundo, χελιδών; strĭgĭlis, stringo, στλεγγίς, στελγίς, στραγγεύω; hăru-spex,
hilla, χόλιξ, χορδή; curvus, κυρ-τός, κυλλός.

SUBSTITUTION: 1. **R** between two vowels is frequently, and 183
final **r** is sometimes, a substitute for an earlier s[1]. But this substitution was prior to any inscription which we have, and may probably
be referred to the fourth century B.C. on the ground of Cicero's statement (*Fam.* 9, 21), that L. Papirius, consul 336 B.C. (=418 U.C),
was the first of his family who ceased to be called Papisius. (Cf.
Pompon. *Dig.* i. 2. § 36.)

This change is noted in

(*a*) stems; e.g. lares for lases (in song of Arval brothers);
aras for asas; ferias for fesias; arena for asena. Compare
nār-is, nās-us; hĕri, χθές, hes-ternus; puer, pŭs-us; ĕr-am,
ĕr-o, sum (for ĕs-um); gĕro, ges-tum; ūr-o, us-tum; &c.
quæro, quæso.

(*b*) dari for dasi; dĭrimere, dĭrhibere from dis-.

(*c*) noun suffixes; e.g. pignŏra, pignus; onĕra, onus, onustus;
vetĕra, vetus, &c.; Venĕris, Venus; Cerĕris, Cerĕs; pulvĕr-is,
pulvis. So also honor has old form honōs; arbŏr, arbōs; robur
had once abl. robōse, and apparently nom. robus.

So also adjectives; e.g. Papīrius for Papīsius; Valĕrius for
Valĕsius; Veturius for Vetusius; Numĕrius for Numīsius; ne-
fārius compared with nefas-tus; Etruria with Etrus-ci; me-
liōrem for meliōs-em (comp. neut. melius); plurima for
plusima.

[The genitive plural suffix -rum is generally held to be for -sam;
and the **r** of the passive voice to be for s; i.e. for se, the passive
having been originally reflexive.]

(*d*) r before m and n appears to have sometimes arisen from s;
e.g. carmen is connected with casmena (old form of camena).
So vĕter-nus (for veter-inus) from vetus; diur-nus compared
with interdius, nudius.

2. For d in the word ad (in composition), and apud, see
§ 160. 10. 11.

3. For l in suffix -ālis, after a stem containing l, see § 176. 6.

---

[1] In some Greek dialects (e.g. Laconian, Elean, Eretrian) ρ is found
for *final s*; e.g. τοῖρ, τίρ, for τοῖς, τίς; and for σ before consonants;
e.g. κορμῆται for κοσμῆται; but not between vowels. See Curtius, *Gr.
Etym.* p. 396, ed. 2.

INFLUENCE: 1. assimilates to itself the final letter of the pre- 184
positions com, in, ad, sub; e.g. corripio, irrogo, arripio, surripio.
(No instances in republican inscriptions.)

2. Changes a preceding tv to d, in quadriduum, quadrupes, &c.,
from quattuor (§ 158). tr, later dr, is found in some early transcriptions of Greek words (§ 148. *c*).

3. dislikes short ĭ (for ĕ) to precede it; comp. legĭs, legĭt,
legĭtur, with legĕris, legĕre, legĕrem; Numĕrius with Numĭsius;
confĕro, contĕro compared with collĭgo, corrĭgo; pario, pepĕri, com-
perio compared with cădo, cecĭdi, concĭdo; pulvis, cucumis with
pulvĕrem, cucumĕrem; anser, anseris with ales, alitis; funus,
funeris with homo, homĭnis; &c.

The only Latin words in which r is preceded by a short ĭ are
vĭr, vĭridis, vĭreo, &c.; Qvĭrītes, Qvĭrīnus; pĭrus, pĭrum; hĭrundo,
hĭrūdo; and dĭr- for dis- in composition; (e.g. dirimo). Comp.
also Hirrus, hirrio. In vir, virtus, &c. i is said by the Roman grammarians to have had the sound of Greek *v*. Cf. § 237.

4. prefers a vowel before it, instead of after it; *e.g.* cer-no,
certus, compared with κρίνω, crēvi, crē-tum; serpo, rēpo; sorbeo,
ῥοφέω; porrum, πράσον; bardus, βραδύς; tertius, τρίτος; corcodilus
(sometimes), κροκόδειλος; caro, carnem, κρέας; tarpessita (sometimes), τραπεζίτης; farcio, φράσσω; Tarsumennus, also Trasumen-
nus. This metathesis appears to have been common to the Latin
with the Æolo-Doric Greek. (Ritschl, *Opusc.* ii. 531.)

5. occasioned the omission of a subsequent s, or of s preceded
by a short vowel; e.g. puer for puerus, tener for tenerus, orator for
orators, &c.

6. rr, rg converted a subsequent suffixed t to s; e.g. curr-o,
cur-sum; merg-o, mersum; &c. (see § 52. 3).

WEAKNESS: 1. is assimilated to a succeeding s, and then 185
often omitted; e.g. prōsa, for proversa (oratio): rusum (also
russum) for rursum (reversum); Tuscus for Turscus (comp. Etrus-
cus); tos-tus for torstus from torr-eo (which was for tors-eo, comp.
τέρσομαι). Pono for por-sino, pos-sino, posno. (Corssen.)

2. is omitted (sometimes) when the following syllable contains
r; e.g. mulie-bris from mulier-; fune-bris from funer- (funos-);
febris from ferveo; pē-jerare for perjerare.

The same dislike of the repetition of r is seen in the retention
(or preference) of -ālis instead of -āris as a suffix when an r precedes; and in the rare occurrence of the future participle (except
futurus) in the genitive plural. Neue (II. 462) mentions only ven-
turorum (Ov.); iturarum, exiturarum, transiturarum, moriturorum
(Sen.); periturorum (Sen. Quintil.).

S.

CHARACTER: as above; but the older form was angular. [186]
Other Italian alphabets, viz. Etruscan, Umbrian, and old Sabellian
had two characters, Σ (or an angular s) and M, for sibilants, apparently the sounds s and sh. The Samnite (Oscan) and Faliscan
agreed with the Roman.

SOUND: a hiss, as English initial s (e. g. in sin), i. e. s sharp. [187]
At one time s between two vowels was probably sounded, as medial
and final s is often sounded in English (e. g. *reason, rose*); i. e. s flat,
which is same as z: hence the change of s to r (§ 183), the position of the organs being very similar for z and r. Final s was at
one time not audible.

POSITION: very frequently final both in nouns and verbs. It [188]
never stands (in Latin words) immediately after an initial consonant; but often before p, c, t.

REPRESENTATION: (i) in Greek by ς; e. g. Sergius, Σέργιος; [189]
Spurius, Σπόριος; Kæso, Καίσων; Crassus, Κράσσος; &c.

(ii) 1. of Greek ς; σοφιστής, sophistes; σπλήν, splen; &c.

2. of Greek initial ζ before Cicero's time; e. g. Ζῆθος, Setus;
ζώνη, sona; &c.

3. ss for Greek medial ζ before Cicero's time; e. g. μᾶζα,
massa; κωμάζω, comissor; μαλακίζω, malacisso; Ἀττικίζω, Atticisso;
&c. (In the Tarentine dialect such forms as λακτίσσω, σαλπίσσω
are said to have occurred.) So the Etruscan Mezentius was in
the older language Messentius.

CORRESPONDENCE: 1. to an original Indo-European s. [190]

2. to Greek ς; e. g. sum (for es-um), εἰμί (for ἐσμί); vestis,
ἐσθής, ἕννυμι; sānus, σάος, σῶς; sūs, σῦς, ὗς; vesper, ἕσπερος;
scūtum, σκῦτος; scīpio, σκῆπτρον; sporta, σπυρίς; &c.

3. to Greek rough breathing; e. g. sal, ἅλς; sălio, ἅλλομαι;
sex, ἕξ; septem, ἑπτά; sĕdeo, sēdes, ἕζομαι, ἕδος; se, suus, ἕ, σφε
(for σϝε), ἑός, σφός; serpo, rĕpo, ἕρπω; simplex, ἁπλόος; silva,
ὕλη; sisto, ἵστημι; sōlus (old sollus), ὅλος; sŏpor, somnus, ὕπνος;
sŏcer, ἑκυρός; sub, ὑπό; super, ὑπέρ; &c.

SUBSTITUTION: 1. st for tt or dt, if the last t was to be pre- [191]
served; e. g. claustrum from claudo; tonstrix from tond-eo; eques-
tris, equester from eques (ĕquĕt-); &c. Cf. § 151. 2.

2. **ss** (or **s**) for **ts** or **ds**; e. g. **clau-si** for **claud-si**; **mi-si** for **mit-si**; **equēs** for **equĕt-s**; **es-se** for **ed-se** (i. e. **ĕdere** *to eat*); **frons** for **front-s** and for **frond-s**; &c.

So also **n** (sometimes) and **r** (rarely) are assimilated to a following **s**, and, it may be, subsequently omitted; e. g. **formōsus** for **formon-sus** (Verg., Ov.); **imperiōsus** or **-ossus** for **imperion-sus**; **viciēs** for **viciens**; **vicēsumus** for **vicensumus**; **trigesumus** for **trigensumus** (see below 4); **mensās** (and other acc. plurals) for **mensams** (**mensans**); **dispessus** for **dispan-sus**; **mostrum** from **monstrum** (see next §).

Prōsa for **proversa** (**prorsa**); **prōsus** for **prorsus**; **rūsus** (or **russus**) for **rursus**. But **mer-sus**, **ver-sus**, &c. (see next §) remain (§ 42).

3. **s** for **t** after **lg**, **rg**, **ll**, **rr**; e. g. **mul-sum** for **mulg-tum**; **mersum** for **merg-tum**; **cur-sum** for **curr-tum**; **pul-sum** for **pell-tum**, &c. (Quintilian, I. 4. 14, speaks of **mertare**, **pultare**, as being the old forms for **mersare**, **pulsare**.) Rarely after single mutes; e. g. **lap-sum** for **lab-tum**; &c. (see § 705 and Preface).

4. **ss** (or **s**) for **dt** or **tt**; (i. e. **dt**, **tt**, become **ds**, **ts** as in preceding paragraph, and then by assimilation **ds**, **ts** became **ss**, of which one **s** was after Cicero's time omitted[1]; e. g. **cessum** for **ced-tum**; **cāsum** (**cassum** Cic.) for **cad-tum**; **mis-sum** for **mitt-tum**; **sen-sum** for **sent-tum**; **divīsum** (**divissum** Cic.) for **divid-tum**; &c. **vicensūmus** for **vicent-tūmus**; **trigensumus** for **trigent-tūmus** (see above 2); &c.

5. **-iss** for **iōs** (cf. § 242) in adjectives of the superlative degree; e. g. **durissimus** for **duriōsimus**; **doctis-simus** for **doctiōs-īmus**, &c. See also the next paragraph and the Preface.

6. **ss** in **prohibessit**, **levassit**, &c. appears to be only indicative of the length of the preceding vowel. Possibly there may have been some confusion with such forms as **complessent**, **recesset**, **levasse**, &c. which contain the perfect suffix **-is**. Moreover an **s** left single would have formed an exception to the general law of Roman pronunciation which changed such an **s** to **r** (§ 183).

For the etymology of **arcesso**, **capesso**, &c. see § 625.

INFLUENCE: 1. Changed a preceding flat consonant to sharp; 192 e. g. **scrip-si** from **scrib-o**; **rexi** (i. e. **rec-si**) from **reg-o**. So (in

---

[1] Quintilian's words (I. 7. 20) deserve quoting; "Quid quod Ciceronis temporibus paulumque infra, fere quotiens s littera media uocalium longarum uel subjecta longis esset, geminabatur? ut 'caussae,' 'cassus,' 'diuissiones:' quomodo et ipsum et Vergilium quoque scripsisse manus eorum docent. atqui paulum superiores etiam illud, quod nos gemina dicimus 'jussi,' una dixerunt."

pronunciation at least) **op-sequor, sup-signo,** though **b** in **sub** (**subs**) sometimes fell away; e.g. **suspicio** (§ 78).

2. changed a preceding **m** to **n**; e.g. **con-scribo, consul,** &c.; or required insertion of **p**; e.g. **hiemps** for **hiems**; **sump-si** for **sum-si**; &c. (but **pres-si** (for **pren-si**) from **prēm-o**).

3. Completely assimilated, or threw out, a preceding **d** or **t** (always), **n** or **r** (sometimes); e.g. **ces-sum** for **ced-sum**, for **ced-tum**; &c. See § 191, 2. But **mons** for **monts**; **ars** for **arts.** See § 42.

4. **ns** lengthens a preceding vowel: see § 167. 2.

WEAKNESS: 1. Initial **s** has fallen off before a consonant in ₁₉₃ some words; e.g. **fallo** compared with σφάλλω; **fungus** with σφόγγος; **tĕgo** with στέγω; **tŏrus** with **sterno,** στόρ-νυμι, στρώννυμι; **tŏno** with στένω; &c., but in most stems the Greek and Latin agree in this matter, and the omission is discernible only by comparison with other languages; e.g. **nix,** νίφει compared with *snow;* **taurus,** ταῦρος with *steer;* **limus** with *slime;* &c.

2. Medial **s** falls away before nasals, liquids, and other flat consonants.

(*a*) before **m**; e.g. **dūmus** for **dus-mus** (comp. δασύς); **Camēna** for **Casmēna**; **pōmerium** for **posmœrium**; **trirēmis** compared with **triresmos** (Duillian inscript.); **dīmota** for **dismota**; **trā-mitto** for **transmitto**; &c.

(*b*) before **n**; e.g. **pōno** for **posno** (comp. **pos-ui** and § 185); **vidĕn** for **vides-ne**; **in** (Ter. *Eun.* 651) for **is-ne,** *art going?*; **satĭn** for **satis-ne**; **ae-num** for **aes-num** (**æs-**).

(*c*) before **d**; e.g. **jū-dex** for **jus-dex**; **īdem** for **is-dem**; **tre-decim** for **tres-decim**; **dīduco** for **dis-duco.**

(*d*) before **l, r**; e.g. **dīlabor, dīripio** for **dis-labor,** &c.

3. **s** between two vowels almost always changed to **r** in early times, see § 183. Consequently no Latin words exhibit **s** between two vowels,

Except (*a*) where **s** is not original, but due to a substitution (often indeed standing for **ss**); e.g. **prōsa, hæ-sum, esūries, ausim, causa** (**caussa,** Cic.), **formōsus,** &c. where it stands for **d** or **t.**

(*b*) compounds of words where **s** was initial; e.g. **de-silio, po-situra, præ-sentia, bi-sextus,** &c.

(*c*) the following words (some of which may perhaps fall under the foregoing classes), viz. **ăsĭnus, băsium, cæsăries, cæsius, căsa, căseus, cīsium, fūsus, lāser, mĭser, nāsus, pŭsillus, quă-**

sillum, quæso (also quæro), rŏsa (comp. ρόδον), vāsa; and some proper names; e.g. Cæsar, Kæso, Lausus, Pisa, Pisaurum, Sisenna, Sosia (gæsum is a Keltic word).

4. Final s became r; (*a*) in the nom. sing. of stems in s (in compliance with the change in the other cases?); e.g. arbor from arbōs-; honor from honōs-; robur from robŏs-; melior from meliōs-; &c.

(*b*) where a vowel originally followed; e.g. puer for puerus, originally puesus. The characteristic r of the passive voice is generally held to be for se.

5. Final s after a vowel at an early period of the language was frequently not pronounced, and thus frequently omitted in writing also. (In the 4th century after Christ the same tendency recurred and remains in Italian, &c.) Instances are

(*a*) nom. sing. of -a stems; e.g. nauta, scriba, &c. compared with ναύτης, &c.; luxuria, spurcitia, &c. with luxuries, spurcities, &c. See Book II.

(*b*) nom. sing. of -o stems; e.g. ille, ipse for illus, ipsus. So perhaps the vocatives domine, fili (= filie), &c. which however most philologers take for the stem itself weakened.

So, frequently in early inscriptions, Cornelio, Fourio, Herenio, &c. for Cornelios, Fourios, Herenios (nom. sing.), the forms with s (both -os and -us) occurring likewise at the same time. In later, chiefly imperial, inscriptions occur, e.g. Philarguru, Secundu, &c.

s with the preceding vowel (ŏ at that time) fell off in puer for puerus, tibicen for tibicenus, &c. Inscriptions (e.g. *S. C. Bacc.*) give Claudi, Valeri, &c. for Claudios, Valerios (nom. sing.), which some refer to a shortened form Claudis, Valeris, as alis for alius; some take to be a mere abbreviation.

(*c*) pote (all genders) for potis; mage for magis (adv.). After l and r we have vigil, pugil for vigilis, pugilis (nom. s. masc. fem.); acer, equester, saluber (m. nom.), &c. for equesteris, saluberis; &c.

(*d*) The nom. pl. of -o stems of all kinds in early inscriptions had frequently s final, which the ordinary language dropped; e.g. Minucieis, Vituries, Italiceis, vireis, publiceis, conscriptes, heisce, hisce, &c. See Book II.

(*e*) The ordinary genitive sing. of -a, -e, and -o stems, e. g. familiæ or familiai, diei or die, domini, is either formed by omission of a final s as in old genitives, familiās (for familiaes); dies, rabies, illius (for illo-ius); or is a locative form in -i (so Bopp, Madvig, and others). Only in late inscriptions occur integritati, Isidi, &c. for integritatis, Isidis, &c.

(*f*) In verbs (2nd pers. sing. of passive voice) **amabare, loquerere, conabere,** &c. for **amabaris** (old **amabares**), &c. So the imperative present (unless taken as the bare stem, cf. *5. b*) is formed from the indicative present; e.g. **ama, amate** for **amas, amatis,** &c.

The old imperative forms **præfamino, progredimino,** &c. are for **præfaminos, progrediminos,** having same suffix as τυπτ-όμενος, and therefore belong to (*b*).

(*g*) In the early poets, so also frequently in Lucretius and once in Catullus, the final **s** before an initial consonant was treated as omitted; e.g. at end of some hexameters, quoted for this purpose by Cicero (*Or.* 48, § 161), **Qui est omnibu' princeps; Vita illa dignu' locoque.** Compare Vergil, *Æn.* XII. 115, **Solis equi lucemque elatis naribus efflant,** copied, with a transposition on this ground, from Ennius (p. 85, Vahlen), **funduntque elatis naribus lucem.**

z.

This letter was common in Umbrian and Oscan. It is found [194] for instance in the Latin transcription of an Oscan law of the time of the Gracchi (*Corp. Inscr. Lat.* No. 197). It is also found in an extract from the song of the Salii given by Varro (*L.L.* VII. 26). In Latin it appears first (unless the above be an exception) in Cicero's time, merely to write Greek words, which were before written with **s** or **ss**.

The introduction of **z** into Plautus must therefore probably be due to a later recension.

In the writers of the 3rd and 4th centuries after Christ **z** is [195] used for **di** in the words **zaconus, zabulus, zeta,** &c. for διάκονος, διάβολος, δίαιτα, &c. So in an Algerian inscription (198 A.D.) **Azabenico** for **Adiabenico.**

The converse is seen in manuscripts giving **glycyrridia, gargaridiare, Medientius** for γλυκύρριζα, γαργαρίζειν and (Etruscan) **Mezentius.**

(In Æolic dialect of Lesbos ζά is found for διά; e.g. ζὰ νυκτός; and so in tragedy, ζάπυρος, ζάχρυσος, &c. So πεζός for πέδιος, &c.). It seems probable that ζ, and, if so, then Latin **z,** was (at least sometimes) sounded like English **j** (which sound soon rises out of ặy) or French **j**; but Curtius, Corssen, and others (not Key or Donaldson) assign it the sound of English **z,** as in modern Greek.

CHAPTER IX.

VOWELS.

The Latin vowels will here be treated in the order which ap- 196
pears to have been followed in the development of the language;
viz. a, o, u, e, i. That is to say, where one vowel has given place
to another, it has been in the direction of a to i, not i to a. Thus a
was capable of changing to o, or u, or e, or i; o to u, or e, or i;
u to e or i; e to i. Changes which *prima facie* seem to be made
in the reverse direction are the result of our regarding, as the
standard form, what is really a later development[1]: e.g. mare, from
the stem (as we now call it) **mari-**; **effectus** from **efficio**, &c. (See
Ritschl, *Rhein. Mus.* (1859) XIV. p. 406. *Opusc.* II. 622, n.) But
see § 234. 5. and 244. And the priority of e to i in the -i stems
rests on but little positive evidence.

A.

CHARACTER: usually as above, but all positions of the middle 197
stroke are found; e.g. bisecting the angle, or bisecting either side
and parallel to, or touching the bottom of, the other.

SOUND: as Continental a; viz. long ă as in *psalm;* short as the 198
broader pronunciation of *pastime.*

POSITION: frequently final   199

1. in nouns; as nom. (ă) and abl. (ā) singular, of a- stems, and
nom. acc. neuter plural (ă) of all stems;

2. in verbs; only 2nd pers. sing. pres. imperative (ă) of a- verbs.

REPRESENTATION: (i) in Greek by *a*; e.g. **Marcus,** Μάρκος; 200
Fabius, Φάβιος; **Publicola,** Ποπλικόλας; **Alba longa,** Ἄλβα λόγγα
(Dionys. H.); &c.

(ii) of Greek *a*; e.g. Ἀλκμήνη, **Alcumena** (Plaut.); Ἀγαμέμνων,
Agamemno; φάλαγξ, **phalanx;** παραπῆγμα, **parapegma;** &c.

of Greek *αι;* e.g. κραιπάλη, **crāpula.**

[1] Corssen contests this, arguing for the priority in some cases of e
to u, and of i to e. *Krit. Beitr.* p. 546 foll. So also Schleicher,
Vergl. Gram. § 49, ed. 2. See also Corssen, *Aussprache,* II. 226, ed. 2.

CORRESPONDENCE[1]: 1. To an original Indo-European A.   201

2. ă to Greek ă (usually); e.g. ăgo, ἄγω; angor, ἄγχομαι; ălius, ἄλλος; ăb, ἀπό; ārgentum, ἄργυρος; dăps, δᾰπάνη; lătĕre, λαθεῖν; păter, πᾰτήρ; călāre, κᾰλέω; sal, sălum, ἅλς, σάλος; &c.

3. ă to Greek ε; e.g. angustus, ἐγγύς; căput, κεφαλή; magnus, μέγας; sălix, ἑλίκη; păteo, πετάννυμι; quattuor, τέσσαρες; măneo, μένω; mălus *bad*, μέλας; &c.

4. ă to Greek ŏ (rare); e.g. salvus, ὁλοός, comp. ὀλοόφρων; hăru-spex, χολάς; to ω; e.g. căpulum, κώπη; ăm-ārus, ὠμός.

5. ā to Greek ā, Doric and, after ρ or a vowel, Attic; otherwise Attic η; e.g. suāvis, ἀδύς, ἡδύς; clāvis (κλαϜ-), κλᾱίς, κληίς; mālum, *apple*, μᾶλον, μῆλον; māter, μᾱτηρ, μήτηρ; plāga, πλᾱγά, πληγή; frāter, φρᾱτήρ; fā-ri, φᾱμί, φημί; ajo, ἠμί; farcio, φράσσω; stāre, ἵστᾱμι, ἵστημι; mācero, μάσσω; pannus, πᾱνος, πῆνος.

6. ā to Greek ω; e.g. lābes, λώβη; ācer, ōcior, ὠκύς.

7. In suffixes, to Greek a or η; e.g. ama-, amābo, τιμάω, τιμήσω; legātis, λέγητε; caritās, φιλό-της; musa, μοῦσα; serva, δούλη; nauta, ναύτης (ναύτας, Dor.); magna, μεγάλα (neut. pl.); &c.

CONTRACTION, HIATUS, &c.: 1. Hiatus is rare; e.g. Gāīus, &c. 202 (§ 139).

2. ā + ŏ to a; e.g. măg-vŏlo, mālo: (on the omission of the g, see § 129. *c*).

3. ă + radical u to au (which then absorbs a short ĭ); e.g. ga-video, gaudeo; căvitum, cautum; ăvĭceps, auceps; &c.

4. ā + ĕ to ā; amāvĕrunt (later amavērunt), amārunt; &c.

5. ā + ĭ to ē; e.g. amāĭtis, amētis; &c.

6. ā + ĭ to ā; e.g. prima-ĭnus, primānus; ama-ĭtĭs, amātis; amāvisse (with I?), amāsse; &c.

CHANGE OF QUANTITY: 1. in the radical vowel of derivatives; 203 e.g. plăcēre, plăcāre; ăgere, amb-āges, ā-ctus (§ 151, note); săgax, săgus, praesăgire; frăg-ilis, suffrāgium; flăgrare, flāgĭtium, flāgito; tăg-, tango, contāges; lăbāre, lābi; cărēre, cārus (comp. Căristia); să-, sător, Sāturnus; făteri, fātum, fāri; păg-, pango, pāci- (pax), pācare, compāges.

1 The instances of *correspondence* of vowels, throughout this chapter, are taken from Curtius' paper, *Ueber die Spaltung des A-Lautes.* (*Berichte d. k. sächsischen Gesellschaft &c.*, Leipzig, 1864.)

2. Lengthened as a means of inflexion; e.g. căveo, perf. cāvi; făveo, fāvi; păveo, pāvi; lăvo, lāvi; (perhaps however for cav-ui, &c.); scăbo, scābi. (For jăcio, jēci, &c. see below § 204.)

3. Lengthened in compensation for extrusion of a consonant; e.g. lāna comp. with λάχνη; arānea with ἀράχνη; mājor for măgior; cāsum for cassum (căd-tum); &c.

4. In final syllables often shortened; e.g. in nom. sing. of -a stems musă, scribă; &c., which were probably originally long, and are sometimes found long in Plautus, Ennius, &c. So technă for τέχνη.

Before -t; e.g. amăt, audiăt, regăt, &c.; all originally long.

Also calcăr, pulvinăr, for calcāre, &c.; bidentăl for bidentāle; &c.

CHANGE OF QUALITY: 1. Radical a changed and lengthened 204 by way of inflexion; e.g. jăcio, jēci; căpio, ͺcēpi; făcio, fēci; ăgo, ēgi; pango, pēgi.

2. Radical a changed after a prefix:

(*a*) ă to ĕ before two consonants or a final consonant; e.g. carpo, discerpo; spargo, aspergo; farcio, confertus; răpio, correptus; jăcio, rejectus; căpio, inceptus; pasco, compesco; scando, conscendo; damno, condemno; tracto, detrecto; pătro, perpĕtro; săcer, consecro; fallo, fefelli, refello.

Ars, sollers; pars, expers; barba, imberbis; ăgo, remex; făcio, artifex, effectus; căput, anceps; căpio, municeps; căno, cornicen, concentus; annus, triennium, perennis; castus, incestus. (But abstractus, subactus, expando, exaggero, incandesco, &c.)

(*b*) a to e before r, or (rarely) some other single consonant. e.g. pătior, perpĕtior; grădior, ingrĕdior; fătisco, defĕtiscor; fătīgo, defĕtigo (also defatigo); păciscor, depĕciscor; păro, impĕro, æquipĕro; părio, pepĕri, compĕrio; hălo, anhēlo. (But compare subtraho, and words compounded with per. post, circum, &c.; e.g. perfacilis, permaneo, posthabeo, &c. Also repāro, exāro, &c.)

(*c*) ă to ĭ before ng; e.g. pango, impingo; frango, confringo; tango, attingo; &c. Before x; e.g. laxus, prolixus.

(*d*) before a single consonant, except r; e.g. răpio, abrĭpio; săpio, desĭpio; căpio, incĭpio; ăpiscor, indĭpiscor; hăbeo, prohĭbeo; stătuo, instĭtuo; făteor, infĭteor; lăteo, delĭtesco; ăgo, prodĭgo; jăcio, inĭcio; făcio, infĭcio; tăceo, contĭcesco; căno, concĭno; măneo, immĭneo; cădo, incĭdo; sălio, insĭlio; &c. (But adămo, adjăceo, &c.)

tango, tetĭgi; cădo, cecĭdi; căno, cecĭni; pango, pepĭgi.

rătus, irrĭtus; dătus, condĭtus, condĭtor; păter, Juppĭter; căput, sincĭput; stăbulum, prostĭbulum; ămicus, inĭmicus; făcetus, infĭcetus; făcies, superfĭcies; făcilis, diffĭcilis.

(*e*) ă to ŭ, only before labials, or before l with another consonant; e. g. căpĭo, aucŭpărĭ, occŭpăre; răpĭo, subrŭpĭo (early Latin); tăberna, contŭbernĭum; lăvo, dĭlŭvĭes; salto, insulto; calco, inculco; salsus, insulsus. So also quătĭo, concŭtĭo, (on account of qu).

3. Radical a to o in derivative; e. g. pars, portĭo; scăbere, scŏbis.

4. ă as final vowel of stem is changed to ĭ before a suffix commencing with a consonant; e. g. domă-, domĭtum, domĭtor, domĭnus; cubă-, cubĭtum, cubĭculum; herbă, herbĭdus; stellă, stellĭger; tubă, tubĭcen.

O.

CHARACTER: In early inscriptions the o is frequently not quite 205 closed.

SOUND: Probably varying between aw English and au French. 206 Compare the modern Italian. These sounds are heard short in English *nŏt* and *ŏmit*.

POSITION: Frequently final; viz. 1. in dat. abl. sing. of nouns 207 with stem in -o; e. g. domino, &c., and in nom. sing. of nouns with stem in -on-; e. g. lectio, sermo, margo, &c. and the words, duo, ego. In the older language o was even more frequently final, owing to the omission of m and s; e. g. optumo, Cornelio, &c. for optumom, Cornelĭŏs (nom.).

2. In first pers. sing. indic. act. of verbs; e. g. amo, amabo, amavero, &c.; and in 2nd and 3rd pers. sing. future imperative active; e. g. amato, &c.

3. In adverbs; e. g. cito, pro, modo, quando, &c.

REPRESENTATION: (i) in Greek; ŏ by ω, ŏ by o; e. g. Kæso, 208 Καίσων; Capitolinus, Καπιτωλῖνος; Roma, 'Ρώμη; Postumius, Ποστούμιος; Cornelius, Κορνήλιος; &c.

(ii) 1. of Greek ω and o; e. g. Λακεδαίμονος, Lacedæmŏnĭs; ἄρκτον, arcton; στόμαχος, stomachus; Παρμένων, Parmeno; Τρώιος, Troius; 'Ρόδος, Rhodos (or Rhodus); &c.

2. ŏ of Greek υ; e. g. λάγυνος, lagōna or lagœna.

3. ŏ is inserted in Latin of second century B.C. where in Greek two consonants touch; e. g. 'Αγαθοκλῆς, Agathocoles; Πατροκλῆς, Patricoles; 'Ηρακλῆς, Hercoles (later Hercules); &c.

5

CORRESPONDENCE: 1. to an original Indo-European A.   209

2. ŏ to Greek ŏ usually; e.g. boāre (bovāre Enn.), βοᾶν; -vŏrus, vorāre, -βορός, βιβρώσκειν; bŏvis, βοός (gen.); dŏlus, δόλος; dŏmus, δόμος; incŏlŭmis, κολούω; cŏma, κόμη; corvus, κόραξ; coxa, κοχώνη; mŏrior, βροτός (for μορτός); ŏdor, ὄζω· ŏvis, ὄις; octo, ὀκτώ; ŏc-ulus, ὄπ-ωπα; orbus, ὀρφανός; os, ὀστέον; vox, ὄψ; portus, πορθμός; pŏtis, πόσις; sorbeo, ῥοφέω; cŏrium, scortum, χόριον; hortus, χόρτος; rŏsa, ῥόδον; ŏrior, ὄρ-νυμι; porro, πόρρω; ab-ŏlere, ἀπ-ολλύναι; &c.

3. ŏ to Greek a; e.g. dŏmāre, δαμᾶν; dŏceo, διδάσκειν; dormio, δαρθάνω; jĕcoris (gen.), ἥπατος; cordis, καρδίας; cornus, κράνον; lŏquor, λακεῖν; marmor, μάρμαρος; quattuor, τέσσαρες; &c.

4. ŏ to Greek ε, chiefly before or after v; e.g. sŏcer, ἑκυρός; volvo, εἴλω (Fελ-); vŏlup, ἔλπομαι; vŏmo, ἐμέω; nŏvem, ἐννέα (for νεFα); ŏb, ἐπί; cornu, κέρας; nŏvus, νέος; cŏqvo, πέσσω; torqveo, τρέπω.

5. ŏ to Greek υ; e.g. nox, νύξ; mŏla, μύλη.

6. ŏ to Greek ω; e.g. gnosco, γιγνώσκω; nos, νώ; vos, σφώ; ŏvum, ᾠόν; ambo, ἄμφω; umbo, ἄμβων; dōnum, δῶρον; ōcior, ὠκύς.

7. in suffixes: ŏ to Greek ŏ; viz. -ŏr- to -ορ-; e.g. oratŏris, ῥήτορος; but also -ηρ-; e.g. datōris (gen.), δοτῆρος; auditōrium, ἀκροατήριον; &c.

-iŏr- to -ιον-; e.g. majŏris, μείζονος; &c.

SUBSTITUTION: 1. ō for au; e.g. Clōdius for Claudius; olla for 210 aula; plostrum for plaustrum; &c. So after a prefix; e.g. plaudo, explōdo; fauces, suf-fōco; &c. (See § 249.)

2. for a in derivatives; e.g. portio from pars, scŏbis from scăbere.

3. for ĕ (?) in derivatives; e.g. tŏga from tĕgo; pondus from pendĕre; &c. (§ 234.5).

CONTRACTION, HIATUS, &c.: 1. o+ā and o+ē remained 211 without contraction; e.g. co-ēgi, co-āctus (but this may be due to the m in com).

2. o+i (probably ī) occurs in cases of o stems; viz. gen. sing. e.g. domino-i, dominī; dat. e.g. domino-i domino; nom. pl. e.g. dominoes, dominois, dominī. Quoi, proin are monosyllabic, though the vowels remain.

3. o + o, or ĕ, or ĭ becomes ō; e.g. copia for co-opia, cōperio for cooperio (but coortus remains uncontracted); coventio, contio; retro-vorsus, retrorsus; cohors, cors; co-igo, cōgo; movisse, mosse; mŏvĭtor, mōtōr; &c.; prōbeat for prohibeat; comptus for coemptus; prōsa for proversa.

Sometimes where a v has stood between the vowels, the resulting contraction becomes ū; e.g. novendinæ (noundinæ old), nundinæ; mŏvĭto, mūto; būbus (rarely bōbus) for bŏvĭbus; &c.

CHANGE OF QUANTITY: 1. in stems; e.g. mŏlestus, mōles 212 (? cf. § 789); vŏcare, vōcem (from vox); sŏnus, sŏnāre, persōna; sŏpor, sōpīre; nŏta, nōtus (but agnĭtus), nōmen.

2. lengthened in compensation for an extruded consonant; e.g. pōno for pŏs-no; glōmus for glŏb-mus; cōnubium for com-nūbium; hoc for hodce; &c.

In formōsus for formonsus; dominōs for dominoms; &c. the length of the o is probably due to ns. Cf. § 167. 2.

3. A final ō is sometimes shortened (see § 281);

(*a*) in the nom. sing. of proper names; e.g. Scipiŏ, &c. So also mentiŏ.

(*b*) in the 1st pers. sing. active present indicative; e.g. vetŏ, putŏ; rarely in other parts of the verb; e.g. dabŏ, cædĭtŏ, oderŏ; &c.

(*c*) in a few other words; e.g. egŏ, citŏ; and sometimes in porro, intro, modo.

4. in final syllables of Latin words ō followed by a consonant is regularly shortened; (*a*) in nom. sing. of stems in -or; e.g. honŏr, sorŏr, cratŏr, majŏr; (*b*) in 1st pers. sing. of passive voice; e.g. amŏr, amabŏr, audiŏr; &c. (*c*) in 2nd and 3rd pers. sing. fut. imper. pass.; e.g. amatŏr, &c.

CHANGE OF QUALITY. The general change of o to u took 213 place about the same time as that of ĕ to ĭ, see § 234. But it was retained after v till later (§ 93) and always in suffix -ŏlus after i or e (infr. 2*b*).

Thus 1. o to u (usually) before two consonants (mn, nc, nd, nt, lt, st); e.g. (*a*) in 3rd pers. plural of verbs; e.g. dederont, dedro (old), dederunt; cosentiont, consentiunt; legunt compared with λέγοντι (Att. λέγουσι). So vivont, vivunt; loquontur, loquuntur, later loquuntur; comfluont, confluunt; &c.

(*b*) in final syllable of stem; e.g. colomna (old form: comp. τυπτόμενος), columna; tirōn-, tirunculus; quæstiōn-, quæstiuncula; homŏn-, homunculus; arbos, arbustum; minor (for minŏs), minusculus; nocturnus compared with νύκτωρ; &c.

(*c*) sometimes in root vowel; e.g. honc, hunc; poplicus, puplicus; Poplius, Publius; Polcer, Pulcer; moltaticod, multatico; oquoltod (*S. C. de Bacc.*), occulto; volt, vult; adolesco, adultus; conctos, cunctos; sesconcia, sescuncia; nontiata, nuntiata; nondinum, nundinum; &c.

2. ŏ to ŭ, (*a*) before a final consonant; e.g. donom, donum; locom, locum; duonoro, bonorum; filios, filius; Cornelio, Cornelius; equos, ecus, later equus; quom, cum; mortuos, mortuus; femor-, femur; corpos-, corpus; cosol, consul; majos, majus (neut.); illo-, illud; &c.

But o remained in æquor, marmor. (In uxor, honor, moneor, major, &c. the o is properly long, and hence is not changed.)

(*b*) in a suffix before l unless followed by i (infr. 5); e.g. popŏlus, popŭlus; parvŏlus, parvŭlus; singŏlis, singŭlis; tabŏla, tabŭla; semŏl, simŭl; conciliabŏleis (A.U.C. 632), conciliabŭlis; Hercŏles, Hercŭles; &c. (The i in singulis &c. is only inflexional.) But after e, i, or v, the o was often preserved; e.g. aureolus, filiolus, Scævŏla; &c.

3. The root vowel is changed in adŭlescens from adŏle-, tŭli for older tŏli, *I bore*. (But stultiloquus, concolor, benivolus, innŏcens, dissŏnus, &c.; ārrogo, evomo, &c. retain o).

4. o to e, (*a*) (sometimes) before two consonants (st, nt, nd); e.g. honŏs-, honestas; majŏs-, majestas; tempŏs-, tempestas; funŏs-, funestus. So in present participle and gerundive ferenti- compared with φεροντ-; faciendus (and faciundus), with presumed common original faciondus; (cf. § 618) &c.

(*b*) as final vowel; e.g. censuerĕ (in *S. C. de Bacc.*) for censueront (censuerunt); ipsĕ, istĕ, illĕ, for ipsŭs (old ipsŏs); &c. So the vocatives; e.g. taure for taurŏs or taurŏ-; and adverbs; e.g. bĕnĕ for bonod; certĕ and certŏ; anxiĕ for anxiod; &c. (In other words where o is final a loss has already taken place (cf. § 42); e.g. cardo, for cardons; rĕgo for rĕgom; &c.)

(*c*) After v the republican language (but see § 93) showed o in some words, where later e was usual; e.g. voster, vorto and its derivatives, vorro, vŏto; later vester, verto, &c., verro, vĕto.

5. ŏ to ĕ: (*a*) before ll; e.g. velle for volĕre; vello, pello, -cello, compared with pĕpŭl-i, vul-sum, (volsella, *pincers*), -culsum; ocellus (for ŏcŏlŏlus) from oculus. (But lapillus from lapid-, &c.; ille for ollus; tollo compared with tuli. In corolla, olla, Pollio or Polio, Marullus for marŏnulus, &c. the o is long.)

(*b*) before r followed by a vowel; e.g. fœderis compared with fœdus; funeris with funus; vulnero with vulnus; &c. (o is presumed as the common original; cf. γένος.)

(*c*) before a single consonant and after ĭ; e.g. socio-, sociĕtas; pĭo-, pĭĕtas; &c.

6. ŏ to (usually) ĭ; in final stem syllable, before a single consonant followed by a vowel, except ĭ not followed by ĭ, and except before **r**; e.g. legĭmus compared with λέγομεν and volŭmus; cardŏn-, cardĭnis; homŏn-, homĭnis; cælo-, cælĭtus; alto-, altitudo; bono-, bonĭtas (compared with ἰσότης, &c.); amico-, amicitia; uno-, unĭcus; armo-, armĭpotens; fato-, fatĭdicus; fago-, fagĭnus; stercos-, sterquĭlinium; incola, inquĭlinus; humo-, humĭlis; simol (later simul), simĭlis; ficto-, fictĭlis (compared with crusto-, crustŭlum, &c.); &c.

So also senatuos, senatuis; Castoris compared with Κάστορος, old Lat. Kastorus.

OMISSION: apparently o in victrix, compared with victŏr-; 214 tonstrina with tonsŏr-, cf. § 209. 7; neptis with nepōt- (nepos).

U.

CHARACTER: In inscriptions always as English V: the rounded 215 form is found in MSS., the earliest extant being the papyrus from Herculaneum.

SOUND: as Italian u; i.e. ū as English u in *brute* (or oo in *pool*, 216 *fool*); ŭ same sound shortened. An owl's cry is written tutu in Plaut. *Men.* 91.

POSITION: ŭ never final, except in inscriptions, chiefly post- 217 Augustan, in which a final s or m has been omitted. ū is final only in some cases of nouns with stems in u; and the adverbs diu, noctu, simĭtu.

It is frequent in suffixes before l, unless l is followed by ĭ (see Book III).

REPRESENTATION: (i) in Greek; 1. usually by ου whether the 218 Latin vowel be short or long; e.g. Regŭlus, Ῥήγουλος; Venusia, Οὐενουσία; Postŭmius, Ποστούμιος; Sŭperbus, Σούπερβος; Vibulanus, Οὐιβούλανος; Vitulum, Οὐίτουλον; Belluti, Βελλούτου (Dion. Hal.); Novum Comum, Νοβουμκώμουμ; Mantua, Μάντουα (Strabo); Appŭleius, Ἀππουλήιος (*Mon. Ancyr.*); &c. For ŭ in suffixes, see § 220. For v after s and g, see § 90.

2. ŭ by o, chiefly before λ, ρ or a vowel (see § 213. 2. *b*); e.g. Amulius, Ἀμόλλιος (Appian), Ἀμούλιος (Plut., Polyæn.); Lŭcullus, Λεύκολλος and Λούκουλλος; Cluentius, Κλοέντιος (Appian); Cŭrius, Κόριος (Polyb.), Κούριος (Plut., App.); Fulvius, Φολούιος (also Φουλούιος, Φούλουιος, Φούλβιος); Coruncanius, Κορουγκάνιος (Polyb.), Κορουγκάνιος (Appian); Saturninus, Σατορνῖνος and Σατουρνῖνος; Mummius, Μόμμιος (Plut.), Μούμμιος (App.): &c. Πόπλιος (Polyb.) really represents the early form Poplius, not Publius (Πούπλιος).

According to Dittenberger (*Hermes*, VI. 282) inscriptions before Christ always give o, not ου.

3. by υ; e.g. Turnus, Τύρνος; Tullius, Τύλλιος (Dion. H.); Capuam, Καπύην (Polyb., Diod., &c.); Romulus, 'Ρώμυλος (Dio C.); &c., but also Τοῦρνος, Τούλλιος (Dio Cass.); Lutatius, Λυτάτιος (Polyb.; others have Λουτ.). Sulla is always Σύλλας.

4. by ε; only in some non-Roman names, e.g Brundusium, Βρεντέσιον; Bruttii, Βρέττιοι (but App. also Βρύττιοι); Nŭmĕrius, Νεμέριος (Inscr., Νουμέριος, Dio, Plut.); Numitor, Νεμέτωρ (Νομήτωρ, Plut., Νουμίτωρ, Strab.).

5. sometimes omitted; e.g. Lentŭlus, Λέντλος (Appian, Plut.); Catŭlus, Κάτλος (Appian, Plut.); Tuscŭlum, Τοῦσκλον (Strabo, Plut.); Figulus, Φίγλος; &c., cf. infr. § 225.

6. ŭ (sometimes) by ευ; e.g. Lucius, Λεύκιος (Mon. Ancyr., Plut.); Lucullus, Λεύκολλος (Appian); Lucani, Λευκανοί (always); &c.

(ii) 1. of Greek υ before Cicero's time (see § 56); e.g. Πύρρος, 219 Burrus; Φρύγες, Bruges (Ennius); Γλυκέρα, Glucera; 'Ησύχιον, Hesuchium; Λυκίους, Lucios; Φιλάργυρος, Pilargurus, Philargurus; Σύρος, Surus; all in Republican inscriptions. So trutina for τρυτάνη. Similarly Plautus must have written sucopanta for συκοφάντης; muropolæ for μυροπῶλαι; sumbolum for σύμβολον; &c. Compare Bacch. 362, "Nomen mutabit mihi, facietque extemplo Crucisalum me ex Crusalo (χρύσαλος)."

2. ŭ of Greek α in suffixes before 1; e.g. κραιπάλη, crapŭla; σκυτάλη, scutŭla (later scytale).

3. ŭ of Greek ŏ; e.g. κόθορνος, cothurnus; ἀμόργη, amurca; πορφύρα, purpŭra; ἐπιστολή, epistŭla; κολεός (Ep. κουλεός), culleus.

4. ŭ of Greek ου; e.g. Λυκοῦργος, Lycurgus; Πεσσινοῦς, Pessinus; Σιποῦς, Sipus (Lucan: but Sipontum, Cic.).

CORRESPONDENCE: 1. to an original Indo-European u; and 220 to a.

2. to Greek υ; e.g. mūcus, mungo, -μύσσω, μυκτήρ; lŭpus, λύκος; ūv-idus, ūmor, ὑγρός; cŭbare, κύπτω; glūbo, γλύφω; fūmus, θύω, θῦμος; ecfūtio, futtilis, χυ-, χέω, χύσις; cluo, inclūtus, κλύω, κλυτός; cucūlus, κόκκυξ (κοκκῦγ-); lūceo, lux, ἀμφι-λύκη, λύχνος; jŭgum, ζυγόν; lūgere, λυγρός; fui, φύω; sus, ὗς; mus, μῦς; rūfus, rūber, ἐρυθρός; &c.

3. to Greek ο; e.g. bulbus, βολβός; upŭpa, ἔποψ; nummus, νόμος; umbilīcus, ὀμφαλός; unguis, ὄνυξ; sūcus, ὀπός; ūter (for quoter), πότερος; fungus, σφόγγος; luxus, λόξος; uncus, ὄγκος.

In suffixes; e.g. gĕnus, γένος; lŭpus, λύκος; lĕgunt, λέγουσι for λέγοντι.

4. to Greek ω; e.g. cŭneus, κῶνος; fūr, φῶρ; ulna, ὠλένη; ŭmĕrus, ὦμος.

5. to Greek *a*; e.g. umbo, ἄμβων; ursus, ἄρκτος; puer, παῖς; hŭmi, χαμαί; sturnus, ψάρ.

6. to Greek ε; e.g. mulgeo, ἀμέλγω; ulcus, ἕλκος; suus, ἑός; tuus, τεός.

7. inserted between two consonants in early Latin in words obtained by oral tradition, not through literature[1]; e.g. Alcŭmena, Ἀλκμήνη; Æsculapius, Ἀσκληπιός; Hercŭles (also Hercoles), Ἡρακλῆς; Tecŭmessa, Τέκμησσα; drăcŭma or drachuma, δράχμη.

SUBSTITUTION: 1. for a radical a (after a prefix) before labials, 221 or 1 with another consonant; e.g. tăberna, contŭbernium; salto, insulto; &c. (see § 204. 2. *e*).

2. ŭ for au; after a prefix; e.g. causa, ac-cŭso; claudo, exclŭdo; &c. Frŭdāre, clŭdus, &c. seem to be earlier forms for fraudare, claudus.

3. for o before two consonants, or a final consonant, or a suffix beginning with l; e.g. honc, hunc; robor-, robur; singŏlus, singŭlus; &c. (see § 213).

4. ŭ for older oi or oe; e.g. oinos, oenus, ŭnus; oitile, ŭtile; moinicipieis, moenia, mŭnicipiis, mŭnia; &c.

5. ŭ for older ou; chiefly after the time of the Gracchi; e.g. jus, judex for jous, joudex; abdŭcit for abdoucit; (see § 251).

CONTRACTION, HIATUS, &c.: u + e and u + i are contracted 222 into u in some cases of substantives with u stems; e.g. senatuis, senatus; senatui, senatu; gradues, gradŭs. In the words huic, cui (for hoic, quoi) and interjection hui, ui is a single syllable, probably pronounced like French *oui* or Engl. *we*.

Before other vowels, and before these in other cases, u remains, usually as vowel, but sometimes as consonant: see § 92.

CHANGE OF QUANTITY: 1. in root syllable; e.g. rŭdis, crūdus; 223 pŭsillus, pŭsio; flŭvius, flŭvidus and flūvidus (both in Lucret.); lŭcerna, lūceo, lux (lūc-); dŭc- (dux), dūco; jŭgum, jūgerum; rŭber, rūfus, rōbigo; pŭtris, pūteo, pūtidus; rumpere (rŭp-), rūpes.

2. lengthened by way of inflexion in perfect tense; e.g. fŭgio, fūgi; fundo (fŭd-), fūdi; rumpo (rŭp-), rūpi; jŭvo, jūvi (for jŭvui?). The u in perfect of verbs with u stems is probably long, but becomes short before the following vowel; e.g. plŭo (for plŭvo, cf. plŭvia), perf. plūi (for plūvi), usually plŭi; &c. (Corssen considers the u in the present also to be properly long.)

[1] Ritschl, *Opusc.* II. 490.

3. lengthened by compensation for an extruded consonant; e.g. dūmus for dus-mus (comp. δασ-ύς).

CHANGE OF QUALITY: 1. The short vowel before a suffix 224 commencing with m, p, or f, is usually written ŭ in præ-Augustan inscriptions, ĭ afterwards. Thus in præ-Augustan inscriptions maxŭmus, optŭmus, proxsŭmus, sanctissŭmus, vīcensŭmus, decŭmus, marĭtŭmus; aestŭmo, recŭpero; aurŭfex, pontŭfex; &c. Jul. Cæsar is said to have first written ĭ, which is somewhat[1] rare in Republican inscriptions, but is exclusively used in the Monum. Ancyr., and is most usual in and after the Augustan age. Quintilian (1. 4, 8) describes this vowel (instancing optimus) as intermediate between u and i. In Greek almost always ι, never υ; e.g. Μάξιμος, Δέκιμος, Ποντίφικες; but also in inscr. Δεκομος, Δεκουμος, Σεπτουμε. Augustus is said to have written sīmus for sumus, *we are*.

The dat. abl. plural of stems in u probably had the ending -ŭbus in all originally, which some retained always; e.g. acŭbus, arcubus, &c.; (but manĭbus, exercĭtĭbus, &c.)

Similarly clŭpeus, mancŭpem, lŭbens are earlier forms than clĭpeus, mancĭpem, lĭbens; &c. In Vergil obstĭpuī for obstŭpuī.

2. Before suffixes not commencing with labials, ŭ becomes ĭ; e.g. cornu, cornĭger; gelu, gelĭdus; arcus, arcĭtenens; &c.

Capŭtalem (*S. C. de Bacc.*), manŭfestus are earlier forms than capĭtalem, manĭfestus.

3. For some other words (e.g. fūnus, fūner-ĭs; vul-sum, vello; &c.) in which u appears to have been only a transition vowel, see § 213. 5. For gerundus &c. see § 618.

OMISSION: The suffixes -cŭlo-, -pŭlo- were shortened to -clo-, 225 -plo- sometimes in prose; e.g. Asclani for Asculani; vinclum for vinculum; nucleus for nŭcŭleus (Plaut.); hercle for hercŭle; and often in verse; e.g. manĭplus, circlus, sæclum, perĭclum, orāclum, spectāclum, tomāclum; &c. So usually assecla, nomenclator; and always, disciplina, simplus, duplus, &c. Lucretius has (once) coplāta for cōpŭlāta. Instances of -glo- are rare, e.g. figlinus for figulinus often; singlāriter for singŭlāriter once (Lucr.). Plautus has always columen for (later) culmen. Comp. § 218. 4.

E.

CHARACTER: as above, but with the horizontal lines sometimes 226 very short. In the very oldest inscriptions probably before 500 U.C. another form, II, is found frequently, but not exclusively. It is also common in the cursive writing of the Pompeian inscriptions, though

---

[1] The earliest instance infĭmo in an inscription of the year 623 U.C. (*Corp. I. R.* 199), which everywhere else has infŭmo, is perhaps a slip of the stonecutter.

rare in any other inscriptions, at least of republican times. (See also F § 95.)

SOUND: ē probably varying between ê and é French. These 227 sounds are heard short as e in Engl. *net*, and (the first) a in *aerial*.

POSITION: frequently final; viz. ē in gen. dat. abl. singular of 228 noun stems in -e, and in 2nd pers. sing. pres. imper. act. of verbs with -e stems: also in pronouns me, te, se, preposition ē, conjunction ne, and adverbs (e.g. docte).

ĕ is final in abl. sing. of nouns with consonant, and (often) -i stems (e.g. patre, puppĕ); in nom. sing. of neuter -i stems (e.g. marĕ); in voc. sing. of o stems (e.g. taurĕ), and nom. sing. masc. of some pronouns (e.g. illĕ); in many parts of verbs, especially the 2nd person (e.g. regĕ, regitĕ, regebarĕ, regarĕ, regerĕ, regerĕ, and 3rd pers. rexerĕ, &c.); also some adverbs, prepositions, &c. (e.g. benĕ, indĕ, -que, antĕ, &c.)

Medial e is frequent before two consonants, or ll; e.g. perfectus, vello; and before r. Cf. § 204, 2, *b*; 213. 5, *b*; 234, 3, *b*.

REPRESENTATION: (i) in Greek, ē by η, ĕ by ε; Mĕnēnius, 229 Μενήνιος; Cornelius, Κορνήλιος; Veturius, Οὐετούριος; Tiberius, Τιβέριος; Metellus, Μέτελλος; &c.

ĕ by α in Calendæ, Καλάνδαι (always); by ε in Puteoli, Ποτίολοι (Inscr. always).

(ii) 1. of Greek η, and ε; e.g. ἠῶος *Ep.*, ἐῷος Att., ēōus, ŏōus; Λῆμνος, Lemnos; ἐλλέβορον, hellebōrum; Περσεφόνη, Persĕphōnē; &c.

2. before vowels, of ει; e.g. βαλανεῖον, balinēum; πλατεῖα, platēa; Αἰνείας, Aenēas; Ἀλεξάνδρεια, Alexandrea (Cic.); Δαρεῖος, Dareus (Cic.); &c. But Ἀλεξάνδρηα, &c. are found in papyri.

3. of Greek ι; e.g. κοχλίας, cochlea; ναυσία (Att. ναυτία), nausea.

CORRESPONDENCE: 1. to an original Indo-European a.   230

2. ĕ to Greek ε (usually); e.g. frĕmo, βρέμω; gĕnus, γένος; sĕdeo, ἕδος; ĕdo, ἔδω; sex, ἕξ; septem, ἑπτά; serpo, ἕρπω; est, ἐστί; ĕt, ἔτι; cervus, κεραός; lĕgo, λέγω; leo, λέων; mel, μέλι; mĕdeor, μέδομαι; mĕdius, μέσος; mens, μένος; pĕto, πέτομαι; rĕpens, ῥέπω; sĕvērus, σέβομαι; quĕ, τε; hĕri, χθές; &c. to Greek η; e.g. fĕra, θήρ; jĕcur, ἧπαρ.

3. ĕ to Greek α; e.g. brĕvis, βρἄχύς (§ 129. 2. *c*); centum, ἑκατόν; cĕrebrum, κάρα; ĕgenus, ἀχηνία; lĕvis, ἐλαχύς; per, παρά; pre-hendo, χανδάνω; sternuo, πταρνύω; über, οὖθαρ; venter, γαστήρ.

4. ĕ to Greek ο; e.g. gĕnu, γόνυ; dentis, ὀδόντος; fel, χόλος; herba, φορβή; sĕrum, ὀρός; pĕdem, πόδα.

5. ē to Greek η; mensis (§ 167), μήν; ne, νή; lien, σπλήν; strēnuus, στρηνής; sēmi-, ἡμι-: to Greek ε; e.g. mē, με; tē, σε.

6. ē to Greek ω; e.g. vēnum, ὦνος.

7. In suffixes ĕ to ε; e.g. legĕ, λέγε; legitĕ, λέγετε; genĕris, γένεος; dextĕr, δεξίτερος; &c. Compare also mĕ-mĭni, μέ-μονα (cf. § 665).

ĕ to *a*; e.g. nomĕn, ὄνομα (ὀνοματ-).

e (old ŭ) to *o*; legent-, λεγοντ-; &c.

SUBSTITUTION: 1. e, for radical a after a prefix, is found before 231 two consonants or a final consonant, or r, or sometimes other single consonants; e.g. tracto, detrecto; pars, expers; căno, cornicen; părio, pepĕri; grădior, ingrĕdior; &c. (§ 204).

2. for radical o, before ll; e.g. vello compared with vulsi; ocellus for ocololus; &c. (§ 213. 5): and after v in vĕster, verto, &c. (§ 93).

3. for suffixed o (§ 213);

(*a*) before r followed by a vowel, or after i before other single consonants; e.g. genĕris from genus (γένος); sociĕtas from socius (stem socio-); &c.

(*b*) before two consonants; e.g. faciendus for faciundus, older faciondus; tempestas from tempos-; &c.

(*c*) in final syllables; e.g. censuere for censueront; ille for illus (illo-); &c.

4. for ae, not frequent till in and after third century after Christ (see § 262).

CONTRACTION, HIATUS, &c.:

1. e+e to ē; e.g. delēverunt, delērunt; delēvĕrat, delērat; 232 deerat, deesse, deest always to dērat, dēsse, dēst; nĕ hĕmo (old for homo), nēmo; prĕhendo, prendo; &c.

2. e+i to e, or (especially if the contraction was not constant) ēi; e.g. delevisse, delesse; dēhĭbeo, dēbeo; mone-is, monēs.

dēin, deinde, dēinceps, (never uncontracted till late); dehinc as monosyllable occasionally; ēi (also ēī), ēidem (dative), often. So also rēi, spēi, fidēi, diēi &c., often written re, spe, fide, die. In Vergil, &c. also aurēi, aureis, aerēi, ferrēi; and Greek proper names as Terēi, Thesēi, Orphēi, Pelēi, &c., sometimes written Teri, &c.

In rēice for rejice, ēicit (Lucr.) for ejicit, ēius (rarely a mono-syllable), Pompēi (voc.) something of the consonantal sound of j may have remained (§ 138). Anteit is used as a trochee, the e being elided. So also ante ea becomes antea.

3. e before **a, o, u,** remained usually a vowel, and without contraction; e.g. **moneas**; **saxeo, saxea, saxeum**; **eunt, eam, eo**; &c.

But in the following, e was probably pronounced as **ĭ,** so as not to form a separate syllable; **eōdem, eādem, eaedem, eōrundem** (Lucr., Verg.); **alveō, alveāria, aureō, aureā** (Verg.); **ostreā, cereā** (Hor.); **alveō, aureō, aureæ; aureā** (Ov.): and Greek proper names; e.g. **Idomeneōs, Peleō, Perseō, Mnestheō**; &c. After the Augustan age this use was confined to proper names and the cases of **balteus, aureus, alveus.**

So, in comic poets, in the cases of the following words, **meus, deus, eo, eam** (both the pronoun and verb).

It is contracted in **neve, neu; ne-uter, neuter**; &c. **revorsus, rursus**; and probably in **seorsum** (sometimes written **sorsum**), **deorsum**; omitted in **n-usqvam, n-ūtiqvam.**

CHANGE OF QUANTITY: 1. in roots; e.g. **rĕgere, rēx (rēg-)**; [233] **tĕgere, tēgula**; **lĕgere, lēx (lēg-)**; **sĕdere, sēdes**; **hĕrus, hēres.**

2. lengthened, as a means of inflexion; e.g. **lĕgo, lēgi**; **ĕdo, ēdi**; **sĕdeo, sēdi**; **vĕnio, vēni**; **ĕmo, ēmi.**

3. lengthened in compensation for the extrusion of a consonant; e.g. **dēni** for **dĕcĭni**; **sē-vĭri** for **sex-viri**; **dumētum** for **dumectum**; &c. In **viciēs** for **viciens**; **vicēsimus** for **vicensimus**; **Hcrtēsia** for **Hortensia**; the long e is probably due to ns. Cf. § 167. 2.

4. In final syllable often shortened; e.g. **bĕnĕ, malĕ, supernĕ, infernĕ,** (compared with **doctē,** &c.); so in the imperatives **cavĕ, vĭdĕ,** (see § 279); and frequently in the comic poets, in verbs with short penult; e.g. **tenĕ, movĕ, tacĕ, manĕ, vĭdĕ, habĕ, jubĕ.**

Monĕt, amĕt, regĕt, (for **monēt,** &c.); **terĕs, equĕs,** &c. (for **terets,** &c.); **vĭdĕn** (for **vidēsne**); **compĕs, desĕs** (for **comped-s,** &c.).

In the ablative of -ĭ stems, and of consonant stems; e.g. **nubĕ, principĕ,** the final syllable was probably once in -ēd; e.g. **nubed, principed.** The earliest forms actually found in inscriptions are **airid, aire, patrē, nominid, coventionid;** and, in and after the time of the Gracchi, e.g. **virtutei, salutei, luci, deditioni, fontei, omnei, parti, vectigali,** &c.

CHANGE OF QUALITY: 1. **ĕ** is found in the old language, in [234] many places where an ĭ is found later. The change began towards the end of 5th century U.C., and was completed, with some exceptions, before Plautus's time (Ritschl, *Opusc.* II. 623); e.g. **sĕmul, fuet, dedet, mereto, tempestatebus, cædete, Fabrecio,** &c. for **simul, fuit, dedit, merito, tempestatibus, cæditis, Fabricius,** &c.

2. ĕ ıs found in a final suffix, where I is found before s or d, e being according to Ritschl (§ 196) the earlier vowel; e.g. facĭle, facĭlis; marĕ, maris; mage, magis; fortasse, fortassis; pote, potĭs; aere, aerid (old abl. but see § 233); rēge, rēgĭs; rĕge, rĕgĭs; amabare, amabarĭs; amabĕre, amaberĭs; fateare, fatearĭs; capĕ, capĭs; &c.

3. ĕ is changed to I, in a final syllable to which a letter or syllable (one or more) is suffixed;—

(*a*) either if **e** be final and the suffix begin with a consonant; ĭlle, ĭllĭc (for ĭllĭce); iste, istĭc (for istĭce); tute, tutĭne, tutĭmet; nunce, nuncĭne; sīce (i.e. sic), sicĭne; unde, undĭque; inde, indĭdem; poste (old form of post), postidea; ante, antidhac, antĭcipo, antistes; bene, benĭvolus, benignus; male, malĭficus, &c.; pave-, pavĭdus; pude-, pudibundus; rube-, rubicundus; mone-, monĭtus; morde-, mordĭcus; habe-, habĭto; pate-, patĭbulum; regĕ, regĭte, regĭto; forte, fortiter; radice, radicĭtus; habe-, habĭlis.

(In nubēs, esuriēs, &c.; amarēs, amēs, monēs, &c., the e is long, arising from contraction with the initial vowel of the suffix. So originally amēt, monēt; &c.)

(*b*) or, if **e** be not final, but the suffix begin with a vowel; e.g. alĕs, alĭtis; pedĕs, pedĭtis; antistĕs, antistĭta, antistĭtem; tibicĕn, tibicĭnis, tibicĭna; agmĕn, agmĭnis; semĕn, semĭno; manceps, mancĭpem (old mancŭpem); biceps, bicipĭtem; vertex, vertĭcis; artĭfex, artĭfĭcis; dĕcem, decĭmus.

But ĕ remains after the vowel ĭ, or before r (or tr); e.g. ariĕs, arietis; tener, tenera; pīpĕr, pīpĕris; ansĕr, ansĕrem; regis, regĕris; genĭtor, genĕtrix; &c.; or if the suffix begin with a consonant; e.g. ales for alet-s; obses (for obsed-s); lamella (for lamen-la) compared with lammĭna; nutrīmen, nutrimentum (but nutrimĭnis); senex, senectus; pedes, pedester; potestas compared with potĭs, pote; patens, compared with patĭna; (comp. vidĕn for vidēsne).

Other exceptions are rare; e.g. fænisex, fænisĕcis; seges, segĕtis; (Pudefacio, &c. are not complete compounds, as is evident from the accent and vowel a being retained; e.g. pudefácis).

4. Radical ĕ changed to I when a syllable has been prefixed; e.g. lĕgo, collĭgo, dilĭgo, &c. (but intellĕgo, neglĕgo, relĕgo; contego, &c.); rĕgo, corrĭgo; ĕmo, adĭmo; sĕco, subsicivus; tĕneo, retĭneo; ĕgeo, indĭgeo; prĕmo, opprĭmo; tĕneo, protĭnus; but decem, undecim, where the penultimate remains, but the final is changed.

But not before r or two consonants; e.g. refero, consentio; &c.

5. The root vowel is (apparently) changed from e to o in some derivatives; e.g. tĕgo, tŏga; sĕqui, sŏcius; prĕcari, prŏcus; pendo, pondus; terra, extorris; sĕrĕre, sors; perhaps rĕgĕre, rŏgus. Probably the **o** is directly from the original a.

6. ĕ to ĭ, frequently through ei as an intermediate sound; e.g. matre, **Maurte, Junone** in old inscriptions, for **matri, Marti, Junoni**; **conscriptes, Atilies** for **conscripti, Atilii** (nom. pl. see Book II); &c. leber, leiber, liber. So **sibe, quase**, are old forms, used by Livy (Quint. I. 7. 24); and **duovir jure dicundo, tresviri auro aere argento flando, feriundo,** etc. apparently are forms retaining the old dative. On the general theory, see § 196.

OMISSION : 1. ĕ, in a root syllable which has received prefixes 235 or suffixes, is sometimes omitted ; e.g. **gigno** for **gigĕno** (or **gigino**); **mălignus** for **malĭgĕnus** ; **gnātus** for **gĕnātus.**

2. Before **r** the vowel ĕ is frequently omitted; e.g. **September, Septembris** ; **ācer, acris** ; **frāter, fratrem** ; **ăger, agrum** ; **infĕrus, infra** ; **dextĕra, dextra** ; **noster, nostra** ; **ludibrium** ; &c.

3. Final ĕ fell off ; (*a*) in neuter nom. acc. of stems in **ăl-** and **ăr-** ; e.g. **calcar, laquear** ; **tribunal, puteal** ; &c. So also **lac** (for **lact,** for **lacte,** nom. sing.) ; **vŏlŭp** for **volupe** ; **simul** for **simile.**

(*b*) in enclitic particles ; e.g. **hic, hæc, hoc,** &c. (for **hice,** &c.), **illic, istic, sic, nunc, tunc** ; **nec, ac,** for **nece, ace,** for **neque, atque** ; **vidĕn** for **vides-ne** ; **potin** for **potis-ne** ; **quin** for **quī-ne, sin** for **sī-ne.** (In **seu, neu** for **sive, nive** (old **seve, neve**), **fili** for **filie,** a contraction has taken place.)

4. On the omission of e in **est** and **es** after a vowel or m, see Book II.

I.

CHARACTER : as above. In the first century B.C., probably not 236 before Sulla's time, began the habit of making a tall I to indicate the long vowel. (See § 59. 2.)

SOUND : as in Italian, viz.: ī as in English *machine ;* ĭ same 237 sound shortened. But in some classes of words, e.g. **vir, qvirites, optimus,** there is some evidence for a modified sound of ĭ, perhaps a fine Germ. ü. See Preface ; also §§ 90, 2 ; 184, 3.

POSITION : ĭ is never final ; except 1. in **quasi, nisi, sicuti** ; 238 and 2. (short or long) in **mihi, tibi, sibi, ubi, ibi.**

ī frequently final ; 1. in gen. and loc. sing. and nom. pl. of o stems (e.g. **dominī**) ; sometimes gen. and dat. sing. of a stems, e stems and u stems (e.g. **musāī, diēī, domuī**) ; dat. sing. of consonant stems, and dat. abl. sing. of i stems (e.g. **nominī, marī**); and dat. sing. of many pronouns ; e.g. **illī** ; 2. some adverbs, once

oblique cases; e.g. herī, vesperī, ubi, uti, si; &c. 3. 1st and 2nd
persons sing. perf. ind. active and present infinitive passive of all
verbs, and 2nd pers. sing. imperative active of I- verbs (e.g. audivī,
audivistī, audirī, audī).

REPRESENTATION: (i) in Greek, 1. I by ι, e.g. Gaius Livius, 239
Γάϊος Λίβιος; Claudius, Κλαύδιος; Titus Otacilius, Τίτος 'Οκτα-
κίλιος (Polyb.); Priscus, Πρίσκος; Opiter, 'Οπίτωρ (Dion. H.);
Capitolium, Καπιτώλιον (Strab., Dion. H., Plut.); Καπιτωλῖνος
(Dion. H., Dio. Cass.); &c.

By ε; e.g. Capitolium, Καπετώλιον (Polyb., Strab., Plut.), Καπε-
τωλῖνος (Diod. S., Dion. H.); Atilius, 'Ατέλιος (Dion. H., 'Ατίλιος
Diod. S.); Tiberis, Τέβερις (Dion. H. but Τίβερις Strab., D. Cass.).
In inscriptions are sometimes found (besides forms with ι) Τε-
βέριος (so always before Tiberius' adoption by Augustus. Dittenberger, Herm. VI. 133), Λέπεδος, Δομέτιος, and others; often
Καπετώλιον, 'Οφέλλιος (but also in Latin Ophellius), λεγεών.

By υ; e.g. Bibulus, Βύβλος (inscr.).

By α in suffixes; e.g. būcīna, βυκάνη (Polyb.).

Sometimes omitted, e.g. Decimus, Δέκμος.

2. I by ι; e.g. Capitolīnus, Καπιτωλῖνος (vide supr.); Albīnus,
'Αλβῖνος; Scīpio, Σκιπίων (Diod. S., Appian, Strabo); Tībur, Τί-
βουρα; Tarracīnam, Ταρρακίναν (Strabo).

By η; e.g. Scīpio, Σκηπίων (Plut.).

(ii) 1. of Greek ι; e.g. Καλλικλῆς, Callicles; Παιγνίον, Paeg-
nium; τραπεζίτης, trapessita; 'Αβδηρίτης, Abderītes; Θέτις, Thetis.

2. I of Greek α in suffixes; e.g. μαχανά (Dor.), machīna; τρυτάνη, trutīna; Κατάνη, Cătīna; &c.

3. I of Greek ει; e.g. πειρατής, pīrata; Νεῖλος, Nīlus; ἀλείπτης,
alipta; 'Αντιόχεια, Antiochia; &c.

4. I inserted in early Latin (cf. § 220. 7) between κν, χν, μν;
e.g. Πρόκνη, Procine; κύκνος, cūcinus; tecīna, τέχνη; mīna, μνᾶ.

CORRESPONDENCE: 1. to original Indo-European ι; and to α. 240

2. to Greek ι; e.g. dīc- in-dīco, causidīc-us, dīco, δίκη,
δείκνυμι; vigintī, εἴκοσι; cio, κίω, κῑνέω; clī-vus, reclī-nare, κλίνη,
κλῑτύς; crī-brum, cer-no, κρίνω; hiemps, χιών; frio, frīco, χρίω;
stinguo, stimulus, στίγω, στιγμή; tri- (e.g. tria), τρεῖς, τρίτος;
dīvus, dies, δῖος, εὐ-δία; video, vīdi; ἰδ-, εἶδον; scindo, σχιδ-,
σχίζω; pilleus, πῖλος; frigus, ρῖγος; quis, τίς; vīs, ἴς (ἶν-); vītex,
vītis, ἴτυς; viola, ἴον; &c.

3. to Greek ε; e.g. in, indo (old, endo), intus, ἐν, ἔνδον,
ἐντός; rīgo, βρέχω; strigilis, στλεγγίς; tinguo, τέγγω.

4. to Greek ει, οι; e.g. fīdo, fīdes, πείθω; quies, κεῖμαι, κοίτη;
pingo, pic-tura, ποικίλος; linquo, reliquus, λείπω, λοιπός.

5. to Greek *a*; e.g. in-, ἀν- (Engl. *un-*); dĭgĭtus, δάκτυλος; pinguis, παχύς; stringo, στραγγεύω.

6. to Greek *o*; e.g. cĭnis, κόνις; imber, ὄμβρος.

SUBSTITUTION: 1. I for ă in root syllable after a prefix, before 241 a single consonant (except r), and before ng; e.g. tango, tetĭgi; căno, concĭno; făcetus, infĭcetus; pango, impingo; &c. (see § 204).

2. (*a*) I for older ĕ in many words· e.g. dedĭt for dedĕt; &c. (see § 234).

(*b*) I for ĕ in root syllable after a prefix; e.g. lĕgo, col-lĭgo; &c.

(*c*) Also in final closed suffix, and in final syllable of stem, to which a letter or syllable is suffixed; either if e be final and the suffix begin with a consonant, or if e be not final, but the suffix begin with a vowel; e.g. marĕ, marĭs; indĕ, indĭdem; ales, alĭtis; &c. (see § 234).

3. I for ŏ in final syllable of stem before a single consonant followed by a vowel, except before l not followed by i, and except before r; e.g. cardŏn- cardĭnis; bono- bonĭtas; &c. (see § 213. 5).

4. I for ŭ in final syllable of stem, but before m, p, f, not until last century of republic; e.g. cornu- cornĭger; maxĭmus for maxŭmus; &c. (see § 224).

5. I appears to have been, at least in many words, preceded by ē, or ei both in root syllables and suffixes, sometimes by both (see §§ 265, 268).

6. I for ai: possibly in the dat. plur. of a- stems: e.g. musis for musais. See § 257.

7. I for æ in root syllable after a prefix; e.g. quæro, inquīro; æquus, inīquus; &c.; cædo, cecĭdi; &c. (§ 262).

CONTRACTION, HIATUS, &c.: 1. I+i, if one be long, is con- 242 tracted to ī; e.g. dii, dī; consilii, consilī; petiit, petīt; audiis, audīs; audivisti, audisti; si vis, sīs; nihil (ne hīlum), nīl; mihi, mī; &c. If both are short, one is dropped; e.g. fugiis, fugĭs; egregi-ior, egregior; navi-ibus navĭbus; etc. (cf. § 144). But tibĭicen tibīcen.

2. i before other vowels usually remained. It absorbed a succeeding vowel in bīga for bijŭga; fĭli for fĭlie; sīs for sĭes; măgĭs for magios; duris-simus for durios-imus; &c., in which comparatives i is perhaps properly long; comp. βελτ-ίων, βελτῖόν-a; &c. (On minor see § 245.)

CHANGE OF QUANTITY: 1. in root syllable; e.g. lībet, līber, 243 lībertas; fīdes, perfīdus, fīdo, fœdus; suspīcere, suspīcio; dīc-, male-dīc-us, dīco; ar-bĭt-er, per-bītĕre; līqvor, also līqvor (once), līqvidus and līqvidus (Lucret. IV. 1259, "līquidis et līquida crassis"); līqvāre, līqvēre, līqvī.

2. in final syllables; e.g. audĭt for audīt; sĭt for sīt (siet); velĭt for velīt; also sometimes audiverĭs for audiverīs (perf. subj. see Book II).

3. final ī is shortened in nisĭ, quasĭ (comp. sīquĭdem), and frequently in mihĭ, tibĭ, sibĭ, ubĭ (always sīcubĭ, nēcubĭ, ubīvĭs, but ubīque), ibĭ (but ibĭdem, alibĭ). So utĭnam, utĭque, from utī.

In Plautus also dărĭ, pătĭ, lŏquĭ; dĕdĭ, stĕtĭ; vĕnĭ, ăbĭ, are found with ĭ short.

CHANGE OF QUALITY: 1. to e before a or o or ĭ; e.g. meĭ, 244 meo, compared with mĭs (old gen.), mihĭ; queo, queam, from quī-re; eo, eam, from īre; eum, eam, compared with ĭs, ĭd. (But audiam, audio, audĭit; &c.) Perhaps the e is even here prior to the ĭ.

2. ŭ is found, from stems (apparently) in e or ĭ, in early Latin before m, f; e.g. testĭ-, testŭmonium; pontĭ-, pontŭfex; carnĭ-, carnufex; dŏcĕ-, dŏcŭmentum; mŏnĕ-, mŏnŭmentum. The forms with ĭ, e.g. testĭmonium are later (cf. § 224).

3. For change of ĭ to j see § 142.

4. For e instead of ĭ, before r, see § 184. 3, 569, 656.

OMISSION: 1. ĭ in suffixes is often omitted between two conso-245 nants; e.g. facultas for facilitas; misertum for miseritum; puertia (Hor.) for pueritia; postus (Verg.) for positus; replictus (Verg.) for replicitus; audacter for audāciter (Quint. I. 6. 17); propter for propiter; fert for ferit; volt for volit; est for ĕdit; valde for valide; caldus (Augustus) for calidus; soldus (Hor.) for solidus; lamna for lammina; alumnus for aluminus; tignum compared with tigillum; tegmen for tegimen; probably benficium, &c. (in Plaut., Ter., Phædr.) for beneficium; &c.

2. In the nom. sing. of -i nouns, but rarely after a short syllable; e.g. ars for artis; ferens for ferentis; Arpinās for Arpīnātis; mendax for mendācis; nux for nŭcis; &c. (see Book II).

3. A radical ĭ is omitted in surgo for surrigo; porgo for porrigo; pergo for perrigo; purgo for purigo; jurgium for jurigium (jus, agere); surpĕre (Luc., Hor.) for surrĭpere.

4. In mĭnor, mĭnus, ĭ is apparently dropped (for min-ior, minius).

INSERTION: 1. ĭ is apparently inserted between consonant stems, and derivative suffixes, e.g. ălĭtus from ăl-ĕre; tĕgĭmen from tĕg-ĕre; fullōnĭcus from fullōn-; hērēdĭtas from hērēd-; &c. But see § 746.

2. in words from Greek. See above, § 239, 5.

CHAPTER X.

DIPHTHONGS.

AU.

SOUND: as in German; i. e. nearly as English *ow*[1] in *cow, town.*

REPRESENTATION: (i) in Greek by αυ; e.g. **Aurunculetus,** 247 Αὐρουγκουλήιος; **Aulus,** Αὖλος; &c.

(ii) of Greek αυ; e.g. Αὐτομέδων, **Automedon;** &c.

CORRESPONDENCE: to Greek αυ; e.g. **augeo,** αὐξάνω; **aurora,** 248 αὔως Æol., (ἠώς Att.); **nauta,** ναύτης; **taurus,** ταῦρος; **caulis,** καυλός.

SUBSTITUTION: 1. for **av** before a short vowel, which is then 249 absorbed; e.g. **cautum** for **cavitum; fautor** for **făvĭtor; auceps** for **aviceps;** &c.

2. for **ab** before **f**; e.g. **aufugio, aufero** compared with **abstuli, ablatum.** But see § 97 n.

CHANGE OF QUALITY: 1. to ō in the older language, but the 25c same words are more frequently found with au retained; e.g. **Clodius** for **Claudius; copa** for **caupa; codex** for **caudex; Plotus** for **Plautus; plostrum** for **plaustrum; lotus** for **lautus; rōdus, (rūdus, rudusculum)** for **raudus, rausculum; olla (ola?)** for **aula;** &c. So (according to Festus) in the country dialect **orum, oriculas** for **aurum, auriculas.** In Plautus **ausculor** for **osculor** (cf. Suet. Vesp. 22).

explodo from **plaudo; suffocare** from **fauces;** &c.

2. into ū; e.g. **frustra** from **fraus; frudare, frude** old forms for **fraudare, fraude; excludo** from **claudo,** sometimes **cludo; accuso** from **causa;** &c.

OU.

SOUND: probably that of the Southern English ō, which is really 251 a diphthong formed of o and u. Cf. § 21.

---

[1] In Phædr. *Append.* 21, A raven (*corvus*) is said to have cried **ave** (**ah-we**, or **au**? cf. § 94). We represent a raven's ordinary cry by **caw.** But Pliny (H. N. 10, § 121) tells of a raven who *sermoni adsuefactus, Tiberium salutabat;* and a *trained* raven is bad evidence.

6

This diphthong is found in inscriptions in a few words regularly before the seventh century U.C., and frequently until after the middle of the same. Afterwards **û** became exclusively used in its place. Thus **Fourius, Loucanam, Loucina, abdoucit, plouruma, poloucta, poublicom, plous, jous, jousit (jussit), joudex, jouranto, noundinum.** Instances of long u before the time of the Gracchi are rare; e.g. **Juno, Junone, Luciom, Lucius,** in some of the earliest inscriptions.

EU.

SOUND: probably pronounced as a diphthong. So in Italian. 252

HISTORY: This diphthong is found in very few Latin words, 253 viz. heu, heus; neu (for neve); seu (for sive); ceu; neuter, for ne uter. Neutiquam (nŭtiquam?) has first syllable short.

It is otherwise found only to represent the Greek ευ; e.g. Εὐρι- 254 πίδης, **Euripides;** Εὖρος, **Eurus; Pseudulus** from ψεύδω; &c.

AI.

SOUND: probably diphthongal; viz. that of a broad English *i*; 255 i.e. as *ai* in *ay* (=*yes*).

HISTORY: This diphthong is found almost exclusively in the 256 inscriptions older than the seventh century U.C. in words afterwards spelt with **æ.** Thus in root syllables we find **aidilis, aide, airid** (i.e. **ære**), **praidad** (**præda**), **quaistores, praitor, Aimilius, aiquom.** Some instances are found in later inscriptions both republican and imperial, chiefly in proper names, especially **Aimilius, Caicilius:** also **Caisar, praifectus;** &c. In final syllables it is found frequently in republican and imperial inscriptions in the genitive and dative singular, rarely in the nominative plural, of stems in **a,** chiefly proper names, but also others; e.g. **faciundai, coloniai, maxsumai, deai, Manliai, Agrippai;** &c. So frequently (making ai two long syllables) in Plautus and Ennius: Lucretius and Vergil appear to have adopted the form as an archaism, or in imitation of Ennius.

CHANGE OF QUALITY: In the dat. abl. plural of **-a** stem 257 probably the original form was **-ais** as in Oscan. In inscriptions are found only **-eis,** and **-is** (§ 266).

AE.

SOUND: the diphthong formed by these two vowels would 258 approach nearly to the sound of a in *hat* lengthened.

REPRESENTATION: (i) 1. in Greek by αι; e.g. Æmilius (see 259 however § 256), Αἰμίλιος; Æbutius, Αἰβούτιος; Kæso, Καίσων; Cæsar, Καῖσαρ; Æqui, Αἴκοι (Strabo); &c.

2. Rarely by ε; e.g. Cæcilius, Κεκίλιος (cf. § 262); Cæcina, Κεκίνας (Plut. but Καικίνας, D. Cass.). This ε is not found in inscriptions till the second century p. Chr. at earliest. (Dittenberger.)

(ii) 1. of Greek αι; e.g. Αἰνείας, Æneas; Παναίτιος, Panætius; Λακεδαίμων, Lacedæmon; αἰγίς, ægis; Παιάν, Pæan; αἰθήρ, æther; &c.

2. of Greek α; e.g. Ἀσκλάπιος (Dor.), Æsculapius (an old genitive Aisclapi is found); πάλλαξ, pælex, (also pelex).

3. of Greek η; e.g. σκηνή, scæna.

CORRESPONDENCE: to Greek αι; e.g. æstas, æstus, αἴθω, 26ι αἰθήρ; lævus, λαιός; scævus, σκαιός; ævum, αἰών, αἰές (Att. ἀεί).

SUBSTITUTION: for ai, which however lingered beside æ. Æ is 261 found first in the *S. C. de Bacc.* in ædem, where in all other words (aiquom, Duelonai, haice, tabelai, datai) ai is retained. Æ is very rare in inscriptions before the time of the Gracchi, but after that time is almost exclusively used in all the longer and more important inscriptions; e.g. the laws, the Mon. Ancyr. &c.

æ, for ē and ĕ, is rare in inscriptions before (at least) the 2nd cent. after Christ. It is frequent in MSS.

CHANGE OF QUALITY: 1. to e both in root and final syllable. 262 A few instances occur in very old inscriptions; e.g. Victorie, Fortune, Diane: so also occasionally in rustic language noted by Varro, edus for hædus, Mesius for Mæsius; Cecilius pretor, ridiculed by Lucilius. But instances in inscriptions (except the Pompeian wall inscriptions) are not numerous till in and after third century after Christ; e.g. prefectus, presenti, aque, patrie, &c.

2. to ī in root syllables after a prefix, e.g. cædo, concīdo; lædo, illīdo; quæro, requīro; æstumo, existumo; æquus, inīquus; &c.

<h2 style="text-align:center">OI, OE.</h2>

SOUND: oi nearly as in English; e.g. *voice*, &c.: oe was also 263 probably sounded as a diphthong.

CHANGE OF QUALITY: Words with ū in the root syllable 264 were in the older language written with oi or œ; and words with œ in the root syllable were also earlier written with oi.

In inscriptions oi is rarely found so late as the first century before Christ: œ (though probably as old as Plautus) is little found in inscriptions before the first century B.C.: u is found in their place in and after the time of the Gracchi.

1. oi, œ to u; e.g. oino, œnus, unus; oinvorsei, universi; ploirume, plœra, plurimi, plura; comoinem, moinicipieis, mœnia, mœniundæ, inmœnes for communem, municipiis, munia, muniundæ, immunes; moiro, mœrum, murum; oitile, œtantur, œtier for utile, utantur, uti; coira, coiravit, cœra, cœravit, cura, curavit; loidos, lœdos, ludos; &c.

2. oi to œ; e.g. foidere, foideratei, fœdere, fœderati; coipint, cœpint, Coilius, Cœlius.

3. some other changes are, nœnum afterwards non; lœbertas, libertas; obœdio from audio.

4. In final syllables, hoice, hoic, quoi (also quoiei), quoique are early forms of huic, cui, cuique: pilumnœ poplœ, for pilumni populi (gen. sing.?), *pike-armed tribe;* Fescenninœ for fescennini (nom. pl.); ab olces for ab illis.

EI.

1. This diphthong is found in inscriptions older than the Gracchi in the following forms, in which ī occurs later. (The *S. C. de Bacc.* has rarely ī, frequently ei.)

(*a*) a few root syllables; e.g. leiber, deivus, deicere, ceivis.

(*b*) dative singular of consonant nouns; e.g. Apolenei, Junonei, virtutei, Jovei. Frequently also in inscriptions later than the Gracchi, in which ī also is found. The dative in e is also found, and more frequently in the earlier than in the later inscriptions.

(*c*) nominative plural of o stems; e.g. foideratei, iei. After the time of the Gracchi both ī and ei are frequent. Earlier forms were ēs, ē, and œ (see Book ii).

(*d*) dative and ablative plural of o stems; e.g. eeis (*S. C. de Bacc.*), also vobeis. -eis is frequently found in this case after the time of the Gracchi. Both -is and -eis occur also from -a stems since that period, but apparently before that period no instance of those cases occurs.

(*e*) also in the datives and adverbs sibei, tibei, ubei, ibei, sei, nei, utei; in which e was probably a still older form.

2. In præ-Augustan inscriptions later than the Gracchi it is found instead of and beside an earlier ī, or e in the classes numbered below (*g*), (*h*).

(*a*) in some root syllables; e.g. deicera, deixerit also (dicere, &c.); promeiserit, eire, adeitur, conscreiptum, veita, leitis, leiteras, meilites, feilia, Teiburtis, eis, eisdem (nom. plur.).

(*b*) in suffixes; e.g. Serveilius, genteiles, ameicorum, discipleina, peregreinus, fugiteivus, peteita (for petita), mareitus, &c.

(*c*) occasionally, but not frequently, as the characteristic vowel of the fourth conjugation; e.g. audeire, veneire, &c.

(*d*) in infin. pass. not commonly till Cicero's time; e.g. darei, solvei, possiderei, agei, &c.

(*e*) in perfect (for an older i or sometimes e); e.g. obeit, fecei, poseivei, dedeit, &c.

(*f*) other verbal forms; e.g. nolei, faxseis, seit, &c.

(*g*) also rarely in the ablative from consonant and i nouns; e.g. virtutei, fontei, &c.

(*h*) nom. and acc. plur. of i stems; e.g. omneis, turreis, &c.

(*i*) genitive singular of o stems; e.g. colonei, damnatei (one or two instances occur a little before the Gracchi).

3. **EI** is but occasionally found in post-Augustan inscriptions.

In the Fast. Triumph. Capit. (C. *I. R.* I. 453 sqq.) cir. 720 U.C. the ablative plur. is almost always in -eis; e.g. Etrusceis, Galleis, &c.

Corssen's conclusion is, that in the root syllable of the words 267 deiva, leiber, deicere, ceivis, in the dat. abl. plur. of -o stems and probably of -a stems, and in the locative forms, as sei, utei, &c., ei was a real diphthong; in all other cases it expressed the transition vowel between ī and ē (*Ausspr.* i. 719. 788. ed. 2). As a diphthong its sound would be nearly that of the English a; e.g. *fate*.

Ritschl's view of the relations of ē, ei and ī is as follows (*Opusc.* 268 II. 626): "*First* period (5th century U.C. to and into the 6th). Predominance of e in place of the later i, and, in fact, both of ē for ī and of ĕ for ĭ. *Second* period (6th century). Transition of e to i (so far as e was changed at all), ĕ changing to ĭ absolutely, but ē to ī with this modification, that where in the case of ē the pronunciation noticeably inclined to i, the habit was gradually adopted of writing ei. *Third* period (1st decad of the 7th century). Accius extends this mode of writing to every ī without exception, in order to obtain a thorough distinction of ī from ĭ, in connexion with his theory of doubling a, e, u to denote the long vowel. Short ĭ remains unaltered. *Fourth* period. Lucilius, recognising the arbitrary and irrational character of this generalisation, confines the writing ei to the cases where ī inclines to ē. Short ĭ remains unaffected by this also."

CHAPTER XI.

OF LATIN WORDS and SYLLABLES.

A Latin word may commence with any vowel or diphthong, 269 semivowel, or single consonant.

But of combinations of consonants the following only are in Latin found as initial; viz.

1. an explosive or **f** followed by a liquid; i.e. **pl, pr; bl, br; cl, cr; gl, gr; tr; fl, fr**: but not **tl, dl, dr**;

e.g. **plaudo, precor; blandus, brevis; clamo, crudus; globus, gravis; traho; fluo, frendo.** (**Drusus** is possibly an exception (cf. § 155); other words in **dr** are Greek or foreign; e.g. **drachma, draco, Druidæ.**)

2. **s** before a sharp explosive, with or without a following liquid; viz. **sp, spl, spr; sc, scr; st, str**;

e.g. **sperno, splendeo, sprevi; scio, scribo; sto, struo.** Also **stlis**, afterwards **lis.** No instance of **scl** is found.

3. **gn** was found in **Gnæus** and in some other words; e.g. **gnarus, gnavus, gnosco, gnascor**, but the forms with **g** are almost confined to the early language (§ 129. 3).

4. The semi-consonant **v** is also found after an initial **q** or **s**; e.g. **qvos, svavis** (§ 89): and in Plautus **scio, dies** are pronounced **scjo, djes** (§ 142).

A Latin word may end with any vowel or diphthong, but with 270 only a few single consonants; viz. the liquids **l, r**, the nasals **m, n**, the sibilant **s**, one explosive, **t.** A few words end with **b, c, d.**

Of these, **b** occurs only in three prepositions, **ab, ob, sub.**

c only where a subsequent letter has fallen away; e.g. **dic, duc, fac, lac, ac, nec, nunc, tunc**, and the pronouns **hic, illic, istic** (for **dice, duce, face, lacte, atque, neque, nunce, tunce, hice, illice, istice**).

d only in **haud, ad, apud, sed**; and the neuters of certain pronouns; e.g. **illud, istud, quod, quid.** In the earliest language it appears to have been the characteristic of the ablative singular; e.g. **bonod patred**, &c. (§ 160. 6).

The following combinations of consonants are found to end 271 Latin words. With few exceptions they are either in nominatives singular of nouns, or the third person of verbs.

1. **s** preceded

(*a*) by certain explosives; i.e. **ps, mps, rps; bs, rbs; cs(=x), ns, lx, rx;**

e.g. **adeps, hiemps, stirps; cælebs, urbs; edax, lanx, calx, arx;** &c. Also the words **siremps, abs, ex, mox, sex, vix.**

(*b*) by a nasal or liquid; i.e. **ns, ls, rs;**

e.g. **amans, frons, puls, ars.** Each of these combinations is unstable (e.g. **homo** for **homons, consul** for **consuls, arbor** for **arbors**); but is here preserved owing to one consonant having been already sacrificed; viz. **amans** for **amants; frons** for **fronts** or **fronds; puls** for **pults; ars** for **arts.** In **trans, quotiens,** the combination is not more stable: comp. **tramitto, quoties.**

2. **t** preceded by **n,** or rarely by **l, r, s;** i.e. **nt, lt, rt, st;**

e.g. **amant, amaverint,** &c. The only instances of the other combinations are **vult, fert, est, ast, post.**

3. **c** preceded by **n,** i.e. **nc.** Only in the following, **nunc, tunc, hinc, illinc, istinc; hunc, hanc; illunc, illanc;** &c.

The division of a word into syllables appears to have been in 272 accordance with the general principles (see § 15)[1]; that is to say,

1. the division was made in the middle of a consonant.

2. the tendency was to pronounce with a vowel as many of the following consonants as were so pronounceable.

3. the admissibility of a particular combination of consonants in the *middle* of a word depends on the laws of phonetics, not on the particular causes, partly etymological, partly accentual (the last syllable, where there is more than one, being in Latin always unaccented, § 296), which controlled the occurrence of consonants at the *end* of a word. But the laws of phonetics in this matter depend on the Roman mode of pronunciation, not on our mode; e.g. **ts, ds** were not stable; &c.

That such was the mode in which the Romans actually pro- 273 nounced is shewn by the following facts:

1. Vowels are affected by the consonants *following* them; viz. **ĕ** before **r** is retained instead of being changed to **ĭ** (§ 234, 204. 184); **ŏ** or **ŭ** before **ll** is changed to **e** (§ 213. 4, also § 204); the short

---

[1] See some discussion of this matter in the Preface.

vowel before l is ŏ or ŭ, not ĭ or ĕ, as before n &c. (§ 176. 2).
So ĕ remains before two consonants (§ 234. 3. *b*).

2. Consonants are affected by the consonants *following;* e.g.
scribtus is changed to scriptus, the pronunciation being script-tus,
not scrib-tus or scri-bdus. (Even in the few cases where a consonant is affected by the preceding consonant, the combination of the
two (or more consonants) in the *same* syllable is presumed; e.g.
dividtum could not have been divid-tum or it would not have become
divissum or divīsum).

3. A syllable with a short vowel is treated as long, if two
consonants *follow* the vowel. This means that though the vowel is
short, the aggregation of consonants occupies as much time in pronouncing, as if the vowel were long. The exception to this rule of
prosody, which a mute and liquid form, is in accordance with the
principle of division of syllables; e.g. patris cannot be divided into
patr-ris but into pat-tris (where the double t represents not twice
t but the two halves of one t, §§ 9. 15).

4. A vowel is often lengthened to compensate for the extrusion
of a consonant *following* (§ 35). The consonant must therefore
belong to the preceding vowel, or that vowel could not be entitled
to the compensation. The so-called compensation is in truth a natural
phonetic effect of the effort to pronounce a difficult combination of
letters.

The division of syllables in *writing*, which is found in inscrip- 274
tions of the eighth and ninth centuries U.C. and the MSS. of the
fourth or fifth century after Christ[1] or earlier (if any), is (though
not quite invariably) as follows:

1. Where a single consonant is between two vowels the division
is before it; e.g. dede | rit, protu | lerint, publi | ce, ma | num, &c.

2. Where two consonants come together the division is between
them; e.g. op | tima, res | ponsum, ig | nota, præs | to, tran | sisse,
&c.

3. Where three consonants come together the division is after
the first two, unless the second and third be a mute and liquid, in
which case the division is before both; e.g. Vols | ci, abs | cedimus,
cons | pexisset, obs | tinati, Quinc | tius, cunc | ta; ins | tructo,
cas | tris, pos | tremo.

4. The letter x is treated as a single consonant; e.g. eni | xa,
di | xit, pro | xumus.

_____

[1] See Mommsen, *Livi Cod. Veron.* p. 163—166. *Mon. Ancyr.*
p. 145. *Stadtrecht d. Salpensa,* &c. p. 505.

(It is obvious that if the division in pronunciation takes place in the middle of a consonant, the writing cannot mark this accurately. That the preference was given to the second half of the consonant is no doubt due to tne fact, that in the case of **p**, **k**, **t** the distinctive power of the sound consists entirely, and in **b**, **g**, **d** considerably, in the slight puff or explosion which follows the separation of the organs (cf. § 57). When three consonants occur together, the writing conforms better to what is above shewn to have been the pronunciation.)

The early inscriptions avoided division of a word altogether. Augustus (Suet. *Aug.* 87) wrote the superabundant letters over or under the word. MSS. in the sixth century (e.g. the Florentine MS. of the Digest) began to follow Priscian's rules, which were borrowed from the Greeks; e.g. **perfe | ctus, i | gnominia**, &c.

CHAPTER XII.

QUANTITY OF SYLLABLES[1].

THAT part of grammar which treats of the Quantity of Sylla- 275 bles is often called *Prosody*, a term which the ancients applied principally to *accentuation.*

If the voice dwells upon a syllable in pronouncing it, it is called a *long* syllable: if it passes rapidly over it, it is called a *short* syllable.

Long syllables are marked in grammars by a straight line over the vowel: thus, **aūdī**.

Short syllables are marked by a curved line over the vowel: thus, **rĕgĕ**.

Two short syllables are considered to occupy the same time as one long syllable.

A *syllable* is long or short, either because it contains a *vowel* naturally long or short; or on account of the position of its vowel.

---

1 Much use in this chapter has been made of Luc. Müller's *De re metrica.*

i. Quantity of vowels not in the last syllable of 276 a word.

__ 1. All diphthongs are long (except before another vowel); e.g. aurum; deīnde; &c.

2. All vowels which have originated from contraction are long; e.g. cōgo for cŏ-ăgo, mōmentum for mŏvĭmentum, tībīcen for tībĭī-cen; &c.

3. The quantity of the radical syllables of a word is *generally* preserved in composition or derivation, even when the vowel is changed; e.g. māter, māternus; cădo, incĭdo; caēdo, incīdo; ămo, ămor, ămīcus, inīmīcus; &c.

Some exceptions will be found under the several vowels, and as regards red and prod (pro), under D (§ 160. 7, 8).

So also almost always where the members of a compound word may be treated as separate words, as quāpropter, mēcum, aliōqui, agrīcultura. But we have sīquidem and quandōquidem (from sī and quandō); and for the compounds of ubĭ, ibĭ, see § 243. 31.

For the quantity of root vowels no rule can be given. The quantity of inflexional or derivative affixes is given in Books II. III.

Greek words usually retain in Latin their own quantity.

ii. Quantity of vowels in the last syllable of a word. 277

(A) *Monosyllables are long.*

Except

(*a*) The enclitics quĕ, nĕ, vĕ, which are always appended to other words.

(*b*) Words ending with b, d, t; e.g. ăb, sŭb, ŏb; ăd, ĭd; ăt, ĕt, tŏt, flĕt, dăt; &c.

(*c*) ĕs (*thou art*), făc, lăc, nĕc, fĕl, mĕl, vĕl, ăn, ĭn, fĕr, pĕr, tĕr, vĭr, cŏr, quĭs (nom. sing.), ĭs, bĭs, cĭs, ŏs (*a bone*). The nom. masculine hic is not frequently short. (ēs in Plaut., Ter.)

(B) *In polysyllables.* 278

1. a and e (*and Greek* ў) *final are short.*

Except a in

(*a*) Abl. sing. of nouns with a- stem; e.g. musā.

(*b*) Imperative sing. act. of verbs with a- stem; e.g. amā.

(*c*) Indeclinable words; e.g. ergā, intrā, quadragintā; but pută (Pers. and Mart.), ită, quiă, ejă.

(*d*) Greek vocatives from nominatives in ās; e.g. Aeneā, Pallā: and Greek nom. sing. of a- stems; e.g. Electrā. Cf. §§ 472. 473.

Except e in   279

(*a*) Gen. dat. abl. sing. of nouns with e- stems; e.g. faciē; so also hŏdiē.

(*b*) Imperative sing. act. of verbs with e- stems; e.g. monē; but in cave (Hor. Ov.), and vide (Phædr. Pers.) it is sometimes short (§ 233. 4).

(*c*) Adverbs from adjectives; with o- stems; e.g. doctē, to which add fĕrē, fermē, ohē; but benĕ, malĕ, infernĕ, supernĕ; tĕmĕre is only found before a vowel. Mactĕ, probably an adverb, also has e short.

(*d*) Greek neut. pl.; e.g. tempē, pelagē; fem. sing. crambē, Circē; masc. voc. Alcidē.

2. i, o, u *final are long.*   28o

Except i in

(*a*) mihĭ, tibĭ, sibĭ, ubĭ, ibĭ, in which i is common, and quăsĭ, nĭsĭ. (See § 243. 3.)

(*b*) Greek nom. acc. neuters sing.; e.g. sinapĭ: vocatives; e.g. Parĭ, Amaryllĭ: rarely dat. sing. Minoidĭ.

Except ŏ in   281

(*a*) citŏ, immŏ, modŏ (and compounds), duŏ, egŏ, cĕdŏ and endŏ (old form of in). Rarely ergŏ. Martial, Juvenal, &c., have introŏ, porrŏ, serŏ, octŏ, &c.; modo has sometimes final o long in Lucretius and earlier poets.

(*b*) In the present tense of the verbs sciŏ, nesciŏ, putŏ, volŏ, used parenthetically, o is sometimes short: and occasionally in and after the Augustan age in other verbs with short penult; e.g. rogŏ, vetŏ, nuntiŏ, obsecrŏ. Instances of other parts of the verb or of long penults are rarer; e.g. estŏ, cæditŏ, oderŏ, dabŏ, tendŏ, tollŏ, credŏ.

(*c*) In Nominatives of Proper names with consonant stems **ŏ** is common, e.g. **Pollio, Scīpio, Cūrio, Naso**; sometimes **virgŏ, nemŏ, homŏ**, and other appellatives in Martial, Juvenal, &c.

Datives and ablatives in **o** are never short, except the ablative gerund once or twice in Juvenal and Seneca.

3. *Final syllables ending in any other single conso-* 282 *nant than* s *are short.*

But the final syllable is long in

(*a*) all cases of **illic, istic**, except the nom. masc.

(*b*) all compounds of **pār**, e.g. **dispār, compār**.

(*c*) **alēc, liēn.**

(*d*) **īit, petīit**, and their compounds (and of course **ît, petît** as contracted perfects).

(*e*) some Greek nominatives in -**er**; e.g. **cratēr, charactēr, aēr**; **æthēr**; and some cases in -**n**; e.g. **sirēn** (nom.), **Æneān** (acc.), **Euclidēn** (acc.), **epigrammatōn** (gen. pl.); &c.

4. *Of the final syllables in* s,   283
         as, os, es, *are long.*

Except

(*a*) **ănăs** (probably); **exŏs; compŏs, impŏs; pĕnĕs.**

(*b*) nom. sing. in -**es** of nouns with consonant stems, which have **ĕtis, ĭtis, ĭdis**, in genitive, e.g. **sĕgĕs, mīlĕs, obsĕs**: but **pariēs, abiēs, ariēs, Cĕrēs.**

(*c*) compounds of **es** (from **sum**), e.g. **abĕs.**

(*d*) some Greek words; e.g. **Iliăs** (nom.), **craterăs** (acc. pl.); **Delŏs** (n. sing.), **Erinnyŏs, chlāmydŏs** (gen. sing.), **Arcadĕs, cra-tērĕs** (nom. pl.); **Cynosargĕs** (neut. s.).

5. us *and* **is** *are short.*   284

Except **ūs** in

(*a*) gen. sing. and nom. and acc. plu. of nouns with -**u** stems.

(*b*) nom. sing. of consonant nouns, when genitive singular has long penultimate, e.g. **tellūs** (tellūris), **palūs** (palūdis), **virtus** (virtūtis).

(*c*) some Greek names; **Sapphūs** (gen. s.), **Panthūs** (nom. s.).

Except ĭs in   285

(*a*) dat. and abl. plural, e.g. mensīs, vobīs, quīs; so gratīs, forīs. Also in acc. (and nom.) plural of -i stems; e.g. omnīs.

(*b*) 2nd pers. sing. pres. ind. of verbs with -ī stems; e.g. audīs: also possīs (and other compounds of sīs), velīs, nolīs, malīs.

(*c*) 2nd pers. sing. of perf. subj. and compl. fut. in which ĭs *is* common; e.g. viderĭs. (But see Book II.)

(*d*) Samnīs, Quirīs. Sangvis sometimes (always in Lucr.), pulvis (once Enn., once Verg.), has -īs.

(*e*) some Greek words; Simoīs, Eleusīs, Salamīs (nom. sing.).

iii   Quantity of syllables by position in the same   286
word

1   A syllable ending with a vowel (or diphthong) immediately   287
followed by another syllable beginning with a vowel, or with h and a
vowel, is short; as, vĭa, praĕustus, contrăhit.

Except

(*a*) In the genitives of pronouns, &c. in -ius; e.g. illīus, where
i is common. In alīus (gen. case) the i is always long: in
solius it is short once in Ter. In utrius, neutrius it is not
found short, but in utriusque frequently[1].

(*b*) the penultimate a in the old genitive of nouns with -a
stems; e.g. aulāī. So also e in dīēī, and, in Lucretius, rēī, and
(once) fīdēī. Also ēī (dat. pronoun), unless contracted eī.

(*c*) a or e before i (where i is a vowel) in all the cases of
proper names ending in ius; e.g. Gāĭŭs, Pompēĭŭs (but see
§ 139).

(*d*) The syllable fĭ in fīo (except before er; e.g. fĭĕri, fĭĕrem).

(*e*) The first syllable of ĕheu! and the adjective dīus. In
Dĭana and ŏhē the first syllable is common.

In Greek words a long vowel is not shortened by coming before
another vowel; e.g. Nerēĭdĭ, Ēōō (but cf. § 229), Aenēās, āĕra,
Maeōtia.

2. A syllable[2] containing a vowel immediately followed by two
consonants, or by x, or z, is long; as, regēnt, strīx.

But if the two consonants immediately following a short vowel
be the first a mute or f, and the second a liquid, the vowel remains

---

[1] See Ritschl, *Opusc.* II. 678 foll.
[2] For the length of the *vowel* itself in some cases see §§ 151 note, 167. 2.

short in prose and in comic poets, though in other verse it is frequently lengthened.

The following combinations occur in Latin words: pr, br, cr, gr, tr[1], dr, fr; pl, cl, fl; e.g. apro, tĕnebræ, vŏlucris, agrum, patris, qvadrīga, vafrum; maniplus, assecla, refluus.

Bl also occurs in publicus, but the first syllable is always long (for pouplicus).

In Greek words other combinations allow the vowel to remain short; e.g. Ätlas, Tĕcmessa, Cŷcnus, Dăphne.

Where the combination is due to composition only, the syllable is always lengthened, just as if the words were separate (cf. § 292); e.g. sŭbruo, abluo.

iv. Effect of initial sounds on the final syllable of ²88 a preceding word.

In verse the final syllable of a word is affected by the vowel or consonants at the commencement of the next word, in something the same way in which one syllable is affected by the succeeding syllable in the same word.

1. A final vowel or diphthong or a final syllable in m is omitted (or at least slurred over) in pronunciation, if the next word commence with a vowel or diphthong or h. See the preface.

Thus vidi ipsum, vive hodie, monstrum ingens are read in verse as of no more length than vid-ipsum, viv-hodie, monstr-ingens.

When est follows a vowel or m the e was omitted (see in Book II.).

But the poets (except the early dramatists) refrain in certain cases ²89 from so putting words as to occasion such an elision[2]. Especially it is avoided when the second word begins with a short vowel; viz.

(*a*) Monosyllables ending in long vowel or m are rarely elided before a short syllable, and, particularly, the following are never so elided; sim, dem, stem, rem, spem, spe, do, sto, qui (plur.):

the following are so elided; cum, tum, num, sum, jam, nam, tam, quam, me, te, se, de, mi (dat.), qui (sing.), ni, si, tu.

(*b*) An iambic word, ending in a vowel, in dactylic verse is not elided before a short syllable or an accented long syllable.

---

[1] Arbĭtro, arbitrium, &c.; genetrix, meretrix, are nowhere found with long second syllable.

[2] These statements are abridged from Luc. Müller, p. 283.

(*c*) A cretic ending in a vowel was very rarely elided before a short syllable, except by Catullus, and Horace in Satires.

(*d*) A spondee ending in a vowel, is rarely elided, by Horace in lyrics, or by Ovid and subsequent poets, before a short syllable, except in first foot; e.g. **certe ego, multi inopes, risi ego** (Lucan, Martial).

(*e*) Of words ending in **m** (counting the last syllable as short) a pyrrich is very rarely elided before a short syllable or accented long syllable, except uninflected particles; e.g. **enim, quidem.** A dactyl is rarely elided before a short syllable by Ovid or later writers.

(*f*) Of words ending in **ă** or **ŏ** a pyrrich or dactyl is rarely elided before a short syllable, except (1) in proper names; or (2) in first foot; or (3) in words ending in **ă**, before a word beginning with **ă**; or (4) in the words **cito, ego, modo, duo.**

An elision at the end of a verse before a vowel in the same verse is very rare in any poet, except in Horace's Satires and Epistles. 290

An elision at end of a verse before a vowel at the beginning of the next verse is found not uncommonly in Vergil, only once or twice in other writers' hexameters. In glyconic and sapphic stanzas it is not uncommon; e.g.

> Aut dulcis musti Volcano decoquit umorem
> et foliis. (Verg.)

> Dissidens plebi numero beatorum
> eximit virtus. (Hor.)

An hiatus is however permitted;   291

Always at the end of one verse before an initial vowel in the next verse except in an anapæstic metre.

Occasionally in the same verse; viz.

(*a*) if there is an interruption of the sense; though it is very rare, when the first of the two vowels is short; e.g.

> Promissam eripui genero, arma impia sumpsi. (Verg.)
> Addam cerea pruna: honos erit huic quoque pomo. (Verg.)

(*b*) in arsis, chiefly at the regular cæsura; e.g.

> Stant et juniperi et castaneæ hirsutæ. (Verg.)
> Si pereo, hominum manibus periisse juvabit. (Verg.)

(*c*) in thesis, a long vowel, especially in a monosyllable, is sometimes shortened instead of elided; e.g.

> Credimus? an qui amant ipsi sibi somnia fingunt? (Verg.)
> Hoc motu radiantis Etesiæ in vada ponti. (Cic.)

(*d*) a word ending in **m** is rarely not elided (there being only about seven instances in arsis, and a few of monosyllables in thesis); e. g.

> Miscent inter sese inimicitiam agitantes. (Enn.)
> Sed dum abest quod avemus, id exsuperare videtur. (Lucr.)

2. A short final syllable ending in a consonant is lengthened by 291 an initial consonant in the word following; e. g.

> Vellitur, huic atro liquntur sanguine guttæ! (Verg.)
> Quo Phœbus vocet errantis jubeatque reverti. (Verg.)

3. A short final syllable ending in a vowel is rarely lengthened 293 before two consonants at the beginning of the next word.

This is done before **sp, sc, st**; more rarely still before **pr, br, fr, tr.** There are a few instances in Catullus, Tibullus, Martial, &c. (none in Lucretius, Vergil, Horace, Propertius, Ovid); e. g.

> Nulla fugæ ratio; nulla spes omnia muta. (Cat.)
> 　　　　　Tua si bona nescis
> Servare, frustra clavis inest foribus. (Tib.)

On the other hand a short final vowel is rarely found before **sp, sc, sq, st, gn.**

Lucilius, Lucretius, Horace in Satires, and Propertius have about 23 instances; Vergil one, and that where the sense is interrupted. Other poets have hardly a single instance: the collocation was avoided altogether. But before Greek words, e. g. **zmăragdus,** and (before z in) **Zăcynthus,** instances are found in many poets.

4. The enclitic **-que** is lengthened in arsis not uncommonly by Vergil (before two consonants, or a liquid or **s**), and by Ovid: very rarely by others; e. g.

> Tribulaque traheæque et iniquo pondere rastra. (Verg.)

So once final **a**;

> Dona dehinc auro gravia sectoque elephanto. (Verg.)

5. Occasionally (in Vergil about 50 times) a short final closed 294 syllable is lengthened by the arsis, though the next word begins with a vowel: this is chiefly in the cæsura, or when a proper name or Greek word follows, or where the sense is interrupted; e. g. (all from Vergil):

> Pacem me exanimis et Martis sorte peremptis
> oratis? Equidem et vivis concedere vellem.
> Desine plura puer, et quod nunc instat agamus.

Olli serva datur, operum haud ignara Minervæ,
Ipse, ubi tempus erit, omnes in fonte lavabo.
Pectoribus inhians, spirantia consulit exta.

In thesis it is very rare; e. g.

Si non periret immiserabilis captiva pubes.   (Hor.)

So also Ennius in arsis has sorŏr, genitŏr, clamŏr, jubăr (masc.); venerŏr; populŭs; servăt, memorăt, versăt, manăt; faciĕt, tenĕt, fierĕt, jubĕt, constituĭt, ponĭt, cupĭt (pres.?), ĭt, tinnĭt, voluĭt, velĭt, and a few others.   In thesis he has clamŏr, ponebăt, essĕt, infĭt. (See Nettleship, *Conington's Vergil, Excurs.* to Book XII.)

v.   Peculiarities in early dramatic verse.

In early dramatic verse the quantity of syllables was not so ??? definitely fixed or observed, as in the later dactylic and other verse. The principal cases of *variation* may be classified as follows[1].

1.   Final syllables, afterwards short, were sometimes used with their original long quantity; e. g. famā (nom. s.), sorŏr, patēr, amēt, sciăt, ponebăt, percipĭt, vendidĭt, amēr, loquār, &c.

2.   Final syllables with long vowels were sometimes used as short; e. g. domŏ (abl. s.), probĕ (adv.), tacĕ, manŭ, virĭ, &c.; conrigĭ, bonăs, forăs, dolŏs, ovĕs, manŭs (acc. pl.), bonĭs, &c. Comp. also § 205, 233.

3.   Syllables containing a vowel followed by two consonants were sometimes used as short.   Such are

(*a*) Syllables in the later language written with doubled consonants (cf. § 58); e. g. ĭmmo, ĭlle, simĭllimæ, Philĭppus, esse, ŏcculto, &c.

(*b*) Some syllables with two different consonants; e. g. ĭnter, ĭnterim, ĭntus, ĭnde, ŭnde, nĕmpe, ŏmnis.   So also (according to some) volŭptas, magĭstratus, minĭstrabit, venŭstas, senĕctus, &c. (better volptas, magstratus, &c.); ĕxpediant, ĕxigere, ŭxorem.

4.   Final syllables ending in a consonant were sometimes not lengthened, though the next word began with a consonant; e. g. (in Terence) enĭm vero, auctŭs sit, sorŏr dictast, dabĭt nĕmo, simul conficiam, tamĕn suspicor, &c.; apud is frequently so used: even studĕnt facere.   This licence is most frequent, when the final consonant is m, s, r, or t; and is due to the tendency of the early language to drop the final consonant (see § 86. 152, 5. 193, 5), and to shorten the final vowel.

5.   On the freer use of synizesis, e. g. tvos for tuos, scjo for scio, &c. see § 92. 142.

[1] See Ritschl *Rhein Mus.* (1859), XIV. 395 sq. and *Opusc.* II. Pref. pp 10, 11: Wagner's Pref. to Plaut. *Aulul.* (1866), and to Terence (1869).

7

CHAPTER XIII.

ACCENTUATION.

ACCENT is the elevation of voice, with which one syllable of 296
a word is pronounced, in comparison with the more subdued tone
with which the other syllables are pronounced[1].

Monosyllables always have the accent.

Disyllables have the accent on the penultimate syllable, unless
they are enclitic.

Words of more than two syllables have the accent on the antepenultimate, if the penultimate syllable is short; on the penultimate,
if it is long.

The Romans distinguish between an acute and a circumflex
accent. The circumflex stands only on monosyllables which have
long vowels; and, in words of more than one syllable, on the penultimate, if that have a long vowel, and the final syllable have a short
vowel.

If the acute be marked by a ´ over the vowel; the circumflex by
a ^, the above rules may be illustrated by the following examples:

Monosyllables; áb, mél, fél; árs, párs, níx, fáx; spês, flôs, môs,
lîs; môns, fôns, lûx.

Disyllables; déus, cítus, árat; déo, Cáto, árant; sóllers, póntus,
pónto, lúnă; lûnă, Rômă, vídit.

Polysyllables; Sérgius, fúscina, crédere; Sérgio, fúscinas, créderent,
Metéllus, fenéstra; Metéllo, fenéstræ; Sabíno, prædíves; Sabínus,
Române, amícus, amâre.

All compound words, whether their parts can or cannot be used 297
as separate words, are accented according to the regular rules; e.g.
anhélo, rédimo; úndique, ítaque (*therefore*); ítidem, útinam, póst-
hac, póstmodo, intrórsus,quicúmque, jandúdum, exadvérsum,qúodsi,
fórsan, &c. So respública or rês pública.

---

[1] This subdued tone is called by grammarians the *grave accent.*
The principal rules of Latin accentuation are given by Quintilian,
I. 5. 22—31.

A few words, called enclitics, always appended to other words, 298 caused, according to the Roman grammarians, the accent to fall on the last syllable of the word to which they were attached. These are -que (*and*), -ne, -ve, -ce, -met, -pte, -dum, and also the separable words, quando, inde; e.g. itáque (*and so*), utíque (*and as*), illíce, hicíne, mihímet, respicédum, éxinde, écquando, &c. So also que in pleráque. In the case of many words called enclitics (owing to their own quantity) the accentuation is the same, whether they be considered as enclitics proper, or parts of a compound; e.g. quandóquidem, scílicet, quibúslibet, quantúmvis, &c.

Prepositions and adverbs used as prepositions (e.g. intra) were 299 regarded as closely attached to the word which they precede, and belong to. In inscriptions they are frequently written as one word with their nouns. The Roman grammarians considered them to have no accent when thus preceding their noun or a word (e.g. adjective or genitive case) dependent on it; e.g. ad éas, adhûc, in fóro, virtútem propter pátris, &c. But if they follow their noun, they are said to retain their own accent; e.g. quæprópter, quácúm, but cum after personal pronouns is said to be enclitic; e.g. nobíscum.

(L. Müller, resting on the usage of dactylic poets as to the cæsura, &c., confines this to the words me, te, se, nos, vos, in company with disyllabic prepositions in -ter, -tra; e.g. inter nós, intra sé).

So also the relative was unaccented, the interrogative accented; e.g. quo díe, *on which day:* quô díe? *on which day?*

Apparent exceptions to the general rules are some words in 300 which the accent remains, notwithstanding the loss of a syllable; e.g.

1. Some words where the accent is on what is now the last syllable; e.g. illíc, prodûc, tantôn, bonân, satín, nostrâs, for illíce, prodûce, tantône, bonâne, satísne, nostrâtis (§ 418), &c.

2. Some where the accent is on the penult instead of on the antepenult; e.g. (gen. and voc.) Valéri, Vergíli, &c. (for Valerie, Valerii; Vergilie, Vergilii; &c.); and the verbs (really not complete compounds) calefácis, mansuefácit, &c.

It would appear[1], though little reference is made to such a doc- 301 trine in the Roman grammarians, that words of more than three syllables must have frequently had besides the principal accent another subordinate one; e.g. numerávimus, sisterêmus, longitûdo, difficultátibus had probably a subordinate accent on the first syllables.

---

[1] See Corssen *Ausspr.* II. p. 242 foll. ed. 1.

7—2

The first part of a compound especially may have retained to some extent the accent which it had as a simple word; e.g. pérgrándis, prætenre, vérsipéllis, úndevigínti.

The frequent omission or absorption of a short vowel, or of a syllable which has according to the general rules the accent, leads to the inference that there must have been a tendency to put the accent nearer to the beginning of the word than the antepenultimate or penultimate syllable[1]. The effort to do this, and the resistance made by the heavy dragging of the unaccented syllables after it, were the cause of the omission, e.g. intellexísti became intelléxti; dehíbeo, débeo; gavídeo, gaúdeo; surrípuit, súrpuit; calcâre, cálcar; armígerus, ármiger; puerítia, puértia; &c.

So the weakening of the vowel in compounds; inquiro for inquæro, concludo for com-claudo, abreptus for ab raptuz, is difficult to explain, so long as the affected syllable is considered as accented.

Similarly the change of ille-ce to illice, illic, suggests doubts as to the truth of the doctrine respecting enclitics, given above § 298.

---

[1] Ib. p. 321 foll.

BOOK II.

INFLEXIONS.

BOOK II.[1]

INFLEXIONS.

CHAPTER I.

OF INFLEXION IN GENERAL.

WORDS may be divided into two classes, those which have 303 *inflexions*, and those which have not.

Nouns, pronouns, and verbs are *inflected:* other words are not.

Inflexions are those alterations or additions, which are made in a 304 word in order to fit it for different functions, as part of a sentence. Thus in **mulier**, *woman;* **mulier-is** *woman's;* **mulier-es**, *women;* **mulier-um**, *women's;* ama-t, *love-s;* ama-sti, *love-dst;* amatus, *love-d;* ama-ns, *lov-ing:* **pu-n-go**, *I prick;* **pu-pug-i**, *I prick-ed;* **pu-n-c-tus**, *prick-ed;* we have the same noun or verb differently inflected.

That part of a word, which is essentially the same under such 305 different uses, is called the *stem.* In the above words **mulier**, **ama**, and **pug** are the stems. The suffix, which forms the inflexion, often affects or is affected by the neighbouring letters of the stem, so that the two melt as it were into one another.

A stem is in Latin rarely used without having, or at least having had, some inflexions; e.g. **consul** is both stem and nominative case; but this is probably because the nominative suffix is incompatible with 1 (see § 176, 5).

---

[1] Throughout this book great and constant use has been made of F. Neue's *Formenlehre* Th. i. (1866); Th. ii. (1861). The authorities, on which the statements in the text are based, will usually be found there. Frequent reference has also been made to Ruddimann's (ed. Stallbaum 1823), Schneider's (1819), G. T. Krüger's (1842), Madvig's (3rd ed. 1857), and Key's (2nd ed. 1858) Grammars. Also to Bücheler's *Grundriss der latein. Declination* (1866); besides Corssen, Ritschl, &c.

Different nouns and verbs and other words have frequently a 306 common part: such common part is called a *root.* Thus the root sta- is common to sta-re, sta-tio, sta-tuo, sta-men, sta-tūra, sta-tim, &c., *to stand, standing, stablish, standing-thread, standing-height, instantly,* &c. A root may be used as a stem, or the stem may contain the root with alterations or additions. The additions made to form a stem from a root are discussed in Book III.

The inflexions of nouns and pronouns are in the main the same, and will be treated of together. The inflexions of verbs are quite distinct, but the formation of certain verbal nouns, though properly belonging to Book III., is generally treated in connexion with the inflexions of the verbs.

CHAPTER II.

OF NOUN INFLEXIONS, AND PARTICULARLY OF GENDER.

THE inflexions of nouns are always additions to, or alterations in, 307 the *end* of the stem. They serve to mark the gender, the number, and the case, of the word.

As regards *gender* a two-fold distinction was made; (1) accord- 308 ing as sex could be attributed or not; (2) according as the sex attributed was male or female.

Names of things, to which sex was not attributed, are said to be of the *neuter* gender: but the Romans, yielding to their imaginations, attributed sex to many things, which really had it not, and thus living creatures are but a small number of the objects, which have names of the *masculine* and *feminine* genders.

The distinction of gender is not marked throughout all the 309 cases. In the nouns put together as the first class, the feminine was perhaps originally different from the masculine and neuter throughout, and it still is so in most cases. The masculine and neuter differ only in the nominative singular, and nominative and accusative plural.

In the second class, the masculine and feminine are alike throughout: the neuter differs from both in the accusative, and usually in the nominative.

The neuter form is always the same in the nominative and accusative cases. In the singular of the first class this form is the same as that of the accusative masculine: in the second class it is the bare stem, unprotected by a suffix, and therefore sometimes withered: in the plural of both declensions it always ends in -a.

The real significance of the inflexions is best seen in adjectives, 310 because they have the same stem modified, if of the first class, to represent all three genders; if of the second class, usually only to represent the masculine and feminine genders as distinguished from the neuter; i.e. sex as distinguished from no sex; e.g. **bonus** (m.), **bona** (f.), **bonum** (n.); **tristis** (m. f.), **triste** (n.); **amans** (m. f. n.), but accusative **amantem** (m. f.), **amans** (n.).

Substantives differ from adjectives as regards their inflexions, 311 chiefly in being fixed to one gender only. But

1. Some substantival stems have a masculine and feminine form; e.g. **Julius** (m.); **Julia** (f.); **equus** (m.); **equa** (f.).

2. A few substantives of the first class are feminine, though with stems in -o; others masculine, though with stems in -a.

3. A substantive of the second class may be masculine, or feminine, or both, the form being indeterminate.

4. Some suffixes of derivation are exclusively used for substantives, and not for adjectives: some again are confined to the masculine gender, others to the feminine. E.g. no adjective is formed with the suffix -iōn: again all abstract substantives, if formed by the suffix -iōn, or -tāt are feminine; if formed by the suffix -ōr are masculine.

It follows from the above, that the gender is not always known 312 by the form.

The test of a substantive's being of a particular gender is the use of an adjective of that particular gender as an attribute to it; e.g. **humus** is known to be feminine, because **dura humus**, not **durus humus** is used.

An adjective, where the form is not determinately significant, is commonly said to be in the same gender, as that of the substantive to which it is used as an attribute.

. But though the sex attributed to the person or thing is not 313 always expressed by the form, the gender was never assigned in defiance of the true sex in persons, nor in animals, if the sex was of importance. Many animals are denoted by a substantive of only one form and only one gender, the masculine or feminine having been originally selected, according as the male or female was most frequently thought of. Animals of the kind generally would be spoken of, without distinction, by this noun, whether it were masculine or feminine; e.g. olōres (m.) *swans* in general; anătes *ducks*, including *drakes*. If a distinction is important, the word mas or femina, as the case may be, is added; e.g olor femina, *the female swan;* anas mas, *the male duck*. Such nouns are called epicœna (Quint. i. 1. 24).

In the same way a feminine, e.g. Ætna, can be spoken of as masculine, if mons be added; a river can be neuter, if flumen be added: and the appropriate change of gender takes place sometimes without the explanatory word being expressed; e.g. Eunuchus acta est, i.e. *the play Eunuchus;* Centauro invehitur magna, i.e. *on the ship Centauros*. So occasionally herba or litera is understood.

The genders assigned to names of persons, animals, or vegetables, 314 and of some other classes of natural objects were as follows:

1. *Names of persons:* Names of males are masculine, of females feminine. Thus proper names of females, derived from the Greek, though retaining the neuter suffix corresponding to their neuter gender in Greek, are in Latin feminine; e.g. in Plautus, and Terence, Planēsium, Glycĕrium, Phronēsium, Stephănium, Delphium.

For *Appellatives*, especially those derived from age or relation- 315 ship, there are separate forms, sometimes from different roots, for the males and females; e.g. mas, femina; păter, māter; ăvus, avia; proăvus, proavia, &c.; filius, filia; puer, puella; nĕpos, neptis, &c.; vir, mulier; mărītus, uxor; vitrīcus, nŏverca; prīvignus, prīvigna; sŏcer, socrus; gĕner, nŭrus; frāter, sŏror; pătruus, amita; ăvuncŭlus, mātertĕra; verna (m.), ancilla (f.); antistes, antistīta; hospes, hospĭta; cliens, clienta; tibīcen, tibicīna; fidīcen, fidicīna. So also many (derived from verbs) with -or for masculine, and -rix for feminine; e.g. tonsor, tonstrix.

Homo, animans (of a rational creature) are masculine; virgo and matrōna, feminine.

Others (all of 2nd class of nouns) are common: viz. conjunx, părens, affinis, patruēlis, sĕnex, jŭvĕnis, ădŭlescens, infans. In Ennius and Nævius puer, nĕpos, and socrus are common. So are ranked hospes (in the poets) and antistes. In none of these, except puer (when used as f.) and verna is the form opposed to the sex.

Other personal appellatives are usually or exclusively masculine, 316 because the offices, occupations, &c., denoted were filled by men, or at least by men as much as by women.

The following are sometimes feminine; cīvis, mūnīceps, con-
tubernālis, hostis, exul, vātes, săcerdos, augur (once or twice),
dux, cŏmes, sătelles, custos, interpres, mīles, vindex, index, jūdex,
testis, præses, hēres, artifex, auctor. Others are used of females,
but without a feminine adjective; e.g. ŏpĭfex, carnĭfex, auspex,
sponsor, viātor, defensor, tutor, auceps, manceps.

So also some with -a stems (see § 335); aurīga, advĕna, &c.

Others are nowhere found applied to females; e.g. cornĭcen,
tĭbīcen, tŭbīcen; latro, fullo, mango, nĕbŭlo.

Some words which are only metaphorically applied to men or 317
women retain their original gender; e.g. mancĭpium (n.) *a chattel*;
acroāma (n.) *a musical performer*, scortum (n.), prostĭbŭlum (n.);
vigĭliæ (f.), excŭbiæ (f.), ŏpĕræ (f.), dēlĭciæ (f.); auxĭlia (n.).

2. *Names of Animals.* For some quadrupeds, with which the 318
Romans had much to do, separate forms are found for the male and
female. The stems in -o are masc., those in -a fem.

Agnus, agna; ăper, apra; aries (m.), vervex (m.), ŏvis (f.);
ăsĭnus, asina; asellus, asella; hircus, căper, capra; cătus (m.),
fēles (f.); cătŭlus, catula; cervus, cerva; cŏlumbus, columba;
ĕquus, equa; gallus, gallīna; hædus, căpella; hinnus, hinna; jŭ-
vencus, juvenca; leo (m.), lea, or (Greek) leæna; lŭpus, lupa;
mūlus, mula; porcus, porca; sīmius, simia (also of *apes* in general);
taurus, vacca; verres, scrōfa; vītŭlus, vitula; ursus, ursa.

(Of these ovis is said to have been also used as masc. in old
sacrificial language. Varro had the expression lupus femina: Cato
had porcus femina; an old law (ap. Gell. 4. 3. 3) agnus femina.)

For most other animals there was only one form; e.g.—

Quadrupeds (besides above); bĭdens (f. *sc.* ovis); bos (m. f.); 319
cămēlus (m. f.); cănis (m. f.); damma (m. f.); ĕlĕphans, elephantus
(m. rarely f.); fīber (m.); glīs (m.); hystrix (f.); lĕpus (m.
rarely f.); lynx (f. rarely m.); mus (m.); mustella (f.); nītella
(f.); panthēra (f.); pardus (m.); quadrŭpes (m. f. n.); sorex
(m.); sus (m. f.); talpa (f. rarely m.); tigris (f. rarely m.); ves-
pertĭlio (m.); vulpes (f.).

Birds: e.g. accĭpĭter (m. rarely f.); āles (m. f.); ănas (f.); anser 320
(m. rarely f.); ăquĭla (f.); ăvis (f.); bŭbo (m. rarely f.); cĭcōnia
(f.); cīris (f.); cornix (f.); cŏtŭrnix (f.); cygnus (m.), ŏlor (m.);
fŭlica and fulix (f.); grăcŭlus (m.); grus (f. rarely m.); hĭrundo
(f.); ībis (f.); luscĭnius (m.), luscinia (f. also of *nightingales* in
general); mĕrŭla (f.); miluus, milvus (m.); noctua (f.); oscen

(m. f.); pălumbes (m. f.), palumbus (m.); passer (m.); păvo (m.);
perdix (m. f.); pīca (f.); stŭrnus (m.); strŭthŏcămēlus (m. f.);
turdus (rarely f.); turtur (m. f.); vultur (m.).

Reptiles: e. g. anguis (m. f.); būfo (m.); chamæleon (m.); 321
cŏlŭber (m.), colubra (f. also of *snakes* generally); crŏcŏdīlus (m.);
drăco (m.); lăcertus (m.), lacerta (f. also of *lizards* generally); răna
(f.); serpens (m. f.); stelio (m.); testūdo (f.).

Fishes: ăcĭpenser (m.); mūgil (m.); muræna (f.); mullus (m.);
piscis (m.); rhombus (m.); sălar (m.); scărus (m.); sōlea (f.).

Invertebrates: ăpis (f.); cĭcāda (f.); ărāneus (m.), aranea (f.
also of *spiders* generally); cīmex (m.); cŭlex (m.); formīca (f.);
hĭrūdo (f.); lendes (pl. f.); līmax (f. rarely m.); mūrex (m.);
musca (f.); păpĭlio (m.); pĕdis (m. f.); pŭlex (m.); sēpia (f.);
vermis (m.); vespa (f.).

3. Almost all *trees* and *shrubs* are feminine. Some of them 322
have -o stems (§ 336), but these are mostly from the Greek.

Of *plants* and *flowers*, some are masculine, the rest chiefly
feminine.

Names of *fruits* and *woods* are often neuter, with stems in -o,
and some *trees* are also neuter, probably because the name was first
applied to the product.

The principal masculine names are: ăcanthus, ămārăcus (also f.),
asparăgus, bōlētus, călămus, carduus, crŏcus, cȳtĭsus (also f.), dūmus, fīcus (also f.), fungus, helleborus (often -um n.), intŭbus (also
intŭbum n.), juncus, lōtus (usually f.), mālus (but as an *apple
tree* f.), muscus, ōleaster, pampĭnus (also f.), raphănus, rhamnus,
rŭbus, rŭmex (also f.), scirpus.

The principal neuter names are ăpium, ăcer, balsămum, lāser,
păpăver (also m.), pĭper, rōbur, sīler, sīser (but in plural siseres),
tŭber (*truffle*): and the *fruits* or *woods* arbŭtum, buxum, &c. (but
castănea, ōlea, bălănus, are also used as fruits, and retain their fem.
gen. So buxus and buxum for *a flute*).

4. Names of *jewels* are mainly feminine and Greek. 323

Masculine are ădămas, beryllus, carbunculus, chrysŏlĭthus (also
f.), ŏnyx (as a *marble*, or a *cup*), ŏpălus, sardŏnyx (also f.), smă-
ragdus, &c.

5. Names of *towns, countries,* &c. have, if of Latin origin, their 324
gender marked by their termination; e. g. masculine; Veji, Puteŏli,
properly the *Veians,* &c.: feminine; e. g. Afrĭca (sc. terra), Itălĭa,
Rōma: neuter; Tarentum, Bĕnĕventum, Reāte, Præneste, Anxur (n.
also m. of the mountain), Tĭbur (n.).

Of Greek nouns many retain their Greek gender (though often with stems in -o), others, owing sometimes to their termination being misunderstood, have other genders: e. g. **Argos** usually neut., but Statius has frequently **patrios Argos, afflictos Argos**, &c.; Livy occasionally **Argi**, as nom. pl.

The Spanish towns are sometimes feminine in -is, e. g. **Illiturgis**; sometimes neuter in -i, e.g. **Illiturgi.**

Some neuter plurals are found; e.g. **Leuctră, Artaxătă, Tigrano-certă.**

6. Names of *mountains* are all masculine, except those with marked feminine terminations (stems in -a or Greek -e); e.g. **Ætna, Ida, Rhŏdŏpē,** &c.; or neuter terminations (nom. in -um, Greek in -e); e. g. **Pēlion, Sōractĕ. Alpes** (pl.) is feminine. ₃₂₅

7. Names of *rivers* are masculine, even those with -a stems, except **Allia, Duria, Sagra, Lēthē, Styx**, which are feminine. But sometimes rivers are made neuter by prefixing flumen and giving a termination in -um; e.g. **flumen Rhenum** (Hor.); **flumen Granĭcum** (Plin.); &c.

8. Names of *winds* are masculine; e.g. **ăquĭlo, Vulturnus**, &c. So also **Etēsiæ** (pl.).

All *indeclinable* words are neuter: e.g. **fas, nefas, instar** (except barbaric names, e.g. **Abraham**); and to this class belong infinitives (e.g. **non dolere istud, totum hœc philosophari**); words used as names of themselves (e.g. **istuc** 'taceo,' **hoc ipsum** 'honesti'); and often the letters of the alphabet (as '**c in g** commutato'); but these last are sometimes feminine, **litera** being expressed or understood. ₃₂₆

CHAPTER III.

OF NOUN INFLEXIONS OF NUMBER.

IN Latin the only distinction in point of number which is marked by inflexions is between one (*singular* number), and more than one (*plural* number). ₃₂₇

The particular inflexions of number will be best treated in connexion with the case inflexions.

Some nouns, in consequence of their meaning, have no plural, others have no singular.

1. The following have ordinarily no plural :

(*a*) *Proper names of persons and places* ; e. g. **Metellus, Roma,** &c.; 328 but **Metelli** of several members of the family; **Camilli** of persons with qualities like **Camillus** : **Galliæ,** of the two divisions of Gaul, **Gallia Cisalpina** and **Transalpina** ; **Volcani** of *gods* with different attributes, or bearing the name of Vulcan, or of statues of Vulcan, &c.

(*b*) *Single natural objects* ; e. g. **sol,** *the sun* ; **tellus,** *the earth* ; but **soles** is used in discussions as to whether there are more *suns* than one, or as equivalent to *days,* &c.

(*c*) *Continua* ; i. e. natural objects which are measured or weighed, not numbered, e. g. **cruor,** *blood* ; **ros,** *dew* ; **æs,** *bronze* ; **frumentum,** *corn* ; **fāba,** *beans,* as a class ; **fumus,** *smoke.* But these are used in the plural, when several *kinds,* or distinct *pieces* or *drops,* are meant ; e. g. **vīna,** *different wines* ; **nīves,** *flakes of snow* ; **fābæ,** *individual beans* ; **æra,** *bronze works of art* ; **carnes,** *pieces of flesh* ; **fumi,** *wreaths of smoke.* In poetry the plural is sometimes used without such a distinction.

(*d*) *Abstract nouns* ; e. g. **justitia,** *justice* ; but not uncommonly the plural is used even in these in order to express the occurrence of the event or exhibition of the quality at several times or in several forms, e. g. **virtutes,** *virtues* ; **cupiditates,** *desires* ; **odia,** *cases of hatred* ; **conscientiæ,** *several persons' consciousness (of guilt)* ; **mortes,** *deaths (of several persons)* ; **otia,** *periods of rest* ; **adventus,** *arrivals* ; **maturitates,** *culminations* ; **vicinitates,** *position of people as neighbours* ; **lapsus,** *slips* ; **calores, frigora,** *times of heat, of cold* ; **similitudines,** *resemblances* ; &c.

2. The following are found only or ordinarily in the plural; 329 though some of them correspond to what in other languages are denoted by singulars.

(*a*) *Names of certain towns or places,* &c.: **Thebæ, Tigranocerta, Leuctra,** **Veji** (originally the *Veians*), **Cannæ** (i. e. *Reeds*): **Gades, Cumæ.** So **Pergama,** *the towers of Troy,* **Tartara.**

(*b*) *Groups of islands and mountains,* &c. ; e. g. **Cyclădes, Alpes, Esquiliæ, Tempe** (properly *glens*).

(*c*) *Bodies of persons* : e. g. **decemvĭri,** *a commission of ten* (though we have **decemvir** also used of *a commissioner*) &c.; **majōres,** *ancestors* ; **prŏcĕres, primores,** *leading men* ; **lībĕri,** *children* ; **infĕri,** *the spirits below* ; **supĕri,** *the Gods above* ; **cælites,** *the heavenly ones* ; **penātes,** *the hearth gods* ; **manes,** *the ghosts* ; **gratiæ** *the Graces* ; **Furiæ,** *the Furies* ; **Diræ,** *Curses* (conceiv d as goddesses) ; &c.

(*d*) *Parts of the body;* e.g. **artus,** *the joints;* **cervīces** (before Hortensius), *the neck* (*neckbones*?); **exta, intestīna, viscĕra,** *the internal organs;* **fauces,** *the throat;* **lactes,** *the lacteal vessels;* **pantīces,** *bowels;* **rēnes,** *kidneys;* **tŏri,** *the muscles;* **praecordia,** *midriff;* **īlia,** *loins.*

(*e*) *Names of feasts or days;* e.g. **Calendæ, Nōnæ, Idus; fēriæ,** 330 *the feast-day;* **nundīnæ,** *market-day;* **Baccānālia,** *feast of Bacchus;* &c.

(*f*) Other *collections* of things, actions, &c.; **altāria,** *an altar;* **ambāges,** *evasion* (but § 415); **angustiæ,** *straits* (sing. rare); **argū- tiæ,** *subtlety;* **antes,** *rows,* e.g. of vines; **arma,** *tools,* esp. *weapons, armour;* **armamenta,** *ship's tackling;* **balneæ,** *the baths,* i.e. *bath- house;* **bīgæ,** *a carriage and pair* (sing. not till Sen.); **cancelli,** *rail- ings;* **casses,** *a hunting net* (properly *meshes,* cf. § 432); **castra,** *a camp* (properly *huts, tents?* castrum is found only as part of proper names, e.g. Castrum Novum); **clathri,** *a grating;* **claustra,** *bars* (sing. in Sen. Curt. rarely); **clītellæ,** *a pack saddle* (*panniers?*); **compĕdes,** *fetters* (but § 446); **crepundia,** *child's rattle,* &c.; **cūnæ, cūnābŭla, incūnābŭla,** *cradle;* **dēlīciæ,** *delight;* **dīvītiæ,** *riches;* **ex- cūbiæ,** *the watch;* **ĕpŭlæ,** *a dinner;* **exsĕquiæ,** *funeral procession;* **exŭviæ,** *things stripped off, spoils;* **facētiæ,** *jokes* (sing. rare); **fălæ,** *scaffolding;* **fasti,** *the Calendar;* **fŏri,** *benches;* **fräces,** *oil dregs;* **grātes,** *thanks* (§ 418); **indūtiæ,** *a truce;* **ineptiæ,** *silliness* (sing. in Plaut. Ter.); **infĕriæ,** *offerings to the shades below;* **infītias,** *denial* (cf. § 369); **insidiæ,** *ambush;* **inĭmīcĭtiæ,** *hostility* (rarely sing.); **lăpĭ- cīdīnæ,** *stone quarries;* **lŏcŭli,** *compartments,* and so *box, bag,* &c.; **lustra,** *a den;* **mănūbiæ,** *booty;* **mīnæ,** *threats;* **moenia,** *town walls;* **nūgæ,** *trifles;* **nuptiæ,** *marriage;* **obīces,** *bolts* (but § 439); **părietinæ,** *ruins;* **phălĕræ,** *horse trappings;* **præstigiæ,** *juggling tricks;* **prĕces,** *prayers* (but § 438); **prīmītiæ,** *first fruits;* **pugillāres,** *writing tablets;* **quadrīgæ,** *a carriage and four* (sing. not till Propert.); **quisquiliæ,** *refuse;* **reliquiæ,** *the remains;* **rĕpāgula,** *bolts,* &c.; **salīnæ,** *saltpits;* **săta,** *the crops;* **scălæ,** *stairs;* **scōpæ,** *a broom;* **sentes,** *thornbush;* **serta,** *a wreath;* **sordes,** *filth* (sing. rare § 421); **suppĕtias,** *supply* (cf. § 369); **tĕnĕbræ,** *the darkness;* **thermæ,** *the warm baths* (cf. **balneæ**); **tesqua,** *wastes;* **valvæ,** *folding-doors;* **vepres,** *thorns* (but cf. § 430); **vindīciæ,** *claims;* **virgulta,** *bushes;* **ūtensīlia,** *necessaries.*

Some of these words are used in one or two cases of the singular. See the references.

3. The following words are used in the plural with a special 331 meaning, besides their use (in most instances) as an ordinary plural:

æ les sing. *a temple,* plur. *a house* (properly, *hearths, chambers?*); **ăqua,** *water;* **aquæ,** *a watering-place:* **auxilium,** *assistance;* **auxilia,** *means of assistance, auxiliary troops:* **bŏnum,** *a good;* **bŏna,** *goods,* i.e. *one's property:* carcer, *a prison;* carcĕres, *the barriers* (in horse races): cōdĭcillus, *a small piece of wood;* cōdĭcilli, *writing tablets:* cōpia, *plenty;* cōpiæ, *supplies, troops:* cŏmĭtium, *the place of tribes-assembly at Rome;* cŏmĭtia, *the assembly:* fĭdes sing. *a harpstring,* plur. *a stringed instrument:* fortŭna, *fortune;* fortŭnæ, *one's posses-sions:* grātia, *thankfulness;* grātiæ, grātes, *thanks:* hortus, *a garden;* horti, *pleasure-gardens, a country house:* impĕdīmentum, *a hindrance;* impedimenta, *baggage:* littera, *a letter* (of the alphabet); litteræ, *a letter,* i.e. epistle: lūdus, *a game;* lŭdi, *Public Games:* nātālis, *a birthday;* nātāles, *one's descent:* ŏpĕra, *work;* operæ, *workmen:* Ops, *a goddess;* opem, *help;* ŏpes, *wealth, resources:* pars, *a part;* partes, *a part on the stage:* rostrum, *a beak;* rostra, *the tribune* or *pulpit at Rome:* tăbŭla, *a plank;* tăbŭlæ, *account books.*

CHAPTER IV.

OF CASE INFLEXIONS IN GENERAL.

IN Latin the distinctions of case are in the singular five, the 332 cases being named *nominative, accusative, genitive, dative, ablative.* In some nouns with stems in -o, besides others derived from the Greek, a sixth form, (not properly a *case,* cf. § 1007), generally called the *vocative* is also found.

In the plural there are only four; viz. nominative, accusative, genitive, and a common form for the dative and ablative.

Another case, distinguished in some other languages, called the *locative,* is in Latin always the same in form, as either the genitive, dative, or ablative.

A similar confusion of forms is found between some of the other cases in some classes of nouns. Originally perhaps there was a different form for each case in each number.

Nouns and pronouns, whether substantival or adjectival, may 333 be conveniently divided according to their case inflexions (called collectively their *declension*) into two great classes, containing respectively—

    I.   Nouns with stems ending in -a, -e, or -o.

    II.   Nouns with stems ending in -u, -i, or a consonant.

All the pronouns, except personal pronouns, belong to the first class, though a few have kindred forms belonging to the second class.

The personal pronouns belong strictly to neither class. They will be treated of as an appendix to the first class.

The chief constant differences between the inflexions of the two classes are these :—

Nouns of the first class have the genitive singular (except in the pronouns), the locative singular, and the nominative plural (except in a few -e stems) alike, and ending in a long vowel or diphthong; the genitive plural in -rum preceded by a long vowel; the dative and ablative plural (except in two -e stems) in -is.

Nouns of the second class have the genitive singular and nominative plural ending in -s, the locative usually the same as the ablative, the genitive plural in -um, the dat. abl. plural in -būs (usually -ĭbŭs).

Some of these differences were not found in the older language. See Chapters VI. and XII.

[The ordinary division of nouns substantive was into five 334 declensions. Of these the 1st contained -a stems (§ 339); the 2nd, -o stems (§ 344 sqq.); the 3rd, consonant (Chap. XI.) and -i stems (Chap. X.); the 4th, -u stems (Chap. IX.); and the 5th, -e stems (§ 340). Adjectives were divided into those of three terminations, -us, -a, um (§§ 339, 344); those of two terminations, -is, -e (Chap. X.), and -or, -us (§ 460); and those of one termination, e. g. felix (Chaps. X. XI.)].

Examples of the regular declensions of the different subordinate classes will be given in the next chapter. Any peculiar forms of inflexion which existed will be found in Chapters VI. and XII., or appended to the mention of the particular word to which they relate.

CHAPTER V.

NOUNS OF CLASS I.

I. GENDER.

As regards the gender of nouns of this class, with comparatively 335 few exceptions, (1) all masculine and neuter nouns have stems in -o; (2) all feminine nouns have stems in -a, or -ē.

8

The exceptions are as follows:

1. Some stems in -ă are masculine; e.g. appellative substantives expressing occupations in which men are exclusively or primarily thought of, viz. accŏla, agrĭcŏla, incŏla; assecla, advĕna, convĕna; aurīga, collēga, convīva, gumia, lanista, lixa, matricīda, parricīda, profŭga, transfŭga, pŏpa, rabŭla, scriba, scurra, verna. And the same termination was given to Greek words in -ηs, e.g. nauta, poëta, Persa, Scytha (see § 475).

Damma is also sometimes masc.: talpa rarely so (§ 319).

So also almost all rivers (§ 325): e.g. Sequăna, Trĕbia, &c, and Hadria (the Hadriatic sea).

A considerable number of proper names, e.g. Numa, Lămia, Ahāla, Pansa, Sulla, Galba, Natta, Tucca, Nasīca, Perpenna, Cinna, Mela, Messalla, Poplicŏla. So also some feminine appellatives were used as family names of men, e.g. Rŭga, Scapŭla, Sūra, Fimbria, Merula, Pīca, Musca, Murēna, Dolabella, Fenestella, Hēmīna, Trăbea.

2. Some words with -o stems are feminine. These are 336 chiefly either names of trees or Greek words, especially names of jewels and towns.

(*a*) alvus (in old language m.); carbăsus, cŏlus (sometimes m.), hŭmus, vannus. For dŏmus see § 394.

(*b*) Names of trees: æsculus, alnus, arbŭtus, buxus, cedrus, cĕrăsus, cĭtrus, cornus, cŏrŭlus, cupressus, cytĭsus (also m.), ĕbĕnus, fāgus, făsēlus, fīcus (rarely m.), fraxĭnus, jūnĭpĕrus, laurus, lōtus (rarely m.), mālus (*apple-tree*), mōrus, myrtus, nardus, ornus, păpȳrus, pīnus, pĭrus, plătănus, pōmus, pōpŭlus, prūnus, quercus, sabūcus, sorbus, spīnus, ulmus. Also bălănus, *acorn*.

(*c*) Jewels: e.g. amethystus, crystallus, sapphīrus, topazus, melichrysos.

(*d*) Towns, &c.; Abȳdus, Ægyptus, Aspendus, Carystus, Chersonēsus, Cyprus, Epĭdamnus, Epĭdaurus, Epīrus, Pĕlŏponnēsus, Rhŏdus, &c.; but Canōpus (m.), Isthmus (m.), Orchŏmĕnus (m.), Pontus (m.). So also Dēlos, Lemnos, &c. are feminine.

(*e*) For Greek appellatives, e.g. ătŏmus, mĕthŏdus, &c., see § 478.

3. Of nouns in -es only dies and mĕrīdies are masculine. 337 Dies however is in the singular number often feminine, especially as *an appointed day*, and almost exclusively fem. when it means *time*, *period of time*.

All neuters (except some pronouns, § 370) have nom. acc. sing. 338 in -um: except vīrus, vulgus (in acc. often vulgum), and the Greek pelăgus, plur. pelagē. (Virus and vulgus have no plural. The authority for vulgus as masc. seems insufficient.)

II. INFLEXIONS OF CASE.

The suffixes for the different cases are usually combined with 339 the final vowel of the stem, so as not always to be readily distinguishable.

1. Declension of stems in -a and -e.

1. The substantive stems in -a (chiefly feminine), and the feminine form of those adjectives which have stems in -o, are declined alike; e.g. mensa (f.), *a table;* scrība (m.), *a clerk;* bŏna (adj. f.), *good;* tĕnĕra (adj. f.), *tender.* There are no neuters of this declension.

2. Stems in -ē of this class (comp. § 407) are all substantives 340 and all feminine: one (dies) is also masculine. All but a few have stems in -ie with a short antepenultimate, and most are words of more than three syllables.

They are as follows: dies, fămes (also famis), fīdes, plēbes (also plebs), res, spes, and (in ablative sing. only) scabrē, squale ;

ăcies, allŭvies (with other derivatives of lăvo), barbăries, cæsăries, căries, conʒĕries, efflgies, ēsŭries, făcies, glăcies, inglŭvies, luxŭries, macĕries, măcies, mātĕries, mŭries (only nom. s.), paupĕries, pernīcies (? permities, Munro, *ad Lucr.* I. 451), prōgĕnies, răbies, rĕqvies (also with stem in -ĕt, § 445), sănies, scăbies, sĕries, spĕcies, sŭperfīcies, tempĕries, and its compound intempĕries ;

and abstract substantives in -īties, viz. ămārities, ămīcities, ăvărities, calvities, cănities, dūrities, lentities, mollities, mundities, nēqvities, nigrities, nōtities, pīgrities, plānities, pullities, segnities, spurcities, tristīties, vastities.

Only two of these words, viz. res and dies, are inflected through- 341 out all cases of both numbers. None (besides dies and res) have any plural, except acies, facies, effigies, species, spes, series, which are found in the nominative and accusative plural; glacies in accus. (Verg.), eluvies in nom. (Curt.). But old forms of spes, viz. speres, nom. acc. plur., speribus, dat. abl. plur., are mentioned as used by Ennius and Varro respectively[1]. Facierum is quoted from Cato. Specierum, speciebus occur in the Digest, &c

---

[1] The stem appears to have been spes- : compare spēr-o. So also perhaps dies-; comp. diur-nus. See also § 405.

The genitive and dative singular are rare[1], except from **dies**, 342
res, spes, fides, and **plebes**.

These cases appear to have ended regularly in **-ei** in and after
the second century after Christ at latest (Gell. IX. 14), but whether
ei was usually one syllable or two is uncertain. Probably it was
a diphthong. Before that time **ei** is proved to be sometimes disyllabic, but in the words **diēī, fidēī** and **fidĕī, rēī** and **rĕī** only. See
§§ 357, 360.

Luxuries, materies, barbaries, intempĕries, effĭgies, and almost all
the words in -ities, have collateral stems in -a (cf. § 932), and these
supply the forms generally used in the genitive and dative singular.

Examples: **mensa**, *a table;* **bona** (adj.), *good;* **luxuria**, *luxury;* 343
res, *a thing;* **acies**, *a point.* All feminine.

	Stems in -a.		Stems in -a *and* -e.	Stems in -e.	
SINGULAR.	Subst.	Adj.	Subst.	Subst.	Subst.
Nom.	mensă	bŏnă	luxŭriă or luxuriĕ-s	rē-s	ăciē-s
Acc.	mensa-m	bona-m	luxuria-m or luxurie-m	re-m	ăcie-m
Gen. Loc. Dat.	mensæ	bonæ	luxuriæ	re-i	ăcii or ăciē
Abl.	mensā	bonā	luxuriā or luxuriĕ	rē	ăciē
PLURAL.					
Nom.	mensæ	bonæ	(Plural not used)	rē-s	ăciē-s
Acc.	mensă-s	bona-s			
Gen.	mensā-rum	bonā-rum		rē-rum	(none)
Loc. Dat. Abl.	mensī-s	bonī-s		rē-bus	(none)

2. Ordinary declension of -o stems.

The following is the regular declension of substantives with 344
stems ending in -o, and of adjectives, with the like stems, in the
masculine and neuter gender.

e.g. **ănĭmŭs** (m.), *a soul;* **bellum** (n.), *war;* **bŏnus** (adj.), *good.*

---

[1] Quintilian says (I. 6, § 26), "Nec plurimum refert, nulla hæc an
prædura sint. Nam quid 'progenies' genetivo singulari, quid plurali
'spes' faciet?"

	Masculine		Neuter	
Singular.	Subst.	Adj.	Subst.	Adj.
Nom.	ănĭmŭ-s	bŏnu-s ⎫		
Voc.	ănĭmĕ	bŏn-ĕ ⎬	bellu-m	bŏnu-m
Acc.	ănĭmŭ-m	bŏnu-m ⎭		
Gen. ⎫ Loc. ⎬	ănĭmī	bŏnī	bellī	bŏnī
Dat. ⎫ Abl. ⎬	ănĭmō	bŏnō	bellō	bŏnō
Plural.				
Nom.	ănĭmī	bŏnī ⎫	bellă	bŏnă
Acc.	ănĭmō-s	bŏnō-s ⎭		
Gen.	ănĭmō-rum	bŏnō-rum	bellō-rum	bŏnō-rum
Loc. ⎫ Dat. ⎬ Abl. ⎭	ănĭmī-s	bŏnī-s	bellī-s	bŏnī-s

The vocative masc. sing. of meus, *mine*, is mi. Deus, *god*, had 345 voc. Deus; nom. plur. dī; dat. abl. dīs; but dei and deis are not infrequent in Ovid and later poets, and even in some MSS. of Varro and Cicero.

3. Declension of stems in -ro.

Of stems in -ĕro, (*a*) most drop the final -us of the nominative 346 singular, and -e of the vocative; and (*b*) many omit the e before r in all the cases except the nom. voc. masculine singular.

(*a*) The following only exhibit -us in the nominative singular: nŭmĕrus, ŭmĕrus (or humerus), ŭtĕrus, and (the single fem. stem in -ĕro), jūnĭpĕrus, and the adjectives prŏpĕrus, præprŏpĕrus, præposterŭs, mōrĭgĕrus, trĭquetrus, and usually prospĕrus. The nominative masculine singular of the adjectives cētĕrum, postĕrum, lūdĭcrum, crĕpĕrum is not found.

(Adjectives with long ē in penultimate (e.g. sēvērus), and some Greek forms, e.g. Evandrus, Petrus, exhibit -us. But Ibēri and Celtibēri have for singular Ibēr and Celtibēr, but only once each.)

Vīr, *a man*, and its compounds, e. g. triumvir, semivir (adj.), and the adjective sătŭr (sătŭră, sătŭrum), also drop -us. Lucretius once uses fămŭl for fămŭlus.

Puere is frequently found in Plautus as the vocative of puer.   347

(*b*) The following only retain e before r; viz.—

(1) All those which retain -us in the nominative singular;

(2) **Adulter, sŏcer, gĕner, Lĭber** (*the god Bacchus*), **puer, vesper** (*evening star*), **jugerum** (which last in plural belongs to 2nd Class);

(3) The adjectives **asper** (**aspris**, abl. plur. once in Vergil), **lăcer, lĭber, mĭser, tĕner, gibber, alter**; and **ceterum, posterum, creperum** (above named). Also **exter** (Papin.), **infer** (Cato), **super** (Cato), chiefly used in plural;

Dexter has both forms; e.g. **dexteram, dextram.** (The comparative of **dexter** is always **dexterior.** So also **deterior.**)

(4) Compounds of more than two syllables ending in **-fer** or **-ger**; e.g. **mortifer, ăliger,** &c.

The following are the principal substantives which omit **e**; **ăger, 348 ăper, ārbĭter, auster, cancer, căper, cŏlŭber, culter, făber, lĭber** (*book*), **măgister, mĭnister.** The neuters are chiefly in **-brum, -trum, -crum**, see in Book III. The adjectives omitting **e** are: **aeger, āter, crēber,** (**dexter,** § 347,) **glăber, măcer, nĭger, pĭger, impĭger, intĕger, lŭdĭcrum,pulcher, rŭber, săcer, scăber, sĭnister** (in comparative always **sinisterior**), **tæter, văfer**: also **Āfer, Călăber.**

Examples: **puer** (m.), *a boy;* **vĭr** (m.), *a man;* **făber** (m.), 349 *a workman;* **membrum** (n.), *a limb.*

SINGULAR.		Masculine		Neuter
Nom. ⎱ Voc. ⎰	puĕr	vĭr	făbĕr ⎱	membru-m
Acc.	puĕru-m	vĭru-m	făbru-m ⎰	
Gen. ⎱ Loc. ⎰	puĕrī	vĭrī	făbri	membrī
Dat. ⎱ Voc. ⎰	puĕrō	vĭrō	făbrō	membrō
PLURAL.				
Nom.	puĕrī	vĭrī	făbrī ⎱	membră
Acc.	puĕrō-s	vĭrō-s	fabrō-s ⎰	
Gen.	puerō-rum	vĭrō-rum	fabrō-rum	membrō-rum
		(and vĭru-m)	(and fabru-m)	
Loc. ⎱ Dat. ⎰ Abl. ⎰	puerī-s	vĭrī-s	făbrī-s	membrī-s

On **-um** in the genitive plural of **vĭr** and **faber** see § 365.

4. Præ-Augustan declension of stems in **-uo** (i.e. either **-uo, -vo,** or **-qvo**).

The older language, as shown especially by inscriptions not 350 later than cir. 520 B.C., retained the final **-o** of the stem in the nominative and accusative cases singular; e.g. **fīliŏs, prīmŏs,**

Lūciom, donom. Though this -o was changed to -u generally (§ 213), yet the stems in which it was preceded by v or u or qu retained it until the Augustan age and later (Quintil. i. 7. 26). The change was however made in these stems also in the course of the 1st century after Christ. In words like **ĕqvŭs** the concurrence of u with u was also avoided by writing **ĕqŭs**, or **ĕcŭs**.

e.g. **ĕqvŏs** or **ĕcŭs** (m.), *a horse;* **ævom** (n.), *an age;* **arduŏs** (adj.), *lofty.*

	Masculine		Neuter	
SINGULAR.	Subst.	Adj.	Subst.	Adj.
Nom. ⎱	**ĕqvŏ-s** or **ĕcŭ-s**	**arduo-s** ⎞		
Voc. ⎰	**ĕqvĕ**	**arduĕ** ⎬ **ævo-m**		**arduo-m**
Acc.	**ĕqvo-m** or **ĕcŭ-m**	**arduo-m** ⎠		
Gen. ⎱	**ĕqvī**	**arduī**	**ævi**	**arduī**
Loc. ⎰				
Dat. ⎱	**ĕqvŏ**	**arduŏ**	**ævŏ**	**arduŏ**
Abl. ⎰				
PLURAL.				
Nom.	**ĕqvī**	**arduī** ⎱	**ævă**	**arduă**
Acc.	**ĕqvŏ-s**	**arduŏ-s** ⎰		
Gen.	**ĕqvŏ-rum**	**arduŏ-rum**	**ævŏ-rum**	**arduŏ-rum**
Loc. ⎞				
Dat. ⎬	**ĕqvī-s**	**arduī-s**	**ævī-s**	**arduī-s**
Abl. ⎠				

5. Augustan and Præ-Augustan declension of stems in -io.

In the Augustan and præ-Augustan period substantives with 351 stems ending in -io formed the genitive singular in -i single. So always in the scenic poets, in Lucretius, Vergil, Horace; also in Persius and Manilius. The genitive of trisyllabic words with a short antepenultimate (e.g. **glădius, fōlium**), appears to have been generally avoided by these poets; but **prĕti, vīti** (from **pretium** and **vītium**) occur. Propertius, Ovid, Lucan, and the later poets, used the full form in -ii; e.g. **Mercŭrii, exsīlii, vītii;** but in proper names the contracted form continued to be most common; e.g. **Antoni, Capitōli, Terenti, Līvi.** In inscriptions -ii appears from the end of Augustus' reign, and with increasing frequency after Nero's reign, though -i is also found to the end of the 3rd century after Christ and probably longer (Ritschl. *Opusc.* II. 779).

The vocative sing. masc. of these stems also ended in -i (not -ie), 352 e.g. **Publi.** But the vocative is found only in proper names and in the words **gĕnius, fīlius, vultŭrius** (cf. Gell. 14. 5). The nominative plural rarely had **ii** contracted into **i.** The dative ablative plural had sometimes, especially in neuters, -is for -iis. (See § 367.)

Adjectives always had -ii in genitive. Only those derived from Greek proper names had a distinct form for vocative; e.g. **Cynthie, Delie.**

In stems ending in -aio, -eio the i both formed a diphthong with the preceding vowel, and also was pronounced as English y before a following vowel. (For some exceptions see § 139.) Hence Cicero wrote the i double, -aiio, -eiio ; but this spelling is not now found in the MSS. or in republican inscriptions.

	Substantives.			Adjectives.
SINGULAR.	masc.	masc.	neut.	masc.
Nom.	Claudius	Pompējus		ēgrĕgius
Voc.	Claudī	Pompēī and	consīlium	
		Pompei		
Acc.	Claudium	Pompējum		egrĕgium
Gen. / Loc.	Claudī	Pompēī	consīlī	ēgrĕgiī
Dat. / Abl.	Claudiō	Pompējo	consīlio	ēgrĕgio
PLURAL.				
Nom.	Claudiī	Pompēī	consīlia	ēgrĕgia
Acc.	Claudios	Pompējos		
Gen.	Claudiō-rum	Pompējōrum	consiliōrum	ēgrĕgiōrum
Loc.				
Dat. / Abl.	Claudiīs	Pompēīs	consīliīs or consīlīs	ēgrĕgiīs

The number **353** appears at the right of the Adjectives heading.

CHAPTER VI.

OLD AND EXCEPTIONAL FORMS OF CASES.

(CLASS I.)

1 Singular Number.

NOMINATIVE: *Stems in* -o. On the faint sound of final s and m 354 which led to their omission even in the older language, see §§ 193, 5. 86. Old inscriptions give such forms as **Acilio, Fourio, Fabrecio, pocolo** (for **Acilius, Furius, Fabricius, poculum**). The nominative sing. of proper names with stems in -io are frequently written in old inscriptions without the final syllable; e.g. **Claudi, Valeri, Minuci** (for **Claudius,** &c). This may be merely an abbreviation, due as Ritschl supposes, to a once collateral nominative in -is; e.g. **Cornelis.** Compare **alis, alius** § 373.

ACCUSATIVE: For the omission of the final **m**, see § 86.   355

Stems in -e. Quintilian (IX. 4. 39) speaks of **diee hanc** (if text be right) being found in Cato the censor's writings, "**m litera in** -e **mollita**".

GENITIVE: 1. *Stems in* -a. Instances of the ordinary genitive 356 in -ae are very rare in inscriptions before the time of the Gracchi.

Three old forms of the genitive singular are found, viz. -aes, -ai and -as.

(*a*) The ending -aes occurs frequently in inscriptions after Sulla's time, but chiefly on tombs of freedwomen and slaves, and rarely in other than proper names; e.g. **Juliaes, Dianaes, Anniaes, Faustinaes, dominaes, vernaes**. Some hold it to be intended for the Greek genitive in -ης. Ritschl (comparing a single **Prosepnais** from the 6th century U.C.) holds it to be a genuine old Latin form, and *possibly* used by Plautus (*Neue Plaut. Exc.* I. p. 115).

(*b*) Of the ending -as examples are given from Livius Andronicus, **escas, monetas, Latonas**; from Nævius, **terras, fortunas**; and from Ennius, **vias**. Some so take **molas** in Plaut. *Pseud.* 1100. This form is preserved in one word at all periods, viz. **familia**, when combined with **pater, mater, filius, filia**; e.g. **paterfamilias** (Cato, Cic.), *a father of a household*. **Pater**, &c. **familiæ** (Cic., Liv.) is also used. In the plural we find both **patres**, &c. -**familiæ** (Varr., Cæs., Liv.), -**familias** (Varr., Cic.), -**familiarum** (Cic., Sall.), *fathers* &c. *of households*.

(*c*) The ending -ai (originally the locative according to Madvig) is more common and earlier, and in Plautus and hexameter verse (retaining probably the old pronunciation) is treated as a spondee (-āī). It is frequent in Lucretius, and is also used by Cicero in his poetry, and by Vergil in four words, **aquai, aulai, aurai, pictai**. Republican inscriptions give, e.g. **Duelonai** (i.e. **Bellonæ**), **Glabrai, ejus rei quaerundai et faciundai causa, calcis restinctai**, &c.

2. *Stems in* -e. Four forms of the genitive-ending are found, 357 viz. **ēs; ei; ē; ī**. (See Gell. 9. 14).

·(*a*) -es; viz. **Dies**, Enn. *A.* 401, Verg. *G.* I. 208 (die, Ribbeck), Cic. *Sest.* 12. § 28; **rabies**, Lucr. IV. 1083; **facies**, Claud. Quadrig. (in Sulla's time); **fides**, see below *b*; **pernicies**, said to have been written by Cicero.

(*b*) -ei; viz. **diei**, frequent in prose; **diēī**, Lucr. (often), Verg. *A.* IV. 156, Hor. *S.* I. 8. 35, Phædr. II. 8. 10, Ter. *Haut.* 168, 212, Plaut.; **diēī**, Ter. *Eun.* 801; **rei**, always in Republican inscriptions; **rēī**, Plaut. *Mil. G.* 103, **magnai rei publicai gratia**; Lucr. II. 112,

548; rĕi, Plaut., Ter., Hor.; reī, Plaut., Ter., Lucil., Lucr.; fidei, frequent in prose; fidēī, Enn. *Ann.* 342, Plaut. *Aul.* 121, 575, Lucr. v. 102; fidĕi, Manil. II. 605, 627, Sil. (four times); fidei (fides Wagner), Plaut. *Aul.* 609; spei, frequent in prose; speī, Ter. always; plebei (especially in phrases tribunus plebei, plebeiscitum, &c.) frequent: aciei, *Bell. Afr.* 59 and 60. Mundiciei, *Inscr.* 136, A.D. (cf. Corssen. *Aussp.* I. 54, ed. 2).

(*c*) -ē; viz. die, in several places (in some MSS.) of Cæs., Sall., Liv., also Plaut. *Pseud.* 1158; ·Sen. *Cons. Marc.* 18. 2; compare also postridie, &c.; re, Cæs., Liv. in some MSS.; fide, Poet. ap. C. *Off.* 3. 26; Planc. ap. Cic. *Fam.* 10. 17; Hor. *C.* 3. 7. 4; Ovid. *Met.* III. 341, VI. 506, VII. 728, 737, &c.; acie, Sall.; facie, Lucil., Plaut. *Mil. G.* 1172; requie, Sall.; scabie, Lucil. "'C. Cæsar in libro de analogia secundo hujus die et hujus specie dicendum putat," Gell. 9. 14.

(*d*) -i; viz. dii, Verg. *A.* I. 636; plebi, frequent in phrases above quoted; acii, Cn. Matius; pernicii, Cic. *Rosc. Am.* 45, Sisenna; specii, Cn. Matius; progenii, Pacuvius; luxurii, C. Gracchus; fami, Lucil., Cato; fidi, Augustan legal inscription (*Corp. I. L.* II. 5042).

3. *Stems in* -o. The oldest form was perhaps -oe; e.g. poploe 358 But the inscriptions to the time of the third Punic war give only I; e.g. Barbati, urbani; after that time, till Augustus, -ei is also frequently found; e.g. populei, cogendei, suei, ostiei, pagei, Marcei, Vergilei; but not so frequently in laws as -ī. In Augustus' time -ei went out of use (§§ 265—268). Lucilius wished to establish the distinction of -ī for the gen. sing.; -ei for nom. plur.

The locative has the same form as the genitive and was not improbably identical with it.

DATIVE: I. *Stems in* -a. Early republican and other inscrip- 359 tions have not unfrequently -ai. The disyllabic āī is not found in the dative in any poet.

Forms like Fortune, Diane in very old inscriptions are probably imitations of Greek.

2. *Stems in* -e. Three forms of the dative are found; -ei, ē 360 and i.

(*a*) -ei; viz. diei, often; rēī, Lucr. I. 688, II. 236; rei, *Corp. I. L.* 201, also (at beginning of verse) Ter. *Ad.* 95; rĕi, Hor. *C.* 3. 24. 64; reī, Enn. *Trag.* 361; Plaut., Ter., Lucil.; fidei, often in prose; fidei, Enn. *Ann.* 111 (fide, Vahlen); Ter. *And.* 296, *Eun.* 886, 898 (ed. Umpfenbach); comp. Plaut. *Trin.* 117, 128; fidĕi, Manil. 3. 107, Sil. 2. 561; plebei, Plin. *H. N.* 19. 4. 19, § 54, 18. 3. 4; aciei, Cæs. *Civ.* III. 89, ib. 93; perniciei, Nep. 12. 4.

(*b*) -ē; viz. diē, Plaut.; re, Plaut. *Trin.* 635, 657; fide, *Corp. I. R.* I. 170, Plaut. *Aul.* 659, *Amph.* 391, *Pers.* 193; comp. *Trin.* 117, 128, 142, Hor. *S.* I. 3. 95; pernicie, Liv. 5. 13, § 5; facie, Lucil. "In casu dandi qui purissime locuti sunt, non 'faciei' uti nunc dicitur sed 'facie' dixerunt," Gell. 9. 14.

(*c*) -i; viz. pernicii, Nep. 8. 2; fami, Plaut. *Stich.* 158; facii (cf. Gell. 9. 14); fidi, Fast. Coll. Arval. *ad Kal. Oct.*

3. *Stems in* -o. The oldest form was -oi; e.g. hoic, quoi, 361 populoi. Perhaps also oe in pilumnoe, poploe, Fest. p. 205.

ABLATIVE. In early times the ablative ended in -d; e.g. oquol- 362 tod (occulto); Benventod (Benevento), praidad (præda), sententiad (sententia). The latest inscription containing such ablatives is the *S.C. de Bacc.* B.C. 186. Plautus probably used it or not as he chose. See § 160 and Ritschl, *Neue Plaut. Exc.* I. 106.

Plural Number.

NOMINATIVE: *Stems in* -a. The ending -as is quoted from 363 Pomponius, 'Quot lætitias insperatas modo mi inrepsere in sinum.' (See Ritschl, *N. P. Exc.* I. 117.)

Stems in -o. The earliest forms of ending in inscriptions are -es (not beyond cir. 90 B.C.) and very rarely -e or -oe; e.g. Atilies, magistres, ploirume, Fescenninoe: from 200 B.C. or earlier to about the birth of Christ, more frequently -ei, and from about the Gracchi till cir. 90 B.C. -eis, or sometimes -is; e.g. Italicei, oinvorsei (universi), Q. M. Minucieis, Q. F. Rufeis (i.e. Q. (et) M. Minucii, Quinti filii, Rufi), gnateis, heisce. So in Plautus hisce, illisce.

The ordinary form in -i appears since the Gracchi, and becomes exclusively used in the Augustan age.

The only instances of dual forms (compare the Greek) are duo and ambo, which are the forms used in the masc. and neut. (duæ feminine as in plur).

ACCUSATIVE: Duo, ambo, masc. and neut.; duos, ambos, also masc. (duas, ambas, fem.).

GENITIVE: Future participles except futurus are very rarely 364 found in the genitive plural, probably on account of the unpleasantness of repeated r (§ 185).

1. *Stems in* -a. The ending -um for -ārum (comp. Oscan -azum; Umbr. -arum or -aru; old Greek -αων) is found;

(*a*) in some names derived from the Greek; viz.: amphorum, (e.g. trium amphorum), drachmum.

(*b*) in proper names, especially patronymics, but almost exclusively in dactylic verse (esp. Vergil); e.g. **Lapithum, Dardanidum, Æneadum.**

(*c*) The only strictly Latin words in which it occurs are (masculine) compounds of **gigno** and **colo**, and these are so used in dactylic verses only; e.g. **Grajugenum, terrigenum, cælicolum.** The forms in **-arum** are also used.

2. *Stems in* **-o.** The ending **-um** (apparently similar to the 365 Umbrian and Oscan forms, and the Greek -ῶν) was perhaps the original Italian form, except in the pronouns, and was gradually superseded in Latin by **-ōrum**, which is common in inscriptions of the second century B.C. and later. In and after Cicero's time (see Cic. *Or.* 46) the genitive in **-um** for ordinary language was found only in certain words. Thus it is found:

(*a*) in names of weights and measures (chiefly Greek) in combination with numerals. Thus **nummum** (e.g. **tria millia nummum**; but **nummorum accessionem**), **sestertium, denarium, talentum, medimnum, stadium.**

(*b*) in **deum, divum**, the compounds of **virum** e.g. **quinquevirum, duum virum**, &c. (but in Liv. **decem virorum** is frequent), and in poetry **virum** itself; **liberum** (*children*), **fabrum** (in phrases as **præfectus fabrum**, **collegium fabrum**), **socium** (in prose rarely except of the *Italian allies*, or with **præfectus**), **equum** (often written **ecum**).

(*c*) in names of peoples (in poetry); e.g. **Achivum, Argivum, Teucrum, Celtiberum** (sometimes in prose), **Rutulum, Italum**, &c. Other words, e.g. **fluvium, famulum, juvencum**, are found occasionally.

(*d*) But few instances of neuters are found; e.g. **somnium, armum**, &c., **oppidum** (Sulpicius ap. Cic. *Fam.* 4. 5. § 4).

(*e*) In adjectives instances are few, e.g. **centum doctum hominum consilia, celatum indagator**, &c. (Plaut.); **motus superum atque inferum, meum factum pudet** (Ennius); **prodigium horriferum portentum pavor** (Pacuv.); **amicum, iniquom, æquom** (Ter. *Haut.* 24, 27); &c., and the old phrase **liberum sibi quæsendum** (or **quærendum**) **gratia**, &c. So in Vergil **magnanimum generator equorum.**

(*f*) **Duum** (frequently), **ducentum, quingentum, sescentum**, &c. So usually distributives; e.g. **binum, quaternum** (never **binorum, quaternorum** with **milium**), **senum, ducenum, quadragenum**, &c.

(*g*) For **nostrum, vestrum**, &c., see § 388.

DATIVE, ABLATIVE. 1. *Stems in* -a *and* -o. 1. The oldest form, 366 of which any instances are found, was **-oes**; e.g. **oloes** for **illis.** But the form most used in præ-Augustan inscriptions is **-eis**. The ending **-is** is found since the Gracchi, and, almost exclusively, in and after the Augustan time.

2. Stems in -ia, -io are found sometimes with -is instead of -iis 367 in inscriptions; e.g. **suffragis, præsidis, provincis.** So in Cic. *Rep.* **socis, præsidis, pecunis,** &c. Plautus has **gaudis, filis** (from **filius**); Vergil has **tænis**; Seneca **supplicis**; Martial **denaris.** In *Mon. Ancyr.* both forms occur not unfrequently; e.g. **municipiis, municipis. Gratiis** (Plaut., Ter.), **gratis** (Cic., Mart.).

3. An ending in -bus, as in the second class of nouns, is found 368 in a few words: viz.

(*a*) **Ambo, duo,** always make **ambōbus, ambābus; duōbus, duābus.**

(*b*) **Dĭbus** is found in inscriptions for **Dīs.** (So also **ĭbus, hĭbus,** from **is** and **hic.**)

(*c*) In prose, chiefly in inscriptions and legal expressions, **-ābus** for -is is found in a few substantives; viz. **deabus** (chiefly in phrases, **dis deabusque), filiabus, libertabus** in opposition to the (usually) masculine **filiis, libertis;** rarely, **conservabus, natabus.** In late writers also **animabus, equabus, mulabus,** and (sometimes in inscriptions) **nymphabus.**

A few adjectives occur with this form in Rhenish inscriptions; e.g. **matronis Gabiabus, Junonibus Silvanabus,** &c.

The following words of this class are defective or redundant in 369 certain cases. (All words of this sort which in any way belong to the 2nd class have their peculiarities mentioned, where they occur in the enumeration of that class.) See also § 330.

ævom (n.), also used as acc. m.; **balneum** (n.), also plur. **balneæ,** of the *bath house;* **balteus** (m.), also **balteum** (n.), esp. in plur.; **buxus** (f.), also **buxum** (n.); **cælum** (n.), no plur. except **cælos** once in Lucret., where the meaning compels it; **callus** (m.), also **callum** (n.); **carbāsus** (m.), plur. **carbāsa; cāseus** (m.), also **cāseum** (n.); **cāvum** (n.), *a hollow,* also **cāvus,** m. (sc. **locus); clĭpeus** (m.), also **clĭpeum** (n.); **collum** (n.), also in old language **collus** (m.); **crŏcus** (m.), in sing. also **crŏcum** (n.); **cȳtĭsus** (m. f.), in sing. also **cȳtĭsum** (n.); **dēlīcium** (n.) or **delĭcia** (f.), plur. **dēlīciæ,** sing. not frequent; **dĭca, dĭcam, dĭcas, dĭcīs,** *law suits* (δίκη), no other forms; **ĕpŭlæ** (pl.), also sing. **ĕpŭlum** (n.); **fĭmus** (m.), in sing. also **fĭmum** (n.); **frēnum** (n.), plur. **frēni** (m.) and **frēna** (n.); **hordeum** (n.), of plural only nom. acc.; **infĭtias,** acc. pl. only with verb **ĭre,** used in no other case; **intĭbus** or **intŭbus** (m.), also **intŭbum** (n.); in plur. **jŏci** and **jŏca; jŭgŭlus** (m.), in sing. also **jŭgŭlum** (n.); **jus jūrandum** (n.), both parts of the word are declined, e.g. **juris jurandi, jure jurando,** &c.; **lŏcus** (m.), in plur. also **lŏca,** of *places,* properly speaking; loci, chiefly of places, metaphorically; macte, indecl. adj. or adverb, once in Pliny macti, but not in all MSS.; margărīta (f.), also margărītum (n.); mendum (n.), also menda (f.); nāsus (m.), also in Plaut. nāsum (n.); nauci only gen. sing.; nĭhĭl (n.) only in nom. acc. s.; often contracted nīl: of the fuller form nihilum are used nihili as gen. (or loc.?) *of price;* nihilo after prepositions, comparatives, and as abl. of price; and ad nihilum (in ordinary language we have nullius rei, &c.); ostrea (f.), also ostreum (n.); palātus (m.), usually palātum (n.); pĕdum (n.), *a crook,* only found in acc. s.; pessum, *bottom,* only acc. s. after verbs of motion, e. g. īre, dăre; pilleus (m.),also pilleum (n.); pondo, properly abl. s., also used as indeclinable, '*pounds*'; porrus (m.), also in sing. porrum (n.); pŭteus (m.), also rarely pŭteum (n.); rāmentum (n.), also in Plaut. rāmenta; rastrum (n.), ·also in plur. rastri (m.); rētĭculus (m.), more frequently reticulum; scalper, scalpellus (m.), also scalprum, scalpellum (n.); sībĭlus (m.), also sībĭlum (n.); suppĕtias, acc. pl., no other case; tergus (m.), usually tergum (n.); vallus (m.), usually vallum (n.), acc. sing. after verbs of motion: Tacitus alone has veno. For vīrus, vulgus see § 338.

For numerical adjectives, some of which are indeclinable, see App. D. i.

CHAPTER VII.

PECULIAR DECLENSION OF CERTAIN PRONOUNS AND ADJECTIVES.

Some nouns adjective, and all pronouns adjective (except 370 possessive pronouns, meus, tuus, suus, noster, vester), have for all genders the genitive singular ending in -ius, the dative in -ī. In the other case the inflexions are the same as ordinary stems in -o and -a. The words belonging to this class are ūnus, ullus, nullus, sōlus, tōtus, alter, ūter (and its compounds uterque, &c.), alius, ille, iste, ipse, hic, is, idem, qui and its compounds (quivis, &c.).

Of these alius, ille, iste, is, qui have neuter nom. and acc. ending in -d instead of -m. Other irregularities are named below.

1. tōtus, *whole.*

371

	SINGULAR.			PLURAL.		
	m.	f.	n.	m.	f.	n.
Nom.	totŭs	tōtă	tōtŭm	tōti	tōtae)	
Acc.	tōtum	tōtam	tōtum	tōtōs	tōtās ∫	tōtă
Gen.	tōtīŭs in all genders			tōtōrum	tōtārum	tōtōrum
Loc.) Dat. ∫	tōtī in all genders		)	tōtīs in all genders		
Abl.	tōtō	tōtă	tōtō)			

In the same way are declined **sōlus**, *alone*, **ūnus**, *one*, **ullus** (i. e. **ūnŭlus**), *any at all*, **nullus**, *none*.

Also **altĕr** (*the other*), **altĕra**, **alterum**, gen. **alterius**, dat. **altĕrī**.

ūtĕr, **utră**, **utrum**, *whether*, i. e. *which of two*, gen. **utrius**, dat. **utri**.

altĕrŭter, **alterutra**, or **altĕra utra**, **altĕrutrum**, or **alterum utrum**; gen. **alterius utrius** (post-Aug. **alterutrius**), dat. **altero utri** or **alterutro**.

ūterque, **utrăque**, **utrumque**, *each;* **ŭtercumque**, **utracumque**, **utrumcumque**, *which so ever* (of two).

ūtervīs, **utrăvīs**, **utrumvīs**, *which* (of two) *you please;* **ŭterlĭbet**, **utrălĭbet**, **utrumlĭbet**, *which* (of two) *you like.*

neuter, **neutră**, **neutrum**, *neither.*

ipsĕ (in early writers frequently **ipsus**), **ipsă**, **ipsum**, *he himself.*

The genitive has usually a long penultimate[1]; but all (except 372 **solius**, **utrius**, and **neutrius**) are frequent in poetry with -ius: so **utriusque** always: **solīus** once in Terence.

soli is found as gen. masc. (Cato); **toti** as gen. fem. (Afran.); **nulli** is once or twice used for the masc. and neut. genitive; and **nullo** for the dative; **ulli** once (Plaut.) for gen. masc.; **neutri** is used in the gen. neut. in the sense of *neuter gender*. The feminine datives **unæ**, **nullæ**, **solæ**, **totæ**, **alteræ**, are (rarely) found in early writers to the time· of, and including, Cicero and Nepos. **Toto** for dat. masc. is used once by Propertius.

The genitive **nullius** and abl. **nullo** are rarely used substantively of things, but frequently of persons; **neminis** being only found in præ-Ciceronian writers, and **nemine** being only used by Tacitus and Suetonius, except once in Plautus.

2. **ille**, *that;* **iste**, *that near you* (declined like **ille**); **ălĭŭs**, 373 *another.*

	SINGULAR.			SINGULAR.		
	m.	f.	n.	m.	f.	n.
Nom.	**illĕ**	**illă**	**illŭd**	**ălĭŭs**	**ălĭă**	**ălĭŭd**
Acc.	**illum**	**illam**		**ălĭum**	**ălĭum**	
Gen.	**illīus** in all genders			**ălĭŭs** in all genders (rare)		
Loc. } Dat. }	**illī** in all genders			**ălī** in all genders		
Abl.	**illō**	**illā**	**illō**	**ălĭō**	**ălĭā**	**ălĭō**

The plural is regular in both.

---

[1] In the comic poets -ĭus and -ius are both found. Cicero (*Or.* 3. 47. 183) implies that **illīus** was in his time pronounced **illĭus**; Quintilian

Old forms of **ille** found in Ennius, Lucretius, and Vergil, are **olli** for dat. sing. and nom. pl. masc.; **ollis**, dat. and abl. plural; and in Lucretius **ollas, olla,** acc. plural. **Ab oloes** for **ab illis** is mentioned by Festus; **ollus** and **olla** (nom. sing.) by Varro.

Istus for **iste** is found once in Plautus.

In the præ-Ciceronian phrases **alii modi, illi modi, isti modi,** we have genitives (or possibly locatives); as also in **alii dei, alii generis** in Varro, **alii rei** in Cælius. **Illæ, istæ, aliæ** are found in early writers rarely for dat. fem. sing.; **aliæ** as genitive in Cicero, Livy, and Lucretius (once each). Collateral forms, viz. **alis,** masc. nom. (Catull.), **alid,** neut. nom. acc. (Lucretius), **ali,** dat. sing. (Cat., Lucr.) are also found. The adverb **alibi** appears to be an old locative.

The demonstrative particle **cĕ** was sometimes appended to the 374 cases of **ille** and **iste** which end in -s, and frequently in an abridged form to the others (except genitive plural), especially in Plautus and the early writers; e.g.

	SINGULAR.			PLURAL.		
Nom.	illīc	illæc	} illūc	illīc	illæc	} illæc
Acc.	illunc	illanc		illosce	illasce	
Gen.	illiusce in all genders					
Loc. } Dat. }	illīc in all genders		}	illisce in all genders		
Abl.	illōc	illāc	illōc }			

So also **istīc.**

In nom. sing. **illăce, istăce** for fem., and **illōc, istōc** for neut. are also found.

The initial **i** of **iste, istic** appears to have been sometimes omit- 375 ted; e.g. At **stuc periculum** (Ter. *Andr.* 566); quæ **sti rhetores** (Cic. *Or.* I. 19); quid me **sta res** (Cic. *Fam.* 4. 3. 2); jam **stinc** (Verg. *A.* 6. 389); modo **sto** (Hor. *Epist.* II. 2. 163), &c. See Lachm. *ad Lucr.* p. 197.

3. Hic (stem **ho-**), *this near me,* is declined as follows, the forms 376 in brackets being older forms used by Plautus, &c. (**hosce, hasce, hujusce** also in Cicero; **hæc** for nom. fem. plur. is found in Varro, Lucretius, and twice or oftener in Vergil. **Haice** neut. pl. only in *S. C. de Bacc.*)

(I. 5. 18) that **unius** was in his time **unīus.** Probably these words **illius, unius**) are taken as *instances* only. (Ritschl, *Opusc.* II. 696.)

SINGULAR.

	m.	f.	n.
Nom.	hĭc (hĭce)	hæc	} hŏc (hocc)
Acc.	hunc	hanc (hance)	
Gen.	hūjus or hujusce (hoiusce) in all genders		
Loc.	hĭc (adverb)		
Dat.	huic (hoice) in all genders		
Abl.	hŏc	hāc (hace)	hŏc

PLURAL.

	m.	f.	n.
Nom.	hī (hisce)	hæ (hæc) }	hæc (haice).
Acc.	hōs (hosce)	hās (hasce)	
Gen.	hŏrum (horunce, horunc)	hārum (harunce, harunc)	hŏrum
Loc. Dat. Abl.	hīs (hībus) in all genders		

4. **Is,** *that* (stem i- and eo-), is thus declined.

377

	SINGULAR.			PLURAL.		
	m.	f.	n.	m.	f.	n.
Nom.	ĭs	ĕă } ĭd		eī or iī	eæ } eă	
Acc.	eum	eam		eōs	eās	
Gen.	ējus (in all genders)			eōrum	eārum	eōrum
Loc.	ĭbĭ (adverb)					
Dat.	eī or ēi (in all genders) }			ēis, eīs or iīs		
Abl.	eŏ	eă	eŏ			

Em or im for eum is quoted from the XII. Tables; eæ for dat.
fem. in Cato; eiei, iei for dat. sing. in post-Gracchan and præ-
Augustan inscriptions; eis once for nom. s. masc.; iei, eis, eeis or ieis
for nom. plur. masc. and eieis, eeis, and ieis for dat. and abl. plural
in præ-Augustan inscriptions; ībus sometimes in comic poets and
Lucretius[1]; eābus in Cato for abl. plur. fem.; i and īs in Plautus.
iī and iis were common in post-Augustan inscriptions. Of poets
only the præ-Augustan used any of the cases, except that Horace
has the genitive and accusative in his non-lyrical writings.

Ennius is said to have written sometimes sum, sam for eum,
eam, and sas for eas. (Or perhaps for suas.)

The dat. sing. ei has rarely a short penultimate (ĕi): as ēi it is
frequent in Plautus and Terence and (in the last foot of the hexameter) in Lucretius. As a monosyllable it is also common.

[1] Where ĭbus appears to be long, hībus is probably the right
reading.

9

The suffix -pse is sometimes found in Plautus appended; e.g. 378
eapse, eumpse, eampse, eōpse, eāpse; and in Cicero often in the
phrase reapse (for re eâpse). In ipse (see above) the suffix is made
the vehicle of the case endings.

Idem, ĕădem, Idem, acc. eundem, eandem, Idem (compound of
is-dem) is declined like it, the forms iidem, iisdem however not
being found, and ĕīdem, ĕīsdem not frequently.

For the nom. masc. sing. and plur. eidem, eisdem are found in
præ-Augustan inscriptions. Comp. § 265, 363. Isdem also appears
to have been in use. For neut. s. eidem is found once in a præ-
Aug. inscr.

5. qui (stem quŏ-), *which, what? any,* an (adjective). relative, 379
interrogative, and indefinite pronoun is thus declined. Older forms
found in Plautus, &c. are added in brackets.

	SINGULAR.			PLURAL.		
	m.	f.	n.	m.	f.	n.
Nom.	quī	quæ }	quŏd	quī	quæ }	quæ
Acc.	quem	quam }		quōs	quās }	
Gen.	cūjus (quoius) in all genders			quōrum quārum quōrum		
Dat.	cui (quoi or quoiei) in all genders }			quĭbus (quīs or queis)		
Abl.	quō	quă	quō			

As an indefinite pronoun quă is more common than quæ in fem.
nom. sing. and neut. plur.

Cūjus was treated (in præ-Augustan writers and once in Vergil)
as a declinable genitive, i.e. an adjective with -o stem (e.g. is cuja
res, cujum periculum est. Cūjum pecus? (See the suffix -io in
Book III.) The following forms are found so used: nom. s. cuja
(f.), cujum (n.); acc. cujum (m. n.); cujam (f.); abl. cujā (f.); plur.
nom. cujæ (f.). (Never used instead of quorum or quarum.)
    In Plautus cuius is often a monosyllable.
    Quī is used (1) as an ablative (of all genders, and, occasionally
in early writers, of the plural) with the preposition cum appended
(quicum); (2) as a substantive relative and interrogative (e.g. habeo
qui utar); (3) as an adverbial interrogative, *how?* and (4) occasionally as indefinite, e.g. neuqui, siqui (Plaut.). As a locative
ūbi (for quŏbi) is used.
    The ablat. plur. quīs is found often in Varro, Sallust, and
Tacitus, rarely in Cicero.

Qui like any other adjective can be used substantively, but 380
(owing to the use of quis, quid) it is actually so used in the nom.
singular and neuter acc. sing., as an interrogative rarely, and
chiefly in dependent questions: as an indefinite pronoun, whether
substantively or adjectively, only after si, nisi, nĕ, num.

In the cases named, an allied form **quis**, neut. **quid** takes its place.   **Quis** (1) as an interrogative is generally a substantive (and as such is in early writers predicated of males or females), but sometimes a masculine adjective : (2) as an indefinite pronoun, it is used both as substantive and as masculine and feminine adjective. **Quid** and its compounds are always substantives.

The compounds of **qui, quis** are mainly declined like them, but 381 all have -**quid** (not -**quod**), when used as substantives. Other peculiarities are here named.

Aliqui, aliqua, aliquod, *some*.   **Aliquis** is a subst. and masc. adj.; and is more common than **aliqui**. **Aliquae** as nom. fem. sing. occurs in Lucretius once, and not at all as neut. plur. Abl. **aliqui** is sometimes used in Plautus.

Ecqui, ecqua, or ecquae, **ecquod**, *any?* **Ecquis** is subst. and masc. adj.   The only cases besides the nom. in use are dat. **eccui** ; acc. **ecquem, ecquam** ; abl. m. and n. **ecquo**.   The plural is rare, but the forms **ecqui, ecquos, ecquas**, are found.

Quinam, quaenam, quodnam, *any?* **Quisnam** is also used.

Quidam, quaedam, quoddam, *certain.*

Quicunque, quaecunque, quodcunque, *whatsoever.* The -**cunque** is sometimes separated from **qui**, &c.; e.g. **qua re cunque possum** :

Quilibet, quaelibet, quodlibet, *which you like:*

Quivis, quaevis, quodvis, *which you will.* Sometimes with **cunque** attached; e.g. **quiviscunque**, *whatsoever.*

The following have **quis** instead of **qui** for the nom. sing. masc. 382

Quisquis, *whosoever* or *whatsoever;* **quidquid** or **quicquid**, *whatever*, also a substantive. **Quiqui** (nom. sing.) only in Plautus once. **Quisquis** as adjective is not applied to females. Of the other cases we have only the locative **quiqui** in Plaut. and possibly in **cuicuimodi**: the abl. masc. and neut. **quoquo**; acc. in comic poets **quemquem**; **quiqui** nom. plur. masc.; in Livy **quibusquibus** (dat. pl. perhaps in quotation from ancient document), and **quaqua**, in Tacitus as abl. fem. sing.; elsewhere only as adverb.

Quisquam, n. **quicquam**, *any at all.* Generally used as substantive, but **quisquam** is also used adjectively of females (as well as of males). **Quiquam** as ablative in Plautus. The plural and the feminine singular are not used. **Quodquam** also not used.

Quispiam, quaepiam, quodpiam, *some.* Plaut. has an abl. **quipiam**.

Quisque, quaeque, quodque, *each.* **Quicque** or **quidque** is subst. **quisque** used of a woman in Plautus.

Its compound **unusquisque** is similarly declined.

Quis appears to have stem **qui-**, and to belong to the **-i** stems (see 383 Chap. x). Probably the forms (now partly assumed by **quo-**) were, Nom. **quis**, neut. **quid** (so also **is, id**); Gen. **quis**; Acc. **quem** (the proper accus. of **quo-** being **quom** now used as conjunction), neut. **quid**; Abl. **qui** (hence possibly **quid**, *wherefore*; but comp. τί). Plural nom. and acc. **ques** (old form used by Cato and Pacuvius, cf. § 363), neut. **quia** (used as conjunction); Gen. **cuium** (found in Plautus); Dat. Abl. **quĭbus.**

CHAPTER VIII.

PERSONAL PRONOUNS.

THE substantives, called personal pronouns, are very peculiar in 384 their inflexions, nor are all the cases formed from the same stem.

	1st Person.	*2nd Person.*	*3rd Person.*
SINGULAR.			SING. and PLUR.
Nom.	ĕgo	tu	no nom.
Acc.	me	te	se
Gen. (see below)			
Dat.	mihi or mi	tibi	sibi
Abl.	me	te	se
PLURAL.			
Nom. Acc.	nos	vos	
Gen.	nostrum	vestrum (vostrum)	
Dat. Abl.	nobis	vobis	

SINGULAR. *Accusative.* The forms **med** and **sed** occur as 385 accusatives in some early inscriptions, and **med** and **ted** both as accusatives and ablatives in Plautus; probably **sed** also (*Mil. Glor.* 1275). The **d** is probably the ablatival **d**, incorrectly transferred to the accusative as well[1]. Quintilian also mentions an old form **mehe**. **Tete** was rarely written for **te: sese** frequently for **se.**

Genitive. The old genitive of the 1st and 2nd persons was **mis**, 386 **tis**; the latter is found in Plautus. This was replaced as possessive by the adjectives **meus, tuus**; and as objective by the gen. sing. neut. **mei** (*of my being*), **tui.** So **suus** (adj.), **sui** for the genitive (both singular and plural) of the reflexive pronouns.

[1] Ritschl, *Neue Plaut. Excùrs.* (1869), p. 11.

Dative. **mi** is used both by Cicero and the poets.   387
For **sibi** old forms are **sibe, sibei** (cf. § 265).

Ablative. See above under *accusative.*

PLURAL. *Accusative.* For **nos** we have **enos** in the *Carmen Arvale.*

Genitive. As possessive genitives the adjectives **noster** and **vester** 388 were used; as objective **nostri, vestri,** and rarely **nostrum, vestrum;** as partitive **nostrum, vestrum,** and in the comic poets sometimes **nostrorum, nostrarum, vestrorum, vestrarum.**

To all cases (except **tu** nom.) of these substantive pronouns the 389 particle -met is sometimes added. For **tu, tutĕ** or **tutĭmet** are found.
The adjectives have in the ablative case -met or -pte often appended; e.g. **meopte, suāmet;** rarely in the gen. sing., e.g. **tuĭpte;** and acc. plur., e.g. **suosmet, suāmet.**

CHAPTER IX.

NOUNS OF CLASS II.

THE second main class of nouns contains stems ending in the semiconsonantal vowels u and i, or in a consonant.

i. DECLENSION OF -u STEMS.

The case suffixes, as seen in consonantal stems, are preserved 390 entire only in three or four nouns. They usually combine with the final vowel of the stem. The terminations thus become sing. nom. -us; acc. -um (for -u-em); gen. -ūs (for -u-is); dat. -ui, often -u; abl. -ū (for -ue); plural nom. acc. -ūs (for -u-es); gen. -uum; dat. abl. -ŭbus, generally -ĭbus. Some have collateral stems in -o, which are at least as early as the -u stems (see below).

The few neuter nouns differ only in the nom. acc. sing., 391 which exhibits the bare stem, and the nom. acc. plural which has the vowel a added (-ua). The contracted form of the dat. sing. is alone found now. (The neuters are **cornu, genu, pecu, veru;** also **artua** and **ossua** pl.)

No adjectives have stems in -u; except perhaps compounds of
manus; but these are found only in nom. and acc. sing., except
angvimanus acc. pl. twice in Lucr.

   (*a*) The words which retain the suffixes entire are   352
grūs (usually f., dat. abl. pl. gruĭbus); sūs (m. f., dat. abl. pl.
suĭbus and sŭbus; also sūbus: a gen. sing. sueris is also mentioned);
bōs, stem bŏv- (m. f., gen. pl. boum, and bovom or bovum; dat. abl.
bŭbus rarely bōbus); Jŏv- nom. s. Jup-pĭter (acc. Jŏv-em, so the
other cases: an old gen. pl. Joum is mentioned).

   (*b*) The remaining words are here arranged according to the 393
letter preceding the final u. (But few however of the numerous
verbals in -tu are here given.) All are masculine, except cōlus,
dŏmus, idus (pl.), mănus, portĭcus, quinquatrus (pl.), trĭbus; and
names of women and trees. A few are fem. or neut. as well as masc.

   The dat. pl. is in -ĭbus, unless otherwise stated.

-bu	trĭbus (f. dat. abl. pl. tribŭbus).
-mu	dŏmus (f.) voc. domus, gen. domus (domi only in Plaut.), 394 loc. domui, usually (as from -o stem) domi; dat. domui, rarely domo; abl. domo, sometimes domu. Plur. nom. domus, acc. domos, sometimes domus; gen. domorum (Lucr. Verg.), domuum (Sen. Plin. Tac.), dat. abl. domibus.
-cu	ăcus (m. f. dat. abl. pl. acŭbus); arcus (m. rarely f. dat. 395 abl. pl. arcŭbus: another form of gen. is arci or arqui (Cic. Lucr.), nom. pl. arci); fĭcus (f., only found in gen. and abl. s. and nom. acc. pl.; other cases, as well as these, from a stem in -o which is rarely m.); lăcus (m. dat. abl. pl. usually lacŭbus; laci gen. s. in inscr. of Sulla's time); pĕcu (n. not in gen. s. or dat. abl. pl. see § 458); portĭcus (f.); quercus (f. gen. pl. quercōrum, no dat. s. or dat. abl. pl.); spĕcus (m. also f. dat. abl. pl. usually specŭbus: rarely a nom. s. neut. specus; also nom. pl. speca).
-gu	algu (only as abl. s.); fāgus (f. -u stem only in nom. pl.; other cases from -o stems).
-tu (-su)	æstus (m.); artus (m. dat. abl. plur. almost always ar- 396 tŭbus); astus (m. often in abl. sing.; also, rarely and in silver age, nom. s. and nom. acc. pl.); cæstus (m. also abl. pl. from -o stem); exercĭtus (m.); fastus (m. i.e. *pride;* fastūs, fastibus are also found, rarely, in sense of *calendar*); frētus (m. only in nom. gen. acc. abl. sing.; but a neuter stem in -o is more usual); impĕtus (cf. § 443); mĕtus (m. no gen. or dat. abl. plur.); myrtus (f. only nom. acc. pl.; all cases, except gen. pl., are found from a stem in -o); noctu (f. only abl. s.; generally as adverb;

for -i stem see § 418); **partus** (m. dat. plur. **partŭbus**); **portus** (m. dat. abl. plur. both in -ŭbus and -ĭbus); **angĭportus** (m. only abl. s. and acc. pl.; a neuter with stem in -o is more common); **rictus** (m. rarely **rictum** n. nom.; **ricto** abl. s.); **rītus** (m.); **saltus** (m.); **sĕnātus** (m. for genitive see §§ 399, 463); **singultus** (m.); **sĭtus**, *drought* (m. no plur. or dat. s.; also a stem in -i, § 417); **spīrĭtus** (m.); **testu** (only in abl. sing.; also **testum, testo,** n.); **tumultus** (m.); **vultus** (m. acc. pl. **vulta** twice, Enn., Lucr.).

Also numerous verbal substantives (e.g. **gĕmitus, ictus,** 397 **luctus, nexus, quæstus,** cf. § 800); some of which are found only in the ablative singular; e.g. **arcessītu,** con-**cessu, nātu,** &c., **in promptu, in procinctu, injussu:** others-only in the dative and ablative singular; e.g. **irrī-sui, irrīsu; ostentui, ostentu;** &c. An oscillation be-tween abl. in -u and -o is found in **plebis scito, -scitu; opus est facto, factu,** &c.

-du   **grădus** (m.); **ĭdus** (f. pl.).

-nu   **ānus** (f.); **cornus** (f. besides nom. s. only in abl. s. and 398 nom. pl.; an -o stem in dat. abl. s. and pl.); **cornu** (n. also nom. acc. s. **cornum**); **gĕnu** (n. also an old nom. acc. **gĕnus**); **mănus** (f.); **pĕnus** (f. rarely m.; also two neut. stems, in -o, and, rarely, in -ŏs (§ 458): all are found in sing. but usually **penu** for abl.; in plur. only acc. **penus, penŏra**); **pīnus** (f. has -o stem also; abl. s. always **pinu,** abl. pl. **pinis;** no gen. pl.); **sīnus** (m.).

-lu   **cŏlus** (f. dat. only colo, abl. **colu, colo;** acc. pl. also **cŏlos;** no gen. or dat. abl. plur.); **gĕlus** (m. rare, except in abl. s.; a stem in -o is also used).

-ru   **currus** (m.); **laurus** (f. besides nom. s. only in gen. and abl. sing. and nom. acc. pl.; also a stem in -o declined throughout, but no gen. pl.); **nŭrus** (f.); **pronurus** (f.); **quinquātrus** (f. pl.); **sŏcrus** (f.); **prosocrus** (f.); **tŏnĭtrus** (m. also a neuter stem in -uo); **vĕru** (n. dat. abl. pl. **verubus** and **veribus;** also nom. s. **verum**).

-su   **cŭpressus** (f. besides nom. only gen. abl. s. and nom. acc. pl. both from -u and -o stems); **luxus** (m.); **ossu** (n. only gen. pl. **ossuum,** Pacuv. and nom. acc. pl. **ossua** in inscript.); **sexus** (m. also an indec. n. nom. acc. **secus**). See also, for supine forms, under -tu.

A genitive in -ĭ, chiefly in words with **t** preceding the ĭ, pos- 399 sibly from some confusion with the past participle, was frequent in writers of the sixth and seventh centuries u.c. These instances are given: **adspectī** (Att.); **adventī** (Ter.); **æstī** (Pac.); **exercitī**

(Næv., Att., Varr.); **fructi** (Cat., Ter., Turp.); **gemiti** (Plaut.);
lucti (Att.); **ornati** (Ter.); **parti** (Pac.); **piscati** (Turp.); **porti**
(Turp.); **quæsti** (Plaut., Ter., &c.); **salti** (Att.); **senati** (Plaut.,
Sallust, and was most common in the seventh cent. U.C.); **soniti**
(Cæc., Pac.); **strepiti** (Enn.); **sumpti** (Plaut., Cat., Lucil., &c.);
tumulti (Plaut., Ter., Enn., Sallust); **victi** (Plaut.). In some
other words (see above), though not in **arci**, **laci**, the -o stem is
found in other cases as well as the genitive. [For other forms of
the genitive, see § 463.]

Examples of declension of stems in -**u**.   400

SINGULAR.

Nom.	sū-s	artŭ-s	grădŭ-s ⎫	cornū
Acc.	su-em	artu-m	grădu-m ⎭	
Gen.	su-ĭs	artŭ-s	grădŭ-s	cornū-s
Dat.	su-ī	artu-ī or artū	grădu-ī or grădū ⎫	cornū
Abl.	su-ĕ	artū	grădū ⎭	

PLURAL.

Nom. ⎱ Acc. ⎰	su-ēs	artŭ-s	grădŭ-s	cornu-a
Gen.	su-um	artu-um	grădu-um	cornu-um
Dat. ⎱ Abl. ⎰	sŭ-bŭs and su-ĭbŭs	artŭ-bŭs	grăd-ĭbŭs	corn-ĭbŭs

CHAPTER X.

ii. DECLENSION OF -i STEMS.

NOUNS with stems ending in -i exhibit the following case end-   401
ings, composed partly of the final stem vowel, partly of case
suffixes.

SINGULAR. The nominative has one, sometimes more than
one, of four forms. It ends

(*a*) in -**ēs**. These are almost all feminine.

(*b*) in -**ĭs**, masc. and fem.: neuter in -**e**.

(*c*) in -**s**, after dropping the final vowel; a preceding t or d is
then also dropped as in consonant stems (§ 436). The same form is
used in adjectives for all genders. No neuter substantives have -**s**.

(*d*) in -**r** or -**l**; viz. some stems end in -er for masc.; others,
neuter in -**ăr** or -**ăl**. A few adjectives have -**ar**, or -**ŏr** for all genders. The r or l is the final consonant of the stem.

Accus. -em is found for masc. and fem. in all adjectives, and 402
always or usually in most substantives.   A few substantives have
also -im; very few have -im always, and of these last only vīs and
sitis are found often in the accusative at all.   (The neuter accusative is like the nominative.)

Gen. in -ĭs, *Dat.* -ī,

Loc. Abl. in -ĕ or -ī.   Adjectives with nom. sing. in -ĭs have -ī 403
always, other adjectives, except participles, used as such (see § 419),
have -ī usually.   Most substantives, substantively used adjectives,
and participles have -ĕ.   Neuters with -ĕ, -ĭ, or -r in the nom. sing.
have -ī in the abl.

PLURAL.   *Nom.* -ēs, rarely -īs; *Acc.* -ēs or -īs indifferently (on 404
-eis see § 265, 266).   Neuters have in both cases -ia, that is, -ă suffixed to the stem.   *Gen.* -ium in prose.   In verse the ı is sometimes
omitted for metre's sake in stems ending in -ntɪ, and in a few other
words.   *Dat. Loc. Abl.* -ĭbus.

Some older forms of the cases will be found in Chap. XII., but
the early inscriptions, i.e. before the seventh century U.C., contain
very few instances of -ɪ stems.

(N.B.   In the list given below, the occurrence of an accus. in -im,
or of an abl. in -e from an adjective, or in -i from a substantive,
will be mentioned.   The instances of the nom. plur. in -īs, being
probably not peculiar to particular words, will not be mentioned.)

The origin of the -ɪ stems[1] and of their case-endings[2] is ob- 405
scure.   Very few of these stems appear to correspond with -ɪ stems
in Sanskrit or Greek (e.g. ignis, Sanskr. agni-; poti-, Sanskr. páti-,
Greek πόσι-; angui-, Sanskr. ahi-, Gr. ἔχι-; turris, τύρσις; ovis,
Sanskr. avis, Gr. ὅϊς); many correspond to stems with a, or (Greek)
o or υ as final vowels.   Some are clearly weakened forms of -o
stems (e.g. exanimis, inermis, sublimis, &c., and comp. humilis
with χθαμαλός, imber- (imbri-) with ὄμβρος, nocti- with noctu,
sitis with situs, perhaps also ponti- with pontufex, fusti- with
fustuarium, &c.): others have lost a consonant[3] (e.g. vī- for vīrī-,
cucumi- for cucumis-, tigrī- for tigrid-, and compare clavis with
κλεῖδ-; apis with ἐμπίς, ἐμπίδ-; ἔριν acc. from ἐριδ-[4]).   It is
probable therefore that the -ɪ of these stems is, at least in most
cases, the representative of an earlier vowel, and, according to the

---

[1] See L. Meyer, *Vergl. Gr.* I. 126, II. 117 sqq., 162 sqq.; Schleicher,
Vergl. Gr. p. 384, 432, 452, ed. 2.
[2] See Corssen, *Aussprache,* I. 727, 734, 738 sqq. ed. 2; Bücheler,
Lat. Dec.
[3] Key considers -ɪ to stand for ·ɪc; *Essays,* 215, 236, &c.; *Lat. Gr.*
p. 441, &c. ed. 2.   [4] But see Curtius, *Gr. Etym.* p. 563, ed. 2.

general law of Latin vowel-changes, may therefore often have been immediately preceded by e (long or short). (In the very early inscriptions we have aidiles beside ædilis n. sing., and marte, martei for marti, dat. s., militare for militaris, nom. s.) This conclusion is confirmed by the fact that in numerous stems a nom. sing. is found in -es, as well as in -is; and it would account for the predominance of -e in the ordinary case-endings. It may be noted that none even of the words quoted above, as having the best claim to an original -i, have -im in the accusative sing. (But see § 196.)

The weakness of the -i is shewn by its frequent omission before 406 the nominative suffix s, whenever the effect of an adjoining s on the preceding consonants would not be dangerous to the identity of the stem. Thus loquax, stirps, mens, ars, mus for loquacis, stirpis, mentis, artis, muris (cf. § 192); but sublimis not sublimps; avis not aus; ungvis not unx (comp. ningvis, nivi-, nix); vates or vatis not vās; vestis not vēs; &c. In the words cānis, juvěnis, mensis the i as well as the s is suffixal, and it is not unlikely that some other words (e. g. indoles, vates, &c.) may belong properly to the class of nouns with consonant stems. (See the Preface.)

The origin of the long vowel in the nominatives in -ēs is not 407 clear. Some stems (e. g. plebes, also plebs; fames, also famis) have cases like the first class of nouns (§ 340).

A large proportion of the -i stems have only one syllable besides 408 the -i, or are compounds with no further derivative suffix. Again, a very large proportion have the syllable preceding -i long. And in many of these, two consonants immediately precede the -i, as if the addition of the -i had either forced together the other syllables, or were itself a means, at least in the gen. plur., of giving play to a too heavy mass. (Comp. § 435.)

The chief derivative suffixes are -ăci, -enti, -īli, -āli, -āri.

The following is a tolerably complete list of words of this 409 class, except that some little-used compounds are omitted, and specimens only given of the principal classes of derivatives. In some words there is little or no positive evidence of the stem having -i, and they are placed here or among consonant stems in accordance with such analogies as may be found.

  1. Stems with labial before -i.   410

All retain i or e in nom. sing. except stirps, trabs, plebs, urbs, nix.

  (a) *Stems in* -pi.

-ăpi   apis (f. gen. pl. sometimes apum); gausăpe (f. abl. sing. also has acc. pl. A neuter stem in -o is more usual).

-ŏpĭ	cōpem (adj. no nom. sing.).
-ūpĭ	rūpes (f.).
-uppĭ	puppis (f. acc. regularly -im; abl. often in -ĭ; puppe, though frequent, being later; not before Ovid).
-æpĭ	cæpe (n. only used in nom. acc. sing.; usually stem in -a); sæpes (f. also sæps rarely).
-ĕpĭ	præsēpe (n. also has acc. pl. præsēpes (f.); abl. s. præsepĭo; abl. pl. præsepiĭs; and perhaps acc. s. præsepim).
-lpĭ	Alpes (f. pl.); volpes (f. also volpis once Petron.).
-rpĭ	stirps (f., sometimes as *tree stem* m.; nom. s. stirpis twice, and stirpes once in Liv.); turpis (adj.).

(β) *Stems in* -bĭ.   411

-ăbĭ	trabs (f. trăbes Enn.).
-ŏbĭ	scŏbis (f.); scrŏbis (m. f. also nom. s. scrobs Colum.).
-ābĭ	lābes (f.); tābes (f. only in singular, and that is rare; abl. tabĕ, tabo usually, tabē once in Lucr.).
-ūbĭ	nūbes (f. also nubs Liv. And.); pūbes (f. dat. pubē Plaut. once); impūbis (adj.).
-ēbĭ	plebs (f. sometimes written plæps; also has nom. s. plēbes and (Liv.) plebis; see §§ 340, 357; no plural).
-mbĭ	delumbis (adj. Plin. once); pălumbes (m. f. also pălumbis, besides gen. and acc. sing. and nom. acc. and abl. pl. from a stem in -o; pălumbibus is not found).
-rbĭ	corbis (m. f. abl. in -i twice in Cato); imberbis (adj. older stem in -o); orbis (m. abl. sometimes in -i); urbs (f. sometimes written urps).

(γ) *Stems in* -mĭ.   412

-ămĭ	fămis (f. rare except in gen. s.; other cases from fames, § 340).
-ŭmĭ	cŭcŭmis (m. acc. in -im, abl. in -i; also with stem cŭcŭmis-); incŏlŭmis (adj.).
-ĭmĭ	exănĭmis, semianimis, unanĭmis (adj. also earlier -o stems, which alone are used in plur.).
-āmĭ	infāmis (adj.; acc. infamam once Lucil.).
-ŏmĭ	cōmis (adj.).
-ūmĭ	implūmis (adj.); rumis (f.? old word; only acc. in -im; abl. in -i).

-ēmi	birēmis, trirēmis, &c. (adj. often as subst. f.; abl. rarely in -e).
-īmi	sublīmis (adj. also an early -o stem).
-rmi	abnormis, enormis (adj.); biformis, informis, &c. (adj.); inermis (adj. also an earlier form in -o); vermis (m.).

(δ) *Stems in* -**vi**. (For -qvi see § 414; for -gvi § 415.)   413

-ui	lues (f. also has acc. and rarely abl. s. no plur.); strues (f. no gen. or nom. acc. plur.). For grūs, sūs, see § 392.
-ăvi	ăvis (f. abl. sometimes in -i); grăvis (adj.).
-ŏvi	ŏvis (f. but in ancient formula m.).
-ĕvi	brĕvis (adj.); lĕvis (adj.).
-ivi	nix (f. gen. pl. only in Lamprid. See below ningvis).
-āvi	clāvis (f. acc. sometimes in -im); conclāve (n.); nāvis (f. acc. often in -im; abl. often in -i); rāvis (f. acc. in -im; abl. in -i); svāvis (adj.).
-īvi	cīvis (m. f. abl. often in -i); acclīvis, declīvis, proclīvis (adj. also with -o stems).
-nvi	tenvis (adj.), see § 92.
-lvi	pelvis (f. acc. sometimes in -im; abl. usually in -i).
-rvi	enervis (adj.).

2. Stems with a guttural before -i.   414

(a) *Stems in* -**ci**, -**qvi**.

All drop -i in nom. sing. except those ending in -sci and -qvi.

-qvi	quĭs (pronoun. See § 383. Comp. also is § 377).
-ŏci	præcox (adj. for older præcoquis; also rarely a stem in -o).
-ĕci (-ĭci)	simplex (adj.); dŭplex, &c. (For supplex see § 439.)
-āci	fornax (f.); pax (f.), and numerous verbal adjectives; e.g. audax, dīcax, fĕrax, lŏquax, vīvax, &c.
-auci	fauces (f. pl., also fauce abl. sing.).
-ōci	atrox (adj.); cĕlox (f., but in Liv. m.); fĕrox (adj.); solox (adj., old word); vēlox (adj.).
-ūci	lux (f. abl. sometimes in -i); Pollux (m. old nom. s, Pollūces).
-æci	fæx (f. no gen. pl.).

-ĭcĭ	bĭlĭcem (adj. acc. s.); fēlix (adj.); pernix (adj.); and the verbal forms chiefly feminine, but in plural used also as neuter adjectives; e.g. victrix, ultrix, corruptrix, fautrix, &c.
-ncĭ	deunx (m.); quincunx (m.), &c.; lanx (f. no gen. pl.).
-lcĭ	calx (f. sometimes m., no gen. pl.); dulcis (adj.).
-rcĭ	arx (f.); merx (f., also old nom. s. merces, mers).
-rqvĭ	torqvis (m. rarely f. nom. sing. rarely in -es).
-scĭ	fascis (m.); piscis (m.).

(β) *Stems in -gı, -gvı, -hı.*   415

All retain ı or e in nom. sing.

-ăgĭ	ambāges (f. pl. also abl. s., ambāge; the gen. pl. only in Ovid once, ambagum); compāges (f.); contāges (f. only in Lucr. abl. once contāgē); propages (f. once in Pacuv.); strāges (f.).
-ūgĭ	jūgis (adj.).
-ngvĭ	angvis (m. f. abl. rarely in -ı); bilingvis (adj.); exsangvis (adj.); ninguis (f. once in Lucr. same as nix); pingvis (adj.); ungvis (m. abl. sometimes in -ı).
-ĕhĭ	vĕhes (f. also vehis Colum., gen. pl. vehum in Cod. Theod.).

Examples of declensions of stems with labial or guttural 416 *before -ı. Compare § 447.*

			adj. m. f. n.
SINGULAR.			
Nom.	nūbē-s	nāvĭ-s	audax
Acc.	nube-m	nave-m	audāce-m n. audax
Gen.	nubĭ-s	navĭ-s	audaci-s
Dat.	nubī	navī	audacī
Loc.	nubī	navī ⎫	
Abl.	nubĕ	navĕ ⎭	audacī (rarely audacĕ)
PLURAL.			
Nom.	nubē-s	navē-s	audacē-s n. audaci-a
Acc.	nubē-s or nubĭ-s	navē-s or navī-s	audacē-s or audacī-s n. audaci-a
Gen.	nubi-um	nāvĭ-um	audaci-um
Dat.⎫ Loc.⎬ Abl.⎭	nubĭ-bus	navĭ-bus	audacĭ-bŭs

3. Stems with a dental before -i.

(*a*) *Most stems in* -ti, preceded by a consonant or long vowel, and a few others drop i (and then t also) in nom. sing.; but stems in -sti, and a few others retain it. Two or three have nom. sing. in -əs.

-ăti   nătis (f.); rătis (f.). Comp. also adfatim.

-ŏti   pŏtis, pŏtĕ (only in nom. and both forms alike for all genders and numbers). For compos, &c. see § 443.

-ŭti   cŭtis (f.). Perhaps also intercus, § 443.

-ĕti   hĕbĕs (adj. abl. in -i, but in Celsus once in -e; tĕrĕs (adj.). No gen. pl.; hebetia, teretia occur once.

-ĕti (-iti)   ancĭpĭti-, nom. s. anceps, also (once in Plaut.) ancipes (adj. abl. s. always in -i, no gen. pl.): so also biceps, triceps, præceps (acc. s. præcipəm (Læv. or Liv. Andr.?), abl. præcipe Enn.).

-iti   sĭtis (f. acc. in -im, abl. in -i, no plur. Comp. situs, § 396).

-ăti   crātis (f. nom. s. only in Veget., acc. s. cratim Plaut. and cratem; comp. cratĭcula); grātes (f. pl.; only nom. acc. and once, in Tacitus, abl. grātĭbus); vātes (m. f. also rarely vatis; gen. pl. usually vatum). So Reāte (abl. in -e).   418

    Burgher names (adjectives); e.g. Arpīnas (old form Arpīnatis); Larinās; Fidenās; Antiās; Privernās; &c.: also cūjas (nom. cujatis, Plaut.); nostrās; optĭmās (nom. sing. not found); pĕnātes (m. pl.); summātes (m. pl.); infĭmātis (nom. s.) occurs once in Plaut. [primas, magnas only late]. For sanates see Fest. p. 321, Müll.

-auti   cautes (f.).

-ōti   cōs (f. no gen. pl.); dōs (f. gen. pl. usually in -ium).

-ēti   lŏcŭplēs (adj. abl. s. usually in -ĕ; gen. pl. sometimes in -um); rēte (n. abl. sometimes in -e; acc. s. also retem, m.); tăpēte (n. sing. acc. m. tăpēta, abl. tăpēte (both in Sil. only); plur. nom. acc. tăpētia, tăpēta; dat. abl. tăpētĭbus, tăpētis); trăpētes (m. pl., acc. trăpētas, abl. trăpētĭbus; but forms from a stem in -o are generally used).

-iti   līs (f., older stlis); dīs (adj., contracted for dives), nom. sing. once only (Ter.); mītĭ-s (adj.); Quirĭs (adj.); Samnīs (adj.); vītĭ-s (f.).

-pti   neptis (f. abl. once in -i in Tac.).

-cti   nox (f., also abl. s. noctu, chiefly adverbial); lac (n., also lact (Pliny, *H.N.* xi. 39, 95, &c. ed. Detlefsen) and lacte; abl. s. lacti; no plur.); lactes (f. pl.); vectis (m. abl. rarely in -i).

The neuter names of towns, **Bibracte, Soracte,** have abl. in -e (**Sauracti** Varr. once).

-ntl-   Adjectives and participles.   Abl. sing. usually in -ı when used as epithets, in -e as substantives; participles always in -e as participles proper (e.g. in abl. of circumstances, or with an object). Nom. pl. sometimes in -**is,** usually in -**es;** acc. plur. in -**is** or -**ēs** indifferently; gen. plur. in -**ium,** except, not unfrequently, for metre sake in poetry.   419

Participles (very numerous); e.g. **ămans, mŏnens, sĕquens, præsens,** &c.

Adjectives; e.g. **āmens, clēmens, contĭnens, dēmens, dīlĭgens, ēlĕgans, ēlŏquens, ingens** (abl. always in -i), **innŏcens, insŏlens, lĭbens, pĕtŭlans, præstans, prūdens, rĕcens, rĕpens, săpiens, sons** (nom. s. not used), **insons, vĕhĕmens,** &c.

Substantives have abl. in -**e;** gen. pl. in -**um** occasionally in poets, except from monosyllabic nominatives; **adulescens** (m.); **ănĭmans** (m. f. in plur. n.); **antes** (m. pl.); **cliens** (m. also **clienta** f.); **consentīs** (m. plur.; gen. **consentum**); **dens** (m. gen. pl., according to Varro's express statement **dentum;** but MSS. and later grammarians give **dentium**); **bidens,** *a rake* (m. abl. in -i once in Lucr. at end of verse; *a sheep* f.); **trīdens** (m. abl. in -i sometimes at end of verse); **dextans** (m.); **dodrans,** &c. (m.); **fons** (m.); **frons** (f., in old writers sometimes m.); **gens** (f.); **infans** (m. f.); **lens** (f. acc. s. sometimes in -**im**); **mens** (f. old nom. s. **mentis**); **mons** (m.); **occĭdens** (sc. **sol** m.); **ŏriens** (sc. **sol** m.); **părens** (m. f. gen. plur. often in -**um** even in prose); **pons** (m.); **rūdens** (m. gen. often in -**um**); **sementis** (f. acc. sometimes in -**im**); **sentes** (m. pl. rarely f.); **serpens** (f. generally); **sponte** (abl. s. f.; also rarely **spontis** gen. sing.); **tŏrrens** (sc. **fluvius** m.); **triens** (m.).

-ltl   **puls** (f. gen. pl. only in Arnob.).   420

-rtl   **ars** (f.); **ĭners, sollers** (adj.); **cohors, cors** (f.); **fors** (f. no plur.); **fortis** (adj.); **Māvors, Mars** (m.); **mors** (f.); **pars** (f. sometimes acc. in -**im,** abl. in -i); **expers** (adj. no gen. pl.); **sors** (f. abl. s. rarely **sorti;** old nom. s. **sortis**); **consors, exsors** (adj. no gen. pl.).

-stl   **agrestis** (adj. abl. as substantive (m.) in -e rarely); **cælestis** (adj.); **fustis** (m. abl. often in -i); **hostis** (m. f.); **pestis** (f.); **postis** (m. abl. often in -i); **restis** (f. acc. usually in -**im**); **testis** (m.), *a witness* (m. f.); **tristis** (adj.); **vestis** (f.). So **Præneste** (abl. in -e except once in Propert.).

(β) *Stems in* -di. 421

All in -di preceded by a vowel retain -i or -e in nom. sing. except
fraus.

-ŭdi   rŭdis (adj.); rŭdis (f.); sŭdis (f. not found in nom. s.);
trŭdes (f. plur. rare).

-ĕdi   pĕdis (m. f.).

-ĭdi   fĭdis, *a harpstring* (f. fides once Cic. *Arat.* 381); vĭrĭdis
(adj.).

-ādi   clādes (f. also cladis Liv.).

-audi   fraus (f. sometimes with u for au).

-ōdi   enōdis (adj.).

-ædi   ædes (f. also ædis); cædes (f. also cædis Liv.).

-ēdi   sēdes (f. gen. pl. usually sedum).

-ndi   frons (f. old nom. frondis and fros); glans (f.); grandis
(adj.); juglans (f.); lendes (f. pl.); librĭpens (m.); ne-
frendes (adj. pl.).

-rdi   sordes (f. plur., also sing. sordem; sordis gen. Plaut. once;
sordi once in Ulpian; abl. sorde rare; sordē once Lucr.).
Adjective compounds of cor, stem cord- (abl. s. always
in -i): excors, concors, discors, mĭsĕrĭcors, socors, vēcors.

Examples of declension of stems with a dental before -i. 422
Comp. § 447.

SINGULAR.

Nom.	rătĭ-s	sĕquen-s	ar-s	ædes or ædis
Acc.	rate-m	sequente-m n. sequens	arte-m	æde-m
Gen.	ratĭ-s	sequentĭ-s	artĭ-s	ædi-s
Dat.	ratĭ	sequentĭ	artĭ	ædĭ
Loc. } Abl. }	ratĕ	sequentĕ or sequentĭ (§ 419)	artĕ	ædĕ

PLURAL.

Nom. }	ratē-s	sequentē-s (§ 419) n. sequenti-a	artē-s	æde-s
Acc. }	ratē-s (or ratĭ-s?)	sequentē-s or sequentĭ-s n. sequenti-a	artīs or artēs	ædĭ-s or ædē-s
Gen.	rati-um	sequenti-um	arti-um	ædi-um
Dat. } Loc. } Abl. }	ratĭ-bŭs	sequentĭ-bŭs	artĭ-bŭs	ædĭ-bŭs

4. **Stems ending in -nĭ, -lĭ, -rĭ, -sĭ.**   423

(*a*) *Stems in* -nĭ.

All retain -i in nom. sing. None have nom. sing. in -es.

-ănĭ   immānis (adj.); inānis (adj.); māne (n. indecl. abl. in -e); mānes (m. pl.); pānis (m. no gen. pl.).

-ŭnĭ   clūnis (m. f.); fūnis (m.); mūnis (adj. Plaut.).

-œnĭ   mœnia (n. pl.).

-ōnĭ   effrēnis, infrēnis (adj. stems in -o more frequent); lien (m. also liēnis Cels., gen. pl. in -ium and -um); pēnis (m.); rēnes (m. pl. gen. pl. sometimes in -um. Also a stem rien-).

-ĭnĭ   acclīnis (adj.); crīnis (m.); fīnis (m. f. in plur. rarely f. abl. s. often in -i); affīnis (adj. as subst. m. f.; abl. in -e and -i).

-mnĭ   amnis (m. abl. often in -i); indemnis (adj. post-Aug.); insomnis (adj. Aug. and post-Aug.); omnis (adj.); sollemnis (adj.).

-gnĭ   insignis (adj.); ignis (m. abl. usually in -i); segnis (adj.).

-nnĭ   biennis, sexennis, &c. (adj.); bipennis (adj. also subst. f. abl. in -i); perennis (adj.).

-rnĭ   bicornis (adj.).

(*β*) *Stems in* -lĭ.   424

All retain -i or -e in nom. sing. except neuters in -ālĭ, which sometimes drop it.

-ŏlĭ   indŏles (f. no plur.); sŏbŏles or suboles (f. plur. rare; no gen. pl.). Comp. proles, § 426. Also interpŏlis (adj.).

-ĭlĭ   ăgĭlis, dēbĭlis, făcĭlis, and many other verbal adjectives; grăcĭlis (adj. also a stem in -o, Ter. Lucil.); novensiles (adj. m. pl.); sĭmĭlis (adj.); stĕrĭlis (adj. with -o stem once in Lucr.); strĭgĭlis (f. abl. usually in -i).

-ālĭ   æquālis (adj. also subst. m. abl. in -i); canalis (m. f. abl. in 425 -i); contŭbernālis (m. f. abl. -e and -i); jŭgālis (adj.); nātālis (adj. as subst. m. abl. often in -e: see also § 331); nŏvālis (as subst. f. and -ale n.); quālis (adj.); rīvālis (adj. as subst. m. abl. in -e and -i); sŏdālis (m. abl. in -e and -i equally); tālis (adj.). Proper names, e.g. Jŭvĕnālis, have abl. in -e.

Neuter adjectives used substantively often drop the final -e and shorten final -al; e.g. ănīmăl, Baccānăl, bidentăl, căpĭtal, cervīcăl, Lŭpercăl, pŭteăl, tŏral, tribūnăl, vectīgăl, &c. But fōcāle, penĕtrāle.

Plural names of feasts; e.g. Baccănālia, compĭtālia, Flōrālia, Saturnālia, sponsālia, &c. have gen. pl. sometimes in -ōrum, as if from -o stems. So also vectigāliorum (Varr. Suet.).

-allĭ   callis (m. f.); valles (f. also vallis); convallis (f.).   426

-aulĭ   caulis (m. also cōlis).

-ōlĭ   mōles (f.); prōles (f. the plur. once only, viz. acc. in Colum.).

-ollĭ   collis (m. abl. rarely in -i); follis (m.); mollis (adj.).

-ūlĭ   ĕdūlis, cūrūlis, tribūlis (adj.).

-ēlĭ   fēles (f. also fēlis); mēles (f. also mælis Varr.); crūdēlis, fīdēlis, patruelis (adj.).

-ellĭ   imbellis (adj.); perduellis (adj.); pellis (f.); versipellis (adj.).

-īlĭ   ædīlis (m. aidiles in very early inscr., abl. usually in -e; 427 as adj. once in Plaut.); Aprīlis, Quintīlis, Sextīlis have abl. in -i; bīlis (f. abl. usually in -e); Civilis (as proper name, abl. in -e); vīlis (adj.); exīlis, servīlis, and other derivative adjectives.

Neuter adjectives used substantively: e.g. ancīle (gen. pl. anciliorum), cŭbīle, ĕquīle, hastīle, mantīle, mŏnīle, ŏvīle, sēdīle.

-illĭ   imbēcillis (adj. in Seneca rarely; regular stem in -o); mille (adj. indecl. in sing.).

Examples of declension of stems in -nĭ, -lĭ.   Comp. §§ 451, 461.   428

SINGULAR.

Nom.	ignĭ-s	sĭmĭlĭ-s	simĭlŏ	ănĭmăl
Acc.	igne-m	simile-m		
Gen.	ignĭ-s		simĭlĭ-s	animāl-ĭs
Dat.	ignī			
Loc. Abl.	ignī or ignĕ		simĭlī	animālī

PLURAL.

Nom.	ignē-s	simĭlē-s	simĭlĭ-ă	animālĭ-ă
Acc.	ignī-s or ignē-s	simĭlī-s or simĭlē-s		
Gen.	igni-um		simĭli-um	animālĭ-um
Dat. Loc. Abl.	ignĭ-bus		simĭlĭ-bŭs	animālĭ-bŭs

(γ) *Stems in* -ri. 429

Stems ending in -ri preceded by ŏ usually drop the ĭ in the nom. sing. masc. and drop the ĕ before r in all other cases; those ending in -āri usually drop e or i in the nom. acc. sing. neuter.

äri   Arar (m. acc. in -im; abl. in -i or -e); hĭlăris (adj. also with stem in -o, Plaut. Ter. Cic.); măre (n. abl. sometimes in -e in poetry; pl. only nom. acc. except marum Næv., maribus Cæs. once); bīmăris (adj.); pār (adj. cf. § 454), impar, dispar (adj.).

-ŏri   fŏris (f.); bĭfŏris (adj.); mĕmor (adj. gen. pl. only once used, viz. memŏrum in Verg., no neut. nom. acc.); immĕmor (immemoris nom. Cæcil.); indĕcŏris (adj. no gen. or neut. pl.).

-ĕri   cĕler (cĕleris m. in Cato); Līger (m. acc. in -im; abl. in ₄₃₀ -i or -e); Tībĕris or Thybris (m.); Vĕsĕris (m.).

(-pri)   vepres (pl. in sing. only veprem, vepre; usually m. Probably had n. sing. in -ēs, comp. veprēcula).

(-bri)   bilībris (adj.); bimembris (adj.); cĕlĕber (adj. cĕlĕbris as m. sometimes); December (adj.); febris (f. acc. often in -im; abl. usually in -i); fēnebris (adj.); fūnĕbris (adj.); imber (m. abl. in -i frequently); lŭgŭbris (adj.); mŭliebris (adj.); November, October (adj.); sălŭber (adj. often salubris m.).

(-cri)   ācer (adj. in Næv. and Enn. also as f.; acris is rarely m.); ălăcer (adj. alacris as m. rarely); mĕdiocris (adj.); vŏlŭcer (adj., rarely volucris as masc. adj. cf. § 456).

(-gri)   tigris (usually f., also with stem tigrid-).

(-tri)   linter (or lunter f. rarely m.); pŭter (adj. usually putris); venter (m.); ūter (m.). Also tres (pl.).

(-stri)   aplustre (n. also rare pl. aplustra); bilustris, illustris, sublustris (adj.); bimestris (adj. abl. rarely in -e Ovid); campester (adj. also campestris as m.); equester (adj. equestris as m. once); păluster (adj. also palustris); pĕdester (adj.); sequester (m.; an acc. and dat. abl. s. and nom. pl. from a stem in -o occur rarely); silvester (adj. usually silvestris); terrester (adj. usually terrestris).

-āri   Numerous adjectives, with contemporaneous or subse- 431 quent stems in -io. The neuter when used as substantive often drops e in nom. sing.

articularis, auxiliaris, popularis, &c. (see Book III.).

10—2

mŏlāris (m. sc. dens, abl. in -i); nāris (f.); pugillares (m. sc. codicilli).

Neuters: altāria (pl.), alveăre, calcăr, cochleăre, exemplar (exemplāre Lucr.), lacūnar, lăqueăr, lŭpānăr, pulvīnăr, tālāria (pl.), torcŭlar.

-auri   auris (f.).

-ōri   discŏlor, versīcŏlor (adj.).

-orri   torris ,(m.); extorris (adj.).

-ūri   būris (m. acc. in -im; no abl. found; also with -a stem); sĕcūris (f. acc. often in -im; abl. always in -i).

-urri   turris (f. acc. usually in -im; abl. often in -i).

-erri   verres (m. also verris Varr.).

(δ) *Stems in* -si.   432

All retain -i in the nom. sing., except as, mas, mus, glis.

-ăsi (-ări) măs (m.).

-assi   as (m. rarely assis). So also its compound semis: but bessis, decussis, centussis, &c. (probably adjectives) are parisyllabic. Casses (m. pl. also casse abl. s.); classis (f. abl. often in -i).

-ūsi (-ūri) mūs (m.); plūs (n. abl. s. plure rare, no dat. s.; in plural nom. plūres (m. f.), plūra (n.); gen. plūrium; dat. abl. plūribus; so also complūres (plur.), but compluria once Ter. and so in other old writers (Gell. v. 21).

-ussi   amussim (m. only acc. s.); tussis (f. acc. in -im; abl. in -i).

-essi   messis . (f. acc. sometimes in -im); nĕcesse (indec., used only as secondary predicate, '*a matter of necessity*.' The form necessum is found in præ-Ciceronian writers and Lucr.; necessus as nom. in Ter.; as genitive (according to Lachm. ạd Lucr. 6. 815) in *S. C. de Bacc.*).

īsi (-īri)   glis (m.); vis (f. acc. vim, abl. vi, gen. and dat. rare: in plural acc. vis is found once or twice in Lucr., but the regular pl. is vīres).

-nsi   ensis (m.). Also numerous derivative adjectives; e. g. Castrensis, Narbonensis, &c. So atriensis (m. sc. servus abl. rarely in -e); circenses (m. pl. sc. ludi); Maluginensis (as proper name with abl. in -e); bimensis (adj.). For mensis see § 460.

-xi   axis (m. also written assis; abl. rarely în -i).

Examples *of declensions of stems in* -rl, *and declension of* vis. 433
Comp. § 461.

SINGULAR.		m. f.		n.	
Nom.	imbĕr	ācer (m.)	acri-s (f.) } acre		vis
Acc.	imbre-m	acre-m			vim
Gen.	imbrĭ-s		acrĭ-s		vis (rare)
Dat.	imbrī				vi (rare)
Loc. } Abl. }	imbrī or imbrĕ		acrī		vī
PLURAL.					
Nom.	imbrē-s	acrē-s			vīrē-s
Acc.	imbrĭ-s or imbrē-s	acrĭ-s or acrē-s	} acri-a		virī-s or vire-s
Gen.	imbri-um		acri-um		viri-um
Dat. } Loc. } Abl. }	imbrĭ-bus		acrĭ-bŭs		virĭ-bus

CHAPTER XI.

iii. DECLENSION OF CONSONANT STEMS.

The suffixes for masc. and fem. nouns with stems ending in a 434
consonant are: *Singular* Nom. -s (which however has fallen off or
was intolerable in stems ending in -n, -l, -r): Acc. -em; Gen. -is;
Dat. -ī; Abl. -ĕ. *Plural* Nom. Acc. -ēs. Gen. -um. Dat. Abl.
-ĭbus. For the older forms see Chap. XII.

The locative was usually the same as the ablative, but in some
words what was probably its original form remains, the same as the
dat. (e. g. Carthaginĕ or Carthaginī; tempori (written tempĕrī), rurī).

These suffixes are appended without alteration of the stem
except for nom. sing.

The suffixes of neuter nouns differ from the above only in having
the bare stem, sometimes with the vowel modified, for nom. acc.
sing.; and -ă (instead of -es) suffixed for nom. acc. plural.

A large proportion of the consonant stems have two syllables, 435
the second syllable being a derivative suffix. The final stem con-

sonant is always preceded by a vowel (except in cor, from stem cord-, mensis, volucris), and this preceding vowel generally short¹. (Comp. § 408.) The principal exceptions to this short quantity are the numerous stems in -tāt, -ōn, -ōr and a few in -īc.

The following enumeration is tolerably complete, except that specimens only are given of such classes of derivatives as contain very numerous instances.

1. Stems ending in mutes (and m). 436

Stems ending in mutes form the nominative singular by adding s, but the dentals (t, d) being assimilated to it fall away. A short ĕ preceding the final stem consonant is usually changed to ĭ in other cases than the nom. sing. (§ 234. 3 *b*).

e.g. princep- nom. princeps, acc. princĭp-em; jūdĕc- nom. jūdex, acc. jūdĭc-em; rādīc- nom. rādix, acc. rādīc-em; ĕquĕt- nom. ĕquĕs, acc. ĕquĭt-em; pĕd- nom. pēs, acc. pĕd-em.

Only three substantives are neuter, viz. ālec (also alex f.), căput (with its derivatives occĭput, sincĭput) and cor. The adjectives have no neut. nom. acc. plural.

(*a*) *Labial Stems.* 437

-ăp   daps (f. nom. s. rare; no gen. pl.).

-ŏp   ops (f. nom. s. only as name of goddess); inops (adj.).

-ĕp (-ŭp) auceps (m.); manceps (m. mancĭp- is more usual than the older mancŭp-).

-ĕp (-ĭp) forceps (m. f.); munĭceps (m. f.); princeps (adj. abl. s. always in -ĕ)²; partĭceps (adj. abl. s. always in -ĕ); adeps (m. f. sometimes written adips: no gen. pl.).

-ĭp   stip-em (f. no certain nom. s. or gen. pl.).

-ĕb (-ĭb) cælebs (adj.).

-m   hiemps (f. sometimes written hiems; cf. § 70).

---

¹ Consequently, the accentuation of the syllables is not altered, as it would have been, if the gen. pl. had ended in -ium, or neut. nom. acc. pl. in -ia; e.g. prínceps, príncipum, but princípium, princípia.

² The genitives, municipium once or twice in inscriptions, principium often in MSS. of Livy, forcipium in extract from Lucilius, are probably only mistakes of scribes. So hospitium in good MSS. of Cic. and Liv., obsidium in Liv. and Cæs., judicium, artificium, &c.

(b) *Guttural Stems.*   453

(a) *Stems in* -c:

-ăc   fax (f. no gen. pl.; old nom. s. faces); frăces (f. plur.
       no gen.).

-ŭc   crux (f. no gen. pl.); nux (f.); dux (m. f.); tradux (m.
       rarely f.); rĕdux (adj. abl. in -i except as oblique predi-
       cate); trux (adj. no gen. pl.).

-ĕc   fœnisex (m.); nex (f.); prĕc-em (f. no nom. s.); rĕsex
       (m.); sēmĭnĕc-em (adj. no nom. s.).

-ĕc (-ĭc)   Chiefly masculine. ăpex (m.); cărex (f.); caudex or 439
       cōdex (m.); cīmex (m.); cortex (m. sometimes f.);
       cŭlex (m.); forfex (m. f.); frŭtēx (m.); īlex (f.); illex
       (m.); imbrex (m. f.); lătex (m.); mūrex (m.); ōbĭce
       (only in plur. and abl. sing. f. sometimes m.); pælex or
       pelex (f. probably πάλλαξ); pōdex (m.); pollex (m.);
       pŭlex (m.); pūmex (m.); rāmex (m.); rŭmex (m. f.);
       sīlex (m. f.); sorex (m.); vortex or vertex (m.); vitex (f.).

       Semi-adjectival compounds; e. g. index (m. f.); jŭdex
       (m. f.); vindex (m. f.); artĭfex (m. f.; abl. sing. as
       adjective in -i); carnĭfex (m. f.); ōpĭfex (m. f.); pontĭfex
       (m. f.); auspex (m. f.); extispex (m. f.).

       Adjectives: supplex (abl. i in prose; ĕ frequently in
       metre); bivertex, &c.

       ĭbĭc-em (m. acc. s.); pantices (m. pl.); urpĭcem (m.
       acc. sing.; irpĭces nom. pl.) are not found in nom. sing.

-ĭc   Chiefly feminine. appendix (f.); călix (m., κύλιξ f.); 440
       dicis (gen. s. only in phrase dicis causā or gratiā); fĭlix
       (f.); fornix (m.); fūlix (f. usually fŭlĭcı); larix (m. f.);
       pix (f. no gen. pl.); sălix (f.); vārix (m. f.); vĭc-em (f.;
       no nom. sing. or gen. pl.).

-āc   lĭmax (usually f.). For adjectives see § 414.

-ōc   vox (f.).

-ūc   lux (f. abl. sometimes in -i; no gen. pl.).

-ĕc   ālex or hallex (f. also a neuter form alec or halec);
       vervex (m.).

-ĭc   All fem. cīcātrix; cervix; cornix; cōturnix; coxendix; 441
       lōdix; mātrix; mĕrĕtrix (the adjective has -i stem);
       nātrix; nūtrix; rādix; struix; vibĭc-em (no nom. s.). (Of

cicatrix, cervix, meretrix, instances of an acc. pl. in -is are found).

(β) *Stems in* -g :   442

-ŭg   conjunx, often written conjux (m. f.) ; bijŭgem, quadrijŭgem, &c. (adj. no nom. s., stems in -o more usual).

-ĕg   grex (m.) ; segrĕg-em (adj. acc. s.) ; ăquilex (m.).

-Ig   strix (f. gen. pl. strigium in Vitruv.) ; rēmex (m.).

-ūg   frūgem (f. no nom. sing.; frux and fruges quoted as early forms of nom. s.).

-ĕg   rex (m.) ; lex (f.) ; exlex (adj. only nom. and exlēgem, acc. s., in use).

(c)   *Dental Stems.*

(a) *Stems in* -t :   443

-ăt   ănas (f.), (gen. anitum, C. *N. D.* 2. 48)'.

-ŏt   compŏs (adj.) ; impŏs (adj.).

-ŭt   intercus (adj. not found in abl. s. or nom. acc. or gen. pl.).

-ŭt (-It)   căput (n. abl. in -i, Catull.) ; occĭput (n.) ; sincĭput (n.).

-ĕt   Nom. sing. in -ēs; ăbiēs (f.) ; ăriēs (m.) ; păriēs (m).

     Nom. sing. in -ĕs; interpres (m. f.) ; indĭges (m., rare in sing.) ; perpes (adj. abl. sometimes in -i) ; præpes (adj. abl. sometimes in -i) ; sĕges (f.) ; tĕges (f.) ; impĕtĕ (abl. s. also rarely impĕtis gen. sing.).

-ĕt (-It)   Nom. sing. in -ĕs;

     Substantives: ămes (m.?) ; cæspes (m.) ; fōmes (m.) ; 444 gurges (m.) ; līmes (m.) ; merges (f.?) ; palmes (m.) ; poples (m.) ; stīpes (m.) ; termes (m.) ; trāmes (m.).

     Semi-adjectival: antistes (m. f., also antistĭta f.) ; cæles (m., also in Ovid cælitibus regnis) ; cocles (m.) ; cōmes (m. f.) ; ĕques (m.) ; hospes (m., sometimes in poetry f.; also hospĭta, as f. sing. and neut. pl.) ; mīles (m. f.) ; pĕdes (m. f.) ; præstes (m. f.) ; sătelles (m. f.) ; vĕles (m.).

     Adjectives: āles (mostly as subst. m. f.; gen. pl. usually, because in dactylic verse, alituum) ; Cærĕs *of Cære* (from which Vergil has abl. Cærēte, and gen.

Cærĭtis); dĭves; sospes (also sospĭta, old form seispĭta, as epithet of Juno); sŭperstes.

-ăt A very numerous class of (chiefly abstract) substan- 445 tives (all feminine) in -tāt, e.g. cīvĭtas, æstas, călămĭtas, simultas, hērēdĭtas, tempestas, voluptas, cupĭdĭtas. The genitive plural is occasionally formed in -ium, especially from civitas and the three nouns next following, but from others than civitas rarely before the Augustan age.

sătias (f. usual only in nom. s.; acc. and abl. also in Lucret.).

damnas (adj.; in formula damnas esto, sunto both for nom. sing. and plur.).

-ŏt nĕpōs (m.); săcerdōs (m. f.).

-ūt jŭventūs (f.); sĕnectūs (f.); servĭtūs (f.); virtūs (f.); sălūs (f. only sing.).

-ēt quiēs (f.); inquiēs (f. also in nom. sing. as adj.); requiēs (f. no dative, or plural; also as an -e stem, § 340).

(β) *Stems in -d:* 446

-ăd vās (m. f. no gen. pl.), *bail.*

-ŭd pĕcŭs (f.), *a head of cattle.*

-ĕd pēs (m.); tripēs, cornĭpēs (adj.), &c.; compĕdēs (f. pl. also abl. s., compede, gen. pl. once compedium Plaut.); quadrŭpēs (f. usually, also m. n.; abl. sometimes in -i: nom. pl. quadrŭpĕdia once in Colum.).

-ĕd (-ĭd) obsĕs (m. f.; præsĕs (m. f.); dēsĕs (adj.); rĕsĕs (adj.).

-ĭd capĭs (f.); cassĭs (f.), *a helmet;* cuspĭs (f.); hence tri-cuspide (abl. sing.); lăpĭs (m. rarely f.); promulsĭs (f.).

-rd cor (n. no gen. pl.). Compounds of cor have stems in -i (§ 447).

-æd præs (m. no gen. pl., ancient form of plur. prævĭdes).

-ōd custōs (m. f.).

-aud laus (f., gen. pl. rarely in -ium).

-ūd pălūs (f.); incūs (f.); subscus (f.).

-ĕd hērēs (m. f.); exhēres (adj.); mercēs (f.).

Examples of declensions of mute stems. 447

Compare §§ 416, 422.

SINGULAR.	(adj. m. f. n.)	m. or f.	f.	m.
Nom.	princep-s	jūdex	ætā-s	pēs
Acc.	{princĭp-em (m. f.) {princeps (n.)	judĭc-em	ætāt-em	pĕd-em
Gen.	princĭp-ĭs	judic-is	ætāt-is	ped-ĭs
Dat.	princĭp-ī	judic-ī	ætat-ī	ped-ī
Loc.} Abl.}	princip-ĕ	judic-ĕ	ætat-ĕ	ped-ĕ
PLURAL.				
Nom.} Acc.}	princip-ēs (no neut.)	judic-ēs	ætāt-ēs	ped-ēs
Gen.	princip-um	judicum	ætāt-um (sometimes ætāt-ium)	ped-um
Dat.} Loc.} Abl.}	princip-ĭbŭs	judic-ĭbus	ætāt-ĭbŭs	ped-ĭbus

2. Stems ending in -n.

Stems ending in -n form the nominative singular in one of two 448
ways:

Either the nom. sing. is formed by dropping the final n; thus
stems in -ŏn, -dŏn, -gŏn, and a few others which are all masc. or
fem.: e. g. sermōn-, sermo (m.); lĕgiōn-, legio (f.); grandŏn-,
grando (f.); ŏrīgŏn-, ŏrīgo (f.). In the oblique cases -ŏn becomes
-ĭn.

Or the stem becomes the nom. sing. without alteration or addition. Thus stems in -mĕn, which, except one, are all neuter, and
a few others which are mainly masculine: e. g. agmĕn (n.), gen.
agmĭnis; tĭbīcĕn (m.), gen. tĭbĭcĭnis. Three words, căn-is, jŭvĕnis, sĕn-ex, are exceptional.

-ăn   cănis (m. f., old form cănes (Plaut.). The derivative
         canīcula seems to imply an -i stem).

-ŏn (-ĭn) nom. s. in -o. All except some here named, are femi- 449
         nine. hŏmo (m. also in old language with stems homōn-,
         hemon-); nēmo (m. f. gen. and abl. sing. rare; cf. § 372);
         turbo (m. turben, Tib.); căro (f. no gen. pl. The stem
         is carn- for cărŏn-).

margo (m. rarely f.); ŏrīgo (f.); ăbŏrīgĭnes (m. pl.);
aspergo (f.); compāgo (f.); ambāgine (f. abl. s. only);
indāginem (f., also in gen. and abl. sing.); and other
feminine substantives in -gŏn.

cardo (m.); ordo (m.); grando (f.); hărundo (f.); hirūdo
(f.); testūdo (f.); alcēdo (f.); grăvēdo (f.); ūrēdo (f.);
cŭpīdo (f. sometimes m.); sōlĭtūdo (f.), &c.; and some
other abstract feminine substantives in -īdŏn, -tūdŏn, &c.

-ĕn (-ĭn) flāmen (m.), *a priest;* fĭdīcen (m.); oscen (m., sometimes f.); tībīcen (m.); tŭbīcen (m.); pecten (m.),
glūten (n.); sangven (n.), and more frequently sangvĭs
(m.); pollin-em (m. also gen. and abl. s.). For stem
fĕmen-, nom. fĕmur (n.), see § 454.

And the numerous verbal neuters; e. g. agmen, lēnĭmen,
pŭtāmen, vŏlŭmen, nōmen, &c.; flāmen (n. is little used
except in abl. s. and pl. and nom. acc. pl.); binōmĭnis
(adj. gen. s. no other case); cognōmĭnem (adj. also abl.
sing. and nom. pl.).

-ĕn sĕn-ex (m. sometimes in poetry f.): the other cases do
not contain -ec- (which is seen in senec-tus, senecio, &c.);
jŭvĕn-is (m. f.).

-ŏn All masculine, except abstract substantives in -iŏn, which ₄₅₀
are all feminine, even when used with concrete meaning.

ăgāso (m.); ăquĭlo (m.); bāro (m.); būbo (m. once
fem.); būfo (m.); caupo (m.); cento (m.); cūdŏn-e (m.
only in the abl. case); leo (m.); līgo (m.); mango (m);
mūcro (m.); ŏpĭlio or upĭlio (m.); pāpĭlio (m.); prædo
(m.); pugio (m.); sermo (m.); stellio (m.); vespertilio (m.); titio (m.); and others.

Căpĭto (m.); and other descriptive names of persons.

ternio (m.); sēnio (m.); and other names of numbers.
Anio (also stem in -ĕn with nom. Aniēn).
commūnio (f.); perduellio (f.); rĕgio (f.); lĕgio (f.);
ŏpīnio (f.); dĭcion-em (f. acc. also in gen. and abl. sing.);
and other derivatives from adjectives and present stem of
verbs.
lectio (f.); ōrātio (f.); cænātio (f.); sorbĭtio (f.);
nātio (f.); and màny other derivatives from supine stem
of verbs.

Examples of declension of nouns with -n stems.   451

Compare § 428.

SINGULAR.	m.	n.	m.	f.
Nom.	tĭbīcĕn ⎫	agmĕn	hŏmo	lĕgiō
Acc.	tibicin-em ⎭		homĭn-em	legiōn-em
Gen.	tibicin-ĭs	agmĭn-ĭs	homĭn-ĭs	legion-ĭs
Dat.	tibicin-ī	agmin-ī	homin-ī	legion-ī
Loc.⎫ Abl.⎭	tibicin-ĕ	agmin-ĕ	homin-ĕ	legion-ĕ
PLURAL.				
Nom.⎫ Acc.⎭	tibicin-ēs	agmin-ă	homin-ēs	legiōn-ēs
Gen.	tibicin-um	agmin-um	homin-um	legiōn-um
Dat.⎫ Loc.⎬ Abl.⎭	tibicin-ĭbŭs	agmin-ĭbŭs	homin-ĭbŭs	legiōn-ĭbŭs

3.   Stems ending in -l, -r, -s.

Stems ending in -l, -r, -s are used as the nominative singular 452
without addition or change, except that some neuters change ĕs
into ŭs, and others change ŏr into ŭr, ŏs into ŭs.

(a) *Stems in* -l.   453

-ăl   sāl (m. sometimes in sing. n., no gen. pl.); Hannĭbal;
       Adherbal; &c.

-ŭl   consul (m.); exul (m. f.); præsul (m. f.).

-ĭl   vĭgil (m. sometimes f.); pervĭgil (adj.); pŭgil (adj.);
       mŭgil (m. also mŭgilis). The ablat. sing. when it occurs
       (as in vigil and pervigil) is in -i (cf. § 424).

       sŭpellectil- (nom. s. sŭpellex, f., no plural; abl. s. in i
       frequently); sil (n.).

-ŏl   sōl (m. no gen. pl.).

-ell   fĕl (n.); mĕl (n.). Both drop the second l in the nom.
       sing., and in plural have only nom. acc.

(β) *Stems in* -r. (Some are properly in -s: cf. § 183.)   454

-ăr   Lār (m.); baccăr (n.); jubăr (n.); instăr (n. only in nom.
       acc. sing.); păr (m. f.); compăr (m. f., as adjectives the
       last two have -i stems).

-ŏr   æquor (n.); marmor (n.).

Four neuters change -or- to -ur- for nominative and accusative cases; ĕbur (n.); fĕmur (n., in other cases stems
femŏr- and femĕn-, § 449, are alike used); jĕcur (n., in
other cases stems jĕcŏr-, jŏcĭnĕr-, are alike used, and more
rarely jŏcĭnŏr-); rōbur (n., probably once had stem in -s;
comp. robus-tus; and Cato probably wrote in one place
robus).

-ŭr   augur (m. f., once had stem in -s; cf. augus-tus); furfur
(m.); Lĕmŭres (m. pl.); turtur (m. f.); vultur (m.);
cicur (adj.).
fulgur (n.); guttur (n. rarely m.); murmur (n.);
sulfur (n.). So Anxur (n. m. § 324), Tibur (n.).

-ĕr   ăcĭpenser (m.); agger (m.); anser (m. rarely f.); asser [455]
(m.); carcer (m.); Cĕlĕres (m. pl.); lăter (m.); laver
(f.); Mulcĭber (m. also Mulcĭberi in gen. s.); mŭlier (t.);
Opĭter (m.); passer (m.); prŏcĕres (m. pl., sing. rare);
tŭber (also with stem in -ur), *a kind of fruit-tree* (f.?);
the fruit (m.); vespĕr-e (m. abl.; otherwise with -o stem);
vōmer (m. sometimes in nom. vōmis).

dēgĕner (adj. abl. always in -i); pauper (adj.); ŭber
(adj. abl. almost always in -i), *fruitful*.

ăcĕr (n.); cădāver (n.); cĭcer (n.); gibber (Plin. n.?);
ĭter (n. rare except in nom. acc. sing.); ĭtĭner (n. rare in
nom. acc. sing.); jŭgĕra (n. pl.; in sing. has stem in -o);
păpāver (n. also in Plaut. m.); pĭper (n.); sīler (n.);
sīser (n.); sŭber (n.); tŭber (n.), (1) *a hump*, (2) *a
moril*; ŭber (n.), *a teat*; verbĕra (n. pl. also abl. sing.
verbĕre, and rarely gen. s. verbĕris).

-ĕr (-r)   păter (m.); māter (f.); frāter (m.); accĭpĭter (m.); all
omit e before r in all cases except nom. sing.

-arr   far (n., in plur. only nom. acc.).

-ōr   All, except three, masculine.   [456]

ŏlor (m.); sŏror (f.); uxor (f.); ădor (n. also quoted with
stem in -ŏr); prīmōr-em (acc. m., nom. sing. not found).
ardor (m.); dŏlor (m.); ămor (m.); cruor (m.); ful-
gor (m.); and other verbals from present stem.

actor (m.); auctor (m. f.); ămātor (m.); auditor (m.);
censor (m.); and other verbals from supine stems.   For
adjectives in comparative degree see § 460.

Slave names; e.g. Marcipor, i.e. *Marcus' slave* (por =
puer, old pover), Lucĭpor, Publĭpor, Quintipor, &c. were
disused in Quintilian's time.

-ûr   fūr (m.).

-ēr   vĕr (n.).

-cr   vŏlŭcris (f. Cf. § 430).

(γ) *Stems in* -s.   457

All except **vas, os** (*a bone*), **mensis,** change **s** into **r** before a vowel; i.e. in all cases except nom. sing.

-ŏs (-ŏr)   All neuter, except **lĕpus** and **arbos.**   458

corpus (n.); dĕcus (n.); dēdĕcus (n.); făcĭnus (n., also stem facinĕr-); fēnus (n.); frīgus (n.); lītus (n.); nĕmus (n.); pectus (n.); pĕcus (n. See also § 395); pĕnus (n., more usually f. with stem in -u; see § 398); pignus (n., also stem pignĕr-); stercus (n.); tempus (n., but tempĕri is the best attested spelling for the locative); tergus (n.).

lĕpŭs (m.); arbōs (f. also arbŏr).

tĕnus (indecl.), *stretch?* used as adverb.

-ŭs (-ĕr)   nom. sing. -us; other cases, -ĕr. Originally -ŏs, § 213. 5.

ăcus (n.); fœdus (n.); fūnus (n.); gĕnus (n.); glōmus (n.); jūgĕrum (n. gen. pl. and jugeribus dat. abl. pl.; the other cases from an -o stem); lătus (n.); mūnus (n. in nom. acc. pl. both munera and munia); hŏlus (n.); ŏnus (n.); ŏpus (n.); pondus (n.); raudus (n.); rūdus (n.); sĕcus (n. only nom. acc. sing.); scĕlus (n.); sīdus (n.); vellus (n.); viscus (n.); ulcus (n.); vulnus (n.).

Vĕnus (f.); vĕtus (adj.).

-ēs (-ĕr)   nom. s. -ēs (gen. -ĕrĭs).   459

Cĕrēs (f.); pūbēs (adj.); impūbēs (adj., oftener impū-bis, neut. impūbe).

-ĭs (-ĕr)   cĭnis (m. rarely f.); cŭcŭmis (m., also with stem cucumi-§ 412); pulvĭs (m. rarely f., also pulvīs). In oblique cases -ĭs becomes -er; e.g. pulvis, pulvĕrem (§ 184. 3).

-ās   vās (n., plural vāsă, vasōrum, vasīs, from stem in -o, of which the singular is found in early writers), *a vessel;* fas (n.), nefas (n., both only in nom. acc. sing.).

-oss   ŏs (n. See also § 398), *a bone;* exŏs (adj. once in Lucr.).

-ōs (-ōr)   All masculine except ōs, *a mouth.*   460

lĕpōs (m.); hŏnōs (also hŏnŏr); lăbōs (more frequently lăbŏr; once in Verg. lăbōr); cŏlōs (also cŏlor); păvŏs (usually **pavŏr**); **ŏdōs** (also **ŏdŏr**); **rūmŏr** (cf. **rumus-culus**); **flōs** (m.); **mōs** (m.); **rōs** (m.); **ōs** (n., no gen. pl., dat. and abl. rare).

Adjectives of the comparative degree; e.g. **mĕliŏr** (m. f.), **mĕliŭs** (n.); **dūriŏr** (m. f.), **dūriŭs** (n.); &c. have ablat. sing. rarely in -**i**. Instances of the neuter also in -**or** are found in writers of the seventh century U.C.; e.g. **prior, posterior bellum** in Valerius Ant., Claudius Quad. &c.

-ūs (-ūr)   **tellŭs** (f.).
    crŭs (n.); **jŭs** (n., gen. dat. abl. pl. very rare); **pŭs** (n.); **rŭs** (n.); **tŭs** (n.): (the last three have in plural only nom. and acc.).

-æs (-ær)   **æs** (n.; the gen. dat. abl. plural are very rare).

-ens   **mensis** (m.); **mensium** and **mensuum** genitive pl. are sometimes found in MSS. but **mensum** usually.

Examples of declension of stems in -**l**, -**r**, *and* -**s**.   461

Compare § 433.

SINGULAR.	m.	m.	adj.	m.
Nom.	consŭl	pătĕr	mĕliŏr (m. f.) meliŭs (n.)	hŏnōs or honŏr
Acc.	consŭl-em	pătr-em	meliŏr-em (m.f.) melius (n.)	honŏr-em
Gen.	consul-ĭs	patr-ĭs	melior-ĭs	honor-ĭs
Dat.	consul-ī	patr-ī	melior-ī	honor-ī
Loc. Abl.	consul-ĕ	patr-ĕ	melior-ĕ (rarely meliorī)	honor-ĕ
PLURAL.				
Nom. Acc.	consul-ēs	patr-ēs	meliŏr-ēs (m.f.) meliŏr-ă (n.)	honŏr-ēs
Gen.	consul-um	patr-um	melior-um	honor-um
Dat. Loc. Abl.	consul-ĭbŭs	patr-ĭbŭs	melior-ĭbŭs	honor-ĭbŭs

SINGULAR.	n.	n.	n.	n.
Nom. } Acc. }	cădāvĕr	rōbŭr	ŏpŭs	tempŭs
Gen.	cadavĕr-ĭs	robŏr-ĭs	opĕr-ĭs	tempŏr-ĭs
Dat.	cadaver-ĭ	robor-ĭ	oper-ĭ	tempor-ĭ
Loc. } Abl. }	cadaver-ĕ	robor-ĕ	oper-ĕ	tempor-ĕ (cf. § 434)
PLURAL.				
Nom. } Acc. }	cadaver-ă	robor-ă	oper-ă	tempor-ă
Gen.	cadaver-um	robor-um	oper-um	tempor-um
Dat. } Loc. } Abl. }	cadaver-ĭbŭs	robor-ĭbŭs	oper-ĭbŭs	tempor-ĭbŭs

CHAPTER XII.

OLD OR EXCEPTIONAL FORMS OF CASES (CLASS II.).

Singular Number.

ACCUSATIVE. On the omission of the final **m** see § 86. Its 462 omission in writing was gradually given up during the 6th century U. C.

GENITIVE. On the omission of the final **s** see § 193. 5. Cicero, in his poems, and Lucretius appear to be the last who made use of this omission.

1. *Stems in* -**u**. Four endings, besides the regular -ŭs, are 463 mentioned, viz.:

(*a*) -uos, e. g. **Senatuos** four times in the *S. C. de Baccanalibus*. Augustus is said to have written **domos**. Ritschl conjectures **domuos**.

(*b*) -uis, the uncontracted ending is mentioned as used by several writers; e.g. **senatuis** (Sisenna); **anuis** (Ter. Varr.); **partuis, fructuis, domuis, victuis, graduis, rituis** (Varr.). Gellius (4, 16) believed that Varro and Nigidius Figulus wrote so always.

(*c*) **-uus** as found in MSS. (e.g. of Pliny the elder) was probably merely so written to denote the length of the û. It is found also in the nom. acc. plur.

(*d*) **-i**, see § 399.

2. *Stems in* **-i.** **Partus** is found on the Bantine bronze A.U.C. 464 621—636.

3. *Consonant stems.* An ending in **-us** is found in some inscriptions, but rarely later than 100 B.C.; e.g. **Castorus, Venerus, Cererus, Honorus, Cæsarus, patrus, nominus, hominus, prævaricationus.**

An ending **-es** is found in **Salutes, Apolones** (before the 2nd Punic war), and **Ceres.**

DATIVE. *Consonant and* **-i** *stems.* **-e** is found in inscriptions 465 chiefly before the end of the sixth century U.C.; (*a*) e.g. **Junone, matre, salute, Diove;** also in one **-i** stem **marte.** It appears to have been retained in some phrases; e.g. **solvendo ære alieno; jure dicundo,** even in Livy and Suetonius.

(*b*) **-ei** in præ-Augustan inscriptions; e.g. **Apolenei, legei, hæredei, Diovei, Hercolei,** &c. The only instances from **-i** stems seem to be **fraudei, martei, urbei.**

Both **-ei** and **-e** appear in the oldest inscriptions; **i** not till the time of the Gracchi. Corssen with others holds **-ei** to be the original dative suffix, **-i** the locative.

ABLATIVE. 1. *Stems in* **-u** *and stems in* **-i.** The ablative 466 probably ended in **-ûd** and **-id** (older **-ed**). But no certain instances occur in inscriptions except **navaled, marid** in the Duillian inscription.

In one or two instances we have **uu** to denote long **u**; e.g. **pequlatuu, arbitratuu.**

From **-i** stems we have, in præ-Augustan inscriptions, both **-ei** and **-i**; e.g. **partei, parti; fontei, omnei, sorti.**

2. *Consonant stems.* In these it ended in early times in **-e** and 467 **-id.** Thus in very old inscriptions we have **airid** and **aire; patre, nominid.** In the Duillian inscr. also **-ed;** e.g. **dictatored.** (But the copy which we have is post-Augustan, and, as Ritschl thinks, not even a faithful copy of the original.) In the *S. C. de Bacc.* is **coventionid.** (No later examples.) Hence the ablative occasionally appears with **i,** the **d** having fallen off; e.g. **deditioni, por-**

tioni (præ-August. inscrip.); **carni, věněri, oneri** (Plaut.); .**rationi, mucroni** (Lucr. in elision), &c.   But since the time of the Gracchi the ablative in -**ě** is much the most common even in inscriptions.

Plural Number.

NOMINATIVE AND ACCUSATIVE.   1. -**uus** sometimes in in- 468 scriptions and MSS. for -**ūs** (see Detlefsen's edition of Pliny, *H. N.*).

2. *Consonant stems.*   A few instances are found in MSS. of the ending -**is.**

GENITIVE.   1. *Stems in* -**u.**   The contraction of -**uum** is rare; 469 but **currum** (Verg.), **passum** (Lucil. Mart.) are found; **exercitum** in Mon. Ancyr., **magistratum** (Liv. *Cod. Veron.*).

2. *Consonant stems.*   Varro speaks of old forms **boverum, Joverum** for **boum, Jovum**; and Charisius speaks of the annalist Cælius having used **nucerum**, and Gellius, the historian, **regerum, lapiderum,** (from **nux, rex, lapis**).   Possibly such forms are due to a collateral stem in -**is** (-**ěr**); as in **cucumis**, §§ 405, 459; **sus** gen. sing., **suer-is** (Plaut.).   But they may arise from the simple addition of -**um** to the gen. sing.; e.g. **nucis-um** would become **nucerum.** Compare **familias** sing., **familiarum** plural.

DATIVE AND ABLATIVE.   The final **s** was omitted or not 470 pronounced in early poetry before a word beginning with a consonant.

The early form was in -**ebus**; e.g. **tempestatebus.**

CHAPTER XIII.

GREEK NOUNS. CLASS I.

GREEK nouns in the præ-Augustan period generally received 471 slight changes, especially of vowels, to adjust them to the Latin usage.   These forms were generally retained by the prose writers, but the Augustan poets, especially Propertius, Ovid and (later)

Statius, often introduced the Greek forms instead; and many words
not in common use are found in the Greek form only[1].

i. Stems in -a.

The Greek nouns corresponding to the Latin -a stems, ended in 472
the nom. sing. as follows: masc. -ᾱς (-ās), fem. -ᾱ (-ā), after a vowel
or r: otherwise, masc. -ης (-ēs), fem. -η (-ē). If Latinized all
become simply -ă.

In oblique cases the Greek declension has (usually) -ā, -ē in the 473
vocative, -ān, -ēn in the accusative singular. But the Latin vocative in -ă and acc. in -am (or -em, from Greek gentile names) are
often found even when the nominative retains the Greek form.
Stems in -tes had vocative (Greek, as well as Latin) -tă, e. g. Thy-
esta; also -tē, e. g. Boōtē. Patronymics in -des had vocative -dē,
e. g. Tȳdīdē, Ǣcīdē, Alcīdē; sometimes -dā, e. g. Ǣcīdā, Cecrōpīdā
(Ovid), Anchīsiādā (Verg.); accusative always -dēn, e.g. Laertia-
dēn, Pēlīden. So also feminine nouns with nom. s. in -ē; e. g. Cir-
cēn, Priēnēn.

The genitive, dative, and locative almost always take the Latin
form -æ. But Propertius, Ovid and later poets usually make the
genitive in -ēs from nominatives in -ē. So also Quintilian in names
like musīcē. A dative in -ē is rarely found except in some (not
early) inscriptions, e. g. Bæbiæ Phœbe; Juliæ Stratonice, &c.

The ablative of stems in -ēs and -ē is usually -ē.

The plural is almost always in the Latin form. (Names of 474
peoples &c. often have -um for -arum. See § 364.)

The following examples will serve to show the variety in the 475
nominative case singular.

1. *Greek nouns in -ᾱς (-ās), or -ης (-ēs). Masculine.*

(a) *Appellatives.* Sȳcŏphanta, pŏēta, nauta, pīrāta always.
Similarly athlēta, bibliopōla, propōla, cĭtharista, and in Plaut.
trapessīta (τραπεζίτης); danista (δανειστής). In Cicero, anagnostes,
geōmetres, sophistes. Later dynastes, choraules, alīptes, comētes,
pyctes, tetrarches, pyrītes, &c. So satrăpes (acc. usually satrăpam).

---

[1] "Nunc recentiores instituerunt, græcis nominibus græcas declina-
tiones potius dare, quod tamen ipsum non semper fieri potest. Mihi
autem placet rationem latinam sequi, quousque patitur decor."
QUINTILIAN (I. 5. 63).

(*b*) *Gentile names.* Persa (Plaut.), Perses (Cic.); Scythes (Cic. Hor.), Scytha (Lucan). In Cicero Abdērītes, Crotoniātes, Epīrōtes, Stagīrītes.

(*c*) *Names of men.* Hermia (Cic.), Mīda (Ter.), Marsya (Hor. Ov.), Pausānia (Cic.), Phædria (Ter.), Perdicca (Curt.), Æēta (Ov.), Prusia (Cic. Liv.). On the other hand Archias, Amyntas (Cic.); Prusias (Liv.); Æneas, &c.

Anchīses, Achātes, Thyestes. Patronymics rarely have -ă. Thus Hēraclīdes, Alcīdes, Asclēpiădes, Pelīdes. But Atrīdă is found (Hor. Ov.). Lucretius has two patronymics from Latin names: Memmiădæ (dat. sing.), *son of Memmius;* Scīpiădas (nom. s.;. Scipiadam acc. s. Hor.; Scipiadæ gen. s., Prop., Hor.; Scipiadas acc. pl., Verg.), *son of Scipio.*

2.   *Greek nouns in -ā (-ă) or -η (-ē). Feminine.*   476

(*a*) *Appellatives.* Apŏthēcă, aulă, bibliothēcă, tragœdiă, comœdiă, prōră, māchæră, purpŭră (πορφύρα), ancŏră (ἄγκῡρᾰ), nauseă (ναυσίᾱ), epistŭla (ἐπιστολή), scæna (σκήνη), always. In Cicero, grammaticē, dialectică, rhetŏrĭcă, mūsică: in Quintilian grammaticē, &c.

(*b*) *Names of places.* Ætnă, Cretă, Libyă, Spartă, Idă, Ĭthăcă, &c., but in Ovid usually Ætnē, Cretē, &c.   Thessălonĭca (Cic.); Thessalonice (Liv. Plin.).   Always Cyrēnē, Meroē.

(*c*) *Names of women.* For Ἀλκμήνη Alcumēna (Plaut.), Alcmēna (Cic.), Alcmēnē (Ovid). In Cicero, Varro, &c., Andrŏmăcha, Antiŏpa, Eurōpa, Hěcăta, Hělěna, Sěměla, &c. In poets usually Andromāchē, &c.   But nympha (Cat. Verg. Ov.), nymphē (Ov.). Always Běrěnīce, Hēbe, Daphne, Persěphŏne, Phœbe, Rhŏdŏpe, Thūle, Tisĭphŏne, &c.

ii. Stems in -o.   477

The -o stems in Greek had -ος (-ŏs) in nom., -ον (-ŏn) in accus. (and neuter nominative) singular.   The Latin form (-um) for the accus. is often found, even when a Latinized nominative (-ŭs, sometimes -er for -ěrus) is not found.   The other cases rarely received any other than a Latin form.

The following are instances of the usage:

SINGULAR. 1. *Appellatives* (Feminine), e.g. methŏdus, periŏ-   478 dus, atŏmus, antidŏtus, dialectus, always.   So trimětrus or trimě-ter; tetramětrus, or tetraměter; on the other hand diamětros (also diamětrus), perimětros, barbĭtos (m. and f.); phasēlos, *a boat,* fasēlus, *a boat, a bean.*

2. *Names of plants*, &c., e.g. acanthus (m.), aspărăgus (m.), asphŏdĕlus (m.), hyacinthus (m.), hellĕbŏrus (m. more frequently hellĕbŏrum, n.), papўrus (f.), &c. But lōtŏs (f.), aspalăthŏs, &c. *Precious stones* (mostly feminine), amethystus (f.), zmaragdus (m.), electrum (n.), topazos (f.), &c. *Animals*, arctos (f.); scorpios or scorpius (m.), camēlus (m. f.), &c.

3. *Names of towns and islands* (feminine), e.g. Abўdus, Corinthus, Lampsăcus, Păphus, Cўprus, Rhŏdus, Tĕnĕdus, Epīrus, &c. The forms in -os (-ον) in the poëts chiefly. Always Ægyptus, but (nom.) Imbros, Lemnos, Dēlos, Sămos, Sestos, Tyros, &c.

Names of rivers and mountains (masculine), Pēnēus, Caystrus, Mæander, Parnassus, &c. Also Penēos, &c. Usually Pelion (n.) and nom. Olympus (m.), Caucăsus (m.), acc. Olympum, Caucasum.

4. *Names of men.* Usually Latinized, especially those in -ρος (-rus), preceded by a consonant; e.g. Teucer, Mĕleager, rarely Meıeagros, Antĭpăter, Alexander, Menander, sometimes Menandros, Evander, sometimes Evandrus. So we have as accusatives Daidălon, Sĭsўphum, &c.

The genitive is sometimes in -u; e.g. Menandru, Apollodoru.

Panthūs, voc. Panthu is a contracted form (Πάνθοος, Πάνθοε).

Greek words in -εως (-eōs), are either completely Latinized; e.g. Tyndarĕůs, Pēnĕlĕůs, or sometimes have nom. -ōs, acc. -ōn or -o, e.g. Andrŏgeos (gen. Andrŏgeo, and Andrŏgei in Vergil).

So also a few names of places, viz.: Athos, Ceos, acc. Athŏn (Cat. Ov. Verg.), Atho (Liv. Plin.), Ceo (Cic.). Coos (Mela), Cŏŭs (Liv.) for Κόως, Κῶς, has acc. Coum (Plin. Tac.), abl. Coo (Cic. Plin.).

For some stems in ευ- (eu-) see § 482.

PLURAL. The Nominative rarely in -œ; e.g. Adelphœ (Ter.), 479 canēphŏrœ, arctœ, cosmœ (Cic.), Solœ, lotœ (Plin.). The Greek genitive in -ων (-ōn) is found sometimes with liber as the name of a book; e.g. Vergil's Būcŏlĭcon, Georgĭcon; Manilius' Astronŏmĭcon; rarely otherwise; e.g. Colonia Theræon, for Theræorum (Sall.).

On the genitive in -um, e.g. Pelasgum, Grajum, see § 365.

CHAPTER XIV.

GREEK NOUNS. CLASS II.

GREEK nouns of this class, as of the first class, frequently retain 480 such of their Greek inflexions as are not very dissimilar to the Latin inflexions. Plautus, Terence and Cicero for the most part Latinize the inflexions. Propertius, Ovid and the post-Augustan poets very frequently retain the Greek vowels and -n (for -m) of the acc. sing. and short pronunciation of the final syllables. Intermediate between these two parties stand Vergil and Horace, who with Corn. Nepos, Pliny and other post-Augustan prose writers share the same tendency as Ovid, but use many of the Latin forms. The Greek forms in all writers are much more frequent in proper names than in appellatives.

1. Stems in -o, -eu, -y.   481

-o   (*a*) Masculine. nom. in -ōs; acc. -ōem or (poet.) -ŏă; gen. -ōĭs; dat. -ōī. Plural nom. -ōĕs; acc. -ŏăs; gen. -ōum; dat. abl. -ōĭbus? (-ōĭsin once in Ovid).

e.g. hēros, Minos.

(*b*) Feminine. All cases in -o, except gen. -ūs. Ovid occasionally has accusative in -on. The early poets (Ennius, Pacuvius, Accius, and once Plautus), treated them as having stems in -ōn (e.g. Dīdōnem, &c.). So also the late writers, e.g. Servius, Macrobius.

e.g. Allecto, Argo, Callisto, Călypso, Dīdo, Echo, Hēro, Io, Ino, Manto, Theăno, Sappho.

·eu   Masculine. Nom. -ēūs; voc. -ēū; acc. -eum or (poet.) 482 ĕă[1]; gen. -ei or (poet.) -eōs; dat. abl. -eo. The poets (e.g. Verg. Ov. Prop.), often treat -ei, -eo as one syllable (see § 232).

_____

[1] Cicero in a letter to Atticus (6. 9. § 1) had used the expression "In Piræa cum exissem," and, Atticus having commented on it, Cicero replies (7. 3. § 10), "Venio ad 'Piræea,' in quo magis reprehendendus sum, quod homo Romanus 'Piræea' scripserim, non 'Piræum,' sic enim omnes nostri locuti sunt, quam quod 'in' addiderim."

e. g. **Atreus, Cepheus, Erechtheus, Mnĕstheus, Nēreus, Orpheus, Pēleus, Perseus, Prŏmētheus, Pīrææus, Prōteus, Tēreus, Thēseus, Typhœeus, Tyndăreus,** &c.   For metre's sake we have in acc. **Idŏmĕnĕă, Ilĭōnĕa** (Verg.), **Căpănĕă** (Stat.).

The plural is rarely found; e. g. accus. **Megareos** (Quintil.), **Phineăs** or **Phinēās** (Mart.).

The name of the Macedonian king Perseus had an e-stem used in Cicero, and an -eu stem used in Livy. Other writers generally follow Livy. Thus in Cicero, nom. **Perses**; acc. **Persen**, rarely **Persem**; gen. dat. **Persæ**; abl. **Persa**. In Livy, nom. **Perseus**; acc. **Perseum and Persea**; gen. **Persei**; dat. abl. **Perseo**.

In Horace are found **Achillĕī, Ulixĕī.**

The Greek ἀμφορεύς (m.), is in Lat. always **amphōra** (f.).

-y   Nom. **-ys** Voc. **-y** (in poets); acc. **-yn** or **-ym**; gen. **-yis** or **-yos**; dat. **-yi**; abl. **-ye**.   483

e. g. **chĕlўs** (f.), **Cotys** (m.), **Erīnys** (f.), **Hălys** (m.), **Phorcys** (f.), **Tēthўs** (f. dat. **Tēthўi** once Catul.).

2. Stems in -e and -i.   484

-e   (*a*) Masculine. Nom. s. **-ēs**[1]. Acc. **-em** or more frequently (especially in post-Augustan writers), in **-ēn**. Gen. usually in **-i**[2], sometimes **-is**. Abl. in **-ĕ**, rarely **-ē**. In plural these stems are often treated as if they ended in **-a**[3].

-ce   e. g. **Pharnăces.**

-che   e. g. **Lăches.**

-te   e. g. **Acestes, Achātes, Bŏōtes, Euphrātes, Hippŏcrătes, Iphĭcrătes, Isŏcrătes, Mithridates, Orestes, Phraētes, Pŏlўcrătes, Sōcrătes, Thyestes, Tīrĭdātes, Tīmŏcrătes, Xĕnŏcrătes,** &c.

A genitive in **-æ** is occasionally found in the poets; e. g. **Antĭphătæ, Bootæ, Orestæ, Thyestæ.**

---

[1] These stems properly end in -*os*, or -*es*; e. g. Σώκρατες, γένος. The final *s*, which is changed to **r** in Latin (§ 183 *b*), is omitted in Greek.

[2] In Greek inscriptions such forms as Σωκράτου, Καλλικράτου, Καλλισθένου, &c., (instead of Σωκράτους, &c.), occur, even in Attic.

[3] Forms like Σωφάναι, Πραξιτέλαι, &c. occur in Greek since Plutarch.

-de   e.g. Alcĭbĭădes, Aristīdes, Carneădes, Dĭŏmēdes, Eurīpĭdes, Gănўmēdes, Hypĕrīdes, Miltiădes, Pălāmēdes, Parmĕnĭdes, Simonĭdes, Thūcўdĭdes. Proper patronymics belong to the first class, § 475.

-ne   e.g. Artăphernes, Clisthĕnes, Demosthĕnes, Diogĕnes, Xĕnŏphanes.

-le   e.g. Achilles (see § 482), Aristŏteles, Hercŭles, Praxĭtĕles, Thales (see § 494); Agăthŏcles, Empĕdŏcles, Thĕmistŏcles, Pĕrĭcles.

        A few instances of acc. in -ă are found from stems in -cle, e.g. Pĕrĭclea, Strătŏclea (Quintil.); Pythŏclea, Sŏphŏclea (Sen.); Eteoclĕă (Stat.).

-se (-ze) e.g. Gotarzes, Oaxes, Ulixes (see § 482), Xerxes, Vologēses (some cases of a stem in -o are found from the last-named).

        (β) Neuters. Nom. acc. sing. -ŏs or -ŭs. Nom. acc. 485 pl. -ē (no other cases). e.g. cētŏs, mēlŏs, pĕlăgŭs; Tempe (plur. only). Pelăgus (n.), and cetus (m.), are also used with -o stems. So also ĕrĕbum (acc.), erebi, (gen.), erebo; chao (dat.), căcŏĕthes (adj. n.).

        (*a*) Feminine (chiefly, except names of rivers). Nom. 486 in -is. Acc. in -im or -in, abl. -ī.

        Appellatives: e.g. băsis (acc. also in -em), cannăbis, phthĭsis, părălўsis, pŏēsis, pristis, tigris (also with stem in -id).

        Names of Persons. e.g. Sesostris (m.), Mephītis (f.), Alcestis (f.).

        Names of Places. e.g. Amphipŏlis, Neăpŏlis, &c.; Chărybdis, Hispălis, Leptis, Memphis, Sўbăris, &c., also the plurals Gadīs, Sardīs, Syrtīs, Trallīs.

        Names of Rivers. Masculine. e.g. Albis, Bætis (abl. also in -ĕ), Ligĕris, Līris, Tamĕsis, Tănais, Tigris (see also § 501), Tībĕris; Vesĕris, Visurgis.

        A gen. pl. in -ŏn occurs in the word mĕtămorphoseōn as part of the title of Ovid's work.

        (β) Neuter. Nom. in -i. Cappări, gummi (or cummi), 487 sināpi, &c. These three are also found with nom. in -is, acc. in -im.

3. Consonant stems.

    The Greek forms are: Singular gen. -ŏs (Lat. -is); acc. -ă 488 (L.:t. -em); Plural nom. -ĕs (Lat. -ēs). Other differences apply only to particular stems.

(a) *Labial stems:*   489

-ăp   e. g. Lælaps (m.).

-ŏp   e. g. Æthiops (m.), Pĕlops (m.).

-ōp   e. g. Cȳclops (m.).

-ȳph   e. g. gryps (m. In plur. also gryphi, gryphorum, gryphis).

-ăb   e. g. Arabs (m., also nom. Arăbus; abl. Arăbō).

-ȳb   e. g. Chălybs (m.).

(b) *Guttural stems:*   490

-āc   e. g. anthrax (f.), Cŏrax (m.).

-ŏc   e. g. Cappădox (some cases from stems in -o in post-Augustan writers).

-ȳc   e. g. Eryx (m. acc. Erycum; abl. Eryco Cic. Tac.).

-ic   e. g. chœnix (f.), Cĭlix (adj.), hystrix (f.).

-āc   e. g. thōrax (m.), Ajax (m.), Thrax (m.), Phæax (m.).

-ȳc   e. g. Ceyx (m.), bombyx (m.).

-ȳch   e. g. ŏnyx (m. f.), sardŏnyx (f.).   491

-nc   e. g. lynx (f. rarely m.).

-ȳg   e. g. Phryx (m.), Styx (f.), Iāpyx (m.).

-ȳg   e. g. coccyx (m.).

-ng   e. g. Sphinx (f.), syrinx (f.), phălanx (f.).

(c) *Dental stems:* (a) *stems in* -t.   492

-āt   (1) Neuter. Nom. s. in -ă: Plural nom. in -tă; gen. in -tōrum; dat. abl. in -tĭs, sometimes in -tĭbus.

         e. g. dīplōma, emblēma, ĕpĭgramma, părăpēgma, pĕri-strōma, plasma, pŏēma, prŏblēma, tŏreuma. The early scenic poets and Sueton. treated schema as having an -a stem with short penult (but Nævius has schēmătĕ): Varro is said to have used schēmăsĭn as the dat. plur. In Plautus glaucŭmam (acc.) for γλαύκωμα (n.).

         (2) Neuter. Nom. s. in -ăs; e. g. artŏcreas, būcĕras, ĕrȳsĭpĕlas.

-ĭt   Nom. s. in ĭs; e. g. Chăris (f.).   493

         Neuter. Nom. s. in -ĭ; e. g. oxȳmĕli, hydrŏmĕli.

-ōt   Nom. s. in -ōs; e. g. Ægŏcĕros (m.), rhīnŏcĕros (m.),   494 Eros (m.).

-ēt   Nom. s. in -ēs; e. g. lĕbes (m.), magnes (m.); Crēs, Dăres, Thăles, Chrĕmes, Phĭlŏlăches, &c. The last three have also forms as from -ĭ stems; e.g. **Thălem, Thăli, Thăle** (§ 484. It has vowel, not dental, stem in Herodotus and Attic Greek).

-ĕth   Nom. s. in -ĕs; e.g. **Parnes.**

-ant   Nom. s. in -as, rarely in -ans; acc. in -anta, often in 495 poets; vocative sometimes in -ā; e.g. **Calchā, Pallā.**

       e.g. **ădămas** (m.), **gīgas** (m.), **ĕlĕphas** (m. the other cases most frequently formed as from a stem in -anto); **Atlas** (m.), **Calchas** (m.), **Cŏrўbantes** (m. plur.), **Pallas** (m.), **Thoas** (m.).

       For the Greek forms **Acrăgas** (m.), **Tăras** (m.) in prose we have regular -o stems; e.g. **Agrigentum, Tărentum.**

-ont   Nom. s. in -ōn. All masculine.   496

       e. g. **hŏrīzon, scazon, Anacreon, Autŏmĕdon, Chăron, Phaĕthon, drăco, chămæleon, Creon, Antĭphon, Xĕnŏphon.**

       The last three words, and others ending in -phont, have in Plautus and Terence and sometimes in Cicero stems in -phōn, nom. -pho, only; e.g. **Ctēsĭpho,** acc. **Ctesiphōnem,** &c.

-unt   Nom. s. in -us.   497

       e.g. **Pessĭnus** (m.), **Sĕlīnus** (f.), **Trăpezus** (f.). For Σιποῦς Cicero has **Sipontum**; Lucan and Silius **Sipūs** (m.); so in Livy and Pliny, **Hydruntum** (Ὑδροῦς). **Acheruns** (Plaut., Lucr.), **Acheron** (Cic. &c.).

-ent   Nom. s. in -is; e.g. **Sīmoïs.**

-ynth   Nom. s. in -ns; e.g. **Tīryns**

    (β) *Stems in -d.*

     In nom. sing. -d gives place to -s.   498

-äd   Nom. s. in -ăs. All feminine; e.g. **hebdŏmas, lampas** (acc. s. generally **lampăda**); **Pallas** (dat. s. **Pallădĭ** once); **Arcas, Cўclas, Drўas, Hămădryas, Hўas, Ilias, Mænas, Nŏmas, Orēas, Pleias, Thyas.**

       A few instances of gen. pl. in -ōn occur; e.g. **hebdŏmădon, Arcădon** (Varr.); and of dat. pl. in -ăsin; e.g. **Hămadrўăsin,** &c. (Prop.) ; **Trŏăsin, Lemniăsin** (Ovid).

-ŏd   Nom. s. in -ūs; e.g. **trĭpūs** (m.), **dăsўpus; Melampus,** 499 m. (voc. **Melampu,** once in Stat.). From **Œdĭpus** (m.) the following forms are found, chiefly in Seneca (*Trag.*) and Statius: nom. -ūs, -ŏdes; voc. -ĕ; acc. -um (Cic.), -ŏda? -ŏdem, -ŏden; gen. -ŏdis (Cic., Stat.), -ŏdæ (Sen., Stat.); dat. -ŏdæ; abl. -ŏde (Cic.), -ŏdā.

-ўd   Nom. s. in -ўs; voc. in -ў in poets; e.g. chlămys (f.), pĕlămys (f.), Iăpys.

-ĭd   Nom. s. in -ĭs; voc. in poets (not Plaut. or Ter.), fre- 500 quently in -ĭ. Other Greek forms are frequent; dat. sing. in ĭ occurs once, viz. Mĭnōĭdĭ (Catul.).

As regards the acc. s. these stems fall into two classes:

(1) Acc. s. in -ĭdem in prose and præ-Augustan poets; in -ĭdă in post-Augustan poets. All feminine.

Appellatives: e.g. ægis, aspis, canthāris, endrŏmis, ĕphēmĕris, hērōis, pĕriscĕlis, prŏboscis, pўrămis, pyxis, tўrannis (acc. s. in -ĭdă once in Cicero).

Names of persons: e.g. Amăryllis, Bacchis, Chrўsis, Dōris, Lāis, Lўcōris, Phyllis, Thāis.

Patronymics, &c.: e.g. Brīsēis, Cadmēis, Colchis, Gnōsis, Mĭnōis, Prĭămēis, Salmōnis, Tītānis.

Names of countries: e.g. Aulis, Chalcis, Locris, Persis, Phōcis.

(2) Acc. s. in -im or, sometimes, esp. in Augustan 501 and post-Augustan poets, -in. So all masculines and some feminines. An abl. or dat. s. in -ī is found in some; e.g. Eupŏli, Osīri, Phălări, Thĕti, Sĕmīrămi.

Appellatives: e.g. ĭbis (f., also in plur. ĭbes, ĭbĭum), īris (f.), tigris (both river and animal, also declined as if with stem in -ĭ. Dat. abl. plur. only tigrĭbus).

Names of persons. Masculine; e.g. Alexis, Adōnis (in Plautus once acc. Adoneum), Daphnis, Eupŏlis, Nabis, Păris (the last three have acc. also in -ĭdem), Mœris, Thyrsis, Zeuxis, Anŭbis, Busīris, Osīris, Serāpis.

Feminine; e.g. Isis, Sĕmīrămis, Procris, Thĕtis.

Names of countries: e.g. Phăsis (f.), Phthiōtis (f.) have also acc. in -ĭdem or -ĭdă.

-ĭd   Nom. s. in -ĭs; e.g. apsis (f.), crēnis (f.). (From κρηπῐδ- 502 we have only an -a stem, crĕpĭda.)

(d)   *Stems in* -n.   503

These generally retain -n in nominative (except some in -ōn); acc. s. frequently in -ă; plur. in -ăs.

-ŏn   Nom. s. usually in -ŏn; gen. s. sometimes in -nŏs; e.g. cănon (m.), dæmon (m.), gnōmon (m.), sindon (f.), Arīon (m.), Gorgon (f.), Memnon (m.), Ixīon (m.).

Some have also nom. s. in -o; e.g. Agămemno (m.),
Amphĭo (m.), Lăcĕdæmo (f.), Măcĕdo (m.), Strymo (m.).

Iāsŏnĭ dat. sing. in Statius.

-ĕn   e.g. Phĭlŏpœmen.

-ăn   Masculine; e.g. pæan, Alcman, Acarnan, Tītan (rarely 504
             declined as with -o stem), Pan (acc. s. always Pāna).

-ŏn   Mostly masculine.
             Names of persons and things. Nom. s. usually in -o; 505
             e.g. arrhăbo (sometimes f.), myŏpăro, sipho, Apollo (also
             e.g. Apollĭnem), Lăco, Amphĭtruo, Drŏmo, Phormio, Simo,
             Trānio, Dio, Hiĕro, Milo, Parmenio, Plato, Pyrrho, Zeno.
             So also stems in -phŏn, see § 496.
             But Trīton, Tĕlămon, Chiron.

             Names of places. Nom. s. usually in -on; e.g. Cŏlŏphon
             (m.), Mărăthon (f.), Sĭcўon (f.), Băbўlon (f.), Călўdon (f.),
             Hĕlĭcon (m.), Cithæron (m.), (Rŭbĭco (m.), is not a Greek
             word). For Ancon, Crŏto (m.), we have often -a stem,
             viz. Ancōna, Crŏtōna.

-ĕn   e.g. attăgen (m. Also a stem in -a, attagena); Sīren (f.), 506
             splen (m.), Trœzen (f.).

-ĭn   e.g. delphin (m. usual nom. delphīnus); Eleusīn (f.),
             Trāchĭn (f.). Rarely nom. s. in -s; e.g. Sălămis (f.).

     (e)   *Stems in* -s *or* -r: exhibit simple stem in nominative.   507

-ăr   e.g. nectar (n.).

-or   all masculine, e.g. rhētor (m.), Amyntor, Antēnor, Castor,
             Hector, Mentor, Nestor.

-ŭs (ŭr)   Nom. s. in -us; e.g. Lĭgus.

-ĕr   Nom. s. in -ĕr; e.g. āer; (m. acc. s. usually ăĕră, but
             aĕrem in Cato and Celsus); æther (m. acc. always
             æthĕră).

-ēr   e.g. chăracter (m.), crăter (m.) acc. crātēra (Cic.). Also
             with stem in -a; nom. s. cratēra and creterra. For pan-
             ther, stater, we have always panthēra, statēra.

CHAPTER XV.

ADVERBS AND CONJUNCTIONS.

ADVERBS and Conjunctions are indeclinable words, some of 508 them cases of existing words, others cases of lost words, others words with case-suffixes, different from those in common use in Latin, others mutilated remnants of fuller expressions.

They are here arranged according to the final letter of the ending, which sometimes is a suffix, sometimes part of the stem or some modification thereof.

-ā   Abl. sing. fem. from -o or rather -a stems. (Cf. § 1120.) 509

ea, *in that direction;* hac, illac, and (Plaut., Ter.) illa; alia; qua, quaque, quanam, qualibet; nequaquam, *by no means;* usquequaque, *everywhere;* utralibet, *in whichever direction you please.* These ablatives are often used with tenus; e.g. eatenus, *thus far,* hactenus, quatenus, quadamtenus, aliquatenus. So circa, *about;* juxta, *close;* erga, *towards.*

Supra (supera Lucr. often), *above;* infra, *below;* extra, *outside;* intra, *within;* ultra, *beyond;* citra, *on this side;* contra, *against.* (See § 160. 6.) So frustra (in Plaut. sometimes frustrā; ne frustra sis, *not to deceive you*), *in vain.*

So with prepositions, which in the ordinary language take an accusative; e.g. antea (antidea old), antehac (antidhac old), *before;* postea (postidea old), posthac, *afterwards;* interea, *meanwhile;* praeterea, praeterhac, *besides;* propterea, *therefore;* quapropter, *wherefore.* These expressions may be compared with paucis post diebus, &c.

-ă   Apparently accusatives plur. neut.   510

ita, *thus* (comp. iti-dem); quiă, *whereas;* aliuta (in old law), *otherwise:* it stands to aliud, aliut in same relation as ita to id.

-æ   præ, *in front* (old locative?).

-ō   Adverbs chiefly of manner (e.g. certo for certod; comp. 511 οὕτως, οὕτω).

(1) from substantives.

ergo, *on account of, therefore* (ἔργῳ); extemplo, *at once*
(extempulo, diminutive of extempore); illico, *on the spot,
instantly* (in loco); mŏdo, *only, just now* (lit. *in measured
terms*); numero (præ-Ciceron.), *just* (Pl. *Amph.* 180),
quickly (Varr. *R. R.* 3. 16. 7), usually *too soon* (lit. *by
number?*); oppĭdo (præ-August.), *very* (lit. *on the plain,*
cf. ἐπιπέδως); postmodo, *afterwards* (cf. § 528); præsto,
at hand; prŏfecto, *really* (for pro facto?); propemodo (Pl.
Ps. 276), *almost* (cf. § 528).

(2)   From noun adjectives and participles.

arcano (Plaut.), *secretly;* assiduo (Plaut.), *constantly;*
certo, *for a certainty;* cĭto, *quickly;* continuo, *straight-
way;* crebro, *frequently;* denuo, *afresh* (de novo); directo,
directly, straight; falso, *falsely;* fortuito, *by chance;* gra-
tuito, *gratuitously;* liquĭdo, *clearly;* manĭfesto, *palpably;*
merĭto, *deservedly;* mutuo, *mutually;* necessario, *necessarily;* omnĭno, *entirely* (as if from an adj. omninus); per-
petuo, *perpetually;* precārio, *on sufferance;* rāro, *seldom;*
secrēto, *secretly;* sedŭlo, *actively;* sērio, *seriously;* sēro,
late; subĭto, *suddenly;* supervacuo (post-Aug.), *superfluously;* tŭto, *safely;* vēro, *indeed, no doubt.*

bipertīto, tripertito, quadripertito, *divided into two,
three, four;* improvīso, *unforeseen;* inaugurāto, *without
taking auspices;* inopīnato, necopīnato, *unexpectedly;* &c.

(3)   *Ablatives of order.*

primo, *in the first place;* secundo, tertio, &c.; postrēmo,
ultimo, *in the last place;* immo (imo, *at the bottom?*) *at
the least, nay rather.*

(4)   *Direction towards a place.*

eo, *thither;* eodem, *to the same place;* eousque, adeo,
so far; quo-ad, *as long as;* huc (for hoc), *hither;* adhuc,
hitherto; illo, illuc (illoc Plaut.), *thither;* isto, istuc (istoc
Plaut.); alio, *elsewhither;* quo, *whither;* quonam, quo-
vis, quocumque, quoquo, quousque; aliquo, *somewhither;*
citro, *to this side;* ultro, *further;* intro, *inwards;* retro,
backwards; utro (rare), *to which of the two sides;* utro-
que, *in either direction;* neutro, *in neither direction.*
porro, *further* (πόρρω); quocirca, cf. § 160. 11.

-o-vorsus or o-vorsum, lit. *turned towards;* but vorsus and vorsum 512
were used indifferently and not inflected.

horsum, *hitherwards* (ho-vorsum); quorsus, quorsum,
whitherwards? istorsum, illorsum (Cato ap. Fest.),
aliorsum, aliquovorsum, utroquevorsum, altrovorsum
(Plaut., &c.), qvoqvoversus (Cic.), qvoqveversum (Cæs.).

controversus (adj.), *in dispute* (*turned against*); **introrsus, introrsum; retrorsum, dextrorsum, sinistrorsum.**

deorsum, *downwards;* **seorsum,** *separately* (**se-vorsum,** *turned to itself,* or *turned aside*); **sursum,** *upwards;* **prorsum, prorsus,** *forwards;* **rursum, rursus,** *backwards again.* (**Susum, prosum, rusum (russum),** are forms also found in Plaut., Lucret., &c.)

-do   **quando,** *when* (**quam-do**); **aliquando,** *sometimes;* **quando-** 513 **que,** *whenever, some time or other;* **quandocumque,** *when-soever;* **endo,** also **indu,** old forms of **in;** (comp. **induperator** for **imperator,** Enn., Lucr.; **indigeo, indipiscor,** &c.).

-ū   **diu,** *for long;* **interdiu** (**interdius** Cato, Plaut., cf. 514 § 828), *in the daytime;* **noctu,** *by night;* **simītu** (also, in an Augustan inscription, **simitur**), *at the same time;* **dudum,** *a long time* (for **diu-dum**).

-ō   Apparently old forms of ablative. (Comp. **facilumed** in 515 *S. C. de Bacc.*) From adjectives with -o stems both positive and superlative.

e. g. **ægre,** *hardly* (**ægro-**); **blande,** *soothingly* (**blando-**); **certe,** *surely* (**certo-**); **considerate,** *with consideration* (**considerato-**); **docte,** *skilfully* (**docto-**); **plane,** *quite* (**plano-**); **ornate,** *in ornate manner* (**ornato-**); **promisce** (Liv. 5. 48); **recte,** *rightly* (**recto-**); **sane,** *of course* (**sāno-**); **valde,** *very* (**valido-**); **vere,** *truly, actually* (**vero-**); &c.

ardentissime, *most eagerly;* **audacissime,** *most boldly;* **creberrime,** *very frequently;* **doctissime,** *very skilfully;* **maxime,** *especially;* **minime,** *least of all;* **pænissume** (Plaut.), *very nearly;* &c.

apprīme (præ-Ciceronian), *exceedingly* (**ad-primo**); **fēre, ferme** (superlative of **fere?**), *almost.*

-ĕ   (1) From -o stems; **běně,** *well* (**bono-**); **male,** *badly* 516 (**malo-**); **inferne,** *below* (**inferno-**); **superne,** *above* (**su-perno-**). Perhaps here belong **těměre,** *rashly;* **mactě,** *blest.* (Some take **macte** for a vocative; but it appears to be invariable in form, though used with a plural (cf. however, Plin. *H. N.* 11. 12), or as an oblique predicate.)

(2) From other stems; **abunde,** *abundantly;* **ante** (for **antid**), *before;* **forte,** *by chance* (abl. of **fors**); **facílě,** *easily* (**facili-**; comp. **dulce ridens,** &c.); **impūne,** *with impunity* (as if from adj. **impunis**); **mágě** (cf. **mágis,** § 545), *more;* **pæne,** *almost;* **rěpente,** *sudaenly* (**repenti-**); **rīte,** *duly;* **sæpe,** *often;* **sponte,** *of its own accord* (abl. of a nom. **spons**); **sublime,** *aloft* (**sublimi-**); **vŏlŭpe** (or better **volup**), *with pleasure* (almost always with **est**).

So the ablatives māne, *in the morning;* lūce, *by day-light;* nocte, *by night;* magnopere, *greatly* (magno opere).

hercle, *'pon honour* (for hercules. See Syntax).

-rĕ   A form of que (compare quispiam, quisquam); nem-pe, 517 *indeed* (nam-pe, comp. namque); quippe, *indeed* (for qui pe? comp. utique); prŏpe, *near* (comp. proximus, § 754, *a*).

-vĕ   Perhaps for vel. Sive (old seve, hence seu), *or if;* neve 518 (neu), *or not.*

-cĕ   ceu, *as* (for ceve, ce being of pronominal origin?).   519

hīc, illīc, &c., see § 524. 3; ecce, *behold* (for ence); sīc, *thus* (cf. § 524).

-qvŭ   Appended to pronouns (a kind of reduplication); e.g. 520 quisque, *each;* quandoque, *whenever;* quicumque (qui-quomque), *whosoever;* ubīque, *everywhere;* undique, *from all sides;* utique, *anyhow;* usque, *ever;* uterque, *each.* Also absqve, *without* (abs); atque (ac), *and also* (for ad-que, cf. p. 50); nĕque (nec), *not;* namque, *for.*

-ptĕ   e.g. suopte; see § 389. For pŏte? comp. utpote, *as.*   521

-dĕ   i.e. the preposition de shortened by losing the accent?; 522 e.g. inde, *thence* (im-de); indĭdem, *from the same place;* deinde, exinde, *thereupon;* proinde, perinde, *just so;* sub-inde, *immediately afterwards, repeatedly;* unde, *whence* (quom- or cum-de); undīque, *from all sides;* undĕcum-que, *whencesoever;* quamde (Enn., Lucr.), *than.*

-nĕ   sīne, *without;* pōne, *behind* (for pos-ne comp. § 535, and for -nĕ comp. supernĕ from supernus).

nē, *not, lest;* nē (wrongly written næ), *verily* (comp. 523 vaì, νή); nĕ interrogative particle, perhaps the same as nē. Comp. nĕ-fas, nĕ-quis, nĕ-vis, § 728.

-ī (rarely ĭ)   (1) Ablative cases of manner.   524

qui, (interrogative and relative like ut), *how, in which case;* quin, *why not?* but (qui-ne); aliōqui, alioquin, ce-teroqui, ceteroquin, *in other respects* (the final n is of obscure origin); nequiquam, *by no means;* atqui, *but;* perhaps also quippe; si, *if* (abl. or loc. of pronoun, *in which case*); nĭsĭ, *unless* (for ne si); quĭdem, *indeed;* sī-quĭdem, *if indeed, since;* quăsĭ, *as if* (quam si); sīc, *thus* (si-ce, *in which* or *this way*); ni, *not* (for ne, nei), also used as = nisi; quidni, *why not?* ŭtī (ut), *how* (for quo-ti); utīque, *any how;* utĭnam, *O that!* ne utīquam (nūtiquam), *by no means.* (For itĭdem *see* §§ 510, 531.)

(2) præfiscĭni (also præfiscine), *without offence* (præ fascino-, *for* i.e. *to avert bewitchments*); proclīvī (or pro-clivĕ), *downward* (proclivi-, old stem proclivo-); brevi, *in few words* (brĕvi-).

(3) Locative cases; illi, isti (Plaut., Ter.); illic, istic, *there* (illo-, isto-); hic, *here* (ho-); prīdem, *some time ago;* and perhaps hĕri (in Quintilian's time herĕ), *yesterday;* peregri, more commŏnly peregre, *abroad, from abroad;* temperi, *in good time* (tempos-); and others; see in Syntax.

-bi   **ibi,** *there* (is); inibi, *therein;* postibi (Plaut.), *thereupon;* 525 interibi (Plaut.), *in the meantime;* ibīdem, *in the same place;* ŭbĭ, *where* (for quobi, cubi); ubīque, *everywhere;* ubīcumque, *wheresoever;* si-cŭbi, *if anywhere;* ali-cubi, *somewhere;* alĭbi, *elsewhere* (ali-); utrŭbi, *at which of two places* (utro-); utrŭbīque, *at both places.*

-b   ab (abs), *from;* ŏb (obs), *opposite to;* sŭb (subs), *under.*

-am   jam, *now;* etiam, *also* (et jam); quŏniam, *since* (quom 526 jam); nunciam (Plaut.), *now* (nunc jam); nam, *for,* (*? now*); quam, *how, as;* quamquam, *however, although;* ălĭquan-do, *sometimes;* aliquamdiu, *for some time;* nŭti-quam (§ 524), *not at all;* uspiam, usquam, *any where;* nusquam, *no where;* præquam, *compared with;* tam, *so;* tamquam, *as if;* tandem, *at length.*

cōram, *face to face* (com, os-); clam, *secretly* (comp. oc-cul-o, *conceal*); obviam, *opposite* (obvio-; or ob viam, comp. obiter); pălam, prŏpalam, *openly* (pad-? pandĕre); perpĕram, *badly* (per-per-am? *thoroughly?*); promiscam (Plaut.), *promiscuously;* protīnam (Plaut.), *immediately.*

So the compounds with fāriam; e.g. bifariam, *divided in two* (bi-); trifariam, quadrifariam; multifariam, *in many places;* plurifariam, *in several places.*

-dam   quondam, *at one time.* (Comp. quidam, *a certain one.*) 527

-om (um)   Probably accusative cases.

dōnĭcum (Plaut., donique Lucr., donec commonly), 528 *until;* dum, *while;* dū-dum, *a long time* (diu dum); interdum, *for a time;* quidum, *how so?* primumdum, *first of all;* appended to imperatives, e.g. agedum, *come now;* manedum, *stop pray;* &c.; num (in questions), *now?* nunc (i.e. num-ce), *now;* etiamnum, *evennow;* quom, cum, *when* (quo-); quom (sometimes in præ-Augustan inscr.), com (in composition), cum (prep.), *with* (comp. ξύν); quon-dam, *at one time* (quom-dam); quandocumque, *whensoever;* tum, tunc, *then;* umquam, *ever* (um for quom; cf. § 121. 3); numquam, *never* (ne umquam); nonnunquam, *at times.*

actŭtum, *instantly* (*on the move?* actu-); circum, *round* (circo-); clancŭlum, *secretly* (clam, cf. § 862. *c*); commŏdum, *suitably, just now* (commodo-); dēmum, *at length:*

12

extrēmum, *for the utmost* (i.e. *last*) *time* (extremo-); in-
cassum, *to no purpose* (in cassum); mĭnĭmum, in phrase
quam minimum, *as little as possible* (minimo-); nimium,
too much; nœnum (generally contracted to nōn), *not* (ne
ūnum); părum, *little;* părumper, *for a little while;* plerumque, *for the most part* (plero-, que); postmodum
(Liv.), *afterwards* (cf. § 511. 1); postrēmum, *for the
hindmost* (i.e. *last*) *time* (postremo-); potissimum, *especially* (potissimo-); prīmum, *for the first time* (prīmo-);
propemodum, *almost* (cf. § 511. 1); ĭtĕrum (§ 888), *for
the second time;* tertium, quartum, &c.; ultimum, *for the
furthest* (i.e. *last*) *time;* secundum, prep. *following, along*
(sequondo-). For rursum, adversum, &c. see § 512.

Impræsentiārum, *at the present time* (for in præsentia 529
rerum? cf. § 28. 2).

-em   propĕdiem, *very shortly* (for propē dĭē, *on a near day?*)

-tem   autem, *however;* ĭtem, *likewise* (comp. ita, itidem); 530
           saltem, *at least.*

-dem   quĭdem, equidem (for et quidem?), *indeed;* prīdem, *some- 531
           time ago;* tandem, *at length* (tamdem); tŏtĭdem, *just so
           many;* ĭtĭdem, *likewise* (ita); ĭdentĭdem, *repeatedly* (for
           ĭdem ĭtĭdem? or ĭdem et ĭdem?). (Comp. ĭdem, *the
           same,* for is-dem; tantusdem.)

-im   denotes *at* or *from a place;* hin-c, *hence* (him ce); illim, 532
           istim, illinc, istinc, *thence;* im in inde (§ 522), *thereupo:;*
           exim, exin, exinde, *therefrom;* dein, deinde, *thereupon;*
           inter-im, *meanwhile;* ōlim, *in those times,* i.e. *formerly* or
           hereafter (ollo = illo); ĕnim, *for* (i.e. in im?); utrinque,
           on both sides (utro-).

           altrinsecus (for altrimsecus; Plaut.), *on the other side;*
           extrinsecus, *from outside;* intrinsecus, *from within;* fo-
           rinsecus (Col., Plin.), *from out of doors* (comp. foris).

-t-im (sim) Formed from or similarly to past participles; e.g. cæsim, 533
           edgewise (cædere); carptim, *by pieces, separately* (lit.
           plucking at it, carpere); cautim, *cautiously* (cavēre); con-
           fertim, *compactly* (confercīre); confestim, *immediately*
           (confĕrīre? cf. § 704); conjunctim (conjun-
           gere); contemptim, *scornfully* (contemnere); cursim,
           swiftly (currere); dispersim, *dispersedly* (dispergere);
           efflictim, *desperately* (efflīgere, *to kill,* hence efflictim amāre,
           to love to death); exsultim, *friskingly* (exsĭlīre); furtim,
           by stealth (fur, *a thief,* furā-ri); incīsim. *in short clauses*
           (incīdere); juxtim, *close at hand* (comp. juxta); mixtim,
           mingling (miscēre); partim, *partly* (parti-); passim, *here
           and there* (in a scattered way, pandere); pĕdĕtentim,

feeling the way (pede **tendĕre**); **præsertim**, *especially* (*putting in front*, **præsĕrĕre**); **punctim**, *pointwise* (**pungĕre**); **raptim**, *hurriedly* (**rapĕre**); **sensim**, *gradually* (lit. *perceptibly*, **sentīre**); **stătim**, *immediately* (lit. *as you stand*, **stă-**, **stāre**); **strictim**, *slightly* (lit. *grazing*, **stringere**); **tractim**, *in a long-drawn way* (**trahĕre**); **vīcissim**, *in turns* (**vīci-**); **ūbertim**, *plentifully* (**uber-**), &c.

-ăt-im   (1) From verbs with -a stems; e.g. **acervatim**, *in heaps*, 534 *summarily* (**acervā-re**); **centŭriatim**, *by centuries* (**centuriā-re**); **certatim**, *vying with one another* (**certā-re**); **cītātim**, *at full speed* (**citāre**); **dătatim** (datatim ludere, *to play at ball*), *giving and regiving* (**dătā-re** frequentative of **dăre**); **grăvatim**, *with difficulty* (**gravāri**); **mĭnūtatim**, *by bits* (as if from **minutare**); **nōmĭnatim**, *by name* (**nomināre**); **prīvatim**, *individually* (**prīvāre**); **prŏpĕratim**, *hurriedly* (**properāre**), &c.

(2) From nouns (compare **barbatus**, &c.); e.g. **căter- vatim**, *in troops* (**caterva-**); **gĕnĕratim**, *taking classes* (**genus**); **grădatim**, *step by step* (**gradu-**); **grĕgatim**, *in flocks, herding together* (**grĕg-**); **membratim**, *limb by limb* (**membro-**); **ostiatim**, *from house to house* (**ostio-**); **paullatim**, *little by little* (**paullo-**); **pectĭnatim**, *combwise* (**pecten-**); **regionatim**, *region by region* (**regiōn-**); **singillatim** *one by one* (comp. **singulo-**); **summatim**, *slightly, summarily* (*taking the tops*, **summo-**); **turmatim**, *by squadrons* (**turma-**); **vīcatim**, *street by street* (**vico-**); &c. Plautus used also **tuatim**, *after your fashion* (**tuo-**); Sisenna had **nostratim**, and **meatim** is mentioned by the grammarians.

-ū̆t-im   **mĭnūtim**, *in small pieces* (**minuĕre**); **tolūtim**, *full trot* (*raising the feet*, **tollĕre**); **trībūtim**, *tribe by tribe* (**tribu-**).

-ī̆o-im   **vīritim**, *man by man* (**vīro-**).

-t   **ast**, *but; at* (for **ad**?), *but* (also **atque, atqui**); **aut**, *or* 535 (comp. αὖτε); **ĕt**, *and* (comp. ἔτι); **ŭt** (for **uti**), *as* (**prout, præut, sicut, velut**); **post**, *after* (also **pos, poste, postidea**; comp. **ante, antidea**). **Săt** is shortened for **satis**. For -**met** see § 389.

-d   Old ablative suffix? cf. § 160. 6; **ăd** (cf. § 160. 10), *to;* 536 **ăpŭd**, *at; haud* (or **hau**), *not; sed, but* (properly *by itself*?). **Quŏd**, *because*, is neut. acc. (comp. ὅτι), but in **quod si**, **quod quia, quod utinam** is by some taken to be an old ablative (see Ritschl, *N. Plaut. Exc.* p. 57).

-n   **quĭn**, *why not?* (**qui ne**); **sĭn**, *but if* (**sī ne**, *if not?*): 537 (comp. **viden, audin**, &c.); **ăn**, *whether; forsan, forsĭtan* (**fors sit an**), *perhaps;* **tămĕn**, *yet;* **ēn**, *lo!* **ĭn** (cf. § 513), *in.*

-1   prŏcŭl, *off*, *afar*; sĭmŭl, older semol (for simile), *together*; sĕ- 538
     mĕl, *once*; vĕl, *or* (probably imperative of volo, hence *choose*).

-ur   Igĭtur, *therefore*; quor or cŭr, *wherefore* (for qua re). 539
     For sinitur see § 514.

-ĕr   Suffix of comparative degree: sŭper, *above* (*higher*; sub,
     up); desuper, insuper. Per, *through*; ter (for tris, cf.
     § 429), *thrice*; quăter, *four times.*

-pĕr   nŭper, *lately* (novumper); părumper, *for but little time* 540
     (parum); paullisper, *for a little while* (paullo-); quan-
     tisper (Pompon.), *for how long* (quanto-); tantisper, *for
     so long* (tanto-); semper, *always* (sim-, *whole?* comp.
     simplex, simul).

-tĕr   (1) From adjectives with -o stems: duriter (also dure), 541
     hardly (dūro-); firmiter (also firme), *firmly* (firmo-);
     hūmāniter, inhumāniter (also humane, inhumane), *polite-
     ly, impolitely* (humano-); largīter (also large), *lavishly*
     (largo-); longīter (Lucr.), *far* (longo-); nāvīter, ignāvi-
     ter (also nāvē, ignave), *skilfully, unskilfully* (gnavo-);
     luculenter (also luculente), *brilliantly* (for lūcŭlentĭter
     from luculento-); pūrĭ-ter (Catull., but commonly purē),
     purely (puro-); turbulĕnter (also turbulentē), *confusedly*
     (for turbulentiter from turbulento-); violen-ter, *violently*
     (violento-; the -i stem is not till Augustan time). Also
     from præ-Ciceronian writers are quoted: æquiter, ami-
     citer, ampliter, aspĕriter, avăriter, avĭditer, blandìter,
     iracunditer, mæstiter, misĕriter, munditer, parciter, præ-
     clāriter, prīmiter, prognāriter, propĕriter, proterviter,
     sæviter, sevēriter, superbiter, torviter, and a few others.
     Also in Varro, cadūciter, prŏbiter.

     (2) From adjectives with -i stems, and one (supplex)
     with consonant stem: acrĭ-ter, *eagerly* (acri-); ălĭ-ter,
     otherwise (ali-, § 373); aman-ter, *lovingly* (for amanti-
     ter); atrōci-ter, audac-ter, brĕvi-ter, celĕrĭ-ter, clemen-
     ter (for clementi-ter), concordi-ter, constan-ter (for
     constanti-ter), cupien-ter (Plaut., Enn.), decen-ter,
     demen-ter, dilĭgen-ter, elĕgan-ter, felīci-ter, ferven-ter
     (Cæl. ap. Cic.), frequen-ter, grăvi-ter, indulgen-ter,
     laten-ter, lēni-ter, lĕvi-ter, mediocri-ter, memŏri-ter,
     with good memory, misericordi-ter, pări-ter, salūbri-ter,
     scien-ter, simĭli-ter, simplĭci-ter, sollemni-ter, soller-ter
     (for sollerti-ter), supplĭci-ter, tenvi-ter, vernīli-ter, vigi-
     lan-ter, utĭli-ter, and others from stems in -nti, of which
     -ti is dropped before the suffix.

     (3) From other words: circi-ter, *about* (circo-); in-
     ter, *between* (in); præter, *beside* (præ); prop-ter, *near*
     (prŏpe); sub-ter, *beneath* (sub).

nĕquĭ-ter, *badly* (nequam). Oblter (not ante-Augustan), *on the way*, is apparently ob iter (comp. obviam).

-s abs (ab, a), *from;* bis, *twice* (cf. § 76); cĭs, *on this side* 542 (comp. ci-tĭmus); ex, *out* (ec in compounds, cf. § 113 and e); mox, *presently;* obs (ob), *on, opposite;* subs (sub), *under* (in subs-traho, &c.); trans, *beyond;* uls, *beyond* (comp. ul-timus); us-quam, us-piam, *anywhere;* vix, *scarcely.* Deinceps, *next*, is like particeps, but indeclinable.
siremps (old), *alike*, according to Ritschl, for si (=.sic) re ipsa, m being inserted as in rumpo, cumbo.

-ĭs alias, *at other times;* cras, *to-morrow;* fŏras, *(to) out of doors* (cf. § 1110).

-ŭs mordĭ-c-us, *with the teeth* (mordĕ-, mordĕre); sĕc-us, *other-* 543 *wise;* tĕnus, *as far as* (subst. acc. s. *extent?* cf. § 1086); prōtĕnus, *immediately.* Emĭnus, *from a distance;* commĭnus, *hand to hand*, are probably compounds of manus, *hand.*

-tŭs *from;* same as Greek -θεν (γράφομεν, scrĭbim*us*). 544 antĭquĭ-tus, *from of old* (antiquo-); divĭnĭ-tus, *from the Gods* (divino-); fundĭ-tus, *from the bottom* (fundo-); hūmānĭ-tus, *after the manner of men* (humano-); in-tus, *from within* (in); pĕnĭ-tus, *from the interior* (pĕno-); prīmĭ-tus, *at first* (primo-); publĭcĭ-tus (Plaut., Ter. &c.), *on the public account* (publico-); rādĭcĭ-tus, *from the root* (radīci-); stirpĭ-tus, *from the stock* (stirpĭ-); sub-tus, *underneath* (sub). From præ-Ciceronian writers also are quoted, medullĭ-tus, *from the marrow* (medulla); immortālĭ-tus, ŏcŭlĭ-tus, pugnĭ-tus, and from Varro communĭ-tus.

-ĕs pĕnes, *in the possession of* (comp. pĕnĭtus).

-is for -Ios, the stem or neuter acc. of the comparative 545 suffix; e. g. nĭmĭs, *too much* (for nimios-); măgĭs (măgĕ, *sometimes*), *more* (for magios-); sătis (also sat), *enough.* Fortassis (fortassĕ), *perhaps.* Perhaps the same is the origin of -is in paulis-per, tantis-per, quantis-per, § 540.

Fŏris, *out of doors;* imprimis, *in the first place;* ingrā- 546 tĭs, *thanklessly* (gratiis); multimodis, *manywise;* quotan-nis, *yearly*, are locatives or ablatives.

-iens post-Augustan -iēs; the regular suffix for numeral ad- 547 verbs: tŏtiens, *so often* (tot); quŏtiens, *how often* (quot); aliquotiens, *sometimes;* plūriens, *often* (plŭs-); quinquiens, *five times* (quinque); sexiens, *six times* (sex); septiens, *seven times* (septem); dĕciens, *ten times* (decem); vīciens, *twenty times* (for vicintiens, cf. § 28; from viginti); duo-detrīciens, *twenty-eight times;* quinquāgiens (in Plaut. *Men.* 1161, quinquagensiens), *fifty times* (quinquaginta); centiens, *a hundred times* (centum); quadringentiens, *four hundred times* (quadringenti), and others. See App. D.

CHAPTER XVI.

INFLEXIONS OF VERB. INTRODUCTION.

LATIN verbs have inflexions to denote differences of voice, 548 person, number, mood, and tense.

1. There are two *voices*, the Active and the Passive (sometimes called Reflexive or Middle).

Some verbs have both voices, some have only the active, except in the third person; others, called deponents, have only the passive, but with the signification (apparently) of the active. (Cf. § 1215.)

2. Two *numbers*, the Singular and Plural.

In a few verbs no plural is found.

3. There are three *persons* (First, Second, Third) in each number. In the imperative mood there is no form for first person singular.

A few verbs are used only in the third person.

4. Three *moods*, Indicative, Subjunctive (often called Con- 549 junctive), Imperative.

5. (*a*) Six *tenses*, in the Indicative mood, active voice:

(*a*) Three, denoting incomplete action; the Present, Future, and Imperfect (sometimes called respectively, present imperfect, future imperfect, past imperfect).

(*b*) Three, denoting completed action; the Perfect, Completed Future, and Pluperfect (sometimes called respectively, present perfect, future perfect, and past perfect).

(*b*) In the Subjunctive mood there are only four distinct tense forms, called Present, Imperfect, Perfect, and Pluperfect. In the Imperative there are only the present and future.

Some verbs in the active and all verbs in the passive have in the 550 Indicative only three simple tense-forms, those of incomplete action, and in the Subjunctive only the present and imperfect. The deficiency of the tenses of complete action in the Passive voice is supplied by participles in combination with certain tenses of the verb of *being*.

Certain verbal nouns are from their mode of formation and 551 use usually treated in connexion with the verb. These are (*a*) Two indeclinable substantives, called *Infinitives* (or the Infinitive Mood). They are the Present infinitive, denoting incomplete action, and the Perfect, denoting completed action.

(*b*) Three verbal adjectives, called *Participles*, the Present and Future belonging to the active voice; the Past participle belonging to the passive voice.

(*c*) A verbal substantive and adjective, called the *Gerund* and *Gerundive*, usually classed, the first with the active, the second with the passive voice.

(*d*) Two *supines*, i.e. the accusative and ablative (or dative) of a verbal noun.

The forms of the verb proper are often called collectively the Finite Verb; the verbal nouns above named are sometimes called the Infinite Verb.

The following are the usual English equivalents of the several 552 tenses and verbal substantives connected with the verb: (See Book IV. Ch. XVIII. XX.)

FINITE VERB.

Indicative.	Active.	Deponent.	Passive.
Present. Sing. 1.	ămo	prĕcor	ămor
	I am loving	*I am praying*	*I am being loved*
	or *I love*	or *I pray*	or *I am loved*
Future. Sing. 1.	ămābo	prĕcābor	ămābor
	I shall love	*I shall pray*	*I shall be loved*
3.	ămabit	prĕcābitur	ămābitur
	He will love	*He will pray*	*He will be loved*
Imperfect.	ămābam	prĕcābar	ămābar
Sing. 1.	*I was loving*	*I was praying*	*I was being loved*
	or *I loved*	or *I prayed*	or *I was loved*
Perfect. Sing. 1.	ămāvi	prĕcātus sum	ămātus sum
	I loved or *I have	I prayed* or *I	I was loved* or
	loved	*have prayed*	*I am loved*
Comp. Future.	ămāvĕro	prĕcātus ĕro	ămātus ĕro
Sing. 1.	*I shall have	I shall have	I shall have*
	loved	*prayed*	*been loved*
Sing. 3.	ămāvĕrit	prĕcātus ĕrit	ămātus ĕrit
	*He will have	He will have	He will have*
	loved	*prayed*	*been loved*
Pluperfect.	ămāvĕram	prĕcātus ĕram	ămātus ĕram
Sing. 1.	*I had loved*	*I had prayed*	*I had been loved*

Subjunctive.

Present. Sing. 1.	**ămem**	**prĕcĕr**	**ămĕr**
	I be loving or *I love*	*I be praying* or *I pray*	*I be loved*
Imperfect.	**ămārem**	**prĕcārer**	**ămārer**
	I were loving or *I loved*	*I were praying* or *I prayed*	*I were being loved* or *I were loved*
Perfect.	**ămāvĕrim**	**prĕcātus sim**	**ămātus sim**
	I have loved	*I have prayed*	*I were loved* or *I am loved*
Pluperfect.	**ămāvissem**	**prĕcātus essem**	**ămātus essem**
	I had loved	*I had prayed*	*I had been loved* or *I were loved*

Imperative.

Present. Sing. 2.	**ămā**	**prĕcāre**	**ămāre**
	love	*pray*	*be loved*
Future. Sing. 2.	**ămāto**	**prĕcātor**	**ămātor**
	Thou shalt love	*Thou shalt pray*	*Thou shalt be loved*

VERBAL NOUNS.   553

Infinitive.

Present.	**ămārĕ**	**prĕcāri**	**ămāri**
	to love	*to pray*	*to be loved*
Perfect.	**ămāvissĕ**	**prĕcātus esse**	**ămātus esse**
	to have loved	*to have prayed*	*to have been* or *to be loved*

Participles.

Present.	**ămans**	**prĕcāns**	
	loving	*praying*	
Future.	**ămātūrus**	**prĕcātūrus**	
	going to love	*going to pray*	
Past.		**prĕcātus**	**ămātus**
		having prayed	*having been* or *being loved*
Gerund.	**ămandum**	**prĕcandum**	
	loving	*praying*	
Gerundive.	**ămandus**	**prĕcandus**	
	to love or *to be loved*	*to pray* or *to be prayed*	

Every single word in the Latin (finite) verb is·a complete sen- 554
tence, the verbal stem being used, not by itself, but in combination
with abbreviated forms of pronouns of the first, second, and third
persons.

The principles, on which all verbs are inflected, are the same. The differences in detail which are found are due, some to the nature or ending of the stem of the particular verb, some to the unequal preservation of parts of an originally fuller system of inflexions.

The inflexions for tense, mood, person, number, and voice are 555 attached to the stem in the order now given. The forms of the present tense, indicative mood, singular number, active voice, are the simplest, and arise from the union of the stem and personal pronouns. All other parts of the verb contain modifications for tense, mood, number, and voice; and of these the modifications for tense and mood are made between the stem and personal pronoun, and the inflexions for number and voice appended after them.

Thus **rĕg-ĕr-ē-m-us** is the 1st pers. plur. active, imperfect subjunctive of a verbal stem meaning *rule*. **Rĕg** is the stem, **ĕr** denotes past time, **ē** the mood of *thought* (instead of *fact*), **m** the speaker himself, **us** the action of others with the speaker. And, if for **-us** we have **-ur**, the speaker and others are passive instead of active.

These inflexions will be discussed in regular order, beginning, at the end of the word, with the most characteristic and universal inflexions.

CHAPTER XVII.

INFLEXIONS OF PERSON AND NUMBER.

THE suffixes, which denote person and number in the active 556 voice, are the same in all tenses of the indicative and subjunctive moods, except in some persons of the perfect, and in the first person singular of the present and completed future of the indicative mood.

In the passive voice the inflexions for this purpose are the same in all tenses of the indicative and subjunctive moods, which are expressed by simple forms. (The tenses denoting completed action are expressed by compound forms.)

These suffixes are as follows, the initial vowel being given in 557 the oldest form (cf. § 196) in which, apart from early inscriptions, it appears in any verbs. For earlier forms, see § 234, and compare §§ 570, 581.

		Active.	Passive.	Perfect Active.
Singular.	1st person	-om	-or	-(ī)
	2nd ,,	-ĭs	-ĕr-ĭs	-(is)tī
	3rd ,.	-ĭt	-ĭt-ŭr	-ĭt
Plural.	1st ,,	-ŭm-us	-ĭm-ŭr	-ĭm-ŭs
	2nd ,,	-ĭt-ĭs	-ĭmĭnī	-(is)t-ĭs
	3rd ,,	-ont	-ont-ŭr	-(er)unt

The short initial vowel of the suffix (ŏ, ŭ, ĕ, ĭ) is absorbed 558 by an immediately preceding a, e, or ĭ; except (1) in the 1st pers. sing., if the m is not retained; (2) in the 3rd pers. pl. present, if -unt follow -i. In a few other verbs (sum, do, fero, volo, edo) some of these suffixes drop the initial vowel in the present tense.

FIRST PERSON.

The -m in the 1st person singular and plural is the same as is 559 seen in the oblique cases of the pronoun me.

Singular. -m is dropped (see § 86) in the singular of the pre- 560 sent indicative of all verbs (e.g. reg-o) except two; viz. sum (for ĕs-om), *I am,* and inqua-m, *quoth I;* also in the completed future of all verbs, and in the future indicative of all verbs with stems ending in -a or -e, and of some with stems ending in -i; e.g. ămābo, mŏnēbo, ībo.

In a- verbs the final a is contracted with the initial of the suf- 561 fix; e.g. am-o for ama-om; do for da-om. Other vowel verbs retain their characteristic vowel; e.g. trĭb-u-o, mŏn-e-o, aud-i-o, căp-i-o. But three ĭ verbs change i to e; viz. ĕo (stem i-), queo (stem qui-), and its compound nĕqueo. Inquam has apparently a stem in ă, which except in 1st sing. pres. passes into ĭ.

In the perfect indicative the personal suffix has dropped off al- 562 together. The final i has another origin. (See § 658.)

In the passive voice the only change from the active is the 563 addition of r, if the m has dropped away, or the substitution of it for m if the m has been retained in the active. This r is generally considered to be a substitute for s, the proper passive inflexion being, as is supposed, the reflexive pronoun[1] se.

---

[1] A passive formed by a reflexive pronoun ıs seen in Germ. *Das versteht sich von selbst;* French *Le corps se trouva;* Ital. *Si loda l'uomo modesto* ('The modest man is praised'); Span. *Las aguas se secaron* ('The waters were dried up'). KEY, *Lat. Gr.* § 379.

Plural. The vowel before **m** is weakened (see § 241) to ĭ in 564 all verbs with stems ending in **u**, or in **ĭ**, or in a consonant, except in the present indicatives of three verbs; viz. **sŭmus**, *we are*, **vŏlŭmus**, and their compounds, and the old form **quæsŭmus** (stem **quæs-**), *we pray*, where we have the older vowel **u**. **dă-mus** retains the radical **a**. With these exceptions the suffix is the same in all tenses of all verbs, except when the initial vowel is absorbed by a preceding **a**, **e**, or **ĭ**.

The final **-us** is the part of the suffix which distinguishes the 565 plural number. By some it is considered to arise from the pronoun of the second person, by others from the pronoun of the third person; so that *we* (-mus) would be expressed by *I, thou,* or by *I, he;* by others again it is considered to be the same as the **s**, which is used to mark the plural of nouns.

In the passive the final s is changed to **r**.

SECOND PERSON.

The consonant contained in the suffix of the second person is **s** 566 in the singular, (changed before another vowel to **r** in the passive), and **t** in the plural. The perfect indicative has **t** in the singular also. The personal pronoun of the second person sing. in Latin (**tu**), and the Doric dialect of Greek (τύ) exhibits this **t**; in the Attic dialect of Greek it exhibits **s** (σύ).

Singular. In the present tense of **fĕro, vŏlo, ĕdo,** the short 567 vowel (ĭ) is omitted or absorbed; hence **fers** (for **fĕrĭs**), **vīs** (for **vŏlis, vīlis, vils**), and **ēs** (for **ĕdĭs, eds**). **es** (**ēs** Plautus and Terence, **ĕs** in subsequent poets) is also the 2nd pers. sing. present indicative of **sum**.

All **a-, e-,** and **ī-** verbs have the final syllable long; viz. **ās, ēs, ĭs.** (Not so the verbs with ĭ; e.g. **capio, capĭs.**)

In the perfect indicative the suffix for the second pers. sing. 568 ends in **-isti**, of which ending **-ti** is the proper personal suffix. (For the rest of the ending see § 658.)

In the passive **-ĕris** (at first sight) appears to be formed by 569 placing the characteristic passive **r** before the personal suffix; the true theory however is no doubt that the passive suffix, with a short preceding vowel, being placed after the personal suffix caused the s between two vowels to change to **r**, necessitating also the change of the vowel i to e before **r**. The passive suffix itself (i.e. **s** for **se**, § 183) was allowed to remain **s**, instead of being changed to **r**, as usually, in order to avoid having two r's close together.

-re (e.g. **amabare**, cf. § 193. 5. f. 234. 2) is more common than 570 **-ris** (e.g. **amabaris**) in Plautus, and, except in present tense, in Cicero and Vergil. It is frequent in Horace, rare in Livy; and is usually avoided by all writers where the form would then be the same as the present infinitive active. Hence -ris is retained in pres. indic. with rare exceptions in verbs which have an active voice; but in deponents (where there is no risk of confusion, as the infinitive ends in i) -re is frequent in Plautus, sometimes found in Cicero; -ris is usual in Vergil and Horace.

Plural. The plural suffix -ĭtĭs contains the personal pronoun 571 of the second person (t), and the syllable -ĭs, which is either a pronoun of the second person in its other form, or a suffix of plurality.

In the present tense of the four verbs named above (§ 567) the initial ĭ of the suffix is again omitted: fertĭs, vultĭs, estĭs, for fĕrĭtĭs, vŏlĭtĭs (§ 213 *a*), ĕdĭtĭs (§ 151. 2), *ye eat*, and for (originally) ĕsĭtĭs, *ye are.* So also in dă-tĭs.

In the perfect s is simply suffixed to the singular form.

In the passive voice the suffix -ĭmĭnĭ is probably a masculine 572 plural participial form. The Greek present passive participle is of the same form; viz. -ŏmĕnŏs, plur. ŏmĕnoi. Originally, perhaps, estĭs was used with it, as in the perfect passive. (This form may have been resorted to because of the unpleasant forms which the course observed in forming the passive of other persons would have produced; e.g. regĭtĭs-er, amātĭs-er would become rĕgĭtĕrĕr, amātĕrĕr, or, if the analogy of the 2nd pers. sing. were retained, regĭtĕrĭs, amātĕrĭs, which would then have come to regetrĭs, amātrĭs (§ 235. 2), or rĕgĭter, amāter (§ 184. 5); both of which forms look more like adjectives or adverbs than verbs.)

THIRD PERSON.

The -t in the suffix of the 3rd person, both singular and plural 573 in all tenses, is a demonstrative pronoun, found in the Greek (so-called) article, and in iste, tot, talis, tantus, &c.

Singular. In the present tense of sum, ĕdo, fĕro, vŏlo, the short 574 vowel before -t is not found; viz. est (both for sum and ĕdo), fert, vult, or (older) volt.

The third person sing. active of a-, e-, and i- verbs was originally long, as may be inferred from the passive voice (amāt-ur, monēt-ur, audīt-ur), and is actually found not unfrequently in Plautus, and sometimes in Augustan poets.

In the perfect active the suffix is the same as in the present 575 (-ĭt). Plautus sometimes, and more rarely Augustan poets, have this -ĭt long.

To form the passive, -ur is suffixed to the active form.

Plural. The plural suffix is usually -unt, but in præ-Augustan 576 inscriptions, in Plautus, and Varro, the older -ont was retained after **v** (or **u**); e.g. **vivont, confluont, loquontur.** The forms **nequinont** and **sont** are also found (for **nequeunt, sunt**). Of this suffix the **t** is probably the same as in the singular; the origin of the **n** is uncertain.

The passive is formed (as in the singular) by suffixing -ur to the active form.

The perfect suffix is the same as the present, the ending being 577 er-unt, of which the -er is the same (cf. § 184. 3) as the -is (before t) of the second person. The penult (-er) is usually long, but the dactylic poets, beginning with Lucretius (not Ennius) often, and others occasionally, shorten it; e.g. **dormiĕrunt, locāvĕrunt, subēgĕrunt**, &c. (Plaut.), **ēmĕrunt** (Ter.); **dedĕrunt, fuĕrunt, exiĕrunt**, &c. (Lucr.).

For -erunt is rarely found -eront (cf. Quint. I. 4. 16); but -ēre 578 is found in some of the earliest inscriptions, and is not uncommon in Plautus and Terence, rare in Cicero and Cæsar, but frequent in dactylic poets and Livy.

In the completed future indic. the suffix-vowel is **i** instead of 579 **u** (-erint for -erunt); probably in order to avoid confusion with the perfect.

CHAPTER XVIII.

INFLEXIONS OF MOOD.

1. *Indicative Mood.*

THE indicative mood contains no special inflexions to distin- 580 guish it. The imperative and subjunctive moods are distinguished from it by certain modifications.

2. *Imperative Mood.*

(*a*) *Present.* The imperative *present* appears to consist of 581 shortened forms of the indicative present. The final **s** is thrown off, and -**i** is changed to -**ĕ** (or rather, as the form originally ended

in -es, the s is simply thrown off, cf. § 234. 2). Hence the active
rĕgĭs (older rĕgĕs) becomes rĕgĕ; rĕgĭtis (older rĕgĕtĕs), regĭte;
the passive rĕgĕrĭs (older rĕgĕrĕs), rĕgĕrĕ: the 2nd pers. plural
rĕgĭmĭnĭ is the same as in the indicative. But from verbs with
vowel stems in a-, e-, ī- (not ĭ-) the s is thrown off in the singular
without further change; e.g. amā, monē, audī. The exceptional form
nolī is formed from the 2nd pers. sing. of the *subjunctive* present.

In the verbs dūco, fĕro (and their compounds), făcĭo (with 582
compounds which retain the radical a), and dīco, the final e of the
singular was always dropped after Terence's time; e.g. dūc, fĕr,
făc, călefac, dīc. In Plautus and other poets the imperatives often
occur before words beginning with a vowel, in which case it is
difficult to decide between duc and duce; &c.

ēs or ĕs (from sum, cf. § 720), ēs fro n ĕdo were used for the
imperative 2nd pers. sing. as well as for the indicative.

In verbs with short penult, and having vowel stems in a-, e-, i-, 583
and also in the compounds of eo, the imperative-forms in Plautus
and Terence often shortened the final vowel (cf. § 295); e.g. com-
mŏdă, mŏnĕ, jŭbĕ, ădĭ, ăbĭ; especially in colloquial forms; e.g.
mănĕdum, tăcĕdum, mŏnĕsis, vĭdĕsis.

(*b*) *Future.* The *future* imperative active is distinguished by 584
a suffix, originally -ōd[1]. In the form which is common to the
second and third persons, e.g. reg-ĭt-ō, and the form for the third
person plural, e.g. regunto, the -d has fallen off, as in the ablative
case of nouns (cf. § 160. 6). The suffix appears to have been
simply added to the present indicative forms of the third person
singular and plural. (The use of this form for the second person
singular was probably due to -t being a characteristic of the second
personal pronoun.) The plural second person is formed by ap-
pending -e (for -es, later -is) as the sign of plurality in this person to a modified form of the singular; e.g. rĕg-ĭt-ōt-e (for rĕg-
ĭt-ōd-e). Others (e.g. Schleicher) consider the -tote to be simply
the demonstrative pronoun doubled (as in the Vedic Sanskrit -tāt).

The passive forms substitute -r for the final -d; e.g. regĭt-or 585
for rĕgĭt-od; regunt-or for rĕgunt-od.

The form in -to (for t-od) was apparently at one time also used 586
as passive; e.g. censento, initianto, in præ-Augustan inscriptions;
and from deponents; e.g. arbitranto, partiunto, utunto, &c., some
of which verbs however had once an active voice, of which these
forms may be relics.

---

[1] Only one instance is actually found in Latin; viz. in Festus,
p. 230 *b*. 14, 'Si nurus...sacra divis parentum estod.' The Oscan had
this d; e.g. estud, licitud. (See Ritschl, *Neu. Plaut. Exc.* I. p. 100.)

In Plautus, Cato, and old inscriptions, a form in -mino is 587 (rarely) found for the 2nd and 3rd pers. sing. of the imperative of deponents; e.g. **profite-mino, præfa-mino, progredi-mino, fru-i-mino.** One instance of a passive verb **denuntiamino** is found. This old form is formed just like the 2nd pers. plur. indicative in -mini.

3. *Subjunctive Mood.*

The subjunctive is characterised by a lengthened vowel imme- 588 diately before the consonant of the personal suffix.

Present. This vowel is **ā** in the present tense of all verbs, except verbs with **ā-** stems, in which it is **ē**; e.g. **reg-ā-mus, regāmur; moneāmus, moneāmur; audiāmus, audiāmur; tribuāmus, tribuāmur**; but **amēmus, amēmur.** Except also some in which it is **ī**; viz. **sim, sīs,** &c. from **sum; velim, velis,** &c. from **vŏlo**; and the compounds of both; e.g. **possim, absim,** &c. **nolim, malim.**

So also (besides the more usual forms) **edim, edīs, edit, edīmus,** 589 **edītis, edint** (Plaut. esp. in phrase ' habeo quod edim,' Cat., Hor.); **comedim, comedis, comedint** (Plaut.), **exedint** (Plaut.); also from **duo** (an old form of **do**?[1]), **duim, duis, duit, duint** (Plaut., Ter., and old law language); **interduim** (Plaut.); **perduim, perduis, perduit, perduint** (Plaut., Ter., chiefly in phrase 'Di te perduint,' which is also used by Cicero); **creduis, creduit** (Plaut., who has also forms from this verb with the more regular **ā**; e.g. **duas, creduas, creduant, accreduas.** Cf. **fuat,** § 722).

Sum and its compounds had an older form **siem, sies** (see 590 § 722), from which **sim, sis,** &c. are contracted. The **-es, -et** is perhaps only the older form of the personal suffix **-is, -it.** (But comp. Gr. εἴην, Sansk. *syâm.*)

Imperfect and Pluperfect. The long vowel in these tenses is **ē** in 591 all verbs; e.g. **rexissēmus, amavissēmus,** &c.

Perfect. The vowel (assumed to have been originally long) is **ī**, 592 which however, probably from confusion with the completed future, is in dactylic poets as often short as long. The pertinent instances are as follows:

Perf. subj. **-ĕrī- dederītis** (Enn.); **fuerīs** (Hor. in hexam.); **respuerīs** (Tib.); **dederīs, crediderīs, contulerīs** (Ovid).

---

[1] The forms **interduo,** Pl. *Capt.* 694, **concreduo,** Id. *Aul.* 577, are used apparently as completed futures ind.; **concredui** in Pl. *Cas.* 2. 8. 43, as a perfect indic. In Plin. *H. N.* 21. 3. 5, is **duitur** (comp. fut. pass.:), for which **duitor** (imper. pass.) is usually read. See Neue II. 339; Schöll, *Leg.* XII. *tab. reliq.* p. 82.

	-ĕrĭ-	ēgerĭmus, respexerĭs (Verg.), dixerĭs (Hor. in hexam.).
Comp. Fut. Ind.	-ĕrĭ-	dederĭtis, transierĭtis, contigerĭtis (Ovid), fecerĭmus (Catull. in a hendecasyllable), dederĭs, occiderĭs, miscuerĭs, audierĭs (Hor. in hexam.), dederĭs (Prop., Ov. several times).
	-ĕrĭ-	viderĭmus (Lucr.); viderĭtis, dixerĭtis (Ovid); suspexerĭs, revocaverĭs (Verg.); vitaverĭs, detorserĭs, acceperĭs, cœperĭs (Hor. in hexam.).

In Plautus and Terence there appears to be no instance incompatible with the rule of ĭ for perf. subj., ĭ for compl. fut. indic. (See Neue II. 196.)

The forms for the subjunctive appear best explicable by assuming the proper suffix to be ĭ (seen in the Greek optative), which was contracted with a preceding ā to ē. Thus amas, ama-ĭ-s, amēs; amāra-s (an assumed indicative, see below, § 610), amāra-ĭ-s, amārēs; amāvissa-s (an assumed indic.), amāvissa-ĭ-s, amāvissēs (or esses for esa-ĭ-s may be supposed to have been suffixed at once). But as ĭ suffixed to the present indicative of other than ā verbs would have given still the same form when contracted, an ā (seen in the Greek subjunctive) was substituted in all such cases. Sis and velis, &c. retain the ĭ, because they have other points of difference from the indicative. [593]

CHAPTER XIX.

CLASSIFICATION OF INFLEXIONS OF TENSE.

THE inflexions of tense are divisible into two classes; viz. those which are common to several tenses or forms, and those which are peculiar to the particular tense. [594]

The inflexions common to several tenses or forms may be referred to three forms of the verbal stem, called the Present stem, the Perfect stem, and the Supine stem.

1. The *present* stem is very often identical with the verbal 595 stem, but not unfrequently is more or less modified. From this present tense are formed all the tenses and verbal forms which express incomplete action; viz. both in Active and Passive voice,—

Indicative.   Present, Future, Imperfect.
Imperative.   Present, Future.
Subjunctive.   Present, Imperfect.

Also the following verbal forms :

Present Infinitive ;
Present Participle, (none in Passive) ;
Gerunds and Gerundive.

2. The *perfect* stem is sometimes identical with the verb-stem 596 and with the present stem, but usually is considerably modified. From this perfect stem are formed all the tenses denoting completed action; viz. in the Active voice,—

Indicative.   Perfect, Completed Future, Pluperfect.
Subjunctive.   Perfect, Pluperfect.

Also the perfect Infinitive.

3. The *supine* stem is always a modification of the verbal stem, 597 and from it are formed certain verbal nouns, of which the forms called the supines, and the passive past participle, and future participle active are generally treated in connection with the verb.

The past participle passive is used with certain tenses of the verb to form the perfect and pluperfect passive both in the indicative and subjunctive.

In accordance with the order of discussion which has been thus far followed, the inflexions of the derivative tenses, being nearer to the end of the word (§ 555), will be discussed before the formation of the stem to which they are appended.

CHAPTER XX.

TENSES FORMED FROM THE PRESENT STEM.

Present. The present indicative is formed simply by suffixing 598 the inflexions of number and person. The present subjunctive has the mood inflexion as well.

Future. The future indicative is in consonant, in i- verbs and 599 in u- verbs a modified form of the present subjunctive. The first person singular is the same: the other persons have long ē where the present subjunctive has ā; e. g. fut. **reges, reget**; pres. subj. **regas, regat.** In the 3rd pers. sing. act. the final syllable was short in the ordinary language (§ 152. 7).

Cato the Censor is said (Quint. I. 7. 23) to have written **dice, facie,** 600 for **dicam, faciam,** and so in other verbs. Probably this statement refers only to the future indic. not to the present subjunctive.

This ē probably arises from suffixing ī (compare the Greek 601 optative) to the present subjunctive of these verbs; e. g. **reg-ā-mus, reg-ā-ī-mus, regē-mus**; just as amemus, pres. subj. was formed (§ 593). But this formation would not do for a- and e- verbs; because in a- verbs such a form (e. g. amēmus) is already used for the pres. subj.; and in e- verbs, it (e. g. monēmus) would be identical with the present indicative.

Accordingly in a- and e- verbs there is a different mode of 602 forming the future indicative; viz. by suffixing ĭb- to the present stem, with the final vowel of which it is contracted; e. g. ama-, ama-ĭb-, amāb-; 1st pers. plu. amab-ĭmus, mon-e, mone-ĭb-, monēb-; 1st pers. plur. **monēbĭmus.**

A similar future (besides the ordinary form in -am, -es, -et), is 603 not unfrequently formed from i- stems in early writers (Plautus, Terence, &c.); e. g. **aperĭbo, adgredĭbor** (comp. **adgredīri** for **adgredi**), **largĭbere, opperĭbor, scĭbo,** &c. But of these forms none are found so late as the first century B.C., except **ĭbo, quĭbo, nequĭbo,** which are the only forms in use at any time (with a few doubtful exceptions). **Lenĭbo** is also found in Propertius. **Veniet** (from **vēn-eo**) for **vēnĭbit** is found however in the lex Thoria (642 A.U.C.), and in Gaius; **exiet** in Seneca.

The verb do has a short penultimate dăbo. Its compound reddo 604 (which usually has reddam), has reddĭbo (i.e. red dabo) in Plaut.: who has also exugebo, as if from an e- stem exuge-.

The verb sum and compounds have apparently merely a different 605 form of the present for the future; viz. ĕr-o, 1st pers. plur. ĕr-ĭmus (compare pres. sŭmus for ĕs-ŭm-us). Most philologers consider ero, &c. to be for esio, the i being similar to that of the present subj.

Imperfect. The imperfect indicative has in all stems a long a 606 (except in 3rd sing. act. §§ 152. 7. 574) preceding the personal inflexions, and in all stems but one (that of ĕs-, *be*) b prefixed to this long a. Moreover in all stems but dă- the vowel preceding bā is long.

The long a, which is always found, serves to distinguish the imperfect from the future where the forms are otherwise similar; e.g. amabāmus (for amabaimus), amabĭmus; monebamus, monebĭmus; ībāmus, ībĭmus; dăbāmus, dăbĭmus; ĕrāmus, ĕrĭmus. It is apparently a sign of past time, and as such is found in the pluperfect also.

In consonant stems the suffix is -ēbā-, and this is usually found 607 also in verbs with i stems; e.g. reg-ēbā-mus, audi-ēbā-mus. But this long e is not found in eo, queo, and their compounds, and is not unfrequently absent in the earlier language (Plautus, Ter., Varr., &c.); e.g. scībam, nescībam, āībam, &c., gestībat, grundībat, insanībat, mollībat, præsagībat, servības, stabilībat, venībat. So also, apparently for metrical reasons, in the dactylic poets (Catull., Lucr., Verg., Ovid, Sil., Stat.); e.g. audībant, lenībat, sævībat, redimībat, molībar, ferībant, &c.

Probably the suffix was originally the same as the future suffix 608 of a- and e- verbs with ā added, i.e. -ĭb-a-. The form -ēbā-, seen in consonant and most i- verbs, is difficult to explain. It is generally supposed to have been erroneously borrowed from the e- stems.

Imperfect subjunctive. This tense had the suffix -ĕr (for ĕs). 609 which with the modal suffix ē made -ĕrē. The first vowel coalesced with a preceding a, e, or ī; e.g. reg-ĕr-ēmus, tribu-ĕr-ēmus, amār-ēmus, mon-ĕr-ēm-us, aud-īr-ēmus, and caused the omission of a preceding ĭ; e.g. capĭ-, capĕrem.

In sum, ĕdo, vŏlo, fĕro, and their compounds, the vowel ĕ was dropped out; e.g. 1st pers. plur. es-sem-us (for es-es-ēmus, or ĕdĕs-ēmus); vel-lēm-us (for vŏl-ĕr-em-us); fer-rem-us (for fĕr-ĕrēm-us). Do has dărēmus.

13—2

The suffix -ĕr (ĕs) is probably from **sum**. So that **reg-** with the 613 imperfect of sum, is reg-eram; hence reg-era-i-m, regerem.

The *imperative* tense suffixes have been already discussed (§§ 581—586).

The *present infinitive active* has the suffix -ĕrĕ (for -ĕsĕ, §§ 183, 611 193. 3), in which the first e coalesces with a preceding ā, e, or ĭ; e.g. reg-ĕre, tribu-ĕre; amāre, mon-ēre, aud-īre. Căpĕre as căp-ĕrem, § 609.

In sum, ĕdo, vŏlo, fĕro, and their compounds, the first vowel e 612 was dropped out, as in the imperfect subj. Hence the infinitives, are esse (for edese), velle (for vŏlere), ferre (for ferere). The infinitive is generally considered to be the dative or locative case of a verbal noun with stem ending in s- or si-; e.g. dicer-e for daikas-ai, viver-e compared with Sanskrit jīvas-ai. The final e (= ai) would be originally long.

The *present infinitive passive* has the suffix i appended to the 613 stem in verbs, whose stem ends in a consonant or in ĭ or in u; e.g. reg-ī, tribu-ī, cap-ī (but fieri from stem fī-; ferrī from fĕr-). In other vowel verbs ī takes the place of the final e of the active infinitive; e.g. aud-īr-ī, mon-ēr-ī, am-ār-ī. So also dă-rī from do.

A further suffix -ĕr is found appended to these forms (e.g. figier, 614 amārier, &c.), in old legal inscriptions (not after the *S. C. de repetundis*, 631 U.C.); and frequently in Plautus, Terence, Lucretius, Cicero (in poetry), and not uncommonly in Vergil and Horace, only occasionally in later poets. But the shorter form is more common even in the first named poets. In inscriptions it occurs first in the *S. C. de repetundis* (darei, beside abducier, avocarier).

The forms in -ier (-ārier, -ērier, -īrier) are probably the original 615 forms, and arose by the addition of the ordinary passive suffix r in the form -ĕr to the active infinitive, whose final ĕ took the form ot ĭ before er. The final r was then dropped on account of its ill sound after another r (§ 185), and ie contracted to ī. Thus amārĕ-ĕr, amari-er, amari.

If the same course had been followed in consonant, and in -ĭ verbs, then owing to the penultimate vowel of the active infinitive being short (e.g. ducĕre), the syllable ĕr would have recurred (e.g. ducerier). The Romans therefore preferred to omit the first (§ 28); i.e. to append -ier immediately to the final consonant of the stem; (e.g. duc-ier, capier). The only instance of the retention of at least some part of the first er is in fer-rier for fererier. Analogy afterwards reduced ducier, &c. to duci.

Present Participle. The suffix is -enti, nom. sing. -ens; e.g. 616
reg-ens, tribu-ens, audi-ens. But in the verb eo and its compounds,
an older form of the suffix, viz. **-unti,** is retained; but the nom.
sing. is usually **-iens.** The form **nequeuntes** (from **nequeo**) occurs
once.

In -a and -e verbs the suffix coalesces with the final stem vowel;
e.g. **amans, monens.**

Gerund and Gerundive. The suffix is **-endo-,** which as a sub- 617
stantive is called a gerund, as an adjective, gerundive; e.g. **regendum, tribuendum, audiendum; amandum, monendum.**

An older form in **-undo** (probably for an earlier **-ondo),** is com- 618
mon in inscriptions to the end of the 7th century, U.C.; in Plautus,
Terence, and Sallust; and, after i, and in the words **gerundus** and
ferundus, frequently in the MSS. of Cæsar, Cicero, and Livy.
Some law phrases always (or at least usually), retained the form;
e.g. **rerum repetundarum; familiæ erciscundæ, finibus regundis, de
jure dicundo.** But after u or v the suffix is found only in the form
-endo (cf. § 213. 4. *a. c*).

Old Futures in -so, -sim¹.

In the older language, of Plautus and ancient laws and formu- 619
laries, a future indicative in **-so (-sso),** subjunctive in **-sim (-ssim),**
infinitive in **-sĕre (-ssĕre),** and pass. indic. in **-sĭtur (-ssĭtur)** is
found. Instances of the indicative and subjunctive active of this
formation are very frequent. (In some instances it is not clear to
which mood the word belongs.)

1. From verbs *with* -a *stems:* amasso (ind.), amassis, amas-
sint (subj.), appellassis (subj.), celassis (subj.), cœnassit (ind.),
occœptassit (ind.), reconciliasso (ind.), creassit (subj.), curassis,
curassint (subj.), accurassis (ind.), decollassit (ind.), indicasso
(ind.), indicassis (subj.), invitassītis (ind.), exoculassītis (ind.),
fortunassint (subj.), irritassis (ind.), locassim (subj.), locassint
(ind.), mactassint (subj.), mulcassītis (ind.), servassit, servassint
(subj.), peccasso, peccassis, peccassit (ind.), and many others.

Passive: turbassitur (ap. Cic.), mercassitur (Lex. Thor.).

Infin. Act.: averruncassere (Pacuv.), reconciliassere, impetrassere
(four times), oppugnassere (Plaut.), depoculassere (or depeculassere),
deargentassere, depeculassere (or despeculassere) (Lucil.).

¹ The fullest discussions of these forms are by Madvig (*Opusc.* II.
p. 64 foll.), Lübbert (*Gram. Stud.* Breslau, 1867), and Neue (II.
421 sqq.).

2. From verbs *with* -e *stems*, preserving the vowel: **habessit** (subj.), **prohibessis, prohibessit** (subj.), **prohibessit, prohibessint** (ind.), **cohibessit** (subj., Lucr. 3. 444), **licessit** (subj.).

3. From verbs *with* -i *stems:* **ambissit, ambissint** (Pl. *Amph.* 69. 71. ex conj.).

4. In verbs *with consonant* or -i *stems*, and *some with* -e 620 *stems*, the -so, -sim is attached immediately to the final stem consonant:

(*a*) -e *stems:* **ausim** (subj.), **noxit** (subj.), **sponsis** (subj.), **auxitis** (subj.), **jusso, jussis, jussit** (ind.), **jussim** (subj.).

Also passive **jussitur** (Cat.).

(*b*) -i *stems:* **faxo** (ind.), **faxis, faxit** (ind. subj.), **faxim, faxīmus** (subj.), **faxitis** (ind. subj.) frequently, **faxint** (subj.), **effexis, defexis** (ind.), **capsis** (ind.), **capsit** (subj.), **capsīmus** (ind.); **accepso, occepso, recepso** (ind.); **incepsit, occepsit; injexit** (ind.), **objexim, objexis** (subj.); **adspexit** (subj.), **respexis** (ind.); **rapsit** (ind.), **surrepsit** (subj.); **excussit** (subj.).

Passive: **faxitur** (ap. Liv.); and perhaps **nanxitur** (Fest.).

(*c*) *Consonant stems:* **axim, adaxint** (subj.), **transaxim, axit; incensit; excessis** (subj.); **clepsit** (ind.); **occisit** (ind.); **dixis** (subj.), **induxis, adduxit** (subj.); **comessis** (subj.); **afflixint** (subj.); **amissis** (ind. subj.); **empsim** (subj.), **adempsit** (ind.), **surrempsit; parsis** (subj.); **rupsit** (ind.); **serpsit; exstinxit** (subj.); **taxis** (subj.); **adussit** (ind.).

Of all these forms **faxo, faxis, ausim, ausis,** almost alone are 621 found after the time of Terence, who himself has only **excessis, appellassis** besides. But the following other instances occur: **cohibessit** (Lucr.); the phrase, **di faxint** (Cic.); **recepso** (Catull.); a few infinitives in Lucil.; **jusso** (Verg., Sil.); and one or two instances in the antiquarians Varro and Fronto. The style of the laws, &c. in Livy and Cicero does not of course belong to the age of their (real or feigned) recorders.

These forms are apparently to be explained as a future indica- 622 tive, subjunctive, and infinitive, formed by the suffix s as in the Greek future to the stem, a short i or sometimes e of the stem being omitted; e.g. leva-, levaso; prohibe-, prohibeso; sponde-, spond-so, sponso; faci, fac-so; dic-, dixo. The double s in the forms from a- and (a few) e- verbs is either a mode of marking the place of the accent, or due to a mistaken etymology, as if the form were analogous to **amasse** from **amavisse**, &c. Possibly both causes may have combined. Moreover a single s between two vowels was in the præ-Augustan language rare (cf. § 191, 193).

The subjunctive is formed by the regular suffix ĭ; the infinitive by
-ĕre, as in the present infinitive.

The use of these forms is analogous to that of the forms in 623
-ero, -erim, but is confined to those classes of sentences in which
those forms differ least from a future indicative, or present subjunctive; viz. (1) the indicative in the protasis (not the apodosis) of
a sentence; (except faxo, which might be either a simple or completed future): (2) the subjunctive in modest affirmations, wishes,
prohibitions, purpose, and in dependent sentences for the future,
never for the perfect indicative (as the form in -erim frequently
is). In all these classes the English language ordinarily uses an
incomplete tense (present or future). The infinitives in -sere might
be taken as either simple or completed futures.

(The ordinary explanation of these forms, viz. that e. g. levasso 624
is for leva-v-eso (= levavero) has much in its favour; but it meets
with great difficulties[1] in such forms as cap-so, rap-so, prohibesso,
&c.; and it does not really account for the double s. For levaveso
would become leva-eso, levaso, levāro; or if it became levav-so,
as is assumed, it would be contracted into levauso or levuso (le-
vauro, levuro) not levasso. Comp. § 94.)

The verbs arcesso, capesso, facesso, lacesso, are probably (Key, 625
Lat. Gr. p. 88) similar formations from arcio (i.e. adcio), capio,
facio, lacio, and have been treated as verb stems, and thus received
new inflexions of tense and mood. Incesso is probably from in-
cedo; petesso from peto (pet- or petĭ-) is also found.

[1] Not removed, I think, either by G. Hermann (*Dissertatio de Mad-
vigii interpretatione*, Lips. 1844), or Curtius (*de verbi latini fut. exact.*,
Dresden, 1844); or Key (*Lat. Gr.* § 566, 1209 f.); or Schleicher (*Vergl.
Gr.* p. 830, ed. 2); or Lübbert (*ubi supr.*). My view agrees partly with
Madvig's (p. 64, 65), and partly with Corssen's (*Ausspr.* II. 37 sq. ed. 1.
See also I. 319, ed. 2). A somewhat different view is given by Merguet
(*Die Entwickelung der Lat. Formenbildung*, 1870, p. 224). Pott deci-
dedly rejects the view that these forms are from the perfect, not the
present, stem (*Etym. Forsch.* II. Th. 4 (1870), pp. 269, 272).
[Gossrau (*Lat. Gr.* § 174, *Anm.* 1) derives these forms from a perfect
in -si. Nettleship (*Academy*, 15 July, 1871) has taken (independently)
a similar view to mine].

CHAPTER XXI.

OF VERB STEMS, ESPECIALLY THE PRESENT STEM.

A VERB often exhibits a different stem in the present tense from 626 that which appears to be presumed in the perfect or in the supine. The changes, which belong strictly to the formation of the perfect or supine themselves, or follow from that formation according to the laws of Roman pronunciation, will be found in Chapters XXIII. XXIV.

Verbs may be divided into consonant verbs and vowel verbs according as the present stem ends in a consonant or in a vowel.

(In the following enumeration the different instances will be classified according to the last letter of the verb stem; and sometimes the perfect and supine added in illustration.)

i. Consonant verbs.

1. Most consonant verbs exhibit in the present stem no altera- 627 tion of the regular stem of the verb; e.g. reg-, reg-o; cæd-, cæd-o, &c.

2. Other consonant verbs exhibit such alteration;

(*a*) The stem is *reduplicated* to form the present tense; e.g. 628
gĕn- (gĕno old form), gigno for gĭ-gĕno (gĕn-ui, gĕn-ĭtum); stă-, sisto (stĕti, stătum); să-, sĕro for sĕso (sēvi, sătum).

(*b*) The radical *vowel* is *lengthened*; e.g. 629

dŭc-, dūco; dĭc-, (cf. dĭc-āre, causidĭc-us), dīco; fĭd-, fīdo; nŭb- (cf. pronŭbus), nūbo. (Probably Key is right in supposing the radical vowel to be always short, and a long vowel (e.g. scrībo, lūdo, &c.) to be due to the formation of the present stem).

(*c*) n *is suffixed* to the stem of the verb; e.g. to stems end- 630 ing in

M. tem-, tem-no.

R. cer-, cer-no; sper-, sper-no; star-, ster-no. In these verbs the perfect and supine have the r transposed; crē-, sprē-, strā-.

A. dă-, dă-no (old form of do).

I. lĭ-, lĭ-no; quĭ-, nequĭ-nont (old form for nequeunt); ĭ-, ⁶³¹ ŏbĭnunt (old form for ŏbeunt); sĭ-, sĭ-no; and its compound pōno for pŏsĭno (old perf. pŏsīvĭ, sup. pŏsĭtum).

So apparently frūniscor from frugv-, fruor. Conquin-isco (con-quexi) may be for conquic-n-isc-o, or may have vowel stem conquĭ-u-isc-o and belong here; see § 635.

Festus speaks also of ferinunt, solinunt for ferunt, solent.

(*d*) A *nasal is inserted* before the final stem consonant; e.g. to ⁶³² stems ending in

P or B. cŭb-, cumbo (also cŭba-); rup-, rumpo.

C or QV. lĭqv-, lĭnqvo; vic-, vinco; năc-, nanc-isc-or (nactus or nanctus).

G. frag-, frango; pag-, pango (old păgo); pŭg-, pungo (in the compounds the stem contains n in all tenses); rig-, ringor; tăg-, tango (old tăgo). In some verbs the nasal is retained in the perfect and dropped only in the supine stem: fĭg-, fingo (finxi, fictum); mĭg-, mingo (minxi, mictum, also minctum); pĭg-, pingo (pinxi, pictum); strĭg-, stringo (strinxi, strictum). In other verbs the nasal is constant in the verb stem; e.g. jungo, junxi, junctum (from jŭg-, comp. jūgum). So ninguit from nigv- (nix).

D. fĭd-, findo (fĭdĭ, fissum); fud-, fundo (fūdĭ, fūsum); scĭd-, scindo (scĭdĭ, scissum); tŭd-, tundo (tŭtŭdĭ, tūsum, or tunsum). Perhaps also frendo (frendĭ, frēsum) may have fred- for stem (but cf. § 168. 3).

In mētior, mensus (properly a vowel verb) the n appears to ⁶³³ have been dropped in the present stem.

In pīso, a collateral form of pinso, the n is dropped in present and supine stems.

(*e*) sc- (isc) *is suffixed* to verbal stems, especially to vowel stems ⁶³⁴ in -e, and gives often the special meaning of *beginning* or *becoming*. This *inchoative* form sometimes exists alone, sometimes is used besides the ordinary stem, sometimes is found in a compound, but not in the simple verb. The perfect and supine, if any, are the same as those of the ordinary stem (real or assumed). A very few stems carry the suffix -sc- throughout all the tenses.

To Consonant stems: ăl- (ălĕre), ăl-esc-ere; dĭc-, di-sc-ĕre (for ⁶³⁵ dic-sc-ĕre), dĭdĭci; frun-, frun-isc-i (frūnitum); gĕm- (gemĕre), ingem-isc-ĕre (ingĕmui); herc- (or erc-), herc-isc-ĕre (herctum); măn- (perf. mĕmĭni), commĭn-isc-i (commentum); păc-, păc-isc-i (pactum); păs-, pasc-ĕre (for pas-sc-ere, comp. πατ-έομαι); trĕm-(tremĕre), contrĕm-isc-ĕre (contrĕmui); perg- (pergĕre), experg-

isc-ĭ (experrectum); vĕd- (comp. ĕdĕre), ve-sc-ĭ (for ved-sc-ĭ);
vigv- (vīvĕre), revīv-isc-ĕre (revixi); ulc-, ulc-isc-ĭ (ultum).   For
escit, see § 722.

Poscĕre (pŏposci); compesc-ere (compescui; comp. pasco) retain sc throughout; miscēre (for mig-sc-ere; comp. μίγ-νυμι) appears
to contain the same suffix, but with an -e stem.

So perhaps conquĭniscere, conquexi (see § 672).

To Vowel stems: **A.** īrā-, ira-sc-ĭ (īrātum); lăbă-, laba-sc-ere 636
(also lăbāre); nā-, na-sc-ĭ (nātum); vespĕrā-, vespera-sc-ĕre (ves-
perāverat, Gell.); vĕtĕrā- (inveterāre, tran.), vetera-sc-ĕre, also
inveterā-sc-ĕre (intrans., inveterāv-, tran. and intran.).

O. no-, no-sc-ĕre (nōvi).

E. ăcĕ- (ăcēre), ăce-sc-ĕre (ăcui), and many others from -e 637
stems, with perfect in -ui; see §§ 677—680.

ægre- (ægrēre, rare), ægre-sc-ĕre; albĕ- (albēre, rare), albescĕre;
arde- (ardēre), exarde-sc-ĕre (exarsi); auge- (augēre), auge-sc-ĕre
(intrans.); calve- (calvēre rare), calve-sc-ĕre; cāne- (cānēre),
cane-sc-ĕre; fronde- (frondēre), fronde-sc-ĕre; refrīge-, refrigescĕre
(refrixi); flavĕ- (flavēre), flāve-sc-ĕre; hærĕ- (hærēre), inhære-sc-
ĕre (inhæsi); hĕbĕ- (hĕbēre), hĕbe-sc-ĕre; hūme- (hūmēre), hume-
sc-ĕre; lactĕ- (lactēre), lacte-sc-ere; livĕ- (livēre, rare), live-sc-
ĕre (rare); lūce- (lucēre), illuce-sc-ĕre (illuxit); măce- (măcēre,
rare), măce-sc-ĕre; mūcĕ- (mucēre), muce-sc-ĕre; splendĕ- (splend-
ĕre), splende-sc-ĕre; turgĕ- (turgēre), turge-sc-ĕre.

crē-, cre-sc-ĕre (crēvi); quiē-, quie-sc-ĕre (quiēvi); suē-,
sue-sc-ĕre, mansuescere, &c. (suēvi).

I. dormī- (dormire), obdormi-sc-ĕre (obdormīvi); oblīvi- (comp. 638
livēre, intrans.), oblīvi-sc-ĭ; scī- (scīre), scī-sc-ĕre (scīvi).

ăpĭ-sc-ĭ (aptum); cŭpĭ- (cŭpĕre), concupi-sc-ĕre (concupīvi);
fătĭ- (?), făti-sc-ĕre and fati-sc-ĭ (fessum); făcĭ- (făcĕre), profici-
sc-ĭ (profectum); gli-, gli-sc-ĕre; hi- (comp. hi-āre), hi-sc-ĕre;
nanci- (nanciam, old fut.), nanci-sc-ĭ (nactum); săpĭ- (săpĕre),
resĭpi-sc-ĕre (resĭpui and rĕsĭpīvi).

For a number of inchoatives formed directly from noun stems
see in Book III. (§ 978).

(*f.* 1)   The guttural is omitted in some stems which probably 639
ended in -gv; e.g. conīgv-, conīveo (conīvi or conixi); flugv-, fluo
(fluxi, adj. fluxus, subst. fluctus); frugv-, fruor (fructus); strugv-,
struo (struxi, structum); vigv-, vīvo (vixi, victum).

Of these coniveo properly belongs to the vowel verbs.

(*f.* 2) Other stems vary between -gv and -g; e.g. stingvo, stingo; 640
tingvo, tingo; ungvo, ungo; ningvit, ningit. Similarly urgveo, urgeo.

(*g*) In **trăho** (**traxi, tractum**), **věho** (**vexi, vectum**), the **h** re- 641 presents a fricative guttural, which becomes partially assimilated in the perfect and supine, and is weakened in the present.

(*h*) **s** is changed, between vowels (according to the general 642 law, § 193. 3), to **r**; e.g. ges-, **gěro** (**gessi, gestum**); haus-, **haurio** (**hausi, haustum**); hæs-, **hæreo** (**hæsi, hæsum**); quæs-, **quæro** (**quæsīvi, quæsītum**); quěs-, **quěror** (**questus**); ūs-, **ūro** (**ussi, ustum**).

Of these **haurio, hæreo** properly belong to the vowel verbs.

(*i*) A few verbs have **ll** in present stem, but not in perfect; 643 the supine appears however to show the effect of **ll** (cf. § 705).

cŏl-(?), **percello** (**perculi, perculsum**); pŏl-(?), **pello** (**pepŭli, pulsum**); tŏl-, **tollo** (**tetŭli**); **vello** retains **ll** in perfect (**velli, vulsum**); **sallo**, *salt*, is a byform of **sălio** (**salsum**).

ii. Vowel verbs.

1. *Verbs with stems ending in* a: 644

(*a*) Most of these verbs have the stem ending in **ă-**, and preserve it in all tenses; e.g.

Flā-, flāre, (**flāvi, flātum**); **fā-, fāri**, (**fātus**); in which a is radical. In **nā-, nāre** (**nāvi, nātum**), the **ā** is constant, but the derivative **nāto** shows that **ă** is radical. In **strā-, sterněre** (**stravi, strātum**); **tlā-, tollěre** (**tetuli, latum** for **tlātum**); the present-stem is consonantal.

Derivative verbs with a- stems are very numerous; e.g. **amā-, ămāre; creā-, creāre; nuntiā-, nuntiāre; leva-, levāre**, &c.; all have perfects in **-āvi, ātum**.

(*b*) *Verbs with stems ending in* ă-; e.g.   645

dă-, dăre, (**dědi, dătum**), but **dās** has **ā**.

In all other verbs of this class, the final a- combines with the initial vowel of the suffixes in tenses formed from the present stem, so as to exhibit **ā**; e.g.

Stă-, stāre (**stěti, stătum**, but sometimes **stātum**) where **ă** is radical. **crěpă-, crepāre; cŭbă-, cubāre; dŏmă-, domāre; frĭcă-, fricāre; mĭcă-, micāre; eněcă-, enecare**, (but **necă-** usually in simple verb); -**plĭcă-** and -**plĭcă-** (cf. §§ 677, 688), **plicāre; secă-, secāre; sŏnă-, sonāre** (also **soněre**); **tŏnă-, tonāre; větă-, vetāre**; all which have perfects in -**ui**, and most of them usually supines in -**ĭtum**.

Also lăvă-, lavāre (and lavĕre); jŭvă-, juvāre; which vocalise and contract the radical v with -ui of the perfect; and contract or omit it in the supine (cf. §§ 669, 688).

(*c*) In some verbs derivative stems in ā are found besides other 646 derivative stems in e or i; e.g.

Artāre, old artīre; bullāre, later bullīre; densāre, old densēre; fulgurāre, old fulgurīre; impetrāre, impetrīre, especially in sacrificial language; singultāre, old singultīre; tintinnāre, tintinnīre.

2. Of *verbs with stems ending in* o, the only traces are nō-, 647 which has the inchoative suffix in the present tense, noscĕre (nōvi, nōtum), where the root has ŏ, comp. nŏta (subst.), nŏtāre, cognĭtum, &c.; pō- (pōtum), the frequentative pōtā-, potāre being otherwise alone in use.

3. *Verbs with stems ending in* u:

(*a*) Most have stems in ū, which however becomes short 648 before the initial vowel of the suffixes; e.g. acŭ-, acŭere, acŭis, acŭisti, acŭas, acŭēbam, acŭĕrem, &c. The supine has ū. (See list in § 690.)

Plu- is apparently contracted for plŭv- (plŏv-), (cf. § 684). And the same may be the case with all: comp. fluo, flŭv-ius.

(*b*) ruo has rŭ- in supine of compounds (but rūta (n. pl.) according to Varro: see § 691). pŭ- is found only in adj. pŭtus and frequentative pŭtāre.

(*c*) A few verbs have u vocal in supine, but consonantal usually 649 (see § 94. 2), in present and perfect.

loqv-, lŏqvi (locūtum); seqv-, sĕqvi (secūtum); solv-, solvere (solvi, sŏlūtūm); volv-, volvĕre (volvi, vŏlūtum).

4. *Verbs with stems ending in* e: 650

(*a*) Few verbs have the stem ending in ē, and these are monosyllables, where e is radical; e.g.

dele- (compound), delēre; flē-, flēre; nē-, nēre; -plē, -plēre. All these have perfect and supine in -ēvi, -ētum.

Other verbs with ē (-ēvi, -ētum) have consonantal present stems; crē-, crescĕre; also crē-, cernĕre; -ŏlē-, -olescĕre (also aboleo, abolēvi, abolĭtum; and adŏlesco, adultum); qviē-, qviescĕre; svē-, svescĕre; sprē-, spernĕre.

(*b*) In most verbs with stems in -e, the e is short, as may be 651 inferred from the perfect being in -ui (for -eui), and supine in -ĭtum (old -ĕtum, cf. § 234. 1), which in some verbs was reduced to -tum. Contraction with the initial vowel of suffixes gives ē in most forms of the present stem; e.g. monēre, monēs, monēmus, monēbam, monēbo, monērem, monētur (monĕt, as amăt, audĭt). In the imperative (2nd pers. sing. act.) of verbs with short penult, it is in early Latin not uncommonly used as short; e.g. tĕnĕ (§ 233. 4); e.g. mŏnĕ-, monēre (monui, monĭtum), and many others; see §§ 677—681.

căvĕ-, căvēre (căvi for căvui, căvĭtum contracted to cautum), and others; see § 669.

(c) Many verbs have e (probably ĕ) in present stem, but drop 652 it entirely and show consonantal stems in the other parts of the verb. (If the vowel had not been dropped, and a perfect in -si or supine in -sum had been formed, there would have been a tendency in the s to become r. Where -si, -sum follows a vowel now, a consonant has been omitted, § 193. 3).

morde-, mordēre (momordi, morsum), and others, in § 666.

vĭde-, vĭdēre (vīdi, vīsum); sĕde-, sedēre (sēdi, sessum); prande-, prandēre (prandi, pransum).

arde-, ardēre (arsi, arsum); and many others in §§ 672—676.

(d) Some have a present stem in -e, besides another (older or 653 poetic) consonantal stem; e.g.

fervēre, fervēre; fulgēre, fulgĕre; ŏlēre, *emit scent*, ŏlēre; scătēre, scătĕre; strīdēre, strīdĕre; tergēre, tergĕre; tuēri, -tui; ciēre, -cīre. (Among other forms the 1st persons fervo, fulgo, olo, scato, strido, tergo, fervĭmus, &c. appear not to occur.)

5. *Verbs with stems ending in* i:　　654

(a) Some verbs with radical i, and many derivatives have ī, and retain it through all the tenses;

scī-, scīre; cī-, -cīre (also ciēre); i-, īre; qui-, quīre. In these the i is radical.

audī-, audīre; dormī-, dormīre; and many other derivatives.

In all these the perfect is in - īvi, and, in the derivative verbs and scio, the supine is in -ītum. For the others see § 696.

(b) Some verbs have ī in present stem, but drop it and show 655 a consonantal stem in other parts; e.g.

amĭcī-, amĭcīre (amicui, amictum); farcī-, farcīre (farsi, fartum); fulci-, fulcīre (fulsi, fultum); hausī-, haurīre (hausi, haustum); mētī- (for mentī-), mētiri (mensum); ordī-, ordīri (orsum); -pĕrī-, ăperīre (ăpĕrui, ăpertum); rĕperīre (rĕpperi, rĕpertum).

and other compounds (Chap. xxx.); sæpĭ-, sæpīre (sæpsi, sæptum); sancĭ-, sancīre (sanxī, sanctum, rarely sancītum); sarcĭ-, sarcīre (sarsi, sartum); sentĭ-, sentīre (sensi, sensum); vĕnĭ-, vĕnīre (vēni, ventum); vincĭ-, vincīre (vinxi, vinctum). Sepĕli-, sepelīre has perfect sepelivi, supine sepultum. (But see Pref. p. c.)

ŏri-, ŏrīri (orsum); pŏti-, potīri show in some tenses a present stem either in ĭ or consonantal. (See Chap. xxx.)

(*c*) Some verbs have the stem ending in ĭ, which fell away 656 before ĭ or ĕr; and as final in imperative, was changed to (or if e was the original, remained) ĕ (§ 234. 2). The ĭ is generally dropped in the supine stem.

căpĭ-, căpĕre (cēpi, captum); cœpĭ-, cœpĕre (cœpi, cœptum); făcĭ-, făcĕre (fēci, factum); fŏdĭ-, fŏdĕre (fōdi, fossum); fŭgĭ-, fŭgĕre (fūgi, fut. part. fŭgĭtūrus); grădĭ-, inf. grădī (gressum); jăcĭ-, jăcĕre (jēci, jactum); -licĭ-, -licĕre (-lexi, -lectum); mŏrĭ-, inf mŏrī (also mŏrīrī, fut. mŏrĭturus); părĭ-, părĕre (pepĕri, partum. old pres. part. părens); pătĭ-, inf. pătī (passum); quătĭ-, quătere (-quassi, quassum); răpĭ-, răpĕre (răpui, raptum); -spĭcĭ-, -spĭcĕre (-spexi, spectum).

Two have ī in other tenses than those derived from the present; cupĭ-, cŭpĕre (cŭpīvi, cŭpītum; in Lucr. also cupīret); săpĭ-, săpĕre (sapīvi, rĕsĭpui and rĕsĭpīvi).

(*d*) A few verbs have consonant stems in present, but ī stems 657 in other parts; pĕt-, pĕtĕre (pĕtīvi, pĕtītum); rŭd-, rŭdĕre (rŭdīvi); quæs-, quærĕre (quæsīvi, quæsītum); arcesso, capesso, facesso, lacesso, incesso, all have inf. -ĕre, perf. -īvi, sup. -ītum; trī-, tĕrĕre, (trīvi, trītum). So ēvĕno is found for ēvĕnio.

CHAPTER XXII.

TENSES FORMED FROM THE PERFECT STEM.

THE suffixes for the tenses formed from the perfect stem; i.e. 658 for the perfect, completed future, and pluperfect in indicative, and perfect and pluperfect in subjunctive, are the same in all verbs; viz.

Comp. Future -ĕr-; Pluperf. Ind. -ĕr-ā; Perf. subj. -ĕr-ī; Pluperf. subj. -iss-ē. The perfect indicative has a suffix -is which however is not found in the 3rd pers. sing. and the first pers. plural; in which the same personal suffixes as in the present indicative are used. This suffix -**is** in the first pers. sing. loses its **s**; in the third pers. plural, being followed by a vowel, changes to -**er**.

The perfect infinitive is formed by the suffix **is-se**. This is 659 apparently composed of the suffix **is-** just mentioned, and -**se** for -**ese** as in the present infinitive. (Comp. **esse** from **sum**, §§ 611, 612.)

The great resemblance of these suffixes to the parts of the verb 660 **sum**, which are used to form the same tenses in the passive voice, suggests (and the suggestion has been generally adopted) that they are identical in origin.

This theory would give a complete explanation of the pluperfect and the completed future indicative, with the exception that the 3rd pers. plural of the latter has **ĕrint** instead of **ĕrunt**, perhaps in order to avoid confusion with the the 3rd pers. plur. perfect indicative.

The perfect subjunctive would be explained by assuming as the suffix an older form of **sim**; viz. -**ĕsim**, or with the usual change, -**ĕrim**.

The perfect indicative and infinitive and pluperfect subjunctive seem to require the assumption of a long **ī** being suffixed to the perfect stem before the respective parts of the verb sum were added[1]. Thus **audivissem**, **audivisse** would stand for aud-īv-ī-essem, audiv-ī-esse, **rexissem**, &c. for rex-ī-ssem, &c.

In the perfect indicative the 2nd pers. sing. e.g. **audivisti** would stand for aud-īv-ī-esti (the personal suffix -**ti** being lost in the simple verb **sum es**), 2nd pers. plu. e.g. **audivistis** for aud-īv-ī-estis; 3rd pers. plur. e.g. **audiverunt** for aud-īv-ī-ĕsunt. The 3rd pers. sing. may have the simple personal suffixes, or may have been reduced from a fuller form; e.g. **au-divi-est**, **audivist**, **audivit**. The -**it** is sometimes found long. The first person singular, e.g. **audivi**, may then be for aud-iv-ī-esum, **audivism**, **audivim**. And the 1st person plural may have had a similar pedigree.

It must however be observed that the resemblance to the parts of the stem **es-**, on which this theory rests, is in some degree deceptive, for it consists largely in personal and modal suffixes, which even on another hypothesis might be expected to be the same. And the rest of the suffixes is, as has been seen, in some tenses but poorly eked out by the simple stem **ĕs**.

The perfect stem when formed by a suffixed **v** (§ 681), is fre- 661 quently modified by the omission of the **v** in all tenses and persons

---

[1] The same view is taken and certain Sanskrit forms compared by Corssen, *Ausspr.* I. 614 sqq. ed. 2.

and both numbers, except in the 1st pers. sing. and plu., and 3rd pers. sing. of the perfect indicative. The vowels thus brought together are contracted, (excepting -ie, and sometimes -ii); e.g. ind. perf. amasti, amastis, amārunt; pluperf. amaram, &c.; comp. fut. amāro, &c.; subj. perf. amarim, &c.; Plup. amassem, &c.; infin. amasse: so flesti, fleram, &c.; and (though here the v omitted is radical) mosti, commosti, &c. (from moveo), and derived tenses.

But we have some instances of uncontracted forms; e.g. audieram, &c.; audiero, &c.; audiisti as well as audisti, &c. And such forms occur not unfrequently from peto, eo, and their compounds.

Nŏvero (1st pers. sing. ind.) always retains the v. (But cognoro, norim, noris, &c.) And so does the shortened form of the 3rd pers. plu. perf. ind. of verbs with ā stems; e.g. amāvēre. The infinitive being amāre, the perfect, if contracted, would be liable to confusion with it.

In dēsĭno, pĕto, eo, and their compounds the omission of v, 662 usually, (in the compounds of eo almost always), takes place even in the excepted persons; viz. in the 1st pers. sing. and plural, and third pers. sing. of the perf. indicative; e.g. desii, desiit, desiimus. In other verbs with -i stems, -iit is sometimes found; -ii hardly ever; -iimus never.

The contracted forms are sometimes found from the above-mentioned three verbs; pĕtī (Sen., Stat.); pĕtīt (Verg., Ov., Lucan, Sen., &c.); dēsīt (Sen., Mart.); dēsīmus (Sen. *Epist.*); rĕdī (Sen.); ābī, inī (Stat.); īt (Ter., Verg., Ov., &c.); ăbīt (Plaut., Ter., Sen.); perīt (Lucr., Phædr., Sen.); adīt, obīt, redīt, &c.

Apparently irritāt, disturbāt, are used as contracted perfects in Lucretius.

In the older poets, and occasionally in Vergil and Horace, in 663 tenses formed from perfect stems in -s, an i between two ss is omitted and the sibilant written once or twice, instead of thrice; e.g. promisse (Cat.) for promisisse; despexe (Plaut.) for despexisse; surrexe (Hor.) for surrexisse: consumpsti (Prop.) for consumpsisti; dixti (Plaut., and twice or thrice in Cic.) for dixisti; erepsēmus (Hor.) for erepsissemus; extinxem (Verg.) for extinxissem.

Percepset for percepisset (Pacuv. ap. C. *Off.* 3. 26); faxem, Pl. *Pseud.* 499, are the only instances of such a form from perfects not in -si. The latter passage is generally considered corrupt.

CHAPTER XXIII.

OF THE PERFECT STEM.

THE perfect stem is formed in one of five different ways, some 664 of which are peculiar to, or invariably found in particular classes of verbs. All are used without any distinction of meaning. Some verbs have two or even more forms of the perfect stem.

The five ways are: (i) Reduplication; (ii) Lengthening the stem vowel; (iii) Suffixing -s; (iv) Suffixing either -u or -v; (v) Using the stem of the verb without change.

In the following enumeration the present stem is added where it differs from the verbal stem. All the verbs, whether consonant or vowel stems, are arranged under the class to which their final *consonant* belongs: except monosyllabic vowel stems, and u stems, which are arranged separately.

i. Perfect stem formed by reduplication.

The first consonant of the stem is prefixed with a short vowel, 665 which is e, if the stem vowel is a or e, and, if not, is the same as the stem vowel. In the præ-Ciceronian language the vowel of the prefixed syllable appears to have been (always?) e, whatever the stem vowel might be. And Cicero and Cæsar are said to have used memordi, spepondi, pepugi (Gell. 6 (7), 9).

If the stem vowel is a, it is changed to e before two consonants, to i before one; æ is changed to ĭ. Before single l ĕ and ŏ become ŭ.

If the stem begins with sp, sc, st, the second consonant is treated as the initial consonant, and the s prefixed to the reduplication syllable.

Gutturals. dĭc-, (Pr. disc- for dic-sc-), dĭ-dĭc-i; parc-, pĕ-perc-ĭ; 666 posc-, pŏ-posc-i; păg-, (Pr. pang-; comp. păc-isci), pĕ-pĭg-i; pŭg-, (Pr. pung-), pŭ-pŭg-i; tăg-, (Pr. tang-), tĕ-tĭg-i.

Dentals. căd-, cĕ-cĭd-i; cæd-, cĕ-cīd-i; pĕd-, pĕ-pēd-i; pend- (also pend-e-, intran.), pĕ-pend-i; scĭd-, (Pr. scind-), scĭ-cĭd-i (old); tend-, tĕ-tend-i; tŭd-, (Pr. tund-), tŭ-tŭd-i (Ennius is said to have used contŭdit).

14

mord-ĕ-, mŏ-mord-i; pend-ĕ- (see above); spond-ĕ-, spŏ-pond-i; tond-ĕ-, tŏ-tond-i.

Nasals. căn-, cĕ-cĭn-i (but compounds suffix -u, § 679, except 667 once, oc-cĕ-cĭni); măn-, mĕ-mĭn-i; tĕn-e-, te-tĭn-i, quoted from Pacuvius and Accius (usually tĕn-ui).

Liquids. fall-, fĕ-fell-i; pŏl-, (Pr. pell-), pĕ-pŭl-i; tol-, (Pr. toll-), tĕ-tŭl-i (in præ-August. poets; tŏli in some præ-Ciceronian inscriptions; usually tŭli-).

curr-, cŭ-curr-i; părĭ-, pĕ-pĕr-i.

Vowels. dă-, dĕ-di; stă- (Pr. stă-), stĕ-ti; stĕ- (Pr. si-st-), stĭ-ti.

ii. Perfect stem formed by lengthening the stem vowel.   668

If the stem vowel be ă, it is changed to ē (except in scăbĕre).

Labials. rŭp-, (Pr. rump-), rūp-i; scăb-, scāb-i; ĕm-, ēm-ĭ. căpĭ-, cēp-i.

Gutturals. lĭqv-, (Pr. linqv-); līqv-i; vic- (Pr. vinc-), vīc-ī; ăg-, ēg-i; frăg-, (Pr. frang-), frēg-i; lĕg-, lēg-i (but some compounds suffix s, § 673); păg-, (Pr. pang-), pēg-i.

făcĭ-, fēc-i; jăcĭ-, jēc-i; fŭgĭ-, fūg-i.

Dentals. ĕd-, ēd-i; fud-, (Pr. fund-), fūd-i; ŏd-, (Pres. obsolete; comp. ŏdium), ōd-i.

sĕdĕ-, sēd-i; vĭdĕ-, vīd-i; fŏdĭ-, fōd-i.

Nasals. vĕnĭ-, vēn-ī.

Semivowels. jŭvă-, jūv-i; lăvă-, (lăv- old), lāv-i.   669

căvĕ-, cāv-i; făvĕ-, fāv-ī; fŏvĕ-, fōv-i; mŏvĕ-, mōv-i; păvĕ-, pāv-i; vŏvĕ-, vōv-i.

The lengthening of the vowel in the verbs, which have **v** for their final consonant, is probably due to the absorption of a suffixed **v** (§ 681); e.g. căvi for cav-vi or căvui. In a similar way vīci, vīdi, vēni may have arisen from an absorption of a reduplication, for vĕvīni, &c.

iii. Perfect stem formed by suffixing s.

If the present stem ends in a vowel, the vowel is dropped before 670 the suffixed s. None of the verbs whose present stem ends in a have their perfect formed by s suffixed.

(This suffix is supposed to be (with the personal suffix) es-i, the ancient perfect of the stem ĕs, and is apparently identical with the suffix of the first aorist in Greek.)

Labials. P. B. carp-, carp-s-i; clĕp-, clep-s-i (old); nūb-, nup-s-i; rĕp-, rep-s-i; scalp-, scalp-s-i; scrīb-, scrip-s-i; sculp-, sculp-s-i; serp-, sərp-s-i.

jŭbĕ-, ju-ss-i (jou-s-i old form: probably jŭbeo is for jŏveo); sæpī-, sæp-s-i.

M. A euphonic **p** is generally inserted before **s**; **m** is once 671 assimilated.

cōm-, comp-s-i; so also dēm-, prōm-, sūm-; prĕm-, pres-s-i (for pren-s-i); tem- (Pr. temn-), temp-s-i.

Gutturals. lc, rc, lg, rg throw away the guttural before s. 672

C. QV. cŏqv-, cox-i; dīc-, (Pr. dīc-), dix-i; dŭc-, (Pr. dūc-), dux-i; parc-, par-si (also pĕ-perc-i); so conqvīnisco has conquex-i (for conquinx-i? comp. mix-tum from misceo).

lŭcĕ-, lux-i; mulcĕ-, mul-s-i; torqvĕ-, tor-s-i.

farcī-, far-s-i; fulcī-, ful-s-i; sancī-, sanx-i; sarcī-, sar-s-i; vincī-, vinx-i.

-līcī-, -lex-i; -spīcī-, -spex-i.

G. GV. cing-, cinx-i; fīg-, fix-i; fing-, (sup. fic-t-), finx-i; -flīg-, 673 flix-i; flŭgv-, (Pr. flu-), flux-i; jung-, junx-i; -lĕg- (in compounds dīlĕg-, intellēg-, neglēg-), lex-i (rarely intel-lēg-i, neg-lēg-i); merg-, mer-s-i; ming-, minx-i; ēmung-, ēmunx-i; ningv-, ninx-it; pang- (or pǎg-), panx-i (usually pēgi or pĕpĭgi); ping-, (supine pic-t-), pinx-i; plang-, planx-i; -pung-, -punx-i; rĕg-, rex-i; sparg-, spar-s-i; stingv-, stinx-i; string-, (sup. strict-), strinx-i; strugv-, (Pr. stru-), strux-i; sŭg-, sux-i; tĕg-, tex-i; tingv-, tinx-i; vigv-, (Pr. vīv-), vix-i; ungv-, unx-i.

algĕ-, al-s-i; augĕ-, aux-i; frīgĕ-, frix-i; fulgĕ-, ful-s-i; in-dulgĕ-, indul-s-i; lūgĕ-, lux-i; mulgĕ-, mul-s-i; conigvĕ-, (Pr. cōnīve-), conix-i; tergĕ-, (terg- old), ter-s-i; turgĕ-, tur-s-i; urgĕ-, ur-s-i.

H. trǎh-, trax-i; vĕh-, vex-i.

Dentals. The dental falls away or is assimilated before **s**, but 674 the preceding vowel is lengthened (cf. § 191. 2, 4).

T. flect-, flex-i; mitt-, mī-s-i; nect-, nex-i; pect-, pex-i. sentī-, sen-s-i; quǎtī-, quas-s-i (e.g. concŭtī-, concus-s-i).

D. cēd-, ces-s-i; claud-, clau-s-i; dīvĭd-, dīvī-s-i; læd-, læ-s-i; lūd-, lū-s-i; plaud-, plau-s-i; rād-, rā-s-i; rōd-, rō-s-i; trūd-, trū-s-i; vǎd-, vǎ-s-i.

14—2

ardĕ-, ar-s-i; rīdĕ-, rī-s-i; svādĕ-, svā-s-i.

Nasals.　mănĕ-, man-s-i.　　　　　　　　　　　　　675

Liquids, &c.　vell-, vul-s-i (post-Augustan cf. § 683); gĕs-, (Pr. gĕr-), ges-s-i; ūs-, (Pr. ūr-), us-s-i.

hæsĕ- (?), (Pr. hære-), hæ-s-i; hausī- (Pr. hauri-), hau-s-i. (Cf. p. 247 and Preface.)

Semivowel.　rāvī-, -rau-s-i (rare).

iv. (*a*) Perfect stem formed by suffixing u¹ (vowel).　　676

Labials.　P. B.　strĕp-, strep-u-i.

crĕpā-, crĕp-u-i (very rarely -crepāvi); cŭbă-, (Pr. also cumb-), cŭb-u-i (rarely cubāvi).

albe-, (Pr. also albesc-), alb-u-i; hăbĕ-, hăb-u-i; lŭbĕ-, lŭb-u-it; rŭbĕ-, (Pr. also rubesc-), rŭb-u-i; sĕnĕ-, (Pr. senesc-), sĕn-u-i; sorbé-, sorb-u-i; stŭpĕ-, (Pr. also stŭpesc-), stŭp-u-i; tābĕ-, (Pr. also tābesc-), tāb-u-i; tĕpĕ-, (Pr. also tĕpesc-), tĕp-u-i; torpĕ-, (Pr. also torpesc-), torp-u-i.

răpī-, răp-u-i; rĕsĭpī-, (Pr. resipisc-), rĕsĭp-u-i (also rĕsĭpīvi).

M.　frĕm-, frĕm-u-i; gĕm-, gĕm-u-i; trĕm-, trĕm-u-i; vŏm-, vŏm-u-i.

cŏmă-, dŏm-u-i; tīmĕ-, tīm-u-i.

Gutturals.　C.　frĭcă-, frĭc-u-i; mĭcă-, mĭc-u-i (but dimicāvi); 677 ēnĕcă , ēnĕc-u-i, (also ēnĕc-ā-vi); -plĭcă-, plĭc-u-i, (also plĭc-ā-vi); sĕcă-, sĕc-u-i.

ăcĕ-, (Pr. also acesc-), ăc-u-i; arcĕ-, arc-u-i; dĕcĕ-, dĕc-u-i; dŏcĕ-, dŏc-u-i; flaccĕ-, (Pr. also flaccesc-), flacc-u-i; jăcĕ-, jac-u-i; lĭcĕ-, lĭc-u-it; lĭqvĕ-, (Pr. also lĭqvesc-), lĭc-u-i; marcĕ-, (Pr. also marcesc-), -marc-u-i; nŏcĕ-, nŏc-u-i; plăcĕ-, plăc-u-i; tăcĕ- (-tĭcesc-), tăc-u-i.

G.　ĕgĕ-, ĕg-u-i; langvĕ-, (Pr. also langvesc-), -lang-u-i; pĭgĕ-, pĭg-u-it; rĭgĕ-, (Pr. also rīgesc-), rĭg-u-i; vĭgĕ-, (Pr. also vĭgesc-), vĭg-u-i.

Dentals.　T.　mĕt-, mess-u-i² (old and rare); stert-, stert-u-i; 678 tĕr-, -tĕr-u-i (once in Tibull.; usually trīvi).

─────

¹ The suffix -ui or -vi is supposed by most philologers to be for fui. Thus the Umbrian ambre-fust is said to correspond to ambiverit. But, if vi and fui are from the same root, they are probably sister forms only.
² Messui is perhaps a secondary derivative, and stands in the same relation to meto, messum that statui does to sto, statum.

vĕtă-, vĕt-u-i (in Pers. once vĕt-ā-vi).

lătĕ-, (Pr. also lātesc-), lăt-u-i; obmūtĕ-, (Pr. obmūtesc-), ob-mūt-u-i; nĭtĕ-, (Pr. also nītesc-), nĭt-u-i; innōtĕ-, (Pr. innōtesc-), innōt-u-i; ŏportĕ-, ŏport-u-it; pænĭtĕ-, pænĭt-u-it; pătĕ-, (Pr. also pătesc-), păt-u-i; pūtĕ-, (Pr. also putesc-), pūt-u-i.

D. candĕ-, (Pr. also candesc-), cand-u-i; crūdĕ-, (Pr. crudesc-), crūd-u-i; mădĕ-, (Pr. also mădesc-), măd-u-i; pŭdĕ-, pud-u-it; sordĕ-, (Pr. also sordesc-), sord-u-i; obsurdĕ-, (Pr. obsurdesc-), obsurd-u-i.

Nasals, Liquids, &c.   N. -cĭn-, -cĭn-u-i (but căn-, cĕcĭnī); gĕn-, 679 (Pr. gĭgn-), gĕn-u-i.

sŏnă-, sŏn-u-i; tŏnă-, tŏn-u-i.

ēmĭnĕ-, emĭn-u-i; mŏnĕ-, mŏn-u-i; sĕne- (Pr. usually sĕnesc-), sĕn-u-i; tĕnĕ-, tĕn-u-i; ēvănĕ- (Pr. ēvănesc-), ēvăn-u-i.

L. ăl-, ăl-u-i; cŏl-, cŏl-u-i; consŭl-, consŭl-u-i; mŏl-, mŏl-u-i; ŏl-, (also ŏlĕ-), ŏl-u-i; vŏl-, (Pr. inf. velle), vŏl-u-i.

călĕ-, (Pr. also călesc-), căl-u-i; calle-, (Pr. also callesc-), call-u-i; coalĕ-, (Pr. coalesc- intrans.; comp. ălo trans.), coăl-u-i; dŏlĕ-, dŏl-u-i; pallĕ-, (Pr. also pallesc-), pall-u-i; sĭlĕ-, (Pr. also sĭlesc-), sĭl-u-i; stŭdĕ-, stŭd-u-i; vălĕ-, (Pr. also vălesc-), văl-u-i.

ēvĭlĕ-, (Pr. ēvĭlesc-), ēvĭl-u-i.

sălĭ-, săl-u-i (rarely sălĭi).

R. sĕr-, sĕr-u-i.   680

ārĕ-, (Pr. also āresc-), ăr-u-i; cărĕ-, căr-u-i; clārĕ-, (Pr. also clāresc-), clăr-u-i; crēbre-, (Pr. crēbresc-), crēbr-u-i; dūrĕ-, (Pr dūresc-), dūr-u-i; flōrĕ-, (Pr. also flōresc-), flōr-u-i; horrĕ-, (Pr. also horresc-), horr-u-i; mātūre-, (Pr. mātūresc-), mātŭr-u-i; mĕrĕ-, mĕr-u-i; nĭgre-, (Pr. also nĭgresc-), nĭgr-u-i; părĕ-, păr-u-i; terrĕ-, terr-u-i.

ăpĕrĭ-, ăpĕr-u-i; ŏpĕrĭ-, ŏpĕr-u-i; sărĭ-, săr-u-i (also sărīvi).

S. deps-, deps-u-i: nex-, nex-u-i; pŏs-, (Pr. pōn), pŏs-u-i; tex-, tex-u-i.

censĕ-, cens-u-i; tors-, (Pr. torrĕ-), torr-u-i.

Semivowels.   ferv- (also fervĕ- and ferve-sc-), ferb-u-i (also fervi).

iv. (b) Perfect stem formed by suffixing v (consonant).   621

The consonantal **v** is suffixed to vowel stems only (except pasco?), and the preceding vowel is always long.

All regular verbs with stems in ā- or ī- (unless otherwise mentioned) have their perfect stem formed in this way. So also

Labials. cŭpĭ-, (Pr. cŭpĭ-, except once cupīret), cupī-v-ĭ; săpĭ-, (Pr. săpĭ-), sapī-v-ĭ.

Dentals. pĕtī-, (Pr. pĕt-), petī-v-ĭ; rŭdī-, (Pr. rŭd-), rudī-v-ĭ.

Sibilant. arcessī-, (Pr. arcess-), arcessī-v-ĭ; căpessī-, (Pr. capess-), capessī-v-ĭ; făcessī-, (Pr. facess-), facessī-v-ĭ; incessī-, (Pr. incess-), incessī-v-ĭ; lăcessī-, (Pr. lacess-), lacessī-v-ĭ; pŏsī-, (Pr. pōn-), posī-v-ĭ (always in Plaut., Ter., also in Cato, Catull.: for posui see § 680); quæsī-, (Pr. quær-), quæsī-v-ĭ.

păs-, (Pr. pasc-, for pas-sc-), pă-v-ĭ (cf. § 93. 2).

Monosyllabic vowel verbs: (also oleo, quiesco).   682

A. să-, (Pr. sĕr-), sē-v-ĭ; strā-, (Pr. stern-), strā-v-ĭ.

O. no-, (Pr. nosc-), nō-v-ĭ.

U. fu- (§ 719), fŭ-v-ĭ (Plaut. but usually fuī); comp. plu-(§ 648), plŭvi (also plui).

E. crē-, (Pr. cer-n-), crē-v-ĭ; crē-, (Pr. cre-sc-), crē-v-ĭ; flē-, flē-v-ĭ; dēlē-, delē-v-ĭ; nē-, nē-v-ĭ; -ŏlē- (e.g. abole-sc-o, adole-sc-o, obsole-sc-o), -ŏlē-v-ĭ; -plē-,-plē-v-ĭ; quiē-, (Pr. quiesc-), quiē-v-ĭ; sprē-, (Pr. sper-n-), sprē-v-ĭ; svē- (Pr. sve-sc-), svē-v-ĭ.

I. cĭ-, (Pr. ciē-, also cī-), cī-v-ĭ; ĭ-, (Pr. ind. 1st pers. eo), ī-v-ĭ; lĭ-, (Pr. lin-), lī-v-ĭ and lē-v-ĭ; qui-, (Pr. ind. 1st pers. queo), quī-v-ĭ; scī-, (Pr. sci-sc-); besides the regular ī verb, scio), scī-v-ĭ; sĭ-, (Pr. sin-), sī-v-; trī-, (Pr. tĕr-), trī-v-ĭ (cf. § 678).

v. **Perfect stem, same as present stem.**   683

This is frequent (1) in the compounds of verbs of which the simple has a reduplicated perfect (see Chap. xxx.); (2) by the dropping of v, in perfects, in -īvi, -ēvi, -āvi (see §§ 661, 662); (3) regularly in verbs with -u stems, which with other, chiefly consonantal, stems are here named:—

Labials. bĭb-, bĭbĭ; lamb-, lambĭ.

Gutturals. ĭc-, īcĭ.

langv-e, langvi (cf. § 669); conigvĕ-, (Pr. cŏnīve-), conīvi (also conīxī).

Dentals. **T.** vert-, vertĭ.

D. -cand-, -candĭ; cŭd-, cŭdĭ; -fend-, -fendĭ; fīd-, (Pr. find-), fīdĭ (probably for fēfīdĭ); mand-, mandĭ; pand-, pandĭ; prehend-, prehendĭ; scand-, scandĭ; scĭd-, (Pr. scind-), scĭdĭ (scicĭdĭ old); sīd-, sīdĭ-; retund-, retundĭ.

prand-e, prandĭ; strīd-e, strīdĭ.

Liquids and Sibilants.

L. psall-, psall-i; vŏl-, (Pr. vell-), vell-i (rarely vulsi).

R. verr-, verr-i.

compĕr-i-, compĕr-i; repĕrĭ-, rĕppĕr-i (both probably compounds of a perfect pĕpĕri).

S. pins-, (also pĭs-), pins-i; vīs-, vīs-i.

Vowels. 5S4

U, vowel and consonant.

ăcŭ-, acu-i; argŭ-, argu-i; bătŭ-, batŭ-i; exŭ-, exu-i; fu-, fu-i (in Plautus sometimes fŭ-vi); grŭ-, gru-i; imbŭ-, imbu-i; indŭ-, indu-i; lŭ-, lu-i; mĕtŭ-, mĕtu-i; mĭnŭ-, mĭnu-i; plŭ-, plu-i, also plŭvi; nŭ-, nu-i; spŭ-, spu-i; stătŭ-, stătu-i; sternŭ-, sternu-i; sŭ-, su-i; trĭbŭ-, trĭbu-i.

solv-, solv-i; volv-, volv-i.

ferve-, ferv-i (also ferbui).

I. ădi-, (Pr. ind. 1st pers. sing. adeo), ădi-i; so usually the compounds of eo; inqui-, (Pr. ind. inquam), inquii; sălī-, sal-i-i (rare, usually sălui).

Among those verbs which have **no perfect active** in use 635 the following non-derivative verbs may be mentioned.

Labials. glŭb-.

Gutturals. **C.** fătisc-; gli-sc-; hi-sc-.

ămĭc-i (see however Chap. xxx.).

G. ang-; clang-; frīg-; ling-; verg-.

Dentals. **D.** fīd-, (fīsus sum); frend-.

aud-e, (ausus sum).

Liquids. fĕr-, (Pr. inf. ferre: perfect in use, tŭli); fŭr-; gavīd-, (Pr. gāud-e-, gavīsus sum).

Vowels. **E.** vi-e-.

I. ai-, (Pr. ind. ajo); fī-, (Pr. ind. fio).

CHAPTER XXIV.

OF THE SUPINE STEM.

THE supine stem has a common base with the stem of the past 685
and the future participles, and that of some verbal substantives, to
which class the supines themselves belong; e.g. supine, ama-t-u-;
past part. amā-t-o-; fut. part. amā-t-ūro-; subst. denoting *agent*,
amā-t-ōr-; denoting *action* amā-t-iōn-. This common base, which
will be here spoken of as the supine stem, is -t- suffixed to the stem
of the verb.   When the verb-stem ends in a vowel, the vowel is, if
long, generally retained; if short, almost always changed, (except
in monosyllables), to ĭ (§ 241), or omitted altogether.   A few
verbs which have a consonant stem, have -ĭt- instead of -t- in the
supine, as if from a vowel stem.   When the verb-stem ends in a
consonant, or loses its final vowel, the -t is, when following certain
consonants, changed to -s.   A few other instances of this softening
admit of special explanation.

The verbs here will be classified according as they do or do not
exhibit a vowel before the supine suffix, and, subordinately to that,
according to the final vowel or consonant of the verb stem.

N.B. The supine itself will be here named whenever either supine,
past participle, or verbal substantive in -tu exists: otherwise such
other form from the same base, as does exist.

i. Verbs with a vowel preceding the supine suffix. 687

   A. 1.   Verbs having ā in supine stem; na- (for gĕnă? Pr.
inf. nasci), nātum; strā-, (Pr. stern-), strā-tum; tlā-, (Pr. toll-),
lā-tum; āmā-, āmā-tum; and all other verbs with derivative ā
stems.

   frĭcā-, frĭcā-tum (also fric-tum); mĭcā-, -mĭcā-tum; nĕcā-,
nĕcā-tum (but cf. § 700); sĕcā-, secāturus (once).

   2.   Verbs having -ă in supine stem; dă-, dă-tum; ră-, (Pr. inf. 688
rĕri: for the vowel, cf. § 668), rătum; să-, (Pr. sĕr-), să-tum; stă-,
(Pr. inf. stāre; also sistĕre), stă-tum (but in some compounds
stā-turus).

3. Verbs having -ĭ (for -ă) in supine stem; crĕpă-, crĕpĭ-tum; cŭbă-, (Pr. also cumb-), cŭbĭ-tum; dŏmă-, dŏmĭ-tum; -plĭcă-, -plĭcĭ-tum (also plĭcă-tum); sŏnă-, sŏnĭ-tum (sonā-turus, once); tŏnă-, tŏnĭ-tum (intonā-tus, once); vĕtă-, vĕtĭ-tum.

In jŭvă-, jŭ-tum (rarely juvā-turus); lăvă- (also lăv-), lau-tum; the ĭ is absorbed by the v preceding.

O. no-, (Pr. nosc-), nŏ-tum; pŏ-, (whence pŏtare frequentative) 689 pŏ-tŭs; cognŏ- (cf. § 647), (so also agno-), cognī-tum.

U. 1. Verbs having ū in supine stem; ăcŭ-, ăcŭ-tum; argŭ-, 690 argŭ-tum; dĭlŭ-, dĭlŭ-tum; exŭ-, exŭ-tum; glŭ- (Pr. glūtă-, frequentative) glŭ-tus, adj.; ĭmbŭ-, ĭmbŭ-tum; indŭ-, indŭ-tum; metŭ-, metŭ-tum (Lucr. once); mĭnŭ-, mĭnŭ-tum; -nŭ-, nŭ-tum (abnuĭturus in Sall.); spŭ-, spŭ-tum; stătŭ-, stătu-tum; sŭ-, sŭ-tum; trĭbŭ-, trĭbŭ-tum; tŭ- (Pr. tue- usually), tŭ-tum.

lŏqv-, locŭ-tum; seqv-, sĕcŭ-tum; solv-, solŭ-tum; volv-, volutum.

fru- (for frugv-) has rarely fruĭtūrus (usually, fruc-tum).

2. Verbs having -ŭ in supine stem; rŭ-, rŭ-tum, (but rūtum 691 according to Varr.; fut. part. is ruĭ-tūrus); pŭ-, (whence pŭtāre frequentative), pŭ-tus (adj.); clŭ-, (almost always clue-), -clŭtum (inclŭtus).

E. 1. Verbs having -ē in supine stem; crē-, (Pr. cern-, also 692 Pr. cresc-), crētum; dēlē-, dēlē-tum; fē-, (Pr. fētă-, frequentative), fē-tus (adj.); flē-, flē-tum; nē-, nē-tum (Ulp.); -olē- (Pr. obs-, exolesc-), -ŏlē-tum; -plē-, plē-tum; quiē-, quiē-tum; svē-, (Pr. svesc-), svētum; sprē-, (Pr. spern-), sprē-tum. Perhaps also fer-re, frē-tus.

2. Verbs having -ĕ in supine stem; vĕgĕ-, vĕgĕ-tus (adj.); 693 viĕ-, viĕ-tum (Hor., but viē-tum Ter. Lucr.).

3. Verbs having ĭ (for -ĕ) in supine stem; ăbŏlē-, ăbŏlĭ-tum; cĭĕ-, cĭĕ-tum; cărĭ-, cărĭ-turus; dŏlē-, dŏlĭ-turus; exercē-, exercĭtum; hăbē- (and compounds dēbē-, præbē-), hăbĭ-tum; jăcē-, jăcĭ-turus; lĭcē-, lĭcĭ-tum; lŭbē-, lŭbĭ-tum; mĕrē-, mĕrĭ-tum; mĭsĕrē-, mĭsĕrĭ-tum (rarely misertum); mŏnē-, monĭ-tum; nŏcē-, nŏcĭ-tum; părē-, parĭ-turus; pĭgē-, pĭgĭ-tum; plăcē-, plăcĭ-tum; pŭdē-, pŭdĭtum; sŏlē-, solĭ-tum; tăcē-, tăcĭ-tus (adj.); terrē-, terrĭ-tum; vălē-, valĭ-turus; vĕrē-, vĕrĭ-tum. Sorbē- has subst. sorbĭ-tio.

căvē-, căvĭ-tum (old: usually cau-tum); făvē-, fau-tum (for favĭ- 694 tum; cf. făvĭtor Plaut.). So also fŏvē-, fŏ-tum; mŏvē-, mŏ-tum; vŏvē-, vŏtum.

I. (1) Verbs having -ī in supine stem; audī-, audī-tum; and 695
others which have -īvī in perfect, except those in § 655.

blandī-, blandī-tum; largī-, largī-tum; mentī-, mentī-tum; mōlī-,
mōlī-tum; partī-, partī-tum; potī-, potī-tum; sortī-, sortī-tum.

sancī-, sancī-tum (sanc-tum more frequently); pĕrī-, pĕr-ītus,
adj. (but in comp. -per-tum); opperī-, opperītum (also oppertum);
oblīvi-, oblītum (for oblīvitum) probably has stem in ī. Perhaps
also pinsī- (usually pins-), pinsī-tum (see Chap. XXX.).

cŭpī-, cŭpī-tum; pĕtī-, (Pr. pĕt-), pĕtī-tum; quæsī-, (Pr. quær-),
quæsī-tum; rŭdī-, (Pr. rŭd-), rŭdī-tum; trī-, (Pr. tĕr-), trītum;
arcessī-, (Pr. arcess-), arcessī-tum; so also lacessī-tum, capessī-tum,
facessī-tum.

(2) Verbs having -ĭ in supine stem; cĭ-, (Pr. cie-), cĭ-tum 696
(sometimes -cī-tum); ĭ-, (Pr. ind. eo), ĭ-tum); lĭ-, (Pr. lĭn-), lĭ-
tum; quĭ-, (Pr. ind. queo), quĭ-tum; sĭ-, (Pr. sĭn-), sĭ-tum.

fŭgĭ-, fŭgĭ-tum; ēlĭcĭ-, elĭcĭ-tum (but illicĭ-, illec-tum, &c.),
mŏrĭ-, mŏrĭ-turus; orī-, ŏrĭ-tūrus (sup. or-tum); părĭ-, părĭ-tŭrus
(sup. par-tum); pōsĭ-, (Pr. pōn-), pōsĭ-tum.

Consonant stems. ăl-, ălĭ-tum (more usually al-tum); frĕm-, 697
frĕm-ĭ-tum; gĕm-, gĕm-ĭ-tum; gĕn- (Pr. gĭgn-), gĕnĭ-tum; mŏl-,
mŏl-ĭ-tum; strĕp-, strĕp-ĭ-tum; vŏm-, vŏm-ĭ-tum). In Columella
(no where else) pecto has pectĭtum.

[Of these supines in -ĭtum from consonantal stems, alĭtum is a 698
post-Augustan form, used perhaps to distinguish the participle of
alĕre from its use as the adjective al-tus. A like cause may be
given for the form molĭtum, to distinguish from multus; fremĭtum,
gemĭtum, vomĭtum would, without the ĭ, have to lose their characteristic m (fren-tum, gen-tum, von-tum), or assume the ugly forms
fremptum, gemptum, vomptum (cf. § 70). And gemitum, genĭtum,
would in the former case become identical. Genitum is probably
from gĕnă- (comp. gna-sc-or); and strepitum may have had a present stem strĕpă- once. Comp. the words in § 688. All have perfects in -ui.]

ii. Verbs with a consonant preceding the supine 699
suffix.

1. Verbs which retain -t-.

Labials. P.   carp-, carp-tum; clĕp-, clep-tum; rĕp-, rep-tum;
rŭp-, (Pr. rump-), rup-tum (rumptum, Plaut.); scalp-, scalp-tum;
sculp-, sculp-tum; sarp-, sarp-tum; serp-, serp-tum.

ăpĭ-, (Pr. api-sc-), ap-tum; căpĭ-, cap-tum; răpĭ-, rap-tum; sæpĭ-, sæp-tum.

B. glūb-, glup-tum; nŭb (Pr. nūb-), nup-tum; scrīb-, scrip-tum.

M. ĕm-, em-p-tum; tem-, (Pr. temn-), tem-p-tum.

Gutturals. After a preceding consonant (except n), the guttural 700 usually falls away.

C. Qv. Coqv-, coc-tum; dĭc-, (Pr. dīc-), dĭc-tum; dŭc-, (Pr. dūc), duc-tum; herc- (? Pr. herciscere), herc-tum; ic-, ic-tum; lĭqv-, (Pr. linqv-), -lic-tum); vic-, (Pr. vinc-), vic-tum.

frĭcă-, fric-tum (also frĭcā-tum); ēnĕcă-, ēnĕc-tum; sĕcă-, sectum (also sĕcāturus).

arcĕ-, arc-tum or ar-tum; dŏcĕ-, doc-tum; misce-, mix-tum (for misc-tum? but cf. § 635: in MSS. often mis-tum); torqvĕ-, tor-tum.

ămīcī-, amic-tum; farcī-, far-tum; fulcī-, ful-tum; sancī-, sanctum (also sănčī-tum); sarcī-, sar-tum; vincī-, vinc-tum.

făcī-, fac-tum; jăcī-, jactum; nancī-, (Pr. nanci-sc-), nanc-tum or nac-tum; -spici-, -spec-tum.

G. GV. (For stems ending in -lg-, -rg, see § 706); ăg-, ac- 701 tum; cing-, cinc-tum; fīg-, (Pr. and Perf. fing-), fic-tum; -flīg-, -flic-tum; flugv-, (Pr. flu-), fluc-tus subst., also fluxus adj.; frăg-, (Pr. frang-), frac-tum; frīg-, fric-tum; frugv-, (Pr. fru-), fructum; fung-, func-tum; jung-, junc-tum; lĕg-, lec-tum; ling-, lictum; mĭg-, (Pr. ming- and mej-), mic-tum and minc-tum; -mung-, -munc-tum; păg-, (Pr. pang-), pactum; pĭg-, (Pr. and Perf. ping-), pic-tum; plang-, planc-tum; pung-, punc-tum; rĕg-, rec-tum; rig-, (Pr. ring-), ric-tus subst.; stingv-, stinc-tum; strĭg-, (Pr. and Perf. string-), stric-tum; strugv-, (Pr. stru-), struc-tum; sŭg-, suctum; tăg-, (Pr. tang-), tac-tum; tĕg-, tec-tum; tingv-, tinc-tum; ungv-, unc-tum; vigv-, (Pr. vīv-), vic-tum.

augĕ-, auc-tum; lūgĕ-, luc-tus subst.

-licĭ-, -lec-tum (except elicĭ-tum).

H. trăh-, trac-tum; vĕh-, vec-tum.

Dentals. See §§ 707, 708. 702

tend-, ten-tum (also tensum; probably the supines of tendo and teneo are mixed); comĕd-, comes-tum (rarely).

Nasals, Liquids, &c. 703

N. Căn-, can-tus subst.; -măn-, e.g. commĭn-isc-, commen-tum.

tĕnĕ-, tentum; vĕnī-, ven-tum.

L. ăl-, al-tum; cŏl-, cul-tum; consul-, consul-tum; cccŭl-, occul-tum; vol- (Pr. inf. velle), vultus, subst. *expression.*

adŏle (Pr. adolesc-), adul-tum (see Chap. XXX.).

sălĭ-, sal-tum; sĕpĕlĭ-, sĕpul-tum.

R. cĕr-, (Pr. cern-), cer-tus adj. (also crē-, crē-tus); sĕr-, -sertum (also serta, n. pl. *garlands*).

ŏrĭ-, or-tum (cf. § 696); ăpĕrĭ-, aper-tum; părĭ-, par-tum.

S. deps-, deps-tum; fĕs-, (Pr. fĕri-¹?), fes-tum (e.g. infes-tus, 704 manĭfes-tus) ; gĕs-, (Pr. gĕr-), ges-tum; păs-, (Pr. pasc-), pas-tum; pĭs-, pis-tum; quĕs-, (Pr. quĕr-), ques-tum; tex-, tex-tum; ŭs-, (Pr. ŭr-), us-tum; tors-, (Pr. torre-), tos-tum.

hausĭ-, (Pr. hauri-), haus-tum; pŏsĭ-, (Pr. pōn-), pos-tum (sometimes).

2. Verbs with t suffixed: but softened to s by the 705 influence usually either of a preceding dental, or of two consonants of which the first is a liquid. A vowel preceding -sum is always long. (Other cases are but few; and the sum may be partly due to the active perfect (if any) having -si, as it has in all these exceptional cases, except censui, and there the s of the stem is perhaps a substitute for an earlier **t**.)

Labials. lăb-, lap-sum; jŭbĕ-, jus-sum (for jŏvĕ-, jousum?).

prem-, pres-sum (for pren-sum).

Gutturals. The guttural usually drops out.   706

C. QU. parc-, par-sum.

mulcĕ-, mul-sum.

G. fig-, fixum (but fictum in Varr. Lucr.); flugv-, (Pr. flu-), fluxus adj. (fluc-tus subst.); merg-, mer-sum; sparg-, spar-sum.

mulgĕ-, mul-sum; tergĕ-, ter-sum.

Dentals. The dental either drops out, the preceding vowel 707 being therefore lengthened, or is assimilated. N.B. All dental stems have -sum (see § 702).

---

¹ Fĕrīre seems a suitable verb to which to refer infestus and manifestus, confestim; (comp. also festinare); and festus itself is in meaning allied to fērīæ, which Festus (p. 85) derives a feriendis victimis; comp. fœdus fĕrīre, *to strike a bargain.* The differing quantities of e are however noticeable in this last etymology. Fendere, to which these forms are often referred, both ought to make, and does make, fensus, not festus.

T. flect-, flexum; mĕt-, mes-sum; mitt-, mis-sum; nect-, nexum; nict-, (Pr. nĭt-), nixum or nī-sum; pect-, pexum (in Columella, pectĭtum); -plect-, -plexum; vert-, ver-sum ; ūt-, ū-sum.

fătĕ-, fas-sum.

sentĭ-, sen-sum; mentĭ-, (Pr. mētĭ-), mensum; senti-, sen-sum.

fătĭ-, (Pr. fatisc-), fes-sus adj.; pătĭ-, pas-sum; quătĭ-, quas-sum. 708

D. căd-, că-sum; cæd-, cæ-sum; cēd-, ces-sum; claud-, clausum; cūd-, cū-sum; divĭd-, divī-sum; ĕd-, ē-sum (rarely comes-tum, from comĕd-); -fend-, -fen-sum; fīd-, fī-sum; fĭd-, fissum; frend-, fres-sum or frē-sum; fud-, (Pr. fund-), fū-sum; læd-, læsum ; lūd-, iū-sum ; mand-, man-sum ; ŏd-, -ōsum (e.g. per-ōsus, exōsus); pand-, pan-sum or pas-sum; pend-, pen-sum; plaud-, plau-sum; prehend-, prehen-sum; răd-, ră-sum; rŏd-, rō-sum; scand-, scan-sum; scĭd-, (Pr. scind-), scis-sum; tend-, ten-sum (also ten-tum); trūd-, trūsum; tud- or tund-, tu-sum or tun-sum.

arde-, ar-sūrus; aud-e-, au-sum; gavĭd-e-, (Pr. gaude-), gāvīsum; morde-, mor-sum; pende-, pen-sum; prand-, pran-sum; rīde-, rī-sum: sĕde-, ses-sum; sponde-, spon-sum; suāde-, suā-sum; tæd-e-, tæ-sum; tonde-, ton-sum; vĭde-, vī-sum.

ordĭ-, or-sum; fŏdĭ-, fos-sum; grădĭ-, gres-sum (ad-gre-tus is said to have been used by Ennius).

Nasals, Liquids, &c.   709

N. māne-, man-sum.

L. -cell-, -cul-sum; fall-, fal-sum; pell-, pul-sum; sall-, salsum; vell-, vul-sum.

R. curr-, cur-sum; verr-, ver-sum.

S. cense- (perhaps a derivative from census), cen-sum; hæse- (?) (Pr. hære-), hæ-sum.

hausī- (Pr. hauri-), hau-sūrus (also haus-tum, see p. 247).

Many verbs have no supine or other words of this formation in use.

The supines are respectively the accusative and ablative (or in 710 some uses apparently the dative), of a verbal noun in -u. They are called respectively active supine, or supine in -um, and passive supine or supine in -u.

From this so-called supine stem are formed, as has been said, the future participle active by suffixing -ūro-, sing. nom. -ūrus (m.); -ūra (f.), -ūrum (n.); and the past participle passive, by suffixing the ordinary case endings of the second class; e.g. sing. nom. -us (m.), -ă (f.), -um (n.).

These participles, in the appropriate gender and number, are used in the nominative case with the finite tenses of the verb sum, and in the accusative as well as the nominative with the infinitive of the same verb to supply the place of certain tenses for which there is no special form. The future participle thus supplies additional future tenses in the active voice especially in the subjunctive: the past participle supplies the perfect tenses of the passive voice, whether the passive voice have a strictly passive meaning, or, as in deponents an active or reflexive meaning.

A few instances are found in which the real formation of these 711 compound expressions appears to have been forgotten. Thus Gracchus is said to have used the expression "Credo ego inimicos meos hoc dicturum" (for dicturos); Valerius Antias to have written "Aruspices dixerunt omnia ex sententia processurum" (Gell. i. 7. 10).

For the future infinitive passive is sometimes used a combination of the supine in -um and the passive infin. of eo, viz. iri, impersonally; but Plautus has (*Rud.* 1242), "Mi istæc videtur præda prædatum irier;" and Quintil. ix. 2. 88, "Reus parricidii damnatum iri videbatur."

From Claudius Quadrigarius is quoted "hostium copias iri occupatas futurum" (for occupatum iri). (Gell. i. 7. 9.)

CHAPTER XXV.

OF THE TRADITIONAL CLASSIFICATION OF VERBS.

As the ordinary classification of verbs is often referred to, it 712
may be convenient here to give a brief account of it. It is as old as
Charisius at least, who wrote probably in the fourth century after
Christ.

Verbs are generally divided according to their form into four
classes, called *Conjugations*.

The four conjugations are distinguished by the vowel which
immediately precedes re in the infinitive mood; which in the 1st
conjugation is ă: in the second ē[1]: in the third ĕ, not usually belonging to the stem: in the fourth ĭ.

The distribution of the verbs among these conjugations is as
follows.

I. First conjugation contains all vowel verbs, whose stem ends
in ă; as ăm-o, *I love*, infin. ămā-re.

II. Second conjugation contains all vowel verbs whose stem
ends in ē; as mone-o, *I advise*, infin. mŏnē-re.

III. Third conjugation contains all verbs whose stem ends in
a consonant, or in u, or a variable i (called I above, § 656); as

    rĕg-o, *I rule*, infin. rĕg-ĕre.

    trĭbu-o, *I assign*, infin. trĭbu-ĕre.

    căpi-o, *I take*, perf. cēp-i, infin. căpĕ-re.

IV. Fourth conjugation contains all vowel verbs whose stem
ends in ĭ, as audĭ-o, *I hear*, infin. audī-re.

[1] i. e. ē according to the ordinary doctrine: but see §§ 650—652.

The following are the regular forms of the perfect and supine 713
in the several conjugations according to the ordinary description.

In the 1st conjugation the regular perfect is formed by the
addition of **vi** to the stem, the regular supine by the addition of
tum, e. g. **āmā-vi, amā-tum.**
The exceptions are few: two verbs **do, sto** have a reduplicated
perfect **dĕdi, stĕti**: two others, **jŭvo, lăvo,** lengthen the stem vowel
e. g. (**jūvi, lāvi**): the others add **ui** to the stem, the final a being
omitted; e. g. **crĕpa-, crĕp-ui.** None form the perfect in **si** or **i**
simple. None form the supine in **sum.**

In the 2nd conjugation the regular perfect is formed by the
addition of **ui** to the stem, the regular supine by the addition of
ītum, the final stem vowel **e** being omitted, as **mone-, mon-ui.** The
exceptions are numerous, and of all kinds: the larger number adding **si.** Many have the supine in **sum.**

In the 3rd conjugation all the forms are much used, some
having even the long characteristic vowel of the other three conjugations, e. g. **sterno, strāvi; sperno, sprēvi; tero, trīvi.** These are
clearly instances of a vowel stem in the perfect and supine super-
seding a consonant stem. Many have the supine in **sum.**

In the 4th conjugation, the regular perfect is formed by the
addition of **vi** and the regular supine by the addition of **tum** to
the stem; e. g. **audī-vi, audī-tum.** The exceptions are few: one
lengthens the stem vowel (**vĕni-o, vēni**): one simply adds the personal inflexions (**compĕri-o, compĕr-i**). Three have perfect in **ui**;
viz. **aperio, operio,** and **salio,** nine have perfect in **si.** Two, viz.
eo and **cio,** have short **ĭ** in supine. None form the perfect by reduplication, except perhaps **repĕri-o, reppĕr-i.** Several have supine
in **sum.**

CHAPTER XXVI.

EXAMPLES OF THE COMPLETE INFLEXIONS OF VERBS.

In this chapter are given specimens of the complete inflexions of verbs: first, of the tenses formed from the present stem; secondly, of the tenses formed from the perfect stem; and lastly of the verbal nouns, which have the same base as the so-called supines, and assist in supplying defective tenses.

For the present stem the different persons in each number are given in full, of one consonant verb (rĕgo), and of one verb (ămo) belonging to the class of vowel verbs which is most numerous, and has inflexions most different from consonant verbs, viz. a stems. Specimens, less full, of four other classes of vowel stems, viz. in u, ī, ĭ and ĕ are given on pp. 228, 229. The omitted forms can be easily supplied by comparison with the forms of rego and amo.

The tenses formed from the perfect stem and the verbal nouns classed under the supine stem have the same inflexions generally, whatever be the verbal stem, except so far as regards the formation of the perfect and supine stems themselves. And the differences in the formation of these do but very partially coincide, as has been seen (ch. XXIII. XXIV.), with the classification of verbal stems. The specimens given on pp. 230, 231 are therefore only an arbitrary selection of the most striking sorts.

PRESENT STEM. *Consonant Conjugation.*

Active Voice.   Passive Voice.
Present.

	Indic.	Subjunc.	Indic.	Subjunc.
Sing. 1.	rĕg-o	rĕg-am	rĕg-ŏr	rĕg-ăr
2.	reg-ĭs	reg-ās	reg-ĕr-ĭs	reg-ăr-ĭs
3.	reg-ĭt	reg-ăt	reg-ĭt-ŭr	reg-ăt-ŭr
Plur. 1.	reg-ĭm-ŭs	reg-ām-ŭs	reg-ĭm-ŭr	reg-ăm-ŭr
2.	reg-ĭt-ĭs	reg-āt-ĭs	reg-ĭmĭn-ī	reg-āmĭn-ī
3.	reg-unt	reg-ant	reg-unt-ŭr	reg-ant-ŭr

Future.

Sing. 1.	rĕg-am	rĕg-ăr
2.	reg-ēs	reg-ēr-ĭs
3.	reg-ĕt	reg-ĕt-ŭr
Plur. 1.	reg-ēm-ŭs	reg-ēm-ŭr
2.	reg-ēt-ĭs	reg-ēmĭn-ĭ
3.	reg-ent	reg-ent-ur

Imperfect.

Sing. 1.	rĕg-ēb-am	rĕg-ĕr-em	rĕg-ēb-ăr	rĕg-ĕr-ĕr
2.	reg-eb-ās	reg-er-ēs	reg-eb-ār-ĭs	reg-er-ēr-ĭs
3.	reg-eb-ăt	reg-er-ĕt	reg-eb-āt-ŭr	reg-er-ēt-ŭr
Plur. 1.	reg-eb-ăm-us	reg-er-ēm-ŭs	reg-eb-ăm-ŭr	reg-er-ēm-ŭr
2.	reg-eb-āt-ĭs	reg-er-ēt-ĭs	reg-eb-āmĭn-i	reg-er-ēmĭn-ī
3.	reg-eb-ant	reg-er-ent	reg-eb-ant-ur	reg-er-ent-ŭr

Imperative Mood.

		Active.	Passive.
Present.	Sing. 2.	rĕg-ĕ	reg-ĕrĕ
	Plur. 2.	reg-ĭt-ĕ	reg-ĭmĭn-ī
Future.	Sing. 2 3	rĕg-ĭt-o	rĕg-ĭt-ŏr
	Plur. 2.	reg-ĭt-ŏt-ĕ	(none)
	3.	reg-unt-o	reg-unt-ŏr

Verbal Noun-Forms.

		Active.		Passive.
Infinitive (Present)		rĕg-ĕr-ĕ		rĕg-ī
Participle (Present), Nom.		rĕg-ens		
Gerund	Nom. } Acc. }	rĕg-end-um &c.	Gerundive } nom. masc. } sing. }	rĕg-end-us &c.

PRESENT STEM. *Principal Vowel Conjugation.* 715

	Active Voice.		Passive Voice.	
		Present.		
	Indicative.	Subjunctive.	Indicative.	Subjunctive.
Sing. 1.	ăm-o	ăm-ēm	ăm-ŏr	ăm-ēr
2.	am-ās	am-ēs	am-ār-ĭs	am-ēr-ĭs
3.	am-ăt	am-ĕt	am-āt-ŭr	am-ēt-ŭr
Plur. 1.	am-ăm-ŭs	am-ēm-ŭs	am-ăm-ŭr	am-ēm-ŭr
2.	am-āt-ĭs	am-ēt-ĭs	am-āmĭn-ī	am-ēmĭn-ī
3.	am-ănt	am-ent	am-ant-ŭr	am-ent-ŭr
		Future.		
Sing. 1.	ăm-āb-o		ăm-āb-ŏr	
2.	am-āb-ĭs		am-āb-ĕr-ĭs	
3.	am-āb-ĭt		am-āb-ĭt-ŭr	
Plur. 1.	am-āb-ĭm-ŭs		am-āb-ĭm-ŭr	
2.	am-āb-ĭt-ĭs		am-āb-ĭmĭn-i	
3.	am-āb-unt		am-āb-unt-ŭr	
		Imperfect.		
Sing. 1.	ăm-āb-ăm	ăm-ār-ĕm	ăm-āb-ăr	ăm-ār-ĕr
2.	am-āb-ās	am-ār-ĕs	am-ab-ār-ĭs	am-ar-ēr-ĭs
3.	am-āb-ăt	am-ār-ĕt	am-ab-āt-ŭr	am-ar-ēt-ŭr
Plur. 1.	am-āb-ăm-ŭs	am-ar-ēm-ŭs	am-ab-ăm-ŭr	am-ar-ēm-ŭr
2.	am-āb-āt-ĭs	am-ar-ēt-ĭs	am-ab-āmĭn-ī	am-ar-ēmĭn-ī
3.	am-ab-ant	am-ar-ent	am-ab-ant-ur	am-ar-ent-ŭr

		Imperative Mood.	
		Active.	Passive.
Present.	Sing. 2.	ăm-ā	am-ār-ĕ
	Plur. 2.	ăm-āt-ĕ	am-āmĭn-ī
Future.	Sing. 2 } 3 }	ăm-āt-o	am-āt-ŏr
	Plur. 2.	am-āt-ōt-ĕ	(none)
	3.	am-ant-o	am-ant-ŏr

		Verbal Noun-Forms.	
		Active.	Passive.
Infinitive Present.		ăm-ār-ĕ	ăm-ār-ī
Participle Present Nom.		ăm-ans &c.	
Gerund.	Nom. } Acc. }	am-and-um &c.	Gerundive } nom. masc. } sing. } ăm-and-ŭs &c.

15—2

PRESENT STEM.	Other Vowel Conjugations.		ACTIVE VOICE. 716

Indicative Mood.
Present.

Sing. 1.	trĭb-u-o	căp-i-o	aud-i-o	mŏn-e-o
2.	trib-u-ĭs	cap-ĭs	aud-ĭs	mon-ēs
3.	trib-u-ĭt	cap-ĭt	aud-ĭt	mon-ĕt
Plur. 1.	trib-u-ĭm-ŭs	cap-ĭm-us	aud-īm-ŭs	mon-ēm-ŭs
2.	trib-u-ĭt-ĭs	cap-ĭt-ĭs	aud-īt-ĭs	mon-ēt-ĭs
3.	trib-u-unt	cap-i-unt	aud-i-unt	mon-ent

Future.

Sing. 1.	trĭb-u-am	căp-i-am	aud-i-am	mon-ēb-o
2.	trib-u-ēs	cap-i-ēs	aud-i-ēs	mon-ēb-ĭs
&c.	&c.	&c.	&c.

Imperfect.

Sing. 1.	trĭ͞o-u-ĕb-am	căp-i-ēb-am	aud-i-ēb-am	mon-ēb-am
2.	trĭb-u-ĕb-ās	cap-i-ēb-ās	aud-i-ēb-as	mon-ēb-ās
&c.	&c.	&c.	&c.

Subjunctive Mood.
Present.

Sing. 1.	trĭb-u-am	căp-i-am	aud-i-am	mŏn-e-am
2.	trĭb-u-ās	cap-i-ās	aud-i-ās	mon-e-ās
&c.	&c.	&c.	&c.

Imperfect.

Sing. 1.	trĭb-u-ĕr-em	căp-ĕr-em	aud-īr-em	mŏn-ēr-em
2.	trib-u-ĕr-ēs	cap-ĕr-ēs	aud-īr-ēs	mon-ēr-ēs
&c.	&c.	&c.	&c.

Imperative Mood.
Present.

Sing. 2.	trĭb-u-ĕ	căp-ĕ	aud-ī	mŏn-ē
Plur. 2.	trib-u-ĭt-ĕ	cap-ĭt-ĕ	aud-īt-ŏ	mon-ēt-e

Future.

Sing. 2 3	trib-u-ĭt-o	cap-ĭt-o	aud-īt-o	mon-ēt-o
Plur. 2.	trib-u-ĭt-ōt-e	cap-ĭt-ōt-ĕ	aud-īt-ōt-e	mon-ēt-ōt-ĕ
3.	trib-u-unt-o	cap-i-unt-o	aud-i-unt-o	mon-ent-o

Verbal Noun-Forms.

Inf. Pr.	trĭb-u-ĕr-e	căp-ĕr-e	aud-īr-e	mŏn-ēr-e
Part. Pr.	trĭb-u-ens	căp-i-ens	aud-i-ens	mŏn-ens
&c.	&c.	&c.	&c.
Gerund.	trĭb-u-end-um	căp-i-end-um	aud-i-end-um	mŏn-end-um
&c.	&c.	&c.	&c.

PRESENT STEM.   *Other Vowel Conjugations.*   PASSIVE VOICE.

Indicative Mood.

Present.

Sing. 1. trĭb-u-ŏr	căp-i-ŏr	aud-i-ŏr	mŏn-e-ŏr
2. trĭb-u-ĕr-ĭs	cap-ĕr-ĭs	aud-ĭr-ĭs	mon-ĕr-ĭs
3. trĭb-u-ĭt-ŭr	cap-ĭt-ŭr	aud-ĭt-ŭr	mon-ĕt-ŭr
Plur. 1. trĭb-u-ĭm-ŭr	cap-ĭm-ŭr	aud-ĭm-ŭr	mon-ēm-ŭr
2. trĭb-u-ĭmĭn-ī	cap-ĭmĭn-ī	aud-ĭmĭn-ī	mon-ēmĭn-ī
3. trĭb-u-unt-ŭr	cap-i-unt-ŭr	aud-i-unt-ŭr	mon-ent-ŭr

Future.

Sing. 1. trĭb-u-ăr	cap-i-ăr	aud-i-ăr	mon-ēb-ŏr
2. trĭb-u-ēr-ĭs	cap-i-ēr-ĭs	aud-i-ēr-ĭs	mon-ēb-ĕr-ĭs
&c.	&c.	&c.	&c.

Imperfect.

Sing. 1. trĭb-u-ēb-ăr	căp-i-ēb-ăr	aud-i-ēb-ăr	mon-ēb-ăr
2. trĭb-u-ēb-ăr-ĭs	cap-i-ēb-ar-ĭs	aud-i-ēb-ăr-ĭs	mon-ēb-ăr-ĭs
&c.	&c.	&c.	&c.

Subjunctive Mood.

Present.

Sing. 1. trĭb-u-ăr	căp-i-ăr	aud-i-ăr	mŏn-e-ăr
2. trĭb-u-ăr-ĭs	cap-i-ăr-ĭs	aud-i-ăr-ĭs	mon-e-ăr-ĭs
&c.	&c.	&c.	&c.

Imperfect.

Sing. 1. trĭb-u-ĕr-ĕr	căp-ĕr-ĕr	aud-ĭr-ĕr	mon-ēr-ĕr
2. trĭb-u-ĕr-ēr-ĭs	cap-ĕr-ēr-ĭs	aud-ĭr-ēr-ĭs	mon-ēr-ēr-ĭs
&c.	&c.	&c.	&c.

Imperative Mood.

Present.

Sing. 2. trĭb-u-ĕr-ĕ	căp-ĕr-ĕ	aud-ĭr-ĕ	mŏn-ēr-ĕ
Plur. 2. trĭb-u-ĭmĭn-ī	cap-ĭmĭn-ī	aud-ĭmĭn-ī	mon-ēmĭn-ī

Future.

Sing. 2.⎫ trĭb-u-ĭt-ŏr 3.⎭	cap-ĭt-ŏr	aud-ĭt-ŏr	mon-ēt-ŏr
Plur. 3. trĭb-u-unt-ŏr	cap-i-unt-ŏr	aud-i-unt-ŏr	mon-ent-ŏr

Verbal Noun-Forms.

Infin. Pres. trĭb-u-ī	căp-ī	aud-ĭr-ī	mŏn-ēr-ī
Gerundive. trĭb-u-end-ŭs	căp-i-end-ŭs	aud-i-end-ŭs	mŏn-end-ŭs
&c.	&c.	&c.	&c.

PERFECT STEM.

	Present stem.	Verb stem.	PERFECT STEM.

I. Reduplication.

1.	tang-	tăg-	tĕ-tĭg-
2.	pend- (or pend-ĕ-)		pĕ-pend-
3.	mord-ĕ-	mord-	mŏ-mord-

II. Lengthening of stem-vowel.

4.	ăg-		ēg-
5.	jŭv-ā-	jŭv-	jūv-
6.	vĭd-ĕ-	vĭd-	vīd-
7.	căp-ĭ-	căp-	cēp-

III. Addition of -s-.

8.	carp-		carp-s-
9.	cŏm-		com-p-s-
10.	rĕg-		re-x-
11.	mulg-ĕ-	mulg-	mul-s-
12.	læd-		læ-s-
13.	quăt-ĭ-		quas-s-
14.	haur-ĭ-	haus-	hau-s-

IV. (a) Addition of -u-.

15.	dŏm-ă-	dŏm-	dom-u-
16.	mŏn-ĕ-	mŏn-	mŏn-u-
17.	tex-		tex-u-

(b) Addition of -v-.

18.	ăm-ā-		ămā-v-
19.	flē-		flē-v-
20.	sue-sc-	suē-	suē-v-
21.	aud-ī		audī-v-
22.	pĕt-		pĕtī-v-
23.	sĭn-	sĭ-	sī-v-

V. Without change of stem.

24.	trĭbu-		trĭbu-
25.	solv-		solv-
26.	vert-		vert-
27.	find-	fĭd-	fĭd-

Suffixes of tense, mood, person, appended to PERFECT STEM.

Indicative.		Subjunctive.
Perfect.	Comp. Fut.	Perfect.

-ī	-ĕr-o	-ĕr-im	1 Sing.
-is-ti	-ĕr-ĭs		2
-ĭt	-ĕr-ĭt		3
-ĭm-us	-ĕr-ĭm-us		1 Plur.
-is-tĭs	-ĕr-ĭt-is		2
-ĕr-unt	-ĕr-int		3

Pluperfect.

Indicative.	Subjunctive.	
-ĕr-am	-is-sem	1 Sing.
-ĕr-ās	-is-sēs	2
-ĕr-ăt	-is-sĕt	3
-ĕr-ām-ŭs	-is-sēm-ŭs	1 Plur.
-ĕr-ăt-ĭs	-is-sēt-ĭs	2
-ĕr-ant	-is-sent	3

Infinitive Perfect.

-is-se

SUPINE STEM.

718

Present stem.	Verb stem.	SUPINE STEM.
1. tang-	tăg-	tac-t-
2. pend- (or pend-ĕ-)		pen-s-
3. mord-ĕ-	mord-	mor-s-
4. ăg-		ac-t-
5. jŭv-ā-	jŭv-	jū-t-
6. vĭd-ĕ-	vĭd-	vī-s-
7. căp-ĭ-	căp-	cap-t-
8. carp-		carp-t-
9. cŏm-		com-p-t-
10. rĕg-		rec-t-
11. mulg-ĕ-	mulg-	mul-s-
12. læd-		læ-s-
13. quăt-ĭ-	quăt-	quas-s-
14. haur-ĭ-	haus-	hau-s-
15. dŏm-ā-	dŏm-	dom-ĭt-
16. mŏn-ĕ-	mŏn-	mŏn-ĭt-
17. tex-		tex-t-
18. ăm-ā-		ămā-t-
19. flē-		flē-t-
20. sue-sc-	suē-(?)	suē-t-
21. aud-ī-		audī-t-
22. pĕt-		pĕtī-t-
23. sĭn-	sĭ-	sĭ-t-
24. trĭbu-		trĭbū-t-
25. solv-		sŏlū-t-
26. vert-		ver-s-
27. find-	fĭd-	fis-s-

Noun suffixes appended to SUPINE STEM.

ACTIVE VOICE.

Future participle.
-ūr-ŭs(m.), -ūr-ă(f.), -ūr-um(n.).sing.nom. &c.   &c.   &c.

Future infinitive.
-ūrŭs(-ă, -um) { esse / fuisse

SUPINES.

-um, i.e. accusative case of verbal noun with u- stem.
-ū, i.e. ablative, or sometimes dative, case of same.

PASSIVE VOICE.

Past participle.
-ŭs (m.), -ă (f.), -um (n.).   sing. nom. &c.   &c.   &c.

With this participle in the proper gender and number are used certain tenses of the verb sum, *I am*, in order to form the perfect tenses of the passive verb, viz.

Indicative.   *Subjunctive.*

	Comp.			
	Perf.	Fut.	Perf.	
-ŭs (-ă, -um)	sum	ĕro	sim	1 Sing.
	ĕs	ĕris	sīs	2
	est	ĕrĭt	sit	3
-ī (-æ, -ă)	sŭmus	ĕrĭmus	sīmus	1 Plur.
	estis	ĕrĭtis	sītis	2
	sunt	ĕrunt	sint	3

	Pluperfect.		
	Indic.	*Subjunc.*	
-ŭs (-ă, -um)	ĕram	essem	1 Sing.
	ĕrās	esses	2
	ĕrăt	esset	3
-ī (-æ, -ă)	ĕrāmus	essēmus	1 Plur.
	ĕrātis	essētis	2
	erant	essent	3

Perf. pass.   infinitive.
-ŭs (-ă, -um)   esse

CHAPTER XXVII.

INFLEXIONS OF THE VERB sum, *I am*, AND COMPOUNDS.

THE tenses, &c. of the verb of *being* are partly from the root ⁷¹⁹ es, whence es-um, Gr. εἰμί (for ἐσμί), and partly from the root fu- (whence fio), Gr. φύω.

N.B. The parts of tenses not here given are quite regular.

		Indicative.	*Subjunctive.*		
			usual form.	old forms.	
Present Sing.	1.	s-um, *I am*	s-ĭm	s-i-em	fu-am
	2.	ĕs, *Thou art*	s-ĭs	s-i-ēs	fu-ās
	3.	es-t, *He is*	s-ĭt	s-i-ĕt	fu-ät
Plur.	1.	s-ŭm-us, *We are*	s-ĭm-ŭs		
	2.	es-t-ĭs, *Ye are*	s-ĭt-ĭs		
	3.	s-unt, *They are*	s-int	s-i-ent	fu-ant
Future Sing.	1.	ĕr-o, *I shall be*			
	2.	er-ĭs, *Thou wilt be*			
Plur.	3.	er-unt		usual forms.	
Imperf. Sing.	1.	er-am, *I was*	es-sem		f-ŏr-em

Perfect Sing.	1.	fu-ī, *I was* or *have been*	fu-ĕr-im
	2.	fu-ĭs-tī	fu-er-ĭs
	3.	fu-ĭt	fu-ĕr-ĭt
Plur.	1.	fu-ĭm-us	fu-er-ĭm-us
	2.	fu-ĭs-ti-s	fu-er-ĭt-ĭs
	3.	fu-ĕr-unt	fu-er-int

Comp. Fut.
  Sing. 1. fu-ĕr-o, *I shall have been*
  Plur. 3. fu-er-int
Pluperf. Sing. 1. fu-er-am, *I had been*   fu-ĭs-sem

Imperative.

Present Sing. 2. ĕs, *be*   Future Sing. 2 and 3. es-t-o
  Plur. 2. es-t-ĕ   Plur. 2. es-t-ŏt-ĕ
                                              3. s-unt-o

Infinitive.

Present. es-sĕ.   Past. fu-ĭs-sĕ.   Future. fŏ-rĕ or futurus essĕ, or fuissĕ.

Participle.

Present. (s-ens or ens) only in   Future. fŭt-ūr-ŭs, -ă, -um.
  compounds.

Es in pres. ind. is always long in Plaut., Terence. 720

When **est** came after a vowel or **m**, the e was omitted both in 721 speaking and writing (**nata st, natum st, oratio st**). So e. g. in Cicero, and (according to L. Müller) always both in scenic and dactylic verse. The same was not unfrequently the case with **es** after a vowel, and perhaps after **m** also; e. g. **nacta's, lignum's.** In the comic writers a short final syllable in s also coalesces with **est**; e. g. **factust, opust, similist,** for **factus est, opus est, similis est**; occasionally with **es**; e. g. **nactu's, simili's,** for **nactus es, similis es.** (Ritschl.)

An old form for the fut. indic. was **escit, escunt;** (apparently an 722 inchoative form). It is found once in Lucretius.

The form for the pres. subj. **siem,** &c. (§ 590) is frequent in Plautus, Terence, and early inscriptions; Cicero speaks of it as used in his time (*Orat.* 47, § 157). **Fuam,** &c. is also frequent in Plautus and other scenic poets, except Terence, who like Vergil uses it once only. The compounds occasionally have **-sies, -siet, -sient.**

The perf. and tenses formed from it are in Plautus occasionally 723 **fūvit, fūverit,** &c. So also Ennius has **fūisset** (ap. Gell. 12, 4. 3).

Like **sum** are inflected its compounds, viz. **absum** (perf. **abfui** or 724 **afui**), **adsum** or **assum** (perf. **adfui** or **affui**), **desum** (de-est, de-eram, &c. pronounced **dēst, dēram,** &c.), **insum, intersum, obsum, præsum** (3rd pers. sing. **præst**), **prōsum** (**prōd-** before a vowel; e.g. **prod-es, prod-ero**), **subsum, supersum.** Of these **adsum** and **præsum** alone have a present participle **absens, præsens.**

Possum, *I can,* compounded of **pŏte sum,** usually retains the 725 t before a vowel (e. g. **pŏt-es, pŏt-est, pŏtestis, pot-ero, pŏteram**), but assimilates it before s (e. g. **possŭmus, possunt,** &c.). The imperf. subj. is **pos-sem,** inf. **posse** (in Plaut. **potessem, potesse**), perf. ind. **potui** (probably for **potīvi,** the perfect of an active form of **potior**: comp. **posivi, posui**). It has no participle, **potens** being used merely as an adjective, *powerful.* **Possiem, possies,** &c. later **possim, possis,** &c. are frequent in Plautus and Terence.

The full forms, **potis sum, es, est, eram, ero, sim,** &c. are found in præ-Augustan poets; especially **potis est** in Terence, Lucretius, and once in Vergil; **pote fuisset** once in Ter. **Potis** and **pote** are also used as direct predicates without the verb.

Potestur, possitur, poteratur, are quoted as used occasionally with passive infinitive in early writers (Pacuvius, Cæl. Ant. &c.). **Potestur** also in Lucr. 9. 1010.

CHAPTER XXVIII.

INFLEXIONS OF SOME IRREGULAR VERBS.

Indicative Mood.	Do,	Volo,	Nōlo (Ne-volo),	Mālo 726 (Ma-volo for mag-volo),
Present Tense.	*give.*	*be willing.*	*be unwilling.*	*prefer.*
Sing. 1. do		vŏlo	nōlo	mālo
2. dās		vīs	non vīs	māvīs
3. dăt		vult	non vult	māvult
Plur. 1. dāmus		vŏlŭmus	nōlŭmus	mālŭmus
2. dătis		vultis	non vultis	māvultis
3. dant		vŏlunt	nōlunt	mālunt
Future Sing. 1. dăbo		vŏlam	(not used)	(not used)
2. dăbis		vŏles	nōles	māles
Imperf. Sing. 1. dăbam		vŏlēbam	nōlēbam	mālēbam
Perf. Sing. 1. dĕdi		vŏlui	nōlui	mālui
Subjunctive Mood.				
Pres. Sing. 1. dem		vĕlim	nōlim	mālim
Plur. 1. dēmus		vĕlīmus	nōlīmus	mālīmus
Imperf. Sing. 1. dărem		vellem	nollem	mallem
Imperative.				
Pres. Sing. 2. dā			nōlī	
Plur. 2. dăte			nōlīte	
Future Sing. 2. dăto			nōlīto	
Plur. 2. dătōte			nōlītōte	
3. danto			nōlunto	
Infinitive.				
Present. dăre		velle	nolle	malle
Future. dătūrum esse				
Participle.				
Present. dans		vŏlens	nōlens	(not used)
Gerund. dandum		volendum		
Gerundive. dandus				
Perfect. dătus				

Of these verbs **do** alone has a passive voice. The forms **der** and 727 **demur** are not actually found anywhere.

For the subjunctive forms **duim**, &c. see § 589.

In præ-Augustan language the 3rd pers. sing. and 2nd pers. plural was 728 **volt, voltis.** In conversational language **si vis, si vultis** became **sīs, sultis.**

For **non vis, non vult** Plautus has frequently **nĕvīs, nĕvult**; on the other hand, for **nolis, nolit, nolint, nollem** he has sometimes the full forms **non velis**, &c. (In Martial IX. 7 **nonvīs** occurs.)

Also in Plautus frequently **māvŏlo** (once also in Terence), **māvŏlet, mavĕlim, mavelis, mavelit, mavellem.**

Eo (stem i-), *go.*	Fio (used as passive of facio), *become.*	Edo, *eat.*	Fero, *bear.*	Feror, *be borne.* 729
ĕo	fīo	ĕdo	fĕro	fĕrŏr
īs	fīs	ĕdis or ēs	fers	ferrĭs
ĭt	rĭ̵	ĕdĭt or est	fert	fertŭr
īmus		ĕdĭmus	fĕrĭmus	fĕrĭmŭr
ītis		ĕdĭtis or estis	fertis	fĕrĭmĭni
ĕunt	fīunt	ĕdunt	fĕrunt	fĕruntŭr
ībo	fīam	ĕdam	fĕram	fĕrăr
ībĭs	fīēs	ĕdēs	fĕrēs	fĕrĕris
ībam	fīēbam	ĕdēbam	fĕrēbam	fĕrēbar
īvi	factus sum	ēdi	tŭli	lātus sum
ĕam	fīam	ĕdam or ĕdim	fĕram	fĕrăr
ĕāmus	fīāmus	ĕdāmus or ĕdīmus	fĕrāmus	fĕrāmur
īrem	fīĕrem	ĕdĕrem or essem	ferrem	ferrer
ī	fī	ĕde or ēs	fĕr	ferre
īte	fīte	ĕdīte or este	ferte	fĕrĭmĭni
īto		ĕdīto or esto	ferto	fertor
ītōte		ĕdītōte or estōte	fertōte	
ĕunto		ĕdunto	fĕrunto	fĕruntor
īre	fīĕri	ĕdĕre or esse	ferre	ferri
ĭtŭrus esse	factum iri	ēsūrus esse	lātūrus esse	lātum iri
iens		ĕdens	fĕrens	
G. ĕuntis				
		ēsūrus	lātūrus	
ĕundum -di -do	făcĭendus	ĕdendus	fĕrendus	
-eundus (in comp.)				
	factus			lātus

Ambio is the only compound of eo, which is inflected regularly like 730 a verb of the fourth conjug.

Futurus sim, fore, futurus esse, frequently supply the place of parts of fio. 731 Fierem, fieri, in Plautus and Terence often have the stem i long.

Of the compounds with prepositions the following forms occur: con-fit, confieret, confierent, confieri; defit, defiunt (Gell.), defiet, defiat, defieri; ecfieri; infit, interfiat, interfieri; superfit, superfiat, superfieri.

In the passive we find **estur** for **edītur** (3 pres. ind.), and **essē-** 732
tur (once in Varr.) for **ĕdĕrētur** (3 pers. imperf. subj.). The contracted forms are also found from **comĕdo**, and some (**exest, exesse,
exesset**) from **exĕdo**.

Quĕo, nĕquĕo, are declined like eo, but have no imperative, par- 733
ticiple, or gerund. (**Nequeuntis** is quoted once from Sallust.) Only
the present indic. and subj. are at all frequent.

Quis and quit (pres. act.) are only used after **non**, as **non quis**
(for **nequis**), **nonquit** (for **nequit**). With the passive infinitive
there are a few instances in early writers of passive forms, **quitus
sum, quitur, queatur**; **nequita est, nequitur. Queatur** also in Lucr.
I. 1045. Cf. § 725.

CHAPTER XXIX.

LIST OF DEPONENT VERBS.

THE following verbs are used as deponents. Sometimes they, 734
especially the past participle, are used in a passive as well as an
active sense. Instances of this are here mentioned. Sometimes the
deponent use is exceptional, and the active form with corresponding
passive usual. Such deponents have here the name of the authors,
who use them, simply appended. A few rare words are omitted.
Compounds also are usually omitted.

Adjūtari (Pac., Afran.; adjūtare Plaut., Ter.); ădūlari (adulāre
Lucr., Cic. poet.); æmulāri; altercāri (altercāre Ter.); alucināri;
ampullāri; ancillāri (old); ăpisci (*pass.* once, Plaut.; so ădeptus
Sall., Ovid, &c.; indīpiscĕre Plaut.); ăprīcāri; ăqūari; arbītrāri
(*pass.*, Plaut., Cic. once; arbitrāre Plaut.); archītectāri; argūmen-
tāri; argūtāri; aspernāri; assentīri (also *pass.*, and assentire frequent
in Cic., also Ov., Tac.); assentāri; auctiōnāri; aucūpāri (aucupāre
scenic poets); augūrāri (augūrāre, Plaut. &c., Verg.; auguratus
pass., Cic., Liv.); auspĭcāri (auspicāre early writers; auspicātus
pass., Ter., Cic., Liv.); auxīliāri; bacchāri; baubāri; bellāri
(Verg.); blandīri (eblandītus *pass.* Cic.); călumniāri; calvi; căvil-
lāri; causāri; circŭlāri; cōmissāri; cōmītāri (*passive* Lucr., Ov.,
Plin.; *pass. part.* frequently Cic., Liv. &c.; comitāre Ov.); com-
mentāri (*pass. part.* Cic.); commīnisci (*pass. part.* Ovid); commū-
nīcāri (Liv.); compĕrīri (Ter., Sall.); expĕrīri (*pass. part.* Cic.,
Liv. frequently, Tac.); contiōnāri; conflictāri (rarely as *pass.*; con-
flictāreTer.); cōnāri; consīliāri; conspĭcāri (*pass.*Sall.); contechnāri;
contemplari (contemplare Plaut. often); convīciāri; convīvāri; crī-
mĭnāri (*pass.* Cic.; criminare Plaut.); cunctāri (*pass. part. impers.*

Tac.); despĭcārī (*pass. part.* Plaut., Ter.); dīgladiārī; dignārī
(dignare Att., Cic. poet.; *pass. part.* Cic., Verg.); dŏmĭnārī; elu-
cubrārī (rare); ĕpŭlārī; exĕcrārī (*pass. part.* Cic.); expergĭscī; fǎbrĭ-
cārī (Plaut., Corn., Cic., Tac.; *pass.* Quintil.; *part. pass.* Ov., Liv.,
Suet., Tac.; fabricare Hor., Ov., Sen. &c.); fābŭlārī; fāmŭlārī;
fātērī (*pass.* Cic.?); confĭtērī (*part. pass.* Cic., Sen., Quint., &c.);
prŏfĭtērī (*part. pass.* Ov., Sen.); fătiscī (Lucr.); fēnĕrārī (*part.
pass.* Plaut., Ter., Scævol.; fenerare Ter., Sen., Plin., &c.); fēriārī;
fluctuārī (Liv., Sen.; fluctuare Plaut., Corn., Cic., Verg.); fārī
(effatus *pass.* Cic., Liv.); frūmentārī; frunīscī (old); fruī; frustrārī
(*pass.* Sall., *pass. part.* Vell.; frustrāre once Plaut.,); frŭtĭcārī (Cic.;
fruticare Col., Plin.); fungī (perfunctum *pass.* Cic.); fūrārī; gestĭ-
cŭlārī; glōriārī; grādī; græcārī; grassārī; grātĭfĭcārī; grātārī;
grātŭlārī; grăvārī; hăriŏlārī; hēluārī; hortārī[1]; hospĭtārī; jăcŭlārī;
imāgĭnārī; ĭmĭtārī (*pass. part.* Cic. poet., Ov., Quint.); infĭtiārī;
injūriārī; insĭdiārī; interprētarī (*pass. part.* Cic., Liv., &c.);
jŏcārī; īrascī; jurgārī (?Hor., jurgare Ter., Cic.); jŭvĕnārī; lābī;
lætārī; lamentārī; largīrī; latrōcĭnārī; lēnōcĭnārī; lĭbĭdĭnārī; lĭ-
cēri; lĭcĭtārī; lignārī; lŏqvī; lūcrārī; luctārī (luctare Enn., Plaut.,
Ter.); lūdĭfĭcārī (ludificare and *pass.* Plaut. often); lūxŭriārī
(usually luxuriare); māchĭnārī (*part. pass.* Sall.); mandūcārī (old);
mātĕriārī; mĕdērī; mĕdĭcārī (medicare more common); mĕdĭtārī
(*pass. part.* Plaut., Cic., Liv., Tac.); mendĭcārī (Plaut.; oftener
mendicare); mentīrī (*pass. part.* Ov., Quint., Plin.; ementītus *pass.*
Cic.); mercārī (*pass. part.* Prop., Plin.); mĕrērī, *to deserve* (frequent; rarely *to earn;* mĕrēre just the reverse: of the compounds
emerere, commerere are more frequent than the deponent forms);
mētārī (*part. pass.* Hor., Liv.); mētīrī (*part. pass.* Cat., Cic.);
mĭnĭtārī (minitare Plaut. rarely); mĭnārī (interminatus *pass.* Hor.);
mīrārī; mĭsĕrārī; mĭsĕrērī (miserēre Lucr.; cf. ch. xxx.); mŏdĕrārī
(*pass. part.* Cic., Sall.); mŏdŭlārī (*pass. part.* Ov., Suet., &c.);
mœchārī; mōlīrī; mŏrī; mŏrārī (morare Plaut. rarely); mōrĭgĕrārī;
mūnĕrārī (also munerare); murmŭrārī (rare; commurmurari Cic.);
mūtuārī (*pass. part.* Plin.); nancīscī (*fut.*, nanciam Gracchus);
nascī; naucŭlārī (Mart. once); nĕgōtiārī; nictari (Plin., nictare
Plaut.); nīdŭlārī (Plin. once); nītī (enisum est *impers.* Sall.);
nixārī (Lucr.); nŭgārī; nundĭnārī; nŭtrĭcārī (also nutricare);
nūtrīrī (Verg. once; usually nutrire); oblīvīscī (*pass. part.* Verg.,
Prop.); obsĭdiārī; ŏdōrārī; ōmĭnārī (abominatus *pass.* Hor., Liv.);
ŏpĕrārī; ŏpīnārī (opinare Enn., Pacuv.; *pass. part.* Cic.); ŏpĭtŭ-
lārī; oppĕrīrī; opsōnārī (Plaut., opsonare usually); ordīrī (exorsus
pass. Plaut., Cic., Verg.); ŏrīrī; oscĭtārī (also oscitare); oscŭlārī;
ōtiārī; pābŭlārī; pǎcīscī (*pass. part.* Cic., Liv.); pālārī; palpārī
(Plaut., Hor., also palpare); pandĭcŭlārī; părāsītārī; partīrī (par-

---

[1] In form frequentative: the simple verb in the 3rd pers. (hŏrĭtur)
is quoted from Ennius.

tire Plaut., Lucr., Sall., *pass. part.* Cic., Liv., Verg., &c.;- dispertire, impertire usually); pasci, of animals (sometimes pascĕre; frequently pascens; depasci *pass.* Cic. once); pāti; pătrōcĭnāri; pĕcŭlāri; percontāri; pĕrĕgrīnāri; pĕrīclītāri (*pass. part.* Cic., once); phĭlōsophāri (philosophatum *pass. impers.* Plaut. once); pignĕrāri, *take in pledge;* pĭgrāri (pigraris 2 *fut. perf.* Lucr.); piscāri; -plccti (amplectĕre, complectĕre rare; *pass. part.* rare); pollĭcēri (*pass. part.* Ov.); pollĭcĭtārī; pŏpŭlāri (populare Verg., *pass.* Liv., *pass. part.* often); pŏtīri (potīre, *to put in possession,* Plaut. once); prædāri; præmiāri (rare); præsāgīri (once Plaut.; præsagire is usual); præstōlāri; prævārĭcāri; prĕcāri; prōcāri (rare); prœliāri; prōfĭcisci; prooemiāri; pūnīri (Cic.; usually punire); quadrŭplāri; quĕri; rādīcāri; rătiōcĭnāri; rĕcordāri; rĕfrāgāri; rĕlĭquāri; rēri; rīmāri; ringi; rixāri; ructāri (Varr., Hor.; usually ructare); rustĭcāri; săcrĭfĭcāri (Varr.; sacrificare usually); sciscĭtāri; scĭtāri; scortāri; scrūtāri (*part. pass.* Sen.; perscrutare Plaut.); scurrāri; sectāri (rarely *pass.*; insectare Plaut.); sĕqui (*pass.* Com. once; obsĕcūtum *pass. impers.* Plaut.); sermōcĭnāri; sōlāri; sortīri (sortire Enn., Plaut., *pass. part.* Cic., Prop.); spătiāri; spĕcŭlāri; stăbŭlāri (stabulare Verg., Stat.); stĭpŭlāri; stŏmāchāri; svāviāri (or saviari); subsĭdiāri; suffrāgāri (suffragare old); suppĕtiari; suspĭcāri (*pass.* once Plaut.); testĭfĭcāri (*part. pass.* Cic., Ov.); testāri (testatus, and compounds often passive, Cic., Ov., Quint.); trĭcāri (once extrīcari Plaut.; usually extricare, intricare); tristāri; trūtīnāri; tuburcĭnāri; tuĕri (*pass.* Varr.; tutus *pass.* almost always; tuĕre rare and old); tūtāri (*pass.*; Plaut., Cic. rarely); tŭmultuāri (*pass. impers.* Ter., Cæs., Liv.; tumultuare Plaut.); ulcisci (*pass.* Sall. once; *pass. part.* Liv.); ūrīnāri; ūti (the active utĕre in Cat. &c.); vădāri (*part. pass.* Plaut. once); văgāri (vagare old); vātĭcīnāri; vēlĭfĭcāri (velificare Prop., Plin. once; *part. pass.* Juv.); vēlītāri (Plaut.); vēnāri; vĕnĕrāri (venerare Plaut.; *part. pass.* Verg., Hor.); vĕrēcundari; vĕrēri; vergi (Lucr., Lucan); vermĭcŭlāri; vermīnāri (also verminarè); versāri; vesci; vilĭcāri old (vilicare Cic. once); vĭtŭlāri.

The following are used as past participles in the same sense as the active inflexions. 733

ădultus; cēnātus; coălĭtus (Tac.); concrētus; conspīrātus (Cæs., Suet.); conflagrātus (Corn.); deflagratus (Cic.); eventum (subst.); fluxus; invĕtĕrātus; jūrātus (conjuratus); nupta; occāsus (post, ante, ad, occasum solem Plaut.); ōsus (Sen., exōsus, perōsus often generally); plăcĭtus; pōtus (also *pass.*); præterĭtus (of time and the like); pransus (Cic., Liv., Hor.); qviētus (reqvietus Liv., Sen., &c.); svētus (and comp.); tăcĭtus.

CHAPTER XXX.

LIST OF VERBS, WITH THEIR PERFECTS, SUPINES,
&c.

The following list contains all verbs of the Latin language, with certain exceptions, which exceptions are—

1. All verbs with a- or i- stems, which have their pres. infinitive in -āre, -īre (-āri, -īri), perf. in -āvi, -īvi (-ātus, -ītus, sum), and supine in -ātum, -ītum. (Lists of both, tolerably complete as regards i- stems, will be found in Book III.)

2. All verbs with e- stems, which have perfect in -ui, but no supine. (They are generally intransitive, and are named in Ch. XXII.)

3. Most inchoatives, which either have no perfect or supine, or one of the same form as the simple verb. (They are all named either in Ch. XX. or Book III.)

4. Verbs compounded with prepositions. But such are named as differ from the form of the simple verb in perfect or supine, or which agree with it in having a reduplication in the perfect.

5. A few verbs, with e- or i- stems, which have no perfect or supine, are given in an appended list at the end of the chapter.

The supine is not much used, but is here mentioned wherever it or a perfect participle is known, as this is similarly formed.

N.B. Where the English translation as given here, whether with or without a preposition, allows of the immediate addition of an object, the verb is transitive (though it may perhaps also be intransitive), e.g. arcesso, *send for;* lædo, *hurt,* are transitive. Where it requires the addition of an English preposition, the verb is intransitive, e.g. nŏceo, *be hurtful.*

Present.	Perfect.	Supine.	Pres. Infinitive.	Stem.

accerso. See arcesso.

ăcuo, *sharpen* ăcui ăcūtum ăcuĕre ăcū-

ăgo, *do, drive* ēgi actum ăgĕre ăg-

ădĭgo, ădēgi, ădactum, adĭgĕre.   So the other compounds,

Except: cōgo (cŏēgi, cŏactum, cōgĕre), dēgo, which has no perf. or supine, prōdĭgo which has perf. only, and circumăgo, perăgo, which retain a in pres., &c. sătăgo is really two words: perf. egi satis.

aio, *say* aj-

The following forms only are preserved, pres. ajo, ăis, ăit (āis, āit in Plaut.), ajunt.

Imp. ajēbam, &c. complete.   In Plaut. and Ter. āibam.   Pres. subj. ajas, ajat.   The part. aiens is used only as adj.

algeo, *be cold* alsi algēre alg-ĕ-

The participle in compar. neut. alsius occurs in Cicero[1].

ălo, *nourish, raise* ălui altum ălĕre ăl-

ălĭtum is found in post-Augustan writers.

ămĭcio, *clothe* ămictum ămĭcīre ămĭc-ī-

amĭcui and amixi are both said to have been used for perf. Fronto has inf. amicisse.

ango, *throttle, vex* angĕre ang-

ăpiscor, *fasten to one-* aptum ăpisci ăp-ī-

self, get

More usual in compound ădĭpiscor, ădeptus sum, ădĭpisci.   See also cœpio.

arceo, *inclose, keep off* arcui adj. artus arcēre arc-ĕ-

artus, only used as adj. *confined, narrow:*

exerceo, *exercise,* exercui, exercĭtum, exercēre.   So also coerceo.

arcesso, *fetch, send* arcessīvi arcessītum arcessĕre {arcess-

for   {arcess-ī-

Another form is accerso.   In pass. inf. arcessīri sometimes occurs.

ardeo, *be on fire* arsi ardēre ard-ĕ-

Fut. part. arsūrus.

arguo, *charge (with* argui argūtum arguĕre argŭ-

crime &c.)

[1] A positive alsis (not alsus) would suit also alsia (Lucr. v. 1015).

argūtus, rare, except as adj. *sharp.* Fut. part. argulturus (once
   in Sall.).

Present.	Perfect.	Supine.	Pres. Infinitive.	Stem.
audeo, *dare*		ausum	audēre	aud-ĕ-

ausus sum is used for perf., *I have dared.* ausus also (rarely)
   passive part. (Verg. Tac.).

ăve, imperat. *hail* (in Quintilian's time hăvĕ) also ăvēto, plur. ăvēte:
   inf. ăvēre.   Martial has ăvē.

ăveo, *long*	no perf. or sup.		ăvēre	ăv-ĕ-
augeo, *increase*(trans.)	auxi	auctum	augēre	aug-ĕ-
endow				
bātuo, *beat, fence*	bātui		bātuĕre	bātŭ-
(with a weapon)				
bĭbo, *drink*	bĭbi		bĭbĕre	bĭb-
cădo, *fall*	cĕcĭdi	cāsum	cădĕre	căd-

occĭdo, occĭdi, occāsum, occĭdĕre.   The other compounds,
   except rēcĭdo and (rarely) incĭdo, have no supine.

cædo, *fell, cut, slay*	cĕcĭdi	cæsum	cædĕre	cæd-

occĭdo, occĭdi, occīsum, occĭdĕre.   So all the compounds.

căleo, *be hot*	călui	(călĭtūrus)	călēre	căl-ĕ-
calvor, *play tricks* (also as passive)			calvi	calv-

Only in early writers for later calumnior.

-cando, *light*, only in compounds.   cand·-
   e. g. accendo, accendi, accensum, accendĕre.

căno, *sing, play*	cĕcĭni	(cantus	cănĕre	căn-
(on a harp &c.).		subst.)		

concino, concĭnŭi, concentum, concĭnĕre.   So occĭno (also once
   occecini), incino and præcĭno.   No perf. found of other compounds.

căpesso, *undertake*	căpessīvi	căpessītum	căpessĕre	căpess- capess-ĭ-
căpio, *take*	cēpi	captum	căpĕre	căp-ĭ-

concĭpio, concēpi, conceptum, concĭpĕre.   So the other compounds, except antecapio, antecepi, anteceptum, antecăpĕre.

căreo, *be in want*	cărui	(cărĭtūrus)	cărēre	căr-ĕ-
căro, *card* (wool), very rare.			cărĕre	căr-
carpo, *nibble, pluck*	carpsi	carptum	carpĕre	carp-

decerpo, decerpsi, decerptum, decerpĕre.   So the other compounds.

Present.	Perfect.	Supine.	Pres. Infinitive.	Stem.
cǎveo, *be ware, be*	cǎvi	cautum	cǎvēre	cǎv-ĕ-

ware of

cavitum is written twice in a seventh century (U.C.) inscription.

| cēdo, *give way, yield* | cessi | cessum | cēdĕre | cēd- |

up

cĕdo, *give*, said to be old imperative 2nd per. sing. The plural
cette (for cĕdĭte) only in early scenic poets.

-cello, *strike?* only in compounds: celsus adj. *high*   cell-
percello (*strike down*), percŭlī, perculsus, percellĕre.
excello (*distinguish myself*) has (in Gellius) a perf. excelluī. Of
antecello and præcello no perf. or sup. are found. excelsus,
præcelsus, *lofty*, are used as adj.

| censeo, *count, recom-* | censui | censum | censēre | cens-ĕ- |

mend

| cerno, *sift, distin-* | crēvi | {crētum
{certus, adj. *sure* | cernĕre | {cĕr-
{crē- |

guish, decide, see

The meaning *see* is confined to pres., imp., and fut. tenses.
decerno, decrēvi, decrētum, decernĕre. So the other compounds.

| cieo}
-cio} *stir up* | cīvi | cĭtum | {ciēre
{-cīre | {ci-ĕ-
{ci- |

The -ı stem is rare in the simple verb: the -e stem rare in the
compounds. accio makes (once) accītus; excio, excītus and
excītus; concio, concĭtus, and (once) concĭtus; percio, percĭtus.

cingo, *gird*	cinxi	cinctum	cingĕre	cing-
clango (rare) *clang*			clangĕre	clang-
claudo, *shut*	clausi	clausum	claudĕre	claud-

conclūdo, conclūsi, conclūsum, conclūdere. So the other compounds.

| clĕpo (old), *steal* | clepsi | cleptum | clĕpĕre | clĕp- |
| clueo, *be spoken of* | | -clūtum | cluĕre | clu-e- |

In Seneca (once) cluo. -clutus only in compound inclutus.

| cŏlo, *till, pay atten-* | cŏlui | cultum | cŏlĕre | cŏl- |

tion to

So the compounds excŏlo, excŏlui, excultum, excŏlĕre, but
accŏlo, incŏlo have no supine.
occŭlo, *hide*, occŭlui, occultum, occŭlere, is probably from a different stem.

| cœpio, *begin* | cœpi | cœptum | cœpĕre | cœp-ĭ- |

Pres. ind. and subj. only in Plaut. Fut. cœpiam in Cato.
Imperf. subj. cœpĕrem once in Ter. Otherwise only perfect
stem in use with present meaning as well as perfect. But
cœptus and œpturus are also used. (Cœptus sum often with
a pass. infin.; but also cœpi.) The verb is apparently from
co-ăpio (apiscor).

Present.	Perfect.	Supine.	Pres. Infinitive.	Stem.
compesco. See pasco.				
conquinisco, *stoop down*	conquexi, old and rare		conquiniscĕre	cf. §§ 631, 635.
consŭlo, *consult*	consŭlŭi	consultum	consŭlĕre	consŭl-
cŏqvo, *cook*	coxi	coctum	cŏqvĕre	cŏqv-
crēdo. See do.				
crĕpo, *rattle*	crĕpui	crĕpĭtum	crĕpāre	crĕp-ă-
cresco, *grow*	crēvi	crētum	crescĕre	crē-

Though cresco is intransitive, it has a part. crētus, *sprung from.*

cŭbo, *lie, lie ill*	cŭbŭi	cŭbĭtum	cŭbāre	cŭb-ă-

cubāvi is occasionally found.

cūdo, *hammer*	cūdi	cūsum	cūdĕre	cūd-

-cumbo, *lie,* only in compounds, as strengthened form of cŭbo.
accumbo, accŭbui, accŭbĭtum, accumbĕre.

cŭpio, *desire*	cŭpīvi	cŭpītum	cŭpĕre	cŭp-ī-

cupīret once in Lucr.

curro, *run*	cŭcurri	cursum	currĕre	curr-

The compounds frequently retain the reduplication, e.g. accŭ-
curri, dēcŭcurri, excŭcurri; more usually (in Cicero and Livy)
drop it, e.g. accurri.

dēleo. See līno.

depso, *knead*	depsui	depstum	depsĕre	deps-
dīco, *say*	dixi	dictum	dīcĕre	dīc-
disco, *learn*	dĭdĭci		discĕre	dĭc-

Compounds retain reduplication, e.g. ēdisco, *learn by heart,*
ēdĭdĭci.

dispesco. See pasco.

dīvĭdo, *divide*	dīvīsi	dīvīsum	dīvĭdĕre	di-vĭd-
do, *give* (see	dĕdi	dătum	dăre	dă-

The half-compounds circumdo, *surround,* pessumdo, *ruin,* să-
tisdo, *satisfy,* venumdo, *expose to sale,* follow do precisely.

crēdo, *entrust, believe,* vendo, *sell,* reddo, *give back,* and the compounds with monosyllabic prepositions have consonant stems:
e.g. crēdo, crēdĭdi, crēdĭtum, crēdĕre. So also accrēdo, accrēdĭdi.
The compound with præ exists only in prædĭtus, *endued.*

The reduplication is retained in the compounds, except usually in abscondo.

For the passives of **vendo, perdo** (except past part. and gerundive) **veneo** and (usually) **pereo** are used.

Present.	Perfect.	Supine.	Pres. Infinitive.	Stem.
dŏceo, *teach*	dŏcŭi	doctum	dŏcēre	dŏc-ĕ-
dŏleo, *be in pain*	dŏlui	(dŏlĭtūrus)	dŏlēre	dŏl-ĕ-
dŏmo, *tame*	dŏmui	dŏmĭtum	dŏmāre	dŏm-ă-
dūco, *draw, lead, account*	duxi	ductum	dūcēre	dūc-
ĕdo, *eat*	ēdi	ēsum	ĕdĕre	ĕd-

Supine sometimes essum.   Comĕdo has also (rarely) comestum.

ĕmo, *buy* (orig. *take*) **ēmi**   emptum   ĕmĕre   ĕm-

ădĭmo, ădēmi, ademptum.   So other compounds, except
(1) cŏĕmo (cŏĕmi, coemptum), perĕmo, interĕmo, which retain e.
(2) the earlier compounds cōmo, dēmo, prōmo, sūmo, which make compsi, comptum, &c.

ĕo, *go* (see Ch. XXVIII.) **īvi**   ĭtum   īre   ĭ-

Compounds always omit **v** (e.g. ădii), in 1st pers. perf., and usually in other persons of perfect and thence derived tenses.

vēneo, *be for sale,* is a compound of eo.   It has no supine.

exuo, *strip off* **exui**   exūtum   exuĕre   exu-
(clothes, &c.)

făcesso, *cause, make* **făcessīvi**   făcessītum   făcessĕre   {facess-
off   {facess-ĭ-
făcio, *make, do*   fēci   factum   făcĕre   făc-ĭ-

For the passive, in tenses formed from present stem, **fio** is used.

prŏfĭcio, *make progress,* prŏfēci, prŏfectum, prŏfĭcĕre.   So the other compounds with prepositions.   But calefacio being only half compound (§ 300) retains a.

prŏfĭciscor, *set out* (*on a journey*), *travel,* prŏfectum, prŏfĭcisci.

fallo, *deceive, elude* fĕfelli   falsum   fallĕre   fall-
refello, *refute,* refelli, refellĕre.

farcio, *stuff*   farsi   fartum   farcīre   farc-ĭ-
rĕfercio, rĕfersi, rĕfertum, rĕfercīre.   So also differtus.

făteor, *acknowledge*   fassum   fătēri   făt-ĕ-
confĭteor, confessum, confĭtēri.   So prŏfĭteor.   diffĭteor has no part. perf.

Present.	Perfect.	Supine.	Pres. Infinitive.	Stem.
fătisco	} *gape, droop*	(fessus adj.	{fătiscere	făt-ĭ-?
fătiscor (old)		*weary*)	{fătisci	

dēfĕtiscor, defessum, defetisci.

făveo, *be favourable*	făvi	fautum	făvēre	făv-ĕ-
-fendo, *strike*, only in compounds.				fend-

defendo, *ward off, guard*, defendi, defensum, defendĕre. So also
offendo, *strike against.*

fĕrio, *strike* (see ico)			fĕrīre	fĕr-ĭ-

(percussi, percussum are often used as perfect and supine.)

fĕro (Ch. XXVIII.),	(tŭli)	(lātum)	ferre	fĕr-
bring				

Perfect and supine are borrowed from tollo.

affĕro,	attŭli,	allātum,	afferre;
aufero,	abstŭli,	ablātum,	auferre;
diffĕro,	distŭli,	dīlātum,	differre;
offĕro,	obtŭli,	oblātum,	offerre;
rĕfĕro,	rēttuli,	rĕlātum (or	rĕferre;
		rarely rellatum)	

rĕfert, *it is of importance* (probably for rəi fert) is used as
impersonal.

suffĕro,	(sustĭnui)		sufferre.

sustŭli as perf. of suffero is rare.

ferveo, *boil, glow*	{fervi		fervēre	ferv-ĕ-
	{ferbui			

A consonantal stem (e.g. fervit, fervĕre) frequent in præ-Aug.
and Aug. poets.

fīdo, *trust*		fīsum	fīdĕre	fīd-

fisus sum is used for perf., *I have trusted.*

fīgo, *fix*	fixi	fixum	fīgĕre	fīg-

fictus as past participle in Varro, *R. R.* and Lucr.

fio, *become* (see Ch. XXVIII.),			fĭĕri	fĭ-

The compound infit, *he begins*, only in this one form (poetical).

findo, *cleave*	fĭdi	fissum	findĕre	fĭd-
fingo, *form, invent*	finxi	fictum	fingĕre	fĭg-
fleo, *weep*	flēvi	flētum	flēre	flĕ-
flecto, *bend*	flexi	flexum	flectĕre	flect-
-flīgo, *strike*, only in compounds.				

afflīgo, *strike against, knock down*, afflixi, afflictum, afflīgĕre.

So the other compounds, except **profligo,** *put to rout,* **prōflīgāvī,**
prōflīgātum, prōflīgāre.

Present.	Perfect.	Supine.	Pres. Infinitive.	Stem.
flŭo, *flow*	**fluxi**		**flŭĕre**	**flŭgv-**

(**fluxus,** adj. *loose,* **fluctus,** subst. *a wave*)

fŏdio, *dig*	**fŏdi**	**fossum**	**fŏdĕre**	**fŏd-ĭ-**

Inf. **fodīri, effodiri** are found in the older language.

fātur, *he speaks*		**fātum**	**fāri**	**fa-**

The following only found: pres. ind. **fātur;** fut. **fābor, fabitur;**
perf. **fatus est;** pluperf. **fatus eram, erat;** imper. **fāre,** inf.
fari; part. **fantem,** &c. (no nominative, except in phrase
fans atque infans, Plaut.), **fatus, fandus,** and **fatu.**

In compounds we have also -**famur,** -**famini;** -**fābar,** -**fārer,** &c.,
and in comp. imperat. &c., **præfato, præfamino.**

fŏveo, *keep warm,*	**fŏvi**	**fŏtum**	**fŏvēre**	**fŏv-ĕ-**
cherish				
frango, *break in pieces*	**frēgi**	**fractum**	**frangĕre**	**frăg-**

Compounds as **confringo, confrēgi, confractum, confringĕre.**

frĕmo, *roar, snort*	**frĕmui**	**frĕmĭtum**	**frĕmĕre**	**frĕm-**
frendo, *gnash* (with the teeth)		{**fressum** / **frēsum**	**frendĕre**	**frend-**
frĭco, *rub*	**frĭcŭi**	{**frictum** / **frĭcātum**	**frĭcāre**	**frĭc-ā-**
frīgeo, *be cold*	**frixi**		**frīgēre**	**frīg-ĕ-**
frīgo, *roast,* (corn, &c.)		**frictum**	**frīgĕre**	**frīg-**
fruor, *enjoy*		**fructum**	**frui**	**frugv-**

fruitum once (Ulpian), fut. part. **fruĭtūrus** once (Cic.). An
old form **fruniscor, frunitum** is quoted from early writers.

fŭgio, *flee, fly from*	**fūgi**	(**fŭgĭtūrus**)	**fŭgĕre**	**fŭg-ĭ-**
fulcio, *prop*	**fulsi**	**fultum**	**fulcīre**	**fulc-ĭ-**
fulgeo, *flash*	**fulsi**		**fulgēre**	**fulg-ĕ-**

A consonantal stem e.g. **fulgit, fulgĕre** is found in præ-Aug.
poets; twice in Vergil.

fundo, *pour, rout*	**fūdi**	**fūsum**	**fundĕre**	**fŭd-**
(an enemy)				
fungor, *get quit, dis-*		**functum**	**fungi**	**fung-**
charge (an office, &c.)				

fuo, *grow?* see **sum,** Ch. XXVII.

fŭris, *thou ragest*			**fŭrĕre**	**fŭr-**

Only **furis, furit, furunt, furebas, furebat, furĕre, furens** are
found.

Present.	Perfect.	Supine.	Pres. Infinitive.	Stem.
gaudeo, *be glad*		gāvīsum	gaudēre	gavĭd-ĕ-
gavisus sum, *I rejoiced*				
gĕmo, *sigh, groan*	gemui	gĕmĭtum	gĕmĕre	gĕm-
gĕro, *carry, perform*	gessi	gestum	gĕrĕre	gĕs-
gigno, *beget, produce*	gĕnui	gĕnĭtum	gignĕre	gĕn-

In old language (Lucr. Varr.), sometimes gĕno is found.

glisco, *swell, kindle*			gliscĕre	glī-
glūbo, *peel*		gluptum	glūbĕre	glūb-
grădior, *step*		gressum	grădi	grăd-ĭ-

Compounds, as aggrĕdior, *attack*, aggressum, aggrĕdĭ. Inf. aggredīri, progredīri, pres. aggredīmur are found in Plaut.

-gruo only in compounds.   gru-
congruo, *agree*, congrui, congruĕre. So also ingruo, *impend*.

| hăbeo, *have* | hăbui | hăbĭtum | hăbēre | hab-ĕ |

So the compounds dēbeo, *owe*, debui, debitum, dēbĕre; præbeo, *afford*, præbui, præbitum, præbēre (in Plautus dehibeo, præhibeo): prōbeo (Lucr.) for prohibeo.

hæreo, *stick* intr.	hæsi	hæsum	hærēre	hæs-ĕ- (or hær-ĕ?)
haurio, *drain, draw*	hausi	haustum	haurīre	haus-ī-
(water)				

In Varr. once haurierint. Fut. part. haustūrus (C. *Fam.* 6. 6. 9) and hausūrus, Verg. *A.* IV. 383; Stat. *Ach.* I. 667; Sil. VII. 584, XVI. 11; and perhaps Sen. *Ep.* 51. 6, exhausurus.

hisco, *gape, open the mouth, to speak*			hiscĕre	hi-
jăceo, *lie*	jăcui	(jăcĭturus)	jăcēre	jăc-ĕ-
jăcio, *cast*	jēci	jactum	jăcĕre	jăc-ĭ-

abĭcio, abjēci, abjectum, abĭcĕre. So the other compounds (see § 144). Dissĭcio for dis-jacio.
porrĭcio, *offer (sacrifices)*, &c, porrectum, porrĭcere (without perf.).

| īco (or īcio?), *strike* | īci | ictum | īcĕre | īc- |

Of the present (rare), only icit, icitur, icimur occurs: (fĕrio is generally used instead). The perfect is often in MSS. written iecit.

imbuo, *steep, imbue*	imbui	imbūtum	imbuĕre	imbŭ-
incesso, *attack*	incessīvi		incessĕre	{incess- {incess-ī-
indulgeo, *yield*, intr.	indulsi		indulgēre	indulg-ĕ-

(Indult-um &c. appears not to be used before the 3rd century or later.)

Present.	Perfect.	Supine.	Pres. Infinitive.	Stem.
induo, *put on* (clothes), &c.	induī	indūtum	induĕre	indŭ-
inquam, *quoth*	inquiī			{ inqvă- or inqvī-

The following forms only occur. Pres. ind. inquam, inquĭs, inquit, inquĭmus, inquiunt. Fut. inquies, inquiet. Imperf. inquiebat. Perf. inquiī, inquisti, inquit. Imperat. 2nd sing. inque, inquĭto, plur. inquĭte.

īrascor, *grow angry*		īrātum	īrasci	īrā-

īrātus sum, *I am angry:* succensui, *I was angry.*

jŭbeo, *bid*	jussī	jussum	jŭbēre	jŭb-ĕ-
jungo, *yoke, join*	junxī	junctum	jungĕre	jung-
jŭvo, *help, delight*	jūvī	jūtum	jŭvāre	jŭv-ă-

fut. part. jŭvātūrus. Adjŭvo has adjūtūrus.

lābor, *slip, glide*		lapsum	lābi	lāb-
lăcesso, *provoke*	lăcessīvī	lăcessītum	lăcessĕre	{lăcess- lacessī-
-lăcio, *entice.* Only in compounds.				lacī-

allĭcio, allexi, allectum, allĭcĕre. So illĭcio, pellĭcio.

ēlĭcio, ēlĭcui, ēlĭcĭtum, ēlĭcĕre. Prōlĭcio has no perfect or supine.

lædo, *strike* (rare),	læsī	læsum	lædĕre	læd- burt

collīdo, *dash together,* collīsī, collīsum, collīdĕre.

lambo, *lick*	lambī (once)		lambĕre	lamb-
langveo, *be faint*	langvī		langvēre	langv-ĕ-
lăvo, *wash*	lāvī	{lăvātum lautum lōtum	lăvāre	lăv-ă-

A consonantal stem (e.g. lăvit, lăvĕre, &c.) is frequent in præ-Augustan and Augustan poets.

For compounds see luo.

lĕgo, *pick up, choose,* *read*	lēgī	lectum	lĕgĕre	lĕg-

collĭgo, *collect,* collēgī, collectum, collĭgĕre. So compounds generally:

Except that (1) allĕgo, *choose besides,* perlĕgo, *read through,* prælĕgo, *read to others,* rĕlĕgo, *read again,* sublĕgo, *pick up, substitute,* retain e.

(2) dīlego (or dīlĭgo), *love*, intellĕgo, *understand*, neglĕgo, *neg-*
lect, retain e and have perf. in -xi, e.g. neglexi. (Rarely
intellēgi, neglēgi.)

Present.	Perfect.	Supine.	Pres. Infinitive.	Stem.
lĭbet, *it pleases*	{lĭbuit / lĭbĭtum est			

Only used in 3rd pers. Rarely in plural. Also participle lĭbens,
(The stem vowel was in early times u; e.g. lŭbet.)

lĭceo, *be on sale*	lĭcui	lĭcĭtum	lĭcēre	lĭc-ĕ-
lĭceor, *bid for*	lĭcĭtus sum		lĭcēri	lĭc-ĕ-
lĭcet, *it is permitted*	{lĭcuit / lĭcĭtum est		lĭcēre	lĭc-ĕ-

Only used in 3rd pers. Rarely in plural. Licēto, lĭcens, lĭcĭtus,
also found.

lingo, *lick*		linctum	lingĕre	ling-
līno, *besmear*	lēvi	lĭtum	lĭnĕre	lĭ-

līvi is also found.

In post-Augustan writers, we have līnio, līnīvi, līnītum, līnīre.

dēleo, *blot out*, delēvi, delētum, delēre, probably belong to this
stem.

linqvo, *leave*	līqvi	linqvĕre	līqv-

The compound, rĕlinqvo, rĕlīqvi, rĕlictum, rĕlinqvĕre, is more
usual.

līqveo, *be clear, fluid*	lĭcŭi	līqvēre	līqv-ĕ-
līqvor, *melt*, intr.		līqvi	līqv-
lŏqvor, *speak*		lŏcūtum	lŏqvi	lŏqv-
lŭceo, *be light, beam*	luxi		lūcēre	lūc-ĕ-
lūdo, *sport*	lūsi	lūsum	lūdĕre	lūd-
lūgeo, *mourn*, trans.	luxi	(luctus subs.)	lūgēre	lūg-ĕ-
luo, *pay, expiate*	lui		luĕre	lŭ-

Compounds retain the original meaning, *wash* (luo=lăvo), and
have past part. e.g. dīluo, dīlŭi, dīlūtum, dīluĕre.

-mănĭscor or -mĕniscor, only in compounds.   {măn- / or mĕn-

Only perfect stem (with present meaning) in use. Memĭni, *I*
remember. Imperative memento, mementote.

commĭniscor, *devise*, commentum, commĭnisci. So also rĕmĭnis-
cor, *call to mind*.

mando, *chew*	mandi (once)	mansum	mandĕre	mand-
măneo, *remain, await*	mansi	mansum	mănēre	măn-ĕ-

ēmĭneo, *project*, ēmĭnui, ēmĭnēre (no supine).
immĭneo, *impend*, promĭneo, no perf. or supine.
permăneo is like măneo.

Present.	Perfect.	Supine.	Pres. Infinitive.	Stem.
mĕdeor, *be a remedy*			mĕdērĭ	mĕd-ĕ-
mĕreo, *earn*	mĕruĭ	mĕrĭtum	mĕrēre	mĕr-ē-
mergo, *sink*, trans.	mersĭ	mersum	mergĕre	merg-

ēmergo, *emerge*, is intrans., but has part. perf. emersus, *having emerged.*

mētĭor, *measure*		mensum	mētīrĭ	mēt-ī-
mĕto, *mow*		messuĭ (rare)messum	mĕtĕre	mĕt-

The perfect is found only in quotations from Cato and Cassius Hemina.

mĕtuo, *fear*	mĕtuĭ		mĕtuĕre	mĕtŭ-

mĕtūtus, once in Lucret.

mĭco, *quiver, flash*,	mĭcuĭ		mĭcāre	mĭc-ā-

ēmĭco, ēmĭcŭĭ, fut. part. emĭcāturus.
dīmĭco, dīmĭcāvĭ (dīmĭcuĭ twice in Ovid), dīmĭcātum.

mingo	minxĭ	mictum	mingĕre	mĭg-

Another form of the present is mejo.

mĭnuo, *lessen*	mĭnuĭ	mĭnūtum	mĭnuĕre	mĭnŭ-
misceo, *mix*	miscuĭ	mixtum	miscēre	misc-ĕ-

The supine is sometimes written mistum.

mĭsĕreor, *feel pity*		mĭsĕrĭtum	mĭsĕrērĭ	miser-ĕ-

misertum is rarely found.

mĭsĕreo is very rare: miseret and (in early writers) miserētur, miserescit are used impersonally.

mitto, *let go, send*	mīsĭ	missum	mittĕre	mitt-
mŏlo, *grind*	mŏluĭ	mŏlĭtum	mŏlĕre	mŏl-
mŏneo, *warn*	mŏnuĭ	mŏnĭtum	mŏnēre	mŏn-ĕ-
mordeo, *bite*	mŏmordĭ	morsum	mordēre	mord-ĕ-
mŏrior, *die*	mortŭus sum		mŏrĭ	mŏr-ī-
	fut. part. mŏrĭtūrus			

Inf. morīrĭ, emorīrĭ several times in Plaut. once in Ter. once in Ovid.

mŏveo, *move*, trans.	mōvĭ	mōtum	mŏvēre	mŏv-ĕ-
mulceo, *stroke*	mulsĭ	mulsum	mulcēre	mulc-ĕ-

Permulctus is also found besides the more usual permulsus.

mulgeo, *milk*	mulsĭ		mulgēre	mulg-ĕ-

mulctu abl. in Varro. mulctrum, *milking-pail.*

Present.	Perfect.	Supine.	Pres. Infinitive.	Stem.
-mungo only in compound				mung-

ēmungo *wipe* (nose), ēmunxi, ēmunctum, ēmungĕre.

| nanciscor, *gain* | | {nanctum
{nactum | nanciscī | {nanc-ĭ-
{năc- |

C. Gracchus is said to have used a future nanciam.

nascor, *be born*   nātum   nascī   gna-
    Originally gnascor, whence agnātus, cognātus, prognātus. But
    ēnascor, ēnātŭs.

nĕco, *kill*   nĕcāvi   nĕcātum   nĕcāre   nĕc-ā̆-
    necui once in Phædrus and Ennius: ēnĕco, *stifle completely*,
    ēnĕcŭi and ēnĕcāvi (both rare), ēnectum, ēnĕcāre.

necto, *link together*   nexi   nexum   nectĕre   nect-
    nexui is probably from nexo, nexĕre which is quoted from early
    writers.

neo, *spin*   nēvi   nētum (Ulp.) nēre   nē-
neqveo. See qveo.

| ningit
ningvit } *it snows* | ninxit | | ningĕre | {ning-
{ningv- |

nītor, *lean, strive*   {nixum
{nīsum   nīti   gnict-
    fut. part. nīsūrus: so also compounds.

    Originally gnītor, *kneel*, from gĕnu, *knee*. Nixus generally in
    sense of *leaning*, nisus, *striving*. Conitor, adnitor, enitor
    have both forms frequently (in sense of *bearing children* always
    enixa). Innisus, obnisus, subnisus are infrequent: and in
    poetry all the compounds of nisus are rare.

-nīveo only in compound.   nĭgv-

    conīveo, *shut eyes,* {conīvi (both (no supine) cōnīvēre
       wink,   {conixi} rare)
nŏceo, *be hurtful*   nŏcui   (nŏcĭturus) nocēre   nŏc-ĕ-
nosco, *get to know*   nōvi,   nōtum   noscĕre   gnō-

    The perf. means *got to know*, and so *know*.

    nōtus only as adj. *known*: fut. part. is not used.

    agnosco, cognosco, have supines agnĭtum (fut. part. agnōturus
       once, Sall.), cognĭtum:

ignosco, ignōtum, fut. part. ignoturus (quoted from Cato and Cic.;
    ignosciturus from Piso): dignosco, internosco, have no supine.

Present.	Perfect.	Supine.	Pres. Infinitive.	Stem.
nūbo, *put on a veil* (as a bride), *marry*	nupsi	nuptum	nūbĕre	nūb-

Part. nupta, *married.*

-nuo, *nod*, only in compounds: but nūtus is used as subst.   nū-
annuo, annui, annuĕre.

abnuo has (once in quotation from Sall.) fut. part. abnuĭturus.

oblīviscor (orig. *cover with black*), oblītum   oblīvisci   ob-līv-ĭ-
forget

occŭlo, *conceal.*   See cŏlo.

ŏdi, *I hate*   ŏd-

Only perfect stem with present meaning in use. Fut. part.
ōsūrus. A perf. form odivi, once (used by M. Antony).
Exosus, perosus, are used with an active meaning.

-ŏleo, *grow*, is only used in compounds, and is a different word
from ŏleo, *smell* (intrans.).   ŏl-ĕ-

ăbŏleo, *destroy*, ăbŏlēvi, ăbŏlītum, ăbŏlēre.

ăbŏlesco, *decay*, ăbŏlēvi, no supine, ăbolescĕre. So also ĭnŏlesco.

ădŏlesco, *grow up*, ădŏlēvi, ădolescĕre, adultus, adj. *grown up.*

ădŏleo (*increase?*), *offer (in sacrifice), burn* {adolēvi ădultum
                                                   {ădŏlui   ădŏlēre

obsŏlesco, *wear out*, intr. obsŏlēvi, obsolescĕre, obsŏlētus, adj.
worn out. So also exŏlesco.

ŏleo, *smell* (intrans.) ŏlui   ŏlēre   ŏl-ĕ-

A consonantal stem (olat, olant, subolat, præolat, olēre) is
found rarely in the comic poets.

ŏportet, *it behoves* ŏportuit   ŏportēre   ŏport-ĕ-

Only used in 3rd pers. sing.

oppĕrior. See -pĕrio.

ordior,   *commence,*   orsum   ordīri   ord-ī-
trans.

ŏrior, *rise*   ortum   ŏrīri   ŏr-ī

fut. part. ŏrĭtūrus: gerundive ŏriundus used as adj. *sprung from.*
Pres. ind. ŏrĕris, ŏrĭtur, ŏrĭmur, imperf. subj. orirer, orērer.
The compound adorior has in pres. ind. adŏrīris, adŏrītur.

ŏvo, *triumph*   ŏv-ā-

The only forms found are ovet, ovāret, ovans, ovātus, ovandi.

păciscor. See pango.

Present.	Perfect.	Supine.	Pres. Infinitive.	Stem.
pænĭtet, *it repents*	**pænĭtuit**		**pænĭtēre**	**pænĭt-ĕ-**

Rarely personal. **pænitendum** and (in quotations from Sall. and Acc.) **pænĭturum** (for **pænitĭturum?**) are also found. **Pæni-tens** as adj. *penitent.*

pando, *spread out,* open	**pandĭ**	**passum**	**pandĕre**	{ pand- { pǎd-

Dispando has **dispansum, dispessum. Expando, expansum.** The simple **pansum** once in Vitruvius.

pango, *fasten*	**pēgi**	{ pactum { panctum	**pangĕre**	{ pǎg- { pang-

Panxi is found twice (in Ennius and Columella).

compingo, compēgi, compactum, compingĕre. So **impingo.**

oppango, oppēgi, oppactum, oppangĕre. **Depango, repango** also retain a.

pǎc-isc-or, *bargain,*	**pĕpĭgi,**	**pactum**	**pǎcisci**	**pǎc-**

Compǎciscor or **compĕciscor** has **compactum** or **compectum.**

In the XII Tables **paco** (for **pago**), *bargain,* is found.

parco, *spare*	**pĕperci**		**parcĕre**	**parc-**

Fut. part. **parsurus.** Plautus always, and Terence sometimes, has **parsi.**

comperco, compersi, compercĕre. Imperco, reperco (or **reparco**) found in present only.

pǎreo, *appear, be obedient*	**pārui**	(**pārĭturus**)	**pārēre**	**pǎr-ĕ-**
pǎrio, *get, bring forth*	**pĕpĕri**	**partum**	**pǎrĕre**	**pǎr-ĭ-**

Fut. part. **pǎrĭturus.**

Pǎrens, *a parent,* is an old participle of this verb.

compĕrio }
compĕrior (rare) }, *ascertain,* **compĕri, compertum, compĕrīre.**

rĕpĕrio, *find,* **reppĕri, rĕpertum, rĕpĕrīre.**

pasco, *pasture, feed*	**pāvi**	**pastum**	**pascĕre**	**pǎs-**

The active is rarely used of the animals *feeding* except in pres. participle.

Dēpasco follows **pasco.**

Compesco (lit. *pasture together?*), *confine,* **compescui, compescĕre** (no supine). So **dispesco** (rare), *separate.*

Present.	Perfect.	Supine.	Pres. Infinitive.	Stem.
pătior, *suffer*		passum	păti	păt-ĭ-

perpĕtior, perpessus sum, perpĕti.

păveo, *quake with* *fear*	păvī		păvēre	păv-ĕ-
pecto, *comb*	pexī (once)	pexum	pectĕre	pect-
pēdo	pĕpēdī		pēdĕre	pēd-
pello,*push,drive back*	pĕpŭlī	pulsum	pellĕre	pell-

appello (esp. of a ship, *put in*), appŭlī, appulsum, appellĕre.
So the other compounds. Rĕpello always has reppŭlī or
rēpŭlī.

pendeo, *hang*, intr.	pĕpendī	pensum	pendēre	pend-ĕ-
pendo, *weigh*, *pay*, *value*	pĕpendī	pensum	pendĕre	pend-

originally *hang*, trans. So suspendo, *hang up*.

-pĕrio only in compounds, except perītus, *skilled.*   pĕr-ĭ-
Comp. perīculum, πειράω.
ăpĕrio (ab perio?), *uncover, open,* ăpĕrŭi, ăpertum, ăpĕrīre.
expĕrior, *try,* expertum, expĕrīri.
ŏpĕrio (ob perio?), *cover,* ŏpĕrŭi, ŏpertum, ŏpĕrīre.
opperior, *wait for,* oppertum and opperītum, oppĕrīri.

pĕto, *seek, aim at*	{pĕtīvī {pĕtiī	pĕtītum	pĕtĕre	{pĕt- {pet-ĭ-
pĭget, *it vexes*	{pĭguit {pĭgĭtum est		pĭgēre	pĭg-e-

Only used in 3rd pers. sing. The gerund and gerundive are also
found.

pingo, *paint*	pinxī	pictum	pingĕre	{pĭg- {ping-
pinso,} pīso, } *pound*	{ pinsuī { pinsī	{pinsitum {pistum	{pinsĕre {pīsĕre	pins- pīs-

Pinsībant once in Ennius. Hence pinsitus, often in Columella's
prose, has perhaps ī. Pinsui, pisi occur once each.

plăceo, *be pleasing*	plăcui	plăcītum	plăcēre	plăc-ĕ-
plango, *beat* (esp. the breast in grief)	planxī	planctum	plangĕre	plang-
plaudo, *clap* (the hands, &c.)	plausī	plausum	plaudĕre	plaud-

explōdo (*hiss off*, i.e. *drive away by hissing*), **explōsi, explōsum, explōdĕre.** So the other compounds. **applaudo** does not change the vowel.

Present.	Perfect.	Supine.	Pres. Infinitive.	Stem.
plecto, *strike, punish* (rare except in passive)			**plectĕre**	**plect-**
-plecto, *twine*		**plexum**	**-plectĕre**	**plect-**

Only in perf. part. and compounds, which are always of deponent form, except in one or two instances of imperatives in præ-Ciceronian writers.

amplector, *twine oneself round, embrace,* **amplexum, amplecti.** So **complector.** Of other compounds only participles, **implexus,** *entwined,* **perplexus,** *entangled,* are found.

-pleo, *fill,* only in compounds   **plē-**
Compounds as **compleo, complēvi, complētum, complēre.**

plīco, *fold*   **plīcātum**   **plīcāre**   **plīc-ā-**
(rare except in compounds)

applīco, *apply, put in* (*to share*)   {**applīcāvi, applīcātum, applĭcui, applĭcĭtum,**}   **applīcāre**

So the other compounds: the præ-Augustan writers used almost always -āvi, -ātum.

pluo, *rain*   {**pluit plūvit** (frequent in Livy)}   **pluĕre**   **plŭv-**

pollūceo, *offer in sacrifice*   **polluctum**   **pollucēre**   **pollūc-ĕ-**

pōno, *place*   **pŏsui**   **pŏsĭtum**   **pōnĕre**   **pŏ-sĭ-**
Posīvi frequent in Plautus; also in Cato. **Posit, poseit** (3rd pers. sing.) are also found in præ-Augustan inscriptions. **Postum** (simple and compound) is frequently found in poetry.

posco, *demand*   **pŏposci**   **poscĕre**   **posc-**
Compounds retain reduplication, as **dēpŏposci, expŏposci.**

possĭdeo. See **sĕdeo.**
possum, *be able*   **pŏtui** (see Ch. XXVIII.)   **pŏtesse**   **pŏtes-**

pŏtior, *be master*   **pŏtītum**   **pŏtīri**   **pŏt-ī-**
In pres. ind. almost always **pŏtĭtur, potīmur;** imp, subj. **potērer** or **potīrer.** In Plaut. inf. once **poti:** also act. perf. **potīvi.**

pōto, *drink*   **pōtāvi**   **pōtum**   **pōtāre**   **pōt-ā-**
Pōtātum is rare; fut. part. **pōtāturus** and **pōturus.**
pōtus, *that has drunk.*

prandeo, *dine*   **prandi**   **pransum**   **prandēre**   **prand-ĕ-**
pransus, *having dined.*

Present.	Perfect.	Supine.	Pres. Infinitive.	Stem.
prĕhendo, *lay hold of* prĕhendi		prĕhensum	prĕhendĕre	prehend-

Often contracted into prendo, &c.

| prĕmo, *press* | pressi | pressum | prĕmĕre | prĕm- |

comprĭmo, compressi, compressum, comprĭmĕre. So the other compounds.

prŏfīciscor. See facio.

| psallo, *play on a* stringed instrument | psalli | | psallĕre | psall- |

| pŭdet, *it shames* | {pŭduit
{pŭdĭtum est | | pŭdēre | pŭd-ĕ |

pudĭturum and gerund and gerundive are also found. Pudens as adj. *modest.*

| pungo, *prick* | pŭpŭgi | punctum | pungĕre | {pŭg-
{pung- |

Compounds have for perfect -punxi.

| qværo, *seek, inquire* | qvæsīvi | qvæsītum | qværĕre | {qvæs-
{qvæs-ī- |

conqvīro, conqvīsivi, conqvīsītum, conqvīrĕre. So the other compounds.

In the 1st pers. sing. and plur. there is an old colloquial form, qvæso, qvæsŭmus, *prythee.*

| qvătio, *shake,* trans. | | qvassum | qvătĕre | qvăt-ĭ- |

concŭtio, concussi, concussum, concŭtĕre. So the other compounds.

qveo, *be able* (Ch. XXVIII.)	qvīvi	qvītum	qvīre	qvī-
qvĕror, *complain*		qvestum	qvĕri	qvĕr-
qviesco, *rest*	qviēvi	qviētum	qviescĕre	qvi-ē-
răbo, *rave* (rare)			răbĕre	rab-
rādo, *scrape*	rāsi	rāsum	rādĕre	rād-
răpio, *snatch, hurry away,* trans.	răpui	raptum	răpĕre	răp-ĭ-

arrĭpio, arrĭpui, arreptum, arrĭpĕre. So the other compounds.

| rávio, *be hoarse,* once in Plaut. | (ir-rauserit Cic.); (rausurus Lucil.) | | | rāv-i- |

rĕfert. See fĕro

| rĕgo, *keep straight, rule* | rexi | rectum | rĕgĕre | rĕg- |

Compounds as arrĭgo, *raise,* arrexi, arrectum, arrigĕre.

Except pergo, *continue*, perrexi, perrectum, pergĕre,
whence expergiscor (*begin to stretch myself out*), *awake myself*,
experrectum (expergĭtum in Lucil. Lucr.).

surgo (sub-rego) *rise*, surrexi, surrectum, surgĕre.

Present.	Perfect.	Supine.	Pres. Infinitive.	Stem.
reor, *think*		rătum	rērĭ	ră-
reor has no present part.				
rēpo, *creep*	repsi	reptum	rēpĕre	rēp-
rīdeo, *smile, laugh*	rīsi	rīsum	rīdēre	rīd-ĕ
ringor, *shew the teeth, snarl*		(rictussubs.)	ringi	rĭg-
rŏdo, *gnaw*	rōsi	rōsum	rōdĕre	rŏd-
rŭdo, *roar, bray*	rŭdīvi (rare)		rŭdĕre	{rŭd- {rŭd-ĭ-

Persius has rŭdere.

rumpo, *break*	rūpi	ruptum	rumpĕre	rŭp-

In Plautus the m is sometimes retained, e.g. dirrumptum, cor-
rumptor (subs.).

ruo, *tumble, dash*	rui	-rŭtum	ruĕre	rŭ-

Generally intrans. The past part. found only in phrase rŭta cæsa
(has ŭ long, according to Varro, but in compounds it is
always short; e.g. dirŭtum).

fut. part. (post-Augustan) ruĭturus.

sæpio, *hedge in*	sæpsi	sæptum	sæpīre	sæp-ĭ-
salio } *salt* sallo }		{ salitum { salsum	sallĕre	{ sal-i- { sall-

An inf. salire is not certain. Nor is the quantity of the first
two syllables in salitum. Both forms of the verb are found
in MSS. with l and ll.

sălio, *leap*	sălŭi	(saltus subst.)	sălīre	săl-i-

Desĭlio, desilui, desĭlīre. So the other compounds.

The forms salīvi, salii are rare both in simple and compounds.

sălve, *hail!* also salvēte inf. salvēre and fut. salvēbis. (The present
salveo once in Plautus, perhaps in joke, salve being probably
originally an adverb.)

sancio, *hallow, ordain*	sanxi	sanctum	sancīre	sanc-ĭ-

sancītum (rarely). Sancierat is quoted from Pompon. Secundus.

17

Present.	Perfect.	Supine.	Pres. Infinitive.	Stem.
săpio, *have a savour*	săpīvī		săpĕre	săp-ĭ-
of, be wise				

desĭpio, *be foolish*, no perf. or sup., desĭpĕre.

rĕsĭpisco, *recover senses*, rĕsĭpŭi and rĕsĭpĭvi, rĕsĭpiscĕre.

sarcio, *patch*	sarsi	sartum	sarcīre	sarc-ĭ-
sărio, *hoe*	sarui (once)	sarītum	sarīre	sar-ĭ-

Also written sarrio. Perf. also sarivi.

sarpo, *trim*		sarptum	sarpĕre	sarp-
scăbo, *scratch*	scăbi (rare)		scăbĕre	scăb-
scalpo, *scrape*	scalpsi	scalptum	scalpĕre	scalp-

Compounds follow sculpo.

scando, *climb*	scandi	scansum	scandĕre	scand-

ascendo, ascendi, ascensum, ascendĕre. So the other compounds.

scindo, *tear, cut*	scĭdi	scissum	scindĕre	scĭd-

A perfect scicĭdi is quoted from Nævius, Attius, &c.

Exscindo has no perfect. The other compounds follow scindo.

scisco, *enact*	scīvi	scītum	sciscĕre	scī-

A strengthened form of scio.

scrībo, *write*	scripsi	scriptum	scrībĕre	scrīb-
sculpo, *carve* in stone,	sculpsi	sculptum	sculpĕre	sculp-
&c.				

Another form of scalpo.

sĕco, *cut*	sĕcui	sectum	sĕcāre	sĕc-ă-

fut. part. sĕcātūrus (once in Colum.).

sĕdeo, *sit*	sēdi	sessum	sĕdēre	sĕd-ĕ-

Possĭdeo, *occupy*, possēdi, possessum, possĭdēre. So the other compounds, except sŭpersedeo, *refrain*, circumsĕdeo, which do not change the e. Dissĭdeo, præsĭdeo have no supine.

sentio, *feel, think*	sensi	sensum	sentīre	sent-ĭ-

Assentior, assensus sum, is used as deponent (besides assentio).

sĕpĕlio, *bury*	sĕpĕlīvi	sĕpultum	sĕpĕlīre	sĕpĕl-ĭ-
sĕqvor, *follow*		sĕcūtum	sĕqvi	sĕqv-
sĕro, *sow, plant*	sēvi	sātum	sĕrĕre	să-
sĕro, *put in rows*		(serta, *garlands*).	sĕrĕre	sĕr-

Compounds as consĕro, consĕrŭi, consertum, consĕrĕre.

Present.	Perfect.	Supine.	Pres. Infinitive.	Stem.
serpo, *crawl*	serpsi	serptum	serpĕre	serp-

Another form of rēpo. Cf. Greek ἕρπω.

sīdo, *settle*, intr.	sīdi		sīdĕre	sīd-

sēdi and sessum from sŏdeo are the usual perfect and supine, and so the compounds.

sīno, *put, leave, suffer*	sīvi	sītum	sīnĕre	sī-

In subj. perf. sīrim, sīris, sīrit, sīrint.

Dēsīno, dēsii in post-Augustan writers (desisti, desiit, pluperf. dēsiĕram, perf. subj. dēsiĕrim), dēsītum, dēsīnĕre. (Cicero and Cæsar generally use destiti for perf.)
Dēsītus sum used before a passive infin. *I ceased.*

sisto, *set, stay*, trans.	stīti (rare)	stătum	sistĕre	stă-

desisto, destīti, destītum, desistere. So the compounds, all intransitive. The reduplication is retained. Sisto is rarely intrans. and then has perf. stĕti (from sto). So also circumstĕti.

sŏleo, *be wont*		sŏlitum	sŏlēre	sŏl-ĕ-

Perf. sŏlitus sum, *I was accustomed.*

solvo, *loose, pay*	solvi	sŏlūtum	solvĕre	solv-

Sometimes in Augustan poets sŏlui.

sŏno, *sound*	sŏnui	sŏnitum	sŏnāre	sŏn-ă-

fut. part. sŏnātūrus (once in Hor.). In præ-Augustan poets sometimes sonĕre, sonit, sonunt.

sorbeo, *sup up, suck in*	sorbui	(sorbītio, subst.)	sorbēre	sorb-ĕ-

absorbeo, absorbui, absorbēre. So other compounds. Rarely a perfect (post-Augustan) in si; absorpsi, exsorpsi.

spargo, *scatter, be-sprinkle.*	sparsi	sparsum	spargĕre	sparg-

Compounds as conspergo, conspersi, conspersum, conspergĕre.

spĕcio, *look*, only in Plautus. (But spīcio Plaut. *Mil.*)   spĕc-ĭ-
aspĭcio, aspexi, aspectum, aspĭcere. So the other compounds.

sperno, *reject, despise*	sprēvi	sprētum	spernĕre	{ spĕr- / sprē- }

17—2

Present.	Perfect.	Supine.	Pres. Infinitive.	Stem.
spondeo, *pledge* oneself	spŏpondi	sponsum	spondēre	spond-ĕ-

Despopondi twice in Plautus.

spuo, *spit*	spui	spūtum	spuĕre	spŭ-
stătuo, *set-up, settle* (*with oneself*)	stătui	stătūtum	stătuĕre	statŭ-
sterno, *throw on the ground, cover*	strāvi	strātum	sternĕre	{ stăr- { strā-
sternuo, *sneeze*	sternui		sternuĕre	sternŭ-
sterto, *snore*	stertui		stertĕre	stert-
stingvo (rare), *stamp, extinguish*			stingvĕre	stingv-

Exstingvo, exstinxi, exstinctum, exstingvĕre. So the other compounds.

sto, *stand*	stĕti	stătum	stāre	stă-

Fut. part. stăturus in Lucan.

Præsto, *be superior, show, warrant*, præstĭti, præstatum (also præstĭtum), præstāre. The other compounds have fut. part. -staturus (constăturus Luc. Mart., perstăturus Stat.) but no supine: disto, has no perf. or supine: those with disyllabic prepositions retain e in the perf. (e.g. circumstĕti).

strĕpo, *make a din*	strĕpui	strĕpĭtum	strĕpĕre	strĕp-
strīdeo, *hiss, screech*	strīdi		strīdēre	strīd-ĕ-

A consonantal form (e.g. stridunt, stridĕre) is found in Augustan poets; also Plin. Epist.

stringo, *strip, graze, draw tight*	strinxi	strictum	stringĕre	{strĭg- {string-
struo, *heap up, build*	struxi	structum	struere	strŭgv-
svādeo, *recommend*	svāsi	svāsum	svādēre	svād-ĕ-
svesco, *accustom one-self*	svĕvi	svētum	svescĕre	svē-

An old form of present indic. 1st pers. plur. suēmus (as from sueo).

sūgo, *suck*	suxi	suctum	sūgĕre	sūg-
sum, *be*	see Ch. XXVII.		esse	ĕs-
suo, *sow, stitch*	sui	sūtum	suĕre	sū-
tăceo, *be silent*	tăcui	tăcĭtum	tăcēre	tăc-ĕ-
tædet, *it wearieth*	tæsum est			tæd-ĕ-

For perf. pertæsum est is more common. Tædescit, obtædescit, pertædescit, distædet are also used impersonally.

Present.	Perfect.	Supine.	Pres. Infinitive.	Stem.
tango, *touch*	tĕtĭgi	tactum	tangĕre	tăg-

Attingo, attĭgi, attactum, attingĕre.   So the other compounds.
In Plautus rarely tago, attĭgo.

tĕgo, *cover*	texi	tectum	tĕgĕre	tĕg-
temno, *despise*	tempsi	temptum	temnĕre	tem-
tendo, *stretch, tend*	tĕtendi	tentum	tendĕre	tend-

In post-Augustan writers sometimes tēnsum.   Compounds have
-tēnsum occasionally.

tĕneo, *hold*	tĕnui	tentum (rare)tĕnēre	ten-ĕ-

Perfect tetĭni is quoted from Pacuvius and Accius.

Supine and cognate forms are little used, except in the compounds, detĭnĕo, obtĭneo, and rĕtĭneo.   Contentus only as adj.
content.

dētĭneo, dētĭnui, dētentum, dētĭnēre.   So the other compounds.

terreo, *frighten*	terrui	terrĭtum	terrēre	tĕrr-ĕ-
tergeo, *wipe*	tersi	tersum	tergēre	terg-ĕ-

A consonantal stem (e. g. tergit, terguntur) is also found sometimes.

tĕro, *rub*	trīvi	trītum	tĕrĕre	tĕr- trī-

attĕruisse in Tibull. (once).

texo, *weave*	texŭi	textum	texĕre	tex-
tingo, tingvo, } *dip, dye*	tinxi	tinctum	tingĕre tingvĕre	tingv-
tollo, *lift up, remove*	(sustuli)	(sublatum)	tollĕre	toll-

tŭli (in præ-August. poets tĕtŭli, in some old inscriptions toli) and
latum (for tlatum) are the proper perf. and supine: but as
these are taken by fĕro, tollo takes the perf. and supine of its
compound sustollo.

The compounds have no perf. or supine.

tondeo, *shear*	tŏtondi	tonsum	tondēre	tond-ĕ-
tŏno, *thunder*	tŏnui	tŏnĭtum	tŏnāre	tŏn-ā-

intŏno has part. intŏnātus (once Hor.).   The other compounds
follow tŏno.

torqveo, *twist, whirl* torsi	tortum	torqvēre	torqv-ĕ-
torreo, *roast*	torrui	tostum	torrēre	tors-ĕ-

	Present.	Perfect.	Supine.	Pres. Infinitive.	Stem.
	trăho, *drag*	traxi	tractum	trăhĕre	trăh-
	trĕmo, *tremble*	tremui		trĕmĕre	trĕm-
	trĭbuo, *assign, grant*	trĭbui	trĭbūtum	trĭbuĕre	trĭbū-
	trūdo, *thrust*	trūsi	trūsum	trūdĕre	trūd-
	tŭĕor, *look at, protect*		{tūtum {tuĭtum	tuēri	tu-ĕ-

tūtus, adj. *safe*.

Tūtātus sum (from tutor) is generally used as perfect; tūtus or (post-Augustan) tuitus sum are rare. Contueor, intueor have (post-Augustan) contŭĭtus, intŭĭtus sum. A present with stem in -u (e. g. tuĭmur, contuor, &c.), is frequent in præ-August. poets and Seneca's tragedies.

	tundo, *thump*	tŭtŭdi	{tūsum {tunsum	tundĕre	tŭd-

Contundo, contŭdi, contŭsum, contundĕre. So pertundo. Obtundo, retundo have both -tunsum and -tūsum. Perfect of retundo always retundi.

	turgeo, *swell*	tursi		turgēre	turg-ĕ-

tursi is quoted from Ennius (once); obtursi from Lucilius (once).

	vādo, *go*			vādĕre	văd-

Invādo, invāsi, invāsum, invādĕre. So other compounds.

	văleo, *be strong*	vălui	(vălĭtūrus)	vălēre	văl-ĕ-
	vĕgeo, *stir up* (old word)		(vĕgĕtus adj.)	vĕgēre	vĕg-ĕ-
	vĕho, *carry*	vexi	vectum	vĕhĕre	vĕh-

Pres. part. and gerund also used intransitively, *riding*.

	vello, *pull, pluck*	velli	vulsum	vellĕre	vell-

Vulsi both in simple and compounds is sometimes found in post-Augustan writers.

vendo, *sell*. See do.
vēneo, *be sold*. See eo.

	vĕnio, *come*	vĕni	ventum	vĕnīre	vĕn-ĭ-
	vĕreor, *be awed at*		vĕrĭtum	vĕrēri	vĕr-e-
	vergo, *incline*			vergĕre	verg-
	verro, *brush*	verri (rare)	versum	verrĕre	verr-
	verto, *turn*	verti	versum	vertĕre	vert-

So the compounds generally, but

dīvertor, *put up* (at an inn), dīverti (perf.), dīversum, dīverti (inf.).

rĕvertor, *return,* perf. revertī, reversum, revertī (inf.), reversus, *having returned.*

prævertor, *attend to first,* is entirely deponent: prævertō, *be beforehand with,* is very rare.

Present.	Perfect.	Supine.	Pres. Infinitive.	Stem.
vescor, *feed oneself*			vescī	vesc-
vĕto, *forbid*	vĕtŭī	vĕtĭtum	vĕtāre	vĕt-ă-

Persius has a perfect vetāvī.

vĭdeo, *see*	vīdī	vīsum	vĭdēre	vĭd-ĕ-

vĭdeor, vīsum, vĭdērī, very common in sense of *seem.*

vĭeo, *plait* (twigs, &c.)		vietum	vĭēre	vĭ-ĕ-

part. viētus (Ter. Lucr., but viĕtus, Hor.), *shrivelled.*

vincio, *bind*	vinxī	vinctum	vincīre	vinc-ĭ-
vinco, *conquer*	vīcī	victum	vincĕre	vĭc-
vīso, *visit*	vīsī		vīsĕre	vīs-
vīvo, *live*	vixī	victum	vīvĕre	vīgv-
ulciscor, *avenge oneself on, avenge*		ultum	ulciscī	ulc-
ungo, \ ungvo, / *grease*	unxī	unctum	{ungĕre {ungvĕre	ungv-
vŏlo, *will*	vŏluī		velle	vŏl-

So its compounds nōlo, mālo; see Ch. XXVIII.

volvo, *roll*	volvī	vŏlūtum	volvĕre	volv-

Sometimes voluī in Augustan poets.

vŏmo, *vomit*	vŏmuī	vŏmĭtum	vŏmĕre	vŏm-
vŏveo, *vow*	vōvī	vōtum	vŏvēre	vŏv-ĕ-
urgeo, *push, press*	ursī		urgēre	urg-ĕ-
ūro, *burn*	ussī	ustum	ūrĕre	ūs-

Combūro, combussi, combustum, combūrĕre, is a compound of com with an older form buro, seen in bustum, *tomb.*

Other compounds (exūro, &c.) follow the usual form.

ūtor, *avail oneself, make use*		ūsum	ūtī	ūt-

The following verbs also have no perfect or supine.

(1) e- verbs:

ægreo, *be sick*	frondeo, *be in leaf*	polleo, *be powerful*
albeo, *be white*	hĕbeo, *be blunt*	renīdeo, *shine*
äveo, *be greedy*	lacteo, *be a suckl'ng, have milk*	scăteo, *bubble forth*
calveo, *be bald*	līveo, *be bluish pale*	splendeo, *be bright*
cāneo, *be hoary*	măceo, *be lean*	squāleo, *be rough*
flāveo, *be yellow*	mæreo, *grieve*	tābeo, *waste away*
fœteo, *stink*	mūceo. *be mouldy*	ūmeo, *be wet*

(2) i- verbs:

cæcutio, *be blind*	prūrio, *itch for*	ineptio, *be silly*
		desideratives
dementio, *rave*	singultio, *sob*	cenatŭrio, *have an appetite*
glocio, *cluck*		emptŭrio, *wish to buy*
		partŭrio, *be in labour*

BOOK III.

WORD-FORMATION.

BOOK III[1].

WORD-FORMATION.

CHAPTER I.

ELEMENTS OF WORD-FORMATION.

WORDS are formed either directly from roots or from other
words. The elements of formation are four: *reduplication, internal
change, addition of suffixes, combination of two or more words into one.*
Two or more of these modes of formation may be called into use
in forming a word; and especially, almost all words, whatever other
change the root may have undergone, exhibit some suffix or other.

i. *Reduplication* is the repetition of the root syllable, either to
express repeated action or simply to give additional emphasis to the
root. In Latin there appear but few instances of reduplication.
The following are probably such:

1. Reduplication of a closed syllable:

bar-bar-us, *foreign* (from βάρβαρος); **car-cer** (n.), *a prison, a
barrier* (for the vowel cf. § 204. 2); **cin-cin-nus**, *a curl* (comp.
κίκιννος); **cur-cŭl-io**, *a weevil* (for the change of liquid cf. § 185. 2);
fur-fur (m.), *bran;* **gur-gŭl-io**, *the windpipe* (cf. § 852); **marmor**
(n.), *marble;* **mur-mur** (n.), *a murmur* (comp. μορμύρειν); **quisquis,**
whosoever; **tin-tin-nāre**, *to tinkle* (cf. § 646); **tur-tur** (m. f.), *a
dove;* **ŭl-ŭl-a**, *a screech-owl;* **ŭl-ŭl-are**, *to howl, wail* (comp. ὀλ-ολ-
ύζειν). Similarly **per-per-am** (adv.), *badly* (§ 526).

2. Reduplication of an open syllable; or rather, of the initial
consonant, with a vowel appended:

bĭ-bĕre, *to drink;* **cĭ-cāda**, *a grasshopper;* **cĭ-cātrix** (f.), *a scar:*
cĭ-cer (n.), *chickpease;* **cĭ-cōnia**, *a stork;* **cĭ-cŭr**, *tame;* **cĭ-cŭta,**
hemlock; **cŏcus** (qvoqvus), *a cook;* **cŭ-cŭlus**, *a cuckoo* (comp. κόκκυξ);
cŭ-cŭmis (m.), *a cucumber;* **cŭ-curbĭta**, *a gourd;* **jĕ-jūnus**, *fasting;*

---

[1] In this book much use has been made of the lists in Leo Meyer's
Vergleich. Gram. (1861—1865) especially the second volume. *Corresponding* Greek words have been usually taken from Curtius (see
above, p. 24 n.).

mamma, *a breast;* **mĕ-mor,** *mindful;* **pă-pāver** (n.), *a poppy;* **pă-pilla** (diminutive of an assumed **papa**), *a teat;* **pī-pīre,** *to chirp;* **pŏ-pŭlus,** *a people;* **qvi-sqvīliæ,** *refuse* (comp. κο-σκυλ-μάτια, and for the omission of **s** § 193); **sŭ-surrus,** *a whisper* (comp. σῦρίζε ν); **tĭ-tillare,** *to tickle;* **tĭ-tŭbāre,** *to stumble.*

For the use of reduplication to form the *present* stem of verbs see § 628; and to form the *perfect* stem, § 665 sqq.

ii. *Internal change* is frequently found accompanying the addition of suffixes, or composition, but is then due mainly to the consequent shifting of the accent, or to the influence of neighbouring consonants. The usual changes have been set forth in Book I. There appear to be but few instances in Latin, in which there is clear evidence of internal change being employed as the main element in the formation of a word. Compare however, e.g. **tŏga** with **tĕg-ĕre; sĕd-es** with **sĕd-ēre; fīdes** with **fīdĕre; prŏc-us** with **prĕc-ari** (§§ 233. 1, 234. 5, &c.); **dūc-ere** with **dŭc- (dux); dīcere** with **malĕdĭcus,** &c.; **vōc-,** nom. **vox,** with **vŏcare.** For the change of vowel in forming the perfect tense see § 668.

But if, as is probable, the primary form of roots admits of short vowels only, then all instances of (apparent) roots with long vowels fall under this head (unless the long vowel is a compensation for omitted consonants); e.g. **lux, pax,** &c., **scrībere, lūdere,** &c.

iii. *Suffixes* are of three kinds: (1) Suffixes of inflexion, (2) stem-suffixes (included under *inflexions* in Book II.), (3) derivative suffixes.

(1) *Suffixes of inflexion* are those which are employed to form the several cases and numbers of nouns, and the persons, moods, tenses, voice, &c. of verbs.

(2) *Stem-suffixes* are those which form the distinguishing marks of the several declensions of nouns, and the several conjugations (or classes) of verbs. In nouns of the first class they are **a, e, o;** in nouns of the second class **u, i** or **e;** in verbs **a, u, e, i.** A large class of nouns, and the most primitive verbs, have no stem-suffix.

The application of the stem-suffixes in Latin nouns coincides to a large extent with the distinction of gender: in verbs it coincides, at least as regards the **a** and **e** stems, to a noticeable degree with the distinction of transitive and intransitive action. The absence of a stem-suffix in many nouns is the result of the shifting of the accent, and consequent slurring of the end of the word, the consonant stem being thus reduced by one syllable from what was, or would otherwise have been, their full form (with a stem-suffix); e.g. **præceps** for **præcĭpĭts,** &c. In other nouns of the same class (consonant stems) there appears to be no clear ground for assuming the previous existence of a stem-suffix. (A similar loss or weakening of the stem-suffix is held by Corssen[1] to have occurred in the consonant verbs, **regis, regit, regere**, &c., being properly divided **regĭ-s, regĭ-t, regĕ-re**, &c. for earlier **raga-sa, raga-ta**, &c.)

Many noun-stems and many verb-stems are apparently formed directly from the root by the addition of these stem-suffixes. In some a reduplication or an internal change, especially of the vowel, occurs also. The formation of one word, compound or simple, from another is often effected by the substitution of the stem-suffix appropriate to one part of speech for that appropriate to another.

Words of simple form which contain no known derivative suffix are presumably formed in this way directly from the root. Instances may be collected from the lists given in this book.

The following are *examples* of the formation of nouns from 744 roots or from other words by the addition or substitution of no other than a stem-suffix. The majority of verbs are so formed (see Chap. x.).

A. **advĕna**, *a stranger* (advenī-re); **convīva**, *a guest* (conviv-ēre); **funda**, *a sling* (fund-ĕre); **mŏla**, *a mill* (mŏl-ĕre); **scrība**, *a clerk* (scrīb-ĕre); **tŏga**, *a cloak* (tĕg-ĕre); **trăha**, *a sledge* (trăh-ĕre).

O. **ahenobarbus**, *bronze-beard* (barba-); **condus**, *a store-keeper* (cond-ĕre); **cŏqvus**, *a cook* (cŏqv-ĕre); **fīdus**, *trusty* (fīd-ĕre, fīde-s); **jŭgum**, *a yoke* (comp. jungĕre); **mergus**, *a diver* (merg-ĕre); **nescius**, *ignorant* (nescī-re); **prŏfŭgus**, *deserting* (prŏfŭgĕ-re); **prŏmus**, *a butler* (prŏm-ĕrĕ); **rŏgus**, *a funeral pile* (rĕg-ĕre, comp. erĭgĕre, *to erect*); **sŏnus**, *a sound* (sŏn-ĕre and sŏnāre).

U. **ăcus**, *a needle* (ăc-, comp. ăc-u-ĕre); **currus**, *a chariot* (curr-ĕre); **dŏmus**, *a house* (comp. δέμ-ειν, *to build*, dŏmāre, *to tame*).

I (or E). **abnormis**, *abnormal* (norma-); **bilingvis**, *two-tongued* (lingva); **nūbes**, *a cloud* (nūb-ĕre, *to cover*, comp. νέφ-ος); **rūpes**, *a rock* (rump-ĕre, *to break*); **sēdes**, *a seat* (sĕd-ēre); **vĕhes**, *a cartload* (vĕh-ĕre).

[Without stem-suffix. **dux**, *a leader* (dūc- comp. dūc-ĕre); **incus**, *an anvil* (incūd-ĕre); **obex**, *a bolt* (obicĕ-re); **plānipes**, *flatfooted* (pĕd-).]

(3) *Derivative suffixes* are those additions (not being recognisable roots) which are interposed between the root and the stem-suffix; or, when there is no stem-suffix, between the root and the suffix of inflexion. If they are themselves recognisable as roots, the formation of the word belongs to the sphere of

(iv)   *Composition* (which is treated of in Chapter XI.).

Interjections, some of which are words, some mere natural sounds, will be enumerated in the last Chapter.

[1] *Aussprache*, II. 50, foll. ed. 2.

CHAPTER II.

DERIVATIVE SUFFIXES.

DERIVATIVE suffixes may originally have been words, but are 745
now merely sounds or combinations of sounds which have no
separate use or separate meaning, but modify the meaning of the
word to which they are suffixed. The same suffix does not usually
express precisely the same modifications, and different suffixes often
seem to have the same effect: compare -tūdŏn, -tia, -tāt, &c. Frequently indeed the use of a suffix may have proceeded from a fan-
cied or imperfectly apprehended analogy; and the ending of a word,
which is partly composed of stem-consonants or stem-vowels, and
partly of a suffix, has been apparently taken for an entire suffix, and
as such applied to other stems. Compare montānus, § 830, mon-
tuosus, § 814. Sometimes the sense of the suffix has been obscured,
and a further suffix is added to realize what the former suffix once
expressed; e.g. puella is diminutive of puera, but afterwards supplanted puera as the ordinary term for a girl, and thus puellula was
formed for a *little* or *very young girl*.

A light vowel, ŏ, ŭ, ĕ, more frequently ĭ, is often found between 746
the last consonant of the stem and the suffix. Its origin is not
clear. Sometimes it appears to be part of the suffix; e.g. -ĕc (-ĭc)
in sĕnex, pŭmex, &c.; more frequently it appears to be the stem-
suffix weakened; e.g. candĭdus from cande- (see the words given in
§ 816), altitūdo from alto-; sometimes it appears to owe its birth
to analogy with other words; sometimes to a desire to ease the pronunciation, or avoid the destructive effect of contiguous consonants;
or even to render possible the use of the word in verse. It is
indeed possible that it may be an expression of the slight sound
occasioned by opening the organs, in order fully to articulate the
final consonant (cf. § 9).

It has most frequently been treated in the following lists as the
weakened stem-suffix; but its occurrence in words formed from
consonant stems is by no means unusual, and seems to conflict with
this theory of its origin. If these consonant stems are the stunted
remnants of forms which originally were vowel stems, this weakened vowel may be the relic of the fuller form. (So in French the

final t of the Latin 3rd pers. sing. is preserved only before a vowel; e.g. a-t-ıl, and its meaning lost to the popular consciousness). If otherwise, one of the other explanations must be resorted to.

The long vowel, found not uncommonly in the same part of 747 a derivative, is sometimes part of the suffix; e.g. dum-ētum for dum-ec-tum; sometimes due to contraction of the stem-suffix with a short initial vowel of the suffix; e.g. the suffix -īno appended to the stems Roma-, divo-, tribu-, mari-, ĕge- gives Romānus, divīnus, tribūnus, marīnus, egēnus: the suffix -īlī appended to ancŏra-, tribu-, fide-, civi- gives ancorālis, tribūlis, fidēlis, civīlis. Sometimes it is due to following a false analogy; e.g. mont-ānus, anser-ī-nus, &c., virgīn-ālis, rēg-ālis, &c.[1]

In other respects the ordinary laws of consonant and vowel changes (given in Book I.) are observed.

In the following lists many words, which so far as our know- 748 ledge goes are primitive, are given along with the derivatives, partly because of the difficulty and consequently arbitrary nature of an attempt to separate them, partly because, as was said above, the ending of a primitive word appears sometimes to have been supposed to be a suffix, and consequently to have been applied as a suffix in the formation of other words. The word-endings therefore, under which the Latin words are here arranged, are not necessarily, though they are usually (except as regards a long initial vowel, cf. § 747), suffixes.

These suffixes are sometimes simple, i.e. consisting of a single vowel, or a single consonant with a vowel; sometimes compound, i.e. consisting of two consonants with one or two vowels. Compound suffixes are usually the result of adding a suffix to a stem which is itself a derivative; but sometimes the suffix, though originally compound, has come to be treated as if it were a simple suffix; e.g. -unculo: sometimes it may be really a word which has ceased to be used separately, and only appears now to be suffixal; e.g. -ginta, § 794, and perhaps -gno, -mōnio, -cīnio, &c.

The primary arrangement of noun-endings is according to the 749 consonant or vowel which immediately precedes either the stem-suffix, or, in consonant nouns, the suffix of inflexions. Subordinately to this, first come all word-endings which have the stem-suffix of nouns of the first class (o being used, for convenience sake, as inclusive of a); secondly, word-endings of the second class. The simplest endings, among which are those beginning with short vowels, are put first; then such compound endings as have a conso-

[1] Key, *Lat. Gr.* §§ 227. 232.

nant before the same short vowel; then simple endings with long vowels; lastly, compound endings with the same long vowel. The order of the consonants and vowels is the same as in Books I. and II.: the order of the words is alphabetical.

The lists are intended to be fairly complete, except in those classes of derivatives which contain too numerous instances to be conveniently or usefully given. Of these a full and typical selection is given. But the lists do not as a rule, though they do sometimes, contain,

(1) Words found only in writers later than Suetonius.

(2) Words only quoted by Nonius or Festus, or other grammarians, and some others of early or rare use.

(3) Words (especially technical or scientific words), found only and seldom in Cato, Varro, Vitruvius, Celsus, Pliny the elder, Columella, Petronius. Many such are however given.

(4) Compounds with prepositions, if the simple form is also found.

(5) Words borrowed from the Greek.

CHAPTER III.

LABIAL NOUN-STEMS.

i. *Stems ending in* -po, -pi, -p.

-po 1. Adjectives: **crispus**, *curling;* **lippus**, *blear-eyed;* **obstīpus**, 750 *bent.*

2. Substantives:

(*a*) Masculine: **capus**, *a capon;* **cippus**, *a post* or *upright block;* **lŭpus**, *a wolf* (comp. λύκος, § 66); **napus**, *a turnip;* **pūpus**, *a boy;* **rumpus** (Varr.), *a vine branch;* **scăpus**, *a stem* (comp. scōpæ, scīpio, σκῆπ-τρον); **scirpus**, *a rush;* **scrūpus**, *a rough stone* (scrūpulus more common); **stloppus**, *a slap;* **struppus**, *a cord* (from στρόφος?); **verpus**, *a circumcised man.*

pŏpa, *a sacrificing priest* (i. e. cŏqva, cf. § 118); **Agrĭppa.**

(*b*) Feminine: **alăpa**, *a slap;* **cōpa**, *a barmaid* (comp. caupo, κάπηλος); **culpa**, *a fault;* **cūpa**, *a tub;* **lappa**, *a bur;* **mappa** (a Punic word according to Quint.), *a napkin;* **nĕpa**, *a scorpion* (African

word?); pulpa, *fleshy substance;* pūpa, *a girl;* rīpa, *a stream bank;*
scōpæ (pl.), *twigs* (see scapus); sāpa, *must boiled down to a third*
(comp. ὀπός); stuppa, *tow* (comp. στυππεῖον); talpa (rarely m.),
a mole; vappa, *flat wine* (comp. văp-or, văp-ĭdus); vespa, *a wasp*
(comp. σφήξ).

(*c*) Neuter: gausăpum, *a frieze cloth* (cf. § 410); palpum,
stroking (only found in acc. and abl.); rapum, *a turnip.*

-pho   lympha, *water* (comp. νύμφη).

-pi   ăpis (f.), *a bee* (comp. ἐμπίς, *a gnat*); cæpe (n.), *an
onion;* cōpis, *plentiful* (com, ŏp-; comp. inops); puppis
(f.), *a ship's stern;* rūpes (f.), *a rock* (rump-ĕre); sæpes
(f.), *a hedge* (comp. σηκός, § 66); stirps (f.), *a stock;*
turpis, *foul;* volpes (f.), *a fox* (comp. ἀλώπ-ηξ).

-p   ădeps (m. f.), *fat* (comp. ἄλειφα, *ointment,* cf. § 174. 4);
daps (f.), *a banquet* (comp. δάπτειν *to devour,* δαπάνη,
δεῖπνον); ops (f.), *help* (comp. ἄφ-ενος); stips, *a small gift in coin.*

Compound stem-ending: only pŭlo, § 860.

ii. *Stems ending in -bo, -bi, -b.*

-bo 1. Adjectives: ăcer-bus, *unripe, bitter* (comp. ācĕri, ăcies, 751
&c.); albus, *white;* balbus, *lisping;* gibbus, *humped*
(comp. κύπ-τειν); orbus, *bereft* (comp. ὀρφ-ανός); prŏ-
bus, *honest;* sŭper-bus, *haughty* (sŭper).

2. Substantives:

(*a*) Masculine: barbus, *a barbel;* bulbus, *a bulb* (βολβός);
cĭbus, *food;* cŏlumbus (also columba, f.), *a pigeon;* glŏbus, *a ball;*
limbus, *a border* or *fringe;* lumbus, *a loin;* mor-bus, *disease* (mŏr-i);
nimbus, *a rain-cloud* (comp. νέφ-ος, nūbes); rŭbus, *a bramble;*
tŭbus, *a pipe.*

Galba (see Suet. *Galb.* 3; some compare Germ. gelb, *yellow*);
scrīb-a, *a clerk* (scrīb-ĕre, § 744).

(*b*) Feminine: barba, *a beard;* fāba, *a bean;* glēba or glæba, *a sod;*
herba, *grass* (comp. ferre, φορβή, φέρειν, and § 134); jŭba, *a mane;*
obba, *a beaker;* teba, *a hill* (old Sabine word); sorbus, *a service-
tree;* tŭba, *a trumpet* (comp. tŭbus); tuṛba, *a crowd* (comp.
tur-ma).

(*c*) Neuter: lībum, *a cake;* plumbum, *lead* (comp. μόλυβδος);
sēbum, *fat;* sorbum, *a service-berry;* tābum, *corrupt matter;* verbum, *a word* (comp. Ϝερ-, ἐρεῖν, § 91).

-bi　　corbis (m. f.), *a basket;* lābes (f.), *a spot* (comp. λώβη, 752 *outrage*); nūbes (f.), *a cloud* (comp. nĕbŭla, νέφ-ος); orbis (m.), *a round;* pălumbes (m. f.), *a dove* (comp. cŏlumbus and § 66); plebs (f.), *the common people* (comp. plĕ-nus, pŏ-pŭl-us, πλη-θύς, &c.); pūbes (f.), *hair of commencing manhood;* scŏbis (f.), *sawdust* (scăb-ĕre); scrŏbis (m. f.), *a ditch;* tābes (f. § 411), *decaying matter* (comp. τή-κειν); urbs (f.), *a city* (comp. orbis).

-b　　cælebs (adj.), *unmarried.*

Compound stem-endings: -bundo, § 818; -bŭlo, -bĭli, -tĭbĭli, §§ 861, 875, 876; -bĕro, -bĕri, §§ 886, 901; -brio, § 941.

iii. *Stems ending in* -mo, -mi, -m.

-mo　　1. Adjectives: 753
al-mus, *nourishing, kind* (ăl-ĕre); firmus, *firm;* līmus, *sideways,* e. g. limis oculis, *out of the corners of the eyes* (for lic-mus: comp. oblīqvus); ŏpīmus, *fat, rich;* sīmus, *flat-nosed;* pătrīmus, *having father living* (patr-); matrīmus, *having mother living* (matr-).

bīmus, *two years old;* trīmus, quadrīmus are probably compounds of hīm-, which appears uncontracted in hiem-p-s.

2. Substantives:

(*a*) Masculine: ănĭ-mus, *soul* (comp. ἄνεμος); ar-mus, *a shoulder joint* (ἄρ-, ἀραρίσκειν); călă-mus, *a reed* (probably from κάλαμος); culmus, *a stalk, haulm;* dūmus, *a thicket* (for dus-mus; comp. δασ-ύς); fīmus, *dung;* fū-mus, *smoke* (cf. § 99. 6); grūmus, *a heap* (of dirt, &c.); hāmus, *a hook;* lī-mus, *slime* (for lit-mus; comp. lĭ-n-ĕre); mīmus, *an imitator* (from μῖμος?); nummus, *a coin* (comp. νόμος); răcēmus, *a bunch of berries* (comp. ῥαγ-, ῥάξ); rā-mus, *a branch* (for rad-mus? comp. rād-ix, ῥαδίνος); rē-mus, *an oar* (comp. ἐρετμόν, § 193); Rĕmus; scalmus, *a thole,* is borrowed from σκαλμός.

(*b*) Feminine: dŏ-mus, *a house* (comp. δέμ-ειν, dŏmĭ-nus); hŭmus, *the ground* (comp. χαμαί); pōmus, *a fruit-tree;* ulmus, *an elm.*

ănĭma, *breath* (see animus); brū-ma, *winter solstice* (for brĕvī-ma, sc. dies); cŏma, *hair of head* (borrowed from κόμη); damma, *a hind;* fā-ma, *fame* (fā-ri); flam-ma, *flame* (for flag-ma; comp. flag-rāre); forma, *shape;* gem-ma, *a bud* (for gen-ma; comp. gĕn-ĭtŭs); gluma, *a husk* (glŭb-ĕre); grō-ma, *a surveyor's rod* (from γνώμων); lăcrĭ-ma, *a tear* (comp. δακρυ-); lā-ma, *a slough* (for lac-ma; comp.

lăcus); lī-ma, *a file;* mamma, *a teat;* nor-ma, *a standard* (perhaps from γνωριμή); pal-ma, *the palm of hand* (comp. παλάμη); par-ma, *a light shield;* plŭma, *a feather;* rīma, *a chink* (comp. ric-tus); Rŏ-ma, *stream-city?* (comp. ru-o, rīv-us, ῥεῦμα: so Cors., Curt.); rŭma, *a breast;* spŭ-ma, *foam* (spu-ere); squāma, *a scale of a fish,* &c.; strŭma, *a tumour;* tama (Lucil.), *a swelling in the leg* (tŭmēre?); trā-ma, *a web;* tur-ma, *a troop* (comp. tur-ba); victi-ma, *a victim* (victo-).

(*c*) Neuter: arma (pl.), *arms* (ἄρ-, see above); pōmum, *an apple, fruit;* vŏlema or volæma (pl.), *a kind of pears.*

-ŭmo or -Imo. On the vowel preceding m see § 224. It may often 754 be that this vowel belongs to the stem, not to the suffix.

(*a*) Superlatives: extrē-mus, *outmost* (for extra-ĭmus); I-mus, *inmost, at the bottom* (for ĭn-ĭmus); inf-ĭmus, *lowest* (inf-ĕr, § 885); mĭn-ĭmus, *least* (comp. mĭn-ŏs-); plŭr-ĭmus (old ploirumus, § 264), *most* (for plo-iŏs-ĭmus, plŭr-imus; with plo- comp. plē-rīque, πολ-ύς, πλε-ίων); postrē-mus, *hindmost, last* (for postera-ĭmus); post-ŭmus, esp. *last born,* usually, *one born after his father's death* (post; but the t may be part of the suffix; cf. § 535); prī-mus (for pris-mus, for pri-os-ĭmus; comp. prior, pris-tinus, and § 193. 2; or directly from pri-, a locative form seen in prī-die; or for pro-imus, comp. πρότερος, πρῶτος); prox-ĭmus, *nearest* (prŏque for prŏpe? comp. namque and nempe, § 517); sum-mus, *upmost* (for sub-mus; comp. sub, sup-er); suprē-mus, *highest* (for supra-ĭmus). In Petron. § 75, ipsimus, ipsima for *master, mistress* (ipso-). So also the adv. de-mum (*downmost*), *at length* (de).

(*b*) Ordinal numbers: dĕcĭmus, *tenth* (for decim-imus); septĭ-mus, *seventh* (for septim-ĭmus); quŏt-umus, *how manyth* (quot; formed by Plautus in imitation of septimus); nō-nus is perhaps for nŏvimĭmus, contracted nōmus, by assimilation of m to the initial n.

-iss-ŭmo or -iss-ĭmo, for -iŏs-umo; i.e. ŭmo, suffixed to the stem of 755 the comparative. For the omission or absorption of the ŏ see §§ 214, 242. For the formation of the comparative § 917. The double s is due partly to the desire to indicate the length of the syllable (which moreover is accented), partly perhaps to preserve the sound of s sharp, instead of s flat or eventually r (cf. §§ 187, 191. 5. 6). For the ordinary explanation see the Preface.

alt-iss-ŭmus, *highest* (alto-, altiŏs-); antīqv-iss-ĭmus, *most ancient* (antiqvo-, antiqvĭŏs-); audāc-iss-ĭmus, *boldest* (audāci-, audāciŏs-); bĕnĕ-fĭcent-iss-ĭmus, *most benevolent* (benefico-, benefĭcentiŏs-, as if from a participial form); dign-iss-ĭmus, *worthiest* (digno-, digniŏs-); dūr-iss-ĭmus, *hardest* (dūro-, duriŏs-); fēlīc-issimus, *happiest* (fēlīci-, felīciŏs-); fertĭl-iss-ĭmus, *most fertile* (fertĭli-, fertĭliŏs-); frŭgālissi-mus, *thriftiest* (frŭgāliŏs-, as if from frugālis, for which frūgi, § 1108, is used); imbēcĭll-iss-imus, *weakest* (imbēcillo- and imbēcilli-, imbēcilliōs-); ips-issumus (Plaut.), *the very man* (ipso-); max-ĭmus, *greatest* (for mags-imus from magis for magiōs-); ōc-iss-imus, *swiftest* (ōciōs-, comp. ὠκύς); neqv-iss-ĭmus, *absolutely good for nothing* (neqvios- from nēqvam); pĕnĭt-iss-ĭmus, *most inward* (pĕnĭtus, adv. but cf. Pl. *Asin.* 42); sēvēr-iss-ĭmus, *strictest* (sēvērō-, severiōs-); verbĕrābĭl-issĭmus (Plaut.), *most thrashable* (verberābĭli-); and many others. See Appendix C.

l-ŭmo } These suffixes are formed in the case of a few superla- 756
r-ŭmo } tives, where the final consonant of the simple adjective is l or r. Probably they are the result of a strong contraction, caused by the desire to avoid s following l or r (cf. § 193. 5. *c*). The double l or r may be the result of assimilation (§ 176. 5), or evidence of the length of the syllable (see last section). Possibly the apparent analogy of altus, altissimus, &c. may have led to acer, acerrimus, &c.

făcill-ĭmus, *easiest* (făcĭli-, faciliōs-). So also difficil-limus; grăcil-lĭmus, *thinnest* (grăcĭli-); hŭmil-lĭmus, *lowliest* (hŭmĭlĭ-); sĭmil-lĭmus, *likest* (sĭmĭli-) and dissimillĭmus.

ācer-rĭmus, *sharpest* (acri-, acriōs- for ācĕrios-); asper-rĭmus, *roughest* (aspĕro-, aspĕriōs-); cĕler-rĭmus, *quickest* (cĕlĕri-, cĕlĕriōs-); crēber-rĭmus, *most crowded* (crebro-, crebriōs- for creberiōs-); dēter-rĭmus, *worst* (deteriōs-, no positive); sălūber-rimus, *most healthful* (salubri-, salubriōs-); vĕter-rimus, *oldest* (veteriōs- from vĕtŭs-). So also māturrĭmus (oftener maturissimus, mĭser-rimus, pulcer-rimus, tĕnerrimus, tæterrimus, văferrimus, and the adverb nŭper-rime, all from o stems; pauperrimus, ūberrimus, from consonant stems.

-t-ŭmo} (*a*) ædĭ-tŭmus (comp. ædituus, § 992, and Varr. *R. R.* 757
-t-ĭmo } 1. 2; Gell. 12. 10), *a sacristan* (ædi-); fīnĭ-timus, *on the borders* (fīni-); lēg-ĭ-timus, *lawful* (lēg-); mărĭ-timus, *by the sea* (mări-).

(*b*) Superlatives:

cĭ-tĭmus, *nearest here* (ci-s; comp. ob-s, ul-s); dex-tĭmus, *on the extreme right* (comp. dex-ter, δεξιά, δεξίτερος); ex-timus, *outmost* (ex); in-timus, *inmost* (in); op-timus, *best* (lit. *overmost, upmost?* ob-s; comp. ἐπί); pes-sĭmus, *worst* (lit. *bottom-most?* pĕd-; or from the stem of pessum?); sinis-timus, *on the extreme left* (only with auspicium; comp. sĭnis-ter); ul-timus, *furthest, last* (ul-s).

sollistimum, only found with tripudium, is by some translated *perfect*, and derived from sollus (Oscan for totus), i.e. sōlus.

(*c*) *Ordinal* numbers from 20th to 90th inclusive. The initial t of the suffix forms with the final t of the stem of the cardinal ss, of which one s was omitted; and in post-Augustan times the pre-

ceding n was omitted (see § 168). Both the c and e of the ordinal
are earlier sounds than the g and i of the cardinal. (Cf. §§ 104, 234).
vīcens-ŭmus, vīcēsĭmus, vīgēsĭmus (all found), *twentieth* (for
vīcentī-tŭmus; comp. viginti, vīcies, and § 28. 2); tricens-umus,
&c. *thirtieth* (triginta); quadrāgēs-imus, *fortieth* (quadrāgintā). So
also qvinqvāgēsimus, sexāgēsimus, septuāgēsimus, octōgēsĭmus,
nōnāgēsimus, and perhaps centes-imus, *hundredth*, for centum-tĭmus,
centuntimus, cententimus (comp. e.g. regendum for regundum).

-ēs-ŭmo   *Ordinal* numbers from 200th upwards to 1000th inclu- 758
sive. The first part of this suffix is due to the mistaken
notion that in the lower numbers ēs was part of the suffix, instead of
(as it really was) the representative of the last part of the cardinal.
It is possible that centēsimus, which no doubt formed the immediate
pattern for the higher numbers, may itself be a product of this false
analogy.

ducent-ēs-ĭmus, *two hundredth* (ducentī-); trecentēsimus, *three
hundredth* (trecentī); qvadringent-ēsimus, *four hundredth* (quadrin-
gentī). So also qvinqvāgēsimus, sexcentēsimus, septingentēsimus,
octingentēsimus, nongentēsimus, mill-ēsĭmus, *thousandth* (mille),
and (in Lucr.) multēsimus, *many-th* (multo-).

-mi   fămes, *hunger* (cf. § 99). Comp. also cŭcŭmis, cōmis, 759
rumis, vermis, &c. § 412.

-m   hiemps, *winter* (cf. § 134, and for the p § 70).

Compound stem-endings: -mento, -mĕt, §§ 792, 806; -mĭno,
-mĕn, §§ 825, 850; -mnio, § 934; -mōnio, § 935.

iv. *Stems ending in* -vo, -uo, -vi.

-vo is found after vowels, or l or r; -uo after other consonants 760
(p, b; c, g; t, d, n; also tr).

-vo   1. Adjectives:
arvus (rare), *ploughed* (see arvum, § 761 c); căvus, *hollow* 761
(comp. cælum, κοῖλος); calvus, *bald;* cur-vus, *curved* (comp. circus, κυρ-τός, κυλ-λός); flāvus, *golden* in colour; fulvus, *tawny*
(comp. fulgere); furvus, *brown, dusky* (comp. fus-cus, φρύνη);
gilvus, *dun* (comp. helvus); gnāvus, *knowing* (comp. gnārus, gno-
scĕre); helvus, *yellow* (comp. χλό-η, χλω-ρός); lævus, *on left-hand*
(comp. λαιός); nŏvus, *new* (comp. νέος); parvus, *small* (comp.
par-cus, παῦρος); prāvus, *wrong;* prī-vus, *single, one's own* (lit.
standing forward; comp. prī-mus, § 754); prōtervus, *frolicsome;*
rāvus, *gray, hoarse;* sævus, *raging;* salvus, *safe* (comp. οὖλος, ὅλος,
sōlus); scævus, *on the left hand* (comp. σκαιός); torvus, *grim* (torqvēre?); vīvus, *living* (cf. § 129 c).

2. Substantives:

(*a*) Masculine : ăcervus, *a heap;* alvus (m. f. § 336), *the belly;* ăvus, *a grandfather;* cervus (*horned;* hence), *a stag* (comp. κεραός); clāvus, *a nail, helm; stripe* on dress (comp. clavis, § 765); clīvus, *a slope* (comp. in-clī-nare, κλίνω); corvus, *a raven* (comp. cornix, κόραξ); dīvus (diva, also deus, dea, and (Lucr. 4. 211) sub diū), *a god, goddess;* făvus, *a honeycomb cell;* milvus (§ 762. 2 *a*); nævus, *a mole* on the body, *a birthmark* (gi-gen-o, comp. gnaivos); nervus, *a sinew, a cord* (comp. νεῦρον); rīvus, *a stream* (comp. ῥεῖν, fut. ῥεύσειν); servus (also adj. and serva, f.), *a slave* (sĕrĕre, *join*). Nerva, a family name.

(*b*) Feminine: calva, *a skull,* or *bald head;* căterva, *a crowd;* clāva, *a club;* gingīva, *the gum* of the teeth; larva (§ 762. 2 *b*); Mīnerva (old Menerva); malva, *the mallow* (comp. μαλάχη, Hesiod); ōlīva (also ŏlea), *olive* (comp. ἔλαιος); silva, *a wood* (comp. ὕλη); stīva, *a plough handle;* valva, *a folding-door;* ulva, *sedge;* volva, *the womb;* ūva, *a grape.*

(*c*) Neuter: ævum, *an age* (comp. αἰών, § 91); arvum, *a field* (comp. arvus, § 761, ăr-āre, ἀρόω, *plough*); ervum, *bitter vetch* (comp. ὄροβος); ōvum, *an egg* (comp. ὠόν, § 91); urvum, *a ploughtail* (comp. curvus and § 121. 3).

-uo   1. Adjectives: 762

(*a*) from verb stems: ambĭg-uus, *on both sides, ambiguous* (amb-ĭg-ĕre); assĭd-uus, *constant* (adsĭd-ĕre); cæd-uus (of a wood), *for cutting* (cæd-ĕre); congru-us, *suitable* (congru-ĕre); contĭg-uus, *touching* (conting-ĕre); contĭn-uus, *continuous* (contĭnĕre); dēcĭd-uus, *falling* (dēcĭd-ĕre); dīvĭd-uus, *parted* (divĭd-ĕre); exĭg-uus, *small,* orig. *precise* (exĭg-ĕre); ingĕn-uus, *free-born* (ingign-ĕre); innŏc-uus, *harmless* (in, nŏc-ĕre); mūt-uus, *by way of change* (mūtā-re); occĭd-uus, *falling:* hence, from the sun, *western* (occĭd-ĕre); pasc-uus, (of land) *for grazing* (pasc-ĕre); perpĕt-uus, *uninterrupted* (perpĕt-cre); præcĭp-uus, *taken in front,* i.e. *chief* (præcĭp-ĕre); prōcĭd-uus (post-Aug.), *falling forward* (prōcĭd-ĕre); promisc-uus (also promiscus), *mixed* (promiscĕre); relĭc-uus (also relicus, § 160. 7), *left behind, remaining* (relinqv-ĕre); rĕsĭd-uus, *sunk to the bottom* like dregs, *left unused* (resĭd-ēre); rĭg-uus, irrĭg-uus, *irrigated* (rĭgā-re); succĭd-uus (not præ-Aug.), *sinking* (succĭd-ĕre); văc-uus (§ 94. 2), *empty* (văcā-re); and others.

(*b*) from substantives, or of obscure origin: ann-uus, *for a year* (anno-); ard-uus, *lofty* (comp. ὀρθ-ός); cern-uus, *headlong* (comp. κραν-ίον); fătuus, *foolish;* menstr-uus, *monthly* (mens-tr-i- from mens-; cf. § 904); mort-uus, *dead* (morti-); strēn-uus, *active;* suus, *his own;* tuus, *your;* vĭd-uus, *widowed* (comp. di-vĭd-ĕre; Germ. wittwe, Engl. widow).

2. Substantives:

(*a*) Masculine: **carduus**, *a thistle;* **lītuus**, *an augur's crook;* **mīluus** (§ 94. 2), *a kite;* **patr-uus**, *a father's brother* (**patr-**).

(*b*) Feminine: **bēlua**, *a beast;* **jān-ua**, *a gate* (**jano-**); **lārua** (§ 94. 2), *a ghost, a mask;* **noct-ua**, *an owl* (**nocti-**); **stăt-ua**, *a statue* (**stătu-**); **trua**, *a spoon.*

(*c*) Neuter: **februa** (pl.), *purgatives* (**febri-**).

-ī-vo   (For some words where the **i** is apparently radical 763 see § 761).

1. Adjectives:

æst-īvus, *of summer* (**æstu-**, *heat*); **adopt-ivus**, *taken by choice* (**adoptā-re**); **căd-ivus** (Plin.), *falling* (**căd-ĕre**); **internĕc-ivus**, *destructive* (**internĕc-ā-re**); **lasc-ivus**, *playful;* **nŏc-ivus** (Phædr., Plin., but **nŏcuus**, Ov.), *hurtful* (**nŏcēre**); **rĕŏĭd-ivus**, *restored* (**rĕcĭd-ĕre**); **rĕdĭvīvus**, a builder's term for *old material;* **sĕment-ivus**, *for sowing* (**sĕmenti-**); **subsĭc-ivus**, *cut off, spare* (**subsĕc-āre**); **tempest-ivus**, *seasonable* (**tempos-**; either the **t** is due to a false analogy with **æstivus**, or the word may be shortened for **tempestātivus**); **vŏc-ivus** (or **văc-ivus**), early form for **văcuus** (**văcā-re**).

2. Substantives: **Grādīvus** (once **Grădivus**), a name of Mars; **săl-iva**, *spittle* (**sal**, *salt*).

-t-īvo   i. e. **-īvo**, appended to the stem of the past participle. 764 (Only **passīvus** exhibits the **s**, and that is not earlier than Appuleius).

1. Adjectives:

(*a*) General: **ac-t-ivus**, *active, practical* (**ăgĕre**); **adoptivus**, *adoptive* (comp. **adoptāre**, frequentative in form); **cap-t-ivus**, *captured* (**capĕ-re**); **collec-tivus** (post-Aug.), *collected* (**collĭg-ĕre**); **condĭ-tivus**, *stored* (**cond-ĕre**); **fes-tivus**, *gay, handsome* (**festo-**); **fŭgĭ-t-ivus**, *run-away* (**fugĕ-re**); **fur-t-ivus**, *stolen* (comp. **fūrā-ri**); **insĭ-t-ivus**, *grafted* (**insĕrĕre**); **instaurā-t-ivus** (Cic.), *renewed* (**instaurāre**); **lūcrā-t-ivus**, *counted as gain* (**lucrā-ri**); **nā-t-ivus**, *born, self-grown* (**na-sc-i-**); **præʳŏgā-t-ivus**, *first-asked* (**præroʳg-āre**); **să-t-ivus**, *for sowing* (**sĕ-rĕre**); **stă-t-ivus**, *stationary* (**stare**); **sec-t-ivus** (Col., Plin.), *split* (**sĕcare**); **subdĭ-t-ivus**, *supposititious* (**sub-dĕre**); **vō-t-ivus**, *vowed* (**vō-vere**); and others little used.

(*b*) Technical terms in rhetoric, grammar, &c.: **defīnī-tivus**, *explanatory* (**defīnīre**); **demonstrā-tivus**, *expository* (**demonstrā-re**); **hortā-tivus**, *hortatory* (**hortā-ri**); **laudā-tivus**, *laudatory* (**laudā-re**); **rătiōcĭnā-tivus**, *of reasoning* (**rătiōcĭnā-ri**); **translā-tivus**, *transferred* (**translāto-**); and others. Similarly in grammar (in Quintilian), ablātivus, accusātivus, gĕnĕtivus, dătivus, nōmĭnātivus, possessivus, rĕlātivus; and others in later writers.

2. Substantives: dōnativum (post-Aug.), *a largess* (dōnā-re).

-vi   ăvis (f.), *a bird;* brĕvis, *short* (comp. βραχύς, § 129); 765
cīvis (m.), *a citizen* (comp. qvi-es, κεῖ-μαι, Curt.);
clāvis (f.), *a key* (comp. claudĕre, κλείς, κληΐς); grăvis, *heavy* (comp.
βαρύς, as glans with βάλανος); lĕvis, *light* (comp. ἐλαχύς, § 129);
nāvis (f.), *a ship* (comp. ναῦς); nĭv- (nom. nix., f.; cf. § 129. 2 c);
snow (comp. νιφ-ετός); pelvis (f.), *a basin;* rāvis (f.), *hoarseness*
(comp. rau-cus); svā-vis, *sweet* (comp. svād-us, ἡδ-ύς); tĕnvis, *thin*
(comp. ten-dĕre, tĕn-er, ταναός).

-ui   grus (f.), *a crane* (comp. γέρανος); lues (f.), *pestilence*
(comp. λοιμός); strues (f.), *a heap* (comp. stru-ere, sternĕre); sus (m. f.), *a pig* (comp. ὗς).

v. *Stems ending in* -fo.

offa, *a morsel;* rūfus, *red;* scrōfa, *a sow;* tōfus, *tufa stone.*   766

CHAPTER IV.

GUTTURAL NOUN-STEMS.

i. Stems ending[1] in -co, -qvo; -cu, -ci, -qvi; -c, -qv.

1. *Stems ending in* -co, -qvo.

-co   1. Adjectives:

æqvus, *level;* averruncus, *averting;* cæcus, *blind;* cascus, 767
old; cōruscus, *flashing;* flaccus, *flabby;* fuscus, *dark coloured;* lusous, *one-eyed;* mancus, *maimed;* parcus, *thrifty;* paucus, *few* (comp.
παῦ-ρος); Plancus (plano-?); priscus, *ancient* (prius); raucus (for
rāvicus), *hoarse* (rāvi-); rĕcĭprŏcus, *backwards and forwards* (rĕco, prŏ-co, derivatives of re and pro; Key, *Essays,* p. 74 sq.); siccus,

[1] On suffixes with -c see Key, *Philol. Soc. Trans.* for 1856.

dry (for sĭtĭ-cus from sĭtĭs, *thirst?*); spurcus, *dirty;* truncus, *lopped;* vescus, *small.*

2. Substantives:

(*a*) Masculine: ăbăcus, *a board* (comp. ἄβαξ); arcus (arqvus), *a bow* (see § 395); circus, *a ring* (κρίκος); cŏcus (coqvus), *a cook;* ēcus (eqvus), *a horse* (comp. ἵππος, § 118); fiscus, *a basket;* floccus, *a flock of wool;* fŏcus, *a hearth;* fūcus (1), *seaweed* (comp. φῦκος, Hom.); (2) *a drone;* hircus, *a goat;* jŏcus, *a joke;* juncus, *a bulrush;* jŭven-cus, *a bullock* (jŭvĕn-); lăcus, *a pool* (cf. §§ 395, 776); lŏcus, *a place;* lūcus, *a grove;* maccus, *a clown* (comp. μακκοᾶν, *to moan*); Marcus, *hammer?* a Roman prænomen; mūcus, *snot* (comp. mungĕre); pīcus, *a woodpecker;* porcus, *a pig;* prŏcus, *a suitor* (comp. prĕcā-ri); saccus, *a bag* (comp. σάκκος); soccus, *a slipper;* sūcus, *juice* (comp. ὀπός, § 107); sulcus, *a furrow* (comp. ὁλκός, ἕλκειν); truncus, *a lopt stem* (see above); vīcus, *a street* (comp. οἶκος); vopiscus (see Plin. 7. 10, § 8).

Roman family names: Murcus; Casca (comp. cascus, *old*); Sĕnĕca (sĕnĕc-, *old*); Tucca.

(*b*) Feminine: fīcus, *a fig-tree;* ruscus (or ruscum, n.?) *butcher's broom.*

ăqva, *water;* arca, *a chest* (comp. arcēre, ἀρκεῖν); bāca, *a berry;* braccæ (pl.), *breeches;* bucca, *a cheek;* esca, *food* (ĕd-, ĕdĕre, esse, *to eat*); furca, *a fork;* jŭvenca, *a heifer* (see above); labrusca, *a wild vine;* mărisca, *a kind of fig;* mīca, *a grain;* mollusca, *a soft nut* (molli-); musca, *a fly* (comp. μυῖα for μυσία?); orca, *a whale, a tun;* Parcæ (pl.), *Fates* (from par-ti-, *the apportioners?* comp. μοῖραι, μέρος: or eulogistic from parc-ĕre, *to spare?*); porca, (1) *a furrow;* (2) *a farrow,* i. e. *a sow* (cf. Key, *Essays,* p. 95); posca, *an acid drink;* rīca, *a woman's veil;* sīca, *a dagger;* spīca, *an ear of corn;* trīcæ (pl.), *trifles;* vacca, *a cow.*

(*c*) Neuter: molluscum, *a fungus* (molli-); naucum (?), *a trifle* (?); tesca (tesqva, pl.), *waste places;* viscum, *mistletoe* (comp. ἰξός).

ĭ-co   i.e. (usually) -co, suffixed to vowel stems.

1. Adjectives: Afrĭ-cus, *of the Afri* (Afro-); belli-cus, *of war* (bello-); cīvĭ-cus, *of a citizen* (cīvĭ-); classi-cus, *of a class,* esp. *the fleet* (classi-); Crēti-cus, *of Crete* (Crēta-); dŏmĭni-cus, *of a master* (dŏmĭno-); fullŏn-ĭcus, *of a fuller* (fullŏn-); Germāni-cus, *of Germans* (Germāno-); lubricus, *slippery;* mangŏn-icus (Plin., Suet.), *of a dealer* (mangŏn-); mĕdĭ-cus, *of healing* (mĕdĕ-, mĕdēri); mŏdĭ-cus, *moderate* (mŏdo-); publi-cus, *public* (pŏpŭlo-, cf. § 69); sonti-cus, *dangerous* (sonti-, *guilty*); tĕtri-cus, *rough* (comp. tætro-?); vāricus (Ov.), *straddling* (vāro-); ūnĭ-cus, *single* (ūno-); urbi-cus, *of the city* (urbi-).

Common in Greek words; e.g. cōmicus, grammăticus, poēticus, &c.

768

2. Substantives:

(*a*) Masculine: vīli-cus (vīlica), *a farm steward* (villa-).

(*b*) Feminine: ălica (halica), *spelt;* brassica, *cabbage;* fabri-ca, *a manufacture* (fabro-); fŏrīcæ (pl.), see Juv. 3. 38; fūlīca (fulix), *a coot;* mäni-cæ (pl.), *gloves, handcuffs* (mänu-); pĕd-ica, *a snare* (pĕd-, *foot*); ridica, *a vineprop;* sīliqva, *a pod;* sublīca, *a pile* for a bridge, &c.; tŭnica, *a shirt;* vŏmi-ca, *a running abscess* (vŏmĕre, cf. § 698).

(*c*) toxĭcum, *poison,* orig. for smearing *arrows* (τόξον).

-tĭ-co   i. e. -co added to real or presumed adjectives in -to.   769

1. Adjectives: dŏmesticus, *of home* (dŏmo-; comp. mŏdestus, § 789; agrestis, § 808); Ligus-ticus, *of the Ligurians* (Ligus-); rus-ticus, *of the country* (rūs-).

2. Substantives: can-ticum, *a song* (can-to-, cănĕre); mantĭca, *a bag;* pertica, *a pole;* scŭtica, *a whip* (comp. scūtum, *a leathern shield*); trī-ticum (*threshed*) *wheat, corn* (trī-to-, tĕrĕre).

-ātĭ-co   1. Adjectives: ăquāticus, *living in* or *near water* (ăqua-);   770 erraticus, *wandering* (errāre); fānaticus, *inspired* (fāno-); lymphāticus, *of the frenzied* (lymphāto-, lympha-); silvaticus, *of a wood* (silva-); vēnaticus, *for hunting* (vēnāri-); umbraticus, *of the shade* (umbra-); vŏlaticus, *winged* (vŏlā-re, *to fly*).

2. Substantives: viāticum, *journey-supplies.* (via-; comp. viātor).

-lĭ-co }
-lcɔ }   1. Adjectives: fămē-licus, *starving* (fămē-); hiu-lcus,   771 *gaping* (hiā-re; cf. § 204. 2 *e*); pĕtu-lcus, *frolicsome* (pĕt-ĕre, cf. § 657, and comp. pĕtŭl-ans).

2. Substantives: bŭbul-cus, *an ox-tender,* i.e. *a ploughman* (bŏv- whence bŭbŭlus, cf. § 76. 2); sub-ulcus, *a swineherd* (su- for sŏv-? or perhaps the word is simply formed in imitation of bubulcus); rēmulcum (only in abl. s.), *a towrope* (probably from Greek; comp. ῥυμουλκεῖν, Polyb.).

-rĭ-co }
-r-co }   vitrĭcus, *a stepfather;* nŏverca, *a stepmother* (nŏvo-; comp. νέος, νεαρός).

-in-qvo}
-īqvo }   Adjectives: ant-īqvus, *ancient* (for antinqvus? from   772 ante, but cf. § 774); long-inqvus, *distant* (longo-); prŏp-inqvus, *near* (prŏpe).

(In oblīqvus the q is radical; comp. līc-īnus, λέχ-ριος).

-āco   mĕr-acus, *pure* (of wine without water; mĕro-); ŏp-   773 acus, *shady;* clo-aca, *a sewer* (cluere old = purgare: comp. κλύ-ζειν).

-ūco   ær-uca, *verdigris* (æs-); căd-ucus, *falling* (căd-ĕre); car-ruca, *a carriage;* ēruca, *a caterpillar, colewort;* festuca, *a stalk;* fistuca, *a pile-driver;* lact-uca, *a lettuce* (lactĭ-); mand-ucus, *a chewer* (mand-ĕre); mastruca (Sardinian), *a sheepskin;* sabucus (sambucus), f., *elder-tree;* verruca, *a wart.*

-īco   The ī seems to be at least in some cases the result of con- 77+ traction with a final vowel; e.g. = oi, ei, &c.

1. Adjectives: ăm-icus, *friendly* (amā-re); ant-icus, *in front* (ante); ăpr-icus, *sunny;* mend-icus, *of beggars;* post-icus, *behind* (post, old poste); pŭd-icus, *shamefast* (pŭdēre).

2. Substantives: formica, *an ant;* lect-ica, *a sedan* (lecto-); lōr-ica, *a breast-plate* (of leathern *thongs;* lōro-); lumbricus, *a worm;* Nas-ica (m.), (năso-); rubr-ica, *red paint, red heading* (rubro-); vēsica, *a bladder;* umbĭl-ícus, *the navel* (comp. ὀμφαλός); urtica, *a nettle* (comp. ŭr-ĕre). See also in § 767. 2 b.

i-āco   Ægypt-ĭ-ăcus, *of Ægypt* (Ægypto-); Cŏrinthiacus, *of Co-* 775 *rinth* (Cŏrintho-); Nīl-ĭ-ăcus, *of the Nile* (Nīlo-).

2. Stems ending in -cu, -ci, -c.

-cu   See § 395. ăcus (m. f.), *a needle* (comp. āc-ĕr, ἀκ-ωκή); 776 arcus (m.), *a bow;* fīcus (f.), *a figtree;* lăcus (m.), *a pool* (comp. lăcūna, lā-ma, λάκ-ος, λάκκος); pĕcu (n.), *a head of cattle;* portĭcus (f.), *a colonnade* (comp. portu-); qvercus (f.), *an oak;* spĕcus (m.), *a cave* (comp. σπέος).

-ci   arx (f.), *a citadel* (comp. arcēre); calx (f.), (1) *chalk,* (2) *a heel;* dulcis, *sweet* (comp. γλυκύς); fascis (m.), *a bundle;* fæx (f.), *dregs;* fauces (m. pl.), *throat;* lanx (f.), *a dish;* lux (f.), *light;* merx (f.), *merchandise;* piscis (m.), *a fish;* torqvis (m.), *a collar* (comp. torqvēre, *to twist*).

-c   crux (f.), *a cross;* dux (m.), *a leader;* fax (f.), *a link;* frăces (m. pl.), *oil-dregs;* nex (f.), *death;* nux (f.), *a nut;* pix (f.), *pitch* (comp. πίσσα and § 839 b); prex (not found in nom. s.) (f.), *a prayer;* trux, *cruel;* vĭc-em (m. f.), *a change;* vox (f.), *a voice.*

-ĕc (-ĭc)   This is a *diminutival* suffix, and forms substantives. 777

ăpex (m.), *the top point;* cărex (f.), *sedge;* caudex, cōdex (m.), *a tree-trunk, wooden tablets;* cīmex (m.), *a bug;* cort-ex (m. f.), *bark of a tree;* cŭlex (m.), *a gnat;* forfex (m. f.), *scissors;* frŭtex (m.), *a shrub;* īlex (f.), *an ilex;* imbr-ex (m.), *a tile* (imbrĭ-); lătex (m.), *water;* mūrex (m.), *the purple fish;*

pæl-ex, **pel-ex** (f.), *a concubine* (a transcription of πάλλαξ); **pŏdex**
(m. **pēd-ĕre**); **poʟex** (m.), *a thumb;* **pūlex** (m.), *a flea* (comp.
ψύλλα); **pŭmex** (m.), *a pumice stone;* **rāmex** (m.), *a (branching)*
bloodvessel (**rămo-**); **rŭmex** (m. f.), *sorrel;* **sĕn-ex** (m.), *an old man*
(comp. ἕνος); **sīlex** (m. f.), *flint;* **sorex** (m.), *a shrew mouse* (comp.
ὕραξ); **vort-ex**, **vert-ex** (m.), *a whirl, the top of a thing* (**vert-ĕre**).

(**Ju-dex**, **arti-fex**, **au-spex**, **simplex**, &c. are compounds; **obices**
from **obīcere**; **illex** from **illīcere**. See § 395.)

-ĭc   **append-ix** (f.), *an appendage* (**append-ĕre**); **fīlix** (f.), *a*   778
fern; **forn-ix** (m.), *a vault* (**forno-**, *an oven*); **larix**,
a larch; **sălix**, *a willow* (comp. ἑλίκη); **var-ix**, *a dilated vein*
(**vāro-**); and a few others (see § 440).

-ăci   1. Adjectives; almost all from verb stems: 779
    aud-ax, *daring* (**audēre**); **căp-ax**, *capacious* (**căpĕ-re**);
contŭm-ax, *obstinate* (**tŭmēre**); **dīc-ax**, *witty* (**dīc-**, comp. **maledīc-us**);
ĕd-ax, *eating away* (**ĕd-ĕre**); **effīc-ax**, *effectual* (**făcĕ-re**); **ĕmax**,
fond of making purchases (**ĕm-ĕre**); **fall-ax**, *deceptive* (**fall-ĕre**);
fĕr-ax, *fruitful* (**fĕr-re**); **fŭg-ax**, *runaway* (**fŭgĕ-re**); **fūr-ax**, *thievish*
(**furā-ri**); **lŏqv-ax**, *talkative* (**loqvi**); **mend-ax**, *lying* (comp. **men-**
tī-ri); **mĭn-ax**, *threatening* (**minā-ri**); **mord-ax**, *biting* (**mor-dēre**);
nŭg-ax, *trifling* (**nugā-ri**); **prŏc-ax**, *forward* in manner (**prŏcā-re**);
pugn-ax, *quarrelsome* (**pugnā-re**); **răp-ax**, *rapacious* (**răpĕ-re**);
săg-ax, *sagacious* (comp. **præ-săgī-re**); **săl-ax**, *lustful* (**salīre**);
sĕqv-ax, *pursuing* (**seqvi**); **perspĭc-ax**, *clear-sighted* (**spĕcĕ-re**); **tăg-**
ax, *light-fingered* (**tag-**, **tangere**); **tĕn-ax**, *tenacious* (**tĕnēre**); **vēr-ax**,
truthful (**vēro-**); **pervīc-ax**, *stubborn* (**vĭnc-ĕre**); **vīv-ax**, *lifefull, long-*
lived (**vīv-ĕre**); **vŏr-ax**, *voracious* (**vŏrā-re**); and some others little
used.

2. Substantives: **forn-ax** (f.), *a kiln* (**forno-**); **pax** (f.), *peace.*
Also (with suffix -āc): **līm-ax** (f.), *a slug* (**limo-**).

-ŏci   Adjectives: **atr-ox**, *cruel* (**atro-**, *black*); **fĕr-ox**, *high-*   780
spirited (**fēro-**, *wild*); **solox**, *coarse* (of wool, only in
Festus); **vēl-ox**, *swift* (**vŏlā-re?**).

    Substantive: **cĕl-ox** (f.), *a yacht* (comp. **cĕl-er**, κέλης).

-ēc   **ālex** (f.), *fish brine;* **verv-ex** (m.), *a wether.*

-ĭci   1. Adjectives: **fēl-ix**, *happy;* **pernix**, *active* (**nī-ti**, cf.   781
§ 707).

-īc   2. Substantives; all feminine.
    cervix, *a neck-bone* (?), *the neck;* **cor-n-ix**, *a crow* (comp.
cor-vus, κορ-ών-η, κόρ-αξ); **cŏturnix**, *a quail;* **cox-end-ix**
(f.), *the hip* (**coxa-**); **jŭn-ix**, *a heifer* (**jŭvĕn-**); **lŏdix**, *a*

blanket; **rād-ix**, *a root* (comp. ῥίζα, and perhaps ῥαδινός, *taper,*
rā-mus); **stru-ix** (f.), *a heap* (**strui-**, **stru-ĕre**); **vībix**, *a weal.*

mātr-ix (f.), *a breeder* (**māter**); **nūtr-ix** (f.), *nurse* (**nutrīre**),
are formed as if analogous to the words in the next section.

-t-r-ĭc ⎰
(-t-r-īcĭ) ⎱ Semi-adjectival feminine substantives corresponding to
nouns in -tŏr. The **t** is the suffix of supine, &c. When
used as adjectives they have -ĭ stems (e. g. **victrīcia**, § 414). 782

accusā-trix (Plaut. twice), *accuser* (**accusā-**); **adjū-trix**, *helper*
(**adjŭva-re**); **al-trix**, *nourisher* (**ăl-ĕre**); **āmā-trix** (Plaut., Mart.),
a mistress (**amā-re**); **bellā-trix**, *a warrior* (**bellā-re**); **cīcā̆trix**, *a
scar;* **conservā-trix** (Cic. once), *preserver* (**servā-re**); **contem-p-trix**,
despising (**contemn-ĕre**); **creā-trix**, *a creator* (**creā-re**); **cul-trix**, *a
cultivator* (**cŏl-ĕre**); **ēdŭcā-trix**, *trainer* (**edŭcā-re**); **expul-trix**, *ex-
peller* (**pell-ĕre, pul-sum**, § 152. 3); **gĕnĕ-trix**, *a mother* (**gĕn-, gignĕre**); **gŭberna-trix**, *directress* (**gubernā-re**); **imperā-trix**, *commander*
(**imperā-re**); **indāgā-trix**, *a tracker out* (**indāgā-re**); **inven-trix**, *discoverer* (**vĕn-ī-re**); **mĕrĕ-trix**, *a courtesan* (**mĕrēre**); **mŏlī-trix** (Suet.),
a contriver (**mŏlī-ri**); **nā-trix**, *a water-snake* (**nā-re**); **obstĕ-trix**,
a midwife (**stāre**, cf. § 645); **oratrix**, *a suppliant* (**orāre**); **receptrix**,
a receiver (**recipere**); **tex-trix** (Mart.), *webster,* i.e. *female weaver*
(**tex-ĕre**); **tons-trix**, *a barber* (**tondēre**, § 160. 3); **venā-trix**, *hunt-
ress* (**vēnāri**); **vic-trix**, *conquering* (**vincĕre**); **ul-trix**, *avenging*
(**ulc-isci**, cf. § 110. 2); and some others.

In Plautus also **cistellatrix**, *a casket-woman* (**cistella-**); **præsti-
giatrix**, *a conjurer* (**præstigia**).

Compound stem-endings: **-cōso, -īcŭlōso**, § 814; **-cundo**, § 820;
-cīno, -ciōn, §§ 840, 853; **-cŭlo, -uncŭlo, -uscŭlo**, §§ 862—864;
-cĕro, -cĕrĭ, §§ 887, 902; **-āceo, -ūceo**, §§ 920, 921; **-cio, -tīcio,
-cīnio**, §§ 930, 931, 936.

---

ii. *Stems ending in* -go, -gvo; -gĭ, -g, -gvi. 783

In most of these words the **g** belongs to the *stem.*

-go 1. Adjectives: **largus**, *bountiful;* **longus**, *long;* **sāgus**
(usually **sāga**, f.), *foretelling* (comp. **săg-āx**); **văgus**, *wandering;* **valgus**, *bow-legged* (comp. **văr-us**).

2. Substantives:

alga, *seaweed;* **bulga**, *a bag* (Gallic word); **călĭga**, *a half-boot*
(comp. **calc-eus**); **fāgus** (f.), *a beech-tree* (comp. φηγός, *oak*); **frāga**
(pl.), *strawberries;* **fŭg-a**, *flight* (comp. φυγή); **fungus**, *a mushroom*
(comp. σφόγγος); **jŭg-um**, *a yoke* (comp. ζύγον, § 141); **merg-us**,

a diver-fowl (merg-ĕre); **mergæ** (pl.), a *two-prong* fork; **nūgæ**
(pl.), *trifles* (comp. **nauco-**); **pāgus**, *a village;* **plāga**, (1) *a region*,
(2) *a snare;* **plāg-a**, *a blow* (comp. **pla*n*g-ĕre**, πλήσσειν, πληγή);
rŏgus, *a funeral pile* (rĕg-ĕre); **rūga**, *a wrinkle;* **săgum**, *a soldier's
blanket*, said by Polybius to be a Celtic word; but comp. σάγη,
harness); **strīg-a**, *a swathe* (comp. **stri*n*g-ĕre**); **tergum**, *a back;*
tŏg-a, *a cloak* (tĕg-ĕre); **virga**, *a switch* (comp. **vir-ĕre?**); **volgus**
(n. § 338), *folk.*

-gvo   **lingva**, *the tongue* (**li*n*gĕre**, *to lick*).

-gi   **ambāges** (f. pl.), *goings round about* (amb, **ăg-ĕre**); com-   784
pāges (f.), *a fastening* (**compa*n*g-ĕre**); **contāges** (f.), *contagion* (com, **ta*n*g-ĕre**); **jūgis** (adj.), *fresh;* **propāges** (f.),
offspring (comp. **propāgā-re**); **strā-ges** (f.), *destruction*
(comp. **sternĕre**, **strā-to-**).

-g   **conjunx**, *a consort* (com, **jŭg-**); **frūg-em** (f. no nom. sing.),
fruit, corn; **grex** (m.), *a flock;* **lex** (f.), *a law* (**lĕg-ĕre**, *to
choose?*); **rex** (m.), *a king* (**rĕg-ĕre**); **strix** (f.), *a screech-owl.*

-gvi   **angvis** (m. f.), *a snake* (comp. ἔχις); **ni*n*gvis** (f. **nix**), *snow*
(comp. νιφ-ετός); **pingvis**, *fat* (comp. παχύς); **ungvis**
(m.), *a nail* (comp. ὄνυξ).

Compound stem-endings: **-gno**, § 826; **-gŏn**, **-āgŏn**, **-īlāgŏn**,
-ūgŏn, **-īgŏn**, § 845; **-gneo**, § 922.

---

iii. *Stems ending in* -ho, -hi.

trăha, *a sledge;* **vĕhes**, *a cart load* (vĕh-ĕre).   785

CHAPTER V.

DENTAL NOUN-STEMS.

i. *Stems ending in* -to (*or* -so *when presumably arisen from
a dental*).

-to   Adjectives of *quantity:*

qvan-tus, *how great* (quam); **qvar-tus**, *fourth* (for   786
qvatvortus from **qvattvor**); **qvīn-tus** (or **qvīnctus**), *fifth* (**qvinqve**);
quŏ-tus, *how great* (*a part*), i.e. *what number* (qvo-, comp. **qvot**);
sex-tus, *sixth* (**sex**); **tan-tus**, *so great* (**tam**); **tŏ-tus**, *so many-th;*
tōtus, *whole.*
Comp. **is-tus** (**iste**), *that;* **ipsus** (**ipse**), *self.*

-to (-so)   1. Adjectives: 787

(a) Participles, expressing *completed action, done* in the case of deponent verbs, and some others (§§ 734, 735); *suffered* in the case of verbs having also an active voice, and in many deponents (§ 734). See full list in §§ 689—709. Also §§ 734, 735.

(b) Participles, or words of similar formation, used as adjectives of quality. (For -āto, &c. see below, § 796.)

al-sus, *cool* (alg-ēre); al-tus, *high* (ăl-ĕre, *to nourish*); ap-tus, *fit* (ăpi-sc-i); artus, *narrow* (arcēre, *to confine*); assus, *roast* (comp. ἄζω); blæsus, *lisping* (comp. βλαισός, *bandy-legged*); brūtus, *brute;* cassus, *empty;* castus, *chaste* (comp. καθᾰρός); cătus, *sharp;* cel-sus, *high* (cell-ĕre, *to strike?*); cer-tus, *sure* (cern-ĕre); crassus, *thick;* cunctus, *all* (covinc-īre); curtus, *docked* (comp. κείρω); dēcrĕpĭtus (*that has cracked off?*), *worn out* (crepāre); densus, *thick* (comp. δασ-ύς); dierectus (Plaut.), *crucified,* usually dierecte; vocative? or adverb? (always trisyll. dis-erĭgĕre?); dīser-tus, *fluent* (dissĕrĕre? *to discuss*); ēlixus, *boiled* (comp. laxus, prolixus); fal-sus, *false* (fallĕre); fastus (nĕfastus), *lawful* (fas); fessus, *weary* (făti-sc-i, *to gape*); fes-tus, *festive* (comp. fēr-iæ); fē-tus, *pregnant* (comp. fē-mina, fē-cundus, § 99); frētus, *relying* (fer-re? cf. § 692); glūtus, *tenacious, soft* (§ 690); grātus, *pleasing;* hirtus, *shaggy;* in-fes-tus, *set on* (cf. § 704. n.); invītus, *unwilling* (for in-vic-tus? comp. Ϝεκ-, ἑκών); ir-rī-tus, *ineffectual* (rēri); justus, *just* (jūs-); lætus, *cheerful;* lassus, *tired;* lātus, *broad* (for tlātus, *borne,* cf. § 176. 3); laxus, *loose;* luxus, *dislocated* (comp. λοξός); lau-tus, *splendid* (lăvāre); lentus, *pliant;* mac-tus, *made great* (comp. magnus); mæstus, *sad* (mærēre); mănĭfestus, *hand-struck,* i.e. *palpable* (§ 704. n.); multus, *much;* mustus, *new;* mūtus, *dumb* (comp. mussāre; also μύειν, *to close* the eyes); ŏbēsus (*overeaten,* i.e.), *fat* (ĕd-ĕre), pætus, *blink-eyed;* pĕr-ōsus, *hating* (cf. p. 252); plautus, *flat;* pūtus, *cleared, quite* (comp. pŭ-tāre, § 964); russus, *red* (comp. ἐρυθ-ρός); sal-sus, *salt* (sălīre); sanctus, *holy, good* (sanc-īre); sentus, *squalid* (comp. sentīna); sī-tus, *placed* (sĭn-ĕre); spissus, *crowded;* stultus, *foolish* (comp. stŏlĭdus); sŭbĭtus, *sudden* (subīre); sublestus (Plaut.), *weak;* tăcĭtus, *silent* (tăcēre); ter-sus, *neat* (tergere, *to wipe*); vastus, *waste, huge;* vĕgĕ-tus, *active* (§ 693).

2. Substantives: 788

(a) Masculine: accensus, *an apparitor* (orig. *supernumerary,* Mommsen, accensēre); cossus, *a worm;* also as proper name (from *wrinkled* skin); dĭgĭtus, *a finger* (comp. δάκτυλος, δεικνύειν, dīcĕre, dĭc-āre, prodĭgium); fūsus, *a spindle;* grossus, *an unripe fig;* guttus (gūtus), *a bottle;* hortus, *a garden* (cf. § 134); lăcertus, (1) *the muscle of the upper arm;* (2) *a lizard;* lectus, *a couch* (comp. λέχος, λέκτρον); līber-tus, *a freedman* (lībĕro-); nāsus (nāsum), *a nose* (comp. nāris); ventus, *wind;* ursus, *a bear* (comp. ἄρκτος).

lānista, *a trainer of gladiators* (comp. cǐthărista, κιθαρισ-τής):
lixa, *a camp-follower.*

Bassus; Cotta (for cocta?); Natta; Pansa, *splay-foot*? (pand-ĕre).
(*b*) Feminine: buxus, *box-tree;* taxus, *yew.*

ămīta, *a father's sister;* ansa, *a handle;* antistǐ-ta, *a priestess*
(ante, stăto-); ărista, *the beard of corn;* ballista, *a military engin?*
(βάλλειν); bēta, *beet;* blatta, *a moth;* capsa, *a box* (cǎp-ĕre?); cā-
tasta, *a platform;* causa, *a cause;* cĕrussa, *white lead* (as if κηρόεσ-
σα?); charta, *paper* (χάρτης); costa, *a rib;* coxa, *the hip* (comp.
κοχώνη); crēta, *chalk;* crista, *a crest;* crusta, *rind, shell,* &c.; cŭ-
curbǐta, *a gourd;* culcǐta, *a pillow;* fossa, *a ditch* (fŏdĕ-re); gutta,
a drop; hasta, *a spear;* hospǐta, *a guest;* impen-sa (sc. pecunia),
expense (impend-ĕre); instǐta, *a flounce* or *band;* jŭven-ta, *youth*
(jŭvĕn-); matta, *a mat;* mensa, *a table;* mēta, *a cone;* multa, *a
fine;* nŏta, *a mark* (cf. § 647); noxa, *hurt* (nŏc-ĕre); offen-sa, *a
striking against* (offend-ĕre); orbǐta, *a wheel track* (orbi-); pausa,
a pause (παύειν); planta, *a sprout, the sole of the foot;* porta, *a gate;*
prætex-ta (sc. toga), *a bordered robe* (prætex-ĕre); prōsa (sc. oratio), *prose* (pro-vert-ere, cf. § 191. 2); rĕpul-sa, *a repulse* (repell-
ĕre); rixa, *a quarrel* (comp. ἔριδ-); rŏsa, *a rose* (comp. ῥόδον);
rŏta, *a wheel;* rūta, *rue* (comp. ῥυτή); sæta, *a bristle;* săgitta,
an arrow; sec-ta, *a party* (sĕcāre or sĕqvi?); sēmǐta, *a path;*
secespita, *a knife;* Sospǐta (epithet of Juno), *Preserver;* sporta,
a basket (comp. σπυρίδ-); tensa, *a sacred chariot;* testa, *a potsherd*
(for tors-ta, from torrē-re?); ton-sa, *an oar* (tund-ĕre); Vesta,
hearth-goddess (comp. ūr-ere, us-tum; Ἑστία); vindicta, (1) *rod*
used in the ceremony of manumission; (2) *revenge* (vindĕc-); vīta,
life; vitta, *a fillet* (comp. viēre); vŏlū-ta, *a scroll* in architecture
(volv-ēre).

(*c*) Neuter: arbŭtum, *wild strawberry;* bus-tum, *a tomb* (comp.
com-būr-ĕre); compǐtum, *a crossroad* (com-pĕt-ĕre?); cŭbǐ-tum, *the
elbow* (cŭbāre); dēfrūtum, *must boiled down* (defervere?); dic-tum,
a saying (dīc-ĕre); dorsum, *a back;* exta (pl.), *heart, liver,* &c. (for
ex-sec-ta?); fā-tum, *destiny* (fā-ri); frētum, *a sea strait;* frustum,
a broken piece (comp. θραύειν, § 99. 6); furtum, *a theft* (fūr-); lētum,
death; lŭ-tum, *mud* (comp. lăv-āre); lūtum, *a yellow dye;* mentum,
the chin (comp. e-mǐnēre, *to project*); ŏmāsum, *bullock's tripe* (a
Gallic word); pas-sum, *raisin wine* (pand-ĕre, *to spread out* to dry);
pen-sum, *a task* (pend-ĕre, *to weigh*); pessum (only acc.), *ground*
(pĕd-, *foot*); porten-tum, *a portent* (portend-ĕre); prătum, *a
meadow;* prosecta (pl.), *parts cut off,* e.g. for sacrifice (prosĕcāre);
pulpǐtum, *a scaffold;* punc-tum, *a point* (pung-ĕre, *to prick*); sæp-
tum, *a fence* (sæp-īre); saxum, *a rock;* scortum, *a whore* (orig.
a hide acc. to Varro; comp. cŏr-ium); scrūta (pl.), *trash;* scūtum,
a leather-covered shield (comp. σκῦτος); sugges-tum, *a platform*
(suggĕr-ere); tec-tum, *a house* (tĕg-ĕre); tes-tum, *a pot-lid* (torrēre); vervactum, *a fallow-field;* virgultum, *a thicket* (virg-ŭl-a-);
vŏ-tum, *a vow* (vŏv-ēre).

-us-to   i.e. -to appended to a suffix in -os, -us (-or, -ur).   789

angus-tus, *narrow* (angŏr-, ang-ĕre; comp. ἄγχειν, *to throttle*); aug-us-tus, *consecrated* (aug-ur-); faus-tus, *propitious* (fă-vōr-); ŏn-us-tus, *laden* (ŏnŭs-); rŏb-us-tus, *strong* (rŏbŏr-); vĕn-us-tus, *pretty* (vĕnŭs-); vĕtus-tus, *ancient* (vetŭs-).

-es-to   i.e. -to appended to a suffix -os or -us.

fūn-es-tus, *deadly* (fūn-ŭs-); hŏn-es-tus, *honourable* (hŏn-ŏ-s); intempes-tus, *unseasonable* (in tempŏs-); mŏd-es-tus, *modest* (modo-; comp. mŏd-ĕr-ā-rī); mŏl-es-tus, *troublesome* (*exhausting*, from mŏl-ĕre, *to grind?*); scĕl-es-tus, *wicked* (scĕlŭs-).

-c-to   i.e. -to appended to the suffix -ĕc, -ĭc.   790

1. Adjectives: senectus (Plaut.), *old* (sen-ec-); hence senecta, sc. ætas, *old age;* ūmectus, *moist* (comp. ŭm-ēre).

2. Substantives: căr-ec-tum, *reed beds* (căr-ĕc-); dŭm-ec-tum (Fest.), old for dumetum (§ 798. 2); frutec-tum (also in Col. frutetum; comp. fruticetum, § 798. 2), *shrubbery* (frŭtĕc-); săl-ic-tum, *a willow bed* (sălĭc-); vīr-ec-tum, *greenery* (vīr-ēre).

-en-to   1. Adjectives: cru-entus, *bloody* (comp. cru-or).   791

2. Substantives: (*a*) feminine: pŏlenta, *pearl barley* (pollĕn-; comp. πάλη); plăcenta, *a cake* (probably from acc. of πλακοῦς).

(*b*) Neuter: arg-entum, *silver* (comp. ἀργός, *white*); carpentum, *a covered two-wheeled carriage;* flu-entum, *a stream* (flu-ĕre); pilentum, *a covered four-wheeled carriage;* tălentum, *a balance* (τάλαντον); ungven-tum, *ointment* (ungvĕn-).

So the names of towns: Agrigentum ('Ακραγαντ-, nom. 'Ακράγας); Bux-entum, *Boxgrove* (buxo-; Πυξοεντ-, nom. Πυξοῦς); Grūm-entum, *Hill-town?* (grūmo-); Laur-entum, *Laurel grove?* (lauro-); Tărentum (Τάρας); comp. Sipontum (Σιποῦς).

-m-en-to   i.e. -to appended to the suffix -mĕn (§ 850).   792
Substantives, (*a*) neuter: usually derived from verbs. Many are used chiefly in the plural.

ălĭ-mentum, *nourishment* (ăl-ĕre); āmentum, *a javelin thong,* (for ăpĭ-mentum, *a fitting?* comp. ap-tus, ἄπτειν); argŭ-mentūm, *a proof* (argu-ĕre); armā-menta (pl.), *tackle* (armā-re); ar-mentum, *a plough beast* (ărā-re); atramentum, *ink* (atro-); auctōrā-mentum, *hire* (auctōrā-rī); blandī-mentum, *soothing* (blandī-re); cæ-mentum, *quarried stone* (cæd-ĕre); calceā-mentum, *a shoe* (calceāre); căpillā-mentum, *hair* (capillo-); coag-mentum, *a joining* (coăg-ĕre); cognō-mentum, *a surname* (cogno-sc-ĕre); complē-mentum (rare), *a filling up* (complē-re); dehŏnesta-mentum, *a disgrace* (dehŏnestā-re); dē-trī-mentum, *a loss by wear* (detĕr-ĕre; comp. detrī-tus); dŏcŭ-men-

19

tum, *a lesson* (dŏcēre); ĕlĕ-menta (pl.), *first principles* (*means of growth?* comp. ŏlescere); ēmŏlŭ-mentum, *gain* (*by grinding;* emŏl-ĕre); expĕrī-mentum, *a test* (expĕrī-ri); fer-mentum, *yeast* (fervere); ferrā-mentum, *an iron implement* (comp. ferrā-tus); fō-mentum, *poultice,* &c. (fŏvēre); frāg-mentum, *a fragment* (fra*ng*-ĕre); frū-mentum, *corn* (comp. frūges); fundā-mentum, *a groundwork* (fundā-re); incĭtā-mentum, *an incentive* (incĭtāre); incrē-mentum, *increase, germ* (incre-sc-ere); instrŭ-mentum, *stock of implements, a means* (instru-ĕre); intertrī-mentum, *waste by rubbing* (cf. detrimentum); irrītā-mentum, *an incentive* (irrītā-re); jū-mentum, *a beast of draught* (ju*ng*-ĕre; comp. jŭg-um); lā-menta (pl.), *lamentation* (for clāmāmenta? cf. § 110. 3); lĕvā-mentum, *a relief* (lĕvā-re); lō-mentum, *a wash* (lăv-āre); māchĭnā-mentum, *a machine* (machĭnā-re); mō-mentum, *motion, impulse* (mŏvēre); mŏnŭ-mentum, *a memorial* (monēre); nūtrī-mentum, *nourishment* (nūtrī-re); ō-mentum, *a fat membrane;* ŏpĕri-mentum, *a lid* (ŏpĕrī-re); ornā-mentum, *an ornament* (ornā-re); pālūdāmentum, *a military cloak;* păvī-mentum, *pavement* (păvī-re, *to beat, ram*); pĕdāmentum, *a prop* for vines, &c. (pĕdā-re, *to put feet to*); pĭg-mentum, *a paint* (pi*ng*-ere); pul-mentum, pulpā-mentum, *meat* (pulpa-); purgā-mentum, *refuse* (purgā-re); rā-mentum, *a scraping, chip* (rād-ĕre); rūdī-mentum, *a trial, beginning* (*foil-exercise?* rŭdis, *a foil?*); sæpi-mentum, *a hedge* (sæpī-re); sar-mentum, *a vine pruning,* i.e. a branch requiring to be pruned off (sarp-ĕre, *to prune*); seg-mentum, *a strip* (sĕcāre); sternŭ-mentum, *sneezing* (sternu-ĕre); strā-mentum, *straw* (ster*n*-ĕre, strā-tus); strig-mentum, *a scraping* (stri*ng*-ere); suffī-mentum, *incense* (suffī-re); tĕg-u-mentum (integumentum), *a covering* (tĕg-ĕre); tempĕrā-mentum, *mixture, moderation* (tempĕrā-re); testā-mentum, *a will* (testā-ri); tō-mentum, *stuffing* (*clippings?* comp. tondēre); tor-mentum, *a hurling engine* (torqvēre); vestī-mentum, *a dress* (vestī-re); and others.

(*b*) Feminine: fulmenta, *a prop;* rāmenta, *a shaving;* both old forms. See the neuters.

ŭl-en-to Sometimes the older -ŏlento; sometimes the later -ĭlento. 793
From real or assumed derivatives in -to, -ti.

Adjectives: corpu-lentus, *fleshy* (for corpŏr-ulentus); escu-lentus, *eatable* (esca-); fraudu-lentus, *cheating* (fraudi-); grācĭlentus, *thin* (comp. grācĭlis); lūcu-lentus, *bright* (lūcĭ-); perhaps also *gainful* for lucru-lentus (lucro-); lūtu-lentus, *muddy* (lŭto-); măcĭ-lentus, *wasted* (măcie-); ŏpŭ-lentus, *wealthy* (ŏpĭ-); potu-lentus, *drinkable* (pōto-); pulvĕr-ŭlentus, *dusty* (pulvĭs-); pūr-ulentus, *festering* (pūs-); sangvīn-olentus, *blood-stained* (sangvĕn-); tēm-ulentus, *drunken* (comp. tēm-ētum); trŭcu-lentus, *fierce* (trŭci-); turbu-lentus, *riotous* (turba-); vīno-lentus, *drunken* (vino-); vio-lentus, *violent* (vi- for vīsi-).

-gintā }
-gintī } Indeclinable adjectives of number, denoting multiples of 794
ten: ֊inti (or -tā) = decem-ti (or -ta).

vī-ginti, *twenty* (dvi-děcem-ti, *two-ten-ty*); trī-gintā, *thirty* (tri-); quadrāgintā (quatvor-. § 158); qvinqvāgintā, *fifty* (qvinqve-); sexāginta, *sixty* (sex); septuāgintā, *seventy* (septem, see below); octōginta, *eighty* (octo); nōnāgintā, *ninety* (nŏvem, see below).

Compare centum, supposed to be for decem-decem-ta.

The formation of the higher cardinal numbers is in some points very obscure. The final vowel—ī in vīginti, ā in the others—is found also in Greek, but is there short; e.g. εἴκοσι, Dor. εἴκατι: τριᾱκοντα, &c. The ā before the guttural in quadrāginta, &c. is also found in Greek; e.g. τεσσαρᾱκοντα, but the origin of none of these vowels is clear. The final i in vīginti may be a *dual* form: the final ā of trīginta, &c. is by some considered to be the same as the ordinary ă of the neuter plural.

Septuaginta, *seventy*, is abnormally formed instead of septenginta, probably to avoid confusion with septingenti, *seven hundred.* (For the u comp. septuennis.) Nōnaginta is probably for nŏvīnaginta, the m being assimilated to the initial n. (Schleicher derives it directly from the ordinal nōno-.)

-cento ⎫
-gento ⎭ Declinable adjectives of number, denoting multiples of *a* 793 *hundred* only used in plural: gento- = centum.

dūcenti, *two hundred* (duo-centum); trěcenti, *three hundred* (tri-); quadringenti, *four hundred* (qvatvor, see below); quingenti, *five hundred* (for qvinqvigenti); sexcenti, *six hundred* (sex); septingenti, *seven hundred* (septem); octingenti, *eight hundred* (octo, see below); nongenti, *nine hundred* (nōn is for nŏvem).

The -in in quadringenti and octingenti has perhaps been suggested by septingenti (where it has its justification in septem; for the i cf. § 204. 2. c) and qvingenti, where it is radical. It may have been adopted to increase the distinction of the hundreds from the tens.

The difference of the vowel before nt in the hundreds compared with the tens, e.g. quadringenti, quadraginta, is probably due partly to the desire for distinction, partly to the fact that the e of a suffix (decem) more easily passes into i (quadraginta) than the e in centum (quadringenti), which is apparently, though perhaps not really (cf. § 794), radical.

-āto   1. Participles from verbs with -a stems (§ 697); e.g. 796 āmātus, &c. *loved* (amā-re); &c.: or adjectives formed as such:

ăcŭle-atus, *furnished with a sting* or *thorn* (acu-leo-); ădīp-atus, *fattened* (aděp-); aer-atus, *of bronze* (æs-); alb-atus, *clad in white* (albo-); ans-atus, *with handles* (ansa-); arm-atus, *armed* (armā-

re); aur-atus, *gilded* (auro-); barb-atus, *bearded* (barba-); brācca-
tus, *breeched* (bracca-); căpill-atus, *hairy* (căpillo-); căpĭt-atus, *with
a head* (căpŭt-); cătēn-atus, *chained* (cătena-); centŭri-atus, *of the
centuries* (centŭria-); cētr-atus, *armed with a short shield* (cetra-);
cincinnatus, *curled* (cincinno-); cŏlumn-atus, *furnished with columns*
(cŏlumna-); cord-atus, *having good sense* (cord-); cŏthurn-atus,
buskined, i.e. *tragic* (cŏthurno-); crēpĭd-atus, *sandalled* (crĕpĭda-);
crēt-atus, *chalked* (crēta-); crist-atus, *crested* (crista-); cūri-atus, *of
the Curia* (curia-); dālĭc-atus, *charming, dainty* (*filtered*, delĭqvāre?);
dent-atus, *toothed* (denti-); dīmĭdi-atus, *halved* (dīmĭdio-); Fāb-atus,
beaned, chiefly as surname (fāba-); fæc-atus, *made from lees* (fæci-);
falc-atus, *sickle-shaped* (falci-); ferr-atus, *iron-covered* (ferro-); gĕnĭcŭl-
atus, *with knees*, i.e. *jointed* (gĕnĭ-cŭlo-); gutt-atus, *speckled* (gutta-);
hast-atus, *armed with spear* (hasta-); littĕr-atus, *lettered*, i.e. *brand-
ed* or *learned* (littĕra-); lŭp-ātus, *armed with* jagged spikes like *wolf's*
teeth (lŭpo-); mōr-atus, *-mannered* (mōs-); numm-atus, *supplied
with money* (numm-); ŏbær-atus, *moneyed over*, i.e. *in debt* (æs-);
ŏcell-atus, *with little eyes* or *spots* (ŏcello-); ŏcŭl-atus, *having eyes*
(ŏcŭlo-); orbĭcŭl-atus, *rounded* (orbĭcŭlo-); palli-atus, *dressed in a
Greek cloak* (pallio-); pālŭd-atus, *with the military cloak on* (comp.
paluda-mentum); palm-ātus, *worked with palm-branches* (palma-);
penn-atus, *winged* (penna-); pīl-atus, *armed with a pike* (pīlo-); pīlle-
atus, *bonneted* (pīlleo-); pinn-atus, *feathered* (pinna-); prætext-atus,
wearing the bordered robe (prætexta-, § 790); torqv-ātus, *wearing a
collar* (torqvi-); trăbe-atus, *wearing the state robe* (tră-bea-); tŭnĭ-
catus, *in a shirt* (tŭnĭca-); visc-atus, *limed* (visco-); vitt-atus, *filleted*
(vitta-); ungvent-atus, *anointed* (ungvento-); and many others.

2. Substantives: arqv-atus, (1) *the jaundice*, (2) *a jaundiced
person* (arquo-, *the rainbow*?); pālātum, *the palate*; victori-atus (sc.
nummus), *a victory-coin* (victoria-).

-ōto   .ægr-ōtus, *sick* (ægro-). See also § 689.   797

-ūto   1. Participles from verbs with -u stems (§ 690); e.g.
          ăcŭ-tus, *sharpened* (ăcu-ĕre); &c.; or adjectives formed
as such, chiefly from substantives with -u stems:

ast-utus, *crafty* (astu-); cinct-utus, *girdle-wearing* (cinctu-);
corn-utus, *horned* (cornu-); dēlĭb-utus, *smeared* (comp. λείβειν);
hirs-ūtus, *shaggy* (comp. hîrto-); nās-utus, *with large*, or, metaphorically, *sharp nose* (nāso-); vers-utus, *adroit* (versu-, *a turning*);
vĕr-utus, *javelin-armed* (veru-).

actūtum (adv.), *instantly* (actu-. See § 528).

2. Substantives: ăluta, *leather*; cĭcuta, *hemlock*; Mātuta, *Goddess of dawn* (comp. māne?); vĕrutum, *a javelin* (veru-). See
also § 788 *b, c.*

-ēto   1. Participles from verbs with stems in -e (§ 692); 798
          e.g. deflētus, *lamented* (deflēre); &c.: also the adjective,
fāc-ētus, *witty*.

2. Substantives: (*a*) masculine or feminine: **bōletus** (m.), *a kind of mushroom* (from βωλίτης?); **Mŏnĕta**, a surname of Juno, in whose temple money was coined: hence *mint;* **rŭbeta,** *a toad* (said to be from rŭbo-, *bramble*). See also § 788 *b.*

(*b*) neuter: (1) **ăcetum,** *vinegar* (ace-sc-ere)**;** **ōletum** (old word), *dung* (ōlēre?); **tăpetum** (cf. § 418), *a carpet;* **tēmetum,** *intoxicating drink* (comp. tēm-ulentus, abs-tēm-ius); **tra̋p-etum** (cf. § 418), *an olive mill.*

(2) Names expressing a *place* where a plant, &c. grows: (But few of these words are used frequently):

aescŭl-etum (Hor.), *an oak forest* (aescŭlo-); **ărundĭn-etum,** *a reed bed* (arundŏn-); **aspr-etum,** *rough place* (aspĕro-, § 347); **bux-etum** (Mart.), *box plantation* (buxo-); **castăn-etum** (Col.), *chestnut grove* (castanea-); **cŭpress-etum,** *a cypress grove* (cupresso-); **dŭm-etum,** *a thicket* (dŭmo-); **fīm-etum** (Plin.), *dunghill* (fīmo-); **frŭtĭc-etum,** *a shrubbery* (frŭtĕc-); **myrt-etum,** *myrtle grove* (myrto-); **ōlĭv-etum,** *an oliveyard* (ōlĭva-); **pīn-etum,** *pine grove* (pīno-); **qverc-etum,** *oak grove* (qverco-); **rōs-etum,** *rose bed* (rōsa-); **sax-ētum** (once Cic.), *bed of rocks* (saxo-); **sentī-c-etum** (Plaut.), *thorn bed* (senti-: formed in analogy with fruticetum?); **sĕpulcr-etum** (Catull.), *a graveyard* (sĕpulcro-); **vĕtĕr-etum** (Colum.), *old fallow land* (vĕtŭs-); **vīn-etum,** *a vineyard* (vīno-); with others used very rarely. So **Argīletum,** *marlbed* (argilla-), popularly misunderstood by the Romans.

-ĭto   1. Participles from verbs with -i stems (§ 695); e. g. 799   aud-itus, *heard* (aud-īre); &c.: and adjectives formed   as such:

ăv-itus, *of a grandfather* (ăvo-); **aur-itus,** *with ears* (auri-); **Cerr-ītus** (for Cereritus), *frenzied by Ceres' influence* (Cĕrĕs-); **crīn-itus,** *hairy* (crīni-); **fortu-ītus** (Hor., Phædr.), *fortuitus,* (Manil., Petr., Juv.), *by chance* (forti-, cf. § 405); **grātu-ītus** (Plaut.), **gratu-ītus** (Stat.), *without pay* (comp. **grātia-**); **măr-itus,** *married, of marriage* (măsi-); **mell-itus,** *honeyed* (mell-); **patr-itus,** *of a father* (patr-); **pell-itus,** *skin-clad* (pelli-); **pĕr-itus,** *skilled* (cf. p. 254); **sci-tus,** *clever, knowing* (scī-re); **turr-itus,** *turreted* (turri-).

2. Substantives: **pītu-ita,** *phlegm* (comp. πτύειν, spu-ĕre); **scrīblita,** *a cake.*

ii. *Stems ending in* -tu, -ti, -t (-su, -si, -s *when presumably arisen from a dental*).

-tu (-su)   Substantives derived mostly from verbs, and generally 800   denoting an *act.* (The accusative and ablative cases are   the so-called supines.) See §§ 397—399 and Book II.   Chap. xxiv.

adven-tus, *an arrival* (advĕn-īre); æs-tus, *heat* (comp. αἴθειν, *to set on fire*); ămic-tus, *a garment* (ămĭc-īre); anfractus, *a circuit, a bend* (am, fra*n*g-ere); anhēl-itus, *panting* (anhēlā-re); appărā-tus, *equipment* (appărā-re); appĕtī-tus, *appetite* (appetī-, appet-ĕre); ar-bĭtr-atus, *judgment, choice* (arbĭtrā-ri); ar-tus, *a joint* (comp. ἄρειν, *to fit*); aspec-tus, *sight* (aspĭcĕ-re); as-tus, *cunning* (§ 396); audĭ-tus, *hearing* (audĭ-re); bālā-tus, *a bleating* (bālā-re); cæs-tus, *a gauntlet* (cæd-ĕre? hence *a strip*); can-tus, *a song* (căn-ĕre); cap-tus, *grasp*, esp. mental (căpĕ-re); cā-sus, *an accident* (căd-ĕre); cen-sus,' *a reckoning* (censēre); coïtus, *a connexion* (co-īre); cœtus, *an assembly* (same as last); cŏmĭtā-tus, *a train* (comĭtā-re); crēpĭ-tus, *a rattling* (crĕpāre); crŭciā-tus, *torturing* (crŭciā-re); decur-sus, *a descent, a course* (decurr-ĕre); delec-tus, *a selection, levy* (dēlĭg-ĕre); ēven-tus, *an occurrence* (ēvĕn-īre); exercĭ-tus, *an army* (exercēre); exĭ-tus, *departure* (exīre); fastus, *pride;* fē-tus, *bearing, offspring* (comp. fē-cundus, fē-mīna); flē-tus, *weeping* (flē-re); fluc-tus, *a wave* (flugv-, flu-ĕre); fruc-tus, *enjoyment, fruits* (frugv-, fru-i); ges-tus, *gesture* (gĕr-ĕre); gustus, *taste* (comp. γεύειν); hăbĭ-tus, *habit* in various senses (hăbē-re); hālītus, *breath* (comp. hālā-re); hiā-tus, *a gape* (hiā-re); ic-tus, *a blow* (ĭc-ĕre); instinc-tus, *instigation* (instingv-ĕre); itus (Lucr., Cic.), *a going* (īre); lessus (old word; only in acc. s.), *wailing;* luc-tus, *grief* (lūgēre); luxus, *luxury;* mercā-tus, *trading* (mercā-ri); mētus, *fear;* mō-tus, *motion* (mŏvēre); mūgī-tus, *lowing* (mūgī-re); necessus (cf. § 432; probably from ne, cēd-ere); nexus, *a bond* (nect-ĕre); or-tus, *a rising* (ŏr-ī-ri); par-tus, *birth* (părĕ-re); pas-sus, *a step* (pand-ĕre, *to stretch*); plau-sus, *a clapping* (plaud-ĕre); portus, *a harbour;* pō-tus, *a drinking* (comp. po-tā-re); progres-sus, *an advance* (progrĕd-ĭ); quæs-tus, *gain* (quær-ĕre); qves-tus, *complaint* (qvĕr-i); ric-tus, *mouthopening* (ring-i); rī-sus, *laughter* (rīdēre); rītus, *a rite;* sal-tus, *a leaping* (săllĭ-re); *a mountain glen* (comp. ἄλ-σος?); sex-us, *sex* (sĕc-āre?); sĭ-tus, *situation* (sĭn-ĕre); spīr-itus, *a breath* (spīrā-re); strĕp-ĭ-tus, *a din* (strĕp-ĕre); sum-p-tus, *expense* (sŭm-ĕre); tac-tus, *a touch* (tang-ĕre); tinnī-tus, *a tinkling* (tinnī-re); transĭ-tus, *a passage* (transī-re); vestī-tus, *dress* (vestī-re); vic-tus, *living, food* (vigv-, vīv-ĕre); vī-sus, *sight* (vĭd-ēre); vol-tus, *expression of countenance, looks*, cf. Cic. *Leg.* I. 9 (velle, vŏlo); ū-sus, *use* (ūt-i); &c.

frĕtus (m.), *a strait;* impĕtus (m.), *an onset* (in pĕtĕre); mĕtus (m.), *fear;* in which t is apparently radical.

-ul-tu   sing-ultus, *sobbing;* tŭm-ultus, *uproar* (tŭm-ēre).

-ātu   From substantives, but formed as if from verbs with -a 801 stems (e.g. consulāre, *to be consul*), denote (1) *the holding office,* (2) *the office itself,* (3) *the body of officers.*

călīb-atus (Sen. Suet.), *celibacy* (cælĕb-); cĭb-atus (præ-Cic. and Plin.), *food* (cĭbo-); consŭl-atus, *a being consul, the consulship* (consŭl-) ; dŭc-atus (post-Aug.), *leadership* (dŭc-) ; ĕqvĭt-atus, *cavalry* (ĕqvĕt-) ; jūdĭc-atus (Cic. once), *judgeship* (jūdĕc-) ; măgistr-atus, *magistracy* (măgistro-) ; pĕdĭt-atus, *infantry* (pĕdĕt-) ; pontĭfĭc-atus, *the pontificate* (pontifĕc-) ; prīm-atus (Varr., Plin.), *primacy* (prīmo-) ; princĭp-atus, *chieftainship* (princĕp-) ; dĕcemvĭr-atus (so triumviratus, &c.), *membership of a commission of ten* (decemvĭro-) ; qvadrīm-atus (Plin., Col.), *age of four years old* (qvadrīmo-) ; re-atus (see Quintil. 8. 3. 34), *condition of an accused person* (reo-) ; sĕn-atus, *a body of old men* (sĕn-, sĕnex) ; summ-atus (Lucr.), *sovereignty* (summo-) ; trĭbūn-atus, *tribunate* (trĭbūno-).

-ti (-sĭ) 1. Adjectives: dĭs, *rich* (contracted from dīves) ; fortis, 802 *brave* (fer-re ; comp. φέρτερος, &c.) ; mītis, *mild* ; pŏtis, *able* (comp. πόσις, *a husband*) ; sons, *guilty* ; tristis, *sad.* Cămer-s, *a man of Camerinum* ; Tībur-s, *a man of Tibur.*

2. Substantives : (*a*) masculine and feminine: amussis (m.), 803 *a carpenter's rule* ; antes (m. pl.) *ranks* ; ars (f.), *art* (comp. ar-tus, *a joint*, ἀρ-αρ-ίσκειν) ; assis, usually as (m.), *a penny* ; axis or assis (m.), *an axle-tree, a board* ; cassis (m. § 432), *a mesh of a net* ; cautēs (f.), *a rock* ; classis (f.), *a class, a fleet* (for κλᾶσις Dor. from καλ-εῖν?) ; cŏhors or cors (f.), *a yard, a company* (com, hor- ; comp. χόρ-τος) ; cōs (f.), *a whetstone* (comp. cautes) ; crātis (f.), *a hurdle of wicker* ; cŭtis (f.), *skin* (comp. scūtum, σκῦτος) ; dens (m.), *a tooth* (comp. ὀδοντ-, nom. ὀδούς) ; ensis (m.), *a sword* ; fătis (only in adfatim, *to satiety*), *a yawn* (comp. fătiscĕre, fătigare) ; fons (m.), *a spring* of water, &c. ; fors (f.), *chance* ; frons (f. § 419), *the forehead* ; fustis (m.), *a cudgel* ; gens (f.), *a race* (gĕn-, gignĕre) ; grātēs (f. pl.), *thanks* (comp. grā-tus, grātia) ; hostis (m. f.), *a stranger, an enemy* ; lens (f.), *a lentil* ; lĭs (for stlĭs, f.), *a strife, a suit* ; mens (f.), *a mind* (comp. rĕ-mĭn-iscī) ; mensis (m.), *a month* (comp. μήν, μήνη) ; mes-sis (f.), *harvest* (mĕt-ĕre, *to mow*) ; mons (m.), *a mountain* ; mors (f.), *death* (mŏr-i) ; nātis (f.) *a buttock* ; neptis (f.), *a granddaughter* (comp. nĕp-ŏt-) ; nox (f.), *night* (comp. νυκτ-, nom. νύξ) ; pars (f.), *a part* (comp. πορ-, ἔπορον aor., pārĕ-re) ; pestis (f.), *destruction* (comp. perd-ĕre, πέρθ-ειν) ; pons (m.), *a bridge* (comp. pondus) ; postis (m.), *a doorpost* ; puls (f.), *pulse* ; rătis (f.), *a raft* (comp. rēmus, *an oar* ; ἐρ-έτης, *a rower*) ; restis (f.), *a rope* ; sēmentis (f.), *seedtime* (semĕn-) ; sentes (m. pl.), *thorns* ; sĭtis (f.), *thirst* ; sors (f.), *a lot* (sĕr-ĕre, *to put in rows*) ; sponte (abl. s. f.), *with a will* ; testis (m.) (comp. τεκ-, τίκτειν) ; (m. f.), *a witness* (comp. τεκ-μήριον) ; tussis (f.), *a cough* (for tŭd-tis from tŭndĕre?) ; vātēs (m.), *a seer* ; vec-tis (m.), *a roller* or *lever* (vĕh-ere) ; ves-tis (f.), *a dress* (comp. ἐν-νύναι, ἐσ-θής) ; vī-tis (f.), *a vine* (vĭ-ēre, *to weave*).

(*b*) Neuters: lac (or lact), *milk* (comp. γαλακτ-) ; rēte, *a net.* 804

-ăt ănas (f.), *a duck* (comp. νῆσσα).

-ŏt   ălĭquŏt, *some;* quŏt, *how many;* tŏt, *so many:* all inde-
            clinable adjectives.

-ŭt (-ĭt)   căpŭt (n.), *a head* (comp. κεφ-αλή).

-ĕtĭ   hĕbĕs, *blunt;* tĕrĕs, *round* (tĕr-ere, *to wear*).

-ĕt   ăbiēs (f.), *a pine;* ăriēs (m.), *a ram;* păriēs (m.), *a wall;*
            sĕgĕs (f.), *standing corn;* tĕgĕs (f.), *a mat* (tĕg-ĕre).

-ĕt (-ĭt)   ăl-es, *winged* (āla-); ăm-es (m.?), *a vineprop* (comp. 805
            ăp-iscī); antistes (m. f.), *a priest* or *priestess* (ante, stă-);
            cæl-es (m.), *a heaven-dweller* (cælo-); cæspes (m.), *turf;* cocl-es
            (m.), *a blind man* (for sco-cul-ĕt-; comp. σκό-τος, Curt., Cors.);
            cŏmes (m. f.), *a companion* (com); dīves, *rich* (comp. divo-); ĕqv-es
            (m.), *a horseman* (ĕqvo-); gurges (m.), *a whirlpool;* merges (f.?),
            a sheaf, also *a pitchfork* (comp. mergæ, *a two-prong*); mīles (m. f.),
            a soldier; pĕd-es (m. f.), *a man on foot* (pĕd-); poples (m.), *the back
            of the knee;* præst-es (m. f.), *protecting* (præ, stă-); sătelles (m.f.),
            an attendant; sospes, *saving, safe;* stĭpes (m.), *a stock* (comp.
            stĭp-ula, *a straw*); sŭperstes, *surviving* (super, stă-); tŭdes (Fest.),
            a hammer (tundere); vēles (m.), *a skirmisher* (comp. vēl-ox).

-m-ĕt(-mĭt) fō-mes (m.), *tinder* (fŏv-ēre); lī-mes (m.), *a balk* 806
            (lī-mo-, *slanting*); palmes (m.), *a vine shoot* (pal-ma,
            a branch); tar-mes (m.), *a woodworm* (comp. tĕr-ebra, τερ-ηδών);
            termes (m.), *a cutting;* trāmes (m.), *a path* (tra-ns).

-en-tĭ   1. Participles present active of verbs: 807

            ăma-ns, *loving* (ămā-); audĭ-ens, *hearing* (audī-); căpĭ-
            ens, *taking* (capĕ-re); gign-ens, *begetting* (gĭ-gn-ĕre); mŏn-ens,
            advising (mŏn-ēre); oblīvisc-ens, *forgetting* (oblīviscī); rĕg-ens,
            ruling (rĕg-ĕre); tribu-ens, *assigning* (tribu-ĕre); and so from all
            verbs.

            2. Adjectives, originally present participles, or formed as such:

            absens, *absent* (abes-se); ăbundans, *abundant* (abundā-re, *to
            overflow*); arrŏgans, *arrogant* (arrŏgā-re, *to claim*); clēmens, *mer-
            ciful;* congru-ens, *suitable* (congru-ĕre, *to agree*); contĭn-ens, *con-
            tiguous* (contĭnēre); dīlĭg-ens, *accurate* (dīlĭg-ĕre, *to love*); ēlĕgans,
            neat; ēlŏqv-ens, *eloquent* (ēloqvī-); ēvĭd-ens, *evident* (ex vĭd-ēre);
            frĕqvens, *crowded;* impŭd-ens, *shameless* (in pŭd-ēre); innŏc-ens,
            harmless (in nŏc-ēre); insŏl-ens, *excessive, haughty* (in sŏl-ēre, *to be
            wont*); insons, *guiltless* (in sons); lĭb-ens, *willing* (lĭb-ēre); lĭc-ens,
            presumptuous (lĭc-ēre); pŏt-ens, *powerful* (pŏt-esse); prægnans, *preg-
            nant* (lit. *before bearing?* præ, gĕn-); præsens, *present* (præ esse);
            præstans, *excellent* (præ-stāre); prūd-ens, *prudent* (pro vĭdēre, *to
            foresee*); rĕcens, *fresh;* rĕpens, *sudden;* săpĕ-iens, *wise* (săpĕ-re, *to

have taste); splend-ens, glittering (splendēre); stellans, starry (stella-); vălens, powerful (vălēre).

3. Substantives, originally participles, &c.:

ădŭlesc-ens (m.), a young man (adulesc-ĕre, to grow); ănĭmans, an animal (ănĭma-, breath); cli-ens (m. also clienta f.), a client (clu-ere, to hear); consentīs (m. pl.), epithet of the twelve chief deities, the Colleagues (com esse); dext-ans (m.), five-sixths (lit. a sixth off, de-sexto-); dodrans (m.), three-fourths, lit. a fourth off (de-qvadro-); infans, an infant (in, fā-ri); occĭd-ens (sc. sol), the west (occĭd-ere, to fall); ōriens, the east (ŏrīrī, to rise); părens (m. f.), a parent (părē-re); rŭdens (m.), a cable; serpens (m. f.), a snake (serp-ĕre, to crawl); sextans, a sixth (sexto-); torrens, a boiling rushing stream (torrē-re, to burn); tri-ens (m.), a trithing, i.e. a third (tri-).

1-en-ti   pestĭ-1-ens, pestilential (pesti-); pĕt-ŭl-ans, saucy (comp. petul-cus from pĕt-ere).

-s-ti   agre-stis, of the fields (agro-); cæle-stis, heavenly (cælo-). 808 Comp. also dŏm-esti-cus, § 769, silv-est-ris, § 904, ĕg-est-ās, pŏt-est-as, § 811.

-āti   Adjectives expressing origin.   809

cūj-ās, of what country (cujo-); infernas, of the lower country (inferno-); infĭm-ātis, one of the lowest rank (infimo-); nostr-ās, a countryman of ours (nostro-); optĭm-ās (§ 418), one of the best party (optimo-); pĕn-ates (m. pl.), household gods (pĕno-, store); summ-ātes (m. pl.), men of the highest ranks (summo-); sŭpernas, of the upper country (superno-).

Similarly from Italian towns: Antiās, a man of Antium (Antium); Ardeas (Ardea); Arpīnas (Arpīnum); Atīnas (Atīna); Căpēnas (Căpēna); Căsīnas (Căsīnum); Fĕrentīnas (Ferentīnum); Fidēnas (Fīdēnæ but Fīdēna, Verg.); Frŭsīnas (Frŭsīno); Lārīnas (Larīnum); Răvennas (Răvenna); Sarsīnas (Sarsīna); Urbīnas (Urbīnum).

-āt   damnas (cf. § 445), condemned (damnā-re); săti-ās, a glut (sătiā-re).

-t-āt   So usually, not tāti-; cf. § 445. For the preceding short 810 vowel, e.g. ītas, see § 213. 6; lĕtas, § 213. 5. c and 42; for its omission § 245. Abstract substantives, derived chiefly from adjectives (from 500 to 600 in number, according to L. Meyer): all feminine.

ăcerbĭ-tas, tartness (acerbo-); ædīli-tas, ædileship (ædīli-); æqvāli-tas, equality (æqvali-); æqvi-tas, fairness (æqvo-); æs-tas, summer (for æsti-tas, æstu-); æ-tas, age (ævo-, § 94); æterni-tas, eternity (æterno-); affīni-tas, relationship by marriage (affīni-);

ăgĭlĭ-tas, *agility* (ăgĭlĭ-); amœni-tas, *pleasantness* (ămœno-); antĭqvĭ-tas, *antiquity* (antĭqvo-); anxie-tas, *anxiety* (anxio-); Appie-tas (formed by Cic. *Fam.* 3. 7), *Appius-ness* (Appio-); aspĕri-tas, *roughness* (aspĕro-); assĭdui-tas, *constant attention, frequency* (assĭduo-); atrōci-tas, *cruelty* (atrōci-); auctōr-i-tas, *advice, authority* (auctōr-); ăvĭdi-tas, *greediness* (ăvĭdo-); bĕnigni-tas, *kindliness, bounty* (bĕnigno-); cæci-tas, *blindness* (cæco-); călămitas (călămo-, *a stalk?* comp. κάλαμος and culmus), *blight, disaster;* cāri-tas, *dearness* (cāro-); cĕlebrĭ-tas, *celebrity* (celebri-); cīvi-tas, *citizenship* (cīvi-); dignitas, *worthiness* (digno-); dŏcĭlĭ-tas, *aptness for being taught* (dŏcĭlĭ-); ēbriĕ-tas, *drunkenness* (ēbrio-); făcĭlĭ-tas, *easiness;* făcul-tas, *doableness, power* (făcĭlĭ-); fămĭliāri-tas, *intimacy* (fămĭliāri-); hērēd-itas, *inheritance* (hērēd-); hōnes-tas, *honourableness* (hōnōs-); hūmāni-tas, *fellow-feeling, politeness* (hūmāno-); immūni-tas, *freedom from public charges* (immūni-); jŭven-tas, *youth* (jŭvĕn-); lĕvĭ-tas, *lightness* (lĕvi-); līber-tas, *freedom* (lībĕro-); mājes-tas, *dignity* (majōs-); mōrōsi-tas, *fretfulness* (mōrōso-); nĕcessi-tas, *necessity* (necesse); pauci-tas, *fewness* (pauco-); pauper-tas, *poverty* (paupĕr-); pie-tas, *dutifulness* (pio-); postĕri-tas, *posterity* (postēro-); prōprie-tas, *proper quality, ownership* (proprio-); qvăli-tas, *quality* (qvăli-); sătie-tas, *satiety* (comp. sătis, sătiāt-); sēcūri-tas, *security* (sēcūro-); simplĭci-tas, *simplicity* (simplici-, nom. simplex); sōcie-tas, *partnership* (sōcio-); tempes-tas, *a season, weather* (tempōs-); vărie-tas, *variety* (vărio-); ūber-tas, *fertility* (ūber-); vēnus-tas, *beauty* (vĕnŭs-); vernīli-tas, *slavishness, coarse jesting* (vernīli-); vĕtus-tas, *old age* (vetŭs-); ūnĭ-tas, *unity* (ūno-); ūnĭversi-tas, *a whole,* either of persons (i. e. *a corporation*) or of things (universo-); vŏlun-tas, *will* (for vŏlenti-tas, § 28); vŏlup-tas, *pleasure* (vŏlŭp, § 516); ūtĭli-tas, *usefulness* (ūtĭli-); and many others.

-es-t-āt　ĕg-es-tas, *want* (ĕg-ēre); pot-estas, *power* (pŏti-); pro- 811 bably formed as if from substantives in ōs- or ŏs- (as honestas, tempes-tas).

-ōti　dōs (f.), *a dowry* (dă-).

-ōt　nĕpōs (m.), *a grandson* (comp. ά-νεψ-ιός, i. e. *common grandson*); săcerdos (m. f.), *a priest* (săcĕro-, da-).

-ūt　sălūs (f.), *safety* (for salvo-t-).

-tūt　Substantives feminine:

juven-tus, *youth* (jŭven-); sĕnec-tus, *old age* (sĕn-ec-); servī-tus, *slavery* (servo-); vir-tus, *manliness* (vĭro-).

-ēti　lŏcŭples, *rich* (perhaps compound of lŏco- and plē-to; cf. 812 Cic. *Rep.* 2. 16). For tăpēte (n.), trăpētes (m. pl.) see § 418 and -ēto, § 798, 1 *b.*

-ĭti   **Quĭrīs,** *a Roman citizen;* **Samnīs,** *a Samnite* **(Samnio-).**
For **dīs, mītis,** &c. see under -ti (§ 802).

Compound stem-endings: **-tŭmo,** § 757; **-tīvo,** § 764; **-tĭco,**
-trīci, §§ 769, 782; **-tāt, -estāt, -tŭt,** §§ 810, 811; **-tŭdōn,** § 847; **-tīno,**
-ter-no, -tīno, -trīno, §§ 827, 829, 840, 842; **-tiōn (-siōn),** § 854; **-tibĭli**
(-sibĭli), § 877; **-tĭli (-sĭli),** § 878; **-tero, -astĕro, -tūro (-sūro),** §§ 888,
889, 893; **-tru, -tĕri, -estĕri, -tĕr, -tōr (-sōr),** §§ 903—905, 908;
-tĭcio, -ĭtio, -ntio, -tōrio (-sōrio), §§ 931—933, 943.

iii. *Stems ending in* -so, -si (for -to, -ti).

-so   See under -to, §§ 787, 788.   813

-ōso   For **-onso** (§ 191. 2), and this again perhaps for **-onti-o**;
comp. γερουσία for γεροντία. The -i probably caused
or assisted the assibilation (§ 143).

Adjectives (said to be 500 in number) expressing *fitness:*
actu-osus, *full of motion* (**actu-**); **æstu-osus,** *burning hot* (**æstu-**):
ambĭti-osus, *ambitious* (**ambĭtu-**); **ănĭm-osus,** *spirited* (**ănĭmo-**);
ann-osus, *full of years, aged* (**anno-**); **ăqv-osus,** *watery* (**ăqva-**);
călămĭt-osus, *disastrous* (for **călămĭtāt-osus**); **call-osus,** *hard-skinned*
(**callo-**); **capti-osus,** *ensnaring, captious* (**captu-** or **captiōn-**); **cări-**
osus, *decayed* (**cărie-**); **clāmosus,** *screaming* (for **clāmōs-osus**); **cōpi-**
osus, *rich* (**cōpia-**); **crīmĭn-osus,** *reproachful* (**crīmĕn-**); **dōl-osus,**
crafty (**dōlo-**); **ēbri-osus,** *a drunkard* (**ēbrio-**); **făm-osus,** *notorious*
for good or ill (**fāma-**); **form-osus,** *shapely* (**forma**); **frăg-osus,** *broken*
(for **frăgōs-osus**); **fructu-osus,** *fruitful* (**fructu-**); **frŭtic-osus,** *full of*
shrubs (**frŭtĕc-**); **gĕnĕr-osus,** *shewing breed, well-born* (**gĕnŭs-**);
grāti-osus, *influential* (**grātia-**); **herb-osus** (poet.), *grassy* (**herba-**);
ingĕnĭ-osus,*clever* (**ingĕnio-**); **invĭdi-osus,** *exposed to odium* (**invĭdia-**);
jŏc-osus, *sportive* (**jŏco-**); **luxŭri-osus,** *luxurious* (**luxŭria-**); **mend-**
osus, *faulty* (**men-da-**); **morb-osus,** *diseased* (**morbo-**); **mōr-osus,**
wayward, cross (**mōs-,** *a whim*); **nĭv-osus,** *snowy* (**nĭvi-**); **nōd-osus,**
knotty (**nōdo-**); **ŏdi-osus,** *troublesome* (**ŏdio-**); **offĭci-osus,** *dutiful,*
obliging (**offĭcio-**); **ŏnĕr-osus,** *burdensome* (**ŏnŭs-**); **ōti-osus,** *at leisure*
(**ōtio-**); **pĕcūni-osus,** *moneyed* (**pĕcūnia-**); **pĕrĭcul-osus,** *dangerous*
(**pĕrīcŭlo-**); **pernĭci-osus,** *destructive* (**pernĭcie-**); **pisc-osus** (rare,
Ov., Verg.), *full of fish* (**pisci-**); **quæstu-osus,** *gainful* (**qvæstu-**);
relĭgi-osus, *scrupulous* (for **relĭgiōn-osus**); **silv-ōsus,** *wooded* (**silva-**);
sqvām-osus, *scaly* (**sqvāma-**); **strīg-osus,** *thin* (? **strīga-,** *a swathe*);
stŭdi-osus, *zealous* (**stŭdio-**); **suspĭci-osus,** *suspicious* (for **suspiciōn-**
osus); **sumptu-osus,** *costly* (**sumptu-**); **vent-osus,** *windy* (**vento-**);
ventri-osus, *potbellied* (**ventri-**); **verb-osus,** *wordy* (**verbo-**); **vermĭn-**
osus (Plin.), *full of worms* (**vermĕn-**); **vīn-osus,** *wine loving* (**vīno-**);
vĭti-osus, *faulty* (**vĭtio-**); and many others.

-c-ōso   belli-cosus, *war-loving* (bello-, comp. bellicus, adj.); 814
           těněbrĭ-cosus (Cic., also tenebrosus, Verg., Ov.), *dark*
           (těněbra-, but Cic. in poetic translation has tenebricus).

-l-ōso   formīdŏ-lōsus, *fearful* (formĭdŏn-, the n being either
           dropped or changed into l).

-ĭc-ul-ōso febr-ĭcŭlosus (Catull.), *feverish* (febri-, febricula-); mět-
           ĭcŭlosus (Plaut.), *in fear* (mětu-); sit-īculosus (Hor.),
           parched (sĭti-); somn-īculosus, *drowsy* (somno-).

-u-ōso   Probably formed on a false analogy with quæstu-osus, &c.:
           monstr-uosus, *prodigious* (monstro-); montu-osus, *moun-
           tainous* (monti-, but cf. § 405); vŏluptu-osus (Plin. *Ep.*),
           pleasurable (voluptāt-).

-ĭ-oso   Probably formed on a false analogy with odiosus, &c.:
           cūr-iosus, *careful* (cūra-); lăbōr-iosus, *laborious* (lăbōs-);
           lusc-ĭt-ĭ-osus (or lusc-iosus), *purblind* (lusco-).

-en-si   Adjectives (some used as substantives) formed from names 815
           of places:

1. From appellatives: amanu-ensis (m. Suet. twice), *a secretary*
(a manu); atri-ensis (m. sc. servus), *house steward* (atrio-); castrensis, *of the camp* (castro-); circ-ensis, *of the circus* (circo-); fōr-
ensis, *of the forum* (fōro-); frětense (sc. mare), *the straits of Sicily*
(frěto-); Lătěr-ensis, properly *of the bodyguard* (lătŭs-); Portu-ensis
(Cod. Theod.), *of the Port*, viz. Ostia (portu-); prāt-ensis, *of the
meadows* (prāto-).

2. From proper names (which are given in brackets in the
nom. case):

Alli-ensis (Allia); Ambraci-ensis (Ambracia); Arīmĭmenses (Arī-
minum); Bononi-ensis (Bonōnia); Cann-ensis (Cannæ); Circei-ensis
(Circeii); Corfini-ensis (Corfinium); Cur-ensis (Cures); Herculan-
ensis (Herculaneum); Hispal-ensis (Hispălis or Hispal); Hispāni-
ensis (Hispānia); Narbon-ensis (Narbo); Osc-ensis (Osca in Spain);
Osti-ensis (Ostia); Sicili-ensis (Sicilia); Veli-ensis (Velia, (1) part of
Palatine; (2) town in Lucania); Volsini-ensis (Volsinii); Utĭc-ensis
(Utĭca); and others.

-i-en-si   Probably from false analogy (with words in preceding
           section). They are rarely used.

Athēn-iensis (Athenæ); Carthăgĭn-iensis (Carthāgo); Corinth-
ienses (Corinthus); Crotōn-iensis (Croto); Latīn-iensis (Latinus?);
Rhŏd-iensis (Rhodus).

Compound stem-ending: ēs-ĭmo, § 758. See also § 918.

iv. *Stems ending in* -do.

-do   1. Adjectives: 816

(*a*) From verbs with -e stems, the final e being changed to ĭ. (The verb has been added in the following list only when not simple in form or evident in meaning.)

ăcĭ-dus, *sour;* albĭ-dus, *white;* algĭ-dus, *cold* (rare, except as name of mountain near Rome); ārĭ-dus, *dry;* ăvĭ-dus, *greedy;* călĭ-dus or caldus (cf. Quint. I. 6. 19), *hot;* callĭ-dus, *crafty;* candĭ-dus, *white;* ēvānĭ-dus, *vanishing* (ēvāne-sc-ĕre); fervĭ-dus, *glowing;* flaccĭ-dus, *flaccid;* flōrĭ-dus, *flowery;* fœtĭ-dus, *stinking;* frīgĭ-dus, *cold;* fulgĭ-dus, *glistening;* grăvĭ-dus, *heavy with child* (grăvə-sc-ĕre); horrĭ-dus, *bristling, fearful;* langvĭ-dus, *languid;* liqvĭ-dus (§ 243), *clear;* līvĭ-dus, *blue, envious;* lūcĭ-dus, *bright;* mădĭ-dus, *wet;* marcĭ-dus, *fading;* mūcĭ-dus, *mouldy;* nītĭ-dus, *shining;* ŏlĭ-dus, *stinking;* pallĭ-dus, *pale;* păvĭ-dus, *frightened;* plăcĭ-dus, *pleased, calm* (plăcēre, *to be pleasing*); pūtĭ-dus, *rotten;* putrĭ-dus, *rotten;* rancĭ-dus, *rancid* (no verb, but present participle in Lucr.); rĭgĭ-dus, *stiff;* rŭbĭ-dus (rŭbidus, Plaut. twice), *red;* sordĭ-dus, *filthy;* sqvālĭ-dus, *squalid;* stŭpĭ-dus, *amazed;* tābĭ-dus, *decaying;* tĕpĭ-dus, *warm;* tĭmĭ-dus, *timid;* torpĭ-dus, *benumbed;* torrĭ-dus, *burning;* tŭmĭ-dus, *swelling;* turgĭ-dus, *inflated;* vălĭ-dus, *strong;* ūmĭ-dus, *damp;* ūvĭ-dus or ūdus, *wet* (ūve-sc-ere).

(*b*) From verbs with -ĭ or consonant stems: cŭpĭ-dus, *desirous* (cŭpĕ-re); fluĭdus (flŭvĭ-dus, Lucr.), *liquid* (flu-ĕre); răbĭdus, *mad* (răbĕre, comp. răbies); răpĭ-dus, *hurried* (răpĕ-re); vīvĭdus, *lively* (viv-ĕre).

(*c*) From substantives or of obscure derivation: absur-dus, *tuneless* (ab, sur-, comp. su-sur-rus, σύρ-ίζειν: and for the meaning Cicero's expression 'vox absona et absurda,' *Or.* 3. 11); bardus, *stupid* (comp. βραδύς); claudus, *lame;* crū-dus, *raw* (crus-, *hard*? comp. crus-ta, κρύσ-ταλλος. κρύ-ος); fīdus, *faithful* (comp. fīd-es, perfīd-us); fœdus, *foul* (comp. fœtēre, fœti-dus); fordus (cf. § 134), *pregnant;* fūmi-dus, *smoky* (fūmo-); gĕli-dus, *icy* (gĕlu-); herbĭ-dus, *grassy* (herba-); hispĭdus, *shaggy* (comp. hir-tus, hirsūtus); lĕpĭdus, *charming* (from presumed lĕpēre; comp. lĕpōs-); limpi-dus (Catull., Col.), *clear* (lympha? comp. λάμπειν); lūridus, *ghastly yellow* (comp. lūror, Lucr.); morbi-dus, *diseased* (morbo-); nūdus, *naked;* sŏlĭ-dus, *firm* (sŏlo-, *ground*); stŏlĭ-dus, *stockish, stupid* (comp. stŏlōn-, *a useless sucker*); svādus, *persuasive* (svādēre); sūcĭ-dus, *juicy* (sūco-); sūdus, *dry* (se, udo-?); sur-dus, *deaf;* tardus, *slow* (comp. trăh-ĕre, *to drag*?); trĕpĭdus, *scarred, flurried* (comp. trĕmĕre); turbi-dus, *disturbed* (turba-); văpĭ-dus, *flat, spoiled* (văpōs-, from a presumed văpēre).

2. Substantives:

(*a*) Masculine: cădus, *a cask;* gurdus, *a dolt* (Spanish word acc. to Quint. I. 5. 57); **hædus,** *a goat;* **lūdus,** *a game;* **mŏdus,** *a measure;* **nīdus,** *a nest;* **nŏdus,** *a knot;* **turdus,** *a fieldfare;* **vĕrēdus** (Mart.), *a hunter* (horse).

(*b*) Feminine: **ălauda,** *a lark* (Keltic); **aplŭda,** *chaff;* **bascauda,** *a basket;* **cassīda** (usually **cassis**), *a helmet;* **cauda,** *a tail;* **cĭcāda,** *a grasshopper;* **crĕpīda,** *a sandal* (from κρηπῑδ-); **merda,** *dung;* **præda,** *booty;* **ræda,** *a four-wheeled carriage* (Keltic; cf. Quint. I. 5. 57); **tæda,** *a torch.*

(*c*) Neuter: **essēdum,** *a gig* (Keltic); **lārīdum (lardum),** *bacon;* **oppĭdum,** *a town* (comp. ἐπίπεδον?); **pĕdum,** *a shepherd's crook;* **vădum,** *a shoal, ford.*

-un-do or **-en-do** I. Verbal adjectives:

(*a*) As gerundive: for use see Book IV. Chap. XIV. and Appendix to Syntax. On their formation see §§ 617, 618. 817

ăma-ndus, *to love* or *to be loved* (**ămāre**); **audi-endus (audīre); capi-endus (căpĕre); gign-endus (gi-gn-ere); mŏn-endus (monēre); nasc-endus (nasci); rĕg-endus (rĕgĕre); tribu-endus (tribu-ĕre);** and so from all transitive verbs (§ 1186).

(*b*) As present participle (without an object accusative) or ordinary adjective:

blandus, *soothing* (comp. **flāre**); **infandus, nĕfandus,** *unspeakable* (**fāri**); **mundus,** *clean;* **ŏri-undus,** *arising* (**ŏrī-ri**); **pandus,** *crooked;* **rŏt-undus,** *round* (comp. **rŏt-āre**); **sĕcundus,** *following,* hence *second* (**sĕqvi**); **volv-endus,** *rolling* (**volvĕre**).

(2) Substantives:

(*a*) Masculine: **fundus,** *a landed estate, the bottom;* also *an authoriser;* **mundus,** *ornaments,* also *the universe* (as transl. of κόσμος).

(*b*) Feminine: **funda,** *a sling* (**fund-ĕre?**); **Kălendæ** (pl.), *the first of the month* (*summoning day?* comp. **călāre,** κάλεῖν); **menda,** (Ov.), **mendum** (Cic.), *a fault;* **mĕrenda** (*dinner*); **sponda,** *a bedstead;* **turunda,** *a paste-ball;* **suggrunda,** *the eaves;* **unda,** *water.*

-ĕb-undo or ⎫
-ĭb-undo ⎭ Adjectives, originally gerundives: 818

frĕm-ĕbundus, *muttering* (**frĕm-ĕre**); **fŭr-ībundus,** *raging* (**fur-ĕre**); **lascīv-ibundus** (Plaut. *Stich.* 288), *playful* (**lascīvī-re**); **lūd-ibundus,** *sporting* (**lūd-ĕre**); **mŏr-ībundus,** *dying* (**mŏrī, mŏrīrī**); **pŭdī-bundus,** *bashful* (**pŭdēre**); **qvĕr-ībundus,** *plaintive* (**quĕri**); **rīdī-bundus,** *laughing* (**rīdēre**); **trĕm-ĕbundus,** *trembling* (**trĕm-ĕre**).

-āb-undo From verbs with -a stems. Many of these forms are found only in Livy and post-Augustan historians. 819

comissā-bundus, *revelling;* **contiōnā-bundus,** *haranguing;* **cunctā-bundus,** *hesitating;* **dēlībĕra-bundus,** *deliberating;* **dēprĕcā-bundus,** *deprecatingly;* **errā-bundus,** *wandering about;* **grātŭlā-bundus,**

making congratulations; hæsĭtā-bundus (Plin. *Ep.* once), *hesitating;* indignā-bundus, *indignant;* lăcrĭmā-bundus, *weeping;* lurchĭnā-bundus (only in Cato; cf. Quint. I. 6. 42), *voracious;* mĕdĭtā-bundus (Just.), *in meditation;* mĭnĭtā-bundus, *threatening;* mīrā-bundus, *in wonder;* noctuā-bundus (Cic. once), *by night* (noctu-; noctuāre not found); oscŭlā-bundus (Suet.), *kissing;* pĕrĕgrīnā-bundus (Liv. once), *travelling about;* plōrā-bundus, *bewailing;* pŏpŭlā-bundus, *wasting;* prædā-bundus, *pillaging;* spĕcŭlā-bundus, *on the watch;* tentā-bundus, *making a trial;* tuburchĭnā-bundus (Cato, see above), *gobbling;* vĕnĕrā-bundus, *shewing reverence;* versā-bundus, *whirling;* vītā-bundus, *avoiding;* vŏlŭtā-bundus (Cic. fragm.), *wallowing.*

-c-undo Adjectives, probably gerundives from *inchoative* stems: 820 all have the preceding syllable long (except rubĭcundus).

fā-cundus, *eloquent* (fā-ri); fē-cundus, *fruitful* (comp. fē-mina, fē-tus); irā-c-undus, *angry* (irasc-i); jū-cundus, *pleasant* (jūv-āre); rŭbĭ-cundus, *ruddy* (rŭbēre); vĕrē-cundus, *bashful* (vĕrēri).

v. *Stems in -du, -di, -d.*

-du See § 397.

-di ædes (f.), *a hearth? a chamber* § 331 (comp. æs-tu-, αἴθειν); 821 cædes (f.), *slaughter;* clādes (f.), *disaster;* fīdis (f.), *a harpstring;* fraus (f.), *cheating;* frons (f.) *a leaf;* glans (f.), *an acorn* (comp. βάλανος and § 765); grandis, *large;* juglans (f.), *a walnut;* lendes (f. pl.), *nits;* pĕdis (m. f.), *a louse;* rŭdis, (1) *rude;* (2) f. *a spoon, a foil;* sēdes (f.), *a seat* (sĕdēre); sordes (f. pl.), *dirt;* sŭdis (f. § 421), *a stake;* trŭdes (f. pl.), *pikes* (comp. trūdĕre?); vĭrĭ-dis, *green* (vĭrēre).

-ŭd pĕcus (f.), *a head of cattle* (comp. pĕcu-, pĕcŏr-). 822

-ĕd (-ĭd) căpis (f.), *a sacrificial bowl* (căpĕre?); cassis (f.), *a helmet;* cuspis (f.), *a spear-point;* lăpis (m.), *a pebble;* promulsis (f.), *a whet for the appetite* (lit. *preliminary draught?*) (pro-, mulso-).

-ōd custos (n.), *a guardian.*

-ŭd palus (f.), *a marsh.*

-ēd cuppes (only in nom. sing.), *a glutton;* hēres (m.), *an heir;* merces (f.), *wages* (comp. merci-).

-d cor (n.), *a heart* (comp. καρδ-ία); laus (f.), *praise;* pes (m.), *a foot* (comp. ποδ-, nom. πούς); præs (m.), *a bail;* vās (m. f.), *a bail.*

Compound stem-endings: -dŏn, -ŭdŏn, -tŭdŏn, -ēdŏn, -ĭdŏn, §§ 846—848; -ēdŭlo, § 865; -ndio, § 933.

CHAPTER VI.

DENTAL NOUN-STEMS (*continued*).

vi. *Stems ending in* -no.

-no or -ino (For all words (except numerals) with long vowel pre- 823
ceding -no see §§ 830—842.)

1. Adjectives:

(*a*) bŏnus, *good;* concinnus, *neat;* dignus, *worthy;* hornus, *of this year* (ho-ver-, *this spring*); mag-nus, *great* (comp. măg-is); nōnus, *ninth* (for nŏvĭ-nus? but see § 754); plă-nus, *level* (comp. πλάξ); pĕrendĭ-nus, *of a day hence* (comp. πέραν, die-); ver-nus, *of spring* (vēr-); ūnus, *one*.

(*b*) Distributive numerals (rarely used in singular): bĭ-nus, *twofold, two each* (bi-); ter-nus or trĭ-nus (ter, tri-); qvăter-nus (qvăter) and (Varr., Plin.) qvadrĭnus (qvatvor); qvī-nus (for qvinqvĭ-nus, qvinc-nus, qvinqve); sē-nus (sex); septē-nus (for septem-nus, septen-nus); octō-nus (octo); nŏvē-nus (for nŏvem-nus); dēnus (for dĕcĭmĭnus? dec-nus); vīce-nus, *twenty each* (for vicent-nus, viginti); trīcē-nus, *thirty each* (trĭgĭnta), &c.; centē-nus, *a hundred each* (for centum-nus, the vowel being assimilated to what is found in others); dŭcē-nus, *two hundred each* (for ducent-nus); trĕcēnus, *three hundred each* (trĕcent-); qvadringē-nus, *four hundred each* (qvadringent-), &c. See Appendix.

(*c*) From names of trees and other materials: ăcer-nus, *of maple* (ăcer-); ădămantĭ-nus, *hard as diamond* (ἀδαμάντινος); ămārăcĭnus, *of marjoram* (ămārăco-); cĕrăsĭ-nus (Petron.), *cherry-coloured* (cĕrăso-); coccĭ-nus, *scarlet* (cocco-); cŏlur-nus, *of hazel* (for cŏrŭlĭ-nus, cŏrŭlo-); ĕbur-nus, *of ivory* (ĕbŏr-); ferrūgĭn-us (Lucr. once), *bluish-green* (ferrūgŏn-; ferrugineus is more usual); qvernus, *oaken* (for qverci-nus, qvercu-). See also salig-nus, &c., § 826.

2. Substantives:　　　　　　　　　　　　　　　　824

(*a*) Masculine: ăcĭnus, *a berry;* agnus, *a lamb;* annus, *a year;* ānus, *a ring;* ăsĭnus, *an ass;* căchinnus, *a laugh* (comp. καχάζειν); circĭ-nus, *a pair of compasses* (circo-); dŏmĭnus, *a lord* (dŏmāre); furnus, *an oven;* ginnus or hinnus, *a mule,* the mother being an ass (comp. γίννος, ἴννος); **mannus**, *a coach horse* (Keltic?); **pampīnus**, *a vine-shoot;* **pannus**, *a piece of cloth* (comp. πῆνος); **pānus**, (1) *thread on the bobbin*, (2) *a swelling* (from πῆνος?); **pugnus**, *a fist* (comp. πύξ, πυγμή); **rīcīnus**, *a sheep tick;* **som-nus**, *sleep* (comp. sŏp-or); **sŏnus**, *a sound;* **sturnus**, *a starling;* **tabanus**, *a gadfly;* **tornus**, *a lathe* (torqvēre, comp. τόρνος). **verna**, *a house slave.*

(*b*) Proper names (some are Etruscan): **Cinna; Perpenna** or **Perperna; Porsenna** (Verg.), **Porsĕna** (Hor., Mart., Sil.); **Saserna; Sisenna; Spurinna; Thalna; Vivenna.** Cf. § 838 *c.*

(*c*) Feminine: **alnus**, *an alder;* **cornus**, *a cornel tree;* **fraxīnus**, *an ash tree;* **ornus**, *a mountain ash;* **vannus**, *a winnowing fan.*

acna, *a plot* 120 *feet square;* **angīna** (L. Müll.), *quinsy* (comp. ἀγχόνη, **angĕre**); **antemna**, *a sailyard;* **fiscĭ-na**, *a rush basket* (fisco-); **fuscĭna**, *a three-pronged spear* (comp. **furca**); **gĕna**, *a cheek* (comp. γένυς, *a jaw*); **nundĭ-næ** (pl.), *market-day* (nōno-, die-); **pāgĭna**, *a leaf of a book*, &c. (comp. **pangĕre**); **pătĭ-na**, *a dish* (pătēre? comp. πατάνη, Sicil. βατάνη); **penna**, *a wing* (in old Latin **pesna** or **petna**; comp. πέτεσθαι); **perna**, *a ham;* **pinna**, *a feather;* **pugna**, *a battle* (comp. **pugnus**); **runcina** (generally given as **runcīna**), *a planing instrument* (comp. **runcāre**, ῥυκάνη); **sanna**, *a grimace* (comp. σαννᾶς); **sarcĭna**, *a bundle* (sarcīre, *to close*); **sqvatina**, *a skate-fish* (comp. **sqvālus**, *a fish*); **transenna**, *a net;* **ulna**, *an arm* (comp. ὠλένη); **urna**, *a pitcher* (comp. **ūrĕre**, *to burn*).

(*d*) Neuter: **cornum** (more frequently **cornu**), *a horn* (comp. κέρας); **fascĭnum**, *a charm* (comp. βάσκανος); **lignum**, *firewood* (līg-āre?); **pastĭnum**, *a two-pronged fork;* **pĕnum** (§ 398), *a store of provisions*, &c.; **reg-num**, *a kingdom* (rĕg-ĕre); **scamnum**, *a bench* (comp. **scab-illum**); **signum**, *a seal;* **stagnum**, *a pool, pent up water?* (comp. στεγανό-); **stannum**, *an alloy of silver and lead;* **tignum**, *a beam.*

-mīno ⎫
-mno ⎬ This suffix in Greek forms participles middle and passive; 825
       ⎭ e.g. τυπτ-όμενος, τυψ-άμενος, τετυμ-μένος, &c.

ær-umna, *sorrow* (αἰρομένη, *excited* mind); **al-umnus**, *a nursling* (ăl-ĕre); **autumnus**, *Autumn* (*the increasing* year, auctu-); **Clitumnus**, a river in Umbria; **cŏlumna**, *a column* (comp. **cul-men**, **cel-sus**); **da-mnum**, *a loss* (properly *a gift*, dă-re; or akin to δαπάνη); **fēmina**, *a woman* (comp. **fe-tus**, &c. § 800); **gĕmĭnus**, *twin;* **lāmmĭna** (lamna), *a plate of metal;* **termĭnus**, *a bound* (comp. τέρμα); **Vert-umnus**, the god of *change* (**vert-ĕre**).

The same suffix is seen in the 2nd pers. plur. of indicative and subjunctive passive of tenses formed from present stem: e.g. amā-

20

mini, amabīmini, amabāmini, amēmini, amarēmini, § 572: and in
an old sing. imperative form; e.g. præfamino, § 587.

Compare also -měn, § 85c.

-gĭno ⎱   Some are probably compounds with stems of gen-, 826
-gno ⎰   gi-gn-ĕre; others have a c turned into g by the influence
of the nasal; others are formed on their analogy.

ābie-gnus, *of fir* (ăbiĕt-); ăpru-gnus (Plaut., Plin.), *of wild
boar* (ăpro-); běni-gnus, *kindly, liberal* (*well-born*? běně-gĕn-); faba-
ginus (Cato), *of beans* (făba-); īlig-nus, *of holm oak* (īlĕc-); ŏleā-
ginus, *of the olive* (ŏlea-); māli-gnus, *stingy* (măle-gĕn-); prīvi-gnus
(subst.), *born from one parent only*, i.e. *a stepson* (prīvo-gen-);
sălig-nus, *of willow* (sălĭc-).

For terrigena, &c. see § 995; for magnus, dignus, § 823.

-tĭno   Adjectives: anno-tinus, *a year old*? (anno-); cras-tinus, 827
of to-morrow (cras); diū-tinus, *long continued* (diu);
horno-tinus, *of this year* (horno-); pris-tinus, *of former times*
(prius; comp. magis for magius); sēro-tinus (Plin., Col.), *late*
(sēro-).

-ur-no   diur-nus, *by day* (dius-, dies-, § 341 n., comp. nūdius; or 828
for diov-ĕrīnus?); diut-urnus (in Ovid always diūtur-
nus), *for long* (comp. diūt-ius); laburnum, *broad-leaved trefoil;*
noctu-rnus, *by night* (noctu-); Sāt-urnus (Saeturnus), *god of produce?* (sāto-, sĕ-rĕre); tăcĭturnus, *silent* (tăcĭto-) vīburnum, *the
wayfaring tree.*

-er-no   căverna, *a cave* (căvo-); cisterna, *a reservoir* (cista-);
fusterna, *the knotty part of a fir-tree* (fusti-, *a club*);
gŭberna (pl.), *rudders* (comp. κυβερνᾶν); hīb-ernus, *in winter*
(hiĕm-, cf. § 86. 5); hŏdiernus, *of to-day* (ho-, dius, or die-); infer-
nus, *below* (infĕro-); lăcerna, *a cloak;* Lăverna, *goddess of gain;*
lŭcerna, *a lamp* (comp. lūci-, lūcĕre); sŭper-nus, *above* (sŭpĕro-);
tăb-erna, *a booth* (from tăb-ŭla, *a plank*?). See also § 823 c.

-ter-no   i.e. -no suffixed to stems in -tĕro or -tri, or to adverbs 829
in -ter. In some the t perhaps is radical.

æ-ternus, *for ever* (ævo-, comp. æ-tat-); al-ter-nus, *alternate,
every other* (al-tero-); ex-ternus, *outside* (ex-tero-); frāternus, *of a
brother* (frāter-, comp. φράτερ-); hes-ternus, *of yesterday* (comp.
hĕri, χθές); in-ter-nus, *inside* (in-ter); lanterna (lāterna), *a lan-
tern;* māter-nus, *of a mother* (mater-); nassiterna, *a watering pot*
(said to be from naso-, terno-, *with three noses*); păternus, *of a
father* (păter-); sempĭternus, *everlasting* (comp. semp-er, § 540);
věter-nus, *lethargy* (větŭs-).

-āno   1. Adjectives: 830

(*a*) with ā as *stem* vowel: cānus, *hoary;* sā-nus, *sound* (comp. σάος); vā-nus, *empty* (comp. văc-uus).

(*b*) from appellatives:

ăpĭ-anus, *of bees;* name of Muscatel grape (ăpĭ-); arc-anus, *secret* (comp. arca-, arcēre); Camp-anus, *of the plain, a Campanian* (Campo-); castell-anus, *of a fortress* (castello-); decŭmanus, *of the tenth* (e.g. a tithe farmer; a soldier of the tenth legion, &c.; dĕcŭma-); font-anus, *of the spring* (fonti-); germanus, *of the full blood;* hūm-anus, *of man* (hŏmŏn-); insŭl-anus (Cic. once), *of an island* (insŭla-); Lătĕr-anus, a family name (lătĕr-?); mĕrīdi-anus, *of midday, southern* (merĭdĭe-); mont-anus, *of the mountains* (monti-); mund-anus, *of the universe* (mundo-); nōn-anus (Tac.), *of the ninth* legion (nōna-); oppĭd-anus, *of the town* (oppĭdo-); pāg-anus, *of a village* (pāgo-); prīdi-anus, *of the day before* (prīdie-); prīm-anus, *of the first* legion (prima-); publĭc-anus, *of the public revenue* (publĭco-); pŭte-anus (Plin., Col.), *of a well* (pŭteo-); qvŏtīdi-anus, *daily* (quotidie-); rustĭc-anus, *of the country* (rustĭco-); urb-ānus, *of the city* (urbi-); vĕtĕr-anus, *old, veteran* (vĕtŭs-); vīc-anus, *of a hamlet* (vīco-).

from proper names; (*c*) of places: Afrĭc-anus, *of the province among the Afri* (Afrĭ-ca); Alb-anus (Alba); Allīf-anus (Allifæ); Atell-ānus (Atella); Coriol-anus (Cŏriŏli); Cŭm-anus (Cumæ); Fregell-anus (Fregellæ); Fund-anus (Fundi); Gallĭc-anus, *of the province among the Gauls* (Gallĭca-); Lăbīc-anus (Labĭcum); Pæst-anus (Pæstum); Pŭteŏl-anus (Puteŏli); Rōm-anus (Roma); Saranus, Sarranus, *of Tyre* (Sarra); also a surname of the Atilian clan; i.q. Serranus (Momm. *C. I. R.* No. 549); Silanus, surname of Julian clan (Sila? but cf. Lucr. 6. 1265); Syracus-anus (Sўrăcūsæ); Thēb-anus (Thebæ); Tuscŭl-anus (Tusculum); and others.

(*d*) of persons: Cĭnn-anus (Cĭnna); Sull-anus (Sulla).

(*e*) *Compounds* formed immediately from a preposition and its case:

antĕlūc-anus, *before daylight* (ante lucem); antemerīdi-anus, *in the forenoon* (ante meridiem); antesign-anus, *in front of the standards* (ante signa); circumpăd-anus, *round the Po* (circum Padum); cis-rhēn-anus, *on this side of the Rhine* (cis Rhenum); pōmĕrīdi-anus, *in the afternoon* (post meridiem); subsign-anus, *of the reserve* (sub signis); suburb-anus, *near the city* (sub urbem); transmont-anus, *beyond the mountains* (trans montes); transpăd-ānus; transrhēn-ānus.

2. Substantives: (*a*) ānus (see § 824); Diana, *the goddess of* 831 *the day* (die-); Jānus (for Dianus), *the god of the day;* fānum, *a*

shrine (fā-rī); **grānum,** *a grain;* **lāna,** *wool* (comp. λάχνη); **membr-āna,** *skin* (membro-); **pānus** (see § 824); **qvartāna,** sc. febris, *a quartan ague* (qvarta-); **rā-na,** *a frog* (comp. **rā-vus,** *hoary*); **Silvānus,** *the wood god* (silva-); **Volcanus,** *the fire god.*

-i-āno   Adjectives in -anus, derived from stems, chiefly of proper 832 names, with suffix -io:

Acci-anus, *of Accius* (Accio-); Æmīli-anus, *belonging to the Æmilian clan* (Æmilia-); Asi-anus, *of Asia* (Asia-); Cæsāri-anus, *belonging to Cæsar's* (Cæsareus, *of Cæsar;* e.g. Cæsaris or Cæsarea celeritas, *Cæsar's quickness;* Cæsariana celeritas, *quickness, like Cæsar's*); Ciceron-ianus, *of Cicero* (Cīcĕrōn-); Claudi-anus, *of a Claudius* (Claudio-); Fābi-anus, *of a Fabian,* or *of the Fabian clan* (Fabio-, Fabia-); Mari-anus, *of Marius* (Mārio-); Mīlōn-ianus, *of Milo* (i.q. Milonius); Orcīni-anus (Mart.), *of a dead man* (Orcinus, *a dweller with death,* orco-); Pompei-anus, *of Pompeius* (Pompeio-); prætōri-anus, *of the prætor's camp* (prætorio-); Sejanus (Seio-); Summœnianus, *of a dweller in Underwall* (summœnio-); Tĭbĕri-anus, *of Tiberius;* Terenti-anus, *of Terentius* (Terentio-); Trajanus; and others.

-īt-āno   Probably from the Greek suffix -ίτης, or in analogy 833 therewith. (Properly it denotes *of the people of:*)

Antipolītanus, *of Antipolis* (Antipoli-); Gādītanus, *of Gades,* i.e. *Cadiz* (Gadi-); Massīlītanus, *of Marseilles* (Massilia-); Panormītanus, *of Panormus* (Panormo-); Taurōmĕnītanus, *of Tauromenium* (Tauromenio-); Tōmītanus, *of Tomi* (Tōmo-).

-ōno   1. Adjectives: prōnus, *headlong, with face forward* (pro-). 834

2. Substantives: (*a*) Masc. and neut.: cŏl-onus, *a farmer* (cŏl-ere); donum, *a gift* (dă-re); patr-cnus, *a patron* (patr-).

(*b*) Feminine: annona, *the year's supply of corn* (anno-); Bellona, *the war goddess* (bello-); caupona, *a tavern* (cōpa-, caup-ōn-); cŏrona, *a crown* (Lātona, *a goddess* (comp. Λήτω); matrona, *a married woman* (mātr-); persona, *a mask* (persŏnāre?); Pōmona, *Fruit goddess* (pōmo-).

For octonus, nonus (whence nōnæ, pl. *the ninth day*) see § 823 a.

-œno   ămœnus, *pleasant;* pœna, *a penalty* (comp. pūnīre).

-ūno   1. Adjectives: importunus, *unseasonable* (*without a port?* 835 in, portu-); jējunus, *fasting;* opportunus, *in front of the port, ready at hand* (ob portum).

2. Substantives: cūnæ (pl.), *a cradle* (for cŭbīnæ? cŭb-āre); fortuna, *fortune* (forti-; comp. nocti-, noctu-); lăcuna (or lŭcuna), *a hole* (lăcu-); Neptunus, *the sea god* (perhaps νιπτόμενος, § 825);

Portunus, *god of harbours* (portu-); pruna, *a live coal;* prunum, *a plum;* tribunus, *a tribe's* chief (trĭbu-); Văcuna, a Sabine goddess (comp. văcāre, văcuus).

-æno)   1. Adjectives: aenus (or ăhenus), *of bronze* (for æs- 836
-ēno (nus, from æsi-: the Umbrian has ahesnes); ălienus, *of another,* *alien* (ălio-); ĕgēnus, *needy* (ĕgēre); obscēnus, *illboding;* plēnus, *full* (comp. plēre); sĕrenus, *calm;* terrēnus, *earthly* (terra). Abȳdenus, *of Abydos* (Abȳdo); Cȳzĭcenus, *of Cyzicos* (Cyzĭco). For vicēnus and other numerals see § 823 *b*.

2. Substantives: (*a*) feminine: ăvena, *oats;* camena (casmena acc. to Varro), *a Muse* (comp. car-men); cătena, *a chain;* cēna (cesna, Fest.), *supper;* crŭmena, *a purse;* gălena, *lead ore;* hăbena, *a rein* (hăbēre); hărena, *sand;* læna, *a cloak* (comp. χλαῖνα, § 110. 3); lāniena, *a butcher's stall* (lānio-); lena, *a bawd;* strena, *an omen,* *a new year's gift;* vena, *a vein;* verbenæ (pl.), *boughs* of myrtle, &c. used in religious acts.

(*b*) Neuter: cænum, *mud;* fēnum (fœnum), *hay;* frēnum, *a rein;* vĕnenum, *poison;* venum (only in accus. § 369).

-i-ēno   i.e. -ēno suffixed to stems in -io.   837
        Proper names: Aufīdienus, Avĭdienus, Cătienus, Labienus, Năsidienus, Vettienus, and others.

-ĭl-ēno   cantĭlena, *a tune* (cantu-).

-īno   (In some of the following words the length of the ĭ is 838
        not proved.)

        1. Adjectives: (*a*) from appellatives:

ădultĕrinus, *spurious* (adultĕro-); agninus, *of a lamb* (agno); ănătinus (Plaut., Petr.), *of a duck* (ănăt-); angvinus, *of a snake* (angvi-); ansĕrinus (Plin., Col.), *of a goose* (ansĕr-); ăprinus, *of a wild boar* (ăpro-); ărĭĕtinus (Plin.), *of a ram* (ărĭĕt-); austrīnus, *southern* (austro-); căninus, *of a dog* (căn-); căprinus, *of a goat* (capro-); cervinus, *of a deer* (cervo-); collinus, *of a hill* (colli-); cŏlumbinus, *of a dove* (cŏlumbo-); cŏqvinus, *of a cook* (cŏqvo-); corvinus, *of a raven* (corvo-); dīvinus, *of a god* (dīvo-); ĕqvinus, *of a horse* (ĕqvo-); femĭninus, *of a woman* (fēmĭna-); festinus, *hasty* (comp. con-fes-tim); fūrinus (Plaut. once), *of a thief* (fūr-); gĕnuinus, *of a jaw* (comp. γένυς); *native* (gĭ-gn-ĕre); hircinus, *of a goat* (hirco-); inŏpīnus, *unexpected* (comp. opīnāri); leōninus, *of a lion* (leōn-); lĕpŏrinus, *of a hare* (lĕpŏs-); lŭpinus, *of a wolf* (lŭpo-); mărinus, *of the sea* (mări-); mascŭl-inus, *of a male* (mascŭlo-); mīluinus, *of a kite* (mīluo-); pĕrĕgrinus, *of abroad* (pĕrĕgre); porcinus, *of a pig* (porco-); sōrĭcinus (Plaut. once), *of a shrew mouse* (sŏrĕc-); sŭpīnus, *with face upward*; taurīnus, *of a bull*; ursīnus, *of a bear* (urso-); verrīnus, *of a boar pig* (verrī-); vĕtĕrīnus, *of beasts of burden* (comp. vĕhĕre); vīcīnus, *of the street, neighbour* (vīco-); vītūlīnus, *of a calf* (vītŭlo-); volpīnus, *of a fox* (volpī-); and others.

(*b*) From proper names of places: Albīnus, a cognomen of the Postumian clan (Alba?); Alpīnus (Alpes, pl.); Arīcīnus (Arīcia); Căpītōlīnus (Căpītōlium); Caudīnus (Caudium); Collātīnus (Collatia); Esqvīlīnus (Esqvīliæ); Fĕrentīnus (perhaps for Ferentininus from Ferentinum); Lānŭvīnus (Lanuvium); Lătīnus (Latium); Mĕdullīnus (Medullia); Pālātīnus, but in Martial Pălātīnus (Palatium); Prænestīnus (Præneste); Reātīnus (Reate); Rhēgīnus (Rhegium); Tärentīnus (Tarentum); Vĕnūsīnus (Venusia); and others.

Aventīnus, Qvīrīnus, Sabīnus, are of uncertain origin.

(*c*) From proper names of persons; chiefly from such as were originally appellatives:

They are used as substantives, being surnames:

Albīnus (Albus); Antōnīnus (Antōnius); Aqvīlīnus (Aquila?); Atrātīnus (Atratus?); Augŭrīnus (Augur); Augustīnus (Augustus); Cæsōnīnus (Cæso); Calvīnus (Calvus); Cicŭrīnus (Cīcur); Corvīnus (Corvus); Crispīnus (Crispus); Flāmīnīnus (Flaminius or flāmen?); Frontīnus (Fronto?); Justīnus (Justus); Lactūcīnus (Lactuca); Lævīnus (Lævus); Longīnus (Longus); Luscīnus (Luscus); Măcĕrīnus and Macrīnus (Macer); Mamercīnus (Mamercus); Mancīnus (Mancus); Marcellīnus (Marcellus); Messallīnus (Messalla); Mĕtellīnus (Mĕtellus); Pætīnus (Pætus); Plautīnus (Plautus); Rūfīnus (Rufus); Saturnīnus (Sāturnus); Sextīnus (Sextus or Sestus); Tricipitīnus (triceps); and some others.

Compare orcīnus, *of Orcus* or *death* (Orcus); Plautīnus, *of Plautus* (Plautus).

2. Substantives:

(*a*) Masculine: concŭbīnus (cŏncubina), *a concubine* (com, cŭbāre); inqvīl-inus, *a lodger* (in cŏl-ere); lŭpīnus, *a lupine;* pulvīnus, *a cushion;* sobrīnus (sobrina f.), *a second cousin, sister's child?* (sŏrŏr-).

Cæcīna (Cæcus); Canina (canis?); Porcīna (porca?).

(*b*) Feminine: carpīnus (-īnus?), *the hornbeam;* pīnus (cf. § 398), *a pine tree* (for pic-nus? cf. § 110, 1; and comp. πίτυς); sapinus (-īnus?), *a kind of pine tree;* sīnus (sinum), *a tankard.*

arvīna (Verg.), *grease;* cæpīna (Col.), *an onion bed* (cæpa-); cărīna, *a keel;* carnificīna, *place of torture, torture* (carnifex); fărīna, *meal* (comp. farr-); fŏdīnæ (pl.), *mines* (fŏdĕ-re); gallīna, *a hen* (gallo-); lăpĭcīdīnæ (pl.), *stone quarries* (lapid-, cæd-ĕre); nāpīna

(Col.), *a colza* or *coleseed bed* (nāpo-); ŏpĭfĭcĭna (Plaut.), offĭcĭna, *a workshop* (offĭcĭo-, § 929 *a*); părĭĕtĭnæ? (parĭetĭnæ?), *ruins* (părĭĕt-); piscīna, *a fish-pond* (piscĭ-); pŏpīna, *a cookshop* (cf. cŏqvo-, § 118. 2); porrina (Cato), *a leek bed* (porro-); pruina, *hoarfrost* (comp. pro, præ, πρωΐ); răpīna, *pillage* (răpĕ-re); rāpīna, *turnip* (rāpo-); rēgīna, *a queen* (rēg-); rēsīna, *resin* (ῥητίνη); ruina, *a fall* (ru-ĕre); săgīna, *stuffing, food* (comp. σάττειν); sălīnæ, pl. (also sălinum), *saltpits* (săl-, sălīre); scobina, *a rasp* (scăb-ere); spina, *a thorn* (for spīcīna, from spīca-); văgīna, *a sheath;* urīna, *urine* (comp. οὖρον).

Agrippīna (Agrippa); Faustīna (Faustus); Plancīna (Plancus).

(*c*) Neuter: cătīnum (also catīnus, m.), *a dish;* līnum, *flax;* vīnum, *wine* (comp. vī-tis, vĭēre, *to twine*).

-c-ĭno   Cloācĭna, *goddess of sewers* (cloāca); medĭ-c-īna, *medical* 840 *art* (medĭco-, mĕdēre); mortĭ-cīnus (adj.), *carrion* (mortĭ-).

-t-īno   1. Adjectives: clandestīnus, *secret* (comp. clam); intes-
            tīnus, *internal* (intus); lībertīnus, *of the* class of *freed-
men* (lĭberto-); mātūt-īnus, *in the morning* (mātūta, *the dawn*);
mĕdĭ-ast-īnus, *from the middle of the city,* hence *a drudge* (medĭo-,
ἄστυ); pauper-tīnus (Varr., Gell.), *poor* (paupĕr-); rĕp-ent-īnus,
sudden (repenti-); vesper-tīnus, *of the evening* (vespĕr-).
    For proper names see § 838 *b. c.*

    2. Substantives: cortīna, *a boiling pot;* Lībĭtīna, *goddess of
funerals;* sentīna, *bilge-water.*

-līno   cŭlīna, *a kitchen* (for coc-līna? coqvo-); discĭplīna, *train-* 841
            ing (disc-ĭp-ŭlo-, discĕre); sterqvī-līnum (Phædr.), *a
dungheap* (for stercŏrīnum? stercŏs-); tablīnum, *a registry*
(tăbŭla-).

-tr-īno   From stems in -tor. (For the omission of ō compare 842
            the ending -trīc, § 782.)

            doc-tr-īna, *learning* (dŏcēre); lā-tr-īna (lăvātrīna), *a privy*
(lăvāre); pis-tr-īnum, *a mill;* pis-tr-īna, *a bakehouse*
(pīs-ĕre, *to pound*); sū-tr-īna, *a cobbler's shop* or *trade*
(su-ĕre); tex-tr-īnum, *weaving* (tex-ĕre); tons-tr-īna, *a
barber's shop* (tondēre).

vii. *Stems ending in* -ni, -n.
                                                                              843

-ni   1. Adjectives: immānis, *wild* (in, māno-; "in carmine
            Saliari Cerus manus intelligitur creator bonus," Festus,
p. 122, Müll.); Inānis, *empty;* mūnis (rare), *obliging* (comp. mūnus); omnis, *all;* segnis, *lazy;* sollemnis, *customary.*

2. Substantives: **amnis** (m.), *a river;* **clūnis** (m. f.), *a haunch;* **crīnis** (m.), *hair;* **fīnis** (m. f.), *a boundary* (for **fid-nis, find-ere**); **fūnis** (m.), *a rope;* **ignis** (m.), *fire;* **māne** (n.), *the morning;* **mānes** (m. pl.), *the spirits below;* **mœnia** (n. pl.), *walls;* **mūnia** (n. pl.), *duties* (same as **mœnia**); **pānis** (m.), *a loaf of bread;* **pēnis** (m. for **pes-nis**; comp. πέος, πόσ-θη); **rēnes** (m. pl.), *kidneys.* On **cănis** (m. f.), *a dog,* see § 448.

-**ŏn** (-**ĭn**) Substantives: **căro** (f.), *flesh* (comp. κρέας); **hŏmo** (m. ⁸⁴⁴ also **hĕmo**, § 449, and with old stem in -**ōn**), *a man* (**hŭmo-,** *ground*); **nēmo,** *no one* (**ne, hĕmɔ**); **turbo** (m.), *a whirl* (comp. **turba-**).

-**gŏn** (-**gĭn**) Substantives: **aspergo** (f.), *a sprinkling* (**adsparg-ere**); ⁸⁴⁵ **margo** (m.), *a brink* (comp. **merg-ĕre,** *to dip*); **virgo** (f.), *a girl* (**vīro,** *a man?* or **vīr-ēre,** *to be fresh.* Curtius and Corssen connect it with the root of ὀργ-άω).

-**āg-ŏn** (-**āgĭn**) All feminine: **ambago** (only abl. s., Manil.), *circuit* (**amb, ăg-ĕre?**); **compāgo,** *a fastening* (**com, pang-ere**); **cŏri-ago** (Col.), *a skin disease* (**cŏrio-**); **farr-ago,** *a mash* (**farr-**); **ĭmāgo,** *a likeness* (comp. **im-ĭtāri;** perhaps for **mimi-tari;** comp. μιμεῖ-σθαι); **indago,** *an encircling* (**indo, ăg-ere?**); **lumb-ago** (Fest.), *loin disease* (**lumbo-**); **plumb-ago,** *blacklead* (**plumbo-**); **prŏpāgo,** *a slip* of a plant, *offspring* (**pro, pang-ere**); **sartago,** *a fryingpan;* **suffrāgo,** *the pastern,* as if *broken* and bent *up* (**sub, frang-ĕre**); **vīrago,** *a bold girl* (**vīro-**); **vŏrago,** *a gulf* (**vŏră-re**).

-**ĭl-āg-ŏn** (-**gĭn**) All feminine: **cartilago,** *gristle* (comp. κρέας); **salsĭlago** (Plin.), *saltness* (**salso-**); **similago** (Plin.), *fine flour* (**sĭmĭla-**).

-**ūg-ŏn** (-**ūgĭn**) All feminine: **ær-ugo,** *bronze-rust, jealousy* (**æs-**); **alb-ugo,** a disease of the eye (**albo-**); **ferr-ugo,** *ironrust* (**ferro-**); **lān-ugo,** *downy hair* (**lāna-**); **sals-ugo,** *saltness* (**salso-**); **vespĕr-ugo** (Plaut.), *the evening star* (**vespĕro-**).

-**ĭg-ŏn** (-**ĭgĭn**) All feminine: **cālĭgo,** *mist* (comp. **clam, cēlā-re**); de**pĕtigo, impĕtigo,** *a scabby eruption;* **fūligo,** *soot;* in**tertrigo,** *a galling* (**inter, tri-, tĕrĕre**); **lent-igo,** *freckles* (**lenti-,** *linseed,* which freckles resemble); **lŏlligo,** *a cuttle fish;* **melligo,** *bee-glue* (**mell-**); **ŏrigo,** *a source* (**ŏrīri**); **porrigo,** *scurf* (**porro-,** *leek?*); **prūrigo,** *itching* (**prūrīre**); **rōbigo** (**rūbigo**), *rust* (**rŭb-ro-,** *red*); **scaturigines** (pl.), *springs* (**scăturīre**); **sīligo,** *white wheat;* **tentigo,** *tension* (**tento-**); **vertigo,** *a turn* (**vertĕre**); **vitiligo,** *a tetter;* **ūligo,** *wet* (**ūdo-**).

-**d-ŏn** (-**dĭn**) **cardo** (m.), *a hinge* (comp. κραδᾶν, *to brandish*); **grando** ⁸⁴⁶ (f.), *hail* (comp. χάλαζα, § 126); **hărundo** (f.), *a reed;* **hĭrundo** (f.), *a swallow* (comp. χελιδών, § 134); **ordo** (m.), *a row.*

-ūd-ŏn (-ūdĭn) hīrudo (f.), *a leech;* testudo (f.), *a tortoise* (testa-, *a potlid.*

-tūdŏn (-tūdĭn) Feminine abstract substantives. All have (appa- 847 rently) a short ĭ before the suffix, except the derivatives from sueto- (in which a syllable has dropped out) and valētudo.

ægrĭ-tudo, *sickness, sorrow* (ægro-); altĭ-tudo, *height* (alto-); amārĭ-tudo (Plin. maj. and min.), *bitterness* (ămāro-); amplĭ-tudo, *wide extent* (amplo-); asperĭ-tudo (Cels.), *roughness* (aspĕro-); assvē-tudo (for assuetitudo), *habit* (ad-svēto-): so also consvetudo, desvetudo, mansvetudo; celsĭ-tudo (Vell.), *highness;* so as a title (Cod. Theod.), e. g. *your Highness* (celso-); clārĭ-tudo (chiefly Tac.), *renown* (claro-); crassĭ-tudo, *thickness* (crasso-); dissĭmĭlĭ-tudo, *unlikeness* (dis;ĭmĭli-); firmĭ-tudo, *firmness* (firmo-); fortĭ-tudo, *courage* (forti-); hăbĭ-tudo, *habit* (for habititudo, from hăbĭto-); hĭlărĭ-tudo (Plaut.), *merriment* (hĭlăro-); lassĭ-tudo, *weariness* (lasso-); lātĭtudo, *breadth* (lāto-); lēnĭ-tudo (rare), *leniency* (lēni-); lentĭ-tudo, *sluggishness* (lento-); lippĭ-tudo, *inflammation in the eyes* (lippo-); longĭ-tudo, *length* (longo-); magnĭ-tudo, *greatness* (magno-); mollĭtudo, *softness* (molli-); multĭ-tudo, *great number* (multo-); nĕcessĭtudo, *necessity, close bond* (nĕcesse); partĭ-tudo (Plaut. twice), *a giving birth* (partu-); pingvĭ-tudo, *fatness* (pingvi-); pulchrĭ-tudo, *beauty* (pulchro-); sanctĭ-tudo (præ-Cic.), *sacredness* (sancto-); sĭmĭlĭ-tudo, *likeness* (sĭmĭli-); sōlĭ-tudo, *loneliness* (sōlo-); sollĭcĭtudo, *anxiety* (sollicito-); svāvĭ-tudo (præ-Cic.), *sweetness* (svāvi-); tĕnĕrĭ-tudo (Varr., Suet.), *softness, tender years* (tĕnĕro-); turpĭ-tudo, *ugliness, disgrace* (turpi-); vălĕ-tudo, *health* (vălēre); vastĭ-tudo (old prayer in Cato), *wasting* (vasto-); vĭcissĭ-tudo, *change* (comp. vicissim): and many others, chiefly words quoted by Nonius from the early dramatists.

-ēd-ŏn (-ēdĭn) All feminine: absūmēdo (Plaut. *Capt.* 901), *consump-* 848 *tion* (absūmĕre, with pun on sumen); alcedo, *king fisher* (comp. ἀλκυών); căpedo, *a sacrificial bowl* (căpĕre; comp. căpĭd-); cuppēdo (Lucr.), *desire* (comp. cuppēdia, *delicacies,* cūpĕ-re); dulcedo, *sweetness* (dulci-); grăvedo, *a heavy cold* (grăvi-); intercăpedo, *an interval* (inter, căpĕre); tĕredo, *a worm,* or *moth* (tĕr-ĕre; comp. τερηδών); torpedo, *numbness* (tŏrpēre); ūredo, *blight* (ūr-ĕre).

-ĭd-ŏn (-ĭdĭn) All feminine: crēpĭdo, *an edge* (from κρηπῑδ-?); cŭpĭdo (f. except as a god), *desire* (cūpĕ-re); formīdo, *dread* (forma-, *making shapes to oneself?*); lĭbido, *lust* (lĭbēre).

-ĕn jŭvĕnis (m.), *a youth;* sĕn-ex (the nom. sing. has a fur- 849 ther suffix), *an old man.*

-ĕn (-ĭn) glūten (n.), *glue* (comp. glūto-, adj.); ingven (n.), *the groin;* pecten (m.), *a comb* (pect-ĕre); pollis (m. no nom. sing.), *fine flour* (comp. πάλη); sangvis (m.) and sangven (n. § 449), *blood;* ungven (n.), *ointment* (ung-ĕre).

-mĕn (-min) All neuter substantives, chiefly derived from verbs. 850 Comp. the suffixes, -mīno, § 825, -mento, § 792.

(*a*) From vowel-verbs with stems ending in -ā, -ū, or -ĭ.

ācū-men, *a point* (ăcu-ĕre); calceā-men (Plin.), *a shoe* (calceā-re); cantā-men (Prop. once), *a spell* (cantā-re); certā-men, *a contest* (certā-re); cōnāmen (Lucr., Ov.), *an effort* (cōnā-ri); curvā-men (Ov.), *a bend* (curvā-re); durā-men (Lucr.), *hardening* (dūrā-re); flāmen, *a blast* (flā-re); also (m.) *a priest;* flū-men, *a stream* (flu-ĕre); fŏrā-men, *a hole* (fŏrā-re, *to bore*); fundā-men (Verg., Ov.), *a foundation* (fundā-re); gestā-men, *a wearing article, a conveyance* (gestā-re); glŏmĕrā-men, *a round ball* (glŏmerā-re); lēnī-men (Hor., Ov.), *a solace* (lēnī-re); lĕvā-men, *an alleviation* (lĕvā-re); mōlī-men, *an effort* (mōlī-ri); nū-men, *a nod, the divine will* (nu-ĕre); nūtrī-men (Ov. once), *nourishment* (nutrī-re); plăcā-men, *a means of pacifying* (plăcā-re); pŭtā-men, *a clipping, shell,* &c. (pŭtā-re); sōlā-men, *a comfort* (sōlā-ri); stā-men, *the warp thread* (stāre); stătū-men, *a stay, prop* (stătu-ĕre); strā-men *a straw* (stra-, sternĕre); suffī-men (Ov. once), *incense* (suffī-re); sufflā-men, *a drag* (sufflāre?); tentā-men (Ov.), *an attempt* (tentā-re); vŏcā-men (Lucr.), *a name* (vŏcā-re); and others.

(*b*) From other verbs, or of uncertain derivation:

abdōmen, *the belly;* agmen, *a train* (ăg-ĕre); albūmen (Plin.), *the white of an egg* (albo-); alumen, *alum;* augmen, *a growth* (aug-ēre); bītūmen, *bitumen;* căcūmen, *a summit;* carmen, *a song, a charm* (comp. cămēna, § 836. 2); cŏlūmen, *a top, support* (comp. cel-sus); crī-men, *a charge* (comp. cre-, cernĕre, κρίνειν); culmen (contr. for columen; rare before Augustan age); discrīmen, *a distinction* (comp. discer*n*-ĕre); dŏcūmen (Lucr. once), *a lesson* (dŏc-ēre); exāmen, *a swarm, the tongue of a balance* (ex-ăg-ĕre); fĕmen-, *a thigh;* ferrūmen, *solder* (ferro-); flē-mīna (pl.), *bloody swellings* (comp. φλέγ-ειν); frag-men, *a fragment* (frang-ere); germen, *a bud;* grāmen, *grass* (comp. grandis, grānum); lĕgūmen, *pulse;* līmen, *a lintel, a threshold;* lū-men, *a light* (lūc-ēre); mō-men (for mŏ-vĭmen), *movement* (mŏvēre); nōmen, *a name,* esp. of the clan; e.g. Cornelius; so also agnōmen, *an additional surname;* e.g. Africanus; cognōmen, *the name of the family;* e.g. Scipio; prænomen, *the individual name;* e.g. Lucius (no-sc-ere); ōmen, *an omen;* rĕg-īmen, *guidance* (rĕg-ĕre); rūmen (rare), *the gullet* (comp. rū-mīn-āre, *to chew the cud*); sagmen, *a tuft of sacred herbs;* sarmen

(Plaut. once), *brushwood* (sarp-ĕre); segmen (rare), *a cutting* (sĕcāre); sēmen, *seed* (sĕ-rĕre); spĕcīmen, *a pattern* (spĕcĕ-re); subtē-men, *the woof* (subtex-ere); sū-men, *an udder* (sūg-ĕre); tĕg-īmen (teg-men), *a covering* (tĕg-ĕre); tor-mina (pl.), *gripes* (torqv-ēre); vermīna, *gripes* (for vermi-min-? vermi-, *a worm*); vī-men, *a withe* (viēre).

-ōn   All masculine (except Juno): many are personal names: 851

(*a*) Appellatives: æro (Vitr., Plin.), *a basket;* ăgāso, *a groom;* āleo (rare), *a gamester* (ālea-); ăqvīlo, *the northwind* (comp. ăqvīlo-, *dark-coloured*); bălātro, *a jester;* bāro, *a dolt;* būbo, *an owl* (comp. βύας); bucco, *a babbler* (bucca-, *a cheek*); būfo, *a toad;* buteo, *a hawk;* calcītro, *a kicker* (calci-); cālo, *a soldier's servant;* căpīto, *a big-headed man* (căpŭt-); căpo, *a capon* (comp. căpo-); carbo, *a coal;* caupo, *a tavern-keeper* (comp. κάπ-ηλος); cento, *a patchwork;* cerdo, *an artisan* (from κέρδος?); cilo (Fest.), *having a long narrow head;* cīnīflo (Hor.), *an assistant at the toilet* (cf. § 992); combīb-o (rare), *a boon companion* (com, bīb-ĕre); cŏmĕd-o (Lucil., Varr.), *a glutton* (comĕd-ĕre); commīlĭt-o, *a fellow-soldier* (com, mīlĕt-); congerr-o (Plaut.), *a playfellow* (com, gerra-); crābro, *a hornet;* cūdo (abl. only; Sil.), *a skin helmet;* dŏlo, *a staff* with a sharp point; ĕpŭl-o, *a feaster* (ĕpŭla-); ĕqviso (Varr.), *a groom* (ĕqvo-); erro, *a runaway* (errā-re); fronto, *with a large forehead* (fronti-); fullo, *a fuller;* gāneo, *debauchee* (gānea-); gerr-o, *a trifler* (gerra-); hēluo, *a glutton;* lābeo, large-*lipped* (lăbio-); latro, *a mercenary* soldier; hence *a brigand* (comp. λᾰτρεύειν); lēno, *a pander;* leo, *a lion* (comp. λέων, λεοντ-); līgo, *a hoe;* lurco, *a glutton;* mango, *a dealer;* ment-o, long-*chinned* (mento-); mirmillo, *a gladiator,* who wore *a fish* (μόρμυρος?) on his helmet; mūcro, *a sharp point;* mūto (i. q. pēnis); nās-o, *with a big nose* (nāso-); nĕbŭlo, *a worthless fellow* (nĕbŭla-); palp-o, *a flatterer* (palpo-); pāvo, *a peacock;* pēro, *a rawhide boot;* pĕtăso, *a leg of pork;* petro, *a hardy rustic* (πέτρα); ponto, *a punt, pontoon* (ponti-?); pŏpīn-o, *a frequenter of eating-houses* (pŏpīna-); præco, *a crier* (præ, vŏc-āre?); præd-o, *a robber* (præda-); pulmo, *a lung* (comp. πλεύμων); rēno, *a reindeer* (Keltic); sabulo, *gravel* (sabulo-); sermo, *conversation* (sĕr-ĕre, *to join,* sĕr-ies); sīlo, *snub-nosed* (silo-); spādo, *a eunuch;* stōlo, *a useless sucker;* strābo, *a squinter;* subulo, *a flute player* (Etruscan); tēmo, *a carriage pole;* tīro, *a recruit;* trīco (Lucil.), *a trickster* (trīca-); udo, *a felt shoe;* vespillo, *a corpse-bearer* at night (vespĕra-); umbo, *a boss* (comp. umbilīcus, ἄμβων); vŏlōnes (pl.), *volunteer soldiers* (vel-le?); unedo (Plin.), *the arbutus.*

Jūno (fem.); comp. also §§ 481, 505.

(*b*) Many are used chiefly or exclusively as cognomina. (In this list the name of the clan is added):

Bucco, of the Pompeian clan (vid. supr.); **Buteo**, Fabian (vid. supr.); Căpīto, Fonteian, &c. (vid. supr.); **Carbo**, Papirian (vid. supr.); **Căto**,

Porcian (Căto-?); Cerco, Lutatian (*tailed*, κερκο-); Cĭcĕro, *vetch man*, Tullian (Cĭcĕr-); Corbŭlo, *basket man*, Domitian (corbŭla-); Culleo, *bagman*, Terentian (culleo-); Dorso, *longback?* Fabian (dorso-); Fronto, a surname in several clans (vid. supr.); Kæso, Fabian, "a cæso matris utero dictus" (Plin. 7. 9. 7); Lăbeo, in several clans (vid. supr.); Latro, Porcian (vid. supr.); Lĭbo, Marian and Scribonian; Lurco, Aufidian (vid. supr.); Mento, Julian (vid. supr.); Nāso, in several clans (nāso-); Nĕro, Claudian (Sabine for "fortis ac strenuus"); Pĕdo, *splayfoot?*, rare (pĕd-); Pĭso, *pease*, Calpurnian (pĭso); Sĭmo, *flat nosed* (sĭmo-); Stŏlo, Licinian (vid. supr.); Străbo, in several clans (vid. supr.); Tappo, Villian; Tŭbĕro, *humpback?*, Cælian (tŭbĕr-, *a boil, lump*, &c.); Varro, *bowlegged*, Terentian (vāro-); Vŏlĕro, Publilian; Vulso, *with smooth face?*, Manlian (vulso-, *plucked?*); and some others (besides those in -iōn).

-iōn   (1) Masculine: (*a*) appellatives: 852

ardĕl-io, *a trifler;* bĭnio, *a deuce* (bĭno-); centŭrio, *a captain* (centŭria-); curcŭlio, *a weevil;* cŭrio, *the head of a curia;* decurio, *a commander of ten* (decuria-); dūplio (old), *the double;* ēsŭrio (Plaut. punning; Petr.), *a hungry man* (ēsŭr-ĭre); gurgŭlio, *the windpipe* (comp. Engl. *gargle*); histrio, *an actor* (Etruscan); lĭbell-io, *a bookseller* (lĭbello-); lūd-io, *a stage player* (lŭdo-); matell-io, *a pot* (mătella-); mŏrio, *a fool* (μωρό-); mūl-io, *a muleteer* (mūlo-); ŏpĭlio, *a shepherd* (comp. ŏvi-, and cf. § 94. 1 *b*); păpĭlio, *a butterfly;* pellio, *a currier* (pelli-); pernio (Plin.), *a chilblain* (perna-?); pugio, *a dagger* (pu*n*g-ĕre); pŭmĭlio, *a dwarf* (pŭmĭlo-); pŭsio, *a little boy* (pŭso-, comp. puĕro-); quīnio, *a cinq* (quīno-) ; restio, *a ropemaker* (resti-); sannio, *a grimacer* (sanna-); scĭpio, *a staff* (comp. σκῆπτρον); scopio, *a grape stalk;* sĕnĕc-io, *an old man* (comp. sĕn-ec-); senio, *a seize* (sex, sĕno-); septentrio, *the north* (septem, trio, *a star?* M. Müller's *Lectures*, II. p. 365); stelio, *a gecko*, a kind of *spotted* lizard (stella-); Tălassio, a cry addressed to a bride; tĕnebrio (Varr.), *a swindler* (tĕnĕbra-); vespertilio, *a bat* (as if from vespertĭlis, *of the evening*); ūnio, *a pearl* (ūno-?).

(*b*) Proper names: Cæpio, Servilian (cæpa-, *onion*); Cŭrio, Scribonian (vid. supr.); Glăbrio, Acilian (glăbro-, *smooth, hairless*); Pollio, Asinian (paullo-); Scĭpio, Cornelian (vid. supr.); Sĕnĕcio, Claudian (vid. supr.).

(2) Feminine: abstract substantives (*a*) derived from verbs:

allŭvio, *inundation* (ad lavāre); căpio, *an acquisition;* collŭvio (Liv.), *sweepings* (com, lăv-are); condĭcio, *terms of agreement* (condīcere, comp. maledĭc-us); contāgio, *contagion* (com, tangĕre); dĭcio (no nom. s.), *rule* (comp. dĭc-, dīcĕre?); internecio, *destruction* (inter, nĕc-are); lĕgio, *a body of soldiers* (lĕg-ere, *to pick up*); oblīvio, *forgetfulness* (oblīvi-sc-i); obsĭdio, *a blockade* (obsĭdēri); occīdio, *massacre* (occīd-ĕre); optio, *a choice;* hence (m.?), *an adjutant* (opt-āre); ŏpīnio, *opinion* (ŏpīnārī); rĕgio, *a district* (rĕg-ĕre, *to mark out boundaries*); rellĭgio, *a scruple* (rĕlĕgere); suspīcio, *suspicion* (suspĭcĕ-re); usucăpio, *acquisition by enjoyment* (usu, căpĕ-re).

(*b*) Derived from noun stems in -i:
commūnio, *sharing in common* (commūni-); consortio, *fellowship* (consorti-); portio, *a share* (comp. parti-); perduellio, *treason* (perduelli-); rĕbellio, *revolt* (rĕbelli-); tālio, *retaliation* (tāli-).

-ciŏn   hŏmun-cio, *a mannikin* .(hŏmŏn-); comp. senĕcion- 353
                (§ 852 *a*).

-tion   Abstract feminine substantives formed from supine stems. 854
Some are used in concrete sense:

(*a*) From supine stems of vowel verbs with long vowel preceding the suffix (the verbs themselves are omitted as self-evident):

accūs-at-io, *an accusation;* advŏc-atio, *legal assistance;* æstĭm-atio, · *a valuation;* ăgĭt-at-io, *movement;* alterc-at-io, *dispute;* ămat-io (Plaut.), *caressing;* ambŭl-at-io, *a promenade;* appell-at-io, *an appeal, a name;* ăqv-at-io, *water-supply;* ăr-at-io, *ploughing;* assent-at-io, *flattery;* attrīb-ūt-io, *assignment;* aud-īt-io, *hearing, hearsay;* capt-at-io, *catching;* căvill-at-io, *raillery;* cĕlĕbr-at-io, *an assemblage;* clārĭg-at-io, *a solemn declaration of war;* cōgĭt-at-io, *thought;* cogn-at-io, *relationship by blood* (com, na-sci); coll-at-io, *a contribution, comparison;* compăr-at-io, *comparison;* concert-at-io, *dispute;* concĭt-at-io, *excitement;* concurs-at-io, *running together;* confarre-atio, *religious marriage* (com-, farreo-, i.e. *eating together the bridal cake*); constĭt-ūt-io, *disposition;* contempl-at-io, *contemplation;* contest-atio, *joining issue, calling witnesses* (com, testārī); crētio, *acceptance of.an inheritance* (cernere); cunct-ăṫio, *delay;* cūr-atio, *management;* damn-atio, *condemnation;* declīn-atio, *turning aside;* defīn-īt-io, *marking off;* dēlēg-atio, *assignment* of debt, &c.; dēmĭnūt-io, *decrease;* denunti-atio, *announcement;* dēspĕr-atio, *despair;* discept-at-io, *discussion;* dissŏl-ūtio, *dissolution;* dŏmĭn-atio, *lordship;* dŭbĭt-atio, *doubt;* ēdŭc-atio, *bringing up;* ērŭd-ītio, *instruction;* existĭm-atio, *judgement, reputation;* exsĕc-ūtio (post-Aug.), *accomplishment;* festīn-atio, *hastening;* frustr-atio, *deceiving;* grăd-ātio, *gradation* (as if from grădārī); grātul-atio, *congratulation;* imĭt-atio, *imitation;* inquīs-ītio, *legal inquiry;* larg-ītio, *bestowal, bribery;* lēg-atio, *the office of an ambassador;* lĭbĕr-atio, *a release;* māchĭn-atio, *contrivance;* mult-atio, *amercement;* mūn-ītio, *a fortification;* mŭt-atio, *change;* nā-tio,*a breed* (na-sci); nŏt-atio, *marking, noticing;* nō-tio,*taking cognisance* (no-sc-ĕre); oblĭg-atio,*engagement;* occŭp-atio, *seizing, business;* ōr-atio, *speech;* part-ītio, *division;* permŭt-atio, *an exchange;* pĕt-ītio, *aiming, candidateship, claim;* postŭl-atio, *demand;* pō-tio, *drinking* (comp. poto-, pō-tare); præst-atio (post-Aug.), *guaranty, payment;* prŏb-atio, *testing;* prŏvŏc-atio, *a challenge, appeal;* pŭt-atio, *pruning;* rĕcord-atio, *remembrance;* recŭs-atio, *refusal;* rĕnunti-atio, *a public announcement of a result;* repræsent-atio, *cash payment;* respir-atio, *taking breath;* restĭt-ŭtio, *restoration;* rŏg-atio, *a legislative proposal, a bill;* sălŭt-atio, *greeting;* sĭmŭl-atio, *pretence;* sŏl-ŭtio, *discharge* of debt, &c.; sort-ītio, *lot-drawing;* stīp-atio, *crowding;* stīpŭl-atio, *a bargain;* supplĭc-atio, *public prayer;* tăbŭl-atio (Cæs.), *a flooring* (tăbŭla-, *a plank*); test-atio (testĭfĭc-atio, Cic.), *giving evidence;* trăl-atio, *transfer;* văc-atio, *exemption;* vēn-atio, *hunting;* and many others.

(*b*) From supine stems, with short vowel preceding suffix:

ăd-ĭtio, *entry* on an inheritance (ădĭ-re); admŏn-ĭtio, *reminding* (admŏnēre); amb-ĭtio, *canvassing* (ambī-re); appăr-ĭtio, *attendance* (appărere); cognĭtio, *knowledge, judicial inquiry* (cogno-sc-ere); dătio, *giving* (dă-re); ēdĭtio, *publishing* (ēdĕ-re); exhĭb-ĭtio (Ulp. &c.), *maintenance;* ĭt-io, *going* (ī-re); mŏn-ĭtio, *warning* (mŏnēre); pŏs-ĭtio, *placing, posture* (pōn-ĕre); ră-tio, *account, reason* (rēri); să-tio, *sowing* (sĕ-rĕ-re); sēd-ĭtio, *a sedition* (sed, īre); sorb-ĭtio, *a supping up, a draught* (sorbēre); stă-tio, *a station, a post* (stāre); sŭperstĭ-tio, *superstition* (*standing over* in awe; super-stāre); vendĭ-tio, *sale* (vendĕre); and others.

(*c*) Either from consonant stems, or contracted:

ac-tio, *action* (ăg-ĕre); adjec-tio, *addition* (adjĭc-ĕre); adop-tio, *adoption* (comp. adoptă-re); affec-tio, *relation, disposition of mind* (affĭcĕ-re); auc-tio, *a sale* (augēre); aversio, *turning away* (vertĕre); in law phrase, per aversionem ĕmĕre, *to buy as a whole* (verrere); cap-tio, *a trick, sophism* (căpĕ-re); cau-tio, *a caution, a legal security* (căvēre); cen-sio, *an assessing* (censēre); circumscrip-tio, *a contour, cheating* (circumscrīb-ĕre); commis-sio, *a contest* (committ-ĕre); comprĕhen-sio, *laying hold of* (comprĕhend-ĕre); concep-tio, *drafting of* law formulæ (concĭpĕ-re); conces-sio, *grant* (concēd-ĕre); conclŭ-sio, *shutting in, a peroration* (conclŭd-ĕre); consen-sio, *agreement* (consentīre); construc-tio, *construction* (constru-ĕre); con-tio, *an assembly, an address to such* (convĕn-īre); contrac-tio, *drawing together* (contrăh-ĕre); defec-tio, *revolt, failure* (dēfĭcĕ-re); devŏtio, *devotion* (dēvŏvēre); dic-tio, *saying* (dīc-ĕre); digres-sio, *digression* (digrĕd-i); distinc-tio, *distinction* (distingv-ĕre); emp-tio, *purchase* (ĕm-ĕre); fĭc-tio, *fashioning, fiction* (fĭng-ĕre); flexio, *a turn* (flectĕre); impres-sio, *an impress, attack* (imprĭm-ere); induc-tio, *a bringing in, drawing* one's pen through (indŭc-ĕre); inven-tio, *discovery* (invĕnīre); lŭ-sio, *playing* (lŭd-ĕre); man-sio, *staying, lodging-place* (mănēre); mis-sio, *a discharge* (mitt-ĕre); mŏ-tio, *moving* (mŏvēre); offen-sio, *stumbling, offence* (offend-ĕre); pas-tio, *pasturing* (pasc-ĕre); pen-sio, *payment* (pend-ĕre); percep-tio, *gathering* (percĭpĕ-re); perpes-sio, *endurance* (perpĕt-ĭ); præsump-tio, *anticipation* (præsūm-ĕre); quæs-tio, *an inquiry* (quær-ĕre); rĕfec-tio (post-Aug.), *restoration, refreshment* (rĕfĭcĕ-re); scrip-tio, *writing* (scrĭb-ĕre); sēces-sio, *a withdrawal* (sēcēd-ĕre); sec-tio, *cutting, sale of a bankrupt estate* (sĕcāre); ses-sio, *a sitting* (sĕdēre); spon-sio, *an agreement, a wager* (spondēre); tac-tio, *touching* (tang-ĕre); trāvec-tio, (1) *carrying across;* (2) *riding post* (transvĕh-ĕre); ul-tio, *revenge* (ulc-īsci); vī-sio, *sight* (vĭdēre); and others.

Compound stem-endings: -inqvo, § 772; -ento, -mento, -lento (-ginta, -gento), §§ 791—795; -enti, § 807; -ensi, -iensi, § 815; -undo, -bundo, -cundo, §§ 817—820; -ĭnĕr, § 905; -nŏs, -nŭs, §§ 911, 913; -neo, -gneo, -āneo, -ōneo, §§ 922, 923; -entia, § 933; -nio, -ṃnio, -mōnio, -cĭnĭo, §§ 934—936.

CHAPTER VII.

LINGUAL NOUN STEMS. L.

i. *Stems ending in* -lo.

-lo   cŏlus (f.), *a distaff;* dŏlus, *craft;* fālæ (pl.), *a scaffold-* 855 *ing;* gĕlum, *frost;* mălus (adj.), *bad;* mōla, *a mill* (mŏl-ĕre); pīla, *a ball;* pĭlus, *a hair;* sălum, *the sea* (comp. săl-, σάλος); sōlum, *the ground;* vŏla, *hollow of hand* or *foot.* (For some with diminutive suffix, e.g. templum, see under -ulo.)

-ŏ-lo   This older form of the vowel before l is retained only 856 after e, i, or v (cf. § 213. 2 *b*). The ŏ is often the final stem vowel of the word to which the suffix is added:

1. Adjectives: aureŏ-lus, *golden* (aureo-); ēbrio-lus (Plaut.), *somewhat drunken,* (ebriŏ-); frīvŏlus, *trifling* (for friqvolus? *rubbed* or *brittle;* comp. frĭc-āre, fri-āre); helvŏ-lus (helveolus), *yellowish* (helvo-); parvŏlus, *very small* (parvo-).

2. Substantives (chiefly in Cicero), mostly diminutives of substantives in -o:

(*a*) Masculine: **alveo-lus,** *a small trough;* **calceo-lus** (rare),
a small shoe; **cāseo-lus,** *a small cheese;* **cūneo-lus,** *a small wedge;*
fīlio-lus, *a little son;* **hārio-lus,** *a soothsayer;* **librārio-lus,** *a bit of a
copyist;* **malleo-lus,** *a small hammer,* a *slip* for planting; **pasceolus,**
a leathern bag (for φάσκωλος?); **pīlleo-lus,** *a small cap;* **sīmio-lus,**
a little ape; **servo-lus,** *a little slave;* **urceo-lus,** *a little pitcher.*

Puteoli, *Little-wells;* Tiberiolus (Tac. *A.* 6. 5), *darling Tiberius;*
Scævŏla (m.), (scæva-, *left-hand*).

(*b*) Feminine; all (except **viola**) diminutives of subst. in -a.

actuariŏ-la (or **-um**?), *a small boat;* **ārāneo-la,** *a small spider;*
ardeo-la, *a heron;* **āreo-la,** *a small open place;* **bestio-la,** *an insect;*
clāvŏ-la, *a scion;* **cōpio-læ** (pl.), *a few troops;* **dēlĭcio-læ** (pl.), *a
little darling;* **fascio-la,** *a small bandage;* **fīlio-la,** *a little daughter;*
glōrio-la, *a bit of distinction;* **hōrio-la,** *a skiff;* **laureo-la,** *a laurel
branchlet;* **luscĭnio-la,** *a little nightingale;* **měmŏrio-la,** *a poor
memory;* **nauseo-la,** *a slight squeamishness;* **sententio-la,** *an apho-
rism;* **sēpio-la,** *a little cuttle fish;* **valvo-læ** (pl.), *double shells* of a
pod; **victōrio-la,** *a small statue* of *Victory;* **vindēmio-la,** *a little vin-
tage;* **vio-la,** *a violet* (comp. ἴον); and others.

(*c*) Neuter: all diminutives of neuter substantives in -o:

atrio-lum, *a small entrance-hall;* **armārio-lum,** *a cabinet;* **bal-
neo-lum,** *a small bath;* **brāchio-lum** (Catull.), *a slender arm;* **com-
mentārio-lum,** *a short essay;* **dēversōrio-lum,** *a small lodging;*
dŏlio-lum, *a small cask;* **flammeo-lum,** *a small bridal veil;* **linteo-
lum,** *a small cloth;* **něgōtio-Ium,** *a bit of business;* **ōtio-lum,** *a bit of
leisure;* **pěcūlio-lum,** *a small private property;* **prædio-lum,** *a small
landed estate;* **sōlācio-lum** (Catull.), *a bit of comfort;* **svāvio-lum**
(Catull.), *a soft kiss;* **tectōrio-la** (pl.), *plaster casts.*

-ŭlo   1. Adjectives[1]:   857
(*a*) Diminutival: all (except **vetulus**) from adjectives
with -o stems: **ācūtu-lus,** *somewhat pointed;* **albu-lus,** *whitish;* **ălĭ-
qvantu-lus,** *somewhat;* **argūtu-lus,** *somewhat subtle;* **ārĭdu-lus**
(Catull.), *a little dry;* **barbātu-lus,** *with a bit of a beard;* **bĭmu-lus**
(Catull., Suet.), *two years old;* **candĭdu-lus,** *fairly white;* **contortu-
lus,** *a bit twisted;* **frĭgĭdu-lus,** *rather cold;* **hĭlăru-lus,** *merry and
little;* **horrĭdu-lus,** *roughish;* **īmu-lus** (Catull.), *lowest;* **lassu-lus**
(Catull.), *a little tired;* **lentŭ-lus,** *rather slow;* **līmātu-lus,** *delicately
fine;* **līmu-lus** (Plaut.), *somewhat askance;* **longu-lus,** *longish;* **pætu-**

---

[1] Comp. the lines made by Hadrian on his death-bed (Hist. Aug.
Hadr. 25):   *Animula vagula blandula,*
                        hospes comesque corporis,
                        quæ nunc abibis in loca,
                        pallidula rigida nudula,
                        nec, ut soles, dabis jocos?

lus, *with a slight squint;* pallĭdu-lus, *growing pale;* paucu-lus, *very few;* prīmu-lus (Plaut.), *first;* qvadrīmu-lus (Plaut.), *little four-years-old;* quant-ulus, *how small?;* rŭbĭcund-ulus, *rather red; scītu-lus* (Plaut.), *stylish;* sīmu-lus (Lucr.), *flattish-nosed;* sordĭdu-lus, *dirtyish;* tābidu-lus, *slowly consuming;* tantu-lus, *so little;* ŭvĭdu-lus (Catull.), *somewhat wet;* vĕnustu-lus, *charmingly pretty;* vĕt-ulus, *little and old* (for vetĕr-ulus); and others.

(*b*) Not (apparently) diminutival; chiefly from verbs: æm-ulus, *emulous;* amp-lus, *large* (*on both sides, around;* amb-, cf. § 70); bĭb-ulus, *thirsty* (bĭb-ĕre); bŭb-ulus, *of oxen* (bŏv-, § 76); cær-ulus, *dark blue* (cf. cæruleus) ; crēd-ulus, *credulous* (crēd-ĕre) ; ēdent-ulus (Plaut.), *toothless* (e denti-); garru-lus, *prattling* (garrīre); pătu-lus, *wide-spreading* (pătēre); pend-ulus, *hanging* (pendēre); quĕr-ulus, *complaining* (quĕr-i); sēdulus (cf. § 990); sing-ŭlus, *one each, single;* strāg-ulus, *for covering* (strāgi-, cf. § 784); strīdu-lus, *whistling* (strīdēre); trĕm-ulus, *quivering* (trĕmĕre).

2. Substantives: (*a*) diminutival: 858

Masculine: mostly from stems in -o: ădŏlescentu-lus, *a young man* (adolescenti-); ămīcu-lus, *a darling friend;* ănīmu-lus, *darling;* annu-lus, *a ring;* calcu-lus, *a pebble* (calci-, *chalk*); circu-lus, *a circle;* cŏlumbŭ-lus, *a little dove;* ĕqvu-lus (ĕcŭleus), *a colt;* fŏcu-lus, *a chafing dish* (fŏco-, *hearth*); fŏrŭ-lī (pl.), *pigeon holes* (fŏrus, *a row*); glŏbu-lus, *a little ball;* hortu-lus, *a small garden;* jŏcu-lus, *a little joke;* lectu-lus, *a couch;* lŏcŭ-lus, *a compartment;* mŏdu-lus, *a small measure;* nĕpōtu-lus (Plaut.), *a little grandson* (nĕpōt-); nīdu-lus, *a little nest;* nummu-lī (pl.), *small coins;* porcu-lus, *a young pig;* puĕru-lus, *a little boy;* rāmu-lus, *a sprig;* rēg-ulus, *a chieftain* (rēg-); saccu-lus, *a small bag;* scrŭpu-lus, *a small stone, a difficulty;* ventu-lus, *a breeze;* vīcu-lus, *a hamlet.*

vernula, *a little slave* (verna-).

Proper names: Lentulus (see § 857 *a*); Prŏculus (prŏcus, *a suitor*); Rēgulus (vid. supr.). Also Barbula (barba, *a beard*).

Feminine: mostly from stems in -a: ætātu-la, *youth* (ætāt-); ămīcu-la, *a darling mistress;* ănīmu-la, *dear life;* āqvu-la, *a little water;* arcu-la, *a casket;* capsu-la, *a bandbox;* căsŭ-la, *a small cottage;* caupōnu-la, *a small tavern;* causu-la, *a petty lawsuit;* cēnu-la, *a light dinner;* cervīcu-la, *a small neck* (cervīc-); clausu-la, *a conclusion* (as if from clausa-); concĭliatrīc-ula, *a soft matchmaker* (conciliatrīc-); făc-ula, *a little torch* (făc-); falcu-la, *a small billhook* (falci-); flammu-la, *a little flame;* formu-la, *a (short) legal form;* glandu-læ (pl.), *glands* (glandi-, *acorn*); guttu-la, *a little drop;* herbu-la, *a little herb;* lăcrĭmu-la, *a tiny tear;* lectīcu-la, *a small sedan;* mensu-la, *a small table;* mercēd-ula, *small wages* (mercēd-); mĕrĕtrīc-ula, *a girl prostitute* (meretrīc-); nŭc-ula, *a small nut* (nŭc-); nūtrīc-ula, *a nurse* (nutrīc-); pallu-la, *a little cloak;* plăgŭ-la, *a bed curtain* (plăga-, *a net*); portu-la, *a small gate,* pūpu-la, *the pupil of the eye* (*image on retina?* pūpa-, *a girl*); quadrīgu-læ (pl.), *a little four-horse team;* rādīc-ula, *a small root* (rādīc-); rīpu-la, *a little bank;* rōtu-la, *a little wheel;* sarcĭnu-la, *a little bundle;* scŭtu-la, a *square* dish (scŭt-; comp. scutra, scutella, and for ŭ scūtica); serru-la, *a small saw;* sextu-la, *the sixth of an uncia;* sportu-la, *a little basket;* tōgu-la, *a little gown;* tonstrīc-ula, *a small hairdresser;* villu-la, *a little country-house;* virgu-la, *a small rod;* vōcu-la, *a weak voice;* and others.

Neuter: căpĭtu-lum, *a small head* (căpŭt-); crustu-lum, *pastry;* muscipulum, *a mouse-trap* (mūsi-, căpĕre, § 992); oppĭdu-lum, *a small town;* postīcu-lum, *a small back building;* prătu-lum, *a small meadow;* răpu-lum, *a little turnip;* saxulum, *a small rock;* scriptu-lum (scripulum, scrupulum, scriplum), $\frac{1}{24}$ oz. (a transl. of γράμμα?); spīcu-lum, *a sharp point* (spīco-, *a point;* comp. spīca); scutu-lum, *a small shield.*

(*b*) Not (apparently) diminutival, or not diminutives of exist- §59 ing nouns:

Masculine: æsculus, *the Italian oak;* angulus, *a corner* (comp. ἀγκύλος, uncus, ungvis, &c.); bājulus, *a porter;* bōtulus, *a sausage;* căpulus, (1) *a hilt,* (2) *a coffin* (căpĕ-re); cătŭlus, *a whelp;* cŭmulus, *a heap* (comp. κυείν, κῦμα); fāmulus (also adj. in Aug. and post-Aug. poetry), *a servant;* fīgulus, *a potter* (fīng-ere); gĕrulus, *a porter* (gĕr-ĕre); lĕgulus, *a picker* (lĕg-ĕre); ŏcŭlus, *an eye* (§ 107); ŏpŭlus, *a kind of maple;* pessŭlus, *a bolt* (from πάσσαλος?); pōpulus, *a people* (comp. plē-nus, πλῆθος, πόλις, &c.); pōpulus (f.), *a poplar;* scōpulus, *a rock* (from σκόπελος?); sītulus (also sītula), *a bucket;* stĭmulus, *a prick* (comp. στιγμή, § 129. *c*); tĭtŭlus, *a title;* tŭmulus, *a hill* (tŭm-ēre); tūtŭlus, *a conical head-dress;* vīdulus, *a portmanteau;* vītulus, *a calf* (§ 91).

assecla, *a follower* (ad sĕqv-i); rab-ula, *a brawler* (răbĕre).

Proper names: Bĭbulus (§ 857 *b*); Catŭlus (vid. supr.); Figulus (vid. supr.); Sĭcŭlus, *a Sicilian;* Tappulus; Trĕmŭlus (§ 857 *b*); Vĭtulus (vid. supr.).   Also Decula; Scăpula (vid. infr.).

Feminine: assula, *a splinter;* căcula (m.), *a servant;* cōpula, *a tie* (com, ăp-isci); ĕpŭlæ (pl.), *a banquet;* fĕrŭla, (1) *fennel giant,* (2) *a rod;* fistula, *a pipe;* gŭla, *the throat* (from the sound); in-fŭla, *a band or fillet;* insula, *an island, a separate block of buildings;* ĭnula, *elecampane;* jugulæ (pl.), *collar-stars* in Orion's belt; mătula, *a pot;* mentula, for mejentula (from mejĕre); mĕrula, *a blackbird;* nĕbŭla, *a cloud* (comp. nūbes, νέφος); pænula, *a cloak;* păpula, *a pimple;* pergula, *a stall* or *booth;* pūsula, *a blister* (from φῦσα, φυσαλλίς; the rarer form pustula is probably from pūs); radula (Col.), *a scraper* (răd-ĕre); rēgula, *a rule* (rĕg-ĕre); scandula, *a wooden shingle;* scăpulæ (pl.), *the shoulder-blades;* spĕcula, *a watchtower* (spĕcĕ-re); stĭpŭla, *a stalk;* tēgŭla, *a flat tile* (tĕg-ĕre):

trāgula, *a javelin*, *a net* (comp. trähere?); ŭlŭla, *a screech-owl*; ungŭla, *a hoof* (ungvĭ-, m.).

Neuter: cingŭlum (also cingulus, cingula), *a belt* (cing-ĕre); coagulum, *rennet* (com, ăg-ĕre, *to make to curdle*); exemp-lum, *a sample* (exĭm-ĕre; cf. § 70); jăculum, *a dart* (jăcĕre); jŭgulum, *the collar-bone* (jŭgo-, jŭng-ĕre); pīpulum, *chirping* (pipāre); rĕpā-gula (pl.), *bolts* (păng-ĕre); spĕcŭlum, *a mirror* (spĕcĕ-re); temp-lum, *a temple* (for tem-ulum; comp. τέμενος and § 70); torc-ulum, *a wine press* (torqvēre).

-pŭlo   (1) Adjectives (comp. the Greek termination -πλοος, 860 e.g. ἁπλοῦς, &c.): simplus (only used as subst., so also simpla, simplum), *single* (comp. sim-plex, semel); dŭplus, *double* (duo); triplus, *triple;* qvadrŭplus, *fourfold;* octuplus, *eightfold.* These words are generally used only in neuter as substantives.

(2) Substantives: discĭ-pŭlus, *a learner* (disc-ĕre); mănĭpulus (maniplus), *a handful, a company* of soldiers (mănu-; comp. ple-, plēnus?); simpŭlum, *a ladle.*

For templum, &c. see § 859; for others, where p is apparently radical, see § 858.

-bŭlo   (*a*) Feminine: fābula, *a narrative* (fāri); fībul?, *a clasp* 861 (fīg-ere); sūbula, *an awl* (su-ĕre); tăbula, *a plank.*

(*b*) Neuter: acētābulum, *a cup* (*for vinegar?* ăcĕto-); conciliā-bulum, *a place for assembly* (conciliāre); incūnā-bula (pl.), *cradle* (in cūna-); infund-ĭbulum, *a funnel* (infund-ĕre); lăt-ĭbulum, *a hiding-place* (lătĕre); mendīca-bulum (Plaut. once), *a beggar* (men-dicāre); nŭcĭfrangĭ-bula (pl.), *nutcrackers* (nŭc-, frang-ĕre); pā-bu-lum, *fodder* (pascĕre); pătĭ-bulum, *a cross* (pătĕre); prostĭ-bulum, *a prostitute* (prostāre); rutabulum, *a poker* or *spoon* (rŭ-ere?); sabu-lum, *gravel;* stă-bulum, *a stall* (stāre); suffī-bulum, *a square white veil,* worn by the Vestal Virgins at a sacrifice (sub fīgĕre?); tin-tinnā-bulum, *a bell* (tintinnāre); trī-bulum, *a thrashing sledge* (trī-, tĕrĕre); trientabulum (Liv. 31. 14), *land assigned in payment of a third* of a debt (trienti-); tūr-ĭbulum, *a censer* (tūs-); vēnā-bulum, *a hunting-spear* (vēnāri); vestĭbulum, *a forecourt* (origin uncertain); vŏcā-bulum, *a name* (vŏcāre).

-cŭlo(clo) 1. Adjectives, chiefly diminutival, and from 1 stems; 862

(*a*) From nouns: acrĭ-culus, *testy;* annĭ-culus, *a year old* (anno-); dulcĭ-culus, *sweetish;* fortĭ-culus, *somewhat bold;* grandĭ-culus (Plaut.), *rather large;* lĕvĭ-culus, *somewhat vain;* mas-culus, *male* (măsi-); mollĭ-culus, *tender;* pauper-culus, *poor* (pauper-); tĕnuĭ-culus, *rather slight;* tristĭ-culus, *somewhat sorrowful;* turpĭ-culus, *ugly;* vernā-culus, (1) *of slaves*, (2) *native* (verna-).

(*b*) From verbs: rīdĭ-culus (deridiculus), *laughable* (rīdēre); reiculus (Cato, Sen.), *refuse* (rējĭcĕre).

(*c*) clanculum (adv.) is adverbial accus. (clam).

21—2

2.   Substantives:

(*a*) Masculine: almost all diminutival:
āmātor-culus (Plaut.), *a lover dear;* ămi-culus, *a dear friend;*
amnĭ-culus, *a streamlet;* angvi-culus, *a small snake;* anser-culus
(Col.), *a gosling;* artĭ-culus, *a joint, knuckle* (artu-); asser-culus,
a small pole; cinctĭ-culus (Plaut.), *a belt* (cinctu-); cŭnĭculus, *a
mine;* hence, *a burrower,* viz. *a rabbit* (cŭneo-); ensĭ-culus (Plaut.),
a small sword; fascĭ-culus, *a packet;* flŏs-culus, *a flowret;* follĭ-
culus, *a small bag, pod;* fontĭ-culus, *a little spring;* frāter-culus, *a
little brother;* fūnĭ-culus, *a thin cord;* grā-çulus, *a jackdaw* (perhaps
the c is radical); ignĭ-culus, *a spark;* lăcus-culus (Col.), *a small
lake* (lacu-); lāter-culus, *a small brick;* lĕpus-culus, *a leveret*
(lĕpŏs-); lĭntrĭ-culus, *a wherry;* mar-culus (martŭlus, Plin. ed.
Detlef.), *a hammer;* mus-culus, *a little mouse, a muscle* (mūsi-);
orbĭ-culus, *a small dish or roller;* pannĭ-culus, *a rag* (panno-);
passer-culus, *a little sparrow;* Păter-culus, *a surname of* Velleian
clan; pēnĭ-culus, *a brush;* piscĭ-culus, *a little fish;* pontĭ-culus, *a
little bridge;* pulvis-culus, *a little dust;* puti-culi (pl., Varr., Fest.),
gravepits (pūteo-); quæstĭ-culus, *a small profit* (quæstu-); rūmus-
culus, *gossip* (rūmōs-); sensĭ-culus (Quint.), *a clause* (sensu-, sen-
sus, *a sentence,* Quint.); scrŏbĭ-culus, *a little trench;* sirpĭ-culus
(surp-, scirp-), *a rush basket* (sirpo-); sur-culus, *a shoot* (said to be
from sŭro-, *a shoot*); testĭ-culus; ventrĭ-culus, *the stomach;* vermĭ-
culus, *a grub;* versĭ-culus, *a short verse* (versu-); utri-culus, *a little
bag;* vultĭ-culus, *a mien* (vultu-).

(*b*) Feminine: diminutives of feminine nouns:
ædĭ-cula, *a chapel;* ănătĭ-cula, *a duckling* (ănăt-); ānĭ-cula, *an
old woman* (ănu-); ăpi-cula, *a little bee;* arbus-cula, *a shrub* (ar-
bŏs-); aurĭ-cula, *the* external *ear;* bŭ-cula, *a heifer* (bŏvi-); cănĭ-
cula, *a bitch, the dog star* (căn-, § 448); cĭcer-cula (cĭcĕr-, n., but
also cĭcĕra-, f.); classi-cula, *a flotilla;* cohortĭ-cula, *a small troop;*
crātĭ-cula, *a gridiron;* cŭtĭ-cula, *the skin;* diē-cula, *a brief day;*
febri-cula, *a feverish attack;* fĭdĭ-culæ (pl.), *a lute, a rack;* lābe-
cula, *a slight stain* (lābi-, lābēs); lenti-cula, *a lentil;* mănĭ-cula,
a little hand (mănu-); māter-cula, *a mother dear;* mŭlier-cula,
a girl; nāvi-cula, *a skiff;* nŏvā-cula, *a razor* (nŏvāre, *to renew?*);
nŭbe-cula, *a little cloud* (nŭbi-, nŭbēs); panĭ-cula, *a tuft* (pāno-,
m.); partĭ-cula, *a little bit;* pellĭ-cula, *a small skin;* plēbē-cula, *the
populace* (plēbe-); resti-cula, *a small rope;* rŭdi-cula, *a mull;*
sĕcūrĭ-cula, *a little axe;* sēde-cula, *a little seat* (sēdi-, sedes); sicilĭ-
cula, *a small sickle;* spē-cula, *a slight hope;* sŭbŭ-cula, *a shirt* (from
sub? comp. ex-u-ĕre); sŭ-cula, *a little pig, a winch* (sui-, n.,
§ 392; also *the* Hyades from a confusion of ὕειν with ὗς); tĕgĕt-ĭ-
cula, *a little mat* (tĕgĕt-); vĕpre-cula, *a small briar* (cf. § 430);
vītĭ-cula, *a little vine;* vulpe-cula, *a little fox* (vulpĭ-, vulpēs);
uxor-cula, *a darling wife.*

(c) Neuter: (1) diminutives from nouns:

conventi-culum, *an assembly* (conventu-); cor-culum, *little heart;* also a surname of Scipio Nasica for his *good sense* (cŏrdi-); corni-culum, *a little horn* (cornu-); corpus-culuḿ, *a particle* (corpŏs-); crĕpus-culum, *twilight* (comp. crĕpĕro-, κνέφας); fēnus-culum, *a little interest* (fēnŏs-); gălĕrĭ-culum (Suet.), *a small cap* (gălēro); gĕni-culum, *a little knee* (gĕnu-); hŏlus-culum, *a bit of vegetable;* jĕcus-culum, *a small liver* (jĕcŏs-); lăter-culum, *a list* (later-, masc. *a brick*); lătus-culum, *a small side;* mūnus-culum, *a small present;* ŏpus-culum, *a small work;* os-culum, *a pretty mouth, a kiss;* ossi-culum, *a small bone;* raudus-culum, *a bit of metal;* rētĭ-culum, *a small net;* tuber-culum, *a small bump;* tus-culum, *a bit of incense;* vas-culum, *a small vessel;* ulcus-culum, *a small sore.*

(2) from verbs (chiefly):

admĭnĭculum, *a prop* (comp. ad mănum); ămĭc-ulum, *a mantle* (where c is radical; ămĭcīre); bă-culum, *a staff* (comp. βάκτρον, βαίνω); cēnā-culum, *a dining-room, an upper room* (cenāre), crĕpĭtā-culum, *a rattle* (crĕpĭtāre); cŭbi-culum, *a chamber* (cŭbă-, cŭbare); curriculum *a course* (curr-ĕre); dēvert-ĭculum, *a bypath, an inn* (devert-ĕre); dīlūc-ulum, *daybreak* (dilūce-sc-ĕre); ēverr-ĭculum, *a drag-net* (ēverrĕre); fer-culum *a bier, a tray* (fer-re); gŭbernā-culum (gubernaclum), *a helm* (gubernāre); hībernā-culum, *a winter lodging* (hibernare); incern-ĭculum, *a sieve* (incernĕre); irrĭdi-culum, *a laughing-stock* (irrĭdēre); jentā-culum, *breakfast* (jentāre); mīrā-culum, *a wonder* (mirāri); ŏper-culum, *a lid* (ŏpĕrire); ŏrā-culum (ōrāclum), *a divine utterance* (ōrā-re); pĕrī-culum (pĕrīclum), *a trial, risk* (comp. pĕrī-tus); perpend-ĭculum, *a plumb line* (as if from perpendere); piā-culum, *an expiation* (piāre); pō-culum (pō-clum), *a cup* (comp. pō-tus), prōpugnā-culum, *a bulwark* (prōpugnā-re); rĕceptā-culum, *a magazine, a retreat* (receptā-re); rĕdĭmī-culum, *a necklace* (rĕdĭmī-re); rĕtĭnā-cula (pl.), *reins* (rĕtĭnēre); sæ-culum (sæclum), *a generation* (a *sowing?* sa-, sĕrĕre); sar-culum, *a hoe* (sārīre); senā-culum (Varr.) *a senate hall* (comp. sĕnātus); spectā-culum, *a sight* (spectāre); spīrā-culum, *a breathing-hole* (spīrā-re); sublīgā-culum, *a waistband* (sublīgā-re); sustentā-culum (Tac.), *a support* (sustentā-re); tabernā-culum, *a tent* (tăberna-); terrĭ-cula (pl.), *bugbears* (terrēre); tŏmā-culum (tŏmaclum), *a sausage* (comp. τομή); torc-ulum, *a press* (torqvēre); vĕh-i-cŭlum, *a carriage* (vĕh-ĕre); vin-culum (vinclum), *a bond* (vincīre); umbrā-culum, *a shady place, a parasol* (umbrā-re).

-un-cŭlo i. e. -cŭlo suffixed to stems (real or presumed) in -ōn.   863

Substantives:

(a) Masculine: ăv-unculus, *a mother's brother* (ăvo-, *a grandfather*); carb-un-culus, *a small coal* (carbōn-); cent-un-culus, *a small patchwork* (centōn-); fūr-un-culus, *a petty thief* (fūr-); hŏm-un-culus, *a poor fellow* (hŏmŏn-); lātr-un-culus, *a footpad, a pawn in draughts* (lātrōn-); lēn-un-culus, (1) *a young pander;* (2) *a skiff;* pect-un-culus, *a small scallop* (pectĕn-); pĕtās-un-culus (Juv.), *a small leg of pork* (pĕt-ă-sōn-); pugi-un-culus, *a small dagger* (pugiōn-); rān-un-culus, *a tadpole* (rāna-); serm-un-culus, *tittle-tattle* (sermōn-); tīr-un-culus, *a young beginner* (tīrōn-).

(*b*) Feminine: chiefly diminutives of substantives in -tiōn (-siōn); frequent in Cicero:

aedīfĭcā-tiun-cula, *a small building;* ambŭlā-tiun-cula, *a short walk;* assentā-tiun-cula, *a bit of flattery;* can-tiun-cula, *a sweet song;* cap-edun-cula, *a small bowl* (capēdŏn-); cap-tiun-cula, *a quibble;* cār-un-cula, *a piece of flesh* (carŏn- nom. cāro); cēnā-tiun-cula (Plin. *Ep.*), *a small dining-room;* commō-tiun-cula, *a slight disturbance;* con-tiun-cula, *a short harangue;* conclū-siun-cula, *a quibbling argument;* contrac-tiun-cula, *a slight oppression;* dŏm-un-cula (Val. Max.), *a small house* (dŏmu-); icūn-cula (Suet.), *a little image* (εἰκόν-); im-agun-cula (Suet. cf. Cic. *Att.* 6. 1. §. 25), *a little likeness* (imāgŏn-); interroga-tiun-cula, *a short question;* lec-tiun-cula, *a little reading;* lĕg-iun-cula, *a small legion* (legiōn-); mor-siun-cula (Plaut.), *a soft bite* (morsŭ-); occā-siun-cula (Plaut.), *a neat opportunity;* offen-siun-cula, *a slight offence;* ōrā-tiun-cula, *a little speech;* posses-siun-cula, *a small possession;* quaes-tiun-cula, *a trifling question;* rā-tiun-cula, *a little account;* rŏgā-tiun-cula, *a little question;* ses-siun-cula, *a little sitting;* vir-gun-cula, *a little girl* (virgŏn-) ; and others.

(*c*)   Neuter: mendaci-unculum (only abl. plur.), *a fib.*

-us-cŭlo   i. e. cŭlo- suffixed to the stem of the comparative degree: 864
alti-us-culus (Suet.), *somewhat high;* compl-us-culi (pl.), *pretty many;* duri-us-culus (Plin.), *somewhat harsh; grandi-us-cula* (f., Ter. *Andr.* 815), *pretty well grown-up;* līqvĭdi-us-culus (Plaut.), *softer;* longi-us-culus, *rather long;* maj-us-culus, *somewhat greater;* meli-us-culus, *somewhat better;* mĭn-us-culus, *rather less;* nitĭdi-us-culus (Plaut.), *somewhat shiny;* plus-culus, *somewhat more, several;* putĭdi-us-culus, *somewhat more disagreeable;* tardi-us-culus, *somewhat slow;* uncti-us-culus (Plaut.), *somewhat unctuous.* So the adverb cĕlĕri-us-cule (Corn.), *somewhat more quickly.*

-ēd-ŭlo-   mŏn-ēdula, *a jackdaw;* nītedula, *a dormouse;* qver- 865
qvedula, *a kind of duck.*

-ull-ŭlo   paullŭlus, *very little,* also as surname.   866

-ell-ŭlo   i. e. ŭlo added to diminutives in ello (for ĕrŭlo); agel-lulus (Catul.), *a little field* (ăgello-); bellulus (Plaut.),

pretty (bello-); cist-ellula, *a little box* (cistella-); lamel-
lula (Petr.), *a metal plate* (lammĭna-); puellula, *a little
girl* (puella); tenellulus, *delicate* (tĕnĕro-).

-ill-ŭlo   i.e. ŭlo suffixed to diminutives in -illo.
ancillula, *a little handmaid* (ancilla-); pauxillulus, *very
small* (pauxillo-).

-llo   (1) Adjectives: aqvĭlus, *dark-coloured;* mŭtilus, *muti-* 867
lated, esp. *having lost a horn* (comp. μίτυλος); nŭb-ilus,
cloudy (nŭbi-): rŭtilus, *auburn,* also as surname; and see
§ 424.

(2) Substantives:
āqvĭla, *an eagle;* jūbilum, *a wild cry;* pūmilus, *a dwarf;*
sandāpĭla, *a common bier;* sībilus, *a hiss, whistle;* sī-
mĭla, *fine wheat flour.*

-allo   cāballus, *a hack;* callum, *thick skin;* galla, *a gall nut;* 868
gallus, *a cock;* intervallum (*part between the palisades*),
interval (inter, vallo-); palla, *a cloak;* vallus, (1) *a winnowing fan*
(vanno); (2) *a stake* (comp. ἧλος, § 91); vallum, *a palisading.*
Proper names: Hispallus (Hispānulus); Messalla (Messānŭla);
Ralla (rānŭla?).

-aullo   paullus, *a little, few* (pauco-): also as surname.

-ollo   ăbolla, *a thick woollen gown* (comp. ἀναβολή); collum,
a neck; cŏrolla, *a garland* (for cŏrōnula); ollus, *that*
(old form of ille, § 373); olla (aula), *a pot;* persolla (Plaut. once),
little mask (for persōnŭla); sollus (sōlus), *alone* (comp. ὅλος, Ion.
οὖλος).

-ul-lo   (1) Adjectives: pullus, *dusky;* sătullus (Varr. once),
sated (sătŭro-); ullus, *any* (ūno-).

(2) Substantives: (*a*) appellatives: ampulla, *a flask* (for am-
pŏrŭla); betulla, *birch-tree;* bulla, *a bubble, a stud;* cŭcullus, *a hood;*
hŏmullus, *a manikin* (for hŏmon-, cf. § 449); lēnullus (Plaut. *Pœn.*
II. 25), *a little pander* (lēnōn-); mĕdulla, *the marrow, pith* (comp.
mĕdio-); mullus, *a mullet;* pullus, *a young animal,* esp. *a chick;*
trulla, *a ladle* (trua-).

(*b*) Proper names: Cătullus for Cătōnulus; Lūcullus; Mărullus
for Mărōnulus; Rullus; Tertullus; Tĭbullus; Tullus.

Sulla for sūrŭla, *little calf* of leg.

-el-lo   Usually arises from the diminutival suffix and assimila- 869
tion of the preceding consonant (§ 176. 1), so that it is
=-ĕrŭlo, -ĕnŭlo, or the doubly diminutival -ŭlŭlo.
Cf. § 213. 5.

1. Adjectives:

bellus, *pretty* (bŏno-); gĕmellus, *twin* (gĕmĭno-); intĕgellus, *tolerably sound* (intĕgero-); miscellus (rare), *mixed* (comp. miscēre); mĭsellus, *pitiable* (mĭsero-); mollĭcellus (Catull.), *soft* (mollĭcŭlo-); nŏvellus, *new* (nŏvo-); pulcellus, *pretty* and *little* (pulcero-); rŭbellus, *reddish* (rŭbero-); tĕnellus, *delicate* (tĕnĕro-).

2. Substantives:

(a) Masculine: ăgellus, *a small field* (ăgero-); ănellus, *a little ring* (ānŭlo-); angellus (Lucr.), *a small corner* (angŭlo-); ăsellus, *an ass's colt* (ăsĭno-); cancellī (pl.), *a grating* or *bars;* cătellus, *a puppy* (cătŭlo-); cultellus, *a small knife* (cultero-); lĭbellus, *a pamphlet, petition,* &c. (lĭbero-); lŏcellus, *a little compartment* (lŏ-cŭlo-); ŏcellus, *a dear little eye* (ŏcŭlo-); pŏpellus, *the rabble* (pŏpŭlo-); porcellus, *a little pig* (porcŭlo-); puellus, *a boy* (puĕro-); rastellus, *a small rake* (rastero-; cf. § 369); vĭtellus, *the yolk of an egg* (vĭtŭlo-, *a calf*).

Proper names: Marcellus (marco-, marcŭlo-); Mĕtellus.

Colŭmella (vid. infr.); Dŏlabella (vid. infr.); Fĕnestella (vid. infr.); Ofella (vid. infr.).

(b) Feminine: cămella, *a wine cup* (cămĕra-, *a vault?*); căpella, *a shegoat* (căpera-); cătella, *a small chain* (cătēna-); cella, *a storeroom;* clĭtellæ (pl.), *panniers;* cŏlŭmella, *a small pillar* (cŏlŭmena-); dextella, *a little right hand* (dextera-); dŏlabella, *a small pickaxe;* (dŏlabra-); făbella, *a short story* (făbŭla); fēmella (Catull.), *a girl* (fēmĭna-); fenestella, *a little window* (fĕnestra-); fiscella, *a small basket* (fiscĭna-); lāmella (Sen.), *a plate of metal* (lāmĭna-); mă-tella, *a pot* (mătŭla-); mĭtella, *a turban* (mĭtera-); numella, *a fetter;* ŏfella, *a little bit;* (offŭla); ŏpella, *light work* (ŏpĕra-); păgella, *a short page* (păgĭna-); pătella, *a small dish* (pătĭna-); prŏcella, *a storm* (comp. procellĕre); puella, *a girl* (puĕra-); scu-tella, *a small dish* (scutra-); sella, *a chair* (sēdi-); sĭtella, *a ballot urn* (sĭtŭla-); sportella, *a little basket* (sportŭla-); stella, *a star* (stēra-? comp. ἀστέρ-, Engl. *star*); tăbella, *a tablet,* pl. for writing or voting (tăbŭla-); tessella, *a little cube* (tessĕra-); tur-bellæ (pl. Plaut.), *a stir* (turba-); umbella, *a sunshade* (umbra-); volsellæ (pl.), *tweezers* (comp. volso-, vellĕre).

(c) Neuter; almost all diminutives of neuters in -ro:

castellum, *a fort;* cĕrĕbellum, *a small brain;* duellum (bellum), *war* (duo); flābellum, *a small fan;* flăgellum, *a scourge;* lăbellum, *a pretty lip* (labro-); lăbellum, *a bathing tub* (lăvabra-); lŭcellum, *a small gain;* măcellum, *meat market* (orig. unknown); plostellum, *a small waggon;* rostellum (Col., Plin.), *a small beak;* săcellum, *a shrine;* scalpellum, *a lancet.*

-illo   In some cases for -inŭlo-; in others from words with 870
1; e.g. ŏvī-, lapĭd-, &c.: in others probably (from false
analogy) appended directly as a dimǐnutival suffix.

1. Adjectives:

aliqvantillus (Plaut. once), *some little* (ălĭquanto-); ŏvillus, *of
sheep* (ŏvī-); pauxillus, *little* (pauco-); pŭsillus, *very small* (comp.
pusus very rare, *a boy*); quantillus, *how very small* (quanto-);
suillus, *of swine* (su-); tantillus, *so very little* (tanto-).

2. Substantives:

(*a*) Masculine: cămillus, *a youth-priest;* căpillus, *the hair* of
the head; cătillus, *a small bowl* (cătīno-); cōdĭcilli (pl.), *a (writing)
note* (cōdĕc-); frītillus, *a dice box;* hædillus, *a little kid* (hædo-);
lăpillus, *a little pebble* (lăpĭd-); lŭpillus, *a small lupine* (lŭpīno-);
pastillus, *a lozenge;* paxillus (Plin., Col.), *a peg;* pēnĭcillus, *a paint
brush* (pēnĭcŭlo-); pugillus (rare), *a handful* (pugǐno-); pulvillus,
a little cushion (pulvīno-); pŭpillus, *a ward* (pŭpo-); villus, *a tuft
of hair.*

Proper names: Cămillus (see above); Faustillus (Faustīno-);
Pulvillus (pulvīno-); Regillus (rēgŭlo-); Rufillus (Rŭfīno-); and
others.   Also Axilla (vid. infr.); Ravilla (rāvus, *gray?*).

(*b*) Feminine: ancilla, *a handmaid;* angvilla, *an eel* (angvī-);
argilla, *white clay* (from ἄργιλλος, comp. ἀργό-, *white*); armillæ
(pl.), *bracelets* (armo-, *shoulder*); axilla (orig. form of āla acc. to
Cic. *Or.* 45, but see § 871), *armpit* (axi-); făvilla, *glowing ash;*
fritilla, *gruel* used at sacrifices; furcilla, *a little fork* (furca-); mămilla, *a breast* (mamma-); maxilla (cf. Cic. *Or.* 45), *a jawbone*
(comp. μαγ-, μάσσω, *knead*); păpilla, *a teat* (comp. păpŭla); pis-
trilla, *a mill* (pistrina-); pŭpilla *a female ward, the pupil* of the
eye (pŭpa-); scintilla, *a spark;* squilla, *a shrimp;* stilla, *a drop* (comp.
stiria, *icicle*); tonsillæ (pl.), tosillæ (C. *N. D.*), *the tonsils;* villa,
a country-house (vīco-?).

Proper names: e. g. Dŏmĭtilla (comp. Domitio-); Drusilla
(Druso-); Livilla (Livia-); Priscilla (Prisco-); Procilla (Proculo-);
Quintilla (Quinto-); Rufilla (Rŭfīno); and others.

(*c*) Neuter: băcillum, *a small stick* (băcŭlo-); bătillum, *a fire-
pan;* oscillum, *a little image* of *a face* (oscŭlum); pistillum, *a pestle*
(comp. pisto-, participle of pins-ĕre); pōcillum, *a cup* (pōcŭlo-);
quăsillum, *a wool basket* (comp. quālo-); sălillum, *a salt-cellar*
(sălīno-); scăbillum (scabellum), *a footstool, castanet played by foot*
(scamno-, cf. § 78.5); sĭgillum, *a seal* (signo-); specillum, *a probe*
(spēc-ĕre; comp. spĕcŭlum); tĕgillum, *a covering* (tĕg-ĕre); tĭgillum, *a little beam* (tigno-); vexillum, *a banner* (vēh-ĕre; comp.
vēlum).

-ālo The long vowel is probably due to the contraction of 871
      longer forms (see Cic. *Or. 45*).

 āla, *a wing* (for axula?); māla, *a jaw* (for maxula?
§ 870, 2, *b.*); mālus, *a mast;* pālus, *a stake;* pāla, *a spade;*
quālum (also plur. quāli), *a hamper* (for quasulum?
comp. quāsillum); scālæ (pl.), *stairs* (for scand-ulæ?);
tālus, *an ankle.*

Proper name: Ahala (comp. āla; and vĕhĕmens with vēmens.

-aulo caulæ (pl.), *holes* (căvo-).

-ōlo cōlum, *a sieve;* sōlus, *alone* (see sollus).

-ūlo cŭcŭlus, *a cuckoo;* cūlus, i.q. ānus; mūlus, *a mule.*

-ælo cælum, *heaven;* cælum, *a graving tool.*

-ēlo } (*a*) feminine. In some the suffix is appended to the 872
(-ello) } simple verb-stem; in some to the past participle; in some
         to other forms. (Lachmann draws from early MSS. the
         use of writing double l if the syllable preceding e be
         short.)

candela, *a candle* (candēre, *to glitter*); cautela (Dig.), *a security*
(cauto-); cicendela, *a glow-worm* (a rustic name reduplicated from
candēla?); clientela, *protection* (clienti-); corruptēla, *a corruption*
(corrupto-); custōdēla (Plaut. and ap. Gaj.), *guardianship* (cus-
tōd-); lŏqvella, *speech* (lŏqvi); mustēla, *a weasel;* nītēla, *a dormouse;* obsĕqvella, *complaisance* (obsĕqvi); qvĕrella, *a complaint*
(qvĕri); sĕquella (rare), *a follower* (sĕqui); suaḍēla, *persuasion*
(suādēre); sūtēla, *an artifice* (sūto-); tēla, *a web* (for texŭla?);
tūtela, *guardianship* (tūto-).

(*b*) neuter: mantēlum, *a cloak;* prēlum, *a press* (prĕm-ĕre);
tēlum, *a dart;* vēlum, *a sail* (for vĕh-ulum?).

-īlo fīlum, *a thread;* hīlum, *a trifle;* pīla, *a pillar;* pīlum, 873
      a pestle, a heavy pike (pīs-ĕre); sīlus (for sīmŭlus?),
      pug-nosed.

ii. *Stems ending in* -li.

With few exceptions all derivatives in -li are, at least primarily,
adjectives.

-li bīlis (f.), *bile;* callis (m. f.), *a path;* caulis or cōlis (m.), 874
     a stalk (from καυλός?); collis (m.), *a hill* (comp. cul-men,
cŏl-umna); fēles (f.), *a cat;* follis (m.), *a bag, bellows;* mæles (f.),

a badger; mille (n)., *a thousand;* mōles (f.), *a shapeless mass;* mollis (adj.), *soft* (comp. μαλ-ακός); pellis (f.), *a skin;* prōles (f.), *offspring* (pro, ŏlere, *to grow*); vallis (f.), *a valley;* vīlis (adj.), *cheap.*

-l   fel (n., stem fell-), gall (comp. χόλος); mel (n., stem mell-), *honey* (comp. μέλι); sal (m. or n.), *salt* (comp. σάλος); sōl (m.), *the sun* (comp. ἥλιος).

-sŭl   consul, *a colleague?*; exul, *an exile.* Comp. præsul, *a dancer in front* (sālĭre).

-ĭli   (*a*) from verbal stems: ăg-ĭlis, *nimble, active* (ăg-ĕre); 875 dēbilis, *weak* (de, hăbĭlis); făcilis, *do-able, easy* (făcĕre); frăg-ilis, *frai* (fraŋg-ĕre); hăbilis, *manageable, apt* (hăbĕre); nūb-ilis, *marriageable* (nūb-ĕre); sorbilis (Cels. &c.), *suckable* (sorbēre); strĭgĭlis (f.), *a scraper* (string-ĕre); ūt-ilis, *useful* (ūt-i).

(*b*) from nouns and others: grăcilis, *thin;* hŭm-ilis, *lowly* (hŭmo-, *the ground*); nōvensiles (pl.), *the New Gods* (opposed to Dii indigetes; comp. nŏvo-); părilis (Lucr., Ov.), *like* (pari-); sĭm-ilis, *like* (comp. sim-plex, sĕm-el, &c., ἅμα); stĕr-ilis, *barren;* ūtensile (chiefly in neut. pl. as subst.), *usable* (ūti-).

-bĭ-li   All from verbs, or verbal forms: usually with a passive 876 signification:

(1) with short vowel preceding suffix:

ālĭbilis, *nourishing, nourishable* (ăl-ĕre); condūcĭbilis, *advantageous* (condūc-ĕre); crēdĭbilis, *credible* (crēd-ĕre); horrĭbilis, *exciting a shudder* (horrēre); impătĭbilis, *insufferable* (in, păt-i); intellĕgĭbilis (Sen.), *mentally cognisable* (intellĕg-ĕre); restĭbilis, *of land sown or tilled every year* (re, si-st-ĕre); stăbĭlis, *steady* (stāre); terrĭbilis, *frightful* (terrēre); vendĭbilis, *saleable* (vend-ĕre); vincĭbilis, *win-able* (vinc-ĕre); ūtĭbilis (Plaut., Ter.), *serviceable* (ūt-i).

(2) with ā preceding suffix:

admīrā-bilis, *wonderful;* æquā-bilis, *equal, equable;* æquĭpărā-bilis (Plaut.), *comparable;* affā-bilis, *affable;* ămā-bilis, *loveable;* commendā-bilis, *praiseworthy;* congrĕgā-bilis (Cic. once), *gregarious;* delectā-bilis (Tac.), *delightful;* desīdĕrā-bilis, *desirable;* detestā-bilis, *execrable;* dŏmā-bilis (Hor., Ov.), *tameable;* dūrā-bilis, *lasting;* ēmendā-bilis, *capable of correction;* exōrā-bilis, *that may be talked over;* făvōrā-bilis, *popular* (favorāre not used); hăbĭtā-bilis, *habitable;* hŏnōrā-bilis (Cic. once), *complimentary;* imĭtā-bilis, *imitable;* impĕnĕtrā-bilis, *impenetrable;* implācā-bilis, *unappeasable;* in-ēnarrā-bilis, *indescribable;* inexōrā-bilis, *inexorable;* inexplĭcā-bilis, *inexplicable;* inexpugnā-bilis, *impregnable;* innŭmĕrā-bilis, *countless;*

insătiă-bilis, *insatiable;* intŏlĕră-bilis, *insupportable;* irrĕpără-bilis, *irretrievable;* irrĕvŏcă-bilis, *irrevocable;* lætă-bilis, *joyful;* laudă-bilis, *praiseworthy;* mĕdĭcă-bilis, *curable, curative;* mĕmŏră-bilis, *memorable;* mĭsĕră-bilis, *pitiable;* mūtă-bilis, *changeable;* nāvĭgă-bilis, *navigable;* optă-bilis, *desirable;* pĕnĕtră-bilis, *penetrable, penetrating* (penetrāre); plācă-bilis, *appeasable;* præstăbilis, *preeminent;* prŏbă-bilis, *probable, acceptable;* sānă-bilis, *curable;* spectă-bilis, *visible, notable;* tractă-bilis, *manageable;* vĕnĕră-bilis, *venerable;* vĭŏlă-bilis, *violable;* and others.

(3) with long vowel (other than ā) preceding the suffix:

dēlē-bilis (Mart.), *destructable;* dissŏlū-bilis, *dissoluble* (dissolvĕre); flē-bilis, *lamentable;* ignō-bilis, *undistinguished* (in, no-sc-ĕre); inexplē-bilis, *insatiable;* mō-bilis, *moveable, changeable* (mŏvēre); nō-bilis, *famous, noble* (no-sc-ĕre); sĕpĕlī-bilis (Plaut. once), *buryable* (sĕpĕlī-re); vŏlū-bilis, *revolving, fluent* (volv-ĕre).

-sĭ-bĭ-lĭ
(for tĭ-bĭ-lĭ) } i.e. bili appended to stem of past participle (except 877 in possibilis):

flexĭbilis, *pliant;* plausĭbilis, *praiseworthy;* persuasĭbilis (Quint.), *persuasive;* possĭbilis (Quint. and Dig.), *possible* (pŏt-, posse); sensĭbilis (Sen.), *perceivable by senses.*

-tĭlĭ
(-sĭlĭ) } i.e. li appended to stem of supine or past participle.   It 878 denotes *possibility* and *quality* (not *action*):

al-tilis, *fattened* (ăl-ĕre); coc-tilis, *baked* (coqv-ĕre); compactilis (Plin.), *thick-set* (comping-ĕre); diffūs-ilis (Lucr.), *expansive* (diffundere); ēlec-tilis (Plaut.), *choice* (elĭg-ĕre); fer-tilis, *fertile* (fer-re); fic-tilis, *made by potters* (fīg-ĕre); fis-silis, *cleavable* (findĕre); flex-ilis, *pliant* (flect-ĕre); fos-silis, *dug up* (fŏdĕ-re); fū-silis, *molten* (fund-ĕre); fut-tilis, *brittle, frothy, untrustworthy* (from obsolete fu-ĕre = fundere? the doubled t being indicative of the length of the syllable); mis-silis, *missile* (mitt-ĕre); nex-ilis, *tied* (nect-ĕre); pen-silis, *hanging* (pend-ere); plec-tilis (Plaut. once), *woven* (plect-ĕre); rā-silis, *scraped* (rād-ĕre); scan-silis (Plin.), *climb-able* (scand-ĕre); sec-tilis, *cut-able, cut* (sĕcāre); sen-silis, *sentient* (sentīre); ses-silis, *fit for sitting, dwarf* (sĕdēre); sŏlū-tilis (Suet.), *capable of dropping to pieces* (solv-ĕre); sū-tilis, *sewed together* (su-ĕre); tac-tilis (Lucr.), *touch-able* (tang-ĕre); tex-tilis, *woven* (tĕg-ĕre); ton-silis, *that may be clipt* (tondēre); tor-tilis, *twisted* (torqvēre); vī-tilis, *platted* (viēre); and some others.

sŭpellex (for supellectilis, *furniture* (properly *coverings?* super lectum; or *odd-gatherings?* super, lĕg-ĕre, comp. Pott, *Etym. For.* II. 545, ed. 2).

-ăt-ĭlĭ   (1) from verbs:

plĭc-ăt-ĭlĭs (Plin.), *that may be folded* (plĭcă-re); vers-ăt-ĭlĭs, *revolving, versatile* (versā-re); vŏl-ăt-ĭlĭs, *winged* (vŏlā-re).

(2) from nouns: 879

ăqv-ātĭlĭs, *living in water* (ăqva-); ferr-ātĭlĭs (Plaut.), of slaves often fettered, *living in iron* (ferro-); flŭvi-ātĭlĭs, *belonging to a river* (flŭvio-); pluviatĭlĭs (Cels.), *of rain-water* (pluvia-); piscatum hamatĭlem et saxatĭlem (Plaut. *Rud.* 299), fishing *with hooks* and *on rocks* (hāmo-, saxo-); umbr-atĭlĭs, *in the shade* (umbra-).

-ālĭ   1. Adjectives: 880

ădĭti-alĭs, *on entering office* (ădĭtu-); æqv-ālĭs, *level* (æqvo-); ambarv-ālĭs (Fest.), *that goes round the fields* (amb, arva); ănĭm-ālĭs, *having life* (ănĭma-); ann-alĭs, *for a year, relating to a year* (anno-); arv-ālĭs, only of the college called Fratres arvales (arvo-); augŭr-alĭs, *of augurs* (augŭr-); austr-ālĭs, *southern* (austro-); bĭpĕd-alĭs, *two feet long* (bĭs, pĕd-); brŭm-alĭs, *of mid-winter* (brŭma-); căpĭt-alĭs, *of the head, deadly* (căpŭt-); centumvĭr-alĭs, *of the court of the Hundred men* (centum, vĭro-); cŏmĭti-alĭs, *of the assembly* (cŏmĭtio-); conjectŭr-alĭs, *conjectural* (conjectūra-); conjŭg-alĭs (Col., Tac.), *of marriage* (conjŭg-); convīv-alĭs, *of a dinner party* (convīva-); corpŏr-alĭs (Sen., Dig.), *of the body* (corpŏs-); crīn-alĭs (Verg., Ov.), *of the hair* (crīni-); Diālĭs *of the day-god*, i. e. *Jupiter* (die-); dōt-alĭs, *belonging to a dowry* (dōti-); ēsŭri-alĭs (Plaut.), *of hunger* (ēsŭrie-); extempŏr-alĭs (Quint., &c.), *extemporaneous* (ex, tempŏre); fāt-alĭs, *of the fates, destined, fatal* (fāto-); fĕr-alĭs, *of the dead;* Flōr-alĭs, *of the Flower Goddess* (flōra-); flŭvi-alĭs (Verg., Col.), *of a river* (flŭvio-); frŭg-ali- (only in comp. and sup.), *thrifty* (frŭg-); fulgŭr-alĭs (Cic. once), *of lightning* (fulgŭr-); fūri-alĭs, *of the furies, raging* (fūria-); gĕnĕr-alĭs, *of a class, general* (gĕnŭs-); gĕni-alĭs, *of the Genius, joyful, nuptial* (gĕnio-); gĕnĭt-alĭs, *of birth* or *generation* (gĕnĭto-); grĕg-alĭs, *of the herd, common* (grĕg-); hiĕm-alĭs, *of winter* (hiĕm-); histriōn-alĭs (Tac.), *of an actor, stagy* (histriōn-); hospĭt-alĭs, *of a guest* or *host* (hospĕt-); illĭbĕr-alĭs, *unworthy of a freeman* (in, lībĕro-); infĭti-alĭs, *consisting of a denial* (infĭtia-); lēg-alĭs (Quint.), *of the law* (lēg-); jŭdĭci-alĭs, *of the courts of justice* (jŭdĭcio-); jŭg-alĭs, *of a yoke* (jŭgo-); jūrĭdici-alĭs, *relating to a question of rightful conduct* (jus- dĭc-ĕre; cf. Corn. I. 14); lībĕr-alĭs, *of a freeman* (lībĕro-), lībr-ālĭs (Plin., Col.), *of a pound* (lībra-); lustr-alĭs, *of purification* (lustro-); mănŭ-alĭs, *for the hand* (mănu-); mărĭt-alĭs, *of married persons* (mărīto-); Marti-alĭs, *of Mars* (marti-); mātrōn-alĭs, *matronly* (matrona-); mōr-alĭs (first formed by Cic.), *of conduct* (mōs-); mort-ālĭs, *subject to death, human* (morti-); mŭr-

alis, *of walls* (mūro-); nāt-ālis, *of birth* (nāto-); nātūr-alis, *natural*
(nātūra-); nāv-alis, *of ships* (nāvi-); němŏr-alis, *of groves* (ně-
mŏs-); nĭv-alis, *of snow* (nĭvi-); nuptĭ-alis, *of a wedding* (nuptia-);
pāc-alis (Ov.), *of peace* (pāci-); părent-alis, *of parents* (părenti-);
(Lucr.) pěnětr-alis, *penetrating* (pěnětrā-re) *innermost* (from an assumed pěnětrum?); plūr-alis (Quint.), *plural* (plūsi-); plūvi-alis,
rainy (plūvia-); princĭp-alis, *of the chief, chief* (princěp-); provin-
ci-alis, *of a province* (prōvincia-); pŭte-alis, *of a well* (pŭteo-);
qvālis, *of what kind* (quo-); qvinqvenn-alis, *happening every five
years* (quinqve, anno-); rătiōn-alis, *having* or *belonging to reason*
(rătiōn-); rēg-alis, *kingly* (rēg-); sesqvĭpěd-alis, *a foot and a half*
in measure (sesquĭpěd-); sŏci-alis, *of companions* or *allies* (sŏcio-);
spēcĭ-alis (Sen., Quint.), *special* (spěcie-); tālis, *such* (to-, comp.
tam, tum); tempŏr-alis, *of time;* also post-Aug. *temporary* (tem-
pŏs-); theātr-alis, *theatrical* (theatro-); triumph-alis, *triumphal*
(triumpho-); vectīg-alis, *of taxes, tax-paying;* vēn-alis, *for sale*
(vēno-); virgĭn-alis, *maidenly* (virgŏn-); vīt-alis, *of life, long-lived*
(vīta-); vōc-alis, *voiceful* (vōc-) and others.

2. Substantives: many of these stems are also used as adjectives, some of which are given above:

(*a*) Masculine: ann-alis, *a history* (anno-); căn-alis, *a conduit*
(comp. canna, *a reed?*); cōmĭti-alis, *an epileptic* (cōmĭtio-); cōntŭ-
bern-alis, *a comrade* (com, tăberna-); Cūri-alis, *a man of the
district* (cūria-); fēti-alis, *a priest ambassador;* mājālis, *a barrow-
hog;* nāt-ālis, *a birthday;* nāt-āles (pl.), *lineage* (nāto-); rīv-alis, *a
rival,* i.e. a person living *on the* same *stream* as another (rivo-);
sŏdalis, *a mate.*

Proper names: Jŭvěn-alis (jŭvěn-); Năt-alis (vid. supr.).

(*b*) Neuter (cf. § 424): ănĭmal, *a breathing thing* (anima-);
augŭr-ale, *the augurial tent* (augŭr-); Baccăn-al, *a place for rites of
Bacchus* (as if from Baccāno-, Baccho-); bĭdent-al, a place consecrated, because struck by lightning (called from *sheep sacrificed,*
bĭdenti-?); căpĭt-al, *a capital crime* (căpŭt-); cervīc-al, *a bolster*
(cervīx-); cŭbĭt-al, *an elbow-cushion* (cubĭto-); dent-alia (pl.),
plough-irons (denti-); fōc-ale, *a neckcloth* (fauci-); front-alia (pl.),
frontlets (fronti-); gěnu-ālia (pl. Ov. once), *garters* (gěnu-); Lŭ-
perc-al, *a place sacred to Pan* (Luperco-); mĭnūt-al, *mincemeat*
(mĭnūto-); pěnětr-ale, *a sanctuary* (see above, § 880, 1); pŭte-al,
a stone curb *round a well* (pŭteo-); qvadrant-al, *a firkin* (really
5¾ gall.; a measure containing *a fourth,* quadranti-, of some other
measure); răm-alia (pl.), *twigs* (rāmo-); scŭt-ale (Liv. once), *a
leathern thong* (scūto-); spons-alia (pl.), *a betrothal* (sponso-);
tŏr-al, *a couch-valance* (tŏro-); trĭbūn-al, *a judgment-seat* (trĭ-
būno-); vectīgal, *a tax* (cf. § 963).

So also many names of feasts; in the plural neuter (cf. § 425). (The time of the year, when fixed, is here added as well as the name of the god or goddess, which however appears sometimes to be an invention of the Roman etymologers. See Mommsen, *Corp. Inscr. Rom.* i. pp. 375—410.)

Agonalia, Jan. 9, Mar. 17, Dec. 11 (*of sacrifice?* ăgĕre; comp. ἀγων?) **Angeronalia,** Dec. 21 (**Angerona**); **Baccanalia** (Βάκχος); **Carmentalia,** Jan. 11 and 15 (**Carmentis**); **Cerialia,** Apr. 19 (**Cĕres**); **Compitalia,** feast of the *Cross Roads* (**compĭto-**); **Consualia,** Aug. 21, and Dec. 15 (**Consus,** stem **conso-**); **Fĕralia** (but **Fĕralia,** Ov.) *all Saints' Day,* Feb. 21. (**fer-re,** *to bring offerings*); **Floralia,** Apr. 21 (**Flora**); **Fontinalia** (**Fontanalia**), *Feast of Water Springs* (**fonti-**); **Fornacalia,** *Oven day* (**Fornax**); **Furrinalia,** Jul. 25 (**Furrina**); **Larentalia** (**Larentinalia**), Dec. 23 (**Acca Larentia**); **Liberalia,** Mar. 17 (**Liber**); **Lupercalia,** Feb. 15 (**Lŭpercus**); **Matralia,** Jan. 11 (**Mater Matuta,** *Mother dawn?*); **Meditrinalia,** Oct. 11 (Varr. L. L. 6. 21); **Neptūnalia,** Jul. 23 (**Neptūnus**); **Opalia,** Dec. 29 (**Ops**); **Paganalia,** *Village festivals* (**pāgāno-**); **Parentalia,** Feb. 13—21, sacred to the dead (**parentāre,** *to sacrifice*); **Portunalia,** Aug. 17 (**Portunus**); **Quirinalia,** Feb. 17 (**Quirinus**); **Robigalia,** Apr. 25, *Mildew day* (**Rōbugo**); **Saturnalia,** Dec. 17—19 (**Saturnus**); **Terminalia,** Feb. 23, *Boundary day* (**Termĭnus**); **Vestalia,** Jun. 9 (**Vesta**); **Vinalia,** Apr. 23, Aug. 19, *Wine day;* **Volcanalia,** Aug. 23 **Volcānus**); **Volturnalia,** Aug. 27 (**Volturnus**).

-ūli   cŭru-lis, *of a chariot* (cf. L. 24. 18), hence (cf. Gell. 3. 18) **sella curulis,** *an official chair* (**curru-**); **ĕd-ūlis** (usually in n. pl.), *eatable* (**ĕd-ĕre**); **pĕd-ulis** (Ulp.), *for the feet* (**pĕd-**); **trĭbu-lis** (subst. m.), *a tribes-man* (**trĭbu-**).   [581]

-ēli   **crūd-elis,** *cruel* (**crūdo-,** *raw*); **fĭde-lis,** *faithful* (**fĭde-**); **infĭdelis,** *unfaithful;* **patru-elis,** *of* (i.e. descended from) *a father's brother* (**patruo-**).

-ili   1. Adjectives: **ăn-ilis,** *of an old woman* (**ănu-**); **cīvīlis,** *of a citizen* (**cīvi-**); **ĕr-ilis,** *of a master* (**ĕro-** or **hĕro-**); **exīlis** (contr. for **exĭgĭlis**), *small;* **făbr-ilis,** *of a workman* (**făbro-**); **gent-ĭlis** (adj., only post-Aug.), *of a clan* (**genti-**); **host-ĭlis,** *of an enemy* (**hosti-**); **jŭvĕn-ilis** (also **jŭvĕnālis,** Verg., Suet.), *youthful* (**jŭvĕn-**); **puĕr-ilis,** *of a boy* (**puĕro-**); **scurr-ĭlis,** *buffoon-like* (**scurra-**); **sĕn-ilis,** *of old people* (**sĕn-**); **serv-ĭlis,** *slavish* (**servo-**); **subtīlis** (for **subtexilis**), suitable for woof (cf. § 113), *fine;* **vĭr-ĭlis,** *of a man* (**vĭro-**).   [582]

2. Substantives: (*a*) masculine: **Æd-ilis,** *commissioner of Public Buildings* (**ædi-**); **Aprilis,** the *opening* month (from the bursting of vegetation, **ăpĕrīre**); **Qvint-ilis,** the *fifth* month, i.e. July (**quinto-**); **Sextilis,** the *sixth* month, i.e. August (**sexto-**).

(*b*) Neuter: **ancīle**, *an oval shield* (for ancīdile; am, cædĕre); **bŏv-ile** or **būbile**, *an ox-stall* (bŏv-, § 76); **căpr-ile**, *a goat-stall* (căpro-); **cŭb-ile**, *a bed* (cŭbāre); **ĕqv-ile**, *a horse-stable* (ĕqvo-); **fēn-ilia** (pl.), *haylofts* (fēno-); **hast-ile**, *a spear shaft, spear* (hasta-); **incīle**, *a cut*, i. e. *a ditch* (for incīdile, incīd-ĕre); **mant-ilia** (pl., also mantēlia), *napkins* (mănu-?); **mŏn-ile**, *a necklace*; **ŏv-ile**, *a sheepfold* (ŏvi-); **Păr-ilia** (pl.), *feast of Pales* (Pali- cf. § 176, 7); **sĕd-ile**, *a seat* (sĕd-ēre, sēdi-); **suovetaur-ilia** (pl.), *a swine-sheep-and-bull sacrifice* (su-, ŏvi-, tauro-).

Compound stem-endings: **-līco**, § 771; **-ŭlento**, § 793; **-ultu**, § 800; **-lenti** §, 807; **-lŏso**, **-īcŭlōso**, § 814; **-līēno**, **-līno**, §§ 837, 841; **-ilāgon**, § 845; **-ullŭlo**, **-ellŭlo**, **-illŭlo**, **-allo**, **-aullo**, **-ollo**, **-ullo**, **-ello**, **-illo**, §§ 865—869; **-lio**, **-ālio**, **-ēlio**, **-illio**, § 937—939, 949.

CHAPTER VIII.

LINGUAL NOUN STEMS (*Continued*).

iii. *Stems ending in* -ro.

-ro   Preceded by **r**. (Stems with other letters, whether radi- 883 cal or suffixal, preceding **r** will be found below.)

(*a*) Masculine: **barrus**, *an elephant;* **Burrus** (cf. § 73); **carrus**, *a waggon;* **cirrus**, *a curl;* **scurra**, *a buffoon.*

(*b*) Feminine: **ăcerra**, *an incense box;* **cerrus**, *the Turkey oak;* **gerræ** (pl.), *trifles* (comp. γέρρον, *a wickerwork*); **marra**, *a weeding hook;* **parra**, *a barn owl?*; **săburra**, *sand as ballast* (comp. sabulum?); **serra**, *a saw;* **terra**, *the earth* (torrēre); **văcerra**, *a log;* **vīverra**, *a ferret.*

(*c*) Neuter: **ferrum**, *iron;* **porrum**, *a leek* (comp. πράσον).

-ăro   **hăra**, *a pigsty;* **hĭlărus** (cf. § 429), *cheerful;* **samara**, 884 *elm seed;* **spărus**, *a hunting spear;* **suppărum**, *a linen under-garment, a topsail;* and (perhaps with ă) **varus**, *a pimple.*

-ŏro   ancŏra, *an anchor* (comp. ἄγκῡρα); foræ (pl), orig. *openings?* only in forās, forīs, *out of doors* (comp. θύρα, θύραζε, θύρασι); fŏrus, generally forī (pl.), *a row of seats,* or *holes;* fŏrum, *a court, market-place;* lŏra, *thin wine;* mŏra (also rĕmŏra, Plaut.), *delay;* tŏrus, *a couch, muscle* of arm, &c.

-ŭro   cămŭrus (adj.), *curved-in;* sătŭr (adj.), *sated;* sătŭra, *a medley,* hence, *a satire;* purpŭra, *purple* (for πορφύρα).

-ĕro   1. Adjectives: 885
æger, *sick;* asper, *rough;* crĕpĕro- (§ 346), *dark* (comp. κνέφας); fĕrus, *savage* (cf. § 99); infĕr (so Cato, but usually in pl.), *below* (comp. infra); intĕger, *untouched, whole* (in, tang-ĕre); mĕrus, *pure, unmixed;* mĭser, *wretched;* nĭger, *black;* nŭpĕrum (acc. m., Plaut.), *recent* (cf. § 540); pĭger, *lazy* (comp. pĭget); prŏ-pĕrus, *hasty;* prospĕrus, *favourable* (pro, spes-?); sŭper (so Cato, but usually in pl.), *above* (sup-er); tĕner, *tender, soft* (*holdable?* tĕn-ēre); văfer, *sly.*

2. Substantives:

(*a*) Masculine: ăger, *a field* (comp. ἀγρός); căper, *a goat* (comp. κάπρος, *wild boar*); ĕrus, *a master;* gĕner, *a son-in-law* (comp. γαμ-β-ρός); nŭmerus, *a number* (comp. νέμ-ειν, *to distribute*); puer, *a boy;* ŭmerus (hŭmerus), *a shoulder* (comp. ὦμ-ος).

(*b*) Feminine: jŭnĭperus, *a juniper tree.*

cămera, *a vault* (from καμάρα?); capra, *a she-goat;* cŭmera, *a chest;* ĕdera (hĕdĕra), *ivy;* ĕra, *a mistress;* ŏpera, *work, attention, a workman* (ŏpi-); phăleræ, *horse-trappings* (from φάλαρα); puera (rare and early), *a girl;* sĕra, *a bolt;* tessera, *a die,* or *square tablet* (comp. τέσσαρες, *four*); vespera, *evening* (comp. ἑσπέρα); vĭpera, *a viper* (for vīvĭ-pĕra? *bringing forth alive,* părĕre).

(*c*) Neuter: flagrum, *a whip;* jŭgerum (cf. § 458), *two-thirds of an acre;* scalprum, *a chisel* (scalp-ĕre); sĕrum, *whey* (comp. ὀρός and § 190); stuprum, *debauchery.*

-b-ĕro   1. Adjectives: crēber, *close* (comp. cre-sc-ĕre, cĕlĕbri-);   886
-b-ro   gibber, *humped* (gibbo-); glăber, *smooth, hairless* (comp. glŭbĕre, *to peel,* γλύφειν, γλάφειν, γλαφυρός); līber, *free* (comp. lĭb-et); rūber, *red;* scăber, *rough, scurvy* (comp. scăb-ies).

2. Substantives:

(*a*) Masculine: cŏlŭber (also colubra, f.), *a snake;* făber, *a smith;* fīber, *a beaver;* Līber, a name of *Bacchus;* lĭber, *the inner bark, a book* (for fli-ber; comp. φλοιός, *bark?* or comp. glăber, γλάφειν). [For Mulcĭber, *Vulcan,* see §§ 455, 901.]

22

(*b*) Feminine: dŏlābra, *a mattock* (dŏlā-re); fībra, *a fibre* (fĭnd-ĕre?); illĕcĕbra, *an allurement* (illĭcĕ-re); lătĕbra, *a hiding-place* (lătēre); lĭbra, *a balance;* palpebræ (pl., Celsus has sing. once), *eyelids* (palpā-re, palp-ĭtā-re); sălĕbra, *a jolting road* (sălīre); scătebra (Verg., Plin.), *a gushing* (scătēre); tĕnĕbræ (pl.), *darkness;* tĕrĕbra, *a borer* (tĕr-ĕre); vertĕbra, *a joint* (vert-ĕre); umbra, *a shadow* (comp. ĭmber, ὄμβρος?).

(*c*) Neuter: candēlabrum, *a candlestick* (candēla-); cĕrĕbrum, *the brain* (comp. κάρα, *head*); crībrum, *a sieve* (cre-, cer-nĕre, κρίνειν); dēlŭbrum, *a shrine* (de, lu-ere, *to expiate?*); flā-bra (pl.), *blasts* (flā-re); lābrum, *a basin* (lăvāre); labrum, *a lip* (lambere); membrum, *a limb;* pollubrum (Fest.), *a thing to sprinkle with* (por, lăv-); prŏbrum, *a disgrace;* vēlābrum, a street in Rome; ventĭlabrum (Col.), *a winnowing-fork* (ventĭlā-re); vŏlūtā-brum, *a wallowing-place* (vŏlūtā-re).

-c-ĕro ⎫ 1. Adjectives: lăc-er, *torn* (comp. λακίς, *a rent*); lūdĭ- 887
-c-ro ⎭   cer, *sportive* (lūdo-); măc-er, *thin* (comp. mac-ies); pulcer, *handsome;* săc-er, *devoted to the gods* (comp. sancīre).

2. Substantives: (*a*) masculine: canc-er, *a crab* (comp. καρκίνος); sŏc-er, *a father-in-law* (comp. ἑκυρός).

(*b*) Feminine: arcĕra (old), *a covered carriage* (arca-).

(*c*) Neuter: ambŭlā-crum, *a walk*, i. e. *place for walking* (ambŭlā-re); fulcrum, *a post* at foot of couch (fulcīre); invŏlucrum, *a wrapper* (involv-ĕre); lŭcrum, *gain* (lu-ĕre, *to pay*); sĕpulcrum, *a tomb* (sĕpĕlīre); sĭmŭlā-crum, *a likeness* (sĭmŭlā-re).

-t-ĕro ⎫ 1. Adjectives: 888
-t-ro ⎭
           alter, *other* (ăli-); āter, *black;* cētĕro- (§ 346), *other;* cīter (rare in positive), *on this side* (cis); dexter, *on the right-hand* (comp. δεξ-ιός); extĕro-, *outside* (ex); neuter, *neither* (ne, ŭtro-); noster, *our* (nos); postĕro-, *after* (pos-te); sĭnister, *on the left;* tæter, *foul;* voster (vester), *your* (vos); ŭter, *whether* (quo-, § 121).

Compare also contra, intra, ultra, frustra, § 509, and the adverbs in -ter, § 541. Also ĭtĕrum, *for the second time.*

2. Substantives:

(*a*) Masculine: admĭnis-ter (also administra, f.), *an attendant;* ădulter (also adultĕra, f.), *an adulterer;* arbĭter (also arbĭtra, f.), *a witness, judge* (ad, § 160. 10, bĭt-ere); auster, *a south-wind* (comp. αὔειν, ŭr-ĕre); cītrus, (1) *the citrus*, (2) *the citron;* culter, *a knife* (comp. κόλος, *docked;* κείρειν, curtus); hister, *an actor* (Etruscan); măgis-ter (also magistra, f.), *a master* (măgis); mĭnis-ter (also mĭnistra, f.), *a servant* (mĭnŭs); sĕqvester, *a stakeholder, mediator* (sĕcus); ŭtĕrus, *the womb*.

(*b*) Feminine: cætra, *a Spanish shield;* cŏlostra (also colostrum), *the first milk;* excĕtra, *a snake;* fĕnestra, *a window* (comp. φαν-, φαίνειν); littĕra, *a letter* (*a painted stroke?* from lĭ-n-ĕre, *to smear*); lutra, *an otter;* māter-tĕra, *a mother's sister* (*a second mother*, mater-, comp. ĭtĕrum, al-ter); mulc-tra (also mulctrum), *a milking-pail* (mulgēre); pătĕra, *a broad dish* (pătēre); scutra, *a flat dish;* and others in (*a*).

(*c*) Neuter: ărā-trum, *a plough* (ărā-re); astrum, *a star* (for ἄστρον); călămis-trum, *a curling-iron* (comp. călămo-, κάλᾰμίδ-, *a reed*); cănistrum (pl.), *a reed basket* (from κάναστρον); căpistrum, *a halter* (căpĕ-re, comp. căpĭd-); castra (pl.; also, as proper name, castrum), *a camp* (properly *huts?* comp. căsa, cas-tus); claus-trum (usually pl.), *a fastening* (claud-ĕre, § 160. 3); fĕretrum, *a bier* (fer-re, comp. φέρτρον); fulge-trum, *a lightning-flash* (fulgere); haus-trum (Lucr.), *a water-lifter* (haurīre); lĭgustrum, *privet;* lus-trum *a purification* (lu-ĕre); *a beast's den* (lūdĕre?); monstrum, *a prodigy* (mŏnēre, for mŏnes-trum, comp. vĕnustas, &c.); plaus-trum, *a cart,* from its jingle or rumbling (plaud-ĕre, *to clap*); ras-trum, *a rake* (rād-ĕre); ros-trum, *a beak* (rōd-ĕre); ru-trum, *a shovel* (ru-ĕre); spec-trum (rare), *a vision* (spĕcĕ-re); talitrum (Suet. *Tib.* 68), *a fillip with the finger?;* trans-trum, *a cross bench* (trans); vērātrum, *hellebore;* vĕretrum (vĕrēri); vĭtrum, *glass.*

-as-t-ĕro⎫
-as-t-ro ⎭ Antoniaster (cf. Prisc. 3. 40), *a little Antony* (Antōnio-); 889
Fulviaster (C. *Att.* 12. 44), ŏleaster, *wild olive* (ŏlea-); părāsītaster (Ter. once), *a bit of a parasite* (parasīto-); pīn-aster, *a wild pine* (pīno-); sĭlīqvastrum, *pepperwort* (sĭlīqva, *a pod*); surd-aster (Cic. once), *rather deaf* (surdo-).

-dro   căliendrum, *a woman's head-dress;* quadra, *a square* (§ 158).

-ĭro   pĭrus (f.), *a pear tree;* pĭrum, *a pear;* vĭr, *a man;* sătĭra, see satura.

-āro   (1) Adjectives: ămarus, *bitter* (comp. ὠμός, *raw*); 890 ăvarus, *greedy* (ăvēre); cārus, *dear;* clārus, *renowned;* gnārus, *knowing* (gno-sc-ĕre); rārus, *rare;* vārus, *crooked.*

       (2) Substantives: āra, *an altar* (§ 183 *a*); tiāra, *a turban* (Persian word?); vāra, *a forked pole.*

-auro   aura, *a breeze* (comp. ἄειν); aurum, *gold;* laurus (f.), 891 *a laurel* (cf. § 398); scaurus, *with swollen ankles.*

-ōro (1) Adjectives: all formed from substantives in -ōs or -ōr.

căn-or-us, *tuneful* (cănŏr-); hŏn-or-us (post-Aug.), *honourable* (hŏnŏr-); ŏd-ōr-us, *possessing scent* (ŏd·ōs-); sŏn-ōr-us, *loud sounding* (sŏnōr-); sŏp-or-us, *sleep bringing* (sŏpōr-).

(2) Substantives: aur-ōra, *the dawn* (comp. αὔως, Aeol. and αὔριον); flōra, *goddess of flowers* (flōs-); hōra, *an hour* (ὥρα, *a season*); lōrum, *a thong;* mōrus (f.), *a mulberry tree* (comp. μορέα, μύρον); ōra, *a coast, region;* prōra, *the prow* (πρῷρα, *the look-out,* προ-ορα).

-ūro 1. Adjectives: dūrus, *hard;* obscūrus, *dusky* (comp 89: σκότος); pūrus, *pure* (comp. pŭ-tus).

2. Substantives: cūra, *care* (căv-, căvēre); flgūra, *form, fashion* (flngēre); mūrus (mœrus), *a wall,* esp. of a city; Sŭbūra, a district in Rome between Esquiline and Viminal (the abbreviation for it was, according to Quint. I. 724, SVC., but this was probably from the pagus Sucusanus included in it); sūra, *the calf* of the leg.

-t-ūro }
-s-ūro } 1. Adjectives; i.e. the future participle active. 89.3

āmāturus, *about to love* (amā-re); dă-turus, *about to give* (dă-re); fŭ-turus, *about to be* (fu-, § 719); mŏrī-tūrus, *about to die* (mŏri); ŏrī-turus, *about to arise* (ŏrīri); ōsurus, *about to hate* (ŏd-); pas-sūrus, *about to suffer* (păt-i); pō-turus, *about to drink* (cf. pŏ-tus); rectūrus, *about to rule* (rĕg-ĕre); and many others. See Book II. Chap. XXIV. XXX.

māturus, *ripe.*

2. Substantives: all feminine, with similar formation to that of the future participle. These words denote the *employment* or *result,* and may be compared with the names of *agents* in -tor.

āper-tura (Vitr., Ulp.), *an opening* (ăpĕrīre); armā-tura, *equipment* (armā-re); cælā-tura (Quint. &c.), *carving* (cælā-re); cæ-sura (Plin.), *a cutting* (cæd-ĕre); cap-tura (Plin., Suet. &c.), *a capture, gain* (căpĕ-re); cen-sura, *the censorship* (censŏr-); coc-tura (Plin., Col. &c.), *cooking* (cŏqv-ĕre); commis-sura, *a joining* (committ-ĕre); compŏsī-tura (Cato, Lucr.), *a fastening* (compōn-ĕre); conjec-tura, *a guess* (conícĕ-re); consī-tura, *a planting* (consērĕre); cul-tura, *cultivation* (cŏl-ĕre); dictā-tura, *the dictatorship* (dictātōr-); fē-tura, *breeding* (comp. fē-tus, fē-cundus); fis-sura (Plin., Col.), *a cleft* (find-ĕre); flex-ura, *a turning* (flect-ĕre); gĕnī-tura (Suet., Plin.), *birth, nativity* (gĭ-gn-ere); jac-tura, *a throwing over, loss* (jăcĕ-re); junc-tura, *a joining* (jung-ĕre); littĕrā-tura, *writing, acquaintance with letters* (littera-); lī-tura, *a blotting* (lĭn-ĕre); men-sura, *a measure* (mētīri); mercā-tura, *trade* (mercā-ri); mis-tura (Lucr.

and post-Aug.), *a mixture* (miscēre); nā-tura, *nature* (na-sc-i);
pŏlī-tura (Plin.), *a polishing* (pŏlī-re); polluc-tura (Plaut.
once), *a feast* (pollūcēre); præfec-tura, *the office* or *territory of a præfectus*
(præficĕ-re); præ-tura, *the prætorship* (prætŏr-); pres-sura (Col.,
Plin.), *pressure* (prĕm-ere); qvæs-tura, *the quæstorship* (quæstor-);
rĕdemp-tura, *an undertaking*, *a contract* (rĕdĭm-ĕre); scalp-tura
(Plin., Vitr.), *a graving* (scalp-ere); scis-sura (Suet., Plin.), *a rent*
(scind-ere); scrip-tura, *a writing*, *a tax on registered* use of public
pastures (scrīb-ĕre); sec-tura (Varr., Plin.), *cutting* (sĕcāre); sĕpul-
tura, *a burial* (sĕpĕlīre); stă-tura, *stature* (stāre); struc-tura, *a
building* (strugv-, stru-ĕre); tempĕrā-tura (Varr. and post-Aug.),
due proportion (tempĕrā-re); tex-tura, *a web* (tex-ĕre); ton-sura,
a shaving (tondēre); vec-tura, *conveyance* (vĕh-ĕre); vēnā-tura
(Plaut. once), *hunting* (vēnā-ri); ver-sura, *a change*, esp. *fresh bor-
rowing* (vert-ĕre); unc-tura (Cic. once), *an anointing* (ung-ĕre);
vol-sura (Varr. once), *a plucking* (vell-ĕre); ūsura, *use*, esp. *of
money* (ūt-i); and others.

-ĕro   1. Adjectives: austērus, *astringent, severe;* plērus (Cato), 894
        most, usually plur. with -que attached, pleri-que; also in
sing. pleraque, plerumque (comp. plūs, plē-nus); prōcērus, *tall;*
sērus, *late;* sĕvērus, *strict* (? seves-=σέβας); sincērus, *uninjured;*
vērus, *true.*

      2. Substantives: cēra, *wax* (comp. κηρός); gălērus, *a skin cap*
(comp. gălea).

-ĭro   1. Adjectives: dirus, *terrible;* mirus, *wonderful.*   895

      2. Substantives: diræ, *curses,* thought as supernatural
beings; ira, *anger;* lira, *a furrow;* spira, *a coil* (comp.
σπεῖρα).

iv. *Stems ending in* -ru, -ri, -r.

-ru   currus (m.), *a chariot* (comp. curr-ĕre); laurus (f.), 896
a bay-tree; nŭrus (f.), *a daughter-in-law* (comp. νυός for
συνσός, Curt.); sŏcrus (f.), *a stepmother* (comp. sŏcĕro-);
vĕru (m.), *a spit.*

ri   auris (f.), *an ear* (comp. audī-re, and § 160. 10); būris 897
(m.), *plough-tail* (from βο-, οὐρά?); extorris (adj.),
exiled (ex, terra?); fŏris (f.), *a door;* hĭlăris (adj.), see hĭlărus;
măre (n.), *the sea;* nāris (f.), *a nostril* (comp. nāso-); torris (m.),
a brand (comp. torrēre); turris (f.), *a tower;* verres (m.), *a
boar-pig.*

-r   far (n., stem farr-), *corn;* fūr (m.), *a thief* (comp. φώρ);
Lar (m.), *a household god;* pār (stem păr-), *equal, a mate*
(cf. § 454); vēr (n.), *spring* (comp. ἔαρ).

-ăr   Substantives: all neuter: baccar, a plant with an aroma-
tic root (from βάκκαρις); jŭbar, *bright light;* instar,
likeness. See also § 454.

-ŏr   Substantives: neuter (on these see § 454): æqvŏr, *a level* 898
surface (æqvo-); ĕbur, *ivory;* fĕmur, *a thigh;* jĕcur, *the
liver* (comp. ἧπαρ); marmor, *marble;* rŏbur, *heart of oak.*
Perhaps also mĕmor (adj.), *mindful,* belongs here (§ 429).

-ŭr   1. Adjective: cĭcur, *tame.*   899

2. Substantives: (*a*) masculine: augur, *a diviner* (probably compound for ăvĭ-ger); furfur, *bran* (perhaps redupl. from
same root as in frĭcāre, *to rub*); Lĕmŭres (pl.), *ghosts;* turtur, *a
turtle-dove;* vultur, *a vulture.*

(*b*) Neuter: fulgur, *a flash of lightning* (fulgere); guttur (rarely
m.), *the throat;* murmur, *a murmuring noise* (redupl.); sulfur,
sulphur.

-ĕri   cĕler, *swift;* pŭtris (§ 430), *rotten* (pŭt-ĕre); vepres 900
(m. pl.), *thorns.*

-ĕr   1. Adjectives: pauper, *poor* (pauco- and pără-re?).

2. Substantives (cf. § 455):

(*a*) Masculine: ăcĭpenser, *a sturgeon;* agger, *a pile* (ad,
gĕr-ĕre); anser, *a gander* (comp. χήν, Germ. *Gans*); asser, *a beam,
post;* carcer, *a prison, barrier;* Cĕlĕres (pl.), *Knights;* lăter, *a brick;*
passer, *a sparrow;* prŏcĕres (pl.), *nobles;* vesper, *evening* (cf. § 885.
2. *b*); vōmer (stem originally vomĭs-), *a ploughshare.*

(*b*) Feminine: lăver, a water-plant ; mŭlier, *a woman.*

(*c*) Neuter: ăcer, *the maple;* cădāver, *a corpse;* cĭcer, *chickpea;*
ĭter, *a journey* (ĭ-, ĭre, *to go*); păpāver, *a poppy;* pĭper, *pepper* (comp.
πέπερι); sĭler, *brookwillow;* sĭser, *skirwort* (comp. σίσαρον).

-b-ĕri
-b-ri   (See § 430). 1. Adjectives: cĕlĕber, *numerous, thronged* 901
in honour (comp. crebro-); December, *tenth;* fēne-bris, *of
interest* (fēnŏs-); fŭnebris, *funereal* (fŭnŭs-); lŭgu-bris,
mournful (lŭgēre; the second u being due to assimilation partly to
the first u, and partly to b); mŭlie-bris, *womanly* (mŭliĕr-);
Nŏvem-ber, *ninth;* Octo-ber, *eighth;* sălŭ-ber, *healthy* (sălūt-); Sep-
tem-ber, *seventh.* (December, &c. are only used of the *month.*)

2. Substantives: fe-bris (f.), *a fever* (for ferv-bris, ferv-ere); imber, *a rain-shower* (comp. ὄμβρ-ος). Mulciber, name of *Vulcan.*

-b-ĕr   sūber (n.), *cork-tree;* tūber (m.), *a fruit tree;* (n.) *a hump* (tŭmēre, see § 455); ūber (adj.), *fruitful;* (n.), *a teat* (comp. οὖθαρ); verbĕra (n. pl.), *strokes.*

-c-ĕri⎫
-c-ri ⎬   Adjectives: ācer, *sharp* (comp. ăcu-, ăcie-); ălăcer, *alert;* 902 mĕdio-cris, *middling,* *ordinary* (medio-); vŏlūcer, *swift* (vŏlāre).

-t-ru   qvinqvātrus (f. pl., also qvinqvatria, n. pl., Suet.), a feast of Minerva kept on 19th March, i.e. *five* days after the Ides (qvinqve); so among the Tusculans, Triatrus, Sexatrus, Septematrus, and among the Faliscans, Decimatrus (Fest. s. v.); tŏnĭtrus (m.), *thunder* (tŏnĭto- from tŏnāre).

-t-ĕri⎫
-t-ri ⎬   1. Adjectives: ĕques-ter, *of horsemen* (ĕquĕt-); pălus- 903 ter, *of the marshes* (pălūd-); pĕdes-ter, *of foot-men* (pĕdĕt-); sĕ-mes-tris, *for six months* (sex, mens-); sĕquester (cf. § 430, and under -tro).

2. Substantives: linter or lunter (f.), *a boat;* venter (m.), *the belly* (comp. γαστήρ); ūter (m.), *a skin-bag* (comp. ŭtĕrus?). Denter, a cognomen of the Livian clan (Liv. x. 1), may belong here.

-es-t-ĕri⎫
-es-t-ri ⎬   i.e. ensi + teri? For the suffix -ensi see § 815, and for 904 the weakening of ns to s § 168.

Adjectives (cf. § 430): campester, *of the fields* (campo-); silvestris, *of the woods* (silva-); terrestris, *of the earth* (terra-).

illustris, *in bright light,* sublustris, *in faint light,* are also probably for illūcenstris, sublūcenstris. Sĕgestre (n.), segestria (f.), *a wrapper,* probably from στέγαστρον.

-t-ĕr⎫
-t-r ⎬   Substantives: accĭpĭter, *a hawk* (comp. ὠκύπτερος); frā- 905 ter, *a brother* (comp. φράτηρ, *a clansman*); māter, *a mother* (comp. μήτηρ); păter, *a father* (comp. πατήρ).

-ĭn-ĕr   i.e. -ĕr appended to suffix -ĕn: ĭt-ĭner (n.), *a journey* (ĭ-, ĭre); jŏc-iner (n.), *a liver* (comp. jĕcŏr). See §§ 454, 455.

-āri   Appended to those stems only which contain l (other- 906 wise āli is appended, § 880).

1. Adjectives: āl-āris (more frequently ālārius), *of the wing* of an army (āla-); ancill-aris, *of a maid-servant* (ancilla-); angŭl-aris, *having corners* (angŭlo-); Apollĭn-aris, *sacred to Apollo*

(Apollŏn-); āquĭlōn-aris, *northerly* (aquĭlōn-); artĭcŭl-aris (Plin.,
Suet., also articularius, Cato), *of the joints* (artĭcŭlo-); auxĭli-aris
(also earlier auxiliarius), *helping* (auxĭlio-); balne-aris (Dig., earlier balnearius), *of the baths* (balneo-); călĭg-aris (Plin., also cali-
garius), *of a soldier's boot* (călĭga-); căpŭl-aris, *of a coffin* (căpŭlo-);
collĭci-aris (Cato), *for gutters* (collĭqvia-); cŏlŭmell-aris (Varr.,
Plin.), *of* or *like pillars* (cŏlŭmella-); consŭl-aris, *of a consul* (con-
sŭl-); cŭbĭcŭl-aris (Cic., also later cubicularius, but cf. § 942. 2), *of
a bedchamber* (cŭbĭcŭlo-); culle-aris (Cato), *sacklike* (culleo-);
ĕpŭl-aris, *of a banquet* (ĕpŭla-); fābŭl-aris (Suet. once), *fabulous*
(fābŭla-); fămĭli-aris, *of a family, intimate* (fămĭlia-); fămŭl-aris,
of a servant (fămŭlo-); fĭgŭl-aris, *of a potter* (fĭgŭlo-); intercăl-
aris (also intercălarius), *intercalary* (intercălă-re); jŏcŭl-aris,
laughable (jŏcŭlo-); līne-aris, *of lines* (līnea-); lūn-aris, *of the moon*
(lūna-); mănĭpŭl-aris, *of a company* (mănĭpŭlo-); maxill-aris (Cels.,
Plin.), *of the jaws* (maxilla-); mīlĭt-aris (also militarius Plaut.
once), *of soldiers* (mīlĕt-); mŏl-aris, *of a mill* (mŏla-); oll-āris
(Mart., also ollārius Plin.), *potted* (olla-); palm-aris (also palma-
rius), *of a palm's breadth, deserving the palm* (palma-); pĕcŭli-aris,
of one's own (pĕcŭlio-); piācŭl-aris, *expiatory* (piācŭlo-); pĭl-aris
(Stat.), *of balls* (pĭla-); plant-aris (Stat.), *of the foot* (planta-);
pollĭc-aris (Plin.), *of a thumb* (pollĕc-); pŏpŭl-aris, *of the people*
(pŏpŭlo-); prœli-aris, *of a battle* (prœlio-); puell-aris, *of a girl*
(puella-); pŭpill-aris, *of a ward* (pŭpillo-); sălŭt-aris, *healthful*
(sălŭt-); saecŭl-aris, *of an age* (saecŭlo-); singŭl-aris, *sole, unique*
(singŭlo-); sōl-aris (Ov., Sen., &c.), *of the sun* (sōl-); spĕcŭl-aris,
of a mirror (spĕcŭlo-); tāl-aris, *of the ankles* (tālo-); triclīni-aris,
of a dining-room (triclīnio-); vall-aris, *of a rampart* (vallo-); vă-
pŭl-aris (coined by Plaut. in imitation of militaris), *of the floggees*
(văpŭlā-re); vēlĭt-aris, *of the light-armed* (vēlĕt-); vulg-aris, *of the
mass, common* (vulgo-).

2. Substantives:

(*a*) Masculine: mŏl-aris, *millstone, grinder* (mŏla-); pugill-ares
(pl.), *writing hand tablets* (pŭgillo-).

(*b*) Neuter: alt-āria (pl.), *a high altar* (alto-?); alve-are (or
alvearium), *a beehive* (alveo-, *hollow*); calc-ar, *a spur* (calci-); că-
pill-are (Mart.), *pomatum* (căpillo-); cŏchle-are, *a spoon* (cochlea-,
snail shell); coll-are (Plaut., Varr.), *a collar* (collo-); exempl-ar, *a
pattern* (exemplo-); lăcun-ar, *a panelled ceiling* (lăcūna-); lăqve-ar,
a ceiling (*dome-like*? as if *drawn in*); lăqveo-, *a noose*); lūc-ar, *a tax
on woods* (lūco-); lŭpān-ar, *a brothel* (lŭpa-, with suffix -āno);
păle-ar, *a dewlap* (pălea-, *cock's wattles*); plant-aria (pl.) *slips* of
trees (planta-); pulvīn-ar, *a cushioned seat* (pulvīno-); sigillaria
(pl.), *feast of images, image market* (sigillo-); spĕcŭl-aria (pl.),
window-panes (spĕcŭlo-); tāl-aria (pl.), *shoes fastened to ankles*
(tālo-); torcŭl-ar, *an oil-press* (torqvēre).

-ōr   1. Adjective: **primōr-** (no nom. s.), *in the first rank* (primo-).

2. Substantives: 907

(*a*) Denoting *quality;* masculine **āc-or,** *sourness* (ācēre); **ægr-or** (Lucr.), *sickness* (ægro-); **alg-or,** *cold* (algēre); **ăm-or,** *love* (ămā-re); **ang-or,** *choking, anguish* (ang-ĕre); **ard-or,** *glow* (ardēre); **căl-or,** *heat* (călēre); **cald-or** (Varr.), *warmth* (caldo-); **cand-or,** *a brilliant white* (candēre); **căn-or,** *tunefulness* (căn-ĕre); **clām-or,** *a shout* (clāmā-re); **clang-or,** *a clang* (clang-ĕre); **crĕm-or,** *broth;* **cru-or,** *gore;* **dĕc-or,** *grace* (dĕcēre); **dŏl-or,** *pain* (dŏlēre); **err-or,** *a straying, error* (errā-re); **făv-or,** *favour* (făvēre); **ferv-or,** *boiling heat* (ferv-ere); **fœt-or,** *a stench* (fœtēre); **frăg-or,** *a crash* (frang-ĕre); **frĕm-or,** *a roaring* (frĕm-ĕre); **fulg-or,** *a glare* (fulg-ere); **fŭr-or,** *rage* (fŭr-ĕre); **horr-or,** *a shudder* (horrēre); **langv-or,** *faintness* (langvēre); **lent-or** (Plin.), *pliancy* (lento-); **lēv-or** (Lucr., Plin.), *smoothness* (lēvi-); **līqv-or,** *a fluid* (līqvi); **līv-or,** *leaden colour, envy* (līvēre); **lŭror** (Lucr.), *sallowness* (comp. lŭrĭdus); **mær-or,** *grief* (mærēre); **marc-or** (Cels., Sen. &c.), *a drooping* (marcēre); **mūc-or** (post-Aug.), *mould* (mūcēre); **nĭd-or,** *a smell;* **nĭgr-or,** *blackness* (nĭgro-); **pæd-or,** *filth;* **pall-or,** *paleness* (pallēre); **păv-or,** *dread;* **plang-or,** *a beating* the breast (plang-ĕre); **pŭd-or,** *shame* (pŭdēre); **pŭt-or,** *rottenness* (pūtēre); **rĭg-or,** *stiffness* (rĭgēre); **rŭbor,** *redness* (rŭbēre); **rŭm-or,** *common talk;* **săp-or,** *flavour* (săpĕ-re); **sŏn-or,** *a din* (sŏnāre); **sŏp-or,** *drowsiness* (comp. sōpĭ-re); **splend-or,** *brightness* (splendēre); **sqvāl-or,** *dirtiness* (sqvālēre); **strīd-or,** *a whistling* or *shrieking* (strīdere); **string-or** (Lucr.), *a shock* (string-ĕre); **stŭp-or,** *amazement* (stŭpēre); **sūd-or,** *sweat* (sūdā-re); **tĕn-or,** *course* (tĕnēre); **tĕp-or,** *warmth* (tĕpēre); **terr-or,** *fright* (terrēre); **tĭm-or,** *fear* (tĭmēre); **torp-or,** *numbness* (torpēre); **trĕm-or,** *a quaking* (trĕm-ĕre); **tŭm-or,** *a swelling* (tŭmēre); **văg-or** (Lucr.), *a squalling* (văgī-re); **văp-or,** *steam* (comp. văpĭdus, and § 121); **vĭg-or,** *vigour* (vĭgēre); **ŭmor,** *moisture* (ūmēre).

(*b*) **ăđor** (n.), *corn;* **ŏlor** (m.), *a swan;* **sŏror** (f.), *a sister;* **uxor** (f.), *a wife* (comp. jŭg-, jŭngĕre).

-t-ōr
-s-ōr } i.e. -ōr appended to the supine stem. All masculine.   908

(*a*) From supine stems of vowel verbs with long vowel preceding suffix: the verbs themselves are omitted as self-evident. A few are formed from substantives:

accūs-at-or, *an accuser;* **ædĭfĭc-at-or,** *a builder, one fond of building;* **æstĭm-at-or,** *an appraiser;* **ăgĭt-at-or,** *a driver;* **āle-at-or,** *a dicer* (ālea-); **ăm-at-or,** *a lover;* **ăr-at-or,** *a husbandman;* **assect-**

at-or, *one of a man's suite;* **aud-ĭt-or**, *a bearer, pupil;* **balne-ăt-or**, *a bathman* (ba!nea-); **bell-at-or**, *a warrior;* **cadŭce-ăt-or**, *an officer with a flag of truce* (cadŭceo-); **căl-at-or**, *a crier, servant;* **călum-ni-at-or**, *a legal trickster;* **capt-at-or**, esp. *a legacy hunter;* **cess-at-or**, *a loiterer;* **circŭl-at-or**, *a huckster, mountebank;* **cōmiss-at-or**, *a reveller;* **compĕt-ĭt-or**, *a rival* (compĕt-ĕre, cf. § 657); **conqvīs-ĭt-or**, *a recruiting officer* (conqvær-ĕre, cf. § 657); **convīv-ăt-or**, *a host;* **cre-ăt-or**, *a creator;* **cunct-ăt-or**, *a loiterer;* **cŭp-ĭt-or** (Tac.), *a desirer* (cŭpĕ-re, cf. § 656); **cūr-at-or**, *a keeper;* **declām-at-or**, *a rhetorician;* **dē-lat-or**, *an informer* (tlā-, tollĕre, cf. § 687); **dict-at-or**, *a supreme commander;* **discept-at-or**, *a judge;* **dispens-at-or**, *a steward;* **dissign-at-or**, *a master of ceremonies, an undertaker;* **dōn-at-or** (Dig.), *a donor;* **ēdŭc-at-or**, *a foster-father, bringer up;* **existĭm-at-or**, *a connoisseur;* **explōr-at-or**, *a spy;* **fāmĭgĕr-at-or**, *a talebearer* (fāma-, gĕr-ĕre); **fēnĕr-at-or**, *a usurer;* **fīn-ĭt-or**, *a surveyor;* **glădi-at-or**, *a swordsman* (glădio-); **grass-at-or**, *a footpad;* **gŭbern-at-or**, *a pilot;* **hort-at-or**, *an inciter;* **ĭmĭt-at-or**, *an imitator;* **impĕr-at-or**, *a commander-in-chief;* **larg-ĭt-or**, *a giver*, esp. *of bribes;* **lā-tor**, *proposer* of a law (cf. § 687); **laud-at-or**, *a panegyrist;* **lībĕr-at-or**, *a deliverer;* **lign-at-or**, *a woodcutter;* **lōc-at-or**, *a lessor;* **mand-at-or**, *a giver of a charge;* **merc-at-or**, *a trader;* **mēt-at-or**, *a fixer of boundaries;* **mŏdĕr-at-or**, *a manager;* **mōlī-tor**, *a contriver;* **mŭn-ĭt-or**, *an engineer;* **narr-at-or**, *a narrator;* **năt-at-or**, *a swimmer;* **nĕgōti-at-or**, *a dealer;* **nōmencl-at-or**, *one who addresses by name* (nōmĕn-, călāre); **obtrect-at-or**, *a disparager;* **ōr-at-or**, *a speaker, a spokesman;* **pābŭl-at-or**, *a forager;* **pĕt-ĭt-or**, *a candidate, a plaintiff* (pĕt-ĕre, cf. § 657); **pisc-at-or**, *a fisherman;* **præd-at-or**, *a pillager;* **prædi-at-or**, *a purchaser of mortgaged estates* (prædium); **prævārĭc-at-or**, *a collusive pleader;* **pugn-at-or**, *a fighter;* **quadrŭpl-at-or**, *a trickster;* **quæs-ĭt-or**, *an inquisitor* (quær-ĕre, cf. § 657); **recŭpĕr-at-ores** (pl.), *judges* in questions of property between citizens and foreigners; **rŏg-at-or**, *a proposer* of a law, *a polling-clerk;* **Sălīn-ăt-or** (usually as surname), *a saltworker* (sălīna-); **salt-at-or**, *a dancer;* **sălut-at-or**, *a visitor;* **sĕn-at-or**, *a senator* (comp. **sĕnex**); **serv-at-or**, *a preserver;* **sīmŭl-at-or**, *a pretender;* **spect-at-or**, *a spectator;* **stĭpŭl-at-or**, *a bargainer;* **test-at-or** (Suet., Dig.), *the maker of a will;* **vēn-at-or**, *a hunter;* **vĕtĕr-at-or**, *an old practitioner* (vetera-sc-ere); **vi-at-or**, *a wayfarer* (via-); **ūrīn-at-or**, *a diver;* and many others.

(*b*) With short vowel preceding suffix: mostly from supine stems:

admŏnĭ-tor, *an adviser* (admŏnere); **appārĭ-tor**, *an official servant* (appārēre); **cognĭ-tor**, *an attorney* (cogno-sc-ĕre); **compŏsĭ-tor**, *an arranger* (compōn-ĕre, cf. § 631); **concĭ-tor**, *exciter* (concīre); **condĭ-tor**, *a founder* (condĕ-re); **crēdĭ-tor**, *a lender* (credĕ-re); **dă-tor** (Plaut.), *a giver* (dă-re); **dēbĭ-tor**, *a debtor* (dēbĕre); **dirĭbĭ-tor**, *a distributor* of voting tickets (dĭrĭbĕre); dŏmĭ-tor, *a tamer* (dŏmāre); exercĭ-tor, *a trainer, a master,* e.g. of a ship or shop (exercēre); fundĭ-tor, *a slinger* (funda-); gĕnĭ-tor, *a begetter* (gĭgn-ĕre, cf. § 698); hŏlĭtor (for hŏlĕrĭtor), *a kitchen-gardener* (hŏlŭs-); jānĭ-tor, *a doorkeeper* (jānua-); insĭ-tor (Prop.), *an ingrafter;* instĭtor, *a factor* (instāre?); mŏnĭ-tor, *an adviser* (mŏnēre); perdĭ-tor, *a destroyer* (perdĕ-re); portĭ-tor, *a toll-taker* (portu-, *harbour;* porta, *a gate*); prŏdĭ-tor, *a betrayer* (prodĕ-re); să-tor, *a sower* (sĕ-rĕre); stă-tor, *a stayer,* epithet of Juppiter; *a magistrate's attendant* (sistĕre); vendĭ-tor, *a seller* (vendĕ-re); vindēmĭtor (also vindemiator), *a vintager* (vindēmia-); vīnĭtor, *a vine-dresser* (vīno-).

(*c*) From consonant stems, or contracted:

ac-tor, *an actor, a plaintiff* (ăg-ĕre); adjŭ-tor, *a helper* (adjŭvāre); al-tor, *a nourisher* (ăl-ĕre); assen-sor, *one who agrees* (assentīre); asser-tor, *a claimant, advocate* (assĕr-ĕre); asses-sor, *a judicial assistant* (assĭdēre); auc-tor, *a founder, recommender, seller* (augēre); can-tor, *a singer* (căn-ĕre); cen-sor, *a valuer, a critic* (censēre); circumscrip-tor, *a cheater* (circumscrīb-ĕre); conjec-tor, *an interpreter,* esp. of dreams, &c. (conĭcĕ-re); consul-tor, *a counseller, a consulter* (consŭl-ĕre); correc-tor, *a corrector* (corrĭg-ĕre); corrup-tor, *a seducer;* cul-tor, *a cultivator, inhabitant* (cŏl-ĕre); cur-sor, *a runner* (currĕre); defec-tor (post-Aug.), *a revolter* (defĭcĕ-re); defen-sor, *a defender* (defend-ĕre); dērĭ-sor, *a mocker* (dērĭdēre); deser-tor, *a deserter* (dĕsĕr-ĕre); dīvĭ-sor, *a distributor* (dīvĭd-ĕre); doc-tor, *a teacher* (dŏcēre); duc-tor, *a leader* (dūc-ĕre); emp-tor, *a purchaser* (ĕm-ĕre); exstinc-tor, *an extinguisher* (exstingv-ĕre); fau-tor, *a patron* (făvēre); fic-tor, *a maker,* e.g. of images (fĭng-ĕre); fos-sor, *a digger* (fŏdĕ-re); impul-sor, *an inciter* (impell-ĕre); interces-sor, *a mediator, interposer* (intercēd-ĕre); inven-tor, *a discoverer* (invĕnīre); lec-tor, *a reader* (lĕg-ĕre); lic-tor, *a magistrate's attendant* (origin uncertain); lŭ-sor, *a player* (lūd-ĕre); men-sor, *a measurer* (mētĭrī); mes-sor, *a reaper* (mĕt-ĕre); pas-tor, *a shepherd* (pasc-ĕre); perfec-tor, *an accomplisher* (perfĭcĕ-re); pic-tor, *a painter* (pĭng-ĕre); pis-tor, *a miller, baker* (pīs-ĕre); pollinc-tor, *an undertaker* (polling-ĕre, *to prepare* a corpse for burial); posses-sor, *a possessor* (possĭdēre); pō-tor, *a drinker* (comp. pō-tus); præcep-tor, *a teacher* (præcĭpĕ-re); præ-tor, *a chief magistrate* (præīre); profes-sor, *a public teacher* (prŏfĭtēri); quæs-tor, *a judge of inquiry, a treasurer* (quær-ĕre); rap-tor, *a robber* (răpĕ-re); rĕcep-tor, *a receiver,* esp. of stolen property (rĕcĭpĕ-re); rec-tor, *a ruler* (rĕg-ĕre); rĕdemp-tor, *a contractor* (rĕdĭm-ĕre); rĕper-tor, *a discoverer* (rĕpĕrīre); rup-tor, *a breaker* (rump-ĕre); scrip-tor, *a writer* (scrīb-ĕre); sculp-tor, *an engraver* (sculp-ĕre); sec-tor, *a cutter, a purchaser* of confiscated goods (sĕcāre); spon-sor, *a surety* (spondēre); svā-sor, *a recommender* (svādēre); sū-tor, *a shoemaker* (su-ĕre); tex-tor, *a weaver* (tex-ĕre); ton-sor, *a barber* (tondēre);

tor-tor, *a torturer* (torqvēre); tŭ-tor, *a guardian* (tuērī); vec-tor,
(1) *a carrier*, (2) *a passenger* (vĕh-ĕre); vic-tor, *a conqueror* (vĭnc-
ĕre); ul-tor, *an avenger* (ulc-isc-ī).

-ūri   sĕcūris (f.), *an axe* (properly *for cutting?* sĕcāre).   909
         gnarūris (adj.), *knowing*, is found in Pl. *Most.* 100
         (gna-ro-).

Compound stem-endings: -rco, -trīcī, §§ 771, 782; -urno, -erno,
-terno, §§ 828, 829; -trīno, § 842; -rio, -brio, -ārio, -tōrio (-sōrio),
§§ 940—943.

iii. *Stems ending in* -s.

-ŏs (-ŏr)   Substantives: (*a*) arbōs (f. also arbŏr), *a tree;* lĕpŭs (m.), 910
            a hare.

(*b*)   Neuter: corpus, *a body;* dĕcus, *a distinction;* dēdĕcus, *a disgrace;* frīgus, *cold* (comp. ῥῖγος); lĭtus, *a shore;* nĕmus, *a grove;*
pectus, *a breast;* pĕcus, *cattle;* stercus, *dung;* tempus, *time.*

-nŏs (-nŏr) Neuter: făcĭ-nus, *a deed* (făcĕ-re); fēnus (fænus), *inte-* 911
            rest of money (*breeding*, comp. fē-tus, fē-mina); pĕnus,
            a store (cf. § 398); pīg-nus, *a pledge* (pang-ere).

-ŭs (-ĕr) (1) Adjective: vĕtus (vĕtĕr, Enn.), *old.*   912

(2) Substantives: neuter: ăcus, *chaff;* fœdus, *a treaty;*
glŏmus, *a ball of thread* (comp. glŏbus); hŏlus (ŏlus), *vegetable;*
lătus, *a side;* ŏpus, *a work;* pondus, *a weight;* raudus, *a piece of
metal;* rūdus, *rubble;* sĕcus (only n. acc. sing.), *a race* or *generation;*
scĕlus, *a crime;* sīdus, *a constellation;* vellus, *a fleece;* viscus, *the
internal organs* of the body; ulcus, *a sore* (comp. ἕλκος).

-nŭs (-nĕr) Neuter substantives: fūnus, *a funeral;* gĕnus, *a race* or 913
            kind (comp. gĭ-gn-ĕre); mūnus, *a gift;* ŏnus, *a burden;*
            vulnus, *a wound.*

            Also Vĕnus (f.), the goddess of *beauty* (comp. vĕnus-
            tus).

-ĕs (-ĕr) Cĕrēs (f.), goddess of corn, &c. (comp. κραίνειν, oĕrus, 914
           § 843); pūbes (adj.), *grown up* (pūbi-).

-ĭs (-ĕr) Substantives: cĭnis (m.), *ashes;* cŭcŭmis (cf. § 412), *a* 915
           cucumber; pulvis (m. rarely f.), *dust.* For vomis, see
           § 900.

-ŏs (-ŏr) 1. Adjectives: **mĭn-or** (adj.), *less* (comp. **mĭn-ĭmus**). 916

2. Substantives: (*a*) masculine:

clāmŏs (cf. Quint. 1. 4. 13, also **clamŏr**), *a shout* (**clamā-re**); **cŏlŏs** (also **colŏr**), *a colour;* **flōs**, *a flower;* **hŏnōs** (also **hŏnŏr**), *an honour, an official post;* **lābōs** (usually **lăbŏr**), *toil;* **lĕpōs**, *pleasantness, humour;* **mōs**, *a custom, a whim;* **ŏdōs** (also **ŏdŏr**), *a scent* (comp. **ŏl-ēre**, *ὄζω, ὄδωδα*); **păvōs** (Næv., usually **păvŏr**), *dread* (**păvēre**); **rōs**, *dew;* **rūmŏr** (comp. **rumus-culus**), *a rumour.*

Compare also the substantives in § 907.

(*b*) Neuter: **ōs**, *a mouth.*

-iōs (-iŏr) Adjectives in comparative degree. These are formed from 917 most noun adjectives and many participles. A list of the principal irregularities will be found in the Appendix.

The original s of the suffix is seen only in the neuter singular nom. acc., and in the superlative forms which are derived from it (§ 755).

ācr-ior, *sharper* (**ācri-**); **æqv-ior**, *fairer* (**æqvo-**); **alt-ior**, *higher* (**alto-**); **ămant-ior**, *more loving* (**amanti-**); **antīqv-ior**, *more ancient* (**antīqvo-**); **aspĕr-ior**, *rougher* (**aspĕro-**); **audāc-ior**, *bolder* (**audāci-**); **bĕnĕfĭcent-ior**, *more benevolent* (with participial suffix, from **benefīco-**); **cĭtĕr-ior**, *on this side* (**citra**); **concord-ior**, *more harmonious* (**concordi-**); **crēbr-ior**, *more crowded* (**crebro-**); **dextĕr-ior**, *on the right side* (**dextro-**); **dētĕr-ior**, *worse;* **dīt-ior**, *richer* (**dīti-**); **dūr-ior**, *harder* (**dūro-**); **ĕgent-ior**, *more needy* (**ĕgenti-**); **extĕr-ior**, *outside* (**extĕro-**); **fēlīc-ior**, *happier* (**fēlīci-**); **fertĭl-ior**, *more fertile* (**fertīli-**); **frūgāl-ior** (for positive frugi indecl. is used); **imbēcĭll-ior**, *weaker* (**imbecillo-**); **industr-ior**, *more active* (**industrio-**); **infĕr-ior**, *lower* (**infĕro-**); **ingent-ior**, *huger* (**ingenti-**); **intĕr-ior**, *inner* (**intra**); **jūn-ior**, *younger* (**jŭvĕn-**); **magnĭfĭc-ent-ior**, *more highminded* (**magnifico-** with participial suffix); **mājor**, *greater* (for **măg-ior**, comp. **mag-nus**); **mĕl-ior**, *better;* **mĭsĕr-ior**, *more wretched* (**mĭsĕro-**); **nēqv-ior**, *naughtier* (**nēquam**); **ōc-ior**, *swifter* (comp. *ὠκύς*); **pējor**, *worse* (for **pĕd-ior**, comp. **pessimus**); **pĭngv-ior**, *fatter* (**pingvi-**); **plūs** (n.), *more* (for **ploiōs**, cf. § 754); **pŏpŭlar-ior**, *more popular* (**pŏpŭlāri-**); **postĕr-ior**, *later* (**postĕro-**); **prĭor**, *former* (pro? cf. § 754); **prŏp-ior**, *nearer* (**prŏpe**); **sălūtār-ior**, *more healthful* (**sălŭtāri-**); **sălūbr-ior**, *more healthy* (**sălubri-**); **sătŭr-ior** (Col.), *fatter* (**sătŭro-**); **sĕn-ior**, *older* (**sĕn-**, nom., **sĕnex-**); **sīnistĕr-ior**, *on the left hand* (**sinistĕro-**); **sŭpĕr-ior**, *upper* (**sŭpĕro-**); **tĕnv-ior**, *thinner* (**tenvi-**); **vĕtust-ior**, *older* (**vĕtusto-**); **ultĕr-ior**, *further* (**ultra**); and very many others.

-ūs (-ŭr) Substantives: (a) feminine: **tellŭs**, *the earth.*   918

(b) Neuter: **crūs**, *a leg;* **jūs**, *right* (comp. **jŭb-ēre** and § 76. 2); *broth* (comp. ζωμόs); **pūs**, *diseased matter;* **rūs**, *the country;* **tūs**, *frankincense* (from θύοs?).

Compound stem-endings: **-issŭmo**, § 758; **-usto**, **-esto**, § 789; **-sti, -estāt**, §§ 808, 811; **-uscŭlo**, § 864.

CHAPTER IX.

VOWEL NOUN-STEMS.

i. *Stems ending in* **-eo.**

-eo   1. Adjectives: 919

ădōr-eus, *of spelt* (**ădōr-**); **æquŏr-eus**, *watery* (**æquŏr-**); **ær-eus**, *of bronze* (**æs-**); **arbŏr-eus**, *of a tree* (**arbŏs-**); **arbŭt-eus** *of the arbutus* (**arbŭto-**); **argent-eus**, *of silver* (**argento-**); **ārundĭn-eus**, *of reeds* (**ārundŏn-**); **aur-eus**, *golden* (**auro-**); **cēr-eus**, *waxen* (**cēra-**); **consangvĭn-eus**, *of the same blood* (**com, sangvēn-**); **corneus**, *of the cornel tree* (**corno-**); *horny* (**cornu-**); **corpŏr-eus**, *of or having a body* (**corpŏs-**); **fēmĭn-eus**, *of a woman* (**fē-mĭna-**); **ferr-eus**, *of iron* (**ferro-**); **flamm-eus**, *flamy* (**flamma-**); **flōr-eus**, *flowery* (**flōs-**); **flūmĭn-eus**, *of a river* (**flū-mĕn-**); **fulmin-eus** *of thunder* (**ful-mĕn-**); **fūm-eus**, *smoky* (**fūmo-**); **grāmĭn-eus**, *grassy* (**grā-mĕn-**); **ign-eus**, *fiery* (**igni-**); **lact-eus**, *milky* (**lacti-**); **lān-eus**, *woolly* (**lāna-**); **lăpĭd-eus**, *pebbly* (**lăpĭd-**); **lŭt-eus**, *muddy* (**lŭto-**); **lūteus** *golden yellow* (**lūto-**); **nĭv-eus**, *snowy* (**nĭvi-**); **oss-eus**, *bony* (**ossi-**); **pĭc-eus**, *pitchy* (**pĭc-**); **plumb-eus**, *leaden* (**plumbo-**); **pulvĕr-eus**, *dusty* (**pulvĭs-**); **rŏs-eus**, *rosy* (**rŏsa-**); **sangvĭn-eus**, *bloody* (**sangvĕn-**); **săx-eus**, *stony* (**saxo-**); **sīdĕr-eus**, *starry* (**sīdŭs-**); **spīc-eus**, *of ears of corn* (**spīca-**); **trītĭc-eus**, *wheaten* (**trītĭco-**); **vīpĕr-eus** *of a viper* (**vīpĕra-**); **virgĭn-eus**, *girlish* (**virgŏn-**); and others.

2. Substantives:

(a) Masculine: **alv-eus**, *a trough, hollow* (**alvo-**); **balt-eus** (or -eum), *a belt;* **calc-eus**, *a shoe* (**calci-** *heel*); **cās-eus**, *a cheese;* **clŭp-**

eus, *a shield;* cull-eus, *a bag* (from Gr. κολεός : comp. cūlus);
cŭn-eus, *a wedge,* lăqv-eus, *a noose;* mall-eus, *a hammer;* mull-eus,
a red shoe (mullo- *red mullet?*); pilleus (also pilleum), *a felt cap*
(comp. πῖλος, *felt*); plŭt-eus, *a board, shed,* &c.; pŭt-eus, *a well;*
urc-eus, *a pitcher.*

(*b*) Feminine : ădōr-ea, *renown* (lit. *corn-reward;* ădōr-); ălea,
a die; ardea, *a heron* (comp. ἐρωδιός); ārea, *an open space;* baxeæ
(pl.), *shoes;* bractea, *a plate of metal;* buccea (Aug. ap. Suet.), *a*
mouthful (bucca-); căpr-ea, *a roedeer* (capro-); fŏvea, *a pitfall;*
frămea, *a spear* (Tac. *G.* 6); gălea, *a helmet* (comp. κῠνέη); gănea,
a restaurant; glārea, *gravel;* grăn-ea, *a corn-mash* (grāno-); lancea,
a light spear; laur-ea, *a laurel tree* or *bay* (lauro-); lĭn-ea, *a flaxen*
thread (līno-); ōcrea, *a greave;* ōlea, *an olive* (comp. ἐλαία); pălea,
straw (comp. Păles); plătĕa, *a street* (from πλατεῖα, *broadway*);
sōl-ea, *a sandal* (sōlo-, *ground*); talea, *a rod;* tĭnea (tinia, comp.
tænia, ταινία), *a bookworm;* trăbea, *a state robe;* vīnea, *a vineyard,*
a shed.

(*c*) Neuter : flammeum, *a bridal veil* (flamma-); hordeum,
barley.

-ăc-eo   1. Adjectives : cret-āceus, *of chalk* (crēta-); ĕdĕr-āceus, 920
of ivy (ĕdĕra-); farr-āceus, *of spelt* (farr-); gallīn-āceus
(gāllīnacius), *of hens* (gallīna-); herb-āceus, *grass coloured*
(herba-); horde-āceus, *of barley* (hordeo-); rōs-āceus, *of*
roses (rōsa-); test-āceus, *of pottery* (testa-); viŏl-āceus
of violes (viŏla-).

2. Substantives : erin-āceus, *a hedgehog* (comp. ĕr, χήρ
Hesych.); must-āceus or *must cake* (musto-); vīn-āceus,
a raisin stone (vīno-).

-ūceo   cāduceus, *herald's staff* (comp. κηρύκειον); pann-ūceus 921
(pannucius), *tattered, wrinkled* (panno-).

-teo   lin-teus, *of linen* (līno-).

-neo   1. Adjectives : ăhē-neus (æneus), *of bronze* (for ahes- 922
neus, from æs-); angvī-neus (rare), *snaky* (angvi-);
ĕbur-neus, *of ivory* (ĕbŏr-); pōpul-neus, *of poplar* (pō-
pŭlo-); quer-neus, *oaken* (quercu- § 110).

2. Substantives : ărān-eus (in Plin. also as adj.), *a*
spider (comp. ἀράχνης); balineum or balneum (cf. also
§ 330), *a bath* (from βαλανεῖον).

-gneo   i. e. gīn-eo, from root of gignĕre; unless the g be
softened for c in the first two words, and in the last
be due to a false analogy.

īli-gneus, *of ilex* (for ilic-gneus, from īlĕc-); sāligneus
(Col.), *of willow* (sălĭc-); vīti-gineus *vine-produced* (vīti-).

-ăn-eo   Adjectives:

(*a*) consent-aneus, *suited* (consentire); dissentaneus, 923 *unsuited* (dissentire), extraneus, *external* (extra); fŏc-aneus (rustic ap. Col.), *of the throat;* applied to a *choking* sprout (fauci-); miscell-aneus (Juv.), *miscellaneous* (miscello-); pĕd-aneus, *an inferior judge* (pĕd-); præcīd-aneus (Cato), *slaughtered before* (præ-cæd-ĕre); prælīg-āneus (Cato), *picked before* (prælīg-ĕre); præsent-aneus (Plin.), *operating quickly* (præsenti-); succēd-aneus or succīdaneus *coming in place of another* (succēd-ĕre or succīdĕre); sicc-āneus (Col.), *dry* (sicco-).

(*b*) Compounds formed immediately from the simple parts: bīpĕd-aneus (Col.), *two feet in measure* (bis pĕd-); circumfŏraneus, *round the forum* (circum fŏro-); collact-aneus, *foster* (com lacti-); mĕdīterr-aneus, *inland* (mĕdio-, terra-); subterraneus, *underground* (sub terra-); sŭpervăc-aneus, *superfluous* (sŭper văcă-re).

t-ăn-eo   i. e. āneo appended to stem of past participle: collec-taneus (Plin., Suet.), *gathered together* (collīg-ĕre); 924 condī-taneus (Varr.), *for preserving* (condĕre or condīre); ŏpertaneus (Plin.), *concealed* (ŏpĕrīre); rejec-taneus (coined by Cic. *Fin.* 4. 26), *belonging to the class of rejected* (reīc-ĕre).

-ŏneo   Idōnĕus, *fit* (ideo, Donaldson); erroneus, *straying* (errōn-).

-leo   1. Adjectives: cærŭleus (cærŭlus), *dark blue* (cælo-, 925 cf. § 176, comp. also cæsio-).

2. Substantives: (a diminutival suffix).

acu-leus, *sting, prickle* (ăcu-); ĕqvŭ-leus, *a colt* (ĕqvo-); hinnu-leus *a fawn* (hinno-); mănŭ-leus, *a long sleeve* (mănu-); nŭc-leus (nŭcŭleus, Plaut.), *a kernel* (nŭc-); trochlea, *a block of pulleys* (from τροχός, comp. τροχαλία). See also § 919. 2.

ii. *Stems ending in* -io.

(For stems in -i see Book II. Chap. x.)

-io   1. Adjectives: chiefly from nouns: 926

(*a*) abstēm-ius, *abstemious* (abs, tēm-; comp. tēm-ŭlen-tus, tēm-ētum); āērius, *in the air* (aer-); æthĕr-ius, *in the æther* (æthēr-); ăl-ius, *other;* anx-ius, *uneasy* (ang-ĕre?); augŭr-ius, *of an augur* (augŭr-); cæs-ius, *gray;* dŭb-ius, *doubtful* (duo-; the b is perhaps parasitical, cf. § 76, or du-bi-us is for du-vi-us, *two-wayed*) ēgrĕg-ius, *select* (e, grĕg-); exĭm-ius, *excepted, extraordinary* (exĭm-ere); fīd-ius, *of good faith,* epithet of Jupiter (fīde-); industr-ius, *active* (indo, stru-ere); injūr-ius, *wrong* (in, jūs-); Mart-ius, *of War* (Marti-); mĕd-ius, *middle* (so dimĭdius, *halved*); nĭm-ius, *excessive* (nĭmis); nox-ius, *hurtful* (noxa-); pātr-ius, *of a father* (patr-); pius, *dutiful;* plŭv-ius, *rainy* (plu-ĕre); rēg-ius, *kingly* (rēg-); saucius, *wounded;* sŏc-ius (mostly subst.), *fellow* (comp. sĕqvi); sŏrōr-ius, *sisterly* (sŏrōr-); sublic-ius, *of piles* (sublĭca-); Vĕnĕr-ius, *of Venus* (Vĕnŭs-); uxōr-ius, *of a wife* (uxōr-).

(*b*) Names of Roman clans: see § iii. infr. p. 363.

2. Substantives: masculine: 927

(*a*) *Prænomina:* see § iii. infr. p. 363.

(*b*) dupond-ius (sc. as), *a two-pound* coin (duo, pondo); fīlius, *a son;* flŭv-ius, *a river* (flu-ĕre); gĕn-ius, *native temper* (*gign*-ĕre); glăd-ius, *a sword;* lūd-ius, *a player* (lūdo-); mŏd-ius, *a bushel* (mŏdo-); nutrīc-ius (also adj.), *a tutor* (nutr-īci-); răd-ius, *a spoke;* Sălii, *Jumpers,* certain priests (săli-re); sīmius (sīmia), *an ape* (sīmo-).

3. Substantives: feminine: 928

(*a*) From verbs or verbal nouns:

axungia (Plin.), *wheel-grease* (axi-, ung-ĕre); corrĭgia, *a shoe-tie* (corrĭg-ĕre); colliqviæ, *gutters* (com, līqvi, comp. lĭqvōr-); dēlĭc-iæ (pl.), *delight* (delĭcĕ-re, *allure*); desĭd-ia, *sloth* (desĭdēre); excŭb-iæ (pl.), *patrol* (excŭbā-re); exēqv-iæ (pl.), *funeral* (exseqvi); exŭv-iæ (pl.), *spoils* (exu-ĕre); fænīsĭcia (also neut.), *haycutting* (fæno-, sĕcāre); fūr-iæ (pl.), *rage* (fūr-ĕre); host-ia, *a victim* (hos-tīre, *to strike*); incūr-ia, *carelessness* (in, cura-); industr-ia, *activity* (indo, stru-ere); indŭv-iæ (pl.), rare, *robings* (indu-ĕre); inĕd-ia, *not eating* (in, ĕd-ĕre); infīt-iæ (pl.), *non-confession* (in, fătĕri); insĭd-iæ (pl.), *plot* (insĭdēre); invĭd-ia, *grudge* (invĭdēre); nox-ia, *a wrong* (noxa-); provinc-ia, *a department* (provinc-ĕre?); redŭv-ia, *misgrowth of nail* (for red-ungv-ĭa, Corss., but comp. exuviæ, indu-viæ); relĭqv-iæ (pl.), *remains* (relĭqvo-); succidia, *a flitch* (sub, cæd-ĕre?); suppĕt-iæ (pl.), *help* (sub, pĕtĕre); via (veha, Varr. *R.R.* 1. 2, § 14), *a road* (vĕh-ĕre); vindēm-ia, *grape-plucking* (vino-, dēm-ĕre?); vindĭc-iæ (pl.), *claim* (vindĭcā-re).

With stems in -ie (-iēs for ia-is?):

allŭv-ies, *overflow;* collŭvies, prolŭvies, &c. (lăv-āre); congĕr-ies, *a heap* (congĕr-ĕre); effĭg-ies, *form* (effĭng-ĕre); ēsŭr-ies, *hunger* (ēsŭrī-re); făc-ies, *a face* (făcĕ-re); măc-ies, *leanness* (măcēre); pernĭc-ies (cf. § 340), *destruction* (pernĕcā-re); prōgĕn-ies, *offspring* (progign-ĕre); răb-ies, *raving* (răb-ĕre); rĕqv-ies, *rest* (reqvi-escĕre); scăb-ies, *scurf* (scăb-ĕre); sĕr-ies, *a row* (sĕr-ĕre); spĕc-ies, *a look* (spĕcĕ-re); tempĕr-ies, *a mixture* (tempĕrā-re).

23

(*b*) From nouns, chiefly from adjectives:

audāc-ia, *boldness* (audācĭ-); ăvĭa, *a grandmother* (ăvo-); bar-băr-ia (barbaries), *uncouthness* (barbăro-); cŏlōn-ia, *a farmer-settlement* (cŏlōno-); cōp-ia, *plenty* (cōpĭ-); concord-ia, *harmony* (con-cordĭ-); cūr-ia, *a body of men* (co-vĭro-?); custōd-ia, *protection* (custōd-); dīvĭt-iæ (pl.), *riches* (dīvĕt-); fallāc-ia, *deceit* (fallācĭ-); famĭl-ia, *a body of slaves, a household* (famŭlo-); fasc-ia, *a bandage, ribbon* (fascĭ-); fĕrōc-ia, *high-spiritedness* (fĕrōcĭ-); host-ia, *a victim* (hostīre, *to strike*); ignāv-ia, *cowardice* (ignāvo-); ignōmĭn-ia, *disgrace* (in, gnōmĕn-? cf. § 129); inert-ia, *inactivity* (inertĭ-); infām-ia, *disgrace* (infāmĭ-); infĕr-iæ (pl.), *offerings to the nether* Gods (infĕro-); injūr-ia, *a wrong* (in, jūs-); inŏp-ia, *scarcity* (inŏp-); insān-ia, *madness* (insāno-); lascīv-ia, *playfulness* (lascīvo-); mā-tĕr-ia (materies), *mother-stuff*, i.e. *matter* (māter-); mĕmŏr-ia, *memory* (mĕmŏrĭ-); mīlĭt-ia, *service in war* (mīlĕt-); mĭsĕr-ia, *wretchedness* (mĭsĕro-); pervĭcāc-ia, *inflexibility* (pervĭcācĭ-); sīm-ia, *an ape* (sīmo-, *flat-nosed*?); sōcord-ia, *indolence* (sōcordĭ-); sollert-ia, *adroitness* (sollertĭ-); sŭperb-ia, *haughtiness* (sŭperbo-); vēment-ia, *vehemence* (vēmentĭ-); vīcīn-ia, *neighbourhood* (vīcīno-); vĭgĭl-ia, *watching, watch* (vĭgĭl-).

Also with stems in -ie:

ăc-ies, *an edge* (ăcu-); paupĕr-ies, *poverty, damage* (paupĕr-).

(*c*) Of uncertain origin:

ascia, *an axe;* bestia, *a beast;* cīcōnia, *a stork;* fēriæ (pl.), *holydays* (cf. § 704. *n*); gavia, *a seamew;* nēnia, *a dirge;* præstīgiæ (pl.), *jugglery;* prosāpia, *stock, race;* stīria, *an icicle;* tībia, *a flute;* tĭlia, *a lime-tree;* vĕnia, *indulgence;* vĭcia, *a vetch.*

With stems in -ie:

cæsāries, *hair of the head;* cāries, *rottenness;* ingluvies, *the gullet* (in, gŭla-?); sānies, *corrupted blood* (comp. sangvis).

4. Substantives: neuter: 929

(*a*) From verbs or verbal nouns:

bĕnĕfĭc-ium, *a kindness* (benefăcĕ-re); collŏqv-ium, *conversation* (collŏqv-ĭ); commerc-ium, *trade* (commercā-rĭ); compendium, *savings* (com, pend-ĕre, *to weigh with*); cōnŭb-ium, *marriage* (com, nŭb-ĕre); contāg-ium, *contagion* (com, tang-ere); defĭŭv-ium (Plin.), *falling off*, e.g. *of hair* (de, flu-ĕre); dēsīdĕr-ium, *longing, regret* (desīdĕrā-re); dīlŭv-ium, *a deluge* (dīlu-ĕre); discĭd-ium, *divorce* (discĭ*n*dere); dīvort-ium, *divorce* (dīvort-ĕre); effŭg-ium, *escape* (effŭgĕ-re); ex-cĭdium, *overthrow* (exscĭ*n*d-ĕre); fastīd-ium, *disgust* (fastīdī-re); flāgĭt-ium, *a crying deed* (flāgĭtā-re); gaud-ium, *joy* (gaudēre for gav-ĭd-ēre; comp. Gaius, § 945); impĕr-ium, *command* (impĕrā-re);

implŭv-ium, *a tank* (implu-ĕre); incend-ium, *conflagration* (incend-ĕre); ingĕn-ium, *disposition* (ĭngign-ĕre); inĭt-ium, *beginning* (inĭre); jurg-ium, *a quarrel* (jurgā-re); lābium, *a lip* (lamb-ĕre); lītĭg-ium, *lawsuit* (lītĭgā-re); obsĕqv-ium, *obedience* (obsĕqv-i); obsĭd-ium, *a blockade* (obsĭdēre); ŏd-ium, *hatred* (Perf. ŏdisse); offĭc-ium, *duty* (ŏpŭs-, făcĕre, cf. opificĭna, § 839; or from offĭcĕ-re, *to do towards*, but the verb is usually in bad sense); opprŏbr-ium, *reproach* (oppro-brā-re); præmium, *a reward* (*a first choice*? præ, ĕm-ĕre); præsăg-ium, *a presage* (præ-sāgīre); præsĭd-ium, *defence* (præsĭdēre); prand-ium, *lunch* (prandēre); prolub-ium, *inclination* (pro, lŭbēre); remĕd-ium, *a remedy* (rĕmĕd-ēri); repŏt-ia (pl.), *renewal of drinking,* i.e. *the second day's feast* (repŏt-āre); repŭd-ium, *divorce* (*repentance*? re, pŭdēre; or re, pĕd-, comp. tripudium); stŭd-ium, *zeal* (stŭd-ĕre); suffrāg-ium, *anything broken off:* hence *a potsherd,* used in voting, *a vote* (sub frang-ĕre); suspend-ium, *hanging* (suspend-ĕre); suspĭr-ium, *a sign* (suspīrā-re); tæd-ium, *weariness* (tædēre); vestĭg-ium, *a footstep, a trace* (vestĭgā-re); and others.

(*b*) From nouns: often from personal names:

ădultĕr-ium, *adultery* (adultĕro-); āpi-um, *parsley* (ăpi-, *bee*); arbĭtr-ium, *a decision* (arbĭtro-); artĭfĭc-ium, *manufacture, art* (artĭfĕc-); aucŭp-ium, *bird-catching* (aucŭp-); augŭr-ium, *an augury* (augŭr-); auspĭc-ium, *auspice* (auspĕc-); bienni-um, *a period of two years* (bienni-); collēg-ium, *a board* (collēga-); conjŭg-ium, *wedlock* (conjŭg-); consĭl-ium, *advice* (consŭl-); convīv-ium, *a dinner-party* (convīva-); cuppēdia (pl.), *delicacies* (comp. cuppes); exĭl-ium, *exile* (exŭl-); gland-ium, *a kernel in pork* (glandi-); herēd-ium, *a plot of two jugera, an inheritance* (hērēd-); hospĭt-ium, *hospitality* (hospĕt-); indĭc-ium, *information* (indĕc-); jejūn-ium, *fasting* (jējūno-); jŭdĭc-ium, *a trial* (jŭdĕc-); mancĭp-ium, *a conveyance of land* (mancĕp-, *a purchaser*); măgĭs-ter-ium, *presidentship* (magĭs-tero-); mendācĭ-um, *a lie* (mendāci-); minĭstĕr-ium, *service* (minĭs-tero); occĭpĭt-ium, *the back-head* (occĭput-); pall-ium, *a cloak* (palla-); partĭcĭp-ium, *a participle* (partĭcĕp-); perjŭr-ium, *false-swearing* (perjŭro-); præcĭpĭtium (post-Aug.), *a precipice, a fall* (præcĭpĭti-); præd-ium, *land* (a thing given as security, præd-); pūlējum, *fleawort, penny royal* (pūl-ēc-); rēmĭg-ium, *rowing, a crew* (rēmĕg-); sacrĭlĕg-ium, *sacrilege* (sacrĭlēgo-); sĕn-ium, *old age* (sĕn-); somn-ium, *a dream* (somno-); sāvi-um, *a kiss* (svāvi-); supplĭc-ium (*kneeling down*), *punishment* (supplĕc-).

(*c*) Compounds formed immediately from the simple parts. (See Chap. xi.)

adverb-ium, *an adverb* (ad, verbo-); æquinoct-ium, *the period when night is equal to day* (æqua-, nocti-); bipāl-ium, *a double mattock* (bis, pāla-); contŭbern-ium, *companionship* (com, tăberna-); dīlūd-ium, *interval between plays* (dis, lūdo-); dŏmicĭl-ium, *home* (dŏmo-, cŏl-ĕre); dīverb-ium, *dialogue* (dis, verbo-); hŏmĭcīd-ium, *manslaughter* (hŏmŏn-, cæd-ĕre); **fordicidia** (pl.), Feast of the *slaughter of cow in-calf,* April 15 (forda-, § 134, cæd-ĕre); **infor-tun-ium** (præ-Cic.), *a scrape* (in, fortŭna-); **interlŭn-ium,** *time of new moon* (inter, luna-); **internŏd-ium,** *space between knots* (inter, nŏdo-); **lectistern-ium,** *couch-covering,* i. e. for a god's banquet (lecto-, sternĕre; comp. **sellisternia,** pl.).; **naufrãg-ium,** *a shipwreck* (nãv-, fra*ng*-ĕre; comp. **naufrãgus**); **parricīd-ium,** *murder* (par-?, cæd-ĕre); **plēnĭlūn-ium** (Plin.), *time of full moon* (plēna-, lūna-); **pōmœr-ium,** *space behind the walls* (post, mūro-); **postlīmĭn-ium,** *return home*;(post, līmen-); **præcordia** (pl.), *the diaphragm* (præ, cordi-); **prīmordia** (pl. in Lucr. also **ordia prima**), *first elements* (primo-, ordī-ri); **prīvilēg-ium,** *an enactment against an individual* (prīvo-, lēg-); **proverb-ium,** *a proverb* (*that has become a word?* pro, verbo-); **puerpĕr-ium,** *childbed* (puero-, pãrĕre; comp. **puer-pĕra**); **rēgĭfŭg-ium,** *the flight of the kings* (rēg-, fŭgĕ-re); **Septi-montium,** *Sevenhills,* as name of Rome and of a feast (septem, monti-); **stillĭcīdium,** *dripping* (stilla-, cãdĕre); **stipend-ium,** *pay* (stĭp-, pendĕre); subsell-ium, *a stool, bench* (sub, sella-); **suburbium,** *the suburbs* (sub, urbi-); **supercīl-ium,** *eyebrow* (sŭper, cīlio-, *above eyelids*); . **tripŭd-ium,** *thrice stamping* (tri-, pĕd-); **tŭbĭlustrium,** *trumpet-purification* on Mar. 23, May 23 (tŭba-, lustrãre); **vēnĭfīc-ium** (§ 28), *poisoning* (vēnēno-, fãcĕ-re).

(*d*) Uncertain:

allium, *garlic;* **ãtrium,** *a hall* (atro-, *black,* Mommsen); **bãsium,** *a kiss;* **cīlium,** *an eyelid, eyelash;* **cīsium,** *a gig;* **convīcium** or **con-vītium,** *abuse;* **cŏrium,** *a hide;* **dōlium,** *a jar;* **ēlŏgium,** *a pithy saying* (for ἐλεγεῖον, Curt.); **fastĭgium,** *a gable top, a slope;* **grĕmium,** *the lap;* **līcium,** *a leash, thread;* **līlium,** *a lily;* **lŏlium,** *tares;* **mīlium,** *millet;* **mĭnium,** *red lead;* **prōdĭgium,** *a prodigy* (comp. **dĭg-itus,** δεικνύειν); **silicernium,** *a funeral feast;* **simpŭvium,** *a sacrificial bowl;* **sīpãrium,** *a curtain;* **sŏlium,** *a seat;* **spŏlium,** *spoil* (cf. § 66).

-c-io }
-ĭc-io}   1. Adjectives, chiefly formed from other derivatives: 930

ædīli-cius, *of an ædile* (æd-īli-); **compĭtãli-cius,** *of the cross-road festival* (compit-ãli-); **cæmĕnti-cius,** *of rubbish* (cæmento-); **gentīli-cius,** *of the clansmen* (gent-īli-); **lãtĕr-icius,** *of brick* (lãtĕr-); **nãtãli-cius,** *of a birthday* (nãtãli-); **pastor-ĭcius,** *of a shepherd* (pas-tor-); **patr-ĭcius,** *of the fathers* (patr-); **Sãturnãli-cius** (Mart.), *of the Saturnalia* (Saturn-ãli-); **sŏdãli-cius,** *of companions* (sŏdãli-); **trībūni-cius,** *of a tribune* (trīb-ūno-); **vēnãli-cius,** *of things for sale,* e. g. *of slaves* (vēn-ãli-). (See also § 926.)

See for proper names in § 946.

2. Substantives (see also § 928)·:
conventicium, *assembly-money* = τὸ ἐκκλησιαστικόν (conventu-);
lānī-cium, *wool* (lāna-); mundicies (§ 357*b*, but comp. § 932; p. 358),
cleanliness; sōlā-cium, *comfort* (sōl-ārī); fīdūcia, *confidence, a mortgage* (fīdo-); un-cia, *a unit* of measure (ūno-).   Cf. § 928.

-īc-io   nŏv-īcius, *new* (nŏvo-)·:

-t-īc-io ⎫
(-s-īc-io ⎭   From past participles (tīcio = -to-īcio?). They denote 921
        the *quality* derived from the past *act.* Few of these words
        are used frequently; and of the quantity of the i (when
        not marked here) there is no positive proof.

advect-icius (Sall.), *imported;* advent-icius, *imputed* (as if from
advento-); ascript-icius (Cic.), *of the class of* ascripti, *enrolled;*
collect-icius, *collected together;* conduct-īcius, *hired;*·commendāt-icius,
commendatory; comment-icius, *invented;* congest-icius, *piled up;* con-
vent-icius, *of an assembly;* e.g. as neut. sub. *the fee for attending;*
dedīt-icius, *surrendered;* demiss-īcius (Plaut. once), *hanging down;*
ēdīt-icius, *nominated;* ēmiss-īcius (Plaut. once), *acting as scouts;*
empticius (Varr.), *bought;* fact-icius (Plin.), *artificial;* fictī-cius
(Plin.), *fictitious;* foss-icius, *dug;* insīt-icius, *ingrafted;* miss-icius,
discharged; multāt-icius, *of fined persons;* perpessicius (Sen.), *patient;*
pignĕraticius (Ulp. &c.), *of a pledge* or *mortgage;* recept-icius, *of
things received;* subdīt-icius, *supposititious;* supposīt-icius, *suppositi-
cious;* surrupt-īcius (Plaut.), *stolen* (surrupto-, i.e. sub, rapto);
trālāt-īcius, *transferred.*

-t-io 1. Adjectives: prŏpi-tius, *favourable* (prŏpĕ) ; ter-tius, 932
third (ter-); vătius, *bent inward* (comp. vārus). See
proper names in § 947.

2. Substantives: (*a*) masculine: nun-tius, *a messenger* (nŏvo-,
vento-, as if participle of ven-īre).

(*b*) Feminine: (1) ia appended to past participles and similar
adjectives; all with long syllable preceding -t:

angus-tiæ, *straits* (angu₃-to-); argū-tiæ, *fine touches* (argu-ĕre);
controver-sia, *a dispute* (controvert-ĕre); făcē-tiæ, *jokes* (făcē-to-);
grā-tia, *pleasingness, thanks* (grā-to-); indūtiæ, *a truce* (orig. uncertain); inep-tiæ (pl.), *trifles, nonsense* (in, ăp-isci); inscī-tia, *awk-
wardness* (in, scīre); mīnūtia (Sen.), *smallness* (mīnu-ĕre); mŏdes-tia,
modesty (mŏdes-to-); mŏles-tia, *troublesomeness* (mŏles-to); nup-tiæ-
(pl.), *marriage* (nūb-ĕre). Also Ostia, town at *mouth* of Tiber (ōs-).

(2) From other adjectives: justī-tia, *justice* (justo-); lautī-tia,
elegance (lauto-); mălī-tia, *mischievousness* (mălɔ-); prīmī-tiæ (pl.),
first fruits (primo-); pŭdīcī-tia, *bashfulness* (pŭdīco-); puĕrī-tia,
childhood (puĕro-); sævī-tia, *cruelty* (sævo-).

(3) Stems in -ĭ-tie, usually with collateral stem in -ĭ-tĭa (§§ 340, 342):

ămārĭ-tĭes (Catull.), *bitterness* (āmāro-); ămīcĭ-tĭa (-e stem once Lucr.), *friendship* (ămīco-); ăvārĭ-tĭa (-e stem once Lucr.), *greediness* (ăvāro-); calvĭ-tĭes (post-Aug.), *baldness* (calvo-); cānĭ-tĭes (-a stem once Plin.), *grayness* (cāno-); dūrĭ-tĭes (also -a stem), *hardness* (dūro-); lentĭ-tĭa (-e stem once post-Aug.), *pliancy* (lento-); mollĭ-tĭa (also -e stem), *softness* (mollĭ-); mundĭ-tĭa (-e stem once Catull.), *cleanliness* (mundo-); nēqvĭ-tĭa (also -e stem), *roguishness* (neqvam-); nĭgrĭ-tĭes (Cels.; -a stem Plin.), *blackness* (nigro-); nōtĭ-tĭa (-e stem Lucr.), *acquaintance* (nōtĭ-); pĭgrĭ-tĭa (-e stem Liv. once), *laziness* (pĭgro-); plānĭ-tĭes (also -a stem), *a level* (plāno-); pullĭ-tĭes (Varr., Col.), *a brood* (pullo-); sĕgnĭ-tĭa (also segnĭ-tĭes), *inactivity* (segnĭ-); spurcĭ-tĭa (-e stem Lucr. once), *smuttiness* (spurco-); tristĭ-tĭa (-e stem Ter. once), *sadness* (tristĭ-); vastĭ-tĭes (Plaut.), *desolation* (vasto-).

(*c*) Neuter: (1) -ĭo appended to supine stems: cŏm-ĭ-tĭum, *place of assembly* (comīre); exercĭ-tĭum (post-Aug.), *exercise* (exercēre); ex-ĭ-tĭum, *destruction* (ex-īre); in-ĭ-tĭum, *beginning* (inīre).

(2) From nouns, or of uncertain origin: calvĭ-tĭum, *baldness* (calvo-); ēquĭ-tĭum, *a stud of horses* (ĕquo-); gurgustĭum, *a hovel;* lautĭa (pl.), *entertainment*, only in Liv. (lauto-?); lotĭum, *urine;* os-tĭum, *a door* (ōs-); ōtĭum, *leisure;* Pălātĭum (in Martial Pālātĭum), *a Roman hill, a palace;* prētĭum, *price;* servĭ-tĭum, *slavery* (servo-); spătĭum, *space;* vĭtĭum, *a blemish, fault, vice* (cf. Cic. *T. D.* 4. 13.).

-en-t-ĭo   i.e. -ĭo or -a appended to stem (in -entĭ) of present par- 933 ticiples or adjectives of like form:

1. Feminine: afflu-entĭa, *abundance* (afflu-ēre); audĭ-entĭa, *a hearing* (aud-īre); bĕnĕvŏl-entĭa, *goodwill* (bene, velle); clĕm-entĭa, *mercifulness* (clem-entĭ-); contĭn-entĭa, *self-control* (contĭn-ere); dīlĭg-entĭa, *accuracy* (dīlĭg-ĕre); ēlĕgantĭa, *neatness* (eleganti); frēqventĭa, *crowd* (frĕqventĭ-); excandesc-entĭa, *bursting into a glow*, i.e. *irascibility* (excande-sc-ĕre); indĭg-entĭa, *need, craving* (indĭg-ĕre); infantĭa, *speechlessness, infancy* (in, fārĭ); intellĕg-entĭa, *intelligence* (intellĕg-ĕre); neglĕg-entĭa, *carelessness* (neglĕg-ĕre); pestĭl-entĭa, *infection* (pestĭl-entĭ-); pĕtŭl-antĭa, *forward conduct* (pĕtŭl-antĭ; comp. petul-cus); prūd-entĭa, *forethought* (prūd-entĭ-, i.e. provĭd-entĭ-); săpĭ-entĭa, *wisdom* (săpĕ-re); sent-entĭa, *an opinion* (for sentientĭa? from sentīre); tēmŭl-entĭa, *drunkenness* (tēmŭl-ento-); vīnŏl-entĭa, *intoxication* (vīnol-ento-); vĭŏl-entĭa, *violence* (viol-ento-); and many others.

So the names of towns; e.g. Placentĭa, Pollentĭa, Valentĭa, &c.

2. Neuter: sĭlentĭum, *silence* (sĭlēre).

-n-d-io   Formed from stem of gerund: crĕpundia (n. pl.), *a child's rattle* (crĕpĕre); fācundia (f.), *eloquence* (facundo-, cf. § 820); īrācundia (f.), *wrathfulness* (īrācundo-); verecundia (f.), *bashfulness* (vĕrērī).

-n-io   contĭci-nium, *time of general silence, evening* (contĭce-sc-   934 ĕre); lăcĭnia, *a flap* of a garment (comp. λακίς, *a rent*); luscĭnia, *a nightingale;* pĕcū-nia, *money (stock of cattle?* from pecu- with suffix -ĭno, see § 747); scrīnium, *a writing-desk* (scrīb-ĕre?); sterqvĭlĭ-nium, *a dung heap* (for stercŏr-ĭl-inium, or (with l for r) for stercor-inium? from stercŏs-). See also proper names in § 948.

-mn-io   calu-mnia, *a false charge* (calv-ĕre).

-ōn-io   aquĭlonius (adj. Plin.), *northern* (aquilŏn-); cŏlonia, *a farmer-settlement* (colōno-); Făvonius, *west wind* (făv-ĕre); flamonium (not flaminium: cf. Momm. *Eph. Epig.* I. 221), *flamen's office;* fullonius (adj.), *of a fuller* (fullōn-); lēnonius (adj.), *of a pander* (lēnōn-); mangonium (Plin. once), *a trimming up* of wares (mangōn-); mulionius (adj.), *of a muleteer* (muliōn-); præconium, *a proclamation* (præcōn-). See also in § 948.

-mōn-io   Substantives: (*a*) feminine: acrĭ-mōnia, *sharpness* (acri-);   935 ægrĭ-mōnia, *sorrow* (ægro-); cærĭ-mōnia, *a sacred rite;* castĭ-monia, *chastity* (casto-); parsĭ-mōnia, *thriftiness* (from participle of parcĕre); quĕrĭ-mōnia, *a complaint* (quĕr-i); sanctĭ-mōnia, *sanctity* (sancto-).

(*b*) Neuter: al-ĭmōnium (also alimōnia, Plaut.), *nourishment* (ăl-ĕre); mātr-ĭmōnium, *marriage* (mātr-); merci-mōnium (Plaut., Tac.), *wares* (merci-); patr-imōnium, *hereditary estate* (patr-); testŭmōnium (testimōnium), *evidence* (testi-); văd-imōnium, *recognizance, appearance on bail* (văd-).

-cĭn-io   i.e. -io suffixed to stem of verbs in -cĭnā (cf. § 967).   936 lātrō-cin-ium, *robbery* (latro-cināri); lēnō-cin-ium, *pander's arts* (lēnō-cīnāri); pătro-cĭn-ium, *protection* (patro-cīnāri); ratiocĭn=ium, *calculation* (rătio-cīnāri); tīrō-cĭn-ium, *pupillage* (tīrōu-; the verb is not in use); văti-cĭn-ium, *prophecy* (văti-cīnāri).

-l-io   i.e. -io suffixed to a diminutival suffix -lo.   937 auxĭlium, *aid* (auxo-, for aucto-? cf. αὐξάνω); concĭ-lium, *a council* (concīre); pĕcū-lium, *property of children or slaves (small stock of cattle,* pecu-); prœlium, *a battle;* qvisqvī-liæ (pl.), *refuse* (§ 118. 4). See also proper names in § 949.

-āl-io   Baccanālia (g. pl. Baccanaliorum, § 425); &c. Cf. p. 335.   938

-ŏl-io   Căpĭtolium, *the Roman Capitol.*   939

-ēl-io   contŭmēlia, *insult* (contumēre?); fīd-elia, *an earthen jar.*

-ĭll-io or -ĭl-io.   See proper names in § 949.

-r-io   1. Adjectives: prŏprius, *one's own;* vărius, *varied.*   940

2. Substantives: cantĕrius, *a gelding* (from κανθήλιος?);
centŭria, *a division composed of a hundred men* (centum, vĭro-?
§ 94. 2); dĕcŭria, *a division composed of ten* (dĕcem-); eqvirria or
ecurria (pl.), *horse-race day* on Feb. 27, Mar. 14 (for eqvi-curr-ia
from eqvo-, curr-ĕre?) glŏria, *glory* (cluĕre? § 127); Lĕmŭria (pl.),
Night of offerings to wrathful spirits, May 9, 11, 13 (Lĕmŭres);
longŭrius, *a long pole* (longo-); luxŭria (luxŭries), *luxury* (luxu-);
macĕria (also early maceries), *a wall;* pēnŭria, *scarcity* (comp. πεῖνα,
hunger); promuntŭrium, see § 943. 2; tŭgŭrium, *a hut* (tĕg-ĕre?);
voltŭrius, *a vulture* (comp. voltur, § 454). See also § 928.

-br-io   1. Adjectives: ēbrius, *drunken;* sobrius, *sober* (comp. 941
σῶς, *safe*).

2. Substantives: Fimbria (proper name); fimbriæ (pl.), *fringe*
(fibro-?); lūdi-brium, *mockery, sport* (lŭdo-); manu-brium, *a handle*
(mănu-).

-ār-io   Very numerous, often with collateral stems in -āri (§ 906), 942
but without any tendency to change to -alio when an r
precedes. Many of these words, named here as substantives, are also
used, less noticeably, as adjectives, or in other genders, or other
special meanings.

1. Adjectives:

advers-arius, *opposed* (adverso-); ær-arius, *of bronze, of money*
(æs-); ăgr-arius, *of land* (agro-); āl-arius, *of the wing* (āla-);
annĭvers-arius, *annual* (anno-, verso-); ăqv-arius, *of water*
(ăqva-); argent-arius, *of silver, money* (argento-); auxĭli-arius
(also auxĭliaris), *auxiliary* (auxĭlio-); calc-arius, *of chalk* (calci-);
cald-arius, *of warm baths* (calda-); caus-ārius, *in ill-health*
(causa-, *an ailment,* Cels., Sen., Plin.); cell-ārius, *of the cellar*
(cella-); classi-arius, *of the fleet* (classi-); contr-arius, *opposed*
(contra); extr-arius, *outside, strange* (extra); fĭdūci-arius, *under
a trust* (fĭducia-); frūment-arius, *of corn* (frūmento-); grĕg-arius,
of a herd (grĕg-); hŏnōr-arius, *of honour* or *of a public office* (hŏ-
nōr-); jūdi-i-arius, *of the law courts* (jŭdicio-); lĕgiōn-arius, *of a
legion* (lĕgiōn-); mănŭfest-arius (Plaut.), *caught in the act* (manu-
festo-); mātĕri-arius, *of timber* (mātĕria-); mens-arius, *of a bank*
(mensa-); mercenn-arius, *for hire* (from mercēd-, with a suffix
-ōn); naumachi-arius (Plin., Suet.), *for a sea-fight* (ναυμαχία);
nĕcess-arius, *necessary* (nĕcesse); numm-arius, *of money* (nummo-);
ŏnĕr-arius, *for burden* (ŏnŭs-); ŏpĕr-arius, *of labour* (ŏpĕra-); pĕ-
cu-arius, *of cattle* (pĕcu-); pisc-arius, *of fish* (pisci-); piscīn-arius,
of a fishpond (piscīna-); prĕc-arius, *on sufferance* (prĕc-); prīm-
arius, *of the first* (prīmo-); qvinusvicenarius, *of twenty-five* (qvino-,
viceno-); qvinqvāgēn-arius, *consisting of fifty* (qvinqvāgēno-); sĕ-

cund-arius, *secondary* (sĕcundo-); sēn-arius, *containing six* (sēno-); stīpendi-arius, *paying a (fixed) tribute* (stīpendio-); sŭbĭt-arius, *hasty* (sŭbĭto-); subsĭdi-arius, *in reserve* (subsĭdio-); sumptu-arius, *of expense* (sumptu-); tăbell-arius, *of the ballot,* see also 2 (*a*) (tăbella-); tālarius, *of dice* (tālo-); tĕmĕr-arius, *rash* (tĕmĕre); tempŏr-arius, *for a time* (tempŏs-); testăment-arius, *of a will* (testămento-); tŭmultu-arius, *of a bustle, hurriedly done* (tŭmultu-); vesti-arius, *of clothes* (vesti-); vīn-arius, *of wine* (vīno-); unci-arius, *of an ounce or twelfth part* (uncia-); vŏlunt-arius, *by free will* (vŏlunti-, or for vŏlunta-tarius); vŏlupt-arius, *of pleasure* (vŏluptāt-; for volupta-tarius); and others.

2. Substantives: (*a*) masculine:

antiqv-arius (post-Aug.), *an antiquarian* (antīqvo-); cēt-arius, *a fishmonger* (cēto-); cĭnĕr-arius, *a haircurler* (cĭnĭs-, *ashes* in which the irons were heated); comment-arius (sc. liber), *a note-book* (commento-); cŭbĭcŭl-arius (Cic., cf. § 906), *a valet* (cubiculo-); dēn-arius (sc. nŭmus), *a ten-as-piece* (dēno-); ēmiss-arius, *a scout* (emisso-); febru-arius (sc. mensis), *the month of purifications* (februo-); horre-arius, *a granary-keeper* (horreo-); jānu-arius (sc. mensis), *the gate-month?* (janua-), or *month of Janus-feast?* (Jano-, Januo-); lĭbr-arius, *a transcriber* (libro-); lĭgn-arius, *a joiner* (ligno-); marmŏr-arius, *a marble mason* (marmŏr-); nŏt-arius, *a shorthand writer* (nŏta-); osti-arius, *a doorkeeper* (ostio-); prōlēt-arius, *a citizen of the lowest class;* pull-arius, *a chicken-keeper* (pullo-); pult-arius (sc. calix), *a cup,* properly for pottage (pulti-); qvadrīg-arius, *a driver of four-in-hand* (qvadrīga-); rēti-arius, *a net-fighter* (rēti-); ror-arius, *a light-armed soldier;* sext-arius, *a pint,* a *sixth* of a congius (sexto-); tăbŭl-arius, *a registrar* (tăbŭla-); tăbell-arius, *a letter-carrier* (tăbella-); tolut-arius (Sen.), *a trotter* (cf. tolutim, § 534); tri-arius, *a soldier of the third line* (tri-); vīc-arius, *a deputy* (vīci-); and others.

(*b*) Feminine: ārēn-ariæ (pl.), *sandpits* (ārēna-); argent-aria, *a bank, a silver mine* (argento-); calv-āria, *a skull* (calvo-, *bald*); ferr-ariæ (pl.), *ironworks* (ferro-); sulpŭr-aria, *a sulphur pit* (sulpŭr-).

So as names of plays (cf. Ritschl. *Parerg. Plaut.* p. 140); e.g. by Plautus: Asĭn-aria (sc. fābula), *of an ass* (ăsĭno-); Aulŭl-aria, *of a pottle* (aulŭla-); Cistell-aria, *of a casket* (cistella-); Frīvŏl-aria, *of cracked crockery?* (frīvŏlo-, cf. Fest. p. 90, Müll.); Mostell-aria, *of a ghost* (mostello-, from monstro-); Nervŏl-aria, *of a little thong* (nervŏlo-); Vidŭl-aria, *of a portmanteau* (vīdŭlo-). By Nævius, Coroll-aria, Tŭnĭcul-aria (tŭnĭcŭla-); by Nonius, Gallīnaria, Tăbellaria, Tŏgŭlaria; by Pomponius, Sarcŭlaria.

(*c*) Neuter: ær-arium, *the treasury* (æs-); æstu-arium, *a tidal bay* (æstu-); armăment-arium, *an arsenal* (armămento-); arm-

arium, *a cupboard* (arma); ăvi-arium, *an aviary* (ăvi-); bell-aria
(Varr.), *pastry* (bello-?); bo-arium (sc. forum), *the cattle-market*
(bŏv-); cĕr-arium, *a fee for sealing* (cēra-); cĭb-aria (pl.), *provisions*
(cĭbo-); cŏlumb-arium, *a dovecot, a set of pigeon-holes* (cŏlumba-);
column-arium, *a tax on pillars* (cŏlumna-); congi-arium, *a quart-
largess* (congius = 5·76 pints); di-arium, *daily allowance* (die-);
dōn-arium, *a temple, an offering* (dōno-); emiss-arium, *an outlet*
(emisso-); frīgĭd-arium, *the cooling-place* (frīgĭda-, sc. aqua); fustuarium, *a cudgelling* (fusti-, cf. § 405); grān-aria (pl.), *granaries*
(grāno-); kălend-arium, *an account-book* (kălenda-); mort-arium,
a mortar (morti-?); pōm-arium, *an orchard* (pōmo-); pulment-aria
(pl.), *condiments, relish* (pulmento-); săcr-arium, *a shrine* (săcro-);
săl-arium, *salt-money, salary* (săi-); sōl-arium, *a sun-dial, balcony*
(sōl-); sŏl-arium (Dig.), *ground-rent* (sōlo-); sūd-arium, *a towel*
(sudā-re, *to sweat*); tăbŭl-arium, *a registry* (tăbŭla-); vīrīd-arium
(or vīrĭdi-arium), *a shrubbery* (vīrĭdi-); vīv-arium, *a preserve*, e.g.
a fishpond (vīvo-); and others.

-tōr-io ⎱ i.e. -io appended to personal names in -tor (or -sor § 908). 543
(-sōr-io) ⎰ Some appear to be formed immediately from the supine
         stem, or past participle:

1. Adjectives:

accūsā-tor-ius, *of an accuser;* ăleā-tor-ius, *of a gamester;* ămā-
tor-ius, *amatory;* ambŭlā-torius (Plin.), *moveable;* bellā-tor-ius, *of
a warrior;* cen-sor-ius, *of a censor;* circŭla-tor-ius (Quint.), *of a
mountebank;* damna-tor-ius, *damnatory;* dēclāma-tor-ius, *declama-
tory;* decrē-tor-ius (post-Aug.), *decisive* (decrēto-); defunc-torius
(post-Aug.), *slight, cursory;* dictā-tor-ius, *of a dictator;* explōra-
tor-ius (Suet.), *of a scout;* gestā-tor-ius (Suet.), *for carrying;* glā-
diā-tor-ius, *of a gladiator;* impĕrā-tor-ius, *of a general;* lū-sor-ius
(post-Aug.), *for playing* (lūsu-?); mes-sor-ius, *of a reaper;* mĕrĭ-
torius, *for hire* (mĕrĭto-); nūgā-tor-ius, *trifling;* objurgā-tor-ius,
reproachful; ōrā-tor-ius, *of an orator;* pas-tor-ius (Ov.), *of a shepherd;* perfū-sor-ius (post-Aug.), *superficial;* piscā-tor-ius, *of a fisherman;* pis-tor-ius (Cels., Plin.), *of a baker;* pō-torius (Plin.), *for
drinking* (pōtu-); præcur-sor-ius (Plin. *Ep.*), *as a forerunner;*
prædā-tor-ius, *predatory;* prædiā-tor-ius, *of purchasers of estates
sold by auction;* profes-sor-ius (Tac.), *of a professor;* pugnā-tor-ius
(post-Aug.), *of a combatant;* quæs-tor-ius, *of a quæstor;* rĕcŭpĕrā-
tor-ius, *of recovery-commissioners;* saltā-tor-ius, *of dancers;* scrip-
tor-ius, *of writers;* sēnā-tor-ius, *of a senator;* spĕcŭlā-tor-ius, *of
scouts;* svā-sor-ius (post-Aug.), *persuasive;* sū-tor-ius, *of a shoemaker;* vĕtĕrā-tor-ius, *of an old practitioner;* and others.

2. Substantives: (*a*) feminine: Agĭtātoria (sc. fabula), name
of a play by Nævius, *of a driver* (agitatōr-); victor-ia, *victory;*
vorsoria, *a turn* (only in Plautus ' cape vorsoriam').

Neuter: aud-ĭtor-ium, *a lecture-room;* adjŭ-tor-ium (post-Aug.), *assistance;* cēnā-toria (pl.), *dinner dress;* condi-tor-ium, *a store-house;* dēvor-sor-ium, *an inn;* dīrīb-ĭtōr-ium, *a ballot-distributing place;* portorium, *a toll (harbour* or *gate* toll? portu-, porta-); præ-tōr-ium, *the general's tent;* promunt-ōr-ium (promuntŭrium, Fleck.), *a headland* (promĭnēre?); rēpŏsĭ-tōr-ium, *a dumbwaiter;* sēclŭ-sōrium (Varr.), *a place of retreat* (secluso-); tec-tor-ium, *plaster of walls* (tecto-); tentōr-ium, *a tent* (tento-); terrĭtorium, *a territory* (terr-ēre? i.e. *a place from which people are warned off*).

-eio   legulejus, *a pettifogger* (as if from lēg-ula-); plēbejus, *of the commons* (plebe-). For proper names see § 951.

Compound stem-endings: -iăco, § 775; -iensi, § 815; -iāno, § 832; -iēno, § 837; -iōn, -ciōn, -tiōn (-siōn), § 852—854.

---

iii. *Proper names with stems ending in -io.*   944

A vast number of Roman names have stems ending in -io. They are properly adjectives, and the suffix -io is probably the same[1] as the genitival suffix seen in illius (illo-ius), cuius (quo-ius; also used as adjective, § 379), &c.[1] Thus Claud-ius is *of Lame,* i.e. (often) *Lame's son* (comp. *John Williams = William's John*).

Most of these names are *clan*-names, i.e. nomina in the strict sense. Some are prænomina. (These have here 'præn.' appended).

The names are selected principally from those occurring in the Corp. Inscr. Lat. Vol. I., especially in the Fasti. Few are post-Augustan only. The quantity of the vowels is marked only when distinct authority for it, either from poetry or Greek transcription, has been found.

p-io   Ampius; Appius (præn.); Oppius; Păpius; Pŭpius; Ulpius. 945

b-io   Albius (albo- *white*); Bæbius; Făbius.(făba-,*bean*); Vībius.

m-io   Memmius; Mummius; Opīmius (ŏpīmo-, *fat*); Postŭmius (postŭmo- *last*); Septĭmius (septĭmo-, *seventh*).

v-io   Băvius; Flăvius (flăvo- *yellow*); Fulvius (fulvo- *tawny*); Gavius (probably same as Gaius: comp. gau-dium, γαῦρος, γαίειν); Helvius (helvo- *yellow*); Līvius (comp. līvēre,

---

[1] Key, *Proc. Phil. Soc.* for 1856, p. 239.

to be blue); Mævius; Nævius (nævo- *wart*); Nŏvius (nŏvo-, *new*); Octāvius (octāvo-, *eighth*), Păcŭvius; Salvius (salvo- *safe*); Servius, præn. (servo-, *slave*); Silvius (silva-, *a wood*); Vitruvius.

f-io   Alfius; Fūfius.

c-io   Accius[1]; Anicius; Apĭcius; Cædicius; Cincius; Cornĭfĭcius 946 *horn maker?* (cornu- făcĕre); Dĕcius; Fabrĭcius (fabro-, *workman*); Genucius; Larcius; Lūcius, præn. (lūc-, *light?*); Maccius (macco-, *buffoon*); Marcius (Marco-); Mĭnŭcius; Mŭcius; Nŭmĭcius; Plancius (Planco-); Poblĭcivs (publico-); Porcius (porco-, *pig*); Roscius; Tuccius (Tucca-); Sulpĭcius; Vinicius.

g-io   Magius; Sergius; Valgius (valgo-, *bowlegged*).

t-io   Aebutius; Antistius (antistĕt-, *priest*); Arruntius; Attius[1]; 947 Cătius (căto-, *sharp*); Cluentius (cluenti- *client*); Curi-atius; Curtius (curto-, *clipt*); Digitius (dĭgĭto- *finger*); Dŏmĭtius (dŏmĭto-, *tamed*); Egnātius; Grātius (grāto-, *pleasing*); Hŏrātius; Hirtius (hirto-, *shaggy*); Hostius; Instantius (instanti-, *urgent*); Juventius (jŭvĕn-, *young*); Lūcrētius; Lūtātius; Matius; Mūnātius; Nautius (nauta-, *sailor*); Plautius or Plōtius (plauto-, *flat*); Pon-tius (for Pomptius? cf. § 951); Pŏtĭtius (pŏtĭto-, *won*); Prŏper-tius; Qvinctius (qvincto-, *fifth*); Sallustius; Scaptius; Sentius; Sextĭus or Sestius (sextō- *sixth*); Stātius; Tĕrentius; Tĭtius (Tĭto-); Trĕbātius; Vegetius (vĕgĕto-, *active*); Vettius.

d-io   Aufĭdius; Calĭdius (călĭdo-, *hot*); Cānĭdia (căno-, *hoary*); Claudius or Clōdius (claudo-, *lame*); Considius (Conso-); Cordius (cord-, *heart*); Falcidius (falci-, *reaping-hook*); Fūfĭdius (Fūfio-?); Helvĭdius (helvo-, *yellow*); Nigidius; Ovĭdius (ŏvi-, *sheep?*); Pĕdius (pĕd-, *foot*); Ventĭdius (vento-, *wind?*); Vettĭdius; Vībĭdius.

n-io   Afrānius; Annius (anno-, *year?*); Antōnius; Apronius; 948 Asinius ('Ασίννιος and 'Ασίνιος) (ăsīno-, *ass*); Autronius; Calpurnius; Caninius; Cānius; Cilnius; Cōmĭnius; Coponius (cŏpōn-, *inn-keeper?*); Coscōnius; Cossinius (cosso-, *wrinkled?*); Ennius; Fan-nius; Feronia, an *Italian goddess*; Flāmĭnius (flāmĕn-, *priest*); Fun-dānius; Furnius (furno-, *oven*); Gabinius; Geganius; Hĕrennius (hĕrēd-, *heir?* comp. mercennarius); Jūnius (jŭvĕn-, *young*); Lĕmō-nia, a tribe; Lĭcīnius (Λικίννιος and Λικίνιος) (lĭcĭno-, *curled upwards*); Mænius; Magulnius; Mānius, præn. (māni-, *morning*); Mĕnēnius; Nōnius (nōno-, *ninth*); Papinius; Pĕtrōnius (petrōn-, *rustic?*); Plīnius; Pompōnius; Pupinia, a tribe; Scrībōnius; Semprōnius;

----

[1] The poet's name is written both Attius and Accius. In Greek "Αττιος only is found.

Sicinius; Sinnius; Stertinius (stertĕre, *snore?*); Svĕtōnius; Tarqvĭnius; Tītĭnius; Trĕbōnius; Vătīnius; Verginius; Vinius (vīno-, *wine?*); Vipsānius; Vŏcōnius; Voltinia, a tribe; Vŏlumnius.

1-io   Acīlius; Ælius; Æmĭlius (æmŭlo-, *rival*); Aquilius or 949 Aquillius (aqvīla-?, *eagle*); Arelius; Atilius; Aurēlius; Cæcīlius; Camilia, a tribe; Carvillius; Cascellius; Cœlius; Cornēlius; Duĭlius or Duellius (duello-, *war*); Foslius or Folius; Gellius; Hostilius (hosti-, *enemy?*); Jūlius; Lælius; Lollius; Lūcīlius (Lūcio-?); Mælius; Mamilius; Mānīlius (Mānio-); Manlius (Μάλλιος and Μάλιος); Orbīlius; Otācīlius; Petilius or Petillius; Pœtēlius; Pollia, a tribe; Pompīlius; Pŏpilius or Pŏpillius (pŏpŭlo-, *people*); Publius, præn. (pŏpŭlo-, *people*); Publilius (Publio-); Qvinctīlius; Rōmilius (Rōmŭlo-); Rŭpīlius; Rŭtīlius; Servīlius; Sextīlius (sexto-); Sīlius (sīlo-, *flatnosed*); Statilius (Stātio-); Tīgellius; Trĕbellius; Tullius (Tullo-); Turpilius (turpi-, *foul*); Vergĭlius; Villius; Vitellius (vītello-, *egg-yolk*).

r-io   Arrius; Cŭrius; Fūrius (fūr- *thief?*); Galeria, a tribe; 950 Hatĕrius; Lăbĕrius; Ligarius; Māmŭrius (Ov.) or Māmūrius (Prop.); Mārius (māri-, *sea*); Massurius (Māsŭrius, Pers.); Mercŭrius; Nĕrius; Numĕrius (præn.); Nŭmitōrius; Păpīrius; Pīnarius; Plætorius; Răbīrius (răbie-? *madness*); Rubrius (rubro-, *red*); Sertōrius; Spŭrius, præn. *illegitimate*; Stăbĕrius; Tībĕrius, præn. (Tībĕri-, *the Tiber*); Titurius; Vălĕrius; Vārius, *spotted*; Verrius (verri-, *a boar*); Vestorius; Vĕturius.

s-io   Cæsius (*bluish grey?* or from cæso-, *slain?*); Cassius (casso-, *empty*); Hortensius (horto-, *garden*); Persius (Persa-, *Persian*); Sōsius; Volusius.

a-io }
or ajo-}   Gajus (comp. Gavius), præn.; Majus (*increasing*, from măg-, § 129. 2. *d*); Stajus.

e-io }
or ejo-}   Appulejus (Appulo-, *Apulian?*); Atejus; Aurunculejus; 951 Canulejus; Cicerejus (L. 41. 28); Consulejus; Coccejus; Egnatulejus (C. *Phil.* 3. 3); Flavolejus; Fontejus; Hirtulejus (hirto-, *shaggy*); Luccejus; Pompejus (comp. pomptis = qvinqve, § 118, 2); Rabŭlejus (rabula-, *pettifogger*); Saufejus; Sejus; Vellejus; Venulejus; Voltejus.

CHAPTER X.

VERB-STEMS.

Simple verbs may be divided into four classes, according as they 952 are formed:

(1) by union of a root directly with the suffixes of inflexion:

(2) by the addition of a verbal stem-suffix to a root:

(3) by the addition of a verbal stem-suffix to a noun-stem:

(4) by the addition of a special derivative-suffix (as well as a verbal stem-suffix) to a root.

Those verbs whose precise origin is obscure may be presumed to belong really to one of these classes.

1. The *first* of these classes contains what are probably the 953 oldest verbs in the language. Many of these verbs exhibit, when the inflexional suffixes are stripped off, a form different from what we may imagine to be the simple root. Such differences are partly due to modifications, either in fact (e. g. **vinc-ere, vic-tum**), or in origin (e. g. **jung-ere**, from root **jug-**), belonging to the present stem only, and therefore in the sphere of inflexion rather than of derivation: and partly due to early modifications of the root in order to suit a different shade or turn of the radical conception (comp. **verr-ĕre** with **vert-ere**). In some cases the apparent root may conceal a compound or derivative origin.

2. The *second* class contains verbs with each of the stem suffixes, e. g. **amāre, cŭbāre; argu-ere, mĭnu-ere; tenēre, cărēre; vĕnīre, fĕrīre**. In some cases the stem-suffix is constant in all parts of the verb; in others it is confined to the present tense. This inconstancy may be accounted for on the presumption that the stem-suffix was originally a tense-suffix only, or that its use was the result of a gradual growth, and therefore precarious and uncertain in its occurrence. In this class of **e** verbs, the **e** is constant only where it is radical.

3. The *third* class contains the great majority of the a verbs and a considerable number of e verbs. In some cases the noun from which the verb might naturally be derived is not found, but the verb is formed on the analogy of others.

4. The *fourth* class can hardly be said to exist at all unless the frequentative verbs (§§ 964—966) be referred to it and not to the third class. The other verbs with derivative suffixes named below (§§ 962, 963, 967—969) may probably be considered as presuming noun-stems as their origin. The suffix sc (§ 978) is more properly an inflexional than a derivative suffix.

The following lists contain chiefly verbs of the third and fourth 954 classes, and those verbs of the second class in which the stem-suffix is constant. The other verbs of the second class (with some exceptions, chiefly of i verbs) and the verbs of the first class are omitted here, being already enumerated in Book II. Chap. xxx. (also in xxi. and xxiii.).

The verbs will be arranged here under their *stem-suffixes* (not in the above-named classes).

i. Verbs with -a stems.   955

(1) from substantives with -a stems:

ancillari, *be a handmaid;* animare, *fill with breath;* aquari, *fetch water;* bullare (also bullire), *bubble;* calumniari, *bring false charges;* cavillari, *jest;* causari, *give as a reason;* cenare, *sup;* centuriare, *divide into centuries;* comare, *furnish with hair* (only in participles); convivari, *banquet with others;* copulare, *unite;* coronare, *crown;* culpare, *blame;* curare, *take charge of;* diffamare, *spread abroad* (fama); effeminare, *make thoroughly womanish;* epulari, *feast;* fabricare, *fashion;* fabulari, *converse;* feriari, *keep holiday;* figurare, *form;* flammare, *blaze;* formare, *mould;* formicare, *creep like ants;* fortunare, *bless;* fugare, *put to flight;* furiare, *drive mad;* gemmare, *bud;* gloriari, *boast;* infitiari, *equivocate;* insidiari, *put an ambush;* lacrimare, *weep;* librare, *balance;* lineare, *make straight;* limare, *to file;* luxuriare, *be rank;* lirare, *plough-in* seed; machinari, *contrive;* maculare, *spot;* materiari, *fell wood;* metari, *measure;* minari, *threaten;* morari, *delay;* multare, *fine, punish;* nauseare, *be sea-sick;* notare, *mark;* nugari, *trifle;* nundinari, *attend market, traffic;* oblitterare, *cover with letters, obliterate;* occare, *hoe;* operari, *be busy;* plantare, *plant;* praedari, *make booty;* pugnare, *fight;* quadrare, *make, or be, square;* rimari, *root out, search* (rima, *chink*); rixari, *quarrel;* rotare, *wheel;* rugare, *wrinkle;* saginare, *fatten;* scintillare, *sparkle;*

scŭrrari, *play the buffoon;* spĕcŭlari, *spy out* (spĕcŭla, *watch tower*); spĭcare (Plin.), *furnish with ears of corn;* spŭmare, *foam;* stillare, *drop;* stĭpŭlari, *make a bargain* (from stĭpŭla, *a straw?* or from diminutive of stips, *a coin?*); tĕrĕbrare, *bore;* trĭcari, *play tricks;* trŭtĭnari, *weigh;* turbare, *disturb;* umbrare, *overshadow;* undare, *swell, wave;* and others.

(2) from substantives with -e stems: 956

glăciare, *turn to ice;* mĕrīdiare (also dep.), *take a noon-day meal.*

(3) from nouns with -o stems; (*a*) from substantives: 957

ăcervare, *pile up* (acervus); ădultĕrare, *pollute* (adulter); æstivare, *pass the summer* (æstīva, pl. *summer quarters*); arbĭtrari, *form a judgment* (arbĭter, *judge*); archĭtectari, *build* (archĭtectus); argūmentari, *adduce proof* (argūmentum); armare, *arm* (arma pl.); auxĭliari, *help* (auxilium); bacchari, *celebrate Bacchic rites, revel;* bajŭlare *carry a burden* (bajulus, *porter*); bāsiare, *kiss* (bāsium); bellāre, *war* (bellum); cachinnare, *laugh* (cachinnus); cælare, *grave* (cælum, *a burin*); calceare (calciare), *shoe* (calceus); cancellare (post-Aug.); *lattice, cross through* (cancelli, pl.); căpistrare, *halter* (căpistrum); carbuncŭlare (Plin.), *have a carbuncle* (carbunculus); circĭnari, *round* (circĭnus, *pair of compasses*); circŭlarī, *form a group* (circŭlus); concĭliare, *unite* (concĭlium); consĭliari, *form plans* (consĭlium); convĭciari, *rail* (convĭcium); cōlare, *filter* (cōlum); crībrare, *sift* (cribrum); cŭmŭlare, *pile up* (cŭmŭlus); cŭneare, *wedge* (cŭneus); damnare, *condemn* (damnum, *loss*); diglădiari, *fight it out* (glădius); dŏmĭnari, *rule* (dŏmĭnus); dōnare, *grant, make a grant to* (dōnum); emendare, *take out faults* (mendum); fămŭlari, *be a servant* (fămŭlus); fermentare, *cause to ferment* (fermentum); flăgellare, *whip* (flăgellum); frēnare, *bridle* (frēnum); frūmentari, *get corn* (frūmentum); fŭcare, *dye* (fŭcus); fŭmare, *smoke* (fūmus); fundare, *establish* (fundus, *bottom*); gŭbernare, *steer* (gŭberna pl.); jŏcari, *joke* (jŏcus); jŭgare, *yoke* (jŭgum); jŭgŭlare, *cut the throat* (jŭgulum); lāmentari, *lament* (lāmenta, n. pl.); lāniare, *butcher* (lanius); lăqveare (not præ-Aug.), *snare* (lăqveus); lignari, *collect wood* (lignum); lŏcare, *place* (lŏcus); lucrari, *make gains* (lucrum); lustrare, *purify, survey* (lustrum); măcĕrare, *steep* (măcer); mĭnistrare, *attend* (mĭnister); mŏdŭlari, *measure* (mŏdŭlus); monstrare, *show* (monstrum); nĕgōtiari, *do business* (nĕgōtium); nōdare, *knot* (nōdus); numerare, *count* (nŭmerus); nuntiare, *announce* (nuntius); oscŭlari, *kiss* (oscŭlum); ōtiari, *have leisure* (ōtium); pābŭlari, *collect fodder* (pabulum); palpare, *stroke* (palpum); pampĭnare, *trim vines* (pampĭnus, *a vine tendril*); pastĭnare, *dibble* (pastĭnum); pŏpŭlare (also -ari), *devastate* (pŏpulus?); prœliari, *battle* (prœlium); prŏcare (rare), *demand* (prŏcus); rădiare, *shoot forth rays* (rădius); regnare, *reign* (regnum); rĕpudiare, *reject* (rĕpudium); scrūtari, *search* (*examine into heaps of old stuff?* scrūta pl.); servare, *take care of* (servus); sībĭlare, *hiss* (sībĭlus); signare, *stamp* (signum); somnĭare, *dream* (somnium); sŏnare, *sound* (sŏnus); spătĭari, *walk about* (spătĭum); spŏlĭare, *despoil* (spŏlĭum); stăbŭlari, *stable, roost* (stăbulum); stĭmŭlare *prick* (stimulus); stŏmăchari, *be irritated* (stŏmachus); stuprari, *debauch* (stuprum); svāvĭare, *hiss* (svavĭum); sulcare, *furrow* (sulcus); sŭsurrare, *whisper* (sŭsurrus); termĭnare, *set bounds to* (termĭnus); triumphare, *triumph* (triumphus); tumulare *cover with a mound* (tŭmŭlus); vallare, *surround with a rampart* (vallum); vēlare, *veil* (vēlum); ventĭlare, *make a small breeze* (ventŭlus); vilĭcare, *to be a farm steward* (vīlĭcus); vitĭare, *spoil* (vĭtĭum); volgare, *publish* (volgus); and others.

(*b*) From adjectives with -o stems :

æmŭlari, *rival;* æqvare, *level;* ălĭēnare, *alienate;* alternare, *do by turns;* antīquare, *reject* a bill; ăprīcari, *bask in the sun;* aspĕrare, *roughen* (asper); averruncare, *avert;* cæcare, *blind;* căvare, *make hollow;* clārare, *make illustrious;* commŏdare, *make serviceable;* contĭnuare, *join;* cŏruscare, *quiver;* crispāre, *curl;* cunctāri, *delay;* curvare, *bend;* curtare, *dock;* densare, *thicken;* dēprāvare, *distort* (prāvo-); dēsōlare, *render desolate* (sōlo-); dignari, *think worthy;* dīlātare, *spread* (lāto-); dūrare, *harden;* explānāre, *make plain;* fēcundare (Verg.), *make fruitful;* festīnare, *hasten;* firmare, *strengthen;* fœdare, *dirty;* fūnestare, *fill with death;* fuscare, *darken;* gĕmĭnare, *double;* grātāri, *show pleasure;* hībernare, *winter;* hĭlārare, *cheer;* hŏnestare, *compliment;* ignōrare, *ignore* (ignarus); incestare, *defile;* infestare, *attack;* infirmare, *weaken;* inqvĭetare, *disquiet;* intĕgrare, *renew* (integer); ītĕrare, *repeat* (comp. iterum, adv.); lăcĕrare, *tear* (lăcer); lætāri, *rejoice;* lætĭfĭcare, *make glad;* lassāre, *weary;* laxare, *loosen;* lībĕrare, *free* (līber); māturare, *ripen;* mēdĭcari, (also -are) *heal;* mendīcari, *beg;* mīrari, *wonder at;* mĭsĕrari, *deplore* (mĭser, *wretched*); mūtĭlare, *lop;* mūtuari, *borrow;* nŏvare, *renew;* nūdare, *make bare;* oblīquare, *turn aside;* obscūrare, *darken;* ŏpīnari, *to think* (comp. nec opīnus); orbare, *bereave;* pācĭfĭcare, *pacify;* pandare, *bend, curve;* pĕrĕgrīnari, *travel;* perpĕtuare (rare), *perpetuate;* piare, *appease;* pĭgrare (Lucr.), pĭgrari (Cic.), *to be lazy* (pĭger); prīvare, *deprive* (prīvus, *single*); prŏbare, *test, show to be good;* prŏfānare, *profane;* prospĕrare, *make prosperous;* prŏpinquare, *approach;* publĭcare, *make public;* quadrŭplari, *be an informer* (lit. *get fourfold* penalty); recĭprŏcare, *move to and fro;* rustĭcari, *live in the country;* rūtĭlare, *make* or *be red;* săcrare, *consecrate* (săcer); sānare, *heal;* sătŭrare, *glut* (sătur); sauciare, *wound;* sĕcundare, *favour;* sĕrēnare, *clear up;* assĕvērare, *assert strongly;* persĕvērare, *persist;* siccare, *dry;* sŏciare, *ally;* sōlĭdare, *make solid;* sollĭcĭtare, *harass;* spissare, *make thick;* sŭpĕrare, *overcome;* sŭpīnare, *bend upwards;* tardare, *delay;* tranqvillare, *calm;* trĕpĭ-

24

dare, *hurry*; truncare, *lop*; văcuare, *empty*; văgari, *stroll about;*
văriare, *diversify*; vastare, *lay waste*; věrecundari, *feel bashful;*
ümectare, *moisten;* and others.

(4)   From substantives with -u stems: 959
æstuare, *be hot, surge;* arcuare, *bend like a bow;* fluctuare (also
depon.), *undulate, waver;* sinuare, *curve;* tümultuare (also depon.),
make a bustle.

(5)   From nouns with -i stems: 960
antestari (for ante-testari), *call witnesses preliminarily* (testi-);
calcare, *trample* (calx, *heel*); cělěbrare, *frequent* (cělěber); cělěrare,
hasten (cěler); compărare, *match* (par: besides the compound of
parare); concordare, *agree* (concors); dītare, *enrich* (dīs); dōtare,
dower (dōs); dŭplĭcare, *double* (duplex); exstirpare, *root out* (stirps);
fraudare, *cheat* (fraus); frēqventare, *resort to* (frēqvens); grăvare,
burden (grăvis); hěbětare, *blunt* (hěbes); interpŏlare, *furbish up*
(interpŏlis); lĕvare, *lighten* (lĕvis); měmŏrare, *relate* (měmor);
mercari, *traffic* (merx); păcare, *appease* (pax); părentare, *sacrifice*
in honour of a parent? (părens); piscari, *fish* (piscis); præcĭpĭtare,
hurl down (præceps); prŏpāgare, *propagate* (propăges); quirītare,
cry in fear (declare oneself a citizen? Quirīs); rěpræsentare, *exhibit,*
pay at once (præsens); sēdare, *settle* (sēdes); sĭmŭlare, *pretend* (sĭmĭlis); suffōcare, *choke, hold under throat* (fauces pl.); supplĭcare,
supplicate (supplex); těnuare, *make thin* (tenvis); testari, *call witnesses* (testis); tristari (Sen.), *be sad;* contrīstare, *sadden* (tristis);
turpare, *be foul* (turpis); vĭrĭdare, *make or be green* (vĭrĭdis); and
some others.

(6)   From nouns with consonant stems: 961
aggěrare, *pile up* (agger); ărǐětare, *butt* (aries); auctiōnari, *hold*
an auction (auctio); auctōrare, *guaranty, hire out* (auctor); aucŭ-
pari, *chase after* (auceps); augŭrari, *augur* (augur); auspĭcari, *take*
omens (auspex); căcŭmĭnare, *point* (căcumen); cognōmĭnare, *sur-*
name (cognomen); cŏlōrare, *colour* (color); contiōnari, *harangue*
(contio); crīmĭnari, *bring a charge* (crīmen); crŭc-ĭ-are, *torture*
(crux, *a cross*); decŏrare, *decorate* (děcus); discrīmĭnare, *distinguish*
(discrīmen); ěqvītare, *ride a horse* (ěqves); exāmĭnare, *weigh* (exāmen, *tongue of balance*); exhērēdare, *disinherit* (exhēres); exŭlare,
be an exile (exul); exŭběrare, *overflow* (über, *abundant*); fēněrare
(also dep.), *lend money* (fēnus, *interest*); ferrūmĭnare, *solder* (ferrūmen); frŭtĭcare (also dep.), *sprout* (frutex); fulgŭrare, *lighten* (fulgur); fulmĭnare, *hurl thunderbolts* (fulmen); fūněrare, *inter* (fūnus);
fūrari, *thieve* (fur); gěněrare, *beget* (gěnus); germĭnare (Plin.),
bud (germen); glŏměrare, *gather into a ball* (glŏmus); glūtĭnare,
glue (glūten); hiěmare, *spend winter* (hiems); hŏnōrare, *honour*
(hŏnor); hospĭtari, *be a guest* (hospes); ĭmāgĭnari, *picture to oneself*

(Imāgo); interprĕtari, *interpret* (interpres); jūdĭcare, *judge* (judex); jūrare, *swear* lit. *affirm right* (jūs); lăbōrare, *labour* (lăbor); lăpĭdare, *stone* (lăpis); laudare, *praise* (laus); lēgare, *appoint formally* (lex); mancĭpare, *sell* (manceps); margĭnare, *furnish with a rim* (margo); mīlĭtare, *serve as a soldier* (miles); mŏdĕrare, *regulate* (as if from a stem mŏdŭs-; comp. modes-tus); mŭnĕrare, *reward* (munus); murmŭrare, *murmur* (murmur); nōmĭnare, *name* (nōmen); nūtrīcare, *suckle* (nutrix); ŏdōrare, *give a smell,* odorari, *scent out* (ŏdor); ōmĭnari, *forbode* (ōmen); ŏnĕrare, *burden* (ŏnus); ŏpĕrari, *work* (ŏpus); ōrare, *speak* (ōs, *mouth*); ordĭnare, *set in order* (ordo); paupĕrare, *make poor* (pauper); pignĕrare, *pledge* (pignus); pondĕrare, *weigh* (pondus); prĕcari, *pray* (prex); pulvĕrare, *bestrew with dust* (pulvis); rĕcordari, *call to mind* (cor n.); refrīgĕrare, *make cool again* (frīgus); remĭgare, *row* (rēmĕx); rōbŏrare, *strengthen* (rōbur); rōrare, *drop, bedew* (ros); rūmĭnare (also dep.), *chew the cud* (rūmen); sălūtare, *greet* (sălūs); scĕlĕrare, *pollute* (scĕlus); sēgrĕgare, *separate* (segrex); sēmĭnare, *sow* (sēmen); spērare, *hope* (spes § 340 n.); stercŏrare, *dung* (stercus); tempĕrare, *proportion, forbear* (tempus); vădari, *bind over by bail* (vas); văpōrare, *steam* (văpor); vēlĭtari, *skirmish* (vēles); vĕnĕrari, *worship* (*regard as charming?* vĕnus); verbĕrare, *beat* (verbĕra pl.); vermĭnare, *to have worms* (vermĭna pl.); vigĭlare, *watch* (vigĭl); ulcĕrare, *ulcer* (ulcus); vulnĕrare, *wound* (vulnus).

-ĭcā   albĭcare, *be white* (albēre); candĭcare (Plin.), *be whitish* 962 (candere); claudĭcare, *be lame* (claudĕre); fŏdĭcare, *dig frequently* (fŏdĕre); varĭcare, *straddle;* prævărĭcari, *act in collusion* (vāro-, *crooked*); vellĭcare, *pluck* (vellĕre). Comp. § 768.

-t-ĭgā   castīgare, *chastise* (casto-); fastīgare, *bring to a point;* 963 fătīgare, *tire* (*make to yawn,* făti-, § 803); vestīgare, *track.* (With this suffix comp. vectigal.)

-tā (-sā)   As if from same stem as past participles : usually express- 964 ing *repeated action,* or *attempt.* In a few cases the simple verb does not exist, or has a different form of past participle. (None are from participles in -āto : compare § 965.)

adjūtare, *help* (adjŭvare); adventare, *come continually* (advĕnīre); ægrōtare, *to be sick* (comp. ægro-); affectare, *aim at* (afficĕre); amplexari, *embrace* (amplecti); aptāre, *fit* (comp. ăpi-sc-i); argūtari, *prate* (arguĕre); artare, *compress* (arcēre); assentari, *flatter* (comp. assentīre); cantare, *sing* (cănĕre); captare, *catch at* (căpĕre); certare, *strive* (cernĕre); cessare, *loiter* (cēdĕre); cĭtare, *rouse* (ciĕre); cœptare, *begin* (cœpĕre); commentari, *debate* (commĭnisci); conflictare, *fight* (conflīgĕre); consultare, *deliberate* (consŭlĕre); crĕpĭtare, *rattle* (crĕpāre); cŭbĭtare, *lie frequently* (cŭbare); cursare, *run about* (currĕre); dătare, *give repeatedly* (dăre); defensare, *defend* (defendĕre); delectare, *delight* (dēlĭcĕre, præ-Cic.); dictare, *say frequently* (dīcĕre); dissertare, *discuss* (dissĕrĕre); dŏmĭtare, *tame* (dŏmare); dormītare, *be sleepy* (dormire); dŭctare, *lead about* (dūcĕre); exercĭtare, *exercise* (exercēre); fŭgĭtare, *flee habitually* (fŭgĕre); gestare, *wear* (gĕrĕre); grassari, *attack* (comp. grădi); gustāre, *taste* (comp. γεύειν); hăbĭtare, *dwell in* (hăbēre); hortāri, *exhort* (cf. p. 237); ītare, *go frequently* (īre); jactāre, *toss*, *boast* (jăcĕre); labefactare, *overthrow*; lactare, *wheedle* (lăcĕre, only in compounds); lapsare, *stumble* (lābi); lătĭtare, *lie hid* (lătēre); mactare, *slaughter* (comp. mactus, as if from măgĕre); mantare (Plaut.), *linger* (manēre); mērĭtare, *use to earn* (mĕrēre); mersare (mertare, old, according to Quint.), *dip* (mergĕre); mōtare, *move about* (mŏvēre); mussare, *mutter* (comp. mŭttīre, μύζειν); mūtare, *change* (comp. mŏvēre); nătare, *swim* (nāre, § 644); nictare, *wink* (comp. cōnīvēre); nixari, *strive* (nīti); nōtare, *note* (noscĕre; comp. cognĭtus); nŭtare, *nod* (nuere, only in compounds); occultare, *conceal* (occŭlĕre); offensare, *strike often*; ostentare, *show off* (ostĕndĕre); păvĭtare, *shake with fear* (păvēre); pensare, *weigh* (pendĕre); plăcĭtare (Plaut. once), *use to please* (plăcēre); pollĭcĭtāri, *make overtures* (pollĭcēri); portare, *carry* (comp. πορ-εύειν); pōtare, *drink* (pōtus); prensare, *grasp* (prendĕre); pressare, *press* (prĕmĕre); pulsare (pultare, old, according to Quintil.), *beat* (pellĕre); pŭtare, *prune, settle, think* (pŭtus); qvassare, *shake* (qvătĕre); raptare, *snatch* (răpĕre); reptare, *creep often* (rēpĕre); responsare, *answer* (respondĕre); restĭtare, *stay behind* (restare); ructare, *belch* (as if from a verb rugĕre; comp. ructus); saltare, *dance* (sălīre); scītari, *inquire* (scīre); sectari, *follow* (sĕqvi, secūtum); spectare, *look* (spĕcĕre); strĕpĭtare, *rustle* (strĕpĕre); temptare, *attempt;* territare, *frighten* (terrēre); tortare, *torture* (torqvēre); tractare, *handle* (trăhĕre); tūtari, *protect* (tuēri); versare, *turn about* (vertĕre); vexare, *harass* (vĕhĕre, vectum); vŏlūtare, *roll* (volvĕre); vŏmĭtare, *vomit often* (vŏmĕre).

-ĭtă   Usually suffixed to the last consonant of the present stem 965 of another verb; sometimes the ĭ may be part of the stem, not of the suffix.

ăgĭtare, *shake* (ăgĕre); bubulcitari (Pl. *Most.* 53), *be an ox-driver* (as if from bubulcare); cēnĭtare, *dine often* (cēnare); clāmĭtare, *shout repeatedly* (clāmare); cōgĭtare, *think* (cōgĕre); dēbĭlĭtare, *weaken* (dēbĭli-, adj.); dŭbĭtare, *doubt* (dŭbio-); febr-īc-ĭtare, *be ill of a fever* (febri- comp. febrĭcŭlosus, § 814); flăgĭtare, *demand;* flŭĭtare, *float* (flu-ĕre); hiĕtare (præ-Cic.), *yawn frequently* (hiāre); imĭtari, *imitate;* impĕrĭtare, *command* (impĕrāre); mĭnĭtari, *threaten repeatedly* (mĭnāri); mōbĭlĭtare, *make moveable* (mōbĭli-); nĕgĭtare, *deny repeatedly* (nĕgāre); nōbĭlĭtare, *make famous* (nōbĭli-); nōmĭnĭtare (Lucr.), *name* (nōmĭnare); noscĭtare, *recognize* (noscĕre); palpĭtare, *throb* (palpāre); părĭtare (Plaut.), *make preparations* (părare); periclitarī, *put to the test* (perīcŭlo-); qværĭtare, *seek earnestly* (quærēre); qvĕrĭtarī, *complain* (qvĕrī); rōgĭtare, *ask eagerly* (rōgare); scǐscĭtarī, *inquire* (sciscĕre); tŭdĭtans (part.), *beating about* (tundĕre); vendĭtare, *offer for sale* (vendĕre); vŏcĭtare, *call often* (vŏcare); vŏlĭtare, *fly about* (vŏlāre). Comp. also crĕpĭtare, cŭbĭtare, dŏmĭtare, exercĭtare, lătĭtare, mĕrĭtare, pǎvĭtare, plăcĭtare, pollĭcĭtarī, strĕpĭtare, terrĭtare, vŏmĭtare, in § 964.

-tĭtā (-sĭtā) i.e. -ĭta suffixed to same stem as past participles or 966 ordinary frequentatives.

actĭtāre, *act often* (ăgĕre); cantĭtare, *sing often* (căntare); cursĭtare, *run about* (cursare); dĕfensĭtare, *frequently to de-fend* (defendĕre); dictĭtare, *say repeatedly* (dictare); ductĭtare, *lead* (ductare); emptĭtare (post-Aug.), *buy up* (ĕmĕre); factĭtare, *do frequently* (făcĕre); gestĭtare, *be wont to carry* (gĕstare); hæsĭtare, *hesitate* (hærēre); lectĭtare, *read frequently* (lĕgĕre); mansĭtare, *stay* (mănēre); missĭtare, *send repeatedly* (mittĕre); mussĭtare, *grumble* (mussare); pensĭtare, *pay habitually*, Cic., *ponder*, Liv., Suet. (pendĕre); pransĭtare, *lunch* (prandĕre); responsĭtare, *give frequent opinions* (respondĕre); scriptĭtare, *write often* (scrībĕre); unctĭtare, *anoint often* (ungvĕre); ventĭtare, *come repeatedly* (vĕnīre); victĭtare, *live* (vīvĕre); visĭtare, *visit* (vīdĕre, vīsĕre). So ūsĭtātus (not used in finite verb, except by Gell.), *customary* (ūti).

-cǐnā   comp. § 936.   Chiefly from stem in -ōn, with n omitted. 967

halucinarī, *dream;* latrōcĭnarī, *practise brigandage* (la-trōn-); lēnōcĭnarī, *be a pander* (lēnōn-); patrōcĭnarī, *be a patron* (patrŏno-); ratiocĭnarī, *calculate* (rătĭŏn-); sermōcĭnarī, *converse* (sermōn-); vātĭcĭnarī, *foretell* (vāti-).

-ŏlā)
-ŭlā}   Compare the nouns with suffix -ŏlo, &c. (§§ 856—867) 968
-ĭlā)   and the verbs in §§ 955—958.

ĕj-ŭlare, *wail, cry* (eja); gesti-cŭlarī, *gesticulate* (gestu-); grāt-ŭlarī, *congratulate* (grāto-, *pleasing*); ŏpĭ-tŭlarī, *assist* (ŏpǐ-, tŭl-; comp. tŭli, ſlātum); pos-tŭlare, *demand* (comp. poscĕre); sorbĭlare, *sip* (comp. sorbēre); strang-ŭlare, *strangle* (comp. string-ĕre, στράγγειν); vāpŭlare, *be beaten;* viŏlare, *use force to* (vi-); vītŭlare, *sacrifice, keep holiday;* ŭlŭlare, *howl* (probably a reduplicated *howl*); ustulare, *singe* (usto-).

-illā   căv-illarī, *jest, banter* (căvilla-); conscrīb-illare (Cat.), 96) *scribble on* (scrīb-ĕre); focillare (or foсīlare), *cherish* (fōco-?); furc-illāre (?), *toss?* (furсa-, furcilla-); obstrigillare, *fetter* (obstring-ere); scint-illare, *sparkle* (scintilla-); sūg-illare, *beat black and blue;* tĭt-illare, *tickle;* văc-illare (vaccillare, Lucr. once), *waddle, hesitate* (vacca-, *a cow*).

-trā   calci-trare, *kick* (calci-); castrare, *geld* (comp. κάστωρ
and Plin. 8. § 109); frustrari, *cheat* (frustra, fraudi-);
lātrare, *bark* (comp. λακ-εῖν?); pătrare, *perform* (patr-); pĕnĕ-
trare, *penetrate* (pĕnŭs, *store*).

Formed from, or parallel to, other verbs; most are compounds: 97·
antīcĭpare, *anticipate* (ante, căpĕ-re); ap- (com-) -pellare, *address* (pellĕre); aspernari, *scorn, spurn* (ab, spernĕre); conspĭcari,
descry (conspĭcĕre); consternare, *dismay* (consternĕre); dĭcare, *dedicate* (dīcĕre); ēdŭcare, *bring up, train* (ēdūcĕre); indāgare, *track out*
(indo ăgĕre? indāgŏn-); instīgare, *goad on* (in, stingvĕre); lăbare,
slip (lābi); lăvarə, *wash* (lăvĕre); lĭqvare, *melt* (lĭqvēre or lĭqvi,
be fluid or *clear*); mandare, *commit, entrust* (mănu-, dăre); mulcare,
beat (mulcēre, *stroke*); nuncŭpare (nōmine căpĕre? cf. § 997); oc-
cŭpare, *seize* (ob, căpĕre); pīpare (cf. pīpīre), *chirp;* plācare, *pacify*
(plăcēre, *be pleasing*); rĕcŭpĕrare, *recover* (re, căpĕre); sēdare,
settle (sĕdēre, *sit*); suspĭcari, *suspect* (suspĭcĕre).

Miscellaneous: chiefly of obscure origin; many have derivative 97t
suffixes similar to noun-stems:

ădŭlari, *fawn on* (ad-ŭlŭlare?); æstĭmare, *esteem;* altercari,
wrangle; ămare, *love;* ampliare, *enlarge* (comp. amplo-); ārare,
plough; auscultare, *listen* (comp. auris, *ear*); autŭmare, *affirm;*
bālare, *bleat;* baubari, *howl;* beare, *bless;* bētare (bītare), *go* (comp.
βαίνειν); blătĕrare, *bluster* (comp. bălătro, *a jester*); boare, *cry
aloud* (comp. βοᾶν); căcare; călare, *summon* (comp. καλεῖν); călī-
gare, *be in darkness;* cēlare, *conceal* (comp. clam); clāmare, *shout;*
clīnare, *bend;* coaxare (Suet.), *croak* (κοάξ); cōnari, *endeavour;*
consīdĕrare, *consider;* contāmĭnare, *stain* (comp. contăg-iōn-); crĕ-
mare, *burn;* creare, *create;* desīdĕrare, *desire;* dissĭpare, *dissipate;*
dŏlare, *hew;* flăgrare, *blaze* (comp. flāre, φλέγειν); formīdare,
dread; frāgrare, *emit a smell;* friare, *rub* (comp. frĭcare); hālare,
breathe; hēluari, *gormandize* (comp. hēluŏn-); hiare, *gape;* incŏ-
hare, *commence;* inqvīnare, *defile* (comp. cæno-, *mud*); instaurare,
renew (comp. instar); invītare, *invite;* irrītare, *irritate;* jentare,
breakfast; jŭvare, *assist;* lībare, *pour out, take* (comp. lībum, *a
cake*); lĭgare, *bind;* lītare, *make a favourable sacrifice;* luctāri,
struggle; lŭcŭbrare, *work by lamplight;* luxare, *dislocate* (comp.
λοξός, *slanting*); mānare, *flow;* mĕdĭtari, *meditate;* meare, *go to
and fro;* mĭgrare, *depart;* mūgīnari, *dally;* narrare, *relate* (gnāro-?);
nĕgare, *deny* (nec); opsōnari, *purchase provisions* (ὀψωνεῖν); optare,
choose; optūrare, *stop up;* ornare, *equip;* oscĭtare, *gape;* pālari,
wander; părare, *prepare;* peccare, *sin;* com-, ex-, sup-pīlare, *plun-
der;* oppīlare, *obstruct;* plōrare, *cry out;* præstōlari, *wait for;* pro-
mulgare, *announce, publish;* prōpīnare, *drink healths* (προπίνειν);
rīgare, *water;* rōgare, *ask;* runcare, *hoe;* screare (Plaut.), *hawk,
hem;* sōlari, *console;* spīrare, *breathe* (spīra-, *wreath?*); stīpare,
crowd; sūdare, *sweat;* suffrāgari, *use a potsherd?* *vote* (suffrāgium);

tāxare, *estimate;* tĕmĕrare, *defile* (comp. tĕmĕre); tĭtŭbare, *totter;* tŏlĕrare, *endure* (tŭlĭ, tollere); trŭcīdare, *butcher;* văcare, *be empty;* vēnarĭ, *hunt;* vĭbrare, *shake;* vĭtŭpĕrare, *blame;* vītare, *avoid;* vŏlare, *fly;* vŏrare, *devour;* ūrīnarĭ, *dive.*

ii. Verbs with -u stems: 972

ăcuĕre, *sharpen* (ăcus, *needle*); mĕtuĕre, *fear* (mĕtus); mĭnuĕre, *lessen* (mĭnus, *less*); stătuĕre, *determine* (stătus, *position*). The verbs exuĕre, *put off;* imbuĕre, *dip in;* induĕre, *put on,* are apparently derived directly from the prepositions ex, in (acquiring a parasitical b from its following u), and indo, the old form of in. Other verbs with -u stems of obscure origin are named in § 684.

iii. Verbs with -e stems: 973

Three only (uncompounded) have more than one syllable before the -e; mĭsĕrerĭ, *have pity;* ŏportere, *behove;* pænĭtere, *repent.*

(1) From adjectives with -o stems:

ægrere, *be sick;* albere, *be white;* calvere, *be bald;* cānere, *be hoary;* clārere, *be bright;* claudere, *be lame;* densēre, *be thick,* *thicken;* flaccēre, *be flabby;* flāvere, *be yellow;* pĭgrere, *be lazy;* sal-vere, *be safe* (? see in Book II. Chap. xxx.).

(2) From substantives with -o stems:

callere, *to have a thick skin, be experienced* (callum); mūcere, *be mouldy* (mūcus).

(3) From nouns with -i stems:

frondere, *have boughs* (frons); lactere, *have milk* (lac); sordere, *be dirty* (sordes pl.); tābere, *waste away* (tabes, also tabum).

(4) From nouns with consonant stems:

flōrere, *be in flower* (flos); lŭcere, *be light* (lux).

For other verbs with -e stems see Book II. Chap. xxiii. and xxx. Many appear to be formed directly from roots.

iv. Verbs with -i stems: 974

(1) From substantives with stems in -a or -o:

bullire (also bullare), *bubble* (bulla); condire, *pickle, preserve* (condus, *storekeeper*); mentiri, *tell lies* (*make for oneself devices?* comp. com-mentum; *also* mens); mētirĭ, *measure* (mēta, *goal*); pūnire, *punish* (pœna); servire, *be a slave, serve* (servus).

(2) From adjectives with -o stems:

blandirĭ, *coax;* ineptire, *be foolish;* insānire, *be insane;* largirĭ, *give bountifully;* lascīvire, *be playful;* lippire, *have sore eyes;* præsā-gire, *foretell;* sævire, *be savage;* sŭperbire, *be haughty.*

(3) From nouns with -u stems, the u being absorbed:
gestīre, *exult* (gestus, *a gesture*); singultīre, *hiccup, sob.*

(4) From nouns with -i stems:
audīre, *hear* (auris, *ear;* for the interchange of r and d cf.
§ 160. 10); dementīre, *be out of one's mind* (mens); dentīre, *cut
teeth* (dens); effūtīre, *pour out* (fūtis, *water-vessel,* according to
Varr.); ērūdīre, *instruct* (rūdis, *a foil?* or rūdis, *rough*); febrīre,
have a fever (febris); fīnīre, *put an end to* (fīnis); grandīre, *make
great* (grandis); hostīre, *hit?* (hostis?); inanīre, *empty* (inānis);
insignīre, *mark* (insignis); irrētīre, *ensnare* (rēte); lēnīre, *soften*
(lēnis); mōlīri, *exert oneself* (mōles); mollīre, *soften* (mollis); mū-
nīre, *fortify* (moenia, pl.); partīre (usually partīri), *part, share*
(pars); potīre, pŏtīri, *be master of* (pŏtis); rāvīre, *make oneself
hoarse* (rāvis); sītīre, *thirst* (sītis); sortīri, *cast lots* (sors); stăbī-
līre, *establish* (stăbĭlis); tussīre, *cough* (tussis); vestīre, *clothe*
(vestis).

(5) From nouns with consonant stems:
custōdīre, *keep* (custos); expĕdīre, *free one's foot* (pĕs); fulgūrīre
(also fulgūrare), *lighten* (fulgur).

(6) Of obscure origin:
ămīcīre, *clothe;* ăpĕrīre, *open* (see pĕrio, Book II. Chap. XXX.);
dormīre, *sleep;* farcīre, *stuff* (comp. φραγ-, φράσσειν); fastīdīre,
loathe; fĕrīre, *strike;* fulcīre, *prop up;* glūtīre, *swallow* (from the
sound); haurīre, *draw;* impĕtrīre (comp. impetrare), *obtain,* esp.
favourable omens; īre, *go;* nūtrīre, *nourish;* ordīri, *commence* (comp.
ord-ŏn-); ŏrīri, *arise* (comp. ὄρ-νυμι); păvīre, *strike* (comp. παίειν);
pŏlīre, *polish;* rĕdĭmīre, *bind;* sălīre, *leap* (comp. ἅλ-λεσθαι); sancīre, *sanction;* sărīre, *hoe;* sentīre, *feel;* sĕpĕlīre, *bury;* sōpīre, *put
to sleep* (comp. somnus); suffīre, *fumigate* (cf. § 99); vĕnīre, *come;*
vincīre, *bind.*

(7) Verbs expressive of *sounds*[1]:
barrīre (Fest.), *roar* of elephant (barrus, *elephant*); blătīre,
babble; crōcīre, *croak* (comp. κρώζειν); frītinnīre (Varr.), *twitter;*
gannīre, *yelp;* garrīre, *chatter;* gingrīre (Fest.), *scream like geese;*
glōcīre, *cluck;* grunnīre, *grunt;* hinnīre, *neigh;* hirrīre (Fest.),
snarl; mūgīre, *low* (comp. μυκᾶσθαι); muttīre, *mutter;* pīpīre (Col.,
also pipare, Varr., pīpiare or pīpulare, Catull.), *pip, chirp;* rugīre
(Spart.), *roar;* tinnīre, *jingle;* vāgīre, *wail.*

-ūtī   balbūtīre, *stammer* (balbo-); cæcutīre, *be blind* (cæco-); 975
frigūtīre (fringuttīre), *twitter, stutter.*

---

[1] Many others, with various stems, will be found in extracts from
later writers in Reifferscheid's *Suetonius,* pp. 247—254, 308—312.

-ūrī   Usually expressing *desire;* formed as if from the supine: 976
cēnātūrīre (Mart.), *be eager for dinner* (cenāre); emptū-
rīre (Varr.), *wish to purchase* (ĕmĕre); ēsūrīre, *be hungry* (ĕdĕre);
hăbĭturīre (?) *desire to have* (hăbēre); mictūrīre (mingĕre); mŏrĭtu-
rīre (quoted from Cic.), *wish to die* (mŏri); nuptūrīre (Mart.),
desire to marry (nūbĕre); pĕtīturīre (Cic.), *wish to be a candidate*
(pĕtĕre); proscripturīre (Cic. *Att.* 9. 10. § 6), *be eager for a pro-
scription* (proscribere); Sullaturīre (Cic. *Att.* 9. 10. § 6), *play the
part of Sulla.*

-ūrī   lĭgurrīre, *lick;* prūrīre, *itch;* scalpūrīre (Plaut. *Aul.* 464. 977
Wagn.), *scratch* (scalp-ĕre); scāturīre, *bubble, gush forth*
(scātere).

v. -sc Inchoative verbs. The following are formed directly 978
from noun stems. (For other verbs with inchoative
suffix see §§ 634—638, 676—680.)

arbŏr-esc-ĕre (Plin.), *grow into a tree* (arbŏs-); dīte-sc-ere
(Lucr., Hor.), *grow rich* (dīti-); dulce-sc-ĕre (Cic., Plin.), *grow
sweet* (dulci-); fermente-sc-ere, *ferment* (fermento-; cf. fermentare); flammescere (Lucr.), *flame* (flamma-); gemma-sc-ĕre, *bud;*
gemm-esc-ere (? Plin.), *become a jewel* (gemma-); grande-sc-ĕre
(Lucr.), *grow big* (grandi-); grăve-sc-ĕre, *grow heavy* (grăvi-);
herbe-sc-ĕre (Cic., in part. pres. only), *grow grassy* (herba-); ignĕ-
sc-ĕre, *burst into flame, kindle* (igni-); intĕgrascĕre (Ter.), *break out
anew* (integro-; comp. integrare, *renew*); jŭvĕn-esc-ĕre, *grow
young* (jŭvĕn-); lăpĭd-esc-ĕre (Plin.), *turn to stone* (lăpĭd-); lasse-
sc-ĕre (Plin.), *become weary* (lasso-); mīte-sc-ĕre, *grow mild, mellow*
(mīti-); molle-sc-ĕre, *grow soft* (molli-); obbrūte-sc-ere, *grow
brutish* (brūto-); pingve-sc-ĕre, *grow fat* (pingvi-); plūme-sc-ĕre
(Plin.), *become fledged* (plūma-; comp. plūmātus); puera-sc-ĕre
(Suet., repuĕrascĕre, Cic.), *become a boy* (puĕro-, as if from a verb
puerāre); radic-esc-ĕre (Sen.), *put forth roots* (rādīc-); rāre-sc-ĕre,
grow thin (rāro-); repulle-sc-ĕre (Col.), *sprout forth* (pullo-); rŏr-
esc-ĕre (Ov.), *dissolve with dew* (rōs-); rūfe-sc-ĕre (Plin.), *become
red* (rūfo-); silve-sc-ĕre, *become woody* (silva-); spisse-sc-ĕre, *become
thick* (spisso-); stĕrĭle-sc-ĕre (Plin.), *become barren* (stĕrĭli-);
tĕnĕre-sc-ĕre (Cels., Plin.; tĕnĕrascere, Lucr.), *grow tender* (tĕnĕro-);
viv-esc-ĕre (Lucr.), *grow lively* (vīvo-); ūve-sc-ere, *grow moist*
(comp. ūvĭdus).

-ss (-ssī) e.g. arcesso, &c. See § 625.

CHAPTER XI.

COMPOSITION.

NEW words may be formed not merely by the addition of 979
a derivative suffix, but by the junction of two or more separately
intelligible words into one. This is called *composition.* The distinctive features of two words being compounded are the loss of their
separate accents, and the possession of but one set of inflexions.

Any two words in syntactical connexion may, if the meaning
be suitable, be the base of a new compound word. So long as the
two words each retain their own proper inflexion or use, however
frequently they may be used together, they are not a proper compound; e.g. **rem gerere, res gestæ,** &c.

Such habitual combinations are called *spurious compounds,* and
are often marked by the fixing of a particular order for the words,
though such order is not absolutely prescribed by general principles; e.g. **pater familias, jus jurandum, respublica, accepti ratio,**
&c. (cf. § 1042).

Compounds are distinguishable from a mere juxtaposition of 980
the simple words of which they are or might appear to be composed,

either (*a*) by the two words not being used together as simple
words, e.g. **ēdūrus, subsimilis, cisrhēnānus, proăvus, qvinqvevir;**

or (*b*) by one or both not being used at all independently,
e.g. **dissimilis, vēsanus;**

or (*c*) by one or both losing their proper inflexions or terminations, e.g. **arcitenens, malevolus, tridens, caprĭfĭcus;**

or (*d*) by a vowel being changed or omitted owing to the two
words being brought under one accent, e.g. **Diespiter, duodecim;**

or (*e*) by the meaning of the compound being different or more
than the meaning of the two words, e g. **supercilium,** *the eyebrow;*
but **super cilium,** *above the eyelid;* **conclāve,** *a chamber.*

The precise form which the compound word assumes is not 981
determined by the previous connexion, but mainly by the class
(verb, adjective, substantive, &c.) to which it is to belong; and,
subordinately to that, by the same causes (known or unknown)
which occasion the selection of particular suffixes of declension or
derivation. To us the particular form thus appears to be frequently

a matter of caprice. There is, however, a tendency for the compound word to take a similar form to the second of the component words.

The combination is always a combination of *stems* or *roots* (sometimes clipt); and the resulting compound, even where it exhibits similar inflexional or derivative suffixes to those of one of the simple words, may most truly be supposed not to have retained such suffixes but to have reproduced them; e.g. palmi-pes is a compound from the stems palma-, ped-, and has received the simple inflexions (i.e. nominative suffix) of the second class of nouns, just as the stem ped- itself has.

But a verb or adjective, compounded with a preposition used absolutely (§ 984), retains the form of the simple stem: a verb compounded of two words in proper syntactical relation with each other takes an a stem.

So far as the inflexional or derivative suffix is concerned, compound words have been already included in the lists in this and the previous book. Here they will be classified and enumerated (or selections made) according to the variety of the elements of which they are composed, and the nature of the connexion.

i. SPURIOUS COMPOUNDS. The following are the combinations which, from the fixity of their use, appear most nearly to approach proper compounds.   982

1. Verbs: (*a*) animum advertere (or animadvertere), *to take notice;* fidei committere, *to entrust;* fideicommissa, *trusts;* fidejubēre, *to bid a person do a thing on your guaranty;* fidejussor, *a (person as) security;* pessum dăre, *to send to the bottom* (comp. pessum ire, abire, premēre); vēnum ire, *to be sold,* vēnum dare, *to sell* (but vēnīre, vendĕre as compounds proper); usucapĕre, *acquire by use.*

Ilicet, *off!* at once (ire licet); scilicet, *let me tell you* (scire licet); vidēlicet, *you may see* = *that is to say* (videre licet), where the re has dropt off by its similarity to li, § 28.

(*b*) The dissyllabic prepositions appear often to form with verbs only improper compounds; e.g. circum dăre, *to throw around,* appears to be in meaning a proper compound in urbem circum dare muro; an improper one in urbi circum dare murum.

Similarly retroagere, retrogradi, &c.; benĕfacĕre, mălĕdicĕre, satisfacĕre, palamfacere, palamfieri.

Compare also inque pediri, jacere indu, inque gravescunt (Lucr.), and the use of per, § 986, p. 384.

2. Nouns: 983

(*a*) Doubled adjective:

altĕrŭter, *one of two;* quisquis, *whosoever;* quŏtusquisque, *how many.*

(Comp. the adverbs: quamquam, utut, *although, however.*)

tertius decimus, quartus decimus, and other compound numerals. So lex quina vicenaria, *law relating to age of twenty-five.*

(*b*) Adjective + substantive: jusjurandum, *an oath* (lit. *a swearing one's right*); res gestæ, *exploits;* res publica, *the common weal;* ros marinus (ros maris Ov.) *rosemary (sea-dew).*

(*c*) Genitive + substantive: accepti (expensi) latio, *entering in book as received (expended)*; agricultura, *farming;* aquæductus, *a water-course;* argentifodinæ, *silver mines;* ludimagister, *a schoolmaster;* paterfamilias, materfamilias, filiusfamilias, &c. *a father,* &c. *of a household;* plēbiscītum, *a commons' resolution;* senatusconsultum, *a senate's decree.* So jurisconsultus, *one skilled in the law.*

(*d*) Genitive + adjective: e.g. verisimilis, *likely (like the truth).*

(*e*) Oblique case and participle; e.g. dicto audiens, *obedient.*

(*f*) Two parallel substantives: e.g. ususfructus, *the use and enjoyment.* So perhaps pactum conventum, *a bargain and covenant* (or *a covenanted bargain?*).

(*g*) Adverb + participle: e.g. grăveŏlens, *strong-smelling;* svaveolens, *sweet-smelling.*

Similarly pæninsula, *an almost-island* (comp. duos prope Hannibales in Italia esse. L. 27. 44).

3. Adverbs: e.g. sæpenumero. *often in number;* tantummodo, *only* (lit. *so much in measure*); hactĕnus (§ 509), *thus far;* quamlibet, quamvis, &c.

itaqve, *therefore;* etĕnim, *in fact,* &c. have each but one accent (cf. §§ 297, 298): magnopere, *greatly;* prorsus (§ 512), *utterly,* &c. have been contracted: sĭqvidem, nĭsi, qvăsi (§ 524), &c. have had the first vowel modified. So nudius tertius (quartus, &c.), *the day* (*two days*) *before yesterday,* is a contracted sentence (nunc dies tertius est). Multimodis, mirimodis = multismodis, &c. Lucr. has also omnimodis. (Cf. Cic. Or. 45.)

ii. COMPOUNDS of prepositions used absolutely, or 984 of inseparable particles.

Such compounds are some verbs and some nouns.

1. Verbs:

(*a*) Common with prepositions; e.g. dissolvere, advenĭre, &c.

(*b*) With inseparable particles: amb, dis, por, red (re), sed (se).
e.g. ambīre, dissolvěre, porrĭgere, resolvěre, sevocāre, &c.

[As the differences turn chiefly on the import of the prepositions and particles, instances are reserved for the Appendix to Syntax.]

(*c*) Rarely with negatives; viz. in, ne; ignoscere, *not recognize, pardon;* nequīre, *be unable;* nescīre, *be ignorant;* nolle, *be unwilling.* With gerundive: in-, ne-fandus, *unspeakable.* For participles see § 986

2. N o u n s: containing either a verbal or nominal stem.   985

(A) Containing a verbal stem, but not being ordinary derivatives from compound verbs:

advěna, *a stranger* (advenīre); acclīnis, *leaning against* (comp. κλίνειν); accŏla, *neighbour* (cŏlěre).

ambāges, *roundabout ways* (ăg-ěre).

anteambulo (post-Aug.), *a forerunner* (ambulare).

convěnæ (pl.), *assembled strollers* (convěnīre); convīva, *a guest* (con, vivere).

in   *not:* inědia, *fasting* (ěd-ěre); innŭbus, *unmarried* (nub-, nŭběre); inscius, insciens, *ignorant* (scīre).

        at: invĭdus, *envious* (vĭd-ēre).

indo   *in, on:* incus, *an anvil* (cūdere); indīgěna, *a native* (gěn-, gignere); indŏles, *growth, temper* (ŏle-scere); industria, *industry* (struěre).

inter   *between:* internuntius, *a go-between* (nŏvo-, věnīre); interpolis, *smoothed out, furbished up* (pŏlīre); intertrimentum, *waste in making* (těrěre); perhaps also interpres, *a broker, interpreter.*

nec (ne)   *not:* necŏpīnus, *unexpected* (opīnāri); nefastus, *forbidden?*; nefrens, *not biting* (frenděre); nescius, *ignorant* (scīre).

obex, *a bolt* (jăcě-re).

perfīca (Lucr.), *a finisher* (făcere); perfŭga, *a deserter* (fŭgě-re).

præcŏqvus, præcox, *early, ripe, precocious* (cŏqvěre); præfīca, *a woman mourner* (præfăcěre, *perform in front?*); præscius, *foreknowing;* præsul, cf. § 874.

prŏfŭgus, *flying* (profŭgěre); prōnŭba, (*veiler beforehand?*), *bridesmaid* (nŭběre); prōvĭdus, *foreseeing* (vĭd-ere).

rědīvīvus (? see § 763); refluus, *flowing back* (fluěre); rěfŭga (Dig.), *a runaway* (rěfŭgě-re).

sŭbŏles (sŏbŏles), *growth, stock* (ŏle-sc-ěre).

transfŭga, *a deserter* (fŭgě-re).

(B)   Containing a nominal stem: 986

ab   **ăbăvus**, *a (distant*, i.e.) *great grandfather;* **abnĕpos**, &c.

ad   **adnĕpos**, *a great-great-great grandson;* so also **at-avus**(?);
         aduncus, *bent forwards* (**unco-**).

amb   *on both sides;* **anceps**, *double-headed, doubtful* (**căpŭt-**).

com   *together;* with adjective stems, also *completely:*

         (1) From adjectives: **cognatus**, *united by birth;* **com-
par**, *well matched;* **compascuus**, *for common pasturage;* **complūres**
(pl.), *several together;* **concăvus**, *hollow;* **condensus**, *very dense;* **con-
dignus**, *quite worthy.*

         (2) From substantives: (*a*) adjectives: **cognōmĭnis**, *of like
name;* **commanipularis**, *in the same company* (**manĭpŭlo-**); **com-
mūnis**, *having common functions, common;* **compos**, *having complete
mastery* (**pŏti-**); **concŏlor**, *of the same colour;* **concors**, *of the same
mind* (**cordi-**); **confīnis**, *having common borders;* **confrăgosus**, *broken;*
consangvīneus, *of the same blood* (**sangvĕn-**); **consŏnus**, *sounding in
unison;* **consors**, *having a common lot* (**sorti-**); **contermĭnus**, *having
common bounds;* **cōpis**, *having complete resources;* **cōpia**, *plenty* (**ŏpi-**).

         (*b*) Substantives: **cohēres**, *a fellow heir* (**hērēd-**); **collēga**, *a
fellow by law;* **collēgium**, *a body formed under same law;* **compes**,
a shackle for the feet (**pĕd-**); **compluvium**, *a cistern to collect rain-
water* (**plŭvia-**); **condiscĭpŭlus**, *a schoolmate;* **congerro**, *a companion
in tricks* (**gerra-**); **conjux**, *one united in marriage* (*yoke fellow*,
jŭgo-); **conservus**, *a fellow slave;* **consobrīnus**, *a child of two sisters*
(**sŏrŏr-**); **consŏcer**, *a joint father in law;* **consponsor**, *a joint surety;*
contŭbernalis, *a companion,* **contubernium**, *companionship* in a shop
or *hut* (**tăberna-**); **convallis**, *a close valley;* **cūria**, cf. § 94. 2.

         So the adverbs: **commĭnus**, lit. *hands together,* at close quarters;
ēmĭnus, *hands off,* i.e. at a distance.

de   As negative: **dēbĭlis**, *weak* (**hăbĭlis**);

         down, e.g. **declivis**, *sloping downwards,* but cf. § 990
         (**clivo-**); **delumbis**, *stooping in the loins? weak* (**lumbo-**);
         deparcus (Nero ap. Suet.), *excessively stingy;*
         off, e.g. **deunx**, *an ounce off* an as, i.e. *eleven-twelfths*
         (**uncia-**).

dis   *in two, divided,* or as negative: (*a*) from adjectives:
         diffĭcĭlis, *difficult;* **dīmĭdius**, *half* (**mĕdio-**); **dispar**, *ill-
matched;* **dissĭmĭlis**, *unlike.*

         (*b*) From substantives: **discolor**, *of various colours*
         (**cŏlōr-**); **discors**, *discordant* (**cordi-**); **dissonus**, *out of
tune* (**sŏno-**).

ē   (*a*) With adjectives, *exceedingly:* ēdūrus, *very hard;* effērus, *very wild;* ēlixus, *sodden* (laxo-).

(*b*) With substantives, *off;* hence = *without:* effrēnare, *to unbridle;* effrēnus, *unbridled* (freno-); ēgĕlĭ-dus, *with the chill off* (gelu-, not compound of gelidus); elingvis, *tongueless* (lingva-); exănimis, *lifeless* (anĭma-); excors, *senseless* (cordi-); exhēres, *disinherited* (hērēd-); exlex, *lawless* (lēg-); exsangvis, *bloodless* (sangvĕn-); exsomnis, *sleepless* (somno-); exsors, *without lot* (sorti-); exspes, *hopeless* (spe-); exsucus (Quint.), *juiceless* (sūco-). Compare its use with verbs in App. to Syntax.

in   *un-* = *not*: adjectives (and thence derived substantives):

(*a*) from existing adjectives and participles: ignāvus, *inactive;* ignārus, *ignorant;* ignōbilis, *unrenowned;* illĕpĭdus, *disagreeable;* illībĕralis, *ungentlemanly;* illĭcĭtus, *unlawful;* illītĕratus, *illiterate;* illōtus, *unwashed;* immansvētus, *untamed;* immātūrus, *unripe;* immĕdĭcabilis, *incurable;* immĕmor, *unmindful;* immĕmŏrābilis, *indescribable;* immĕmŏratus, *unmentioned;* immensus, *measureless;* immĕrens, *undeserving;* immĕrītus, *undeserved;* immĭsĕrĭcors, *pitiless;* impĕrītus, *unskilled,* impĕrītia, *unskilfulness;* impius, *impious;* impos, *powerless* (pŏti-); inaudītus, *unheard;* incæduus, *uncut;* incognĭtus, *unknown;* incŏlŭmis, *unhurt* (comp. -cellĕre, *strike*); incrēdĭbilis, *incredible;* indĕcōrus, *unbecoming* (dĕcōr-); indēfessus, *unwearied;* indignus, *unworthy;* ineptus, *without tact;* infandus, (cf. 984 *c*); inhābĭlis, *unmanageable;* inhospĭtalis, *inhospitable;* inĭmīcus, *unfriendly;* inīqvus, *unlevel, unfair* (æqvo-); insulsus, *insipid* (salso-); intempestivus, *unseasonable;* intestātus, *that has made no will;* invĕrēcundus, *unblushing;* irrĭtus, *in vain* (rāto-); and many others.

(*b*) From substantives: ignōmĭnia, *disgrace* (gnōmĕn-); imbellis, *unwarlike* (bello-); imberbis, *beardless* (barba-); immunis, *without charge* (mūn-ŭs-); implūmis, *featherless* (pluma-); inănĭmis, *lifeless* (anĭma-); incūria, *want of care* (cura-); indemnis (post-Aug.), *without loss* (damno-); inermis, *unarmed* (armo-); iners, *unskilled, sluggish* (arti-); infāmis, *of ill-report* (fama-); informis, *formless* (forma-); infrēnis, *bridleless* (frēno-); ingens, *not of the class? huge* (genti-); inglōrius, *without glory* (gloria-); inhospĭtus, *inhospitable* (hospĕt-); injūria, *wrongful conduct,* injūrius (rare), *wrongful* (jūs-); innŭmĕrus, *numberless* (nŭmĕro-); inops, *helpless* (ŏpi-); insomnis, *sleepless* (somno-); invius, *roadless* (via-); and others.

in   *on*: insignis, *with a stamp on, distinguished* (sign-).

rĕ   *not*: nĕfas, *wickedness* (fas); nĕgōtium, *business* (otium); nēmo, *none* (hŏmŏn-); nullus, *not any* (ullo-).

ob   *over*: oblīqvus, *aslant* (*bent over,* cf. § 772); obscūrus, *shadowed over* (comp. σκό-τος, σκιά); obstīpus, *bent over;* obuncus, *curved over;* occipitium (occiput, Pers.), *the top* or *back head.* Perhaps obscēnus, *inauspicious, foul;* oblongus, *longish,* belong to this class.

per *thoroughly:* with all kinds of adjectives: **perabsurdus,**
peraccommodatus (per fore accommodatum tibi, C. *Fam.*
3. 5. 3), pĕrācer, perăcerbus, perăcutus, perădŭlescens, peramplus,
perangustus, perbŏnus, percontŭmax (Ter.), perēlēgans, perexĭg-
nus, perfăcētus, perfăcĭlis, pergrātus, pergrăvis, perhŏnŏrĭficus,
perhūmānus, perīdōneus, perinsignis, perjūcundus, permagnus, per-
mīrus (per mihi mirum visum est, Cic.); permŏdestus, permultus,
peropportunus, perparvus, perprŏpinquus, perpulcer (Ter.), perrā-
rus, perstūdiosus, persubtīlis, pertīnax (tĕnax), perurbanus, pervĕ-
tus, and many others. Similarly peropus (Ter.), *very necessary.*

through: pervius, *with a way through.*

præ (1) *very:* from adjectives, but few used before Augustan
age: præaltus, præcălĭdus (Tac.), præclārus, prædensus
(Plin.), prædīves, prædulcis, prædūrus, præfĕrox, præfervĭdus,
præfīdens (Cic.), prægĕlĭdus, prægrandis, prægrăvis, prælongus,
præproperus (Cic.), *over hasty;* prærăpĭdus (Sen., Sil.), prætĕnvis,
prætrĕpĭdus, *in a great flurry;* prævălĭdus, and others.

(2) *before:* (*a*) from adjectives: præcānus (Hor.), *prematurely*
(or *very?*) *gray;* præmātūrus, *ripe before the time;* prænuntius,
foretelling; præpĭlātus, *tipped with a ball in front;* præpostĕrus
(Cic.), *behind before, reversed;* præsāgus, *foretelling.*

(*b*) From substantives: præceps, *headlong* (for præcăpĭts); præ-
nōmen, *the commencing name* (nōmĕn-); præsæpe, *an enclosure*
(sæpi-); præsignis, *distinguished.* (signo-); prævius, *on the way in
front* (via-).

pro *forwards:* proăvus, *a great grandfather;* prōcērus, *tall;*
prōclīvis, *sloping forwards;* prōcurvus, *curved forwards;*
prōfundus, *pouring forth? deep;* progĕner, *a grandson-in-law;* prolixus, *stretched out* (laxo-); promulsis, *a preliminary mead-drinking,*
the first course (mulso-); prōmūtuus, *lent in advance;* prōnĕpos, *a
great grandson;* propălam (adv.), *publicly, open in front?* propătŭlus,
open in front; prōtēlum, *a team (lengthened web?);* prōtervus, *forward in manner, saucy;* protĕnus or protĭnus (adv.), *forthwith.*

re *back:* rĕbellis, *insurgent* (bello-); rĕclīnis, *leaning back;*
rĕcurvus, *curved back* (curvo-); rĕduncus, *hooked back*
(unco-); rĕmŏra, *delay* (mŏra-); rĕpandus, *turned backwards*
(pando-); rĕsīmus, *turned up* (sīmo-); rĕsŏnus, *resounding* (sŏno-);
rĕsŭpīnus, *lying on one's back* (sŭpīno).

sub (*a*) *slightly:* from adjectives: subabsurdus, subagrestis,
subalbĭdus (post-Aug.), sŭbāmārus, subcandĭdus, sub-
crispus, subcrūdus, subdiffĭcĭlis, subdulcis (Plin.), subdūrus, sub-
flāvus (Suet.), subfuscus, subgrandis, subhorrĭdus, sublimpŭdens,

subīnānis, sublīvīdus (Cels.), submolestus, submōrōsus, subnīger, subnūbīlus, subobscūrus, subpallīdus (Cels.), subpar, subrancīdus, subraucus, subrīdīcŭlus, subrŭber, subrŭbīcundus (post-Aug.), subrūfus, subrustīcus, subrŭtīlus (Plin.), subsīmīlis (Cels.), subtristis, subturpīcŭlus, subturpis, and some others.

(*b*) *beneath:* subcăvus, *hollow underneath;* sublāmīna (Cato), *an underplate.*

(*c*) *inferior:* subcentŭrio, *an under-centurion;* subcustos, *an under-keeper;* subprōmus, *an under-butler;* subvădes (old word), *under-sureties.* So Plautus coins Sub-Ballio from the name of a man.

sŭper   *above, exceedingly:* superfĭcies, *the surface* (facie-); supervăcāneus, sŭpervăcuus, *superfluous.*

ve   *bad:* vēcors, *foolish* (cordi-); vēgrandis, *small;* vēmens (vĕhĕmens), *violent* (menti-); vēpallidus (Hor.), *very pale;* vēsānus, *not sane.*

iii. Compounds of words in regular syntactical re- 937 lation to each other.

(A) Attribute+substantive: (*a*) numeral+substantive:

bicessis, *a twenty-as* (bi-, decussi-, or vīginti, assi-); bĭcŏlor, *of two colours;* bicornis, *with two horns* (cornu-); bicorpor (rare), *with two bodies;* bĭdens, *with two teeth* (denti-); biduus, *for two days* (die-); biennis, *lasting for two years;* hence biennium (anno-); bĭfŏris, *with two doors* (fori-); biformis, *with two shapes* (forma-); bifrons, *with two fronts* (fronti-); bifurcus, *with two forks* (furca-); bīga, *a two-yoke chariot* (jŭgo-); bigĕner, *from two stocks* (gĕnus-); bĭjŭgis, *yoked two together* (jŭgo-); bilībris, *weighing two pounds* (librā-); bilingvis, *with two tongues* (lingva-); bimăris, *on two seas* (māri-); bĭmestris, *for two months* (mens-); bīmus, *two years old* (hiem-); bipalmis, *two spans in measure* (palma-); bīpĕdālis, *two foot in measure* (pĕd-); bĭpennis, *a two-edged axe* (penna-); bĭpes, *with two feet;* bīrēmis, *with two oars* (rēmo-); bĭsulcus, *forked* (sulco-); bīvius, *with two roads* (via-); and others with bi-.

centīmănus, *hundred-handed* (manu-); centumvīrālis, *of the hundred men* (vīro-); centuplex, *hundred-fold;* centūria, *a company of a hundred* (vīro-? cf. § 94. 2); centussis, *of a hundred asses* (assi-).

dĕcempĕda, *a ten foot rod* (pĕd-); decemscalmus (Cic.), *ten-tholed* (σκαλμός); dĕcennis, *for ten years* (anno-); dĕcussis, (1) *a cross,* (2) *a ten-as piece* (assi-).

25

ducenti (pl.), *two hundred* (centum); dūcēni, dŭcenties, &c.; dŭplex, *with two folds* (comp. plĭcāre); dupondius, *two pound* piece or sum (pondo-); duumvir, duovir, apparently formed forgetfully from some such expression as duumvirûm collegium.

nundīnæ (pl.), *the ninth day*, i.e. *market day* (novem, die-).

primævus, *in early age* (ævo-); primĭgĕnius, *of the first stock* (gĕnŭs-); primipīlus, *a captain of the first pike* (pĭlo-).

qvadragēnārius, *consisting of forty* (see § 942); qvadragēni, *forty each*; qvadragēsimus, *fortieth*; qvadrangŭlus, *four-cornered* (angŭlo-); qvadrīgæ (pl., also qvadrīga sing.), *a four-horse chariot* (jŭgo-); qvadrĭjŭgus (qvadrĭjugis), *four-yoked*; qvadrimestris, *four months* (mens-); qvadrīmus, qvadrīmulus, *four years old* (hĭĕm-); qvadrin-geni (pl.), *four hundred each*; qvadringenti, *four hundred* (centum, cf. § 794); qvadrŭpĕdans, *going on four feet* (pĕd-); qvadrŭplex, *fourfold* (plĭc-, cf. qvadruplus, § 860); and others similar to the compounds with bi-.

qvincunx, *five-twelfths* (uncia-); qvincuplex, *five-fold* (plĭc-āre); qvinqvefolium, *cinquefoil* (folio-); qvinqvennalis, *happening every five years* (anno-); quinqvennis, *five years old* (anno-); qvinqvevir, *one of five commissioners* (cf. duumvir); and some others.

qvŏtidianus, *daily* (qvoti, die).

sembella, *a half-pound* (sēmi, libella-, Varr. *L.L. 5.* 174); semjădăpertus, *half-opened*; semiambustus, *half-burnt*; semjānīmus (semjānimis), *half-alive* (ănĭma-); semibarbarus, *half-barbarous*; semibos, *half an ox*; semicaper, *half a goat*; semicirculus (Cels.), *a half-circle*; semicoctus, *half-cooked*; semideus, *a demigod*; semjer-mus (semjermis), *half-armed* (armo-); sēmĭfer, *half-beast*; semi-Germanus, *half-German*; semĭhians, *half-open*; semĭhŏmo, *half a man*; semihora, *a half-hour*; semĭlixa, *half-suttler*; semimas, *half a male*; seminec- (no nom.), *half-dead*; seminūdus, *half-naked*; semipĕdalis, *a half-foot* in measure; semipes, *a half-foot*; semiplē-nus, *half-full*; semirŭtus, *half-pulled down*; semisĕnex, *an oldish man*; semisomnus, *half-asleep*; semjustus, *half-burnt*; semivir, *half a man*; semivīvus, *half-alive*; semuncia, *a half-ounce*; sestertius, *containing* two and (*the third*) *a half* (semis tertius).

septemgeminus, *sevenfold*; septentrio, *the constellation of the seven stars?* i.e. Great Bear (cf. § 852); septimontium, *the group of seven hills* (monti-); septuennis, *seven years old* (anno); septunx, *seven-twelfths* (uncia-).

sescuncia, *one and a half ounces*; sesqvihora, *one hour and a half*; sesqvilibra, *a pound and a half*; sesqvimensis, *one month and a half*; sesqvimodius, *a peck and a half*; sesqvioctavus, *of a thing contain-ing a whole and an eighth*; sesqvipedalis, *a foot and a half* in mea-sure; sesqvipes, *a foot and a half*; sesqviplāga (Tac.), *a stroke and a half;* sesqviplex, *once and a half* (cf. plic-āre); sesqvitertius, *containing four-thirds.*

Sedigitus, *six-fingered,* a proper name; sevir (sexvir), *one of six commissioners;* sexangulus, *hexagonal;* sexcenti, *six hundred* (centum); sexcentoplāgus (Plaut.), *a six-hundred-stripe man;* sextadecimarius, *of the sixteenth legion* (sextadecima).

teruncius, *a three-ounce,* i. e. $\frac{1}{4}$ of an as (uncia-); tressis, *a three-as* (tri-, assi-); triceps, *with three heads* (caput-); tricuspis, *with three points* (cuspid-); tridens, *with three teeth* (denti-); trifaux, *having three throats* (fauci-); trifilis (Mart.), *with three threads* (filo-); trigēmīnus, tergeminus, *born three at a birth;* trigemmis, *with three buds* (gemma-); trilingvis, *triple-tongued* (lingva-); trilix, *triple-twilled* (comp. lic-ium); trinoctium, *a space of three nights* (nocti-); triplex, *threefold;* tripūdium, *a thrice stamping* (tri-, pēd-?); triqvetrus, *three-cornered* (comp. qvat-tuor, qvadra); triumviri or tresviri (also triumvir, sing. Suet.), *a board of three;* and others similar to the compounds with bi-.

unānīmus, *of one mind* (ānīmo-); unīcaulis (Plin.), *with one stalk* (caulis-); ūnicŏlor, *self-coloured* (cŏlōr-); unīmānus, *one-handed* (mănu-); unīversus, *all together* (*in one row*, versu-?).

(*b*) Ordinary adjective+substantive: 588

æqvilibris, *of equal balance* (libra-); æqvævus, *contemporary* (ævo-); Ahēnŏbarbus, *Bronzebeard,* name of family in Domitian clan; āhēnīpes, *bronzefoot* (pĕd-); æqvănīmītas (Ter.), *equanimity* (animo-); æqvinoctium, *a time when nights are equal* to days (nocti-); ălīqvis, *some* (lit. *an other one*); angustīclāvius (Suet.), *with a narrow border* (clavo-).

celĕrīpes (Cic.), *swift-footed;* flexipes, *with curling foot* (flexo-); plānipes, *with flat foot* (plāno-); sŏlīdipes, *solid-hoofed* (of horses); tardipes, *slow-footed.*

falsīpărens (Catull.), *having a false father* (falso-, parenti-); flexănīmus, *causing a bent soul,* i. e. *soul swaying* (flexo-); grandævus, *of great age* (grandi-, ævo-); grandiscāpius (Sen.), *big-stemmed* (grandi-, scāpo-); lātīclāvius, *with a broad border;* lēvīsomnus (Lucr.), *light-sleeping* (lēvi-, somno-); longævus, *long-lived;* magnānīmus, *high-souled* (animo-); mediastīnus, *a mid-city dweller* (mĕdio-, αστυ-); mediterrāneus, *midland* (terra-); merīdies, *noon* (medio-? or mero-? Cf. § 160, 10); mīsĕrīcors, *pitiful* (misero-, cord-).

multīcāvus, *with many hollows* (căvo-); multiformis, *with many shapes* (forma-); multīfŏrus (Ov.), *many-holed* (fŏro-); multigĕnus (with -o stem, Lucr.); multīgĕner (? no nom. is found of this consonant stem: Plaut.), *of many sorts* (gĕnŭs-); multijugus, *many-teamed* (jūgo-); multīmŏdus, *in many ways* (mŏdo-); multiplex, *manifold* (plic-āre).

nasturtium (*nose-racked*), *cress* (nāso-, torto-, cf. 110. 2);
plēnǐlūnium, *the time of full moon* (plena-, lūna-); prīvǐlēgium, *an
individual law*, i.e. a law against an individual (priva-, lēg-);
soliferreum (Liv.), a javelin *all of iron* (solo-, ferro-); sollers,
skilful (sōllo-, arti-); versǐcōlor, *with changed colour* (cōlōr-); versipellis, *with changed skin* (pelli-); vīvǐrādix, *a quickset* (rādǐc-).

(*c*) Substantive + substantive: 989

The first substantive is used as attributive:

ærǐpes, *bronze-footed* (æs-). So also ālipes (ala-), angvipes
(angvi-), cornipes (cornu-), palmipes (palma-), sōnipes, *with clatter-
ing foot* (sōno-).

angvimanus, *snake-handed;* aurǐcōrnus, *golden-haired.*

caprifǐcus, *goat-fig;* capricornus, *goat-horned;* ignǐcolor, *fire-
coloured;* juglans, *a walnut* (*Jove's acorn?* Jov-, glandi-, Varr.
L. L. 5. 102); manupretium, *cost of handiwork;* rūpicapra, *a rock-
goat,* i.e. a chamois; tauriformis, *bull-shaped.* Perhaps here belongs
regifugium, § 992.

Diespiter, *Father Day* (pater); Juppǐter, *Father Jove* (Jou-,
pāter).

B. Preposition + substantive: 990

amanuensis (Suet.), *a secretary* (a manu); abnormis, *irregular*
(ab norma); abōrǐgǐnes, *the primitive inhabitants* (ab origine); ab-
sōnus, *out of tune* (ab sono); abstēmius, *temperate* (abs temo? = te-
mēto? or for abstemētius?); absurdus, *out of tune* (cf. § 816. 1. *c*);
āvius, *out of the road* (a viā).

acclīvis, *uphill* (ad clivum), or *sloping upwards,* § 986; accūsāre,
to call to account (ad causam); adæqvāre, *to bring to a level* (ad
æqvum); aggregare, *attach* (ad gregem); admīnǐculum, *a prop* (ad
mānum); adumbrare, *to sketch in outline* (ad umbram, *draw by the
shadow*); adverbium, *a word qualifying a verb* (ad verbum); affīnis, *a relation by marriage,* lit. *a neighbour* (ad fīnes); agnōmen, *an
addition to the name* (ad nomen); apprīme (adv.), *up to the first*
(ad primos).

ambarvales (Fest.), *of going round the fields;* amburbialis (Fest.),
of going round the city; amsěgětes (Fest.), *round the crops?*

antēlūcānus, *before daybreak* (ante lucem); antemērīdianus, *before noon* (ante meridiem); antěpīlani (pl.), *in front of the pikes*
(ante pīla); antesignani (pl.), *in front of the standards* (ante
signa).

circumfŏrāneus, *round the forum* (circum forum); cis-Alpinus, *on this* (Roman) *side the Alps* (cis Alpes); cis-Rhēnanus, *on this side the Rhine* (cis Rhēnum); commŏdus, *with full measure* (com mŏdo); conclāve, *a lock-up room* (com clāve).

declīvis, *down from the slope* (de clīvo, or *sloping down*, § 986); dēcŏlor, *discoloured* (de cŏlōre); dēdĕcŏr, *unseemly*, dēdĕcus, *disgrace* (de dĕcŏre); dēdĕcōrus, *disgraceful* (de dĕcōre); dēflōrescĕre, *to lose flower* (de flōre); deformāre, *to put out of shape*, deformis (de formā); dēgĕnĕr, *degenerate* (de gĕnĕre); dēlīrare, *to rave* (de līrā, i.e. *to stray from the furrow*); demens, *out of one's senses* (de mente); denormāre, *to put out of shape* (de normā); dēvius, *off the road, retired* (de viā). But some of these may belong to § 985.

duodeviginti, *two from twenty*, i.e. *eighteen;* undeviginti, *nineteen* (uno-); &c. See Appendix D.

ēgrĕgius, *selected* (ex grĕge); ēlīmĭnāre, *to turn out of doors* (e līmĭne); exsecrāri, *to banish from sacred rites* (or perhaps only strengthened for sacrāre); extempŏralis, *on the moment* (ex tempore); extermĭnāre, *to banish* (ex terminis); extorris, *banished* (ex terrā); extrīcāre, *to free from perplexities* (ex trīcis); extraordĭnarius, *out of the usual order* (extra ordĭnem). But some of these may belong to § 985.

illăqueāre, *to ensnare* (in laqueum, but perhaps belongs to § 984); illustris, *in the light, clear* (in lūce, cf. § 904); inalpīnus, *dwelling among the Alps* (in Alpibus); inaures (pl.), *eardrops* (in aure); inflammare, *set on fire* (in flammam); informāre, *to put into shape* (in formam); inglŭvies, *the crop* or *maw* (in gŭlā); ingurgĭtare, *to plunge* (in gurgitem); insŏlare (Col.), *to place in the sun* (sol-); insomnium (Plin.), *a vision in sleep.*

Interamna, a city in Umbria *between rivers* (inter amnes); intercŏlumnium, *space between columns* (inter columnas); intercus (adj.), *between skin* and flesh (inter cutem); interlūnium, *time between* visible *moons*, i.e. the time of new moon (inter lunas); intermenstruus, *between two months*, i.e. time of new moon (inter menses, cf. § 762. 1. *b.*); interregnum, *time between two reigns* (inter regna); interrex, *commander between two kings* (inter rēges); intervallum (*space between palisades*), *an interval* (valla or vallos?).

obnoxius, liable *for a wrong, exposed* (ob noxam); obvius, *in the way* (ob viam); opportūnus, *before the port, convenient* (ob portum); opprobrare, *to upbraid for shameful act* (ob probrum); obsecrare, *to beseech* (ob sacra).

perduellis, *a public foe* (per duellum, *in a state of war?*); pĕrĕgrīnus, *a foreigner* (from *peregre, abroad*, per agros); perennis, *all through the year* (per annum); perfĭdus, *breaking through faith*, i.e. *treacherous* (per fĭdem); perjūrus, *oath-breaking* (per jūs); permărīnus, *of passing through the sea* (per mare); pernoctāre, *to spend the night*, pernox, *through the night* (per noctem).

pōmĕrīdianus, *in the afternoon* (post meridiem); pōmœrium, *the space behind the walls* (post mœrum); postlīmĭnium, *a return home* (post līmen); poscænia (pl.), *parts behind the scenes* (post scænam). præcordia (pl.), the diaphragm *in front of the heart* (præ corde). proconsul, *a deputy-consul* (pro consule). So also proprætor, proquæstor.

prŏfanus, *in front of the temple,* i.e. *unconsecrated* (pro fano); prŏfānare, *to dedicate* (see also § 958); prŏfestus, *not-feast* (*before a feast?*); promercalis (post-Aug.), *marketable* (pro merce); prospĕrus, *successful* (pro spe or spes-, *according to hopes,* § 341).

sēcūrus, *careless, secure* (se cūrā); sēdŭlus, *without craft?* hence *trustworthy, diligent* (se dōlo?); sēgrex (no nom.), *apart* (sē grĕge).

subbasilicanus, *a lounger under the halls* (sub basilicā); subdialis (Plin.), *in the open air* (sub die-); subdŏlus, *cunning* (sub dōlo); sublīmis (for sublimĭnis), *up to the lintel* (sub līmen, Ritschl.); sublūcanus, *towards morning* (sub lucem); sublustris, *in faint light* (sub lūcem, *towards dawn?*); subsellium, *a stool under a chair?* (sub sellā); subsignanus, *serving under the standards* (sub signis); subsōlanus, *under or towards? the sun,* i.e. *east* (sub sole or solem); subterraneus, *underground* (sub terra); suburbanus, *near the city* (sub urbem).

suppeditare, *to supply (put under feet,* sub pedes, Corss.); subrū̆mare, *to put to the breast* (sub rūmā); suffōcare, *to strangle* (lit. *under-throat*) (fauci-).

sŭpercĭlium, *eyebrow* (super cilium, *eyelid*).

trans-Alpīnus, *beyond the Alps* (trans Alpes); similarly trans-Danuvianus, transmārīnus, transmontanus, trans-Pādānus, trans-Rhēnanus.

C. Nouns collateral to one another: 991.

duodecim, *twelve* (duo + decem); octodecim, *eighteen* (octo +); quindecim, *fifteen* (quinque +); sedecim, *sixteen* (sex +); undecim, *eleven* (uno- +).

suovetaurilia (pl.), *a sacrifice of a sheep, pig, and bull* (su- + ovi- + tauro-).

D. Object + verb: 992.

ăg-   fūmĭgare (*to make smoke,* hence) *to fumigate* (fumo-); lītĭgare, *to go to law; litīgium, a lawsuit* (līti-); nāvĭgare, *to voyage, nāvĭgium, a voyage, a ship* (nāvi-); rēmex, *a rower,* rēmĭgare, *to row* (rēmo-).

ambŭla-   fūnambŭlus, *a rope-dancer* (fūni-).

cæd-   frātrĭcīda, *a brother-slayer* (fratr-); hŏmĭcīda (for homĭ-nĭcīda), *a man-slayer,* homĭcīdĭum, *manslaughter* (hŏ-mŏn-); parrĭcīda, parrĭcīdĭum, *murderer, murder of an equal, treason* (par-?); lăpĭcīdĭnæ (for lapĭdĭcīdĭnæ), *stone quarries* (lapĭd-); tyran-nĭcīda, *a tyrant-killer,* tyrannĭcīdĭum (tyranno-).

cālā-   nomenclātor, *a name-caller* (nōmĕn-).

căpĭ-   auceps, *a birdcatcher,* hence also aucupĭum, aucupāre, &c. (ăvĭ-); mūnĭceps, *a burgher* (mūni-); muscĭpulum, mus-cipula (f.), *a mousetrap* (mūsi-); partĭceps, *a sharer* (parti-); prin-ceps, *a chief* (prīmo-). So also tertĭceps, qvartĭceps, &c. (Varr.).

cŏl-   Æquĭcŭli, *plain dwellers?* (cf. L. 1. 32); agrĭcŏla, *a farmer* (agro-); agrĭcolatio (Col. for the more usual agrĭcultura), *farming;* amnĭcola, *a dweller on the river* (amni-); Appennĭnĭcŏla (Verg.), *a dweller on the Appennines* (Appennĭno-); cælĭcola, *a dweller in heaven* (cælo-); plēbĭcola, *a people-courter* (plēbi-); Pop-lĭcola (publicola, C. *Rep.* 2. 31), *a people-courter* (populo-); rūrĭcola, *a countryman* (rūs-).

crĕmā-   turicremus, *incense-burning* (tūs-).

crĕpă-   pĭlĭcrĕpus, *a ball-rattler* (pĭla-).

dă-   săcerdos, *a priest* (=sacra dans?).

dĭc-   (§ 629): causĭdĭcus, *a pleader* (causa-); falsĭdĭcus, *false speaking* (falso-); fātĭdĭcus, *prophetic* (fato-); jūdex, *a law declarer,* judĭcāre, judĭcĭum (jus-); jurĭdĭcus, *administering justice* (jus-); svavĭdicus, *speaking sweet things* (svavi-); vērĭdĭcus, *truth-speaking* (vero-); vindĭcare, *claim by challenge?* (=vim dīcĕre).

făcĭ-   ædĭfĭcare, *to build a house,* ædĭfĭcĭum, *a house-building,* i.e. *a house* (ædi-); auctĭfĭcus (Lucr.), *growth-causing* (auctu-); dēlēnĭfĭcus (Plaut. &c.), *cajoling* (dēlēnīre); furtĭfĭcus (Plaut.), *theft-committing* (furto-); grātĭfĭcari (cf. § 12. 6. 4), *to be obliging* (grāto-); hŏnōrĭfĭcus, *complimentary* (hŏnŏs-); horrĭfĭcus, *shudder-causing* (horre-); lānĭfĭcus (Tib., Mart.), *woolmaking* (lāna-); luctĭfĭcus, *woeful* (luctu-); magnĭfĭcus, *magnificent* (magno-); mellĭ-ficare, *to make honey* (mell-); mūnĭfĭcus, *present-making* (mūni-); mīrĭfĭcus, *doing strange things* (mīro-); nīdĭfĭcare, *to make nests* (nīdo-); ŏpĭfex, *workman* (ŏp-us-); pācĭfĭcus, *peace-making* (pāci-); pontĭfex, *bridge-maker* (ponti-); sacrĭfĭcĭum, *a sacrifice* (sacro-); saxĭfĭcus, *petrifying* (saxo-); signĭfĭcare, *make signs, show* (signo-); tābĭfĭcus, *wasting* (tābi-); terrĭfĭcus, *terrifying* (terre-); vēlĭfĭcari, *make sail, voyage* (vēlo-); vĕnēfĭcus (for vĕnēnĭfĭcus), *poison-making* (vĕnēno-); versĭfĭcare, *to make verses* (versu-); vulnĭfĭcus, *wound-ing* (vuln-ŭs-); and others.

fĕr-   ærĭfer, *bronze-bearing* (æs-); æstĭfer, *heat-bringing* (æstu-);

āqvīlīfer (Cæs.), *eagle-bearing* (āqvīla-); astrīfer, *star-bearing* (astro-); bācīfer, *berry-bearing* (bacca-); bīpennīfer (Ov.), *carrying a two-headed axe* (bipenni-); cādūcīfer (Ov., for caduceifer), *carrying a herald's staff* (caduceo-); cælīfer, *heaven-bearing* (cælo-); fātīfer, *death-bringing* (fāto-); flabellīfera (Plaut.), *a fan-bearer* (flabello-); horrīfer, *shudder-bringing* (horre-); imbrīfer, *rain-bringing* (imbri-); ōdōrīfer, *scent-bearing* (ōdōs-); sensīfer (Lucr.), *causing sensation* (sensu-); vēnēnīfer (Ov.), *poison-bearing* (vēnēno-); vocīfērarī, *to shout* (vōci-); and many others.

fla-   cīnīflo (Hor.), *an ash-blower?* in some toilet operation? (cīnīs-).

fōdī-   argentifōdīna, *a silver-mine* (argento-); aurifōdīna, *a gold-mine* (auro-).

frāg-   calcīfrāga, *a chalk-crushing* herb (calci-); fœdifragus (for fœderifragus), *league-breaking* (fœdus-); fluctīfrāgus (Lucr.), *wave-breaking* (fluctu-); naufrāgus, *shipwrecked* (nāvi-); saxīfrāgus, *stone-crushing* (saxo-).

    dentifrangibulum, *tooth-cracker;* nucifrangibula (pl.), *nut-crackers* (see § 861).

fraudā-   sociofraudus (Plaut.), *mate-cheating* (sōcio-).

frīcā-   dentifrīcium, *tooth-powder* (denti-).

fūgī-   hērīfūga (m., Catull.), *lord-flying* (hero-); lūcifūgus, *shunning light* (lūci-).

gĕr-   ālīger, *winged* (āla-); armīger, *arm-wearing* (armo-); augur, *bird-manager?* *soothsayer* (āvi-); aurīger, *gold-wearing* (auro-); barbīger (Lucr.), *beard-wearing* (barba-); bellīger, *warring* (bello-); clāvīger, *club-wearing* (clāvo-); famīgĕr-ātor (Plaut.), *a tale-bearer,* famīgĕrātio, *tale-bearing* (fāma-); lānīger, *wool-wearing* (lāna-); mōrīgĕrus, *complaisant* (mōs-); sandālīgĕr-ūlæ (pl., Plaut.), *slipper-carriers* (sandālo-); sētīger, *hairy* (sēta-); spūmīger, *foaming* (spūma-); sqvāmīger, *scaly* (squāma-); and others.

lĕg-   āqvilex, *water-collector?* hence *conduit-master* (āqva-); dentīlĕgus (Plaut.), *picking up teeth* (denti-); flōrīlĕgus (Ov.), *flower-cutting* (flōs-); frūgīlĕgus (Ov.), *fruit-picking* (frūg-); sacrīlĕgus, *stealer of sacred things* (sacro-); sortīlĕgus, *lot-picker,* hence *soothsayer* (sorti-); spīcīlegium (Varr.), *gleaning* (spīca-).

lōqv-   grandīlōqvus, *talking big* (grandi-); largiloqvus, magniloqvus, mendācilōqvus, stultiloqvus, suaviloqvus, vaniloqvus; paucīlōqvium, *little-speaking.*

lustrā-   armilustrium, *purification of arms* (arma-); tubilustrium, *purification of trumpets* (tuba-).

mulge-   caprimulgus, *goat-milker* (capra-).

pără- ŏpĭpărus, *help-providing* (ŏpĭ-).

părĭ- frugĭpărus (Lucr.), *fruit-producing* (frūg-); puerpĕra, puerperium, *child-bearing* (puĕro-).

pend- libripens, *balance-hanger*, i.e. *a scalesman* (libra-); stipendium (for stipipendium), *pay* (stĭp-).

pĕt- agripeta (Cic.), *land-seeker* (agro-); heredipeta (Petr.), *inheritance-seeker* (heredio-).

pŭg- solipuga, *sole-pricker?* a venomous snake (sŏlo-).

răpĭ- pinnirăpus, *a feather-snatcher* (pinna-). (In Plautus bustirăpus, *body-snatcher*, is probably a hasty compound for ex busto rapĕre, or bustum is taken as *a burnt body*.)

rŭp- usurpare, *break a user*, hence *assert a right to*, *make use of*, &c. (usum ru*m*pere. So Key, *Phil. Soc. Trans.* 1855, p. 96).

să- vitisător, *vine-planter* (viti-).

scalp- dentiscalpium, *toothpick* (denti-).

sĕcă- fænisex, *hay-cutter* (fæno-).

sĕqv- pĕdĭsĕqvus, *foot-following*, i.e. an attendant (pĕd-).

sŏn- ærĭsŏnus, *bronze-sounding* (æs-); horrĭsŏnus, *shudder-sounding* (horr-, stem of horr-e-re, horr-or); luctĭsonus (Ov.), *doleful* (luctu-).

spĕcĭ- auspex, *bird-viewer* (ăvi-); extispex, *entrail-viewer* (exto-); hăruspex, *gut-viewer?* (comp. hilla for hirula).

stătŭ- justĭtium, *suspension of law courts* (jūs-); solstĭtium, *sun-staying*, i.e. time when the sun is stayed (sōl-).

stern- lectisternium, *couch-covering* (lecto-); sellisternium, *chair-covering* (sella-), two religious ceremonies.

sŭg- sangvisūga, *a bloodsucker*, *leech* (sangvĕn-).

tĕnĕ- arcĭtenens, *bow-holding* (arcu-).

tĕrĕ- ferrĭtĕrus, ferritĕrium (Plaut.), *iron-rubber*, &c.

tue- ædĭtuus, *a sacristan* (ædi-). First used in Varro's time for older æditumus (Varr. *R.R.* I. 2. I). Lucr. (6. 1275) has ædituentes.

versa- tergiversari, *turn one's back*, *shuffle* (tergo-).

vŏră- carnĭvŏrus, *flesh-eating* (carŏn-).

E. Oblique predicate+verb: 993

æqvīpĕrāre, *to make equal* (æquo-); amplīfĭcāre, *to enlarge*
(amplo-); ludĭfĭcāre, *to make game of* (ludo-); mītĭfĭcāre, *to make
mild* (mīti-); pūrĭfĭcare, *purify* (pūro-).

So perhaps mītĭgare (mitem agere?); lēvĭgare, *make smooth*
(lēvi-); purgare, *cleanse* (puro-).

Here may be put the half-compounds (§ 300) with facere or 994
fĭerī. (The quantity of the e is here marked' only when proof
exists,' and in that case the author's name is added. Ritschl. *Opusc.*
II. 618 sqq. lays down the rule that in the *Scenic* poets the e is long
in verbs with long penult, short in verbs with short penult.)

allĭce-; āre-; cālĕ-, concale-, percălĕ- (Plaut., Lucr. &c. also
cal-, excal-); cande-, excande-; condŏce-; dome- (Petr.); expergĕ-
(Plaut., Lucr.); ferve-, confervē- (Lucr.), deferve-, inferve-, per-
ferve-, sufferve-; frīge-, perfrīgē- (Plaut.); lăbĕ- (Ter.. Ov.), conlăbē-
(Lucr.); līqvĕ- (Verg., Ov.), līqvē- (Lucr., Catull., Ov.), colliqve-,
inliqve-; mădĕ- (Plaut., Verg., &c.), permădĕ- (Plaut.); commŏnĕ-
(Plaut.); obsŏle-; ŏl-; pătĕ- (Plaut., Verg., Ov., &c.), pătē- (Lucr.);
păvĕ- (Ov., Sen.), perpăvē- (Plaut.); pingve- (Plin.); pŭtrĕ- (Ov.),
pŭtrē- (Plaut., Lucr., for which Ritschl pŭtē-); quăte- (Auct. *Ep.
ad Brut.*); rārĕ- (Lucr.); rŭbĕ- (Ov.); stŭpĕ- (Verg., Ov., &c.),
obstŭpē- (Ter., but see edd.); assue-, consue-, desue-, mansue-;
contābē- (Plaut.); tĕpĕ- (Catull., Verg., Hor.), tĕpē- (Catull.);
perterre-; tīmĕ- (Lucr.), pertīmĕ- (Pacuv.); torre- (Col.); trĕmĕ-
(Prop., Verg., Ov., &c.); tŭmĕ- (Prop., Ov.); văcē- (Lucr.),
văcue- (Cic., Nep.).

Compare also deterrĭfĭcus, horrĭfĭcus, terrĭfĭcus, § 992.

cĭnĕfactus (Lucr.) is a bold compound from cĭnĭs- (which would
give cĭnĕrĭfactum), as if there were a verb cĭnēre, *to be ashy.* Similar
non-existent verbs are presumed in dome-, rare-, vace-, vacue- (above).
In allice-, condoce-, dome-, experge-, commone-, quate-, perterre-,
torre-, a neuter signification or passive infinitive appears to be presumed. Either these verbs are formed on a false analogy, or they
may be compared with such phrases as "es lässt sich begreifen,"
"je me suis senti entraîner."

The incompleteness of the composition is seen in the separation
of the parts in ferve bene facit (Cato), perferve ita fit, consul quoque faciunt, excande me fecerunt (all in Varr. *R. R.*), and facit are,
rareqve facit (Lucr.); perhaps in facit putre (Varr. *R. R.* 1. 41. 2).

For fabrefactus see § 997.

Here also may be put the compounds qvīvis, qvantusvis; qvīlĭ- 995
bet, qvantuslĭbet, *what you please, as great as you please.* The
pronoun retains its inflexions, but is treated syntactically, as if it
were expressing an absolute name or quality, and were not really
an object (to vīs) or oblique predicate.

F. Subject+verb:

alienigena (ăllēnĭgĕnus, Val. Fl.), *born of foreigners* (alieno gen-
itus); angvigena, *snake-born;* cæligena (f.), *heaven-born;* caprigenus,
of goat stock; terrigena, *earth-born;* vitigenus, *vine-produced* (vĭti-).
See also § 826.
(Perhaps these should be referred to A, § 988.)
būcĭna, *an ox-horn trumpet* (bos canit; but cf. 997, can-); gal-
licĭnium, *time of cockcrowing* (gallus canit); gelicidium (Cat., Varr.,
Col.), *hoarfrost* (gelu cadit); poplifugium, *people's flight* (pŏpulus
fugit); rēgĭfugium, *king's flight* (rex fugit); rēgĭfĭcus, *royal* (rex
facit); stilllcĭdium, *a dripping* (stilla cadit).

G. Oblique case, or adjective used adverbially, + verb.
The construction presumed is often very loose.

ăg-	jurgāre, *to dispute, scold,* jurgium, *altercation, scolding* (jure ago).
căpĭ-	manceps, *a purchaser;* mancĭpium, *a chattel* (manu capio); nuncŭpare, *to declare* (nomine capio?).
căn-	cornicen, *hornblower* (cornu cano); fĭdĭcen, fidĭcĭna, *a player on the strings* (fĭdĭbus cano); lĭtĭcen, *a trumpeter* (lituo cano); oscen, *a singing* bird (ōre, stem ŏs-, cano); tĭbĭcen, tĭbĭcĭna, *a flute player* (tibiā cano); tŭbĭcen, *a trumpeter* (tŭbā cano).
dă-	mandāre, *commit to a person's charge* (in manum dăre?). Compare crēdere, *trust;* ven-dĕre, *sell* (venum dare).
dĭc-	mălĕdĭcus, *scurrilous* (male dico).
făcĭ-	artifex, *a handicraftsman* (arte facio); bĕnĕficus, *kind* (bene facio); carnĭfex, *a butcher* (carne facio; comp. vĭtŭlā facio, Verg.); mălĕfĭcus, *unkind* (male facio). Here belongs fabrefacere, *to make in workmanlike fashion;* comp. also infabre factus.
fĭd-	used passively: bifĭdus, *cleft in two* (bis findor); multĭ- fĭdus, *with many clefts* (multum findor); quadrĭfĭdus, *four-cleft;* trĭfĭdus, *three-cleft.* benignus, *well-born, liberal;* malignus, *ill-born, stingy* (bene, male, genitus); comp. § 826.
flu-	largifluus, *copious;* septemfluus, *seven-streamed.*
gĕn-	primigenus (Lucr.), primigenius (Varr.), *first-born, pri- mitive* (primus gignor).
părĭ-	prīmĭpăra, *bearing for the first time* (primum pario).
pŏtes-	bellĭpŏtens, *powerful in war* (bello possum); omnĭpŏtens, *all-powerful,* multĭpŏtens, *very powerful* (omnia, multum possum); pennĭpŏtens (Lucr.), *winged* (pennis potens).

sŏnă-   armĭsonus (Verg.), *arm-resounding* (armo-); fluctĭsŏnus (Sil.), *wave-resounding* (fluctu-); fluentĭsŏnus (Catull.), *flood-resounding* (fluento-); raucĭsŏnus (Catull.), *hoarse-sounding* (rauco-); undisonus, *wave-sounding* (undis).

sulcă-   bĭsulcus, *cloven-footed* (i.e. cleft in two by a furrow).

văgă-   montĭvăgus, *wandering on the mountains* (monte văgor); nĕmŏrĭvăgus (Catull.), *wandering in thickets* (in nemoribus vagor); noctĭvăgus, *wandering by night* (noctu vagor); sōlĭvăgus, *wandering alone* (solus vagor).

vŏl-   bĕnĕvŏlus, *well-wishing;* mălĕvŏlus, *ill-wishing* (bene, male, volo).

volă-   altĭvŏlus, *flying on high* (alte volo); vēlĭvŏlus, *sail-flying* (vēlīs volat).

So Adverb (or oblique case) + Participle: 998

alticinctus, *girt-high;* mănĭfestus, *hand-struck?* (cf. § 704); sacrosanctus, *consecrated* (perhaps this belongs to spurious compounds), sollĭcĭtus, *anxious,* lit. *all-excited* (sollo-, ciēre, cf. § 759).

bipartitus, tripartitus, qvadripartitus, *divided into two, three, four* (bis, tris = ter, qvadri = qvatvor, § 184).

CHAPTER XII.

INTERJECTIONS.

INTERJECTIONS may be divided into two classes: (1) imita- 999
tions of sounds, (2) abbreviated sentences or mutilated words.

1. Imitations of sounds. (The probable Greek and English modes of representing the same or similar sounds will be added.)

a or ah } in warning or sorrow. Comp. ă, Engl. *ah!* Germ. *ach.*
or ha }

ējă (heia) in encouragement. Comp. εἶα, Engl. *hey.*

vah   in surprise or indignation. Comp. ὀᾶ.

o   various. Comp. ὤ, ὦ, Engl. *oh!*

iō   a shout in excitement. Comp. ἰου or ἰοῦ, Engl. *yoho!*

ĕhŏ or oho a cry of distress. Comp. Engl. *Ho!* In Terence some-
           times with dum appended.

pro or proh in surprise or indignation; especially in phrases, pro Di
           immortales, &c. Perhaps this is not imitative of a natu-
           ral sound, but is a word.

euoe   for εὐοῖ: a cry in Bacchic rites.

au   in fear and warning.

fu or phui expression of disgust. Plaut. *Most.* 39, *Pseud.* 1294.
           Comp. φεῦ (?), Engl. *fie! faw! foh!* Germ. *pfui.*

phy   in impatience at unnecessary explanation. Ter. *Ad.* 412.
           Probably same as last. Comp. Engl. *pooh.*

hui   various. Perhaps a whistle, which is written in Engl.
           whew.

babæ)
papæ }   in wonder and delight: a quivering of the lips. Perhaps
           imitative of Greek βαβαί, πόποι, παπαῖ. Comp. Herm.
           on *Soph. Phiioct.* 746.

hahahæ   *Laughing.* Comp. ᾰ, ᾱ, Engl. *Haha.*

væ   in grief and anger. Represents a wail. Comp. οὐαί, in
           Alexandrine and later writers, perhaps imitation of the
           Latin; Germ. *weh,* Engl. *woe.* Compare also vah and
           the verb vāgīre.

ŏhē   in annoyance, especially when a person is *sated;* probably
           between a groan and a grunt. Comp. Engl. *ugh.*

hei or ei in grief. It represents a sigh. Comp. ἒ ἔ or ἓ ἓ or ἐή,
           and perhaps αἰαῖ, Engl. *heigh.*

ehem or)
hem or em } the sound of clearing the throat? Comp. Engl. *hem,*
           ahem. In Plautus em is often found in MSS. for en.

st   to command silence. The corresponding sound in
           English, *hist,* is used to attract attention; and *sh, hush* to
           command silence.

attat or atat or } in surprise, vexation, fear, &c.: smacking of the
rarely attatæ   }   tongue against the teeth. Comp. ἀτταταῖ, ἀττα-
           ταταῖ, ὀτοτοτοῖ, Engl. *tut tut.*

heus   a noise to attract attention: a combined whistle and hiss.
           Comp. Engl. *whisht!* and perhaps Germ. *heisa* (= Engl.
           huzza).

bombax   apparently from βομβάξ: expression of wonder.

| euax | a cry of joy. Comp. εὐᾶ, εὐάζειν, and perhaps Germ. *juchhe.* |
| taxtax | the sound of blows. Comp. Engl. *thwack.* |

2. Abbreviated sentences or mutilated words. The following are probably such:

(*a*) Latin:

en	in Plaut. usually **em**, *lo!*
ecce	*lo here!* The **ce** is perhaps the demonstrative particle, cf. § 374. In the comic poets it is frequently combined with the accusative (as if it were equivalent to *see*) of the pronouns **is** and **ille**; **eccum, eccam, eccos, eccas, ecca**; **eccillum, eccillam, eccillut**; once also **eccistam.**
eccere	used similarly to English *there!*

mehercules, mehercule, me-⎱ abbreviations of **me Hercules juvet.**
hercle, hercules, hercle ⎰

medius fidius for **me deus Fidius juvet**, *so help me* the God of Faith.

ecastor	perhaps for **en Castor.**
pol	for **Pollux.**
edepol	said by Roman grammarians to be for **per ædem Pollucis.**
sodes	*prythee.* Said by Cicero (*Or.* 45) to be for **si audes** (cf. Wagner ad Pl. *Aul.* 46).

(*b*) Borrowed from the Greek:

age	*come!* for ἄγε. It is sometimes followed by **dum.**
ăpăge	*off!* for ἄπαγε.
euge	for εὖγε.
eugipæ	originally for εὖγε παῖ?

APPENDICES.

APPENDIX A.

i. THE following Extracts are made in order to give a fuller exposition of some points of Phonetics, and to furnish physiological explanations of some of the phenomena stated in Book 1.

The books chiefly quoted from are, as I believe, the best on the subject, viz.: A. Melville Bell's *Principles of Speech*, London, new edt. 1863. *Visible Speech*, London, 1867. A. J. Ellis *on Early English Pronunciation*, Part I. 1869; Part II. 1869. These books contain much more that is illustrative but not so easily quotable. The *Visible Speech* contains Bell's latest views, which in some points are different from those given in the *Principles*.

The notation of the sounds has been in some cases modified, to make the account intelligible to readers who are not familiar with Bell's or Ellis' notation. (In the *Principles*, Bell uses 'articulations' for 'consonants.' I have substituted the latter term as better known.) I have also occasionally made omissions and transpositions for the sake of brevity and clearness, but have not cared to remove all repetition.

On Nasals. (Comp. § 6.)

ii. ' The letters **m, n, ng** have the same oral positions as **b, d, g** ' but the inner end of the nasal passages is uncovered by the soft ' palate, and while the breath is shut in by the mouth, it escapes ' freely through the nostrils. .

' Though the nasals gain but little percussive audibility by the ' cessation of contact, yet they cannot, any more than the perfectly ' obstructive consonants, be considered finished until the oral organs ' are separated. There is breath within the mouth pressing against ' the conjoined organs, and slightly distending the pharynx, as well ' as a free current in the nostrils: and though the voice may be ' perfectly finished by merely closing the glottis, the consonant ' would be imperfect, if the breath within the mouth were not ' allowed to escape. There is thus a slight, but very slight, effect of ' percussion heard on the organic separation as in *come, sun, tongue,* ' &c.; and when a vowel follows the articulation, this slight pha-

26

'ryngal expression gives a sharpness and closeness of connexion
'to the combination, which would be wanting, if the voice were
'stopped in the glottis before the organic disjunction.

'In finishing these nasal elements, the soft palate must not be
'allowed to cover the nares before the articulating organs are sepa-
'rated; for a momentary closure will convert **m**, **n**, **ng** into
'**b, d, g**. A tendency to compress the breath in this way is especi-
'ally felt in finishing **ng**, in the formation of which the tongue and
'soft palate are already in contact, and so in the position for **g**,
'to which **ng** is consequently more easily convertible than the other
'nasals are to their corresponding shut letters.

'The English nasals are all *voiced* consonants.

iii. 'The French has a series of seminasal sounds represented
'by **an, en, in, on, un** and by various other literal combinations.
'In forming these the soft palate is depressed sufficiently to open
'the nasal passages but not so much as, by contact with the tongue,
'to obstruct the passage into the mouth. Thus having an oral
'as well as a nasal passage they are capable of being affected by
'changes in the position of the mouth. There are four recognized
'varieties of them. The English **ng** on the contrary, has always
'a uniform sound, it is incapable of any change of vowel quality.'
M. Bell, *Principles*, pp. 49, 50, 39.

iv. It may here be noted that **n** and **l** are in several languages
palatalised. Thus Ital. **gl**, Spanish **ll**, Portug. **lh**, all are equal,
or nearly so, to **ly**: French and Ital. **gn**, Span. **nn** (old) now **ñ**,
Portug. **nh** are all equal or nearly equal to **ny**. (Ellis, p. 199.
Brücke, p. 70.)

On held or sustained Consonants.

v. 'The nasal elements and also the letter **l**, are often called
'*semivowels* because they are perfectly sonorous and capable of
'separate and prolonged enunciation like vowels. These semi-
'vowels may each separately form a syllable; **l** and **n** often do so
'in English as in *castle, fasten*, &c.; and **m** has a similar syllabic
'effect in *rhythm, chasm, prism*, &c. In the pronunciation of such
'words care must be taken that no vowel sound is heard between
'the **m** and the preceding consonant.

'The letters of this class are often called *liquids* because they
'flow into other articulations, and seem to be absorbed by them.
'This peculiar quality might perhaps be better understood, were
'we to call it *transparency;* they shew through them the nature of
'proximate consonants. When the liquids occur before voiceless

''consonants, they are so short as scarcely to add any appreciable
'quantity to the syllable; *wilt, bent, brink, lamp,* &c. have thus but
'very little more duration than *wit, bet, brick, lap,* &c. When these
'letters however come before voiced consonants, they form the
'longest syllables in the language, as in *willed, bend, tongues, lambs,*
'*film, helm* which have as long quantity as any syllables containing
'the same vowels can have. The liquids have the same quantity as
'other varied consonants before vowels. They are however longer
'when final.' M. Bell, *Principles,* pp. 167, 8.

On the length of Consonants.

vi. 'Among the consonants there are various degrees of
'quantity. The vocal articulations are essentially longer than the
'non-vocal, but in each class there are varieties.

'Thus: The breath obstructives **p, t, k** are the shortest.

'The breath continuous elements **f, th, s, sh** are the next longer.

'The shut voice consonants **b, d, g** are the next in length.

'The close continuous voice consonants **v, th, z, zh** (i.e. French
'j) are longer still.

'The open continuous voice consonants or liquids **l, m, n, ng**
'are the longest simple consonants.

'**wh, w, y** and **r** are not included because these consonants do not
'occur after vowels, but only as initials in English; and all initial
'letters, whether voice or breath, are alike in quantity.' M. Bell,
Principles, p. 86.

On sharp and flat Consonants. (Comp. § 2.)

vii. Brücke's view is as follows, as stated by v. Raumer:

'The difference between the soft and hard consonants consists
'in this, that the voice sounds with the former and not with the
'latter. When we speak aloud, the voice must actually sound in
'pronouncing the soft consonants: in whispering, the sound of the
'vocal chords falls away altogether, but the place of this is supplied
'in the case of the soft consonants by a rustling in the larynx.' Cf.
Brücke, p. 55. See von Raumer's criticism (*Gesam. Schriften.* p.
450 sq.).

Mr Bell's account is as follows: 'When the glottis is contracted
'to a narrow chink the breath in passing sets the edges of the
'orifice, i.e. the vocal ligaments, in vibration, and creates sonorous
'voice. When the glottis is open, and the supraglottal passage is

' contracted, the breath creates in the latter the non-sonorous rust-
' ling or friction, which is called "whisper." The organic effect
' of the open glottis will be understood by whispering a voiced con-
' sonant, such as **v**. The result is clearly different from the sound
' of the non-vocal consonant of corresponding oral formation, **f**.
' For the former, the fricativeness of the breath is audible from the
' throat, through the oral configuration; for the latter, the breath
' friction is audible only from the lip.' *Visible Speech*, p. 46.

In Lower Germany usually, as in England always, the soft
(flat) consonants are accompanied (in speaking aloud) with the
sound of the voice. But in far the greater part of Germany,
i. e. over almost the whole of South and Mid-Germany, the regular
pronunciation of the soft consonants is, according to von Raumer,
unattended by the faintest sound of the voice. Again, ' many per-
' sons accompany some soft consonants with the sound of the voice,
' and pronounce others without; e.g. some give the sound of the
' voice to **w**, but not to **s**; others to **w** and **s**, but not to soft
' mutes; others again, and this is frequent, to the nasals, but not to
' other consonants.' Von Raumer mentions, that a highly educated
man of his acquaintance, who never voiced the soft consonants,
yet found it inconceivable how people could confuse together such
different sounds as the soft and hard consonants. (p. 454.)   See
also Max Müller, *Lectures*, II. pp. 118, 131.

On the imperfect vocality of Consonants.

viii.   ' All consonants being merely transitional sounds in ordi-
' nary utterance, the voice is not equally sustained from the beginning
' to the end of the vocalized articulation.   In pronouncing the word
' *leave* for instance the vocality of the **v** is clearly heard only at the
' junction of that element with the syllabic sound, the vowel; and
' the initially voiced **v** sinks imperceptibly into its voiceless corre-
' spondent **f**—as if the word were written *leavf*.   This effect does
' not require to be written, as it is inherent in the implied transi-
' tional character of the consonant.

' When a voiced consonant comes before a non-vocal element,
' the murmur of the vocal letter is heard only at the instant of its
' junction with the preceding vowel, and immediately lost in the
' transition to the next element, as in the words *art, purse, else, felt,*
' *lance, cant, lamp, ink,* &c.

' Foreigners in pronouncing English words generally fail to give
' the requisite abruptness to these "liquids" before voiceless conso-
' nants.

'The preceding observations shew that the absolute quantity
'of voice in a vocal consonant depends on the nature of the follow-
'ing element. Five degrees of absolute quantity in the sound of *l*
'will be recognised in the following combinations; arranged from
'shortest to longest: *felt, health, fell'd, realm, fell.*' M. Bell,
Visible Speech, p. 67.

ix. In French such words as *stable, schisme* are not pronounced as in English with the final voiced consonant held or prolonged, but either with the faintest vowel murmur following, thus
making **l, m** initial and consequently shortening the sound, or with
an entire remission of the vocal murmur, i. e. with **l, m** whispered.
See Ellis, p. 52.

x. The same imperfect vocality is noticeable particularly in a
comparison of Icelandic with English **s**.

'**s** is always (in Icelandic) intentionally **s** and never **z**, but **z** is
'sometimes generated, although it is not recognized. Thus **s** final
'after **l, n**, and perhaps in other cases, generates an intermediate **z**.
'For example if we compare *eins, sins* with English *stains, scenes*
'we should see that the difference of the terminations arises from the
'**s** in Icelandic being intentional and predominant, but the **z** gene-
'rated and therefore lightly touched, while in English the **z** is inten-
'tional and predominant, and although the **s** is often prolonged and
'in the church singing of charity children not unfrequently pain-
'fully hissed, it is yet merely generated by a careless relaxation of
'the voice, and its very existence is unknown to many speakers.
'I found also that there was an unacknowledged tendency to pro-
'nounce **s** final after long vowels in the same way.' Ellis, p. 547.

This is only in accordance with English (and Icelandic) habits
of modifying the second consonant to suit the preceding sound.
Latin took the opposite course and expelled **n** when preceding **s**, or
s when preceding **m** or **n**, clearly because **s** was sharp and **m** or **n**
flat (see §§ 191, 2. 193).

On diphthongs. (Comp. § 20.)

xi. 'The common definition of a diphthong "a complexion or
'*coupling of vowels* when the two letters send forth a joint sound,
'so as in one syllable both sounds be heard" (Ben Jonson), is quite
'defective if not absolutely erroneous. Between a coupling of
'sounds and a diphthongal sound the interval is as wide as between
'a mechanical mixture and a chemical combination. The two
'marks of sound which connote a diphthong are neither of them
'sounded, they do but indicate the two limits, from one of which to
'the other the voice passes continuously in uttering the diphthong;

' it is the filling up of the interval so symbolised which constitutes
' the diphthongal sound and accordingly it is not every two vowel
' symbols which can be conjoined to represent a diphthong, but only
' such two as admit of a continuous uninterrupted passage of the
' breath from one limit to the other. A diphthong is a sound of an
' essentially different nature from a vowel or any combination of
' vowels. However rapidly two vowels are made to succeed each
' other they will remain two vowels still and never blend into a
' diphthong. The nearest analogue to the diphthong is the slur in
' vocal music. In general (I do not say always), a diphthong cannot
' be reversed as such; i.e. in the act of reversal it becomes a vowel
' syllable.' J. J. Sylvester, *Laws of verse* (Lond. 1870), p. 50.

A similar definition of a diphthong is found in Brücke, p. 27. See
also M. Bell, *Visible Speech*, p. 78. Ellis, p. 51. Comp. Rumpelt,
Deutsche Gram., p. 33.

xii. ' The general rule for the stress upon the elements of diph-
' thongs, is that it falls upon the first, but this rule is occasionally
' violated. Thus in many combinations with initial i, u the stress
' falls on the second element, in which case, according to some
' writers, the first element falls into y, w, which, however, others
' deny. In iu, ui the stress is properly on the first element. But
' in Italian *chiaro*, *ghiaccio* the i is touched quite lightly, and is almost
' evanescent, so that it would generally be thought enough to denote
' the chi, ghi as palatalised k, g.' Ellis, p. 418.

' There are three principal vowels a, i, u, whence are formed six
' principal diphthongs, each consisting of two vowels connected by a
' gliding sound arising from the continuance of the voice-sound while
' the organs of speech pass from the positions due to one vowel
' to that due to the other. It is this glide which gives the diphthongal
' character. The first element or vowel is usually brief, but it
' generally receives the accent, and it may be long. The second
' element is generally long and occasionally accented. These six
' diphthongs are ai, au, ui, iu, ia, ua. The two first, ai, au, degene-
' rate into the intermediate vowels e, o in various shades, as may be
' satisfactorily proved historically. The two next, ui, iu, generate
' the peculiar middle vowels French eu, u; and the two last
' cause the evolution of the consonants y, w. Of these the diph-
' thongs ui, iu are the most unstable. The pure sound of the
' first occurs in the French oui as now pronounced; it is however
' used as a dissyllable by Moliere[1] and must therefore have been pro-
' nounced as the present French *ouï*. The pure sound of the second,
' iu, is common in Italian as *più*. In both ui, iu, the stress may be

[1] Diez's *Etymological Dictionary*, sub voce. The older *oil* was dissyllabic, from *hoc illud*. (Ellis.)

'laid on either element, and in both the attempt may be made to fuse
'the 'diphthong into a single sound. When the stress falls on the
'second element, an Englishman (but not a Welshman) says *we*,
'*you*. When the organs of speech endeavour to produce a single
'sound, it differs from either, and results in French **eu**, **u** in various
'shades.' Ellis, *Philolog. Soc. Trans.* 1867. *Suppl.* p. 58.

On English r.

xiii. The English pronunciation of **r** is so peculiar, and its effect
on vowels so great that an English student studying vowel sounds
is liable to fall into many mistakes if he does not bear it constantly
in mind. The following passages will explain the matter. The
vowels will be denoted by the numbers in the list on p. 9.

'**R** is produced when the breath is directed over the upturned tip
'of the tongue so as to cause some degree of lingual vibration. In
'order to effect this, the breath must be obstructed at all other
'points, that the force of the stream may be concentrated on the
'tip; and the tongue must be held loosely to enable it to vibrate
'readily. The vibration may be produced in every degree from the
'soft tremor of the English r, which merely vibrates the *edge* of the
'tongue, to the harsh rolling of the Spanish **rr**, which shakes the
'whole organ. The trilled or strongly vibrated **r** is never used in
'English.

'Between vowels as in *merit* the **r** is strongest, but it has only a
'momentary tremor; for consonants between vowels are always
'short in English.

'**r** *initial* has the consonantal vibration, but only of the edge of
'the tongue.

'Final **r** is the 3rd vowel. When the tongue is raised just
'enough to mould the passing stream of air, but not yield to it, we
'have the condition for the final **r**. The aperture for the emission
'of the voice is so free that the vowel quality of the sound is
'scarcely, if at all, affected. When the succeeding word however
'begins with a vowel, the final **r** has generally the effect of medial
'**r**, to avoid hiatus, as in *her own, or else*, &c.' M. Bell, *Principles*,
p. 189.

xiv. 'The open vowel quality of the English **r** draws all pre-
'ceding closer vowels to a greater degree of openness than they have
'before consonants. This is particularly noticeable in the 16th and
'8th vowels, which are regularly changed into the 15th and 7th
'before **r** (3rd vowel). But the 18th and 10th—the closest vowels—
'equally illustrate the tendency. Very few English speakers pro-
'nounce **ee** (18th), and **oo** (10th), distinctly before **r**, at least in

'conversational utterance. Such words as *beard, hereafter, earwig,*
'*merely*, &c.: *cure, your, poor,* &c., are frequently pronounced
'17 to 3, and 8 to 3, instead of 18 to 3, and 10 to 3.' M. Bell,
p. 146.

xv. 'The long form of the 15th vowel, identical with the French
'*ê* in *même, bête,* &c.' (14th vowel acc. to Ellis) 'is the sound which
'is substituted for the 16th vowel, before r (3rd vowel) in English.
'It is heard in no other position in the language. An ear unac-
'customed to analyze vocal sounds may possibly at first fail to
'recognize the same vowel formation in the words *ell* and *ere.* Let
'the reader pronounce the first word of each of the following
'pairs, *omitting* the vowel sound of the r, and joining the *consonantal*
'effect of r to the preceding vowel, and his pronunciation should
'correspond to the second words; or conversely, let him pronounce
'the second word in each pair, *with* the interposition of the vowel-
'sound of r between the consonantal r and the preceding vowel,
'and his utterances should give the first words: *fairy, ferry; chary,*
'*cherry; dairy, Derry; vary, very; mary, merry; airing, erring.*

'But it is not every ear that will be at once competent for this
'experiment.' M. Bell, pp. 126—128.

xvi. In such words as *four, our* we have triphthongs, viz. 3 to
18 to 3, and 3 to 10 to 3.

The difference between this vocal sound of r when separate and
when part of a diphthong (or triphthong) is heard by comparing
lyre, liar; ne'er, greyer; drawer (a thing), *drawer* (a person);
more, mower; your, ewer.

xvii. Mr Ellis' account (abridged) is as follows:

'In English at the present day r has at least two sounds, the
'first when preceding a vowel, is a scarcely perceptible trill with the
'tip of the tongue, which in Scotland and with some English
'speakers, as always in Italy, becomes a clear and strong trill. The
'second English r is always final or precedes a consonant. It is a
'vocal murmur, differing very slightly from the u in *but* (3rd vowel).
'This second r (marked ɹ) may diphthongise with any preceding
'vowel. After the 2nd, 6th and 5th vowels (as in *hard, dwarf,*
'*born*) the effect is rather to lengthen the preceding vowel, than to
'produce a distinct diphthong. Thus *farther, lord* scarcely differ
'from *father, laud:* that is, the diphthongs 2 to ɹ, 5 to ɹ are heard
'almost as the long vowels 2 and 6. That a distinction is made by
'many, by more perhaps than are aware of it, is certain, but it is
'also certain that in the mouths of by far the greater number of
'speakers in the south of England the absorption of the ɹ is as
'complete as the absorption of the l in *talk, walk, psalm,* where it

' has also left its mark on the preceding vowel. The diphthongs
' 15 to 1, 3 to 1 as in *serf*, *surf*, are very difficult to separate from
' each other, and from a long 3rd vowel. But the slight raising of
' the point of the tongue will distinguish the diphthongs from the
' vowel in the mouth of a careful speaker, that is, one who trains
' his organs to do so. No doubt the great majority of speakers do
' not make any difference.' Ellis, p. 196.

' The combination of the vocal r with the trilled r after a long
' vowel is very peculiar in English; compare *dear, deary, mare,*
' *Mary, more, glory, poor, poorer,* with the French *dire, dirai, mère,*
' *Mairie, Maure, aurai, tour, Touraine.*

' The Scotch do not use the vocal r at all, but only the strongly
' trilled r.

' In Italy this strongly trilled r is constant; in France and a
' great part of Germany a trill of the uvula is pronounced in lieu of
' it. This French r (r *grasseyé ou provençal*) is not unlike the Arabic
' *grh* and the Northumberland *burr*. The last is often confused by
' southerners with g, *Harriet* sounding to them like *Hagiet*.' Ellis,
p. 198.

Connexion of u, w, v, b, qu, &c. (Comp. §§ 90, 118. 2.)

xviii. ' When the breath passes between the *anterior* edges of
' the lips in close approximation, the effect of the breathing resem-
' bles the sound of f. The Spanish b is articulated in this way, but
' with vocalized breath, its sound consequently resembling v. When
' the aperture of the lips is slightly enlarged by the separation of
' their anterior edges, and the breath passes between the *inner* edges
' of the lips, the effect is that of the English wh, w; the former
' being the voiceless, the latter the vocal form of the same articula-
' tion. The lips must be in sufficiently close approximation to pre-
' sent a degree of resistance to the breath, or the w will lack that
' faint percussive quality which alone distinguishes it from the
' vowel oo (10th vowel).' M. Bell, p. 52.

' The sound of v consonant in ancient Latin is a matter of
' dispute: it was probably w or bh (i. e. labial v), and more proba-
' bly the latter than the former, because we can hardly imagine w
' generating v except through bh, but the passage from bh to v is
' so easy and slight, that the two parts of Germany which are dis-
' tinguished by the two different sounds at this day profess to pro-
' nounce their w in the same way. Bh is a kind of bat sound readily
' falling into w or v, but the real w has a very moderate domain in

'Europe. The **bh** is thoroughly established in High Germany and
'in Spain, where the old joke of

'felices populi quibus *vivere* est *bibere*

'points at once to the antiquity of the sound in that country in
'which it is still used for both **b** and **v**, and to the probable pronun-
'ciation of **v** in Latin as **bh** at that time. The example of καυνέας
'being heard as **cav' n'eas**=**cave ne eas** would be solved by the
'identity (**kabhne'ās**) in both languages at that time.' [But comp.
§ 94.] 'At the time when the Anglo-Saxons being Christianized
'adopted the Christian Roman alphabet, the Roman **v** consonant
'was certainly [the denti-labial] **v**, a sound which the Anglo-Saxons
'did not then distinguish from **f**.

'An accurate conception of the three sounds **w**, **bh**, **v** is neces-
'sary for the proper understanding of many linguistic relations.
'For **w** the lips are rounded nearly as for **u**, and the back of the
'tongue is raised, but the outer edges of the lips are brought more
'together than for **u**, and the sound of **w**, when continued, is there-
'fore a buzz, a mixture of voice and whisper, and not a pure
'vowel sound. When the buzz is strong, the tremor of the lips is
'very perceptible, and a little more force produces the labial trill
'**brh**. If the voice is removed, we have **wh**, and the back of the
'tongue being raised as before mentioned, the slightest effort suffices
'to raise it higher and produce **kwh**. This gives the relation between
'the gutturals and labials which plays such an important part in
'comparative philology. On the other hand for **bh** the tongue is
'*not* raised, the sound is a pure labial, less like **u**, but easily deduced
'from **w** by lowering the tongue and slightly flattening the lips. It
'is to those used to it an extremely easy and pleasant consonant, pro-
'duced with the least possible effort. By dropping the voice it pro-
'duces **ph**, which is not now used in Europe but was probably a
'value of φ. For **w**, **bh** there must be no contact with the teeth.
'Directly the lower lip touches the upper teeth, an impediment is
'raised to the passage of the air through the mouth, and the breath
'escaping out on both sides, produces a rushing, rubbing, rustling
'sound, distinctive of the "divided" consonants, and known as **v**,
'which on dropping the voice, becomes **f**. But all degrees of con-
'tact between the lower lip and the teeth are possible, producing
'varieties of **f**, **v**, from sounds which can scarcely be distinguished
'from **ph**, **bh**, up to extremely harsh hisses and buzzes. Generally
'then **w** is a consonant framed from **u** by closing the lips too closely
'to allow of a pure resonance for the vowel sound; **bh** is a **b** with
'the lips just slightly opened, or a **v** without touching the teeth,
'that is, a pure labial; **v** is a denti-labial. The **w** is further dis-
'tinguished from **bh**, **v** by having the tongue raised. It is possible
'of course to raise the tongue when sounding **v**; the result is **vh**,

'a very peculiar and disagreeable sound. But if the tongue is raised
'when sounding **bh**, no ear would distinguish the result from **w**.
'The following words may shew these differences. Fr. *ouï, oui;*
'Engl. *we*, Germ. *wie*, Fr. *vie;* usual Scotch *quhen*, English
'*when*, Aberdeenshire *fen;* usual German *schreiben*, faulty German
'*schreiwen;* German *pferd*, now *pfert*, once probably *pphert*, and in
'some Bavarian dialects *p'hert*.' Ellis, pp. 514, 515.

Roman Preference of vo to vu. (Comp. § 93.)

xix. The reason of the Romans retaining this vowel **o** after **v**
instead of allowing it to pass into **u** (§ 213) was the danger of thus
losing either the consonant sound **v** (= **w**) or the vowel **u**.

'The 10th vowel (i.e. **u** = **oo**) has an *articulative* (i.e. conso-
'nantal) effect, when the modifying organs are further approximated
'during the continuance of the sound. By a slight appulse of the
'lips, the vowel **oo** becomes the articulation **w**. Thus if the lips
'be momentarily compressed between the finger and thumb while
'sounding **oo**, the voice will be modified into *woo, woo, woo*, &c.'
M. Bell, p. 151.

'When **w** is before **oo** the combination is rather difficult
'from the little scope the organs have for the articulative action; the
'**w** is in consequence often omitted by careless speakers, *wool* being
'pronounced *ool; woman, ooman;* &c.' M. Bell, p. 171.

On Labialisation. (Comp. § 93. 3.)

xx. The Latin **v** when following **q** or **g** is not really a separate
letter but a modification of **q** or **g**. Thus Mr Ellis speaking of English
says: '**kw** or Labialised **k**, the lips being opened simultaneously
'with the release of the **k** contact and not after it, is an ancient
'element of our own and probably of many other languages. In
'Anglosaxon it is written **cw**, in Latin **qu**, which is the form
'adopted in English. **Gu** bears the same relation to **g** as **qu** to **k**,
'but as the form of the **g** remained unchanged little attention was
'paid to it. It does not exist as part of the Saxon element of
'our language. Initially it is generally used superfluously for **g**.
'Occasionally it has the sound **gw**, as in *language*, itself a loan
'form, *anguish, distinguish*. Usage however varies, some saying
'*lang-gwage, ang-gwish* and others *lang-wage, lang-wish*. The
'Italian *quale, guanto* are apparently *kwuale, gwuanto*...As we have
'**ky, gy** (in the antiquated pronunciation of *card, sky, guide* = *kyard*,
'*skyi, gyide*) and **kw, gw**, so also to our unacknowledged palatal
'modification of **t, d**, viz. **ty, dy** (e.g. in *nature, verdure*, often pro-

' nounced as *na-tyoor*, *ver-dyoor*) correspond an equally unacknow-
' ledged labial modification of t, d, viz. tw, dw, e.g. *between*, *twain*,
' *twelve*, *twist*, *twirl*; *dwindle*, *dwell*, *dwarf*. Many of those who
' have thought on phonetics have been more perplexed to decide
' whether w is here really a vowel or a consonant, than in the corre-
' sponding words, *wean*, *wain*, *wist*, *well*, *war*. The difficulty is
' resolved by observing that the opening of the lips is really *simul-*
' *taneous* with the release of the t, d contact.' Ellis, pp. 206, 208,
209, slightly compressed.

xxi. In French this labial modification is common after most
consonants, e.g. p (*pois*), b (*bois*), m (*mois*); f (*fois*); v (*voix*),
k (*quoi*), g (*goître*); t (*toi*), d (*doit*); n (*noix*), l (*loi*), r (*roi*), s (*soi*).
Ellis, pp. 4—9.

xxii. In Latin it occurs only after k (or q), g, and s, e.g.
svavis, svadeo (So in English *sweet*, *persuade*).

Compare however tvos, fvit, &c. § 92. After initial l and r it
does not occur. In salvus, servus it was probably separately pronounced and hence the first syllable was long, whereas aqva has the
first syllable short. A preceding g was expelled sometimes e.g.
nivis for nigvis, brevis for bregvis, fruor for frugvor, &c. (§ 129. 2.
639). In other words the v was dropped (§ 640).

The Roman grammarians had similar perplexities to those
mentioned in the passage quoted above. See Schneider, *Lat. Gr.*
I. p. 329 sq.

On k, c, q. (Comp. § 57.)

xxiii. The names of the three consonants k, c, q, viz. ka, ce, qu,
all representing the sharp guttural explosive, were pronounced with
a different vowel. Compare this fact with the following. 'K is
' formed by the silent contact and audible separation of the back
' of the tongue and the posterior part of the palate. The precise
' points of contact vary between the different vowels. Before the
' close lingual vowel ee (18th vowel) the position of the tongue is
' much further forward than before ah (2nd vowel) or aw (6th
' vowel). The tongue *could* articulate k from one uniform position
' before all the vowels, but there is a natural tendency to accom-
' modate facility of utterance by these little changes which would
' require an effort to avoid.' M. Bell, p. 217.

The Germans have similar modifications of the continuous consonant. Ch in *ach* is guttural, in *ich* is palatal, in *auch* is labial
(Ellis, p. 206).

Close affinity of ı and ȷ (=**y**). (Comp. § 138. 144. 2.)

xxiv. ' The tongue in forming **y** is almost in the position for the
' vowel **ee**; just as in forming **w** the lips modify the voice almost to
' the quality of the vowel **oo**. The formative apertures are simply
' more close, so that **y** and **w** are articulated forms of the close
' vowel sounds **ee** and **oo**.

'**Y** before **ee** (18th vowel) presents an articulative difficulty.
' Many persons, especially in Scotland, entirely omit the **y** in that
' situation: thus we hear of an old man bending under the weight
' of *ears* instead of *years*.' M. Bell, p. 216.

On Palatalisation (§ 110. 4).

xxv. ' In pronouncing ȷ (= Engl. **y**) the middle of the tongue is
' arched up against the palate; while for **k** the back and for **t** the
' tip of the tongue only come in contact with the palate. When
' then **kȷ** or **tȷ** come together rapidly, the first change is to produce
' a palatal modification of **k** and **t**. For there is an attempt to
' pronounce **k** and ȷ simultaneously. Hence the back of the tongue
' still remaining in contact with the palate, the middle of the
' tongue is also raised, so that both back and middle lie against the
' palate. This is rather a constrained position, and consequently the
' back of the tongue readily drops. The result is the exact posi-
' tion for the palatal modification of **t**, which originating in an
' attempt to sound **t** and ȷ simultaneously brought the tip and
' middle of the tongue to the palate, and this being almost an im-
' possible position dropped the tip. The two consonants **k** and **t**,
' as palatally modified, are therefore ready to interchange. The
' passage from this modification of **t** to **tsh** (= Eng. **ch**) is very
' short and swift. But the organs of different speakers have differ-
' ent tendencies, and in some **s** or **sh** are more readily evolved than
' **tsh** from **t** palatally modified. It must be remembered that
' when the sound is thus spoken of as changing, it is not meant
' that it changes in the mouth of a single man from perfect **k** to
' perfect **tsh**. Quite the contrary. It probably required many
' generations to complete the change, and the transitional forms
' were probably in use by intermediate generations.' Ellis, pp. 204,
205.

On the change of t to s (§ 151. 2).

xxvi. The slight change requisite to convert **t** into **s** is seen in
the following description of their formation.

' In forming **t** the edge of the whole tongue is laid against the

'front and sides of the mouth so as perfectly to obstruct the breath.
'While the tongue is in this position, there must be a continued
'pressure of breath against it, and wherever an aperture is made
'by the removal of any part of the obstructing edge, the confined
'breath will be emitted with a degree of explosiveness more or less
'strong in proportion to the degree of its previous compression be-
'hind the tongue, and also in proportion to the abruptness with
'which the aperture is made.' M. Bell, p. 199.

xxvii. 'The peculiar mechanism requisite to produce the clear
'hissing sound heard in the letter s, is a single and very contracted
'aperture for the emission of the breath over the centre of the fore-
'part (not the tip) of the tongue, when without much elevation
'from the bed of the lower jaw, it is closely approximated to the
'upper gum. The tongue is otherwise in contact with the teeth
'and gum so as to obstruct the breath at all parts but the point,
'which is sufficiently squared to prevent its touching the front
'teeth. The slightest projection of the tip brings it against the
'teeth, and by partially intercepting the breath at that point modi-
'fies the sound into that of th: and the least retraction of the
'tongue from the precise point of the true formation causes the
'middle of the tongue to ascend towards the arch of the palate,
'and modifies the current of breath into that of sh.' M. Bell,
p. 181.

On the change of s to r. (Compare § 183.)

xxviii. 'The articulative position of s giving sibilation to voca-
'lized breath, produces z, which differs in no wise from the oral
'action of s.

'r as pronounced in England, differs from z merely in the nar-
'rowing and retraction of the point of the tongue. In Scotland, in
'Spain, and on the Continent generally, r receives a stronger vibra-
'tion of the whole forepart of the tongue.' M. Bell, pp. 53, 54.

On the pronunciation of r generally, see above § xiii.

Omission of t before l and n. (Comp. § 192. 1. 4.)

xxix. The following passage shews that the pronunciation of t
is peculiar before l and n.

'The correct articulative action of t is the removal of the whole
'tongue from the palate, allowing the breath to escape by a single
'frontal aperture. Such must always be the mechanism of t initial
'or final: but when the liquids l or n follow t in the same word, a

' lateral explosion before 1, and a nasal emission before n are the
' regular and necessary modes of finishing *t* in such cases. Thus in
' *fitly* and *fitness*, &c.: *batch, nettle, little*, &c., *batten, bitten, button,*
' &c., the point of the tongue is kept in contact with the front of
' the palate in forming the tl; and the whole tongue is retained in
' its obstructive position during the utterance of the tn.' M. Bell,
p. 200.

The interchange of l and r. (Comp. § 176. 7.)

xxx. ' r and l are very liable to be confounded where they occur
' in proximate syllables. The vocal aperture for the former is over the
' point of the tongue, and for the latter over the sides of the back
' part of the tongue; and there is a difficulty in passing quickly
' from one to the other of these positions.' M. Bell, p. 193.

Correspondence of Latin f to Greek θ. (Comp. § 99. 6.)

xxxi. The following passages deal with a confusion of f with
the sharp dental fricative, which is the sound ordinarily given to the
Greek θ, though, as stated in the text, probably not its real value,
at least originally.

' A faulty pronunciation of th consists in a movement of the
' lower lip inwards to meet the tongue. This gives so much of the
' character of f to this articulation that it is often difficult to know
' which is the letter intended. F and Th are mechanically much
' alike. The action of the lip for f is precisely analogous to that of
' the tongue for th. Both organs partially obstruct the breath by
' central contact with the teeth; and the breath is in both cases
' emitted through lateral interstices.' M. Bell, p. 177.

' When f and th are pronounced without any vowel, it is very
' difficult to distinguish them at a little distance.' Ellis, p. 213.

APPENDIX B.

The following selection of inscriptions has been made in order to give specimens of the old forms of the language. They are arranged in chronological order, and have all (except No. 20) been taken from, and examined and re-examined on the proof sheets with, the facsimiles given in Ritschl's *Priscæ Latinitatis Monumenta*, and, in the case of No. 9, with that given in the *Corp. Inscr. Rom.* Vol. II. The explanations have been taken chiefly from Ritschl's preface and the *Corp. Inscr. Lat.*, edited by Mommsen (Vol. I., except when otherwise stated). The number of the inscriptions in *Corp. Inscr.*, as well as of Ritschl's plates, is added to facilitate reference. All these inscriptions are in the original in capital letters. The vertical strokes are used to denote the end of the line in the original; but in the modernisation they mark off the cæsura in the saturnian lines.

The blank spaces, and the omission or insertion of dots (to mark the end of the words), have been represented with tolerable fidelity. The dot is sometimes a dot proper (e. g. in iii. iv. xvii.), sometimes a square (e. g. in xiv. xxi.), sometimes a triangle (e. g. in ix. xxii.), sometimes a cross, or square with projecting corners (e. g. in xvi. xxiv.).

I.

Found in a sacred grove at Pisaurum in Picenum on stone. ' End of 5th century.' Ritschl and Mommsen.

Corp. I. R. 173. Ritschl, tab. XLIII. C.

iunone · re | matrona | pisaurese | dono · dedrot |

Junoni reginæ matronæ Pisaurenses dono (donum?) dederunt.

II.

Do. on stone, end of 5th century. Ritschl and Mommsen.

Corp. I. R. 177. Ritschl, tab. XLIII. A.

matre | matuta | dono · diidro | matrona | m · cu
ria · | pola · liuia | deda |

Matri Matutæ dono (donum?) dederunt matronæ, mania Curia, Pola Livia deda (dedant, comp. πεφύκαντι).

The *m* before Curia is the old form with five strokes (see p. 23), for which in modern books M' is substituted.

III.

On a bronze tablet found at Firmum in Picenum, now in the Paris museum, ' of a date nearer to the oldest Scipio inscription than to the second.' Ritschl.

Corp. I. R. 181. Ritschl, tab. XCVII. A.

erentio·l·f | ·aprufenio·c·f | l·turpilio·c·f |
m·albani·l·f | t·munatio·t·f | quaistores |
aire·moltaticod | dederont |

Terentius, Lucii filius,   Aprufenius Gaii filius, Lucius Turpilius Gaii filius, Marcus Albanius Lucii filius, Titus Munatius, Titi filius, quæstores ære multatico dederunt; i.e. from the produce of fines.

IV.

On a bronze tablet, first made known at Rome, but the place of finding is unknown.

Corp. I. R. 187. Ritschl, tab. II. B.

m·mindios·l·fi | p·condetios·ua·fi | aidiles·uicesma.
parti | apolones·dederi |

Marcus Mindius Lucii filius, Publius Condetius, valesi (?) *filius, ædilis vicesimam partem Apollinis dederunt,* i.e. have offered Apollo's twentieth.

V.

On a small stone column found at Tusculum near the tomb of the Furii. ' A faithful copy of an original older than the Scipio inscriptions.' Ritschl.

Corp. I. R. 63. Ritschl, tab. XLIX. B.

m·fourio·c·f·tribunos
militare·de·praidad·maurte·dedet·

Marcus Furius, Gaii filius, tribunus, militari de præda Marti dedit.

VI.

This and VIII. XI. XIII. XIV. are all on stone and taken from the tombs of the Scipios near the Capene gate. This inscription is on L. Cornelius Scipio, son of Barbatus, Consul 495 U.C. ' It probably was written about 500 U.C.' Ritschl.

27

Corp. I. R. 32.   Ritschl, tab. xxxviii. E.   The additions in italics
   are from Ritschl's conjecture.

honcoino · ploirume · cosentiont · r	*omai*
duonoro · optumo · fuise · uiro	*virorum*
luciom · scipione · filios · barbati	
*c*onsol · censor · aidilis · hic · fuet · a	*pud vos*
*h*ec · cepit · corsica · aleriaque · urbe	*m pugnandod*
*d*edet · tempestatebus · aide · mereto	*d votam.*

Arranged by Ritschl as Saturnian metre, as follows (except that
the words are here modernised), the accents denoting the arses, and
the vertical lines the cæsuras.

> *Hunc únum plúrimí con | séntiúnt Római* (i. e. Romæ)
> *bonórum óptimúm fu | ísse virúm virórum,*
> *Lucíum Scipiónem. | Filiús Barbati*
> *consúl, censór, ædílis | híc fúit apúd vós.*
> *Hic cépit Córsicam Áleri | ámque urbém pugnándo;*
> *dedít témpestátibus | aédem mérito vótam.*

VII.

On a bronze tablet fixed to a wall at Tibur in Latium.   'Probably
   at end of 5th century when the final *-os* was giving place to
   -us.'   Ritschl.   The inscription on the second side is probably
   a little later than on the first.

Corp. I. R. 62.   Ritschl, tab. xcvii. B.

on one side,   c · placentios · her°f° | marte · sacr om° |
on the other side, c · placentius · her · f | marte donu · dede |

> *Gaius Placentius, Herii filius.*   *Marti sacrum.*
>   *Marti donum dedit.*

(The small rounds are probably marks of nails.)

VIII.

On L. Cornelius Scipio Barbatus, Consul 456.   'The inscription
   dates not later than 520 U.C.'   Ritschl.

Corp. I. R. 30.   Ritschl, tab. xxxvii. B.

cornelius · lucius · scipio · barbatus · gnaiuod
· patre | prognatus fortis · uir · sapiensque—quoius · forma ·
uirtutei · parisuma | fuit—consol · censor · aidilis · quei · fuit ·
apud · uos—taurasia · cisauna | samnio · cepit—subigit · omne
· loucanam · opsidesque · abdoucit · |

Cornélius Lucius | Scípió Barbátus,
Gnæó patré prognátus | fórtis vir sapiénsque,
Cujús fórma virtu | tí paríssuma fuit,
Consúl, censor, ædilis | quí fúit apúd vós
Taurásiám Cisaunam | Sámnium cépit
Subigit omném Lucaniam, óbsidésque abdúcit.

Mommsen considers *Samnio* to be the ablative, *Taurasia* and *Cisauna* being towns '*in Samnium.*' *Lucanam* sc. *terram*, i.e. *Lucaniam.*

IX.

On a bronze plate found in the mountains of Gibraltar near Alcala de los Gazules by a Polish engineer in A.D. 1867. Published in facsimile and with Commentaries by E. Hübner and Mommsen, *Hermes*, III. 243 sq. Decree made 565 U.C., and inscription is probably of this date.

Corp. I. R. II. No. 5041.

laimilius · l · f · inpeirator · decreiuit | utei · quei · hasten sium · seruei | in · turri · lascutana · habitarent | leiberei · es sent · agrum · oppidumqu | quod · ea · tempestate · posedisent | item · possidere · habereque | iousit · dum · poplus · senatus que | romanus · uellet · act incastreis | ad · xii · k · febr

L. Æmilius, Lucius' son, general, decreed that such slaves of the people of Hasta as dwelt in the tower of Lascuta should be free. With regard to the land and town which they had possessed at that time, he ordered them to continue to possess and hold it so long as the people and senate of Rome should will. Done in the camp 19 *January.*

This inscription though of the same age as the *S. C. de Bacanalibus* is not so antique in spelling, probably owing to the more formal legal nature of the *S. C. de Bac.*

The *ei* in *inpeirator* appears to be an inscriber's blunder. This inscription affords the earliest instance of doubled letters, e.g. *essent*, *vellet*. Cf. § 58. Ritschl has discussed the peculiarities in his *Neue Plautinische Excurse*, 1st Heft. 1869, p. 16 n.

X.

On bronze, found at Tiriolo a village in the country of the Bruttii. Supposed to be written at the time of the event referred to, i.e. 568 A.U.C. See Liv. XXXIX. 8—19. Cic. *Leg.* II. 15, § 37.

Corp. I. R. 196. Ritschl, tab. XVIII.

marcius · l · f · s · postumius · l · f · cos · senatum · consoluerunt · n · octob · apud · aedem | duelonai · sc · arf · m · claudi · m · f · l · ualeri · p · f · q · minuci · c · f · de · bacanalibus quei · foideratei |

esent · ita · exdeicendum · censuere ·⸱neiquis · eorum · sacanal ·
habuise · uelet · sei · ques | esent · quei · sibei · deicerent nece
sus · ese · bacanal · habere · eeis · utei · ad · pr · urbanum | ro
mam · uenirent · dequeeeis · rebus · ubei · eor m · utr a · audita ·
esent · utei · senatu*a* | noster · decerneret · dum · ne · minus ·
senator bus · c · adese*pit* ·   rescosoleretur | bacas · uir
· nequis · adiese · uelet · ceiuis · romanus · neue · nominus · latin
neue · socium | quisquam · nisei · pr · urbanum · adie · sent · is
que · e · senatuos · sententiad dum · ne | minus · senatoribus
· c · adesent · quom · ea · res · cosoleretur · iousisent ce suere
    | sacerdos · nequis · uir · eset · magister · nequeuir · neque ·
mulier · quisquam · ese · t | neuepecuniam · quisquameorum
· comoin   abuise · ue et neue · magistratum | neue · promagi
stratuo · neque · uirum   ier · em quiquam · fecise · uelet |
neue · post hac · inter · sed · conioura   e · comuouise ·
neue · conspondis · e | neue · conprome · siseuelet · neue · quis
quamfidem inter · sed · dedise · uelet | sacra · in · dquol
tod · ne quisquam · fecise · uelet · ncue · in · poplicod · neue · in |
preiuatod · neue · exstrad · urbem · sacra · quisquam · fecise ·
uelet · nisei | pr · ur anum · adieset · isque · de · senatuos ·
sententiad · dum · ne · minus | senatoribus · c · adesent ·
quom · ea · res · cosoleretur · iousisent · censuere | homines ·
plous · u · oinuorsei · uirei · atque · mulieres · sacra · ne · quis
quam | fecise · uelet · neue · inter · ibei · uirei · pl*d*us · duobus ·
mulieribus · ploustribus | ar*f*uise · uelent · nisei · de · pr · urbani ·
senatuosque · sententiad · utei · suprad | scriptumest ·   haice ·
utei · in · couentinoid · exdeicatis · ne · minus · trinum | noun
dinum · senatuosque · sententiam · utei · scientes · esetis ·
eorum · | sententia · ita · fuit · sei · ques · esent · quei ·
aruorsum · ead · fecisent quam · suprad | scriptum · est · eeis ·
remcaputalem · faciendam · censuere atque · utei | hoce ·
in · tabolam · ahenam · inceideretis · ita · senatus · aiquom · cen
suit | uteique · eam · figier · ioubeatis · ubei · facilumed ·
gnoscierpotisit · atque | utei · ea · bacanalia · sei · qua · sunt
· exstrad · quam · sei · quid · ibei · sacri · est | ita · utei · suprad
· scriptum · est · in · diebus · x · quibus · uobeis · tabelai · datai |
erunt · faciatis · utei dismota · sient   in · agro · teurano |

The letters in italics are such as appear from the facsimile to be
those inscribed. But in line 6 *nt* would be very nearly right for
pit. In the 12th and 13th lines I have omitted some letters, which
have been supplied on a modern insertion in the broken plate.

Q. Marcius, Lucii filius, Spurius Postumius, Lucii filius consules senatum consuluerunt nonis Octobribus apud ædem Bellonæ. Scribendo adfuerunt M. Claudius, Marci filius, L. Valerius, Publii filius, Q. Minucius, Gaii filius.

De Bacchanalibus qui fœderati essent ita edicendum censuere: (i.e. decreed the issue to those who were in league with the Romans, of a proclamation in the matter of the feasts of Bacchus) *nequis eorum Bacchanal habuisse vellet. Siqui essent, qui sibi dicerent necesse esse Bacchanal habere, ei uti ad prætorem urbanum Romam venirent, deque eis rebus, ubi eorum verba audita essent, uti senatus noster decerneret, dum ne minus senatoribus centum adessent, quum ea res consuleretur. Bacchas vir nequis adiisse vellet civis Romanus, neve nominis Latini, neve sociorum quisquam, nisi prætorem urbanum adiissent, isque de senatus sententia, dum ne minus senatoribus centum adessent, quum ea res consuleretur, jussisset.*

Censuere, sacerdos nequis vir esset: magister neque vir neque mulier quisquam esset: neve pecuniam quisquam eorum communem habuisse vellet, neve magistratum, neve pro magistratu neque virum neque mulierem quisquam fecisse vellet. Neve posthac inter se conjurasse neve convovisse, neve conspondisse, neve compromisisse vellet, neve quisquam fidem inter se dedisse vellet. Sacra in occulto nequisquam fecisse vellet, neve in publico, neve in privato, neve extra urbem sacra quisquam fecisse vellet, nisi prætorem urbanum adiisset, isque de senatus sententia dum ne minus senatoribus centum adessent, quum ea res consuleretur, jussisset.

Censuere, homines plus quinque universi, viri atque mulieres sacra ne quisquam fecisse vellet, neve interibi viri plus duobus, mulieribus plus tribus, adfuisse vellent, nisi de prætoris urbani senatusque sententia, uti supra scriptum est (i.e. that not more than five persons in all men and women, celebrate the rites, that the five should be two men, and three women. *quisquam* is in apposition to *homines*).

Hæc uti in contione exdicatis ne minus trinum nundinum (i.e. not less than three assembly days); *senatûsque sententiam uti scientes essetis. Eorum sententia ita fuit: siqui essent qui advorsum ea fecissent, quam supra scriptum est, eis rem capitalem faciendam censuere.*

Atque uti hoc in tabulam ahenam incideretis: ita senatus æquum censuit;

Utique eam figi jubeatis, ubi facillume nosci possit;

Atque uti ea Bacchanalia, siqua sunt, extra quam si quid ibi sacri est, ita uti scriptum est, in diebus decem, quibus vobis tabellæ datæ erunt, faciatis uti dimota sint. In agro Teurano.

The document is evidently a letter (*tabellæ*) from the consuls to the local magistrates conveying to them a copy of (as Mommsen thinks, part only of) the decree of the senate, an intimation of the penalty which the senate ordered for a transgression of it, and directions for its publication.

XI.

On the son of P. Scipio Africanus major. Augur 574 A.U.C. 'End of 6th century U.C.' Ritschl. There is a vertical fracture in the middle of the stone, occasioning a loss of several letters.

Corp. I. R. 33. Ritschl. tab. XXXIX. F.

```
quei · apiceinsigne · dial    aminis · gesistei          |
    mors · perfe    tua · ut · essent · omnia  |
    breuia  ·  hor os · fama · uirtusque       |
    gloria · atque · in · genium · quibus · sei      |
    in · longa · licu set · tibe utier · uita        |
    fa · cile · factei superases · gloriam      |
    maior · um  qua · re · lubens · te · ingremiu    |
    scipio · recip t  · terra · publi           |
    prognat · um · publio · corneli         |
```

Qùi ápicem ínsígnem diális | flámínís gessísti,
mors pérfécit túa ut | éssent ómnia brévia :
honós famá virtúsque | glória átque ingénium,
quibús si in lónga lícuís | sét tibi útier (i.e. uti) víta
facilé factís superásses | glóriám majórum.
Quaré lubéns te in grémium, | Scípió, récipit
Terrá, Publí, prognátum | Públió Cornéli (i.e. Cornelio).

XII.

On stone at Sora. ' Not later than 620 A.U.C., perhaps more probably at the very beginning of the century.' Ritschl.

Corp. I. R. 1175. Ritschl. tab. LII. A.

```
a · p · uertuleieis · c · f.            |
quod · re · sua · d  eidens · asper |
afleicta   · parens · timens    |
heic · uouit · uoto · ho c      |
solut       cuma · facta    |
polouctaleibereis · lube      |
te  s  donu · danunt ·        |
hercolei · maxsume ·          |
mereto  semol · te    |
orant · se ·  oti · crebro    |
condemnes ·            |
```

Marcus Publius Vertuleii, Gaii filii
Quod ré suá diffidens | aspere afflicta
Paréns timéns hic vóvit, | vóto hóc solúto,
Decumá factá pollúcta, | liberí libéntes
Donúm danúnt (i.e. *dant*) *Hérculi | máximé mérito*
Simúl te oránt se vóti | crébro cóndémnes.

XIII.

Uncertain which Scipio is meant. ' At beginning of 7th century
U.C.' Ritschl.

Corp. I. R. 34. Ritschl. tab. XLI. Ka.

l·cornelius·cn·f·cn·n·scipio· magna·sapientia |
multasque·uirtutes·aetate·quom·parua |
posidet·hoc·saxsum·quoiei·uita·defecit·non |
honos·honore·is·hic·situs·quei·nunquam |
uictus·est·uirtutei·annos·gnatus·xx·is |
d ei·s datus·ne·quair·atis·honore |
queiminus·sit·mand u

> *Lucius Cornelius, Gnaei filius, Gnaei nepos, Scipio.*
> *magnám sapiéntiám mul|tásque vírtútes*
> *aetáte cúm párva | póssidét hoc sáxum.*
> *quoiei* (i.e. *cui*) *vitá defécit,| nón honós, honórem.*
> *Is híc sitús. Qui núnquam | víctus ést virtúte*
> *annós natús vigínti | is Diti ést mandátus:*
> *ne quaératis honórem | químinus sít mandátus.*

In the words *honos honorem* the first denotes *honour*, the second
office. ' *In whose case life, not worth, fell short of official post.*' The
last line means, *seek not for official post which was not given him.*

XIV.

On three stones. ' At beginning of 7th century, latest of all the
Scipio inscriptions.' Ritschl.

Corp. I. R. 38. Ritschl, tab. XLII. L.

Inscription on Cn. Scipio Hispanus who was prætor 615 U.C.

cn·cornelius·cn·f
||| ||| scipio·hispanus |

|| pr·aid·cur·q· tr·mil·II·xuir·sl·iudik |
x·uir·sacr·fac·*p* |

uirtutesgenerismieismoribusaccum au*i*
progeniemigenuifactapatrispetiei
maiorum optenuilaudem ut sibeime ess ecreatum
laetentur stirpem nobilitauithon or

There are three blocks of stone, on the 2nd and 3rd of which this inscription is written. The first has only one stroke to number it but nothing else. The second has two strokes on the left side and three strokes on the right, apparently to shew where it was to fit to the 3rd tablet, which has also three strokes. The space just before the end of the verses is apparently due to a miscalculation on the part of the stone-cutters.

Gnæus Cornelius, Gnæi filius, Scipio Hispanus, prætor, ædilis, curulis, quæstor, tribunus militum bis, decemvir litibus judicandis, decemvir sacris faciundis.

> *Virtutes generis meis moribus accumulavi,*
> *progeniem genui, facta patris petii,*
> *majorum obtinui laudem, ut sibi me esse creatum*
> *lætentur; stirpem nobilitavit honor.*

Mommsen considers the beginning of the second line is *progenie mi*, and that *progenie* is a dactyl (cf. Lachm. ad Lucr. II. 991); but ?.

These are according to Ritschl the oldest Latin elegiac verses.

XV.

On stone upon Mt. Cælius at Rome. · 'Between 608 and 620 A.U.C. but nearer to the latter than the former.' Ritschl.

Corp. I. R. 541. Ritschl, tab. LI. A.

l·mummi·l·f·cos·duct | auspicio·imperioque | eius · achaia capt·corinto | deleto·romam·redieit | triumphans·ob·hasce | res·bene · gestas·quod | in·bello·uouerat | hanc·aedem·et ·signu | herculis·uictoris | imperator·dedicat |

Lucius Mummius, Lucii filius consul. Ductu auspicio imperioque eius Achaia capta, Corintho deleto, Romam rediit triumphans. Ob hasce res bene gestas, quod in bello voverat, hanc ædem et signum Herculis victoris imperator dedicat.

XVI.

On stone at Aletrium. 'Shortly after 620 A.U.C.' Ritschl.

Corp. I. R. 1166. Ritschl, tab. LII. B.

*l·*betilienus·l·f·uaarus | haec·quae·infera·scripta | sont ·de·senatu·sententia | facienda·coirauit·semita | in·oppido · omnis·porticum · qua | inarcem · eitur · campum · ubei | lu dunt· horologiummacelum | basilicam · calecandam · seedes |

cum · ba · linearium · lac · um · ad | ortam · aquam · in · opi
dumadqu | arduom · pedes · cccxⱳ · fornicesq | fecit · fistulas ·
soledas · fecit | ob · hasce · res · censorem · fecere · bis | sena
tus · filio · stipendia · mereta | ese · iousit · populusque · sta
tuam | donauit · censorino |

A letter or two has been broken away at the beginning of the
9th and 10th lines (of the original).

*Lucius Betilienus, Lucii filius, Varus hæc, quæ infra scripta sunt,
de senatus sententia facienda curavit, semitas in oppido omnes, porti-
cum qua in arcem itur, campum ubi ludunt, horologium, macellum,
basilicam calcandam* (chalking), *sedes, lacum balnearium, lacum
ad portam, aquam in oppidum adque arduum* (i. e. *ad arcem*) *pedes
CCCXL fornicesque fecit, fistulas solidas fecit. Ob hasce res censorem
fecere bis senatus, filio stipendia merita esse jussit, populusque statuam
donavit Censorino* (i. e. under the name of Censorinus, because he
had been twice Censor).

XVII.

On stone.   At Polla in Lucania.   622 A.U.C.

Corp. I. R. 551.   Ritschl, tab. LI. B.

uiam · fecei · ab · regio · ad · capuam · et | in · ea · uia · ponteis ·
omneis · miliarios | tabelariosque · poseiuei · hince · sunt |
nouceriam · meilia · ⱳI · capuam · xxcIIII | muranum · ⱳxxIIII ·
cosentiam · cxxIII | ualentiam · cⱳxxx■ ·   ad · fretum · ad
statuam · ccxxxI■ · regium · ccxxxvII | suma · af · capua ·
regium · meilia · cccxxI■ | et · eidem · prae tor · in |
sicilia · fugiteiuos · italicorum | conquaeisiue i · redideique |
homines · ᴅccccxvII · eidemque | primus · fecei · ut · de · agro ·
poplico | aratoribus · cederent · paastores | forum · aedisque ·
poplicas · heic · fecei

The xxI in the 6th line (as here printed) are in the original
written under the ccc and in the next line.

The black squares are marks of the erasure of some figures by
the stonecutter.

This relates to P. Popillius C. F. Lænas, consul 622 A.U.C.
(Mommsen, Ritschl.)

*I made the road from Rhegium to Capua, and on that road placed
all the bridges, milestones and letter-carriers. From here to Nuceria
51 miles; to Capua 84 miles; to Muranum 74 miles; to Consentia*

123 *miles; to Valentia* 180 *miles; to the strait up to the statue* 231 *miles; to Rhegium* 237 *miles. Total from Capua to Rhegium* 321 *miles. And I the same man, when praetor in Sicily, recovered the runaway slaves of the Italians, and restored the men in number* 917. *And I the same was the first to make the shepherds give up the public land to the farmers, and I erected a public building here.*

The two following inscriptions are on boundary stones erected by the land commissioners under the Sempronian law of Tiberius Gracchus.

XVIII.	XIX.
A.U.C. 622-23. Corp. I. R. 552.	A.U.C. 624-25. Corp. I. R. 554.
Ritschl, p. 49.	Ritschl, tab. LV. Ca.

c·smpr	m·foluius·m·f. ac
ap·claudius·c·f·polc	c·sempronius·ti·f·grac
plicinius·p·f·cras	c·paperius·c·f·carb
III·vir·a·i·a	III·uire·a·i·a

The gap in the first line of each inscription is occasioned by the stones being broken. The first *m* in 18 is imperfect.

18.   *C. Sempronius, Tiberii filius, Gracchus*
        Ap. Claudius, Gaii filius, Pulcer
        P. Licinius, Publii filius, Crassus.
        Tres viri agris judicandis assignandis.

In the later pillar *M. Fulvius Flaccus* and *C. Papirius Carbo* are joined with *C. Gracchus.*

XX.

On bronze, found at Tibur. Not now extant. 'About the middle of the 7th century,' Mommsen. Ritschl thinks it may have been written in A.U.C. 595, supposing L. Cornelius to have been L. Corn. Lentulus, consul in 598, but at any rate before 631.

Corp. I. R. 201. See Ritschl, tab. XLVIII. G, where only a line or two are given copied from Piranesi. [N.B. I have not noted the spaces in this inscription.]

l·cornelius·cn·f·pr·sen·cons·a·d:III·nonas·maias· sub·aede·kastorus | scr·adf·a·manlius·a·f·sex·iulius·l· postumius·s·f· | quod·teiburtes·u·f·quibusque·de·rebus· uos·purgauistis·ea·senatus | animum·aduortit·ita·utei·

aequom · fuit · nosque · ea · ita · audiueramus | ut · uos · deixsis
tis · uobeis · nontiata · esse · ea · nos · animum · nostrum | non ·
in · doucebamus · ita · facta · esse · propter · ea · quod · scibamus |
ea · uos · merito · nostro · facere · non · potuisse · neque · uos ·
dignos · esse | quei · ea · faceretis · neque · id · uobeis · neque ·
rei · poplicae · uostrae | oitile · esse · facere · et · postquam ·
uostra · uerba · senatus · audiuit | tanto · magis · animum · no;
trum · indoucimus · ita · utei · ante | arbitrabamur · de · eieis ·
rebus · af · uobeis · peccatum · non · esse | quonque · de · eieis ·
rebus · senatuei · purgati · estis · credimus · uosque | animum ·
uostrum · indoucere · oportet · item · uos · populo | romano ·
purgatos · fore

Lucius Cornelius, Gnæi filius prætor senatum consuluit ante diem
tertium nonas maias sub æde Castoris. Scribendo adfuerunt Aulus
Manlius Auli filius, Sextus Julius, Lucius Postumius Spurii filius.
Quod Tiburtes verba fecerunt, quibusque de rebus vos purgavistis,
ea senatus animum advertit, ita uti æquum fuit. Nosque ea ita audi-
veramus, ut vos dixistis vobis nuntiata esse. Ea nos animum nos-
trum non inducebamus ita facta esse, propterea quod scibamus ea vos
merito nostro facere non potuisse, neque vos dignos esse, qui ea face-
retis, neque id vobis neque reipublicæ vostræ utile esse facere. Et
postquam vestra verba senatus audivit, tanto magis animum nostrum
inducimus, ita uti ante arbitrabamur de eis rebus a vobis peccatum
non esse. Cumque de eis rebus senatui purgati estis, credimus, vos-
que animum vestrum inducere oportet, item vos populo romano pur-
gatos fore.

XXI.

On stone, found at Capua. 646 A.U.C. Ritschl.

Corp. I. R. 565. Ritschl, tab. LXIII. A.

n · pumidius · q · f	m · raecius
m · cottius · m · f	n · arrius · m · f
m · eppilius · m · f	l · ieioleius · p · f
c · antrac · ius · c · f	c · tuccius · c · f
l sempronius · l · f	q · uibius · m · f
p · cicereius · c · f ·	m · ualerius · l · f · 2m

heisce · magistreis · uenerus · iouiae · muru |
aedificandum · coirauerunt · pedccʊxxet |
loidos · fecerunt · ser · sulpicio · m · aurelio · cof

The last *m* of *murum* has had to be written in the line above,
the mark ꝛ is used here as we should use [. *cof* is a mistake for *cos.*

Hi magistri Veneris Joviæ murum ædificandum curaverunt pedes CCLXX (i.e. 270 feet long) *et ludos fecerunt, Servio Sulpicio Marco Aurelio consulibus.*

The 'magistri' appear to have been the town council.

XXII.

On stone, found at Aeclanum 'circiter 664 U.C.,' Ritschl.

Corp. I. R. 1230. Ritschl, tab. LXX. C.

> c · quinctius · c · f · ualg · patron · munic
> m · magi · min · f · surus · a · patlacius · q · f
> IIII · uir · d · s · sportas · turreis · moiros
> turreisque · a · equas · qum · moiro
> *f*aciundum ·   coirauerunt

C. Quinctius, Gaii filius, Valgus patronus municipii, M. Magius, Minatii filius, Surus, A. Patlacius, Quinti filius, Quattuor viri de senatus sententia portas, turres, muros, turresque æquas cum muro faciundum curaverunt.

'faciundum' is carelessly put for 'faciundas.' The *c* is almost a *g*.

XXIII.

On bronze, found in the ruins of the temple of Saturn at foot of the Tarpeian mount at Rome. Sulla's law *de* XX. *quæstoribus* A.U.C. 673 (674, Ritschl). Cf. Tac. *Ann.* 11, 22.

Corp. I. R. 202. Ritschl, tab. XXIX.

> q · urb · quei · aerarium · prouinciam · optinebit · eam |
> mercedem · deferto · quaestorque · quei · aerarium · prouin
> ciam | optinebit · eam · pequniam · ei · scribae · scribeisque ·
> herediue | eius · soluito · idque · ei · sine · fraude · sua ·
> facere · li · ceto · quod | sine · malo · pequlatuu · fiat · olleis
> que · hominibus · eam | pequniam · capere · liceto
> | cos · quei · nunc · sunt · iei · ante · k · decembreis · primas · de ·
> eis · quei | ciues · romanei · sunt · uiatorem · unum · legun
> to · quei · in | ea · decuria · uiator · appareat · quam ·
> decuriam · uiatorum | ex · noneis · decembribus · primeis
> · quaestoribus · ad · aerarium | apparere · oportetoportebit ·

A part only of the law has been preserved: the above is the first two sections of what has been preserved.

He shall report the salary to the city quæstor, who shall have the treasury as his department, and the quæstor who shall have the treasury department shall pay the money to the clerk and clerks and his heir, and it shall be lawful for him to do so without incurring any risk, so far as it is done without dishonest embezzlement, and it shall be lawful for the men to receive the money.

The present consuls shall before the first of December next choose a messenger from those who are Roman citizens, to act as the messenger in that detachment of messengers which is or shall be bound to attend the quæstors at the treasury after the seventh December next (i.e. the day on which the quæstors entered on office).

XXIV.

On stone, at Rome on the Appian road. 'Of the age of Sulla,' Ritschl.

Corp. I. R. 1006. Ritschl, tab. LXIX. D.

hoc·est·fac·tum·monumentum
maarco·caicilio
hospes·gratum·est·quom·apud
meas·restitistei·seedes
bene·rem·geras·et·ualeas
dormias·sine·qura

Hoc ést factúm monuméntum | Márcó Caecílio.
Hospés, gratum ést cum apúd meas | réstitísti sédes.
Bene rém gerás et váleas: | dórmiás sine cúra.

XXV.

A leaden plate, formerly doubled, found about 500 paces from Rome on the left-hand of the Latin road among the tombs. 'Written at the end of the republic or in the Augustan time.' Mommsen. The formation of the letters is very rough, as that of a person writing hastily on an unyielding material. N.B. The first three letters project in the original. I have not noted the spaces at end of lines.

Corp. I. R. 818. Ritschl, tab. XVII. 30.

quomodomortuos qui·istic | snpultus nst·nnc·loqui |
nn·c snrmonarn potnst·snic· | rhodinn·apud·m·licinium |
faustum·mortua sit·nnc | loqui·nnc snrmonarn pos·sit | ita
uti·mortuos·nnc·addnos | nnc·ad hominns accnptus ᷐nst |
snicrhodinn·aput·m·licinium | accnptasit nttantum ualnat |
quant·um illn·mortuos qnn | isticsnpultus nst·dinnpatnr·

rhodinu | tibu · commundo · uti · sumpur | odio sit · m · licin
io fausto | itum · mhudium amphionum | itum c · popillium a
pollonium | itum uunnonia · hurmiona | itum surgia glycin
na |

In the first line on this page the *nu* in *Rhodine* is in the original
written below (as in XVII). The double ı is an old form of the
letter E (see § 226). So *suıc* is *seic*, i.e. *sic*. In the original, of
course, no i has a dot, but they are often tall, without reference to
the quantity.

*As he is dead who is buried there, and can neither speak nor
discourse, so may Rhodine at M. Licinius Faustus' house be dead,
and not be able to speak or discourse. So as he being dead has
been received neither to the gods nor to men, so may Rhodine at M.
Licinius' be received and have as much strength (or be good for as
much) as the dead man who is buried there. Father Ditis I commend to thee Rhodine, that she may ever be hateful to M. Licinius
Faustus.*

*Likewise (I commend to thee) Marcus Hedius Amphion. Likewise
Gaius Popillius Apollonius. Likewise Vennonia Hermiona. Likewise
Sergia Glycinna.*

N.B. The name of Rhodine occurs thrice to make the impreca-
tion effective.

XXVI.

On bronze, found at Heraclea. Lex Julia municipalis, 709 U.C.
Corp. I. R. 206. Ritschl, tab. XXXIII.

(Two sections only are given here: a considerable number are
extant.)

quae · uiae · in · urbem · rom · propiusue · u · r · p · q · ubei · con
tinente · habitabitur · sunt · erunt · quoius · ante · aedificium
earum · quae | uiae · erunt · is · eam · uiam · arbitratu · eius ·
aed · quoi · ea · pars · urbis · h · l · ob · uenerit · tueatur · isque · aed
· curato · uti · quorum | ante · aedificium · erit · quamque ·
uiam · h · l · quemque · tueri · oportebit · ei · omnes · eamuiam ·
arbitratu · eius · tueantur · neue · eo | loco · ao · consistat · quomi
nus · conmode · populus · ea · uia · utatur
    | aed · cur · aed · pl · quei · nunc · sunt · quei · quomque · post ·
h · l · r · factei · createi · erunt · eumue · mac · inierint · iei ·
indiebus · v · proxumeis | quibus · eo · mac · designatei · erunt ·
eumue · mag · inierint · inter · se · paranto · aut · sortiunto · qua ·
inpartei · urbis · quisque | eorum · uias · publicas · in · urbem
· roma · propius · ue · u · r · p · *m* refi ciundas · sternendas · curet ·

eiusque · rei · procurationem | habeat · quae · pars · quoique ·
aed · ita · h · l · ob · uener it · eius · aed · ineis · loceis · quae · inea ·
partei · erunt · uiarum · reficien | darum · t · uemdarum ·
procuratio · esto · utei · h · l · oportebit

The c in ma*c* might be read g.

*With regard to the roads which are or shall be into the city of
Rome, or nearer to the city of Rome than* 1000 *paces* (*p.q.* is a mistake
for *p.m.* i.e. *passus mille*: there is a correction in the plate), *where
the dwellings shall be continuous, the person, before whose house any of
the said* (earum) *roads shall be, must protect such road according
to the discretion of the ædile on whom that part of the city shall by
this law have devolved; and such ædile shall take care that all
such persons, before whose house it shall be, shall protect at his discretion the road which* (the *que* in *quamque* is really superfluous) *by
this law they shall severally be required to protect, and shall take care
that water* (ao mistake for *aqua*) *do not settle in the place so as to
inconvenience people using the road.*

*The curule ædiles, the ædiles of the commons, both those now and
whosoever shall after the proposal of this law* (post hanc legem roga-
tam) *have been made, or created or shall have entered on that office,
shall within the five next ten days after that they shall have been
elected to* (lit. *marked with*) *that office, or shall have entered on that
office, prepare or settle by lot among themselves in what part of the city
each of them shall see to the reparation and paving of the public roads
into the city of Rome* (roma for romam) *or nearer to the city of Rome
than* 1000[1] *paces, and have the charge of the matter. The ædile to
whom any[2] part of the city shall thus by this law be assigned shall be
charged, as shall be incumbent by this law, with the reparation and
protection of the roads in such places as shall be in that part.*

[1] The letter for 1000 in Ritschl's facsimile is blurred so as to be
illegible.
[2] Literally, *the persons before whose house it shall be and the road
which,* &c. ; *the part which and the ædile to whom,* &c.

XXVII.

On stone, found at Rome. 'At end of Republic,' Mommsen.
Ritschl.

Corp. I. R. 1009. Ritschl, tab. LXXXI.

eucharis · licin*iae · l*
docta · erodita · omnes artes · uirgo · ui*xit · an · xiiii*
heus · oculo · errante · quei · aspicis · léti · dom*us*
morare · gressum · et · titulum · nostrum · perlege
amor · parenteis quem · dedit · natae · suae

ubei se·reliquiae conlocarent·corporis
heic uiridis·aetas·cum·floreret·artibus
crescente·etaeuo·gloriam·conscenderet
propirauit·hóra·tristis·fatalis mea
et denecauit·ultra ueitae spiritum
docta·erodita·paene·musarum·manu
quae·modo·nobilium·ludos·decorauichoro
et·graeca·inscaena·prima·populo·apparui
en·hoc·intumulo·cineremnostri·corporis
infistae·parcae·deposierunt·carmine
studium patronae·cura·amor·laudes·decu*s*
silent·ambusto·corpore·et·leto·tacent
reliqui·fletum nata·genitori·meo
et·antecessi·genita·post·leti·diem
bis·hic·septeni·mecum·natales dies
tenebristenentur·ditis·aeterna dom*u*
rogo·ut·discedens·terr·am·mihi dic*as·leuem.*

The letters printed in italics are supplied from (as is believed)
a transcription previous to the breaking of the stone. See Mommsen.

Two words, *leti, hora,* exhibit the apex, § *59* (3).

Some of the peculiarities are due merely to careless inscribing.
Thus 7. *propiravit* for *properavit;* 9. *denecavit* for *denegavit;* 14.
infistæ for *infestæ.*

In line 18 *genita post* should be taken together; *though born later,
I preceded the day of their death.*

APPENDIX C.

DEGREES OF NOUNS ADJECTIVE.

i. From many adjectives two derivative adjectives are formed
in order to denote the degree of the quality exprest by them. The
simple form is called the *positive.* The *comparative* expresses a
higher degree of the quality in a comparison of two things or
persons. The *superlative* expresses a higher degree in a comparison
of more than two things or persons; as, **dūrus,** *hard,* **dūrior,** *harder,*
dūrissimus, *hardest.*

The comparative is sometimes used to express that the quality
is possessed in *too high* a degree.

The superlative is sometimes used to express that the quality is
possessed in a *very high* degree.

ii. Ordinary formation of Comparative and Superlative.

These derivative adjectives are formed from the positive as follows. (For a more accurate mode of statement see §§ 755, 917.)

1. The comparative is formed by adding ior (for the nom. sing. masc. and fem.) to the last consonant of the stem; i.e. by changing the inflexion i or is of the genitive into ior.

2. The superlative is formed by adding issimus to the last consonant of the stem; i.e. by changing the inflexion i or is of the genitive into issimus. Thus,

dūr-us,	gen. dur-ī,	comp. dur-ior,	superl. dur-issimus.
trist-is,	gen. trist-is,	comp. trist-ior,	superl. trist-issimus.
felix (felic-s),	gen. felic-is,	comp. felic-ior,	superl. felic-issimus.

Some adjectives form their superlative by doubling the last consonant of the stem and adding imus. These are

(a) Adjectives with stems ending in ĕro or ĕri, the e being omitted or retained, as in the positive, § 347.

pulcher, comp. pulchr-ior, superl. pulcher-rimus.

So niger, piger, ruber, tæter, vafer: acer, celĕber, salŭber.

asper, aspĕrior, asperrimus.

So cĕler, dexter (also rarely superl. dextimus), liber, miser, pauper, tĕner, über. Also

vĕtus	no comp.	vĕterrimus
prospĕrus		prosperrimus
sinister	sinisterior	(sinistimus only in augurial language)
no positive	dĕtĕrior	deterrimus
nūpĕrum (acc. Plaut. once)	nūpĕrior	no superl.

matūrus has matur-rimus, as well as the more common form maturissimus.

(sincērus, austērus, procērus, sevērus have superl. in issimus.)

(b) The following adjectives whose last stem consonant is l; fācilis, *easy;* similis, *like;* difficilis, *difficult;* dissimilis, *unlike;* gracilis, *thin, slender;* humilis, *low;* as, facil-is, facil-limus. (Imbecillis has imbecillissimus.)

The vowel preceding mus in superlatives was in the older language (including Cicero) ŭ not i; thus, durissŭmus, facillŭmus, pulcherrŭmus. So almost always in præ-Augustan inscriptions.

28

iii. Irregular or defective adjectives (besides those named in 2. *a*).

1. The following are either deficient in the positive degree or form their comparative and superlative irregularly or from a different stem:

Positive.	Comp.	Superl.
bŏnus, *good*	mĕlior	optĭmus
mălus, *bad*	pējor	pessĭmus
magnus, *great*	mājor	maxĭmus
parvus, *small*	mĭnor	mĭnĭmus (parvissĭmus, Varr., Lucr.)
multus, *much*	plūs (neut. cf. § 432)	plūrĭmus
nēqvam (indecl.), *wicked*	nēqvior	nēqvissĭmus
dīves } *rich* dīs }	dīvĭtior dītior	dīvĭtissĭmus (Cic.) dītissĭmus (Aug. and post-Aug.)
sĕnex, *old*	sĕnĭor	(nātu maxĭmus)
jŭvĕnis, *young*	jūnĭor (sometimes post-Aug. jŭvĕnior)	(nātu mĭnĭmus)
pŏtis, pŏtĕ (§ 417), *able, possible*	pŏtior, *better*	pŏtissĭmus, *best*
(no positive)	ōcĭor, *swifter*	ōcissĭmus
frūgi (indecl.)	frūgālior	frūgālissimus
ĕgens } ĕgēnus }	egentior	egentissimus
bĕnĕvŏlus bĕnĕvŏlens (Plaut.,Ter.) }	benevolentior	benevolentissimus
mălĕvŏlus mălĕvŏlens (Plaut.) }	malevolentior	malevolentissimus
mălĕdīcus mălĕdīcens (Plaut.) }	maledīcentior	maledīcentissimus
bĕnĕfīcus	benefĭcentior	benefĭcissimus (Cato) benefĭcentissimus
mălĕfīcus		malefĭcentissimus
magnĭfīcus	magnificentior	magnĭfĭcentissimus
mŭnĭfīcus		munĭfĭcentissimus
mīrĭfīcus		mirificissimus (Ter. once)
hŏnōrĭfĭcus	honorificentior	honorificentissimus
cītra (adv.), *on this side* (dē, prep. *down from*)	cĭtĕrior dētĕrior, *worse*	cĭtĭmus dēterrĭmus

extra (adv.), extĕr (adj.) Papin.) *outside*, (very rare in sing.) externus } extĕrior		{extrēmus {extĭmus
infra (adv.), infĕr (adj.), *low*) (chiefly used in plur. *the* {infĕrior *beings, places*, &c. *below*))		{infĭmus {īmus
intra (adv.), *within*	intĕrior	intĭmus
post, postĕrus, *next* (in time) {postĕrior, *hinder,* { *later*		{postrēmus, *last* {postŭmus, *last-born*
præ (prep.), *before*	prior	prīmus
prŏpe (adv.), *near*	prŏpior	proxĭmus
supra (adv.), sŭpĕr (adj.), *high*) (chiefly used in plur. *the* {supĕrior *beings, places*, &c. *above*))		{sŭprēmus, *highest,* { *last* (in time) {summus.
ultra (adv.), *beyond*	ultĕrior	ultĭmus

2. The following have superlative, but not comparative: bellus, cæsius, falsus, inclŭtus, invictus, invītus, nŏvus, săcer, văfer.

3. The following have comparative, but not superlative:

Verbals in -ĭlis: except amābilissimus (Cic., Sen.), hăbilissimus (Cels.), mirabilissimus (Col.), mōbilissimus (Cic., Tac.), stăbilissimus (Cato), fertilissimus (Cæs., Liv., Plin. *H. N.*), utilissimus, nobilissimus.

ălăcer, agrestis, arcānus, āter (Plaut.), diuturnus, exīlis, jējūnus, jŭvĕnis, longinquus, oblīqvus, opīmus, proclīvis, proximus (*of kinship*, in Sen., Ulp. &c.), prōnus, sătur, segnis, sĕnex, sērus, silvestris (Plin.), supīnus, surdus, taciturnus, tempestivus, vicīnus.

iv. Adjectives used only in the positive:

Many adjectives, which express an absolute state or quality, e.g. *material* (e.g. aureus), *time* (e.g. nocturnus), *relationship* (e.g. paternus), which does not readily admit the idea of a higher or lower degree, have no comparative or superlative. In some others they are wanting without any such apparent reason.

If a comparison is required in such adjectives the defect is supplied by adding măgis and maxime. Thus, magis mirus, *more wonderful*, maxime mirus, *most wonderful*.

Adjectives used only in the positive are chiefly of the following classes:

1. *Derivatives* ending in -ĭcus, -īnus, -īvus, -ōrus, -tĭmus, -ŭlus, -ālis or -āris, -ĭlis, and (from substantives) in -ātus and -ītus, as cīvĭcus, natūrālis, &c., barbātus, crīnītus.

28—2

Exceptions: rusticior (Sen.); rusticius, as adv. (Hor.).

æqvalior (Liv., Quint.), inæqvalior (Plin. *Ep.*), inæqvalissimus (Suet.); capitalior (Cic.); frugalior, frugalissimus; hospitalissimus (Cic.); liberalior, liberalissimus; mortalior (Plin. *H. N.*); penetralior (Lucr.); regalior (Plaut.); vocalior (Sen., Quint.), vocalissimus (Plin. *Ep.*).

familiarior (Liv.), familiarissimus; popularior (Liv.); salutarior (Cic.).

civilior (Ov.); juvenilior (Ov.); puerilior (Hor.).

2. *Compounds;* as inops, magnanimus, &c.

Except those named above from dico, facio, volo (§ iii. p. 434).

amentior (Cass., Cic., Suet.), amentissimus (Cic.); dementior, dementissimus (Cic.); ingentior (Verg.).

concordior (Plaut.), concordissimus (Cic., Sen.); misericordior (Plaut., Cic.); vecordissimus (*Or. pro Domo*).

inertior, inertissimus (Cic.); sollertior (Cic., Ov.), sollertissimus (Cato, Sall.).

deformior (Cic., Mart., Plin.); insignior (Liv.); perennior (Hor.); immanior (Cic., Verg.), immanissimus (Cic., Plin. *Ep.*).

3. Adjectives *ending in* -us, *preceded by a vowel.*

(*a*) But u often is, or becomes, consonantal, and thus allows a comparative or superlative without difficulty; e.g. in -qvus and -gvis; e.g. antiqvior, antiqvissimus; pingvior, pingvissimus; tenvis, tenvior, tenvissimus.

ardvior, arduissimus (Cato); assidvior (Varr.), assiduissimus (Suet., and as adv. Cic.); exiguior (Col.), exiguissimus (Ov., Plin. *Ep.*); strenuior (Plaut., Lucil.), strenuissimus (Cato, Sall. &c.); vacuissimus (Ov.); perpetuior, perpetuissimus (Cato).

(*b*) industrior (Plaut.); piissimus (condemned by Cic. *Phil.* 13. 19, but used by Antony, Sen., Curt., Tac.); noxior (Sen.). On alsius see p. 240.

4. The following: albus, almus, cădūcus, calvus, cānus, cĭcŭr, claudus, cōmis (comior once in Cic.), compos, curvus, dirus (dirior once in Cic.), fĕrus, gnārus, lăcer, luscus, mancus, mĕdiocris, mĕmor, immĕmor, mĕrus, mīrus (mirior Fest., Varr.), mūtĭlus, mūtus, gnāvus, nĕfastus, par, impar, dispar, rŭdis, trux, văgus.

v. Many participles present and past have comparatives and superlatives.

Neue (II. 91) gives the following lists of participles, with the time of the *first* occurrence of one or other form (i.e. comparative or superlative).

1. Present Participle:

(*a*) In Cicero: amans, appetens, ardens, continens, egens, fervens, flagrans, florens, indulgens, negligens, patiens, temperans, tuens, valens.

(*b*) In Cæs. or Liv. (not in Cic.): obœdiens, patens.

(*c*) In imperial times: abstinens, audens, decens, instans, metuens, obseqvens, reverens.

2. Past Participle:

(*a*) In Cicero: abjectus, acceptus, accommodatus, accuratus, adstrictus, apertus, apparatus, attentus, aversus, celebratus, commendatus, commotus, concitatus, conditus, confirmatus, conjunctus, contemptus, contractus, cultus, cumulatus, demissus, despectus, desperatus, despicatus, disjunctus, dissolutus, distortus, doctus, effusus, erectus, eruditus, exercitatus, exoptatus, expeditus, exploratus, expressus, exqvisitus, exspectatus, fractus, impeditus, incitatus, inqvinatus, instructus, intentus, junctus, munitus, obstinatus, obtusus, occultus, optatus, ornatus, pacatus, paratus, perditus, perfectus, perversus, politus, pressus, probatus, productus, promptus, refertus, remissus, remotus, restrictus, sedatus, solutus, spectatus, suspectus.

(*b*) In Cæs. or Liv. (not in Cic.): auctus, citatus, confertus, conspectus, distinctus, diversus, excitatus, extentus, insignitus.

(*c*) In imperial times: coloratus, compressus, confusus, effectus, elatus, emendatus, fusus, ordinatus.

But the comparative or superlative of many other participles occurs occasionally.

APPENDIX D.

NUMERALS, MEASURES, WEIGHTS, &c.

i. List of Numerals (chiefly from Neue, cf. supr. p. 103).

ARABIC SIGNS.	ROMAN SIGNS.	CARDINAL: answering to the question quot? *how many?* (adjectives).	ORDINAL: answering the question quotus? *which in numerical order?* (all declinable adjectives).	DISTRIBUTIVE: answering to the question quoteni? *how many each?* (all declinable adjectives plural).	NUMERAL ADVERBS: answering the question quotiens (quoties)? *how many times?* (see § 168. 3 *b*).
1	I.	ûnus, a, um	prîmus, a, um *first of two*; prior	singŭli, æ, a	sēmĕl
2	II.	duo, æ, o	secundus; alter	bîni	bis
3	III.	tres, tria	tertius	terni (or trîni, cf. inf.)	têr
4	IIII. or IV.	qvattuor	qvartus	qvâterni	qvâtĕr
5	V.	qvinqve	qvintus	qvîni	qvinqviens
6	VI.	sex	sextus	sēni	sexiens
7	VII.	septem	septimus	septēni	septiens
8	VIII. or IIX.	octo	octâvus	octôni	octiens
9	VIIII. or IX.	nŏvem	nônus	nŏvēni	nŏviens
10	X.	dĕcem	dĕcimus	dēni	dēciens
11	XI.	undĕcim	undĕcimus	undēni	undēciens
12	XII.	duodĕcim	duodĕcimus	dŭŏdēni	duodēciens
13	XIII.	tredĕcim	tertius decimus	terni dēni	terdēciens
14	XIIII. or XIV.	qvattuordĕcim	qvartus decimus	qvâterni dēni	qvâterdēciens

No.	Roman	Cardinal	Ordinal	Distributive	Adverbial
15	XV.	qvindécim	qvintus decimus	qvíni déni	qvindéciens
16	XVI.	sédécim	sextus decimus	séni déni	sédéciens
17	XVII.	septemdécim	septimus decimus	septéni déni	septiens déciens
18	XVIII. or XIIX.	duodéviginti	duodévicénsimus	duodévicéni	duodéviciens (?)
19	XVIIII. or XIX.	undéviginti	undévicénsimus	undévicéni	undéviciens (?)
20	XX.	viginti	vicénsimus	vicéni	viciens
21	XXI.	ūnus et viginti	unus (more rarely primus) et vicensimus	vicéni singuli	semel et viciens
22	XXII.	duo et viginti	alter et vicensimus	viceni bini	bis et viciens
28	XXVIII. or XXIIX.	duodétriginta	duodetricensimus	duodetricéni	duodetriciens
29	XXVIIII. or XXIX.	undetriginta	undetricensimus	undetricéni	undetriciens (?)
30	XXX.	triginta	tricénsimus	tricéni	triciens
40	XXXX. or XL.	qvadráginta	qvadrágénsimus	qvadrágéni	qvadragiens
50	L.	qvinqvaginta	qvinqvagensimus	qvinqvágéni	qvinqvagiens (also qvinqvagésiens, Plaut.)
60	LX.	sexaginta	sexagénsimus	sexágéni	sexagiens
70	LXX.	septuaginta	septuagénsimus	septuágéni	septuagiens
80	LXXX. or XXC.	octóginta	octogensimus	octogéni	octogiens
90	LXXXX. or XC.	nónáginta	nonagensimus	nonágéni	nonagiens
98	XCIX. or IIC.	octo et nonaginta	duodecentensimus	duodecenteni	duodecentiens
99	XCIX. or IC.	undecentum	undecentensimus	undecenteni	undecentiens
100	C.	centum	centénsimus	centeni	centiens
101	CI.	centum et unus	centensimus primus	centeni singuli	centiens semel
124	CXXIIII. or CXXIV.	centum viginti qvattuor	centensimus vicensimus qvartus	centeni viceni qvaterni	centiens viciens qvater
200	CC.	dúcenti, æ, a	ducentensimus	duceni	ducentiens
230	CCXXX.	ducenti(æ, a) triginta	ducentensimus tricensimus censimus	duceni triceni	ducentiens triciens

List of Numerals (*Continued*).

300	CCC.	trĕcenti, æ, a	trecentensimus	treceni	trecentiens
400	CCCC.	qvadringenti, æ, a	qvadringentensimus	qvadringeni	qvadringentiens
500	IƆ.	qvingenti, æ, a	qvingentensimus	qvingeni	qvingentiens
600	IƆC.	sescenti, æ, a	sescentensimus	sesceni	sescentiens
700	IƆCC.	septingenti, æ, a	septingentensimus	septingeni	septingentiens
800	IƆCCC.	octingenti, æ, a	octingentensimus	octingeni	octingentiens
900	IƆCCCC.	nongenti, æ, a	nongentensimus	nongeni	nongentiens
1000	CIƆ.	mille	millensimus	singula millia	milliens
1235	CIƆCCXXXV.	mille ducenti (æ, a) triginta qvinque	millensimus ducentensimus tricensimus qvintus	singula millia ducena tricena quina	milliens ducentiens triciens qvinqviens
2000	CIƆCIƆ.	duo millia	bis millensimus	bina millia	bis milliens
4000	CIƆCIƆCIƆCIƆ.	qvattuor millia	qvater millensimus	qvaterna millia	qvater milliens
5000	IƆƆ.	qvinqve millia	qvinqviens millensimus	qvina millia	qvinqviens milliens
6000	IƆƆCIƆ.	sex millia	sexiens millensimus	sena millia	sexiens milliens
10,000	CCIƆƆ.	decem millia	deciens millensimus	dena millia	deciens milliens
20,000	CCIƆƆCCIƆƆ.	viginti millia	viciens millensimus	vicena millia	viciens milliens
50,000	IƆƆƆ.	qvinqvaginta millia	qvinqvagiens millensimus	qvinqvagena millia	qvinqvagiens milliens
100,000	CCCIƆƆƆ.	centum millia	centiens millensimus	centena millia	centiens milliens
500,000	IƆƆƆ.	qvingentá millia	qvingentiens millensimus	qvingena millia	qvingentiens milliens
100,000,000	CCCCIƆƆƆƆ.	deciĕns centum millia	deciens centiens millensimus	deciens centena millia	deciens centiens milliens

In spelling, on the above table, the terminations of the ordinals -ensimus (instead of the older -ensumus, and later -esimus), and of the adverbs -ens (instead of the later -es), and of millia (not milia), the *Monumentum Ancyranum* has been followed.

In some good MSS. other forms for the distributives of hundreds are (rarely) found; e.g. ducenteni, qvadringenteni, &c., and these forms are mentioned by Priscian.

Multiplicative adjectives are formed with the suffix -plex, *-fold*, viz. simplex, sescuplex (*one and a half fold*), duplex, triplex, quadruplex, qvincuplex, septemplex, decemplex, centuplex.

Others in -plus are generally used in neuter only, to denote a magnitude *twice*, &c. *as great* as another. These are simplus, sescuplus, duplus, triplus, qvadruplus, octuplus.

For derivatives like primānus, *of the first* (legion), see § 830; primarius, *of the first* (rank), § 942, 1; and the names of the numbers, e.g. binio, *two*, see § 852.

Another series (see esp. Frontin., *de aquæduct.*, 26—62) is binarius, *containing two*, ternarius, qvaternarius, qvīnarius, sēnarius, septenarius, octonarius, nŏvenarius, denarius, duodenarius, vicenarius ("lex quina vicenaria," Plaut.), tricenarius, qvadragenarius, qvinqvagenarius, sexagenarius, septuagenarius, octogenarius, nonagenarius, centenarius, ducenarius, trecenarius, qvadringenarius, qvingenarius, septingenarius, octingenarius, millenarius. Comp. § 942, 1.

ii. Signs for Numerals.

In writing numbers a stroke over the (Roman) letters indicates thousands, and top as well as side strokes indicate hundred thousands; e.g. X̄VIII. is duodeviginti millia, X̄X̄CCCC. is viginti millia quadringenti, |X̄|CLXXXDC is deciens centum millia et octoginta millia sescenti (1,180,600)[1]. See also in § xii.

The signs[2] for 50, 100, 1000 were originally the three Greek aspirate letters which the Romans did not require, viz. Ψ, ⊙, Φ, i.e. χ, θ, φ. The Ψ was written ⊥ and abbreviated into L; ⊙ from a false notion of its origin made like the initial of centum; and Φ assimilated to ordinary letters CIƆ. The half of Φ, viz. D, was taken for ½ 1000, i.e. 500; X probably from the ancient form of θ, viz. ⊗, being adopted for 10, the half of it V was taken for 5 (Ritschl[2]). According to others, an outstretched finger, the open hand, and the double hand, were taken, viz. I, V, X for 1, 5, 10; and another position of V (viz. L) for 50[3].

[1] Marquardt, *Röm. Alterth.* III. 2, p. 32.
[2] *Rhein. Mus.* 1869, XXIV. p. 12.
[3] See Mommsen, *Röm. Gesch.* B. 1. kap. XIV.

iii. Inflexions of Numerals.

Unus. For mode of declension see § 371. In the plural it is only used with substantives whose plural *denotes* a singular, e.g. **unæ litteræ,** *one epistle;* **unæ ædes,** *one house (set of rooms,* or *of hearths?);* **uni mores,** *one and the same conduct;* **uni Suevi,** *the single tribe of the Suevi* (or *the Suevi alone*).

Duo. The masc. and neut. are: nom. acc. **duo,** gen. **duorum** or **duum,** dat. abl. **duōbus.** For the m. acc. **duos** is also used. The fem. is: nom. **duæ,** acc. **duas,** gen. **duarum** or **duum,** dat. abl. **duābus.** **Ambo,** *both,* is similarly declined. In expressions like **duodecim, duodeviginti, duoetvicesimus, duo** is not varied.

Nom. and acc. **tres,** n. **tria,** gen. **trium,** dat. **tribus.**

All the other cardinal numbers up to **centum** are undeclined: so also is **mille** when used as an adjective. As a substantive it has a declinable plural **millia, millium, millibus** (cf. § 177): but in the singular is only used in nom. or acc., except ablative (**mille**) in Pl. *Trin.* 959 and (**milli**) Lucil. ap. Gell. I. 16. In expressions like **cæsi sunt tria millia trecenti milites,** we must supply **militum** after **millia.** If the name of the thing, &c. numbered precede, it is usually put in the genitive, e.g. **militum** (not **milites**) **tria millia trecenti cæsi sunt.**

The other cardinal, all the ordinal and the distributive numbers, are declinable adjectives with -o stems. The genitive plural of the cardinals and distributives is usually in -um for -orum (cf. § 365.); e.g. **non plus mille qvingentum æris** (for **qvingentorum nummorum**); **senum septenumque denum.**

iv. Order in compounding Numerals.

In compound numbers, from *thirteen* to *nineteen* inclusive, the smaller is usually prefixed to the larger without et, e.g. **septem decem** (or **septemdecim**), **septimus decimus, septeni deni, septies decies**; but in cardinals and ordinals the order is sometimes reversed, and in cardinals et is sometimes inserted, especially if the larger come first, e.g. **decem septem, decem et septem, septem et decem: decimus septimus** (Sen.).

From *twenty-one* to *ninety-nine,* the rule is that, either the larger should precede the smaller number without et, or the smaller precede the larger with et, e.g. **viginti qvattuor** or **qvattuor et viginti; vicesimus quartus** or **qvartus et vicesimus,** &c.; but in the ordinals and distributives, exceptions to both usages occur, e.g. **qvadragesimum et sextum, sexto tricesimo, qvinqvagena et singula, qvinos vicenos,** &c.; and in cardinals and distributives the conjunction is sometimes inserted even when the larger precedes, e.g. **viginti et septem** (Cic.), **qvadraginta et qvisque** (Liv.), **vicies ac septies,** &c.

From a *hundred and one* upwards, the larger number is usually put first, either without or (except distributives) with a conjunction, e.g. **ducentos (et) qvadraginta (et) qvattuor, qvingentesimum (et) qvinqvagesimum (et) octavum, duceni septuageni, centies (et) qvadragies**; but with a conjunction the smaller (cardinal or ordinal) number sometimes is found preceding, e.g. **qvinqvagintā et ducentā, septimum et qvinqvagesimum ac centesimum.** So also **ducentos et mille, mille et ducentos.**

For *eighteen, nineteen, twenty-eight, twenty-nine,* &c., the subtractive forms (e.g. **duodeviginti, undeviginti, undetrigesimus,** &c.) are most common, but compound forms are also found, e.g. **decem octo, decem et octo** (frequently), **octodecim** (rare); **novem et triginta, qvinqvaginta octo, triginta novem** (Liv.), **octavo decimo** (Tac.), **octoni deni** (Liv.).

v. Use of classes of Numerals.

The *ordinal,* not the *cardinal,* is used in giving the date, e.g. *In the year* 1869 is anno **millesimo octingentesimo sexagesimo nono.**

The *distributives* are used

(1) to denote that the number belongs to each of several persons or things, e.g. **Cæsar et Ariovistus denos comites ad colloqvium adduxerunt,** *took ten companions each;* **pueri senum septenumve denum annorum,** *boys of sixteen or seventeen years old,* i.e. *each was* 16 *or* 17; **ambulare bina millia passuum,** *to walk two miles each time;* **tritici modius erat sestertiis ternis,** *corn was at three sesterces the* (i.e. *each*) *bushel.* If **singuli** is expressed with the persons, &c., the cardinal number may be used with the things numbered, e.g. **singulis denarii trecenti imperabantur,** *each was required to pay three hundred pence.* In this use **terni,** not **trini,** is used.

(2) in expressions of multiplication, e.g. **bis bina,** *twice two;* **ter novenæ virgines,** *thrice nine girls;* **decies centena millia,** *ten times a hundred thousand.* In these expressions the distributive numerals, e.g. **decies centena millia,** do not mean *a million to each person,* but *a hundred thousand taken each of ten times.*

(3) with nouns which have no singular, e.g. **bina castra,** *the two camps;* **trinis hostium spoliis,** *with three sets of spoils from the enemy.* (In this use **uni** not **singuli**; **trini** not **terni** is used.)

(4) Poets use distributives as merely equivalent to cardinals, e.g. **centum quoi brachia dicunt centenasque manus** (Verg. *A.* x. 565), i.e. *a hundred hands in all,* not a hundred in each arm. So also post-Augustan writers use **trinus** (not **ternus**).

(5) In the singular the distributives are sometimes used, chiefly

by poets, e.g. centauri corpore bino, *a double body;* centenāque arbore fluctum verberat assurgens (Verg.), *with an hundred-fold shaft,* i.e. *a hundred oars;* novena lampade, *with nine torches (a torch repeated nine times).*

Every other is expressed by alterni; e.g. alternis diebus, *every second day.*

vi. Expression of Fractions[1].

Fractions are expressed in words in several ways:

1. All fractions, with 1 for numerator, are denoted by ordinal numbers, with or without pars, e.g. $\frac{1}{2}$, dimidium (not dimidia) or dimidia pars; $\frac{1}{3}$, tertia or tertia pars; $\frac{1}{4}$, qvarta, &c.

2. All fractions with a numerator less by one than the denominator are denoted by the cardinal with partes simply, e.g. $\frac{2}{3}$, duæ partes; $\frac{3}{4}$, tres partes; $\frac{4}{5}$, qvattuor partes; $\frac{5}{6}$, qvinque partes.

3. All fractions with 12, or its multiples for a denominator, are denoted by the parts of an as, which is taken as the whole and is equal to 12 unciæ. (See below, § viii.) Hence heres ex asse, *heir to the whole inheritance:* ex triente, *to a third;* ex dimidia et sextante, *to two thirds (a half and a sixth).*

4. Other fractions, not expressible by one of the above methods, are denoted by the cardinal for a numerator, and the ordinal (as in subsection 1) for the denominator, e.g. $\frac{4}{7}$, quattuor septimæ; $\frac{7}{9}$, septem ncnæ.

5. Some fractions are denoted by resolution into their components, e.g. $\frac{3}{4}$, dimidia et quarta; $\frac{2}{3}$, pars dimidia et sexta; $\frac{4}{9}$, pars tertia et nona; $\frac{10}{21}$, pars tertia et septima.

6. Sometimes further division is resorted to, e.g. $\frac{1}{10}$, dimidia qvinta. And dimidia tertia is used for sexta; dimidia qvarta for octava.

7. Sesqui, $1\frac{1}{2}$, is used only in compounds, see § 987 (p. 386).

vii. Money coinage.
(Chiefly from Hultsch, see below, p. 451.)

Coined money was not used at Rome till the time of the Decemviral legislation (303 U.C.=451 B.C.). The coin was called an as, and was supposed to weigh a pound; hence called in distinction from the subsequent as, as libralis or librarius. Coins also existed for the semis, triens, qvadrans, sextans, and uncia. The real weight (of unworn pieces now found) was 9 to 11 unciæ and may be taken

---

[1] Chiefly from Gossrau, *Lat. Sprachlehre,* § 125.

therefore at 10 unciæ. The coinage was of copper (æs), alloyed with tin and lead. Analysis of these pieces gives 7·16 to 7·66 per cent. of tin; and 19·56 to 29·32 per cent. of lead.

In 485 U.C. (=269 B.C.), shortly before the first Punic war, silver was first coined, and at the same time the as was reduced to the weight of 4 unciæ (and then gradually before the end of the 1st Punic war to 2 unciæ) instead of an actual 10, nominal 12, unciæ. Three silver coins were introduced, the **denarius** (often stamped with a **biga**, or **quadriga**, and thence called **bigatus** or **quadrigatus**) = 10 (reduced) asses; the **qvinarius** = 5 asses; the **sestertius** = 2½ asses. The coin equivalent to the reduced as was of copper and called **libella**; the half of this was **sembella**; the quarter (of the **libella**) was **teruncius**. The double as was coined and called **dupondius**; other coins were **tressis** = 3 asses; **decessis** = 10 asses. The denarius was probably $\frac{1}{72}$ pound of silver.

In the year 537 U.C. (=217 B.C.) the copper as was reduced to the weight of one uncia, and to the value of $\frac{1}{16}$ denarius or $\frac{1}{4}$ sestertius. Probably at the same time the denarius, which had been gradually losing, was reduced so as to be equal to $\frac{1}{84}$ pound of silver. The as eventually sunk to the value of $\frac{1}{2}$ uncia.

A new silver coin called **victoriatus**, because stamped on the reverse with a figure of Victory, was introduced probably about the year 228 B.C. At first it was $\frac{3}{4}$ denarius, afterwards by the Clodian law, 104 B.C., it was reduced to be = $\frac{1}{2}$ denarius, and as such was known to Varro, Cicero, &c.

In the time of Nero the denarius was again reduced to $\frac{1}{96}$ pound of silver, and remained at this until Marcus Aurelius. At the same time Nero debased the silver, which hitherto had been fine, by an admixture of 5 to 10 per cent. of alloy. Under Trajan, about the year 100, the alloy was 15 per cent., under Hadrian nearly 20 per cent., under Marcus Aurelius 25 per cent., under Commodus 30 per cent., under Septimius Severus 50 to 60 per cent.

Copper coinage was dropped from about 84 to 74 B.C. until 15 B.C. (Except that some coins by Antony are found.) Then the silver sesterce being given up, a four-as piece was coined instead; and a piece of half the value of the new sesterce, viz. the dupondius. Both these were of brass (the proportions being not quite $\frac{1}{5}$ zinc to more than $\frac{4}{5}$ copper). The as, semis and qvadrans were of copper.

Gold was first coined in 217 B.C.; but sparsely until Sulla, Pompey and Cæsar. Cæsar's coin called **aureus** was fixed as equivalent to 25 **denarii** or 100 sesterces.

The value of these different coins is as follows according to Hultsch. Hultsch's values are reduced to English money on the basis of 1 silver groschen = 1½d. sterling.

	Silver groschen.	Eng. mon.
As libralis (copper) . . .	4·7	5·3*d.*
269—217 B.C.		
As sextantarius (= ⅖ sestertius) (copper)	·8 [1]	·93*d.*
Sestertius (silver) . . .	2·	2⅓*d.*
Denarius (silver) . . .	8·2	9⅓*d.*
217—30 B.C.		nearly
Sestertius (silver)	1·7	2*d.*
Denarius (silver)	7·	8¼*d.*
Aureus (gold) = 25 denarii = 100 sestertii		17*s.*

Hence the following amounts are deduced :

Mille sestertium	£8. 10*s.*
Decies sestertium = 1,000,000 sestertii	£8500.

In intrinsic value the denarius is reckoned by Hussey at 8·62
pence; the aureus, in terms of the English sovereign, at £1. 1*s.* 1½*d.*
If the value of the denarius (fixed at the twenty-fifth of the aureus)
is deduced from this value, it would, of course, be considerably
higher than that given above.

viii. Expression of sums of money.

The denarius which was the silver coin in most currency was
little used in reckoning. The ordinary unit of reckoning was the
sestertius, or nummus, or, in full, sestertius nummus.

Up to 2000, the cardinal numbers are prefixed, e.g. centum sestertii, ducenti sestertii. But for higher numbers, in thousands up
to a million, a neuter substantive in the plural number was used,
sestertia, e.g. duo or septem sestertia for duo or septem millia
sestertium (the short form of the genitive plural being taken for a
neuter substantive); sestertium sexagena millia, sestertium sexagena
millia nummum, sestertium nummum qvinqve millia.

For sums of a million and upwards numeral adverbs are resorted
to, e.g. decies centum (or centena) millia sestertium. Usually the
numeral adverb and sestertium are put alone, e.g. decies sestertium;
similarly duodecies sestertium (1,200,000), ter et vicies (2,300,000).
In these expressions again sestertium was taken to be a neuter substantive, and described as such, but in the singular number only,
e.g. (nom.) sestertium qvadragies relinqvitur (4,000,000); (acc.)
sestertium qvadragies accepi; (abl.) sestertio decies fundum emi,
in sestertio vicies egere (*to be poor in the possession of* 2,000,000
sesterces). Occasionally, when the context is clear, the adverb alone
is put, and sestertium omitted. Sometimes other parts of the full

---

[1] But intrinsically worth from 1·97 to 0·93 silv. gr.

expression are omitted, e.g. decies centena millia, decies centena. (cf. § v. 2.) As an instance of a composite expression may serve, Accepi vicies ducenta, triginta qvinqve milia, qvadringentos decem et septem nummos (C. *Verr.* Lib. I. 14), 2,235,417 sesterces[1].

The sign for a denarius was X, for a qvinarius V, for an as I, for a dupondius II, for a sestertius IIS (for duo + semis). Sometimes a line is drawn through the middle of these signs, and hence printers have substituted for IIS HS. Hence IIS decem = 10 sesterces; IIS decem millia = 10,000 sesterces; IIS decies = 10,00,000. If the numbers were not written in full but denoted by letters an ambiguity might arise, which was however obviated by adding (see § ii.) a top line for thousands $\overline{\text{IIS}}$; and top and side lines for hundred-thousands when the sum was equal to a million or more[2]; e.g. Plin. 33. 3, 17, §§ 55, 56 (ed. Jan.). Auri in aerario populi Romani fuere sex Julio L. Aurelio coss. septem annis ante bellum Punicum tertium, pondo $\overline{\text{XVII.CCCX.}}$, argenti $\overline{\text{XXII.LXX.}}$ et in numerato $\overline{|\text{LXI}|.\text{XXXV.CCCC.}}$; Sex. Julio d. Marcio coss. hoc est, belli socialis initio, auri $\overline{|\text{XVI}|.\text{XX.DCCCXXXI.}}$: i.e. *There was in the Roman treasury in the year* 157 B.C., *in weight* 17,410 (*pounds*) *of gold*, 22,070 (*pounds*) *of silver*, *and in count* (i.e. *in coin*) 6,135,400 *sesterces; in the year* 91 B.C. 1,620,831 (*pounds?*) *of gold.*

The as[3] consisted originally of 12 unciæ, and there were distinct names and signs for each multiple of the uncia and for some fractions of it.

unciæ.		as.	sign.
12	assis or as, *a pound*	1	I
11	deunx (de-uncia), *an ounce-off*	$\frac{11}{12}$	S - - - -
10	dextans (desextans), *a sixth-off*	$\frac{5}{6}$	S - -
9	dodrans (deqvadrans), *a fourth-off*	$\frac{3}{4}$	S - -
8	bessis or bes (dvi-assis), *a two-as*[4]	$\frac{2}{3}$	S -
7	septunx (septem unciæ), *a seven-ounce*	$\frac{7}{12}$	S -
6	semissis or semis (semi-assis), *a half-as*	$\frac{1}{2}$	S.
5	qvincunx (qvinqveunciæ), *a five-ounce*	$\frac{5}{12}$	- - -
4	triens (tri-), *a third*	$\frac{1}{3}$	- -
3	qvadrans or teruncius (qvattvor-), *a fourth*	$\frac{1}{4}$	- -

---

[1] Madvig, *Lat. Gr.* Append. II.

[2] Marquardt, *Röm. Alterth.* Th. III. Abth. 2, p. 32.

[3] See Volusius Mæcianus in *Metrol. Script.* II. p. 61 sqq.; Hultsch's *Preface* to same, pp. xxv. to xxviii.; *Prolegom.* pp. 17—22; Marquardt, *Röm. Alt.* III. 2, pp. 41—44, V. 1, p. 102.

[4] This term must either have been formed when the as was equal to 4 unciæ; or be short for *two-thirds* of an as (cf. § vi. 2).

unciæ.		as.	sign.
2	**sextans** (sexto-), *a sixth*	$\frac{1}{6}$	—
$1\frac{1}{2}$	**sescuncia** (sesqvi-uncia), *one and a half ounce*	$\frac{1}{8}$	- Σ
1	**uncia,** *an ounce*	$\frac{1}{12}$	—
$\frac{1}{2}$	**semuncia,** *a half-ounce*	$\frac{1}{24}$	Σ or £
$\frac{1}{4}$	**sicilicus,** *a Sicilian* farthing	$\frac{1}{48}$	)
$\frac{1}{6}$	**sextula,** *a little sixth*	$\frac{1}{72}$	~ or \\

Of the above the **sicilicus** was not used till imperial times. The **scriptulum** or **scripulum** (γράμμα) was also used for $\frac{1}{24}$ of the **uncia,** $=\frac{1}{288}$ **as.** The fraction $\frac{1}{36}$ **as** was denoted by **binæ sextulæ,** or **duella;** $\frac{1}{144}$ **as** by **dimidia sextula,** or **duo scripula.**

The above-named parts of the **as** were used (as has been said) as mere duodecimal fractions, applicable without any specific concrete meaning to any unit. See below, p. 449.

Though this system had its origin at the time when money was copper, taken by weight, it survived several changes in the monetary system. It has been mentioned that when silver money was first coined the **denarius** was the unit, and equal to 10 asses; the **sestertius** to $2\frac{1}{2}$ asses. Each of these asses was called **libella.** The half of a **libella** was called **sembella** (Varr.) or **singula** (Mæc.); the half of the **sembella** or quarter of the **libella** was called **teruncius.** Pre-sently the **denarius** was made equivalent to 16 asses, and the **sestertius** to 4 asses.

Now in money accounts the **denarius** (of 16 asses) was sometimes taken as the unit; at other times the **sestertius** (of 4 asses). The "*odd pence*" (æs **excurrens**) required to be noted in each case. The **as** and each number of asses up to the **denarius,** the half-**as** and each number of half asses up to the **sestertius,** required a sign. For the 'odd pence,' when the **denarius** was the unit, the old *duodecimal* system was applied, and the sixteenths were expressed by twelfths, and combinations of twelfths, half-twelfths, and quarter-twelfths. For the 'odd pence,' when the **sestertius** was the unit, the old *decimal* system (which was now no longer required for the **denarius**) was applied, and the asses and half-asses up to the **sestertius** were expressed by tenths (**libellæ**), half-tenths, and quarter-tenths.

The following were the modes of expressions used in each case.

'ODD PENCE,' when the **denarius** was the unit. N.B. The crossed X (for denarius) ought to be prefixed to all the signs. In this duodecimal system the half denoted by S contains 6 parts; but $\frac{ō}{12} = \frac{8}{16}$.

asses.		denarii.	sign.	name of sign.	explanation of name.
16	denarius	1			
15	qvindeciære[1]	$\frac{15}{16}$	S———Ɔ	deunx sicilicus	$\frac{11}{12} + \frac{1}{48}$
14	qvattvordeciære	$\frac{7}{8}$	S——ƆƆ	dextans semuncia	$\frac{5}{6} + \frac{1}{24}$
13	tredeciære	$\frac{13}{16}$	S———ƆƆ	dodrans semuncia sicilicus	$\frac{3}{4} + \frac{1}{24} + \frac{1}{48}$
12	duodeciære	$\frac{3}{4}$	S———	dodrans	$\frac{3}{4}$
11	undeciære	$\frac{11}{16}$	S——Ɔ	bes sicilicus	$\frac{2}{3} + \frac{1}{48}$
10	decus (decussis)	$\frac{10}{16}$	S—ƆƆ	septunx semuncia	$\frac{7}{12} + \frac{1}{24}$
9	nonus (nonussis)	$\frac{9}{16}$	SƆƆ	semis semuncia sicilicus	$\frac{1}{2} + \frac{1}{24} + \frac{1}{48}$
8	octus (octussis)	$\frac{8}{16}$	S	semis	$\frac{1}{2}$
7	septus (septussis)	$\frac{7}{16}$	———Ɔ	quincunx sicilicus	$\frac{5}{12} + \frac{1}{48}$
6	sexis	$\frac{6}{16}$	————ƆƆ	triens semuncia	$\frac{1}{3} + \frac{1}{24}$
5	qvinqves (quinquessis?)	$\frac{5}{16}$	————ƆƆ	qvadrans semuncia sicilicus	$\frac{1}{4} + \frac{1}{24} + \frac{1}{48}$
4	qvattrussis	$\frac{4}{16}$	————	qvadrans	$\frac{1}{4}$
3	tressis	$\frac{3}{16}$	——Ɔ	sextans sicilicus	$\frac{1}{6} + \frac{1}{48}$
2	dupundius	$\frac{2}{16}$	Ɔ—	sescuncia	$\frac{1}{8} + \frac{1}{48}$
1	as (assis)	$\frac{1}{16}$	ƆƆ	semuncia sicilicus	$\frac{1}{24} + \frac{1}{48}$

'ODD PENCE,' when the **sestertius** was the unit. In this *decimal* system the half denoted by S contains 5 parts.

asses.		sestertii.	sign. IIS	name of sign.	explanation of name.
4	sestertius	1	S———ƆT	octo libellæ singula teruncius	$\frac{8}{10} + \frac{1}{20} + \frac{1}{40}$
3½	tressis semis	$\frac{7}{8}$	S——Ɔ	septem libellæ singula	$\frac{7}{10} + \frac{1}{20}$
3	tressis	$\frac{3}{4}$	S—T	sex libellæ teruncius	$\frac{6}{10} + \frac{1}{40}$
2½	dupundius semis	$\frac{5}{8}$	S	qvinqvé libellæ	$\frac{5}{10}$
2	dupundius	$\frac{1}{2}$	——ƆT	tres libellæ singula teruncius	$\frac{3}{10} + \frac{1}{20} + \frac{1}{40}$
1½	as semis	$\frac{3}{8}$	——Ɔ	duæ libellæ singula	$\frac{2}{10} + \frac{1}{20}$
1	as	$\frac{1}{4}$	—T	libella teruncius	$\frac{1}{10} + \frac{1}{40}$
½	semis	$\frac{1}{8}$			

5 parts.

---

[1] i. e. quindecim *æro, fifteen in copper*. Comp. the use of **pondo**.

ix. Expression of Interest of Money.

Interest was denoted at first by the proportionate part of the capital, and the parts of the as were made use of for this purpose. Thus the decemviral legislation fixed legal interest at $\frac{1}{12}$ of the capital, fenus unciarium. This is equivalent to $8\frac{1}{3}$ per cent., and if Niebuhr's views be right, that this originally related to the old year of ten months, it would be equivalent to 10 per cent. for a year of twelve months. In 347 B.C. the rate was reduced to semunciarium fænus, i. e. $\frac{1}{24}$ of the capital, i. e. 5 per cent. for the year of twelve months.

In and after Sulla's time, the more common Greek method of reckoning interest *by the month* came in, and the legal rate was $\frac{1}{100}$ of the capital per month, called centesima (sc. pars sortis), i.e. 12 per cent. for a year. Lower rates of interest were denoted by the fractional parts of the as (the centesima being taken as the as), higher rates by distributives (or a combination of distributives and fractions). The following expressions are found either in the *Corpus Juris* or Cicero[1]. Interest is expressed by the plural usuræ, in apposition to the parts of the as:

usuræ unciæ . .	i.e. $\frac{1}{12}$ of the centesima .		= 1 per cent.		
usuræ qvadrantes .	$\frac{1}{4}$	......	= 3	...	
usuræ trientes or tertia centesimæ pars	$\frac{1}{3}$	......	= 4	...	
usuræ qvincunces . .	$\frac{5}{12}$	......	= 5	...	
usuræ semisses or dimidia centesimæ .	$\frac{1}{2}$	......	= 6	...	
usuræ besses or bes centesimæ . . .	$\frac{2}{3}$	......	= 8	...	
usuræ deunces . . .	$\frac{11}{12}$	......	= 11	...	
usuræ centesimæ . .		......	= 12	...	
binæ centesimæ, . .		......	= 24	...	
ternæ centesimæ . .		......	= 36	...	
qvaternæ centesimæ .		......	= 48	...	
qvinæ (centesimæ) .		......	= 60	...	

But the singular is sometimes found, e.g. fenus ex triente factum erat bessibus (C. *Att.* IV. 15). Interest rose from $\frac{1}{3}$ to $\frac{2}{3}$, i.e. per month, = 4 per cent. to 8 per cent. per year.

---

[1] Marquardt, *Röm. Alterth.* Th. III. Abth. 2, p. 50.

x. Measures of Weight[1].

The **as** and its divisions and multiples have been already given, § viii.

The Greek system also was used in the imperial times, the unit being a **denarius**, called from the Greek **drachma**, of which the **libra** (= **as**) contained until Nero's time 84 (so in Celsus and Pliny), afterwards 96. This latter **drachma** was divided into three **scriptula**, the **scriptulum** = two **oboli**, the **obolus** = three **siliquæ**.

If the **libra** be taken as equal to $5053\cdot2$ Engl. grains (so Böckh, Mommsen, Hultsch), it will be about $\frac{7}{8}$ pound Troy (5760 grains). Hence the **denarius** or **drachma** (before Nero's time) was $= 60\cdot16$ grains, i.e. nearly an Engl. drachm (60 grains). After Nero's time the **drachma** was $= 52\cdot6$ grains and the **siliqua** $2\cdot9$ grains.

xi. Measures of length.

The unit of one system was *a finger-breadth*, **digitus**; four finger-breadths made a *palm*, **palmus**; and four palms, a *foot*, **pes**; *a foot and a palm* was **palmipes**; a foot and a half (**sesquipes**) was a *forearm*, **cubitus**. The **ulna** was taken as a third of a man's height, perhaps the length of the whole arm.

But the foot was also divided into twelve parts, and for these the names of the fractions of an **as** were used. *Two feet* was similarly called **dupondius**; $2\frac{1}{2}$ feet was **pes sestertius**.

In land-surveying, the *rod*, **pertica**, contained ten feet, hence called **decempeda**. The **actus** (i.e. the furrow made at one drawing (*driving*) of the plough oxen) measured 12 rods.

The unit of distance was not the single step (**gradus**, $2\frac{1}{2}$ feet) but the **passus**, 5 feet, i.e. the distance from the point where the same foot is taken up to the point where it is put down. A *thousand* paces, **mille passus**, gives the origin of a *mile*. The Greek **stadium** was also used and taken at $\frac{1}{8}$ of a mile (i.e. our furlong).

The **pes** $= 11\cdot6$ Eng. inches or $\cdot97$ Eng. foot; **mille passus** $= 4850$ Eng. feet or $\cdot919$ Eng. mile. The **pertica** $= 9$ feet $8\cdot5$ inches.

---

[1] In §§ x.—xiii. I have chiefly followed Hultsch's *Griech. u. Röm. Metrologie* (1862). See also his *Metrologici Scriptores*, Vol. II. The English equivalents are usually from the tables appended to Smith's *Dict. Antiqq.*

xii. Measures of Surface.

The pes qvadratus (*square foot*), as contrasted with the pes porrectus (*foot in length*), was the unit. But in land-measurement a higher unit was taken, the scripulum (Varro), decempeda qvadrata (Pallad.), i.e. the *square rod*.

The actus qvadratus, often simply actus, contained 144 *square rods*, perticæ; a double actus was a jugerum; a double jugerum formed an heredium; 100 heredia formed a centuria; 4 centuriæ formed a saltus (Varr. *R. R.* 110).

The fractions of the jugerum were denoted by the parts of an as, the sicilicus also being used for $\frac{1}{48}$; the sextula for $\frac{1}{72}$; the scripulum for ($\frac{1}{4}$ of the sextula, i.e. for) $\frac{1}{288}$ of the jugerum.

The pes qvadratus = ·94 Engl. sq. foot: the actus qvadratus = 1 rood 9 perches 231 sq. feet: the jugerum = 2 roods 19 perches 189·9 square feet, i.e. almost $\frac{5}{8}$ of an acre; an heredium was nearly an acre and a quarter.

xiii. Measures of Capacity.

The unit of *liquid* measure was the qvadrantal, which was defined as vas pedis qvadrati, i.e. as *containing a square foot* of wine. The name in and after Cicero's time was superseded by that of amphora (ἀμφορεύς). The amphora contained two urnæ, the urna four congii; the congius six sextarii; the sextarius two heminæ; the hemina two qvartarii; the qvartarius two acetabula. A culeus contained 20 amphoræ.

The duodecimal system was applied to the sextarius, a twelfth of which was a cyathus = uncia. The triens = 4 cyathi, qvadrans = 3 cyathi, sextans = 2 cyathi, &c., are spoken of. (See also Mart. 11, 36; 12, 28.)

The unit of *dry* measure was the modius, which contained two semodii or 16 sextarii. The divisions of the sextarius (hemina, &c.) were the same as of liquid measure.

The sextarius was = ·96 pint Engl. Hence the amphora was about = 5 gall. 6 pints Engl.; the modius = 1 gall. 7·36 pints Engl.

xiv. Division of Time.

The Romans divided time into years, months, days, and hours. A civil day, as recognised in law, was from midnight to midnight; a natural day, from sunrise to sunset. The duodecimal system was applied here also, the natural day being divided into twelfths, called horæ, which were therefore of different absolute lengths according to the time of year. From Dec. 23rd, when the day at Rome was, according to modern reckoning, 8 hrs. 54 m. long, and the Roman hour was 44½ m., the length increased up to 25 June, when the day was 15 hrs. 6 m., and the Roman hour 75½ m. At the equinoxes, 23 March, 25 Sept., the Roman hour was of the same length as our own. The civil day is sometimes spoken of as divided into twenty-four hours.

The night was for military purposes divided into four *watches* (vigilia prima, &c.) of equal length. And a similar division of the day into four parts is also implied by Varro's account of the prætor's marshal crying the 3rd hour, noon, and the 9th hour. Various loose names for different parts of the day and night came into vogue, and are arranged by Censorinus (c. 24) in the following order, starting from midnight:

1. De media nocte; 2. gallicinium; 3. conticinium, *general silence;* 4. ante lucem; 5. diluculum; 6. mane; 7. ad meridiem; 8. meridies; 9. de meridie; 10. suprema; 11. vespera; 12. crepusculum; 13. luminibus accensis, or, anciently, prima face; 14. concubium; 15. intempesta nox; 16. ad mediam noctem; 17. media nox.

xv. Expression of the Date.

(Partly from Madvig. *Suppl. to Gram.*)

The division of time into weeks of seven days with distinct names was not used by the ancient Romans (before the introduction of Christianity). The months were distinguished by the names adopted by us from the Romans, excepting that, before the time of the Emperor Augustus, Julius and Augustus had the names of Quinctilis and Sextilis (i.e. *fifth* and *sixth* month, March being the first). The days of the month were computed from three leading days in each, which were called respectively Calendæ (Kal.), Nonæ (Non.), and Idus (Id.); to these the name of the month was appended as an adjective. The Calendæ was the first day of every month; the **Nonæ** and **Idus** the fifth and thirteenth, except in the months of March, May, July, and October, in which they were the seventh and fifteenth respectively. From these days they counted backwards, the days between the 1st and the Nones being reckoned as so many days before the Nones; the days between the Nones and Ides as so many days before the Ides; and the remaining days of the month as so many days before the Kalends of the *next* month. The day immediately preceding any of these reckoning points was called **pridie Nonas**, &c.; the day next but one before was the *third* day before (in consequence of the Nones, &c. being themselves included in the reckoning), and so on.

There are two abbreviated modes of denoting the date; e.g. the 27th of March might be marked as **vi Kal. Apr.**, or **a. d. vi Kal. Apr.** The first is for **sexto (die ante) Kalendas Apriles**; the second for **ante diem sextum Kalendas Apriles**. The latter expression appears to have originally signified *before (on the sixth day) the Kalends of April;* the exact day being thrown in parenthetically, and attracted from the ablative into the accusative case in consequence of following **ante**. Similarly we find the date sometimes denoted by the number of days preceding a festival; as, **a. d. v Terminalia**, i.e. 19th Feb. (the festival of the god of boundaries being on the 23rd Feb.). This expression was considered as one word, before which **in** or **ex** may stand; as, **Ex ante diem iii Nonas Junias usque ad pridie Kalendas Septembres,** *from the 3rd June to the 31st August;* **differre aliquid in ante diem xv Kalendas Novembres,** *to put off something to the 18th October.*

The readiest way of reckoning the day is, (1) if the date lie between the Kalends and Nones, or between the Nones and Ides, to subtract the number of the day mentioned from the number of the day on which the Nones or Ides fall, and add *one* (for the inclusive reckoning): (2) if the date lie between the Ides and the Kalends, to subtract the number of the day mentioned from the number of the days in the month, and add *two* (i.e. one for the inclusive reckoning, and *one* because the Kalends are not the last of the month in which the date lies, but the first of the following month).

In leap year the intercalated day was counted between **a. d. vi Kal. Mart.** and **a. d. vii Kal. Mart.** and denominated **a. d. bissextum Kal. Mart.**, so that **a. d. vii. Kal. Mart.** answers in the ordinary February to Feb. 23, and **a. d. viii Kal. Mart.** to Feb. 22nd, &c. (Hence the name of leap year, **annus bissextilis**.)

Before the reformation of the Calendar by Julius Cæsar, B.C. 45, the number of days in the months were in March, May, July and October, 31; in February 28; in all the rest 29. Hence, as these four months were two days longer, the Nones and Ides were two days later. This should be remembered in reading Cicero's letters, many of which were written before 45 B.C. After that year the number of days in each month was the same as it is with us to this day.

The following examples suppose the date to be *subsequent to* B.C. 45. The usual abbreviated form is given. [It must be remembered that Kalendæ, Nonæ, and Idus are feminine, and the months *adjectives;* that the date ('*on the first,*' &c.) is in the ablative (Kalendis, Nonis, Idibus) ; and that a. d. vi Non. Mart. &c. is for ante diem sextum Nonas Martias.]

Day of English month.	January (So also Aug. Dec.).	April (So also Jun., Sept., Nov.).	March (So also May, Jul., Oct.).
1	Kal. Jan.	Kal. Apr.	Kal. Mart.
2	a. d. iv Non. Jan.	a. d. iv Non. Apr.	a. d. vi Non. Mart.
4	Prid. Non. Jan.	Prid. Non. Apr.	a. d. iv Non. Mart.
5	Non. Jan.	Non. Apr.	a. d. iii Non. Mart.
6	a. d. viii Id. Jan.	a. d. viii Id. Apr.	Prid. Non. Mart.
7	a. d. vii Id. Jan.	a. d. vii Id. Apr.	Non. Mart.
8	a. d. vi Id. Jan.	a. d. vi Id. Apr.	a. d. viii Id. Mart.
12	Prid. Id. Jan.	Prid. Id. Apr.	a. d. iv Id. Mart.
13	Id. Jan.	Id. Apr.	a. d. iii Id. Mart.
14	a. d. xix Kal. Feb.	a. d. xviii Kal. Mai.	Prid. Id. Mart.
15	a. d. xviii Kal. Feb.	a. d. xvii Kal. Mai.	Id. Mart.
16	a. d. xvii Kal. Feb.	a. d. xvi Kal. Mai.	a. d. xvii Kal. Apr.
30	a. d. iii Kal. Feb.	Prid. Kal. Mai.	a. d. iii Kal. Apr.
31	Prid. Kal. Feb.		Prid. Kal. Apr.

APPENDIX E.

NAMES OF RELATIONS BY BLOOD AND MARRIAGE.

i. By blood.

N.B. = denotes marriage.
| denotes descent.
—   is put between brothers and sisters.

tritavus = tritavia

atavus = atavia

abavus = abavia

proavus = proavia

avus = avia

pater = mater

frater   ego   soror

filius

nepos

pronepos

abnepos

adnepos

trinepos

patruus maximus or abpatruus   avunculus maximus or abavunculus

patruus major or propatruus   avunculus major or proavunculus

patruus.magnus   avunculus magnus

propior sobrino *first cousin once removed*   propior. sobrino *first cousin once removed*

sobrinus *second cousin*   sobrinus *second cousin*

amita   patruus   matertera   avunculus

amitinus *first cousin*   patruelis *first cousin*   consobrinus *first cousin*   amitinus (?) *first cousin*

ii. By marriage.

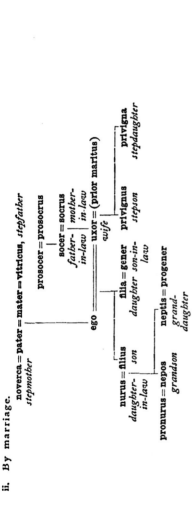

iii. All the names in the above tables denote their relation to *me*. Their relation to others would of course be denoted analogously.

In Table i. are omitted, for clearness' sake, (*a*) all ascendants of the mother, the names being the same as for the ascendants of the father; (*b*) all female relatives, except mother, grandmothers on father's side, sister, and aunts; the names of others can be easily supplied by analogy; e.g. **amita magna**; **amita major** or **proamita**; **propior sobrinā**; **sobrina**; **amitina**; **filia**; **neptis**; **proneptis**; &c.

amitinus, consobrinus, patruelis are properly adjectives, and **frater** (or **soror**) is often used with them. **Consobrinus**, properly *sister's children*, became the ordinary term for any *first cousin*.

In Table ii. the descendants of a **filia** would be described by the same names as those of a **filius**; and **prosocer, prosocrus** would apply to the father and mother of a **socrus** as well as a **socer**.

levir (174, 4) is *a husband's brother*; **glos** (comp. γάλως), *a husband's sister*.

agnatus is *a relative through males*; consequently it includes a **soror, filia, amita**, &c., but not any of their descendants. **Cognatus** is *any relative by blood*; **affinis** *a relative by marriage*.

APPENDIX F.

TABULAR ARRANGEMENT OF CERTAIN PRONOUNS.

i. Correlative (pronominal) adjectives.

Demonstr.	Rel. and Interrog.	Indef. Rel.	Indef.
is, *that.*	**qui**, *which.*	**quisquis, quicunque** } *whosoever.*	**ăliquis**, *some.* **quis**, *any.*
	ūter, *which of two.*	**alteruter**, *one or other of two.* **uterquisque**, *whichever of the two.*	**quilibet, quivis** } *any you please.* **utervis, uterlibet** } *whichever (of two) you please.*
tālis, *such.*	**quālis** {*of which quality, as, of what quality?*	**quāliscunque**, *of what quality soever.*	**quālislibet**, *of any quality you please.*
tantus, *so great.*	**quantus** {*as great, how great?*	**quantuscunque**, *how great soever.*	**aliquantus**, *of some considerable size.*
tantŭlus, *so small.*	**quantŭlus**, *as small.*	**quantŭluscunque**, *how small soever.*	**quantuslibet, quantusvis** } *of any size you please.* **aliquantŭlum**, *a little* (subst.).
tot (indecl.), *so many.* **tŏtĭdem** (indecl.), *just so many.*	**quŏt** (indecl.) {*as many, how many?*	**quotcunque, quotquot**(indecl.) } *how many soever.*	**ăliquot** (indecl.), *some.*
tŏtus (rare), *such in numerical order.*	**quŏtus** {*what in numerical order? which,* &c. (rare).		

Quāliscunque and **quantuscunque** are also used as simply indefinite (non-relative) pronouns; **aliquantus** is commonly only used in the neuter (**aliquantum, aliquanto**), and then as *substantive* or *adverb*.

ii. Correlative (pronominal) adverbs.

tam, *so.*	quam, *how? as.*	quamquam, } *however.*	quamvīs, } *however much*
		quamcunque}	quamlibet } *you please.*
tōtiēs, *so often.*	quōtiēs {*how often?*	quotiescunque, *however*	quotieslibet, *however often*
	{*as often.*	*often.*	*you please.*
ita, } *thus, so.*	ut, *how, as.*	utcunque, *however.*	aliquōtiēs, *sometimes.*
sīc }			

iii. The following are the chief (pronominal) adverbs of place.
(Fuller lists will be found in Book II. Chap. xv.)

ō (= om, accus.?)	de = θεν, gen. (or abl.)	bī or ī, dat. or loc.	ā, abl. fem.
Quō {*whither?* {*whither.*	undē {*whence?* {*whence.*	ubī {*where?* {*where.*	Quā {*by what way?* {*by which way.*
hāc, *hither.*	hinc, *hence.*	hīc, *here.*	hāc, *by this way.*
eō, *thither.*	indē, *thence.*	ibī, *there.*	eā, *by that way.*
istō, istūc, *to your place.*	istim, istinc, *from your place.*	istīc, *there (where you are).*	istāc, *by your way.*
illō, illūc, *to that place.*	illim, illinc, *from that place.*	illīc, *there (where he is).*	illāc, *by that way (near him).*
eōdem, *to the same place.*	indidem, *from the same place.*	ibidem, *in the same place.*	eādem, *by the same way.*
utrōque, *to both places.*	utrinque, *from both sides.*	utrōbīque, *in both places.*	
	undique, *from all sides.*	ubīque, *everywhere.*	
aliquō, *to some place or other.*	alicunde, *from some place or other.*	alicubī, *somewhere or other.*	aliquā, *by some way.*
quōvīs, } *to any place you* quōlibet} *please.*	undēvīs, } *whence you* undēlibet} *please.*	ubīvīs, } *where you please.* ubīlibet}	quāvīs, } *by any way you* quālibet} *please.*
utrōlibet, *whithersoever (of two places) you choose.*			
quōquam, *anywhither (in negative, &c. sentences).*		usquam, *anywhere (in negative, &c. sentences).*	

Tabular Arrangement of Certain Pronouns (*Continued*).

siquā, *if anywhither.* sicunde, *if from any place.* sicūbi, *if anywhere.* siquā, *if by any way.*
nequō, *lest anywhither.* nēcunde, *lest from anywhere.* nēcūbi, *lest anywhere.* nequā, *lest by any way.*
aliō, *to another place.* aliunde, *from another place.* alibi, *elsewhere.* aliā, *by another way.*
quōcunque, } *whitherso-* undēcunque, *whencesoever.* ubicunque, *wheresoever.* quācunque, } *by whatsoever*
quōquō } *ever.* nusquam, *nowhere.* quāquā } *way.*
  usquequaque, *everywhere.*
quōnam, *whither?* quanam, *where?*
adeo, *so far.*
quorsum (i. e. } *whitherwards?*
quōversum) } *whitherwards.*

iv. The following are the chief (pronominal) adverbs *of time.*

Quando { *when?* quamdiū { *how long?* quōtiēs { *how often?*
  { *when.* { *as long as.* { *as often as.*
quom, *when.* aliquamdiū, *for some length* tōtiēs, *so often.*
nunc, *now.* *of time.* aliquōtiēs, *several times.*
tunc, } *then.* quousque, *till when?* identidem, *repeatedly.*
tum } adhuc, *hitherto* (i.e. up to nonnunquam, } *sometimes* (i.e. *not unfrequently*).
antehāc, *before this.* the time *now* present). aliquando, }
posthāc, *after this.* quandōque }
nondum, *not yet.* interdum, *sometimes* (i.e. *occasionally*).
aliās, *at another time.* subinde, *one after the other.*
intērim, } *meanwhile.* unquam, *ever* (after negatives, &c.).
intereā } usque, *ever* (of progressive continuance).
quondam, } *formerly, or hereafter* (olim is from
ōlim } ollus (=ille) and so means *at that time*).

APPENDIX G.

ABBREVIATIONS.

For abbreviations in Inscriptions see Hübner's Index to *Corp. Inscr. Rom.* I. pp. 610—613 *et passim,* also *supra* App. B. For others, esp. *legal* abbreviations, see Keil's *Gram. Lat.* IV. p. 276 sqq.; and Lachmann's *Gaius,* p. 432 sqq.

For abbreviations of *money,* see App. D. viii., of *date,* App. D. xv.

(1) *First Names* (Prænomina).

A.	Aulus.	Mam.	Mamercus.
App.	Appius.	N. *or* Num.	Numerius.
C.	Gaius.	P.	Publius.
Cn.	Gnæus.	Q.	Qvintus.
D.	Decimus.	S. *or* Sex.	Sextus.
K.	Kæso.	Ser.	Servius.
L.	Lucius.	S. *or* Sp.	Spurius.
M.	Marcus.	T.	Titus.
M'.	Manius.	Ti.	Tiberius.

Women's names are expressed by inverted characters; as, Ɔ for Gaia.

(2) *Titles of Persons, &c.*

CES. *or* CENS.	Censor *or* Censores.	PROC. *or* PRO. COS.	} Proconsul.
COS.[1]	Consul *or* Consules.	PRO. PR.	Proprætor.
		PROQ.	Proqvæstor.
D.	Divus.	P. R.	Populus Romanus.
DES.	Designatus.	Q.	Qvæstor.
F.	Filius.	QUIR.	Qvirites.
IMP.	Imperator.	RESP.	Respublica.
LEG.	Legatus.	R. P. P. R. Q.	Respublica Populi Romani Qviritium.
L. *or* LIB.	Libertus, Liberta.		
MAG.	Magister.	S.	Servus.
N.	Nepos.	S. P. Q. R.	Senatus Populusque Romanus.
P. C.	Patres Conscripti.		
P. M.	PontifexMaximus.	S. P. P. Q. R.	Senatus Populus Plebesque Romana.
PR.	Prætor, *or* Prætores.		

---

[1] Not until 3rd cent. p. Chr. was cons. used; in Diocletian's time began the custom of doubling the s (e.g. conss.) to denote the plural (Mommsen, *Liv. Cod. Ver.* p. 189).

Tr. Mil.	Tribunus militum.	X. Vir. Stl.	Decemvir stliti-
Tr. Pl.	Tribunus Plebis.	Judik.	bus (i. e. litibus)
Tr. Pot.	Tribuniciā Potes-		judicandis.
	tate.	XV. V. S. F.	Qvindecimviri sa-
X. V.	Decemvir.		cris faciundis.

The name of the tribe to which a person belonged is sometimes added to the name in an abbreviated form; thus, **Pup.** for **Pupiniā**; **Qvi.** or **Qvir.** for **Qvirinā.** See § 1113, and Cælius' letter in Cic. *Epist. ad Fam.* VIII. 8, § 5.

(3) *Sepulchral.*

D. M. S.	Dis Manibus sacrum.	H. S. E.	Hic situs est.
D. S. P.	De sua pecunia.	O B.	Obiit.
F. C.	Faciundum curavit.	P. C.	Ponendum curavit.
H. C. E.	Hic conditus est.	V.	Vixit.

(4) *In voting on trials.* *In voting on laws.*

A.	Absolvo.	A. P.	Antiquam (legem) probo.
C.	Condemno.	V. R.	Uti rogas.
N. L.	Non liquet.		

(5) *Epistolary.*

D.	Data (est epistola).
S. D.	Salutem dicit.
S. P. D.	Salutem plurimam dicit.
S.	Salutem (dicit).
S. V. B. E. E. V.	Si vales, bene est: ego valeo.
S. T. E. Q. V. B. E. E. Q. V.	Si tu exercitusque valetis bene
	est: ego quoque valeo.
S. V. G. V.	Si vales gaudeo. Valeo.

(6) *In decrees of the Senate.*

D. E. R. I. C.	De ea re ita censuerunt.		
I. N.	Intercessit nemo.	Scr. arf.	Scribendo adfuerunt.
S. C.	Senatus consultum.	V. F.	Verba fecit.

(7) *Miscellaneous.*

A. U. C.	Anno urbis conditæ.	ITER.	Iterum.
D. D.	Dono dedit.	L.	Libertas.
DD.	Dederunt.	M. P.	Mille passuum.
D. D. D.	Dat, dicat, dedicat.	Q. B. F. F. Q. S.	Quod bonum fe-
F. F. F.	Felix, faustum, fortu-		lix faustumque sit.
	natum.		

(8) *Modern Latin.*

A. C.	Anno Christi.	L. B.	Lectori Benevolo.
A. D.	Anno Domini.	l. c.	loco citato.
A. M.	Anno Mundi.	l. l.	loco laudato.
a. C. n.} ante}		leg.	lege, or, legatur.
p. C. n.} post} Christum natum.		L. S.	Locus Sigilli.
c.	caput, capitis, &c. (*chapter*).	MS., MSS.	Manuscriptum (or Ma-
cet.	cetera.		nuscriptus, sc. liber),
cf.	confer, or, conferatur.		Manuscripta, or -ti.
Cod., Codd.	Codex, Codices.	N. B.	Nota bene.
coll.	collato, or, collatis.	N. T.	Novum Testamentum.
comp.	compara, or, comparetur.	obs.	observa, or, observetur.
del.	dele, or, deleatur.	P. S.	Postscriptum.
D. O. M.	Deo optimo maximo.	q. v.	quem, or quod, vide.
ed., edd.	editio, editiones.	sc.	scilicet.
e. g.	exempli gratiâ.	sq., sqq.	sequenti, sequentibus.
etc. *or* &c.	et cetera.	s. v.	sub voce.
h. e.	hoc est.	vid.	vide.
I. C.	Jesus Christus.	viz.	videlicet.
Ictus.	Juris consultus.	v.	versus, versum, &c.
ibid.	ibidem.	v. c.	verbi causa.
id.	idem.	V. cel.	Vir celeberrimus.
i. e.	id est.	V. cl.	Vir clarissimus.
i. q.	id quod.	V. T.	Vetus Testamentum.
L. or Lib., Libb.	Liber, Libri.		

Select Index.

The numbers denote sections, unless *p.* (for *page*) is prefixed.

Lightning Source UK Ltd.
Milton Keynes UK
UKOW040750050613

211805UK00001B/3/P